Delia
SMITH'S
COMPLETE COOKERY COURSE

Delia
SMITH'S

COMPLETE COOKERY COURSE

BBC BOOKS

For dearest Debbie.
Happy 20th!

PHOTOGRAPHY *Simon Smith at Barry Bullough Studios*
(*assisted by Thierry Guinovart*)
FOOD PREPARATION *Catherine Calland*

Published by BBC Books
a division of BBC Enterprises Ltd,
Woodlands, 80 Wood Lane, London W12 0TT

© Delia Smith 1978, 1979, 1981, 1982, 1989
Omnibus edition published 1982
Reprinted 1982, 1983 (five times), 1984 (three times),
1985 (twice), 1987, 1988 (twice)
New edition published 1989
Reprinted 1989 (four times) and 1990
This revised hardback edition published 1992
Reprinted 1992 (three times), 1993 (three times),
1994 (twice), 1995

ISBN 0 563 36429 9 (paperback)
ISBN 0 563 36286 3 (hardback)

Typeset in 11/12 Baskerville
by Datix International Ltd, Bungay, Suffolk
Printed in England by Clays Ltd, St Ives plc
Colour origination by Technik Ltd, Berkhamsted

CONTENTS

Conversion tables · 6

Introduction · 7

Equipment · 9

Eggs · 18

Bread and yeast cookery · 35

Stocks and soups · 61

Pâtés and starters · 85

Fish · 101

Meat:
roasting and pot-roasting · 138

Meat:
casseroles and braised dishes · 158

Poultry · 179

Offal · 206

Vegetables · 226

Rice and other grains · 268

Vegetarian cooking · 288

Pulses · 304

Pasta and pancakes · 324

Herbs · 345

Spices and flavourings · 362

Sauces · 386

Cheese · 411

Salads and dressings · 435

Barbecues and picnics · 455

Cream, ice cream and yoghurt · 472

Pastry · 492

Cakes · 532

Scones and biscuits · 561

Fruits and puddings · 574

Preserving · 604

Left-overs · 624

Index · 633

CONVERSION TABLES

♦

All these are approximate conversions, which have either been rounded up or down. In a few recipes it has been necessary to modify them very slightly. Never mix metric and imperial measures in one recipe: stick to one system or the other. All spoon measurements used throughout this book are level unless specified otherwise.

Oven temperatures		
Mark 1	275°F	140°C
2	300	150
3	325	170
4	350	180
5	375	190
6	400	200
7	425	220
8	450	230
9	475	240

Measurements	
$1/8$ inch	3 mm
$1/4$	5 mm
$1/2$	1 cm
$3/4$	2
1	2.5
$1^{1}/4$	3
$1^{1}/2$	4
$1^{3}/4$	4.5
2	5
$2^{1}/2$	6
3	7.5
$3^{1}/2$	9
4	10
5	13
$5^{1}/4$	13.5
6	15
$6^{1}/2$	16
7	18
$7^{1}/2$	19
8	20
9	23
$9^{1}/2$	24
10	25
11	28
12	30

Weights	
$1/2$ oz	10 g
$3/4$	20
1	25
$1^{1}/2$	40
2	50
$2^{1}/2$	60
3	75
4	110
$4^{1}/2$	125
5	150
6	175
7	200
8	225
9	250
10	275
12	350
1 lb	450
$1^{1}/2$	700
2	900
3	1.3 kg

Volume	
2 fl oz	55 ml
3	75
5 ($1/4$ pt)	150
10 ($1/2$ pt)	275
15 ($3/4$)	425
1	570
$1^{1}/4$	725
$1^{3}/4$	1 litre
2	1.2
$2^{1}/2$	1.5
4	2.25

INTRODUCTION

♦

'What I like about you, Delia, is that all your recipes work — even for idiots like me!' This kind comment was cheerfully whispered to me at a recent book-signing session, by a charming lady who was anything but an idiot, and this started me thinking. How incongruous it is that any published recipe shouldn't actually work. What I feel quite sure of is that problems only arise when recipes assume a lot of knowledge and experience that isn't always there. Cooking is rarely an automatic instinct — we have to learn as we go.

What I myself have learned over the last twenty years or so of writing recipes is that, while experienced cooks do not object to familiar techniques being fully explained, those who are less experienced really value a comprehensive explanation. This can be very reassuring and help to overcome the beginner's first hurdle, which is invariably anxiety. When I wrote the first edition of the *Complete Cookery Course*, it was my ambition to provide just such an all-round basic cookery book so that absolutely anyone, from nine to ninety, male or female, whatever their experience, could cook with complete confidence. Millions of copies — and I have to say thousands of appreciative letters — later, it would seem the book has largely achieved its objective and I count it a great privilege to have been, as it were, 'adopted' on christian name terms in so many families' day-to-day cooking.

This year, however, the *Cookery Course* is all of fourteen years old! And here I am introducing you to a revised edition. What I have set out to do primarily is to communicate what many of the recipes and techniques actually *look* like. It has been a great joy to be able to show the degree of creaminess in a classic Italian risotto, the wafer-like frazzle on perfect pork crackling, or the consummate crunchiness of a roast potato! In all the photographs I have tried to achieve the same criteria of simplicity and clarity as in the text.

Also quite a lot has changed in the past fourteen years, and for that reason the text has been revised and updated, and new recipes added where appropriate.

The past decade has brought huge benefits to the cook: television programmes have helped to familiarise us with cooking from all round the world, bringing an enormous demand for new ingredients which in turn has created a much wider supply. What, fourteen years ago, had to be sought out in specialised food shops is now widely available in supermarkets up and down the country. Almost everyone now has access to good olive oil, fresh herbs, imported cheeses. I found myself over and over again deleting the words 'or if you can't get it . . .'

As a nation we have also become increasingly preoccupied with the subject of healthy eating. This too has meant a new demand for low-fat foods, which has inspired an increased supply. Products like real Greek yoghurt and French fromage frais are helping us all to cut down on too much cream and fat in recipes. I have indicated where these are desirable alternatives and have cut the fat or butter content of recipes where this is in no way detrimental to the recipe. Where it is not possible, I have left well alone, in the firm conviction that it is up to individuals to gauge their own levels of 'healthy' eating. My own philosophy could be summed up thus: I would rather eat a roast chicken *with* butter once a month than eat it three times a week with none. That wise old adage is as true now as it ever was: everything in moderation.

The essence of what this book is about has not changed. First and foremost it is about the principles of good cooking. An eighteenth-century English cook called Hannah Glasse wrote a book with the wonderfully lucid title, *The Art of Cooking Made Plain and Easy*. Two centuries later I would like to re-present my own book, which I hope echoes her title and will help to make the whole art of cooking both plain and easy for anyone who wants to cook in the 1990s.

Thank you for all your appreciation and enthusiasm. Happy cooking!

Delia Smith

EQUIPMENT

$\blacklozenge$

It would be quite unthinkable for a carpenter or a dressmaker or even an amateur gardener to attempt to create anything worth while without the right tools for the job. Yet many people try to cook with second-rate, dilapidated, or sometimes with hardly any equipment at all. Whether you have to cook for a family every day or simply want to cook for pleasure, one thing is certain: good results will be achieved far, far more easily with the right kind of basic equipment.

Good kitchen equipment *is* expensive, but most items last a lifetime and will pay for themselves over and over again. I see so many people attempting to cook with battered saucepans with ill-fitting lids, with blunt knives and makeshift scales – often in the homes of those who have spent a small fortune on the kitchen fixtures. But all the matching units in the world can't compensate for having to peel Brussels sprouts with a table knife.

I don't suggest you can go out and equip yourself with all the essentials in one go. But they should be your priorities as and when you are able to add to your stock, and they should be distinguished from the mountain of gadgetry which clutters up the shops in the name of labour-saving: a great many of these supposedly convenient gadgets are often more expensive than the basic tool and a lot less efficient (even when they are not going wrong).

GENERAL COOKING

$\blacklozenge$

SAUCEPANS

Now there's a subject for a start. The market is inundated with them, all shapes, sizes and colours of the rainbow. But they represent a big investment, so how does a beginner know what to choose? I do think some personal preference comes into this, and often what a person is used to is what he or she likes best. It's probably fair to say that no one particular type of saucepan can answer every type of need. I have several different sorts myself, and below are my opinions on them. But first, one important point, how do you prevent cookware sticking? When it's new, always follow the manufacturer's instructions on how to season new saucepans, frying-pans and casseroles – this will vary depending on the make, but it makes a world of difference.

Heavy-gauge aluminium

Not quite so glamorous as the others to look at, they offer all-round reliability and a good, even conducting of heat. They are easy to keep clean – sometimes the aluminium inside them blemishes, but this is easily remedied by boiling up water in them, to which a little lemon juice or vinegar has been added. They are very hard-wearing and should last a lifetime but *a warning about these saucepans*: food should not be allowed to stand too long in them as the metal can react unfavourably on the food and this has made them a less popular choice in the past few years. There has been some discussion of aluminium as being a health risk, but this has not yet been proven.

Enamelled cast-ironware

These are very heavy and for this reason they hold the heat extremely well – so a much lower heat is needed to keep up a gentle simmer. They come in bright jewel colours and look very attractive. But their heaviness can be a disadvantage: very often two hands are needed to lift a large saucepan full of something. If they are dropped on a hard surface they can chip or even break. I have found that sauces tend to stick and catch if I'm in a hurry and haven't kept the heat as low as it should be. Finally, the inside enamelled surface can become badly stained (though an overnight soak in a biological washing-powder solution does help).

Stainless steel

I know one or two professional cooks who prefer these to anything else, especially now that the bases can be made with layers of steel, copper and aluminium which, sandwiched together, prove an excellent conductor of heat. I have found, though, that the contents of the pan nearest the edges (say, while boiling milk or making a sauce) get hot more quickly than the centre, which means that cooks in a hurry will regularly find the edges of the pan are scorched. The advantages, however, are that they are easy to keep clean, look attractive even after years of use, and are light to handle.

Copper saucepans

I have a set of heavy, handsome copper saucepans hanging up on the wall of my kitchen – and that's where they're staying. I know that the great French chefs swear by them, but I couldn't manage them at all. The brass handles become very hot, and it is easy to forget to use a cloth. Also I found the tinned lining wore down quickly, exposing the copper beneath whose qualities make some foods become rancid more quickly.

Non-stick saucepans

For my own cooking I find it essential to use metal implements, and for that reason alone I can never recommend non-stick pans – all the ones I have ever used very soon abandoned their non-stick surfaces. I have continued over the last ten years to try all the latest non-stick surfaces, but all eventually become affected by too high a heat or the rigours of metal implements.

STEAMERS

I would say that another essential piece of equipment is a steamer. I actually like the classic steamer which sits on top of the saucepan and can take large pudding basins etc. But I also find the fan-shaped steamer very useful: this one sits *inside* a variety of sizes of saucepan and is perfect for steaming vegetables (which sit inside it with the water boiling away underneath).

FRYING-PANS

My choice here is definitely for a heavy, cast-iron pan – there is a particularly good French, imported one which has a matt-black inside coating which remains unharmed by metal utensils. Every cook should have two frying-pans, one with an 8 inch (20 cm) diameter base and another a 10 inch (25·5 cm).

MEAT-ROASTING TINS

Solidity is the important thing here – the cheap, thin-gauge metal ones, when exposed to very high temperatures, simply buckle. And once the base of the tin has become uneven you might as well throw it away. I have now practically abandoned all roasting tins and use oval cast-iron gratin dishes of various sizes.

CASSEROLES

I would definitely recommend cast-iron enamelled ware. One good 4½– 5 pint (2.5–2.8 litre) casserole would be about right for a family of four. The advantage of this kind of casserole is that you can use it on top of the stove as well as inside – and it is attractive enough to be taken straight to the table. The less expensive earthenware casseroles are useful for certain recipes, but these are only suitable for oven cookery.

BAKING

———— ♦ ————

For baking you need: a long straight *rolling-pin* (see the Pastry chapter), a *flour dredger* which sprinkles a dusting of flour over a flat surface very evenly, a *pastry brush* (the flat one rather than the round type), and a set of *pastry cutters*, plain and fluted, which come in sets of seven ranging from 1 inch (2.5 cm) to 3½ inches (9 cm) in diameter.

⅂ SHEETS

⌐, solid and flat, these are a very necessary item as they conduct ⅂eat from underneath, so helping to cook the under-side of a quiche or tart. They are essential for baking biscuits and scones etc.

PATTY TINS

If you are buying these for the first time, make sure you buy tins with a dozen sections and not just nine. If you are slogging through a batch of mince pies you save a lot of time cooking twelve in one go.

QUICHE TINS

Should be as solid as possible, with a loose base. The most useful sizes are 8 inch (20 cm) and 10 inch (25·5 cm) but I also now use a 7½ inch (19 cm) which gives a thicker quiche.

PIES AND TARTS

For these the old-fashioned enamelled pie-plates are best, because being metal they conduct the heat, and cook the pastry, more evenly. One 8 inch (20 cm) and one 9½ inch (24 cm) plate should cover most needs. A deep-rimmed pie-plate with sloping sides, however, is useful for a recipe that calls for depth (like a lemon meringue pie). Here 8 inch (20 cm) diameter is ideal.

BREAD TINS

These come in a bewildering variety of sizes, but except for the most ambitious the old-fashioned bread tins (with pleated corners, rims and double bases) which come in 1 lb (450 g) and 2 lb (900 g) sizes seem to be the most popular. I *do* think a non-stick tin is useful in bread-making. Although it still must be greased, it is much easier to turn the bread out. For a loaf made from 1 lb (450 g) of flour, the base of the tin should be 5¼ inches × 3 inches (19 cm × 9 cm), and for one made with 2lb (900 g) of flour it should be 6½ inches × 3½ inches (16 cm × 9 cm).

WHISKING AND MIXING
———————— ♦ ————————

WHISKS

One of the prime functions of a whisk is to get air into something, and a balloon whisk (especially with egg whites) will obtain the largest volume of all: it whisks very evenly and can disperse lumps in a sauce in seconds.

ELECTRIC HAND WHISK

I have never felt the need to own a free-standing mixer – partly, I think, because I like to get the feel of the ingredients I am mixing. An electric hand whisk allows me to do this, and its other advantage is that it can be used anywhere in the kitchen – in a saucepan or bowl over heat, for instance. A hand rotary whisk is, of course, cheaper, but a lot more hard work. If, however, you want to do a fair amount of bread-making and yeast cooking, a free-standing mixer will save a lot of strenuous kneading.

KITCHEN FORK

I use a wooden kitchen fork for fluffing and separating rice. It is gentler than a metal one, and is also useful for starting off the mixing of bread dough, and perfect for scrambled eggs.

KITCHEN SPOONS

Apart from the metal teaspoons, dessertspoons and tablespoons which are essential, a cook also needs a variety of wooden spoons, including a very useful one with a pointed edge that can delve into the corners and crannies of a saucepan quickly (e.g. for scrambled eggs). Other handy spoons are: a long-handled draining spoon with perforations in it to separate something solid from its liquid; an unperforated, long-handled spoon which will save you burning your arms when you want to baste something in a hot oven; and a ladle.

SLICES AND SPATULAS

FISH SLICE

Something of a misnomer, because this will come in useful when frying all kinds of things. Its flat blade should have plenty of flexibility in it – the rigid ones simply can't slide under such delicate things as fried eggs without damaging them.

KITCHEN TONGS

These will permit you to turn steaks, chops or sausages without piercing them and losing their juices. My husband insists on a pair for his barbecue.

SPATULA

A flat-edged piece of hard rubber with a wooden handle: it clears a bowl of dough or other mixture in seconds and much more effectively than scraping with a spoon.

CUTTING, CHOPPING AND GRATING

◆

KNIVES

A set of good-quality kitchen knives can transform your culinary life overnight – and by this I mean the stainless steel ones with riveted wooden handles (the Swiss make excellent ones). Carbon steel knives are often recommended but are the devil to stop discolouring. There are endless shapes and lengths of knives available, but you can build up your collection gradually with care. My priorities would be a couple of varying cook's knives, a small kitchen knife, a small curved paring knife, a potato peeler, a good carving knife with either a serrated or straight edge (and a carving fork), a palette knife for smoothing icing or cream and lifting biscuits from a baking sheet, and a bread knife (though in fact my palette knife has a serrated edge and cuts bread beautifully).

Keeping knives sharp
This is vital. They ought to be sharpened regularly: a sharpening steel is best for this, although it requires a little practice. I was hopeless at first. The butcher's tip to sharpen little and often is a good one, and remember always to sharpen the whole length of the blade, not just one section. (If you really can't manage a steel, there are knife-sharpening gadgets available: they just tend to wear out knives rather more quickly, that's all.) It also helps to keep knives sharp (and is a lot kinder on the fingers) if you store them on magnetic racks, which can be attached to the wall, rather than in drawers where they can come into contact with other implements. Never use your knives on a plastic or laminated surface – both the surface and the knives will be ruined in no time. Good knives need a *wooden chopping board* with a bit of give in it.

KITCHEN SCISSORS

A good, tightly riveted pair, kept strictly for kitchen use, will come in handy more often than you might imagine. They are so useful for snipping herbs, cutting string on puddings or scaling fish. My pair, made in Finland, are the best I have come across and (rather enterprisingly) they are manufactured for left-handed people as well.

GRATERS

Quite honestly nothing grates as well or as easily as the versatile, four-sided grater with each of its sides offering a different variety of grate. And one of its endearing qualities is that it is so easy to clean. The only other grater I use is a small nutmeg grater, which has a built-in compartment for holding a few whole nutmegs. It hangs on a hook within arm's reach, ready for instant use.

LEMON ZESTER

This is a useful, and inexpensive, item which nothing can really replace. It extracts the outer 'zest' from a lemon, leaving the unwanted pith behind, and is so constructed it can get round the awkward curves of a lemon without difficulty.

GRINDING AND MINCING
♦

MINCER

The cast-iron kind, with a clamp-base, is not really an expensive piece of equipment and is virtually indestructible. It comes with three different blades for different coarseness of mince and – as we shall see later – is invaluable for dealing with left-over meat, making hamburgers and a dozen other recipes, including chutneys. I emphasise the clamp-base because suction bases never seem strong enough – but make sure you have a suitable table edge to clamp it to.

PESTLE AND MORTAR

A mortar is a heavy porcelain bowl and a pestle a rounded porcelain tool that crushes or pounds the substances in the bowl – use it for crushing whole spices or pounding garlic and salt together to a cream. I would not be without mine, and suggest the larger and sturdier kind you can buy the better.

PEPPER MILL

There are plenty of pepper mills around that don't work too well, so it is worth investing in a good, wooden one. The taller it is, the less often you will have to refill it with peppercorns. Elsewhere in the book I have enlarged on the virtues of freshly ground pepper, so let me only say here that it has 100 per cent more fragrance and flavour than the ready-ground stuff.

LEMON SQUEEZER

In this case, the simpler the better. A strong plastic or a tough glass squeezer will do well: some of the plastic ones have a screw-on cup underneath to catch the juice and separate off the pips – so that the juice is easier to pour.

SIEVING, SIFTING, STRAINING

SIEVES

I have three sieves at home. Two of them, in different sizes, are metal ones because I have had to discard so many melted and disfigured plastic ones in the past. The one plastic one I still possess, with its fine mesh, is used almost exclusively for sifting flour.

COLANDER

The same goes for colanders: never get a plastic colander – you are guaranteed a disaster sooner or later when it has been left too near the heat. The small aluminium or enamel ones will be sturdier and safer.

SALAD BASKET

Although practically redundant in the winter, my wire salad basket comes into its own in the summer. When salad leaves require washing, you can put them wet inside one of these enclosed baskets then (outdoors) swing the whole thing, using circular movements, and shake off most of the excess water. Then just leave it somewhere to finish drying.

MEASURING

SCALES

If you have cooked for a lifetime with maybe a fairly modest repertoire, then perhaps you don't have to weigh anything – your 'instincts' are well developed. Lucky you. If you're a beginner or, like me, have upwards of 1500 recipes on file and cannot commit even one of them to memory, then you simply *must* weigh everything to be sure of success. My advice is to opt for a proper pair of balance scales (where the weights go on one side, the ingredients on the other): these are far more accurate than the needle-and-spring kind and sturdy enough to outlast you. Look for the largest pair possible. I have some antique balance scales like this that still register perfect balance. You can now buy a set of metric weights, as well as imperial – so the same scales can cope with either.

MEASURING JUGS

A glass measuring jug, with imperial and metric volumes marked on the side, will tell you in seconds what 3 fl oz is (otherwise it is impossible to know: milk bottles are not advised).

Timing, Testing and Temperature

—————— ◆ ——————

SKEWERS

Unassuming little pieces of equipment, but *vital*. Without one I just don't know how to tell if potatoes or vegetables are cooked, but the 'feel' or give of a skewer as it is inserted into the centre is a sure guide. Flat skewers are essential for kebab cookery.

KITCHEN TIMER

Very often these are incorporated into modern ovens. But if yours does not have one built in, they can be bought separately. Memories are fallible, and a timer can save a lot of hard work from going out of the window.

COOKING THERMOMETER

Sometimes described as a 'sugar thermometer'. Will save a great deal of agonising as to whether the fat is hot enough to put in the chips, or the jam has reached a set. Such information is printed alongside the appropriate temperature on good kitchen thermometers. A *meat thermometer* is a gadget inserted in a joint of meat to help you determine when the joint is ready. However, they can be fallible if they happen to touch and rest against a bone.

There is only one other item I would include in this list. I find my *food processor* does all the work of a mincer and a liquidiser – and more, as it's excellent for shredding, slicing and grating in large quantities. But what you must bear in mind is that the blades do not last for ever, and if the machine is not performing well you probably need to get a new blade. For chopping things evenly, though, I still prefer a wooden board and a sharp knife. I also feel that pastry and cake mixes made in a processor don't incorporate enough air. Otherwise it's very useful. Alternatively a solid 2 pint (1.2 litre) capacity *liquidiser* will take care of the puréeing part.

EGGS

◆

In this book it's the egg – and not the chicken – that comes first. There are good reasons for starting with eggs, not least because they are such a basic ingredient in our cookery and a real understanding of what they are and what they can do is essential before we progress to, say, pastry later.

But there's another reason. Someone who 'can't even cook an egg' is – to the rest of the world – someone who has either despaired of or totally neglected the art of cooking. Yet there is an assumption here that egg cookery is so basic it needs no practice or experience – it's intuitive. I don't believe that. Cooking *can* be easy, but only when you know the proper way to do it. And that's something I hope to demonstrate by starting with eggs. And anyway imagine – if everyone from the age of nine to ninety could make an omelette correctly, they'd never lack for one delicious, interesting and nutritious meal at their fingertips!

WHAT'S IN AN EGG?

◆

Eggs are full of life: they provide nutrients, proteins, fats, vitamins and minerals, nearly everything needed for life. One ingredient that may seem less essential, but as we shall see figures pretty largely in the cooking of an egg, is air. It's that tiny pocket of air that is directly related to the age and quality of an egg.

Nature included this air pocket so that the tiny, developing chick could breathe. However, when eggs are for consumption rather than hatching, they are cooled and stored, and their water content starts to evaporate – and the air pocket gets bigger. It follows therefore that, generally speaking, the larger the air pocket the staler the egg. (I say generally because sometimes a hairline crack, invisible to the human eye, can let air into a very fresh egg: but this is distinctly rare.)

The freshness of an egg is very important in cooking. Stale eggs, with their flat yolks and watery whites, spread themselves miserably to all corners of the frying-pan. Not to mention the ones whose yolks in poaching water completely part company with their whites – while the whites in turn are reducing the water to a mass of foaming bubbles!

CHOLESTEROL

———— ♦ ————

Cholesterol, a by-product of animal fats and dairy foods which has a tendency to build up in our systems, is often cited as a contributory factor in heart disease. Quite apart from the total diversity of opinion among nutrition experts all over the world on the subject, I am certainly not in a position to expound on medical problems. What I can say is that if we only eat what we actually *need* to eat and in a balanced pattern, all the risks of our modern diet are minimised. The root of the problem is that as a (comparatively) affluent nation we have acquired the habit of over-eating and under-exercising. Perhaps the worry ought to be, not am I eating too many eggs or too much butter, but am I eating too much overall? In the end it may be the old answer about moderation being the cure for most ills.

BUYING EGGS

———— ♦ ————

If there's one thing we can thank our membership of the EC for, it's the compulsory date-stamp on egg-boxes. Undoubtedly it has meant that fresher eggs are now more widely available, and if the packing-date on the box does happen to say Week 1 and it's already Week 4, you can tell those eggs have been hanging around the supermarket a bit too long. It is not always easy to work out which Week 33 is, in the middle of a crowded supermarket, but if you buy eggs regularly you should be able to check week by week; or you can get little charts from the British Egg Information Service, Bury House, 126–128 Cromwell Road, London SW7 4ET. All eggs are classified for quality (A, B or C) at the packing station, by the process called 'candling' – originally quite literally by shining a candle behind the egg to detect defects such as blood spots, cracks and blemishes. Class A and B eggs can be sold in shops. Class A have excellent internal quality; Class B have fair internal quality. Boxes containing Class A eggs could have a red band round bearing the word 'Extra'. This means that the eggs have been packed for less than 7 days (the date of packing must be on the box). Class C eggs are used only for manufacturing, i.e. commercially made confectionery.

Now what about size? Eggs are now numbered, by decree of the EC, from 1 (largest) to 7 (smallest), and this system replaced the old categories of large, standard, medium and small. It can be rather confusing when a recipe calls for eggs without specifying which size, but ever since I started cooking I have used 'large' eggs which in practice now mean numbers 1 or 2. In this book, therefore, all recipes are made with no. 1 or 2 sized eggs.

A GUIDE TO EGG SIZES

Pre-EC Sizes	EC Sizes	Weight
Large	Size 1	70 g or over
	Size 2	65–70 g
Standard	Size 3	60–65 g
	Size 4	55–60 g
Medium	Size 5	50–55 g
	Size 6	45–50 g
Small	Size 7	under 45 g

FREE-RANGE EGGS

A very large percentage of the eggs sold in Britain are battery-produced. However, if you're lucky enough to live near an old-fashioned farm where the hens scratch about and run free, you probably can get well-flavoured eggs with rich-coloured yolks. A warning though: many farm gates with their Free Range notices are not to be trusted. Many have their own deep-litter units where hens by no means run free. Also the eggs bought there will be ungraded, often with startling degrees of size difference, and blood spots or hairline cracks are all part of the bargain. If you are lucky enough to get *fresh* free-range farm eggs, these undoubtedly have the best flavour of all.

BROWN OR WHITE?

The only difference between brown and white eggs is the colour of the shell. The contents are identical. In this country we tend to find brown eggs aesthetically pleasing and happily pay extra for them. And I admit, if I had a pretty breakfast tray all set with a fine china egg-cup, I would personally choose a brown egg (preferably with speckles) and of course brown bread to match.

HOW FRESH ARE THEY?

The best place to buy eggs, at least in a town, is from a supermarket with a quick turnover. But once you've bought your eggs, how do you know if they're fresh or not? One reliable way of telling is to place one in a bowl of cold water: if it sits on the bottom in a horizontal position, the egg is very fresh. On the other hand, if it tilts to a semi-vertical position, it is less fresh; and stale if it pops up into a completely vertical position.

By breaking one out into a saucer you can tell at a glance. A fresh egg will have a rounded, plump yolk that sits up proudly: the white will consist of an inner gelatinous circle clinging all round the yolk, with a second outer circle of flatter, more liquid white. When an egg is stale the yolk turns flabby and the white loses its gelatinous inner circle – it looks frankly weak and watery. This is what makes stale eggs more difficult to separate, among other things.

STORING EGGS

It's my opinion that eggs stored in a cool place will remain in good shape for two weeks. During the third week of storage I tend to use them only for cakes or sauces. Eggs in any event don't like extremes of temperature: I prefer not to keep mine in the fridge, if only because most recipes call for eggs at room temperature. This helps to avoid curdling in cake recipes and they are less likely to break if you're boiling them. If you have no practical alternative, then keep your eggs in the lowest part of the refrigerator: near the freezing compartment is usually too cold a position (which is unhappily where most manufacturers of fridges tend to put their egg racks). And remember to remove them several hours in advance to allow them to come to room temperature – for breakfast take them out the night before. The general guidelines then are (i) store them in a spot neither too warm nor too cold, (ii) store them thin end down, and (iii) store them away from strong smells, because the shells are porous and can absorb pungent flavours.

Separated yolks and whites can be kept for a day or two. The yolks, if they're unbroken, can be kept in water: if broken, sprinkle some water on top to prevent a skin forming. The container should be covered closely with foil or cling film and kept in the fridge. It's interesting to note that chilled egg whites when whisked produce a slightly larger volume (though it's up to you to decide if this is any incentive to go to the trouble of separating and chilling the whites first – I know my life is too busy for such refinements!).

BEATING EGG WHITES

The secret of beating egg whites is knowing when to stop, because once they're over-beaten they start to collapse. What happens is this: whisking incorporates air into the whites, making them expand and grow in volume. As you whisk, tiny air bubbles are formed, but as with all bubbles too much air causes them to burst – and naturally with over-beaten egg whites the loss of air will cause a loss of volume.

I find that when you lift the whisk up and the egg stands up in soft peaks, it is time to stop. If you are folding egg whites into another mixture (i.e. for a soufflé or mousse) use just one metal tablespoonful and fold that in first. This slackens the mixture, making it much easier to fold the rest in. For notes on various types of whisk see page 12.

BOILED EGGS

There seem to be almost as many methods of boiling an egg as there are cooks. The aunt of a friend of mine insists that three verses of 'Onward Christian Soldiers' is the correct timing for a perfect egg (but she takes it a trifle *maestoso*, I think). My recommendations would be rather more precise.

To get the best results the eggs should be at room temperature, otherwise the change in pressure within causes them to crack on contact with the heat. (If you find your boiled eggs constantly cracking, try piercing the rounded end first with a needle to release the pressure – it's very easy.) The water for boiling should not be bubbling too fast, just barely simmering. The saucepan should be small enough to prevent the eggs dancing around while cooking. Both these factors can also cause cracking.

I have found the most trouble-free method is to lower the eggs carefully (using a tablespoon) into gently simmering water. Simmer for exactly 1 minute, then remove the saucepan from the heat, put a lid on and leave the eggs for a further 5 minutes for size 4, or 6 minutes for size 1 or 2. This will produce a white that is just set and a soft creamy yolk. If you like them done more or less than this, add or subtract ½ minute from the 5 or 6 minutes. This way there's less chance of them cracking by careering about in the bubbling water and less likelihood of overcooking by boiling too fiercely.

Note For *really* fresh eggs, that is less than 4 days old, allow extra cooking time.

HARD-BOILED EGGS

Place the eggs in a saucepan of cold water, bring them up to a gentle simmer, and simmer for exactly 6 minutes for size 4 eggs or 7 minutes for size 1 or 2 eggs. This gives a hard yolk but with a little creaminess in the centre. *Always* cool them under cold running water to prevent them cooking further or developing a dark ring between the yolk and the white. If, for a particular recipe, you need to peel the eggs while they're still warm – tap gently to crack the eggs all over, peel the shells, and rinse off any reluctant pieces of shell under a warm running tap.

POACHING EGGS

You could assemble a whole catalogue of 'dos and don'ts' on the subject of poaching if you wanted to. French chefs whisk the water to form a sort of whirlpool before dropping the egg in, which is said to help it keep a good shape. Some say add a little salt to the water: others say never, never add salt. Some add a few drops of vinegar, others pour in as much as 3 tablespoons. Salt and vinegar *do* help the white to coagulate, but the method below has proved 100 per cent satisfactory in my experience.

The most important ingredient is really fresh eggs. Start with a small frying-pan, filled to a depth of approximately 1¹/₂ inches (4 cm) barely simmering water. No salt, no vinegar. Keep the heat low enough for there to be just the merest trace of tiny simmering bubbles on the base of the pan, and no more.

Break each egg gently into the water (breaking the eggs into a cup first is all right but unnecessary, I think), and don't attempt to poach more than two at a time unless you're a really experienced hand. Three minutes is just right for size 2 eggs, but you can vary this fractionally according to taste. While they are cooking you can help the tops to cook by basting with the water. To remove, use a slotted spoon and have ready a wad of kitchen paper on which to rest the spoon and egg for a few seconds, to absorb any excess water. Remember to remove the first egg that went in, before the other.

SCRAMBLING EGGS

On this I'm a disciple of Escoffier. And what he did was to melt a walnut of butter in a small solid saucepan over a gentle heat, then swirl it around to coat the pan thoroughly. Have ready two large eggs beaten and seasoned, and put them into the foaming butter. (Whatever you do, don't let it brown.) Now with a wooden spoon – preferably one with a point – stir like mad, getting the point right into the corner of the pan to prevent the egg sticking.

Take the pan off the heat while there's still some liquid egg left, then add another knob of butter which will melt into it as it finishes cooking in the heat of the pan. For a touch of luxury you could stir in a teaspoonful of thick cream along with the second lot of butter!

FRYING EGGS

————— ◆ —————

A very personal thing, how you like your egg fried – but for absolute beginners here is my method, which might prove helpful. For me frying requires a bit more heat than other methods, because I like a faint touch of crispness around the edge of the egg: so – a medium heat, a fresh egg and some hot but not smoking bacon fat, pure lard or groundnut oil (butter goes too brown for frying, I think). Let the egg settle in the pan and start to set; then, using a tablespoon, tip the pan and baste the top of the egg with the fat until it's done to your liking. Lift it out carefully with a fish slice.

BAKED EGGS (EGGS EN COCOTTE)

————— ◆ —————

These are deliciously special, and can be cooked with a variety of other ingredients (such as cheese, cream, lightly cooked chopped vegetables) in the base of the dishes. The most important items are the special dishes in which the eggs are cooked, called ramekins and looking like small ridged soufflé dishes about 3 inches (7.5 cm) in diameter.

The basic method is as follows. Butter the dishes fairly generously and break an egg into each one. Season them with salt and pepper, then put a large knob of butter on top of each yolk. Now stand the dishes in a meat-roasting tin, pour in enough hot water to come half-way up the sides of the dishes, and bake on a high shelf in a pre-heated oven (gas mark 5, 375°F, 190°C) for 15–20 minutes. Then serve straightaway.

OMELETTES

————— ◆ —————

Let me say first that the *size* of your frying-pan is as vital for good omelettes as for many other things. Ideally every cook should possess two or three pans of varying size – a two-egg omelette, for instance, needs a 6 inch (15 cm) pan, while a four-or five-egg omelette calls for a 10 inch (25.5 cm) pan. Too few eggs in a large pan make a thin, dry (and probably tough) omelette. Too many eggs in a small pan make a thick and uncomfortably spongy one. An omelette pan should be rounded at the sides and, best of all, made in enamelled cast-iron or heavy aluminium.

If your omelette is for one person, break two eggs into a basin and on no account over-beat them. This is where so many people go wrong. You don't need an electric whisk or even a hand whisk – just a large fork or, as I observed a Breton lady use when demonstrating an omelette French-style, a knife. She simply stirred the yolks into the whites with the blade of the knife. So – no vigorous beating or whisking.

Next add a seasoning of salt and freshly milled black pepper. Now put your omelette pan on a medium heat to warm through, without anything in it (if you're using butter, this pre-heating the dry pan prevents the butter being over the heat too long and therefore browning). When the pan is hot, throw in a good knob of butter, say ³/₄ oz (20 g), then turn the heat up to its highest and swirl the butter round and round so that it coats the base and sides of the pan completely.

When the butter starts to froth, pour in the eggs and shake the pan to spread them out evenly, then take a fork or a spoon and draw the edges of the omelette towards the centre, allowing the pools of liquid egg on the surface to run into the channels you have made.

Carry on like this until the omelette is almost set but the surface still soft and a little liquid (or, as the French say, *baveuse*). When it's ready, take the pan handle in one hand, tilt the pan onto the edge of a warm plate, then with a fork or spoon in your other hand flip the edge of the omelette over to the centre. Then let it fold over again as you turn it out of the pan.

One tip, if you're using butter, is to add a little of the melted butter to the eggs just before you pour them in. This seems to give the omelette an extra-buttery flavour. The nicest omelettes of all, I believe, are the simplest, and if you're adding a filling, use very little – remembering that the eggs are the most important part. One favourite variation of mine is an omelette made with a few fresh herbs (*omelette aux fines herbes*): use a level tablespoon of very finely chopped parsley and a level tablespoon of very finely chopped leek, or spring onion or chives. Add the herbs to the two stirred eggs 30 minutes before you make the omelette, then proceed as above.

Note Olive oil or a flavoured groundnut oil can be used instead of butter.

OPEN-FACED OMELETTE

This is a quite different sort of omelette – it's never folded but served cut into wedges. In Spain they refer to this as *tortilla* and in Italy *frittata*. Fillings can be varied: a typical tortilla would contain potatoes, peppers, onions and slices of spiced chorizo sausage. In Italy I've eaten it cooked with cubes of cheese and raw chopped spinach leaves. Following is a French version, sometimes known as *Omelette savoyarde*.

OMELETTE SAVOYARDE
♦

(Serves 2 people)

4 eggs
¹/₂ oz butter (10 g)
1 dessertspoon olive oil
2 medium potatoes, peeled and cut into small cubes approx. ¹/₄ inch (5 mm) square
3 rashers bacon, de-rinded and chopped
1 large onion, chopped
2 oz Gruyère cheese (50 g), coarsely grated
salt and freshly milled black pepper

You'll need a medium-sized frying-pan, 10 inches (25 cm) in diameter.

Melt the butter and oil together in the frying-pan. Dry the cubes of raw potato thoroughly in a tea towel, then fry them over a medium heat, tossing them around quite often until they're beginning to turn golden and are almost cooked through (about 10 minutes). Then add the bacon and onion to the pan and continue to cook these for a further 10 minutes or so or until the onion is soft.

Meanwhile pre-heat the grill to its highest setting. Arrange three-quarters of the grated cheese over the other ingredients in the pan, then beat the eggs with a fork (gently and not too much); season them with pepper but only a pinch of salt, because of the bacon.

Next turn the heat right up under the frying-pan and pour in the eggs. Now, using a palette knife, draw the outside of the omelette inward, allowing the liquid egg to escape round the edges. Sprinkle on the rest of the cheese, then place the pan under the grill for a few moments to set the top (the underneath will go on cooking in the heat of the pan). Serve cut in wedges with a crisp green salad as an accompaniment.

Note In the summer this tastes just as good served cold.

EGGS AND LENTIL CURRY

◆

(Serves 3 people)

If I'm in the mood for a simple everyday kind of curry but am a bit short of time, an egg curry always seems to fit the bill. Sometimes for extra flavour I add 2 oz (50 g) of grated creamed coconut, whisking it into the hot water before adding it to the sauce.

6 large eggs
For the sauce
2 tablespoons groundnut oil
1 medium onion, roughly chopped
2 celery stalks, chopped
1 large carrot, thinly sliced
1 small green pepper, de-seeded and chopped fairly small
3 oz whole green-brown lentils (75 g), washed and drained
1 clove garlic, crushed
1 rounded tablespoon flour
1 rounded teaspoon hot Madras curry powder
1/2 teaspoon ground ginger
1 level teaspoon ground turmeric
1 pint boiling water (570 ml)
2 tablespoons natural yoghurt
salt
To garnish
chopped parsley and thin slices of raw onion

First heat the oil in a thick-based saucepan and fry the onion, browning it a little, then add the celery, carrot and pepper, and continue to fry till these have browned a little too (about 5 minutes). Then stir in the lentils and crushed garlic, and after that sprinkle in the flour and spices. Stir to soak up the juices, and keep stirring while you gradually add the boiling water. Add some salt, then put a lid on and simmer gently for about 35 minutes or until the lentils are soft.

While the sauce is cooking place the eggs in cold water, bring them up to simmering point and then simmer for 7 minutes exactly. Now run some cold water over them until they're cool enough to handle, then peel them and slice in half lengthways.

A minute or two before serving, taste the sauce and add more salt if necessary, stir in the yoghurt and add the halved eggs. Then serve the curry with boiled rice sprinkled with chopped parsley and raw onion slices and have some mango chutney to go with it.

POACHED EGGS WITH CREAM AND WATERCRESS

♦

(Serves 2 people)

The sauce for this recipe is a very attractive speckled pale green colour – and the whole thing goes very well either with some plain buttered noodles or on a bed of lightly cooked spinach.

4 large fresh eggs
For the sauce
1¹/₂ oz butter (40 g)
³/₄ oz plain flour (20 g)
10 fl oz milk (275 ml)
2 bunches watercress, trimmed and chopped
1 oz mild cheese (25 g), grated
1 level tablespoon freshly grated Parmesan cheese
2 tablespoons double cream
lemon juice
salt and freshly milled black pepper
extra grated Parmesan cheese, to serve

Make the sauce first by gently melting 1 oz (25 g) of the butter in a saucepan, stirring in the flour and adding the milk by degrees until you have a smooth white sauce. Then season, turn the heat to its very lowest and allow the sauce to cook for about 7 minutes. While that's happening, trim and discard the watercress stalks and chop the leaves roughly. Then melt the extra ¹/₂ oz (15 g) of butter in a saucepan, add the watercress and, again with the heat as low as possible and a lid on, allow the watercress to collapse into the butter – this should take about 5 minutes.

Now add the watercress and all its buttery juices to the sauce, adding the grated cheeses. Stir to melt the cheese, then pour the sauce into a liquidiser and blend it at high speed until you have a green speckled sauce. Next return the sauce to the saucepan, adding the cream and a squeeze (¹/₂ teaspoonful) of lemon juice and a seasoning of salt and pepper.

Keep the sauce warm while you now, quickly, poach the eggs by breaking them into a frying-pan of barely simmering water and giving them approximately 3 minutes. Lift them out with a draining spoon, resting each one on a wad of kitchen paper to drain. Serve them on a bed of noodles or spinach with the sauce poured over and sprinkled with more freshly grated Parmesan.

EGGS AND LEEKS AU GRATIN

◆

(Serves 4 people)

Eggs, leeks and cheese are a really delicious trio and all this simple lunchtime dish needs to accompany it is some crusty wholewheat bread and good butter.

8 large eggs
4 medium leeks, cleaned and chopped
3 oz strong Cheddar cheese (75 g), grated
1 tablespoon grated Parmesan cheese
2 oz butter (50 g)
1½ oz plain flour (40 g)
15 fl oz milk (425 ml)
cayenne pepper
salt and freshly milled black pepper
To garnish
chopped parsley or watercress

For this you'll need a generously buttered, shallow baking dish, approximately 10 inches (25 cm) in diameter, or the oval equivalent.

Select a saucepan that will hold 8 eggs fairly snugly, then cover them with cold water, bring the water to a gentle simmer and allow 7 minutes exactly – then cool them under cold running water. Peel the eggs and slice them in half lengthways.

While the eggs are cooking, make up a sauce using 1 oz (25 g) of the butter and 1½ oz (40 g) of flour. Add these to the milk and whisk over a medium heat until the sauce is thickened and smooth. Then leave it to cook very gently for about 6 minutes on the lowest heat possible.

Next melt the other 1 oz (25 g) of butter in a saucepan, stir in the chopped leeks and let them sweat gently (with a lid on) for 5 minutes – they should have cooked in that time but still have a bit of 'bite' to them.

Now arrange the leeks over the base of the buttered baking dish and place the peeled, halved hard-boiled eggs on top – round side up. Next stir two-thirds of the Cheddar cheese and all the Parmesan into the sauce. Season well and, as soon as the cheese has melted, pour the sauce all over the eggs. Sprinkle the remaining Cheddar on top with a dusting of cayenne, then place the dish under a medium grill until the sauce is bubbling hot and the cheese is nicely toasted. Sprinkle with parsley or garnish with watercress before serving.

PIPÉRADE

♦

(Serves 2 people)

I had this recently in a delightful restaurant in Paris called Chez Philippe, which specialises in dishes like this from the Basque region of France. There they served it with tiny rounds of spicy chorizo sausage and small slices of raw-cured Bayonne ham lightly sautéed. This latter addition could, of course, be replaced by some crisp fried bacon slices.

4 large fresh eggs
2 medium onions, chopped small
1 or 2 cloves garlic, crushed (how much is up to you)
1 lb firm tomatoes (450 g), peeled, de-seeded and chopped in ¼ inch (5 mm) cubes
2 green peppers, de-seeded and cut into ½ inch (1 cm) strips
½ oz butter (10 g)
1 dessertspoon olive oil
½ teaspoon chopped basil
salt and freshly milled black pepper
For the garnish
2 oz chorizo sausage (50 g), cut into rounds and lightly fried in butter
2 oz Bayonne ham (50 g), lightly sautéed in a little butter

For this you'll need a heavy, medium-sized saucepan.

Melt the butter and olive oil in the pan and add the onions, cooking them very gently for 10 minutes without browning. Now add the crushed garlic, tomatoes and peppers, stir everything around a little, season with salt and pepper and basil, and cook without covering for another 20 minutes or so (the peppers should be slightly under-done).

Now beat the eggs thoroughly, pour them into the pan and, using a wooden spoon, stir just as you would for scrambled eggs. When the mixture starts to thicken and the eggs are almost cooked, remove the pan from the heat, continuing to stir, and serve immediately (as with scrambled eggs, do be very careful not to overcook). Serve in the centre of the plate with the sausage rounds and ham slices around the edge.

CHEESE SOUFFLÉ

◆

(Serves 3–4 people)

The one and only secret of success in making a soufflé is to *whisk the egg whites properly* (see page 21). Once you have mastered that, soufflés should never be a problem. But do remember it is in the nature of soufflés to start to shrink straightaway, and always serve them absolutely immediately.

3 large eggs, separated
3 oz cheese (75 g), grated (any hard cheese can be used)
5 fl oz milk (150 ml)
1 oz butter (25 g)
1 oz plain flour (25 g)
a pinch of cayenne pepper
¼ teaspoon mustard powder
a little freshly grated nutmeg
salt and freshly milled black pepper

Pre-heat the oven to gas mark 5, 375°F (190°C).

For this you will need a 1½ pint (850 ml) soufflé dish or a pie-dish. Butter it well.

Place the milk, butter and flour in a medium saucepan over a medium heat and whisk until blended and thickened. Continue to cook for 3 minutes with the heat at its lowest setting, still giving it an occasional stir. Then stir in the cayenne, mustard, nutmeg and a seasoning of salt and pepper, and leave the sauce to cool a little before stirring in the grated cheese. Beat up the egg yolks thoroughly, then stir them in.

Next whisk the egg whites till they are stiff, take a couple of spoonfuls and beat them into the sauce, then fold in the rest gently and carefully so you don't lose all the precious air. Transfer the mixture to the soufflé dish, place it on a baking sheet in the centre of the oven and bake for 30–35 minutes. The soufflé is cooked when a skewer inserted into the centre comes out fairly clean and not too coated with liquid. Be careful not to overcook: it does need to be soft, not dry, in the centre. Serve immediately with a little dish of grated Parmesan cheese and perhaps a sharp lemon-dressed lettuce and watercress salad.

CHILLI EGGS

◆

(Serves 2 people)

These are eggs set in a hot spicy tomato sauce. In the summer 1 lb (450 g) of peeled fresh tomatoes would be best, but in the winter the tinned Italian variety have more flavour than imported tomatoes.

4 large fresh eggs
3 tablespoons olive oil
1 large onion, chopped
1 green pepper, de-seeded and chopped
2 cloves garlic, crushed
½ teaspoon hot chilli powder
½ teaspoon cumin powder
¼ teaspoon dried oregano or 1 teaspoon chopped fresh basil
a few drops of Tabasco
14 oz tin Italian tomatoes (400 g)
4 oz Cheddar cheese (110 g), grated
salt and freshly milled black pepper
To serve
chopped parsley

A heavy, medium-sized frying-pan.

Heat the oil in the frying-pan and fry the chopped onion, green pepper and garlic gently for about 10 minutes until they're nicely softened. Then stir in the chilli and cumin powders and add the oregano along with a few drops of Tabasco. Mix thoroughly and then add the contents of the tin of tomatoes.

Turn up the heat a bit and let the mixture cook (uncovered) for about 10 minutes or until the tomatoes have reduced to a thick pulp, then season with salt and freshly milled black pepper.

Now carefully break the eggs into the pan on top of the mixture. Then sprinkle the cheese all over the eggs, cover the pan with a close-fitting lid or a suitably-sized plate and, lowering the heat, simmer very gently for about 10–15 minutes, or until the eggs are cooked to your liking. Alternatively, you can place the pan under a hot grill until the cheese is browned and bubbling and the eggs just set (7 minutes for soft eggs, 10 for well done). Sprinkle with chopped parsley and serve with lots of bread or toast to dunk into the juices.

ZABAGLIONE

◆

(Serves 4 people)

This very famous Italian classic should be made with Marsala wine, which isn't very expensive, but failing that a sweet sherry or Madeira would do, as would a liqueur like Grand Marnier to give a hint of caramelised orange.

8 egg yolks
4 dessertspoons caster sugar
3 fl oz Marsala (75 ml)

For this you'll need a medium-sized mixing bowl that will sit comfortably over a saucepan containing barely simmering water.

Into the mixing bowl place the egg yolks and sugar and start to whisk them (not on the heat yet) with an electric hand whisk or a balloon whisk until the mixture is pale and creamy – this will take about 4 minutes. Then gradually whisk in the Marsala bit by bit.

Now transfer the bowl to the saucepan – keep the heat very low – and continue whisking until the mixture thickens. This can sometimes be rather slow (10–15 minutes), but don't be tempted to turn the heat up because, if the mixture becomes too hot, it will curdle. Better to keep the whisk in one hand and a crossword in the other, so you don't get too bored! When it does thicken, pour it into four warmed wine glasses and serve straightaway.

LEMON SOUFFLÉ OMELETTE

◆

(Serves 2 people)

This is a light, foamy, lemony pudding literally made in moments.

3 large eggs, separated
grated rind and juice of 1 large lemon
2 dessertspoons caster sugar
¹/₂ oz butter (10 g)
brandy (optional)

A thick-based frying-pan.

First of all, add the lemon rind and juice to the egg yolks, together with the sugar, and whisk until the mixture is slightly thick and creamy. Now start to melt the butter in the frying-pan and turn the heat on the grill to its highest. Whisk the egg whites until stiff, then using a metal spoon lightly and quickly fold them into the yolks.

Now pour the lot onto the foaming butter, then fold and stir a bit to prevent anything sticking to the bottom. After about 10 seconds place the pan under the grill, so that the top can brown nicely. Serve immediately straight from the pan.

If you like to make it more spectacular, warm a small ladle and pour brandy into it. Set light to the brandy, then carry your omelette to the table, pouring the lighted brandy over just before you get there.

JOHN TOVEY'S QUICK HOLLANDAISE SAUCE

◆

(Makes enough for 4 people)

This recipe is excellent for using up egg yolks, and is equally delicious with plain grilled fish or meat – or as an accompaniment to vegetables like asparagus and artichokes. (For a more traditional version of this sauce, see page 394.)

6 oz butter (175 g)
1 tablespoon wine vinegar
2 tablespoons lemon juice
3 large egg yolks
a pinch of salt

Put the butter into a small saucepan and allow it to melt slowly. Place the wine vinegar and lemon juice in another saucepan and bring to the boil. Meanwhile blend the egg yolks and salt in a liquidiser or food processor – then, with the motor still switched on, gradually add the hot lemon juice and vinegar.

When the butter reaches the boil, start to pour this in very slowly in a thin trickle (with the motor running all the time) till all the butter is added and the sauce is thickened. To keep it warm, place it in a basin over some hot water till ready to serve.

SEE ALSO

Aïoli sauce
Alpine eggs
Broccoli cheese soufflé
Crème caramel
Dutch omelette
Eggs en cocotte with soured cream
    and asparagus
Eggs Florentine
Ham, egg and cheese risotto
Home-made mayonnaise

Hot chocolate rum soufflé
Lemon meringue pie
Queen of puddings
Sauce rouille
Sauce tartare
Scotch eggs with fresh herbs
Smoked haddock with cream and egg sauce
Spaghetti alla carbonara
Spanish tortilla
Welsh rarebit soufflé

BREAD AND YEAST COOKERY

◆

FLOUR, YEAST AND BREADS

◆

You may drive out Nature with a pitchfork, but she will ever hurry back, to triumph in stealth over your foolish contempt. HORACE: Epistles

There's a lot of truth in that little Latin quote, and never more so than now when technology tends to dictate, rather than serve, the needs of man. When it comes to the milling of flour and the commercial baking of bread, nature has indeed been driven out, not with a pitchfork but by a mountain of machinery.

In Britain more than 80 per cent of our flour is milled for the convenience of the machines that make factory bread, and not for the pleasure it gives to those who eat it. Alas, the very essence and flavour of the cornfields are contained in that part of the wheat which is discarded by modern millers: even the natural colour of the wheat is bleached out. It's true that the lost nutrients are replaced chemically, but as our modern wrapped-and-sliced white loaf shows only too clearly, nothing can replace the character, texture and flavour of the wheat.

However, it seems that Horace was right – nature is poised for a comeback. It is now quite evident from sound medical opinion the world over that too much 'refined' food isn't very good for us: it lacks the fibre ('roughage') essential to our diet, and it's said to be the cause of serious colonic diseases, not to mention the national preoccupation with constipation. As a result the 'wholefood' movement is losing its cranky image and gathering strength, and more and more people are attempting quite deliberately to adapt to a more wholesome, less refined diet.

First of all we must define what is meant by refined flour as opposed to unrefined 'whole' flour. In the past large bakeries have managed to obscure the real difference: often so-called brown bread has been white with caramel colouring added, and sometimes the odd bit of natural grain was re-incorporated. Now the Trades Description Act stipulates that wholewheat bread *must* be made with 100 per cent wholewheat flour, and so-called 'wheatmeal' bread with 81–85 per cent extraction flour. Nowadays anything brown that is not called either of these is probably of the refined, dyed variety.

A GRAIN OF WHEAT

Let us examine a grain of wheat, then, and see how it is milled into the various types of flour. Each grain contains three basic components. There is the *germ* (the part that germinates and grows into a new wheat plant), and this contains proteins, vitamins, oil and much of the flavour. Next there is the *endosperm*, containing starch, and all round both these are the protective layers of *bran*. The germ accounts for 2 per cent of the grain, the bran layers 13 per cent and the starch 85 per cent. In the days when the whole grain was ground by hand on millstones, the bread contained all the properties above.

MILLING OLD AND NEW

Obviously the bread made with these traditional methods was brown. The trouble started, in my opinion, when white flour (at least, whiter) became fashionable on a wide scale in the late seventeenth century, as a symbol of status and wealth. This 'refined' flour was sifted, or bolted, through a wool-and-linen fabric which got rid of the toughest layer of bran particles: later an even finer flour was obtained by sifting through silk. This fine flour made lighter bread and became a symbol of a more refined life-style. It was of course more suitable for cakes, biscuits and other confections.

By the 1870s the modern mechanical roller-mill had been invented, which automatically separated the bran and the germ from the starch: the starch was then crushed through fine meshes, and finally bleached with chlorine into our modern whiter-than-white flour. The 'status symbol' was available to all, but ironically it was no longer because we wanted it but because we had to have it. The vast machinery that made our national loaf could now only cope with this sort of flour (even the bleaching, which helps to mature the flour, was for the benefit of technology rather than taste; it was banned in several countries because it also happens to destroy the Vitamin E content – in Britain this was put back synthetically).

However technology never has the final word, fortunately. Thanks to pressure from the wholefood movement, which mobilised public opinion, we now have a very wide choice of bread available. Between them the small bakers, the wholefood stores and even the factory giants can supply us with any – even international – kinds of bread. Yet for all this, there is still infinite pleasure in baking your own bread at home. Sometimes even the busiest people bake their own loaves, and often claim they find the whole process relaxing and therapeutic.

FLOUR

— ♦ —

100 PER CENT STONEGROUND WHOLEWHEAT (WHOLEMEAL) FLOUR

As the name suggests, this is flour ground on a traditional millstone. It contains the whole of the grain of wheat. Nothing has been added and nothing taken away. There has been some confusion as to what exactly is the difference between *wholewheat* and *wholemeal*. Whatever terms the millers might use to describe the coarseness of the grinding, so far as consumers are concerned there is *no* difference. I have bought various bags of flour, some labelled wholemeal and others labelled wholewheat: sometimes the texture of one is coarser than the other, sometimes it's identical. Suffice it to say that whatever texture you happen to like is right for you.

80–90 PER CENT EXTRACTION FLOURS

These are unbleached flours in which 10–20 per cent of the grain has been extracted in the milling. Provided these are stoneground, they are natural flours with the bran partially removed. This type of flour is sometimes referred to as 'wheatmeal' and the loaf made from it is called wheatmeal bread – lighter in texture but still with a wholewheat flavour. (If you like making wholewheat bread most of the time but occasionally want the lighter wheatmeal, you can make up your own 85 per cent extraction by using half quantity of wholewheat flour and half of strong white.)

Note Unless the extraction rate is given on the packet and it carries the magic words 'stone ground', the sort of brown flour distributed by some of the larger firms is usually roller-milled white flour with added colour and part of what has been extracted put back.

STRONG WHITE FLOUR

White flours are normally of 70–72 per cent extraction, with hardly any traces of bran or germ left and of course bleached (actually an unbleached variety is available, and this is a pale cream colour).

All flours vary in strength, according to the amount of *gluten* (protein) they contain. This will depend on the variety of wheat, and the type of soil and climate in which it is grown. Strong (or 'hard') wheats are grown in extreme climates, as in Canada or Russia: in this country our wheat, and therefore our flour, is soft. The stronger the wheat, the higher the gluten content and (as we shall see) the better a dough will stretch and expand – which is exactly what we need for bread.

PLAIN FLOUR

Plain household flour is usually a soft flour. It won't give such good results as strong flour for bread, but it is cheaper and quite capable of producing a home-made loaf better than any shop-bought varieties. With less gluten in it, it is the very best type of flour for cakes and short pastries (and, along with self-raising flour, is dealt with in the Pastry chapter).

HOW TO STORE FLOUR

Flour needs a cool, dry place for storage. That's easier said than done in a modern kitchen, I know, but do try to keep it away from a damp steamy atmosphere: a large and roomy enamelled flour-bin is ideal or, failing that, tightly-lidded storage jars will do. Wholewheat flours have a much shorter shelf-life than white flours, because the wheat germ contains oil which can in time develop a rancid flavour. Six weeks is the maximum storage time for wholewheat (so buy in small quantities), and three months the maximum for white flour.

YEAST

◆

In her splendid book *English Bread and Yeast Cookery*, Elizabeth David has this to say:

In Chaucer's England one of the names for yeast or barm was goddisgoode, 'bicause it cometh of the grete grace of God'. These words simply imply a blessing. To me that is just what it is. It is also mysterious, magical. No matter how familiar its action may become nor how successful the attempts to explain it in terms of chemistry and to manufacture it by the ton, yeast still to a certain extent retains its mystery.

Perhaps one of the reasons yeast seems so mysterious is that it is in fact alive. When we buy it it is alive (one hopes) but inactive: under the right conditions, that is with a little warmth and the addition of some water, it is activated and releases the gas that will raise the dough. All this activity ceases only when the dough is placed in the oven and the extreme temperature kills off the yeast.

Yeast is available in three forms: fresh from some bakers or chemists, and dried (granular) or powdered in tins or packets.

FRESH YEAST

This should look firm and moist, cream-coloured and cool to touch. If it's crumbly, dryish and dark in places it is stale and might not do its work. To use it simply mix the required amount into the liquid and mix into the dough straight away. Fresh yeast can be bought in bulk and stored in a deep freezer in, say, wrapped 1 oz (25 g) portions. It will keep in a freezer for three months, or in a refrigerator for three days.

DRIED YEAST

As supplies of fresh yeast are sometimes unreliable I use either dried yeast, which is reconstituted with warm water and sugar, or powdered easy-blend yeast. Ah, but it's not like the real thing, some people will say. But first of all it *is* the real thing, because dried or powdered it's still yeast. Secondly, I have tasted fresh yeast and dried yeast bread side by side, and really couldn't tell the difference. One word of warning though: dried yeast, just like fresh, does become stale. So dried granular yeast must be stored in an airtight container and used according to the date stamp, and if it doesn't produce a 'frothy head' it is not fresh and won't raise the dough.

POWDERED EASY-BLEND YEAST

This kind is the easiest of all to use – no measuring out, no hand-hot water, no waiting for frothy heads. All you do is sprinkle the required amount in with the flour and add the water separately; 2 level teaspoons of powdered easy-blend – exactly the same as 2 teaspoons dried yeast – is the correct amount for each 1 lb (450 g) of flour. But yet another warning! Do inspect the date stamp carefully, as this will not do its work once it becomes stale.

SALT

◆

The quantity of salt you put into bread is determined by three considerations – your own taste, whether you're in a hurry and to some degree whether you use salted or unsalted butter to spread over it. Salt does slow down the action of the yeast (too much can actually kill it), so if you want to increase the salt in any of my recipes do allow extra rising time. Some people omit it altogether for health reasons: too much salt in a diet can exacerbate high blood pressure if this condition already exists.

LIQUID

◆

Water is most commonly used for bread; and occasionally milk or a combination of both. Milk in the mixture gives a softer crust and is better for soft rolls, baps and muffins. Liquid measurements can never be absolutely exact because different types of flour absorb different amounts.

SUGAR

◆

Sugar is always needed to activate dried (but not fresh or powdered easy-blend) yeast. For dried yeast use brown sugar for wholewheat loaves, and white for white bread mixes. Molasses or honey is sometimes used to give a different flavour and a moister loaf.

FATS

———— ◆ ————

Adding a small proportion of fat can very slightly enrich a dough and help it to stay fresh longer. Personally I find butter is best of all, but vegetable fat or lard if you prefer can be used instead. Proper enriched doughs are those that have quite a lot of fat in them, sometimes plus eggs and dried fruit (e.g. hot cross buns, malt loaves). The extra fat retards the growth of the yeast, so an extra quantity of yeast is used in this type of recipe.

HOW A LOAF OF BREAD IS MADE

———— ◆ ————

These notes apply to the traditional method of bread-making. However, later in this chapter, I have also given recipes for quick and simple loaves, dispensing with some of these stages.

FLOUR

This should be at room temperature, even slightly warmer, to speed things up. If your flour feels chilly, warm it in a low oven for 10 minutes (and if the bowl it's in gets too hot, tip it into another).

DRIED YEAST

The water for mixing with the yeast should be hand-hot, i.e. you can place your little finger into the water for a few seconds without it hurting. I find a mixture of half boiling and half cold water gives the right temperature. Measure it out and pour approximately one-third of it into another jug, add the sugar to this, then sprinkle in the dried yeast. Stir once and leave it until it forms a frothy head – this will probably take 10 minutes but might take a little longer. In order to raise the dough it must have at least ¾ inch (2 cm) of froth.

FRESH YEAST

Just add the yeast to the warm water before adding it to the flour.

EASY-BLEND YEAST

Simply sprinkle the powdered yeast into the flour and add the water.

MIXING

Add the salt to the flour and blend it in thoroughly – remember if you add extra salt to allow for extra rising time. Pour the yeast liquid in and mix to a dough, gradually adding the rest of the liquid, bearing in mind that as flours vary you may not need it all or you may well need a spot more. Add enough to make a smooth dough that will leave the bowl clean. If you've overdone the liquid and it's too slippery it doesn't matter a scrap: just sprinkle in some more flour.

KNEADING

For bread dough that has to be kneaded, simply place it on a flat work surface then stretch it away from you, using the heel of one hand to push from the middle and the clenched knuckles of your other hand to pull the other half of the dough towards you – both hands should move simultaneously to stretch out the dough. Then lift the edges over and back to the middle. Give it a quarter-turn and repeat the process. It soon becomes a rather rhythmic operation, and the dough will then start to become very elastic. This is the gluten at work. In simple language, the water meets the gluten and what makes it become springy and alive is a good pummelling. That's why if you're feeling angry bread-making can be most therapeutic! One point to bear in mind here is that refined flour has a larger proportion of gluten, so white bread dough will become more elastic and rise much more than a wholewheat dough. A properly kneaded piece of dough will look plump and rounded with a very smooth surface. If you're lazy, weak or just tired, a Kenwood mixer with a dough hook will do all this for you – as will a Magimix 5300 with a dough blade.

RISING

This is the period the dough must be left for the yeast to do its work: all yeast doughs need at *least an hour at room temperature* before baking or less in a warm place. I used to think how annoying it was that longer rising times produce better bread, though now I do feel it is sometimes more convenient to go away and leave it for a couple of hours. In the end you will make the sort of bread that fits into your own timetable. To speed up the rising it is best to leave the dough in a so-called 'warm' place. I use the plate-warming compartment of my cooker – but some may be too hot for this and care has to be taken because too high a temperature can kill off the yeast. Always cover the dough, either with a folded damp tea towel or with cling film. Alternatively you can completely encase the bowl inside a polythene bag such as a bin-liner (put a few drops of oil in the bag first to prevent the dough sticking). The Flour Advisory Bureau recommends that if no suitable warm place is forthcoming you wrap the bowl in a polythene bag, seal it and sit the whole thing in a larger bowl of warm water. (If you don't cover the dough, heat is lost and a skin can develop and, when you knead again, the dough will be lumpy.)

If you have more time to spare, the dough will rise at room temperature and perhaps be the better for it. You can even allow the dough to rise at a cold temperature, in the lower part of the fridge, covered in the same way. This is useful if you want to mix and knead the dough the night before, leave it to rise in the fridge, and shape and bake next morning. Dough, when risen properly, should have doubled in size and should spring back and feel very slightly sticky when lightly touched with the finger. Remember: the longer the rising time, the more uniformly the yeast will work and the more evenly textured the finished bread will be.

KNOCKING DOWN AND PROVING

Some recipes call for a second rising or 'proving', which is exactly what it is: the yeast proving it is still alive and active. The experts say that sometimes during the first rise a dough will expand unevenly (with a resulting loaf that is partly too open-textured, partly too close-textured). The proving ensures there will be an even rise. Knocking down is simply punching all the gas out of the dough and bringing it back to its original size, to allow it to rise for a second time in the bread tin. Again the dough will need to be covered, so place the tin or shaped loaf inside a sealed polythene bag.

BAKING

Bread tins should always be generously greased. I always use butter for this, and a piece of kitchen paper to spread it evenly all round the tins – especially in the ridges and corners. Always bake bread in a hot oven (from gas mark 6, 400°F, 200°C minimum, to gas mark 8, 450°F, 230°C maximum). Bear in mind it's always better to overcook rather than undercook bread: to test if a loaf is cooked, tap it on the under-side with your knuckles and, if it sounds hollow, it's done. If you like very crusty bread, then after you've turned the loaves out of their tins, pop them back in the oven upside down for 5–10 minutes (to bake the underneath and sides).

COOLING

Always cool bread on a wire cooling tray, otherwise on a flat surface the steam will be trapped and the crust will become soggy. Also a loaf that has not been properly cooled before freezing or storing can taste doughy. If you like very crusty bread don't wrap it or put it in a bread bin (provided you're going to eat it the same day). If you have to eat bread that has been stored for a day, you can revive the crustiness by placing it in a medium oven for 5–10 minutes.

STORING BREAD

———————◆———————

The best way to store a loaf for any length of time is in the freezer. I have a small 4-star freezing compartment above my fridge and I sometimes freeze bread for as little as 3 days – because once de-frosted it really is fresher than if kept in the bread bin for the same time. Otherwise I would recommend a stainless steel or aluminium bread bin, or roll-top container. But all these must have tiny air holes in them to keep bread for a reasonable period: if the moisture is not allowed to escape, mould can develop.

So much for the essential principles of bread-making, which I hope will answer most everyday queries. At the same time I wouldn't want anyone to be side-tracked into too many paths of perfection. Your loaves, buns and rolls may not win a prize at a Master Bakers' contest (I know mine wouldn't), but the pleasure they will give you and your family will make the small amount of effort worth while.

QUICK AND EASY WHOLEMEAL BREAD

———————◆———————

(Makes 1 large or 2 small loaves)

This recipe was inspired by Doris Grant in her excellent book *Your Daily Food*. Although it's quick and easy, it has a wonderful, wholesome, home-made flavour. For those of us who simply don't have the time for kneading, knocking down and proving, this loaf is an absolute gem and the one that I, personally, make most often.

1 lb stoneground wholewheat flour (450 g)
2 teaspoons salt
approx. 12–13 fl oz hand-hot water (355–380 ml)
1 teaspoon brown sugar
2 level teaspoons dried yeast or powdered easy-blend yeast or ½ oz fresh yeast (10 g)
a little extra flour

(For 3 lb/1.3 kg flour simply multiply the rest of the ingredients by three.)

You'll need one 2 lb (900 g) bread tin with a base measurement of 6½ × 3½ inches (16 × 9 cm) or two 1 lb (450 g) bread tins 5¼ × 3 inches (13.5 × 7.5 cm). The tin or tins should be buttered fairly thickly.

Begin by weighing the flour and mixing the salt into it so that it is fairly evenly distributed. Then warm the flour slightly in a low oven for about 10 minutes.

While the flour is warming, prepare the dried yeast (if using) by measuring 3 fl oz (75 ml) of the hand-hot water in a measuring jug. Stir the sugar in and sprinkle in the 2 teaspoons of yeast as well, stir once, then leave for 10–15 minutes until a good 1 inch (2.5 cm) of froth has formed. If you're using fresh yeast simply mix it with the 3 fl oz (75 ml) water to a smooth cream and it's ready. Easy-blend should be sprinkled evenly into the measured flour just before mixing.

Now tip the warm flour into a large mixing bowl, and make a well in the centre. Stir the yeast liquid once – to make sure it's dissolved – then pour it into the well and, starting with a wooden spoon, begin to mix the yeast liquid into the flour to form a dough, gradually adding the rest of the measured water. Finish off the mixing with your hands until you have a smooth dough that leaves the bowl clean, i.e. no bits of flour or dough remain on the side of the bowl. The exact amount of water you need depends on the flour. You can do the mixing with the dough hook of an electric hand whisk (or even in a mixer).

Now transfer the dough to the tin (or tins) by stretching it out to an oblong and folding one edge into the centre and the other edge over that. Fit the dough into the tin, pressing all round the edges so that the surface will already be slightly rounded. Next sprinkle the surface with a generous dusting of flour. Cover the tin with a damp tea towel and leave it to rise in a warm place for 30–40 minutes or at room temperature for approximately an hour.

Meanwhile pre-heat the oven to gas mark 6, 400°F (200°C), and when the dough has risen to within ¼ inch (5 mm) of the top of the bread tin (or to the very top if you are using a shallower loaf tin), bake the bread for 45 minutes if it's the larger size or 35 minutes for the smaller size. After that turn out the bread and return it to the oven, upside down, for a further 5–10 minutes to crisp the base and sides.

The loaves, if cooked, will sound hollow when tapped underneath. Cool the bread on a wire cooling tray and *never* put it away or freeze it until it's absolutely cold.

Note If you want to make a lighter textured loaf by the same method, all you do is use 8 oz (225 g) 100 per cent wholewheat flour and 8 oz (225 g) strong white flour and prepare it in exactly the same way as above.

PLAIN WHITE BREAD
♦

(Makes 2 loaves)

This is, for those who prefer the lighter texture of a plain white loaf (and indeed most people prefer it for toast), a basic white loaf recipe.

15 fl oz hand-hot water (425 ml)
1 teaspoon white sugar
2 level teaspoons dried yeast (or see page 38 for fresh and easy-blend)

1½ lb strong white flour (700 g), warmed slightly
1 level tablespoon salt, or less according to taste
½ oz butter (10 g)
a little extra flour

Two 1 lb (450 g) loaf tins, well-buttered.

Pour 5 fl oz (150 ml) of the hand-hot water into a bowl, then with a fork whisk in the sugar, followed by the dried yeast – and set this mixture aside to froth.

Meanwhile sift the flour and salt into a bowl and rub in the butter. When the yeast is ready, pour it into a well made in the centre of the flour, then pour in the remaining 10 fl oz (275 ml) of warm water. Now mix to a dough, starting off with a wooden spoon and using your hands in the final stages of mixing.

Wipe the bowl clean with the dough – adding a spot more water if there are any dry bits left – and transfer it to a flat work surface (there shouldn't be any need to flour this). Knead the dough for 10 minutes or until it develops a sheen and blisters under the surface (it should also be springy and elastic).

You can now either leave the dough on the surface covered by the upturned bowl or return the dough to the bowl and cover with polythene or cling film. Leave it until it looks as though it has doubled in bulk – 1½–2 hours at room temperature or 45–60 minutes in a warm place.

After that knock the air out, then knead again for 5 minutes. Now divide the dough in half, pat each piece out to an oblong, then fold one end in to the centre and fold the other end in on top. Put each one into a buttered tin, sprinkle each loaf with a dusting of flour, then place them side by side in an oiled polythene bag until the dough rises above the tops of the tins (30 minutes in a warm place or an hour at room temperature). Meanwhile pre-heat the oven to gas mark 8, 450°F (230°C).

Bake the loaves for 35–40 minutes or until they sound hollow when their bases are tapped. Return them, out of their tins, upside down to the oven to crisp the base and side crust. Then cool on a wire rack.

SOURED CREAM SODA BREAD

◆

(Makes 1 loaf)

I have a passion for Irish bread and always bring some back when I visit Dublin. The true Irish way of making this is with soured unpasteurised milk or buttermilk. The latter *is* available but not everywhere, so here I have used soured cream thinned down with water, which works perfectly. I happen to like a really rough soda bread, but if you prefer a lighter one, you can use a wheatmeal flour.

1 lb wholewheat flour (450 g), or for a lighter loaf use the same quantity of 85 per cent wheatmeal flour
2 teaspoons salt
1 teaspoon bicarbonate of soda
5 fl oz soured cream (150 ml)
5 fl oz water (150 ml) plus 2–3 extra tablespoons

Pre-heat the oven to gas mark 7, 425°F (220°C).

A greased baking sheet.

Begin by mixing the flour, salt and bicarbonate of soda thoroughly in a bowl. Then in a jug whisk the soured cream and 5 fl oz (150 ml) water together and stir this mixture into the flour together with 2–3 further tablespoons of water, if it needs it.

Knead the dough lightly (into a round ball) so as to get the surface smooth, then put it onto the prepared baking sheet. Cut halfway through the loaf with a sharp knife, one way, then do the same the other way forming a cut cross, which will form the loaf into four crusty sections.

Bake the loaf in the top half of the oven for 30 minutes – covering the top with foil for the last 5 minutes of the baking time, if the crust looks like it's getting too dark. Cool on a wire rack for a minimum of 15 minutes before eating. This is delicious cut in thick slices, buttered and spread with home-made lemon curd (page 544) or honey.

If you don't like a very crisp crust, wrap the bread in a tea towel while it cools, so that the steam it gives off softens the crust a little.

Note Soda bread is best eaten as fresh as possible: it's not a keeping loaf at all – though I'm sure there won't actually be any left to keep! If you can't get soured cream use 10 fl oz (275 ml) milk and 2 teaspoons cream of tartar in addition to the soda.

OATMEAL BREAD

♦

(Makes 2 small loaves)

This bread has a lovely wholesome flavour, just the thing for a snack lunch with some strong Cheddar cheese; it also makes delicious bacon sandwiches.

4 oz medium oatmeal (110 g)
10 fl oz milk (275 ml)
5 fl oz hand-hot water (150 ml)
1 teaspoon sugar
2 teaspoons dried yeast (or see page 38 for fresh and easy-blend)

10 oz wholewheat flour (275 g), warmed slightly
10 oz strong white flour (275 g), warmed slightly
1 dessertspoon salt
2 oz butter (50 g)
1 teaspoon honey
extra wholewheat flour and oatmeal

A floured baking sheet.

Start this about 4 or 5 hours ahead by combining the oatmeal and the milk in a bowl and leaving them to soak. Then to make the loaves, start by pouring the hand-hot water into a jug. Whisk in the sugar and then the yeast, and leave it for 10 minutes to get a good frothy head.

Then mix the two flours and the salt in a mixing bowl, making sure you mix them together very thoroughly. Then make a well in the centre of the flour.

Next gently warm the butter and honey together in a small saucepan until the butter becomes liquid, then pour this into the well in the flours, followed by the frothed yeast. Finally add the soaked oatmeal mixture, then mix everything together to form a smooth dough that leaves the bowl clean. If it's very stiff you may need a drop more milk. Now transfer the dough to a flat working surface and knead it for about 10 minutes: after that return it to the bowl and cover with a damp cloth or cling film. Leave it like this until the dough has doubled in bulk (about 90 minutes at room temperature or rather less in a warm place). Then knock and punch the air out and knead again for 5 minutes.

Next, divide the dough in half, and make each half into a round shape. Roll each loaf gently in some wholewheat flour, pressing in a light coating, then place both on a floured baking sheet. Use a sharp knife to make ¼ inch (5 mm) deep slashes across the top of each loaf. Place the baking sheet (and contents) inside an oiled plastic bag and let the dough prove for a further 1– 1½ hours (or 45 minutes in a warm place). Meanwhile pre-heat the oven to gas mark 8, 450°F (230°C).

Bake the loaves for 10 minutes, then turn down the heat to gas mark 4, 350°F (180°C), and bake for a further 30 minutes. Cool them thoroughly on a wire rack before cutting or storing.

POPPY SEED ROLLS

◆

(Makes 16 rolls)

Basically these are the familiar soft Vienna rolls – improved, I think, by a liberal sprinkling of poppy seeds.

10 fl oz hand-hot milk (275 ml)
1 teaspoon white sugar
2 teaspoons dried yeast (or see page 38 for fresh and easy-blend)
1 lb strong white flour (450 g), warmed slightly
2 teaspoons salt
4 oz butter (110 g), at room temperature
1 egg, beaten
2 tablespoons (approx.) poppy seeds

One large (or two small) baking sheets, well-greased.

Start by pouring 5 fl oz (150 ml) of the milk into a bowl and whisk the sugar into it with a fork, followed by the dried yeast. Leave this on one side for 10 minutes to froth. Meanwhile sift the flour and salt into a bowl, make a well in the centre, and (when it's ready) pour in the frothed yeast and milk, and the rest of the milk. Mix to form a smooth dough, then turn out onto a working surface and knead for 10 minutes.

After that put the dough back in the bowl, cover with cling film and leave it to rise until doubled in bulk (which will take 1½–2 hours at room temperature or 45–60 minutes in a warm place). Then punch the dough down in the bowl to knock the air out, and gradually work in the softened butter. The dough will now be very sticky, but ignore this and carry on until the butter is evenly worked in.

Next, turn it out onto a lightly floured work surface and knead into a round shape – divide this into sixteen sections. Roll each piece out into a long roll, and literally tie each roll into a knot. Place each roll on the baking sheet and brush with beaten egg. Now pop the baking sheet and rolls into an oiled polythene bag, and leave them to prove until puffy and risen again – about half an hour in a warm place or an hour at room temperature. Meanwhile pre-heat the oven to gas mark 5, 375°F (190°C).

Sprinkle the rolls with the poppy seeds and bake for about 20 minutes or until golden-brown. Cool on a wire cooling rack.

QUICK WHEATMEAL ROLLS

♦

(Makes 12 rolls)

The quick wholemeal bread on page 43 is not suitable for individual rolls because, without kneading, there's no elasticity in the dough and, during the rising time, it spreads itself out too much. This recipe does require 5–6 minutes' kneading but only one rise, so it's still relatively quick.

8 oz wholewheat flour (225 g)
8 oz strong white flour (225 g)
2 level teaspoons salt
10 fl oz hand-hot water (275 ml)
1 level teaspoon brown sugar
2 level teaspoons dried yeast (or see page 38 for fresh and easy-blend)
1 teaspoon butter
a little extra flour

One large or two small well-greased baking sheets.

Measure the flours into a bowl, add the salt and mix thoroughly together. Then warm the flour slightly in a low oven.

To prepare the yeast measure the hand-hot water into a jug, then pour half of it into another jug or bowl. Sprinkle the sugar and then the yeast into one lot of water, stir and leave aside till a good 1 inch (2.5 cm) frothy head has formed.

Now remove the flour from the oven, rub in the butter, then make a well in the centre, stir the yeast liquid and pour it into the well. Pour the other liquid into the yeast jug, to rinse it out, then add this to the flour, gradually stirring with a wooden spoon at first and then finishing off with your hands until you have a smooth dough that leaves the bowl cleanly.

Now transfer the dough onto a flat working surface and knead it thoroughly for about 6 minutes, by which time it will have become very elastic and springy.

Next divide the dough into twelve portions to form the rolls. If you want your rolls to be absolutely the same size, you can weigh the dough, divide the total weight by twelve and then weigh each individual piece. Stretch each piece into an oblong and fold one end into the middle and the other end over that. Then, with the folds underneath, slap the roll into a round ball. Place the rolls onto the well-greased baking sheet, cover with a sheet of oiled polythene, or encase the baking sheet inside an oiled pedal-bin liner. Leave the rolls to rise until they have doubled in size: 35–40 minutes in a warm place or 1–1½ hours at room temperature. Meanwhile pre-heat the oven to gas mark 7, 425°F (220°C).

When the rolls have risen, sprinkle them with flour and bake them on a high shelf of the oven for 20–25 minutes. They should sound hollow when you tap them underneath if they are cooked enough. Cool the rolls on a wire cooling rack.

MUFFINS

◆

(Makes 12)

Muffins always remind me of fireside teas in the depth of winter. I like to cook them on top of the stove, which is the traditional method, but if you haven't got a griddle, use a heavy frying-pan.

8 fl oz milk (225 ml)
2 fl oz water (55 ml)
1 teaspoon caster sugar
2 level teaspoons dried yeast (or see page 38 for fresh and easy-blend)
a little lard
1 lb strong plain flour (450 g)
1 rounded teaspoon salt
a little rice flour or ordinary flour

One large or two small floured baking sheets.

Measure the milk and water into a small saucepan and heat until just hand-hot. Pour it into a jug, add the sugar and dried yeast, mix it with a fork and leave it about 10 minutes to get a real frothy head.

Meanwhile sift the flour and salt into a large mixing bowl, make a well in the centre, then pour in the frothy yeast mixture and mix it to a soft dough – it should leave the bowl cleanly, but if it seems a bit sticky add a spot more flour. On the other hand, if it seems a little dry add just a spot more water.

Now transfer the dough to a flat surface and knead it for about 10 minutes, by which time it should be very smooth and elastic. The dough can go back into the bowl now. Just slip the bowl inside a large, oiled polythene bag, and leave it in a warm place until the dough has doubled in size. This will take about 45 minutes or longer, depending on the temperature.

When the dough has risen, lightly flour the work surface, then tip the dough out and roll it out to about 1/2 inch (1 cm) thick, then using a 3 inch (7.5 cm) plain cutter cut out twelve rounds, re-rolling the dough a couple of times again if it starts to get puffy. Mix the scraps and re-roll to use all the dough up.

Now place the muffins on an ungreased, lightly floured baking sheet, sprinkling them with a little rice flour, then cover with a plastic bag, loosely tied, and leave them to puff up again for about 25–35 minutes in a warm place.

When they are ready to be cooked, grease a thick-based frying-pan or griddle with just a trace of lard. Then heat the pan over a medium heat, add some muffins and cook them for about 7 minutes on each side, turning the heat down to low as soon as they go in. You'll need to do this in three or four batches, but they can be made well in advance.

If you want to serve them in the traditional way, all you do is break them just a little around their waists without opening them, then toast them lightly on both sides. The correct way to eat them is just to pull them apart without cutting and insert a lot of butter. You can store them in an airtight tin for about two days before toasting if you have any left over.

BREAKFAST BAPS

(Makes 12)

These are indeed good at breakfast; they're also good for hamburgers or for filling and taking on a picnic.

1 lb strong white flour (450 g)
1½ teaspoons salt
2 oz butter (50 g)
5 fl oz hand-hot water (150 ml)
5 fl oz hand-hot milk (150 ml)
1 teaspoon granulated sugar
2 teaspoons dried yeast (or see page 38 for fresh and easy-blend)
a little extra milk and flour

Two lightly-greased baking sheets.

Sift the flour and salt into a bowl, and rub the butter in until thoroughly blended. Now blend the water, milk and sugar together in another bowl, whisk in the yeast and leave on one side for 10 minutes to form a good head of froth.

Now make a well in the flour, stir the liquid into it until the mixture forms a smooth dough, then turn the dough onto a lightly floured surface and knead for about 10 minutes – or until the dough is silky smooth and feels very springy and elastic. Return it to the bowl, cover with a damp cloth or cling film and leave it until it's doubled in bulk (about 1½ hours at room temperature, or 50–60 minutes in a warm place). Meanwhile pre-heat the oven to gas mark 9, 475°F (240°C).

Knead the dough lightly and divide it into twelve equal pieces. Form each one into a ball and place them on the baking sheets – you should manage to get six on each baking sheet. Flour your hands and flatten the balls slightly into disc shapes. Then press a deep hole with your thumb in the centre of each bap (this prevents any blistering while it's cooking). Now brush each one with milk and sprinkle on a generous dusting of flour. Then put the baking sheets inside large oiled plastic bags for 20–25 minutes to prove.

Bake for 10 minutes so they are golden-brown under the floury tops. Transfer to a wire rack to cool, and eat them very fresh.

CHAPATTIS

◆

(Makes 12)

This is an anglicised version of the flat bread served with curry in India. Don't be put off because it sounds complicated. It's actually much easier and quicker than it sounds.

8 oz wholewheat flour (225 g)
1 teaspoon salt
about 5 fl oz cold water (150 ml)
a little lard

A frying-pan or griddle.

Simply mix the flour and salt in a bowl, then gradually add enough water to combine the mixture to a non-sticky dough. Transfer the dough to a work surface and knead for about 10 minutes. Then leave it, covered by the upturned bowl, to rest for 30 minutes. After that pre-heat the grill to high, then break up the dough and roll it into walnut-size pieces. Now roll out each piece on a lightly floured surface as thin as possible; just less than 1/8 inch (3 mm).

Next heat a frying-pan or griddle over a medium heat and grease lightly with a piece of lard paper. Put the pancakes on the hot surface, one at a time, and wait until bubbles start to rise in them, rather like cobblestones. Flip over and cook for about 15 seconds, then transfer each one to cook under the grill about 6 inches (15 cm) from the heat. They should immediately inflate to virtually a round ball. Then, when lightly browned, turn and cook the other side. To serve, as the bread collapses, transfer it to a warmed dish, lined with a napkin. Cover and take to the table.

Each chapatti should take about 1/2 minute to cook, so the total cooking time is only about 6 minutes.

BARA BRITH

◆

(Makes 1 loaf)

There are several different versions of this Welsh 'speckled bread'. Many of them don't contain yeast; but, for me, this version is the nicest and if there's any left over it's delicious toasted.

8 fl oz milk (225 ml)
2 oz brown sugar (50 g), plus 1 teaspoon
4 teaspoons dried yeast (or see page 38 for fresh)
1 lb strong plain flour (450 g)

1 teaspoon salt
3 oz butter or margarine (75 g)
1 teaspoon ground mixed spice
1 egg, beaten
12 oz mixed dried fruit (350 g)
clear honey, to glaze

A 2 lb (900 g) loaf tin, well-greased.

First warm the milk in a small saucepan till it's hand-hot, and then pour it into a bowl. Whisk in the teaspoon of sugar, followed by the yeast, then leave it in a warm place to froth for about 15 minutes.

Now sift the flour and salt into a large mixing bowl, stirring in the remaining 2 oz (50 g) of sugar as well. Then rub the fat into the dry ingredients until the mixture looks like fine breadcrumbs. Stir in the mixed spice next, then pour in the beaten egg and frothed yeast, and mix to a dough. Now turn the dough onto a floured surface and knead until smooth and elastic (about 10 minutes), then replace the dough in the bowl and cover with a damp cloth or some cling film. Leave in a warm place to rise until it has doubled in size – about 1½ hours.

After that turn the dough out and knock it down to get the air out, then gradually knead the fruit in and pat out to a rectangular shape. Roll it up from one short side to the other and put it in the loaf tin (seam-side down). Place the tin inside an oiled plastic bag and leave it to rise, until the dough has rounded nicely above the edge of the tin (about 30–45 minutes). Meanwhile pre-heat the oven to gas mark 5, 375°F (190°C).

When the dough has risen and springs back when pressed lightly with a floured finger, remove the bag; transfer the loaf to the oven and bake on the shelf below the centre for 30 minutes. Then cover the top of the loaf tin with foil to prevent it over-browning, and continue to bake for a further 30 minutes. Turn the loaf out, holding it in a tea cloth in one hand and tapping the base with the other. It should sound hollow – if it doesn't, pop it back upside down (without the tin) for 5 minutes more. Cool the loaf on a wire rack, and brush the top with clear honey, to make it nice and sticky, before the loaf cools. Slice thinly and serve buttered.

Note Easy-blend yeast is *not* suitable for this recipe.

HOT CROSS BUNS

(Makes about 12)

It's hard to believe the difference in home-made hot cross buns – they really are far better than any bought from a shop and a lot cheaper into the bargain! (Illus. opposite p. 128.)

2 oz caster sugar (50 g), plus 1 teaspoon
5 fl oz hand-hot water (150 ml)
1 level tablespoon dried yeast (or see page 38 for fresh)
1 lb plain flour (450 g)
1 level teaspoon salt
1 rounded teaspoon ground mixed spice
3 oz currants (75 g)
2 oz cut mixed peel (50 g)
1¹/₂–2 fl oz warmed milk (40–55 ml)
1 egg, beaten
2 oz butter (50 g), melted
For the glaze
2 tablespoons granulated sugar
2 tablespoons water

A greased baking sheet.

First stir the teaspoon of caster sugar into the hand-hot water, then sprinkle in the dried yeast and leave it until a good frothy 'beer' head forms.

Meanwhile sift the flour, salt and mixed spice into a mixing bowl and add the remaining 2 oz (50 g) of sugar, the currants and mixed peel. Then make a well in the centre, pour in the yeast mixture plus 1¹/₂ fl oz (40 ml) of milk (again hand-hot), the beaten egg and the melted butter. Now mix it to a dough, starting with a wooden spoon and finishing with your hands (add a spot more milk if it needs it).

Then transfer the dough onto a clean surface and knead it until it feels smooth and elastic – about 6 minutes. Now pop it back into the bowl, cover the bowl with a lightly oiled plastic bag, and leave it in a warm place to rise – it will take about an hour to double its original size. Then turn it out and knead it again, back down to its original size.

Divide the mixture into twelve round portions, arrange them on the greased baking sheet (allowing plenty of room for expansion), and make a deep cross on each one with a sharp knife. Leave them to rise once more, covering again with the oiled polythene bag for about 25 minutes. Meanwhile pre-heat the oven to gas mark 7, 425°F (220°C).

Bake the buns for about 15 minutes. Then, while they're cooking, melt the sugar and water for the glaze over a gentle heat, and brush the buns with it, as soon as they come out of the oven, to make them nice and sticky.

Note Easy-blend yeast is *not* suitable for this recipe. If you want to make more distinctive crosses, use a flour-and-water paste made with 4 oz (110 g) plain flour and approximately 3 tablespoons water. Roll out thinly and divide into small strips, dampening them to seal.

PIZZA

♦

One of the very nicest ways of eating bread is as a 'pizza' – freshly baked bread dough with delicious fillings melting and bubbling on top. There are, of course, hundreds of variations – tomatoes, cheese, olives, anchovies, chopped peppers, capers, sliced mushrooms, salami – anything and everything can be used. Below is a recipe for a plain pizza dough and then two of my own favourite fillings.

PIZZA DOUGH

♦

3–4 fl oz hand-hot water (75–110 ml)
¹/₄ teaspoon sugar
1¹/₂ teaspoons dried yeast (or see page 38 for fresh and easy-blend)
8 oz strong white flour (225 g)
1 level teaspoon salt
1 standard egg, beaten
1 teaspoon olive oil

First pour 3 fl oz (75 ml) of the hand-hot water into a basin and whisk in the sugar, followed by the yeast; then leave this mixture on one side for about 10–15 minutes until it gets a nice frothy head on it.

Meanwhile sift the flour and salt together in a mixing bowl. Then pour in the frothy yeast mixture and the beaten egg, and mix to a dough. (You may need to add just a spot of extra warm water – it depends on the flour – but, at the end, you should have a soft, pliable dough that leaves the bowl clean.) Then transfer the dough to a working surface and knead for about 10 minutes until it's silky smooth and fairly elastic.

Now replace the dough in the bowl and rub the surface all over with the oil. Then seal the top of the bowl with cling film – or cover with a clean, damp cloth – and put the dough in a warmish place to rise for about an hour, or until it has doubled in size.

Once the dough has risen (that is, doubled in size), knead it again for about 5 minutes, and then it's ready to use. No second rise is needed.

PIZZA WITH PEPPERONI AND MUSHROOMS

◆

(Serves 2–4 people)

1 quantity pizza dough (see page 55)
olive oil

For the tomato sauce
8 oz tin Italian tomatoes (225 g), drained
1 tablespoon tomato purée
1 teaspoon dried basil or oregano
salt and freshly milled black pepper

For the topping
4 oz Italian pepperoni sausage or salami (110 g)
1 small green pepper, de-seeded and finely chopped
1 tablespoon capers
2 oz mushrooms (50 g), thinly sliced
2 tablespoons freshly grated Parmesan cheese

Pre-heat the oven to gas mark 7, 425°F (220°C).

A shallow oblong tin, 10 × 11 inches (25 × 28 cm).

Prepare the pizza dough as described on page 55. Place the dough in the tin and push it out with your hands to line it completely, bringing it up at the edges and pinching it to make a sort of border to contain the filling. If the dough is very springy, be determined with it. Finally brush the base with oil.

Now, for the sauce, either liquidise the tomatoes or simply rub them through a sieve into a bowl. Then stir in the tomato purée and basil, taste and season with salt and freshly milled black pepper. Now spread the mixture all over the pizza base.

Next, skin and thinly slice the pepperoni (if you're using salami, slice thinly and cut the slices in half). Then arrange them over the top of the pizza, sprinkle on the chopped pepper, capers, sliced mushrooms and grated Parmesan, and again trickle a little oil all over the top. Leave the pizza on one side for about 10 minutes before baking in the oven for 15–20 minutes. Check that the bread base is cooked through to the centre by lifting the pizza up with a fish slice and taking a look. It's better to overcook a pizza slightly than to undercook it, and always serve straight from the oven.

PIZZA WITH MOZZARELLA, ANCHOVIES AND OLIVES

◆

(Serves 2–4 people)

Italian Mozzarella cheese is now widely available in most supermarkets, sold in little polythene sachets to keep it moist. It has a wonderful melting quality and provides the perfect creaminess to complement the strong, gutsy flavour of the other ingredients.

1 quantity pizza dough (see page 55)
olive oil
For the tomato sauce
1 Spanish onion, chopped
2 cloves garlic, crushed
2 × 14 oz tins Italian tomatoes (2 × 400 g)
1 teaspoon chopped fresh or ½ teaspoon dried basil
1 large bay leaf
salt and freshly milled black pepper
For the topping
4 oz Mozzarella cheese (110 g), cut in small pieces
2 oz tin anchovy fillets (50 g), drained and chopped
1 dozen black olives, pitted and halved
1 teaspoon dried oregano or 1 tablespoon chopped fresh basil
1 tablespoon freshly grated Parmesan cheese

Pre-heat the oven to gas mark 7, 425°F (220°C).

A shallow oblong tin, 10 × 11 inches (25 × 28 cm).

First prepare the sauce by heating 2 tablespoons of oil in a saucepan and frying the onion until softened and golden. Then stir in the remaining sauce ingredients and simmer gently (uncovered) for about an hour, or until the tomatoes have reduced to a jam-like consistency. Then take the pan off the heat, discard the bay leaf, and leave the sauce to cool.

Prepare the pizza dough as on page 55, then line the tin with it, working it over the base of the tin with your hands to line it completely and bringing it up at the edges then pinching to make a sort of border to contain the filling. Brush the base with oil, cover with the tomato sauce and spread it right up to the pinched edge. Next sprinkle the pizza with the Mozzarella, anchovies, olives, dried oregano and Parmesan, drizzle a tablespoon of oil over the top and leave at room temperature for 10–15 minutes before baking.

Bake the pizza for 15–20 minutes, then lift it up with a fish slice to check that the base is cooked through to the centre. Serve straight away.

QUICK WHOLEWHEAT PIZZA

♦

(Serves 2–4 people)

Wholewheat dough gives a different, somewhat more substantial pizza, something like the 'deep pan' variety. This one is perfect for slicing and taking on picnics, as it travels well and is easily eaten – as a kind of self-contained open sandwich.

8 oz wholewheat flour (225 g)
½ teaspoon salt
1 teaspoon dried mixed herbs
freshly milled black pepper
6 fl oz hand-hot water (175 ml)
1 teaspoon sugar
1 teaspoon dried yeast (or see page 38 for fresh and easy-blend)
For the tomato sauce
1 tablespoon olive oil
1 large onion, chopped
14 oz tin Italian tomatoes (400 g)
1 teaspoon dried basil
1 clove garlic, crushed
1 tablespoon tomato purée
For the topping
2 oz mushrooms (50 g), thinly sliced
2 oz Cheddar cheese (50 g), thinly sliced
2 oz tin anchovies (50 g), drained
6 black olives
a little extra olive oil and dried mixed herbs

A well-buttered 8 inch (20 cm) sandwich tin.

To make the base, combine the flour, salt, herbs and pepper in a bowl, then in a jug measure the hand-hot water and whisk in the sugar and yeast. Leave it to get a frothy head (about 10 minutes), then stir the frothed yeast into the dry ingredients and mix to a smooth dough. Then press it down into the well-greased sandwich tin, bringing the dough up the side of the tin. Now leave to rise, covered with a damp cloth, for about 25 minutes.

While that's happening pre-heat the oven to gas mark 7, 425°F (220°C), and make the tomato sauce. Heat the oil in a saucepan and soften the onion. Stir in the contents of the tin of tomatoes, followed by the basil and garlic, and simmer (uncovered) for 25 minutes or until the sauce has reduced to a very thick, jam-like consistency. Then add the tomato purée.

Now push the dough lightly back up the side of the tin if it has slipped during the rising, and spread the tomato sauce all over the base. Scatter the thinly sliced mushrooms over the top; lay the pieces of cheese over the mushrooms, then add the anchovies, making a rough criss-cross pattern. Next, drizzle a little more olive oil over everything and sprinkle with a few more mixed herbs and the olives.

Bake on a high shelf for about 20 minutes. Then serve piping hot with a crisp salad and some Italian wine to drink.

PISSALADIÈRE

♦

(Serves 2–4 people)

Just over the border from Italy, in the south of France, they have their own version of pizza – Pissaladière. This too is perfect for eating outdoors, perhaps cut into smallish portions for serving with pre-barbecue drinks (some chilled Provençal rosé would be the perfect match).

For the filling
4 tablespoons (approx.) olive oil
2 lb large onions (900 g), thinly sliced
1 fat clove garlic, crushed
salt and freshly milled black pepper

For the dough
8 oz strong white flour (225 g)
1 teaspoon salt
1 teaspoon dried herbs of Provence
freshly milled black pepper
6 fl oz hand-hot water (175 ml)
1 teaspoon brown sugar
1 teaspoon dried yeast (or see page 38 for fresh and easy-blend)

For the topping
2 oz tin anchovy fillets in oil (50 g)
1 dozen (approx.) black olives, pitted and halved
1 teaspoon dried mixed herbs

A Swiss roll tin 13 × 9 inches (33 × 23 cm), brushed with oil.

Make the filling first by heating the oil in a large saucepan. Stir in the onions and crushed garlic, then cook them over a gentle heat (uncovered) for about 30 minutes, stirring occasionally, or until the onions have just about formed a soft mass and show a tendency to stick to the base of the pan. Then take the pan from the heat and taste and season with salt and freshly milled pepper.

While the onions are cooking you can combine the flour, salt, herbs, and some freshly milled pepper together in a bowl. Pour 5 fl oz (150 ml) of the hand-hot water into a separate bowl and, using a fork, whisk in the sugar followed by the yeast. Leave on one side for 10 minutes to froth, then pour this into the flour mixture. Add a further 1 fl oz (25 ml) of hand-hot water and mix to form a dough. Knead well as described on page 55.

Then turn the dough out onto a lightly floured surface and roll out roughly to a shape 13 × 9 inches (33 × 23 cm). Place it in the tin, pushing it up the sides and into the corners with your fingers. Then brush the dough with some extra olive oil, cover with a clean cloth and leave in a warm place for 20–30 minutes to rise a little. Meanwhile pre-heat the oven to gas mark 7, 425°F (220°C).

Now spread the cooked onion filling over the base. Drain the tin of anchovies: reserve the oil and slice the fillets in half lengthways. Arrange them in a diamond-shaped pattern (like lattice-work) all over the onion filling, and stud each diamond with a halved, pitted olive. Sprinkle with the herbs and drizzle the reserved anchovy oil over the lot. Bake on a high shelf of the oven for 20–25 minutes. Serve hot or cold.

SEE ALSO

Crumpets

STOCKS AND SOUPS

◆

I can recall a time, not so long ago, when home-made soups seemed to be in a period of decline: perhaps the combination of increased affluence after the war and the advent of tinned, dehydrated and instant soups gave us less incentive to make our own. Thankfully I feel that home-made soups have now made a comeback. Where once we could overlook the bland uniformity of a ready-made soup at a price, in these days of world shortages and inflation we've grown more critical. I believe that you can spend either money or time on food, and lately many people have found they have had rather more time than money and that 30 minutes' preparation can produce a soup at half the cost of and with twice the flavour of a tin.

If there's one thing that's always evocative of homeliness and comfort it's real soup. But I do emphasise that it must be well made: simply throwing together any old hotch-potch of ingredients and calling it soup is a travesty. Care with the selection, and freshness, of the ingredients will reward you with a soup that is nourishing, satisfying and (particularly in the case of vegetable soups) low on the calories!

Strange, isn't it, that in spite of the advances in food technology there simply is not a tinned or packet soup that comes anywhere near the real thing. For all the recent restrictions on additives and colourings, commercial soups still contrive to taste synthetic.

Stocks are the basis of many soups (and indeed casseroles – see the chapter on these). Like soups, home-made stocks have been eclipsed by the huge range of commercial alternatives, and the dilemma facing us is the same. So first let's see what is involved in making stock at home.

STOCKS

◆

The first thing to say about making basic stock for soups and casseroles is that it is *not* as much bother as it sometimes sounds. For a start a proper stock-pot – the sort that needs endless boiling-up and skimming – isn't really needed in today's family kitchen. One occasional stock-making session is more useful. Freezer owners can freeze any surplus to use later.

All that is actually involved is bones, carcasses or giblets plus a few other ingredients being simmered, totally unattended. A rich brown

61

stock is the only one that requires the bones to be roasted first, and even this doesn't call for any real work. The results will produce goodness and flavour at a minimal cost, and will prove how well spent in these days of chemical flavourings just a few minutes of your own time can be.

Is Home-Made Stock Necessary?

Not always. Especially with many vegetable soups, bearing in mind that most vegetables have lots of good fresh flavour of their own, introducing a meat-flavoured stock can conflict with and spoil the original vegetable flavour. On the other hand, a meaty stock makes the world of difference to clear-based soups (like *Soupe à l'oignon* or *Minestrone*), and I nearly always use some sort of stock to give body to soups made with dried vegetables and pulses (see the Pulses chapter).

Stock Cubes

When this book was first published I wrote that, if I was making a soup containing the delicious juices and flavour of, say, carrots or leeks, I would not really wish to add ingredients like hydrolised protein, ribonucleotides and monosodium glutamate, which are constituents of the average stock cube. Ten years later I find the same ingredients are present, alongside the declaration that there are no artificial colours or preservatives. That statement may well be true, but there are still some odd things lurking in the average stock cube. The problem for me with these 'flavour enhancers' is that they cannot avoid introducing their own chemical flavours to compete with the natural flavour of other ingredients.

So, I am still against using stock cubes. However, of late some instant vegetable stock powders have come onto the market which are acceptable: they are available in health and wholefood shops, but you need to inspect the list of contents in them to discover which ones do not carry these alien tastes. If you cannot get hold of these – and you need some stock in a hurry – what you can do is boil a halved stalk of celery (plus leaves), a halved onion, a small carrot halved lengthways, a few parsley stalks, 6 peppercorns, a bay leaf and some salt in 1 pint (570 ml) cold water for 10 minutes, then strain.

SOME PRINCIPLES OF STOCK-MAKING

SIMMERING

An important word in the vocabulary of stock- and soup-making. Fast boiling can turn a stock very cloudy and murky, or ruin the delicate flavour of a fresh vegetable soup. So always keep everything at a *gentle* simmer.

SKIMMING

When you're boiling bones, giblets or a chicken carcass, a certain amount of scum inevitably rises to the surface. To get rid of this it's important to skim the surface right away. Quite easy to do: just slide a large spoon horizontally across the surface and gently lift off and discard the scum.

REMOVING FAT

Marrowbones, oxtails, neck of lamb etc. all give off a certain amount of fat while they're cooking, and there are two ways of dealing with this. First, if you allow the stock or soup to settle for about 30 minutes after cooking, you can skim some of the fat from the surface as above. What is also helpful here is to lay a double sheet of absorbent paper on the surface, to float as it were, and absorb the fat (sometimes it needs two or three lots to remove the fat completely). The other way, and this de-greases *more* thoroughly, is to leave the whole thing to cool overnight, and next morning you'll find the fat has solidified on the top and you can remove it completely.

REDUCING

If, after straining and de-greasing, you find your stock needs a more concentrated flavour, bring it back to the boil and simmer it without a lid so that some of the liquid evaporates and the stock reduces in volume. Be careful though not to add too much salt initially: the reducing process also concentrates the saltiness. So always season stocks *after* reduction.

STOCK FOR SAUCES

Stocks are also useful for sauces, casseroles or for cooking rice in to give extra body and flavour. A good chicken stock is essential for *Risotto alla Milanese* on page 277.

BROWN BEEF STOCK

◆

Butchers will chop up and sell you marrowbones for just a few pence, or they can sometimes be bought pre-packed in supermarkets.

3 lb beef marrowbones (approx. 1.5 kg), in pieces
2 large carrots, peeled and cut into chunks
2 onions, quartered
3 celery stalks, each cut into three pieces
4–5 pints cold water (2.25–2.8 litres)
a few parsley stalks
1 bay leaf
8 whole black peppercorns
1 blade mace
¼ teaspoon dried thyme
1 teaspoon salt

Pre-heat the oven to gas mark 8, 450°F (230°C).

Begin by placing the bones in a meat-roasting tin, tucking the chunks of carrot, quartered onion and celery in amongst them. Now, without adding any fat, just pop the roasting tin onto a high shelf in the oven and leave it there for 45 minutes, basting with the juices now and then. After that both the bones and the vegetables will have turned brown at the edges.

Now transfer them all to the very largest cooking pot you own, add enough cold water just to cover everything, add the rest of the ingredients and bring to the boil on top of the stove. As soon as it reaches boiling point remove the scum and lower the heat. Put the lid on but not completely (leave a little gap for the steam to escape, thereby reducing and concentrating the stock). Now simmer very gently for about 4 hours. When the stock is ready, strain it into a clean pan, leave it to become quite cold, then remove the congealed fat from the surface. The stock is now ready for use, or for freezing for later use.

Light beef stock

If you want a pale coloured stock, use the same ingredients as above and follow the same instructions but leave out the initial roasting of the bones and vegetables.

PRESSURE-COOKED BEEF STOCK

◆

This method, of course, cuts the cooking time down to an incredible 40 minutes. You can't make such a large quantity, but the resulting stock will have a more concentrated flavour and you can dilute it afterwards.

64

2¹/₂ lb beef marrowbones (1.25 kg), in pieces
2 pints cold water (1.2 litres)
1 small onion
1 carrot, cut into chunks
1 celery stalk, halved (plus leaves)
1 small bunch parsley stalks
1 bay leaf
5 whole black peppercorns
1 small blade mace
1 teaspoon salt

Place the bones (which can be browned in the oven first if you want a brown stock) in the pressure cooker along with the water. Bring to the boil, then remove any scum with a spoon. Now add the remaining ingredients, put the lid on the cooker and bring to pressure. Then place the 15 lb (6.75 kg) weight on and cook for 40 minutes. Reduce the pressure by allowing the cooker to cool slightly, then place it under cold running water to release. Strain the stock, leave to cool, then remove the fat from the surface.

CHICKEN GIBLET STOCK

◆

Chicken giblets can be bought in frozen packets from supermarkets specifically for stock. If you own a freezer it's always useful to have a packet to hand. The general rule is to use 1 pint (570 ml) water per set of giblets, or if you're buying frozen giblets use 6 oz (175 g) giblets per pint (570 ml) water. If you are using fresh giblets and don't need the liver for making a stuffing, do add it to the stock as well – I think it adds a real richness of flavour.

12 oz chicken giblets (350 g), washed
2 pints cold water (1.2 litres)
1 carrot, cut into chunks
1 onion, quartered
1 celery stalk, halved
1 leek, cleaned and sliced
6 whole black peppercorns
a few parsley stalks
2 pinches mixed dried herbs or 1 sprig fresh thyme
³/₄ teaspoon salt

Just put everything into a large cooking pot, bring to the boil, skim the surface to remove any scum, then simmer gently with the lid almost on for 2 hours. After that strain the stock, cool it and remove the fat from the surface before using or freezing.

Chicken carcass stock
Use the same vegetables, herbs and flavourings as in the above recipe, adding them to the cooking pot along with the broken-up carcass of the bird (plus any odd bits of bone and skin). Add enough cold water to cover, then proceed as above.

Pressure-cooked chicken stock
Proceed as above with vegetables, herbs and flavourings and either giblets or carcass, plus 2 pints (1.2 litres) of water. Bring to pressure and cook with 15 lb (6.75 kg) pressure for 30 minutes.

TURKEY GIBLET STOCK
◆

the giblets (including the liver) and neck of the turkey
1 onion, halved
1½ pints cold water (850 ml)
a few parsley stalks
a chunk of celery stalk and a few leaves
1 bay leaf
6 whole black peppercorns
salt

Wash the giblets first, then place them in a saucepan with the halved onion, cover with 1½ pints (850 ml) of water and bring to simmering point. Then remove any surface scum with a slotted spoon, add the remaining ingredients, half cover the pan and simmer for 1½–2 hours. After that strain the stock, and bring up to boiling point again before using to make the gravy.

Turkey carcass stock
For this you need your largest cooking pot. Break up the carcass as far as you can and add to the pot with the same ingredients as for *Chicken carcass stock* (see above). Put in enough cold water to cover, bring up to simmering point, skim and cook for 2 hours. Then strain and make a *Turkey soup*, using 1 lb (450 g) vegetables to each pint (570 ml) of stock. A combination of chopped swede, carrot, onion and leek sweated in some turkey dripping, then simmered in stock for 1½–2 hours before puréeing, makes a delicious soup.

FISH STOCK

— ◆ —

Use this as the basis for all kinds of fish soup, sauces and rice dishes.

1 lb fish trimmings (450 g), whatever your fishmonger can rustle up for you
1 pint water (570 ml)
5 fl oz dry white wine (150 ml)
1 onion, quartered
2 celery stalks, chopped
a few parsley sprigs
1 bay leaf
¼ teaspoon dried thyme
salt and freshly milled black pepper

Simply place the fish trimmings in a large pan, with the water, wine and the rest of the stock ingredients, season with salt and pepper, then bring up to simmering point. Simmer for about 20 minutes (without a lid on), then strain and reserve the stock.

Shellfish stock
This is particularly good and can be made simply with the above ingredients, substituting whatever prawn shells you have left over after peeling prawns for the 1 lb (450 g) of fish trimmings.

SOUPS

— ◆ —

Fortunately soup-making at home calls for very little in the way of equipment and makes only brief demands on your time. The only real essential is to have the freshest ingredients to start with.

SOME PRINCIPLES OF SOUP-MAKING

Sweating
I have found that a better flavour is produced in vegetable soups if the chopped vegetables are stirred into a little melted butter quite thoroughly until they're all glistening and well coated. Then, with a little salt added, they are placed over the gentlest heat possible and the pan is covered. The heat then draws out the natural juices and the vegetables become softened before the liquid is added. Care is needed for this, because too much heat will cause the vegetables to brown and spoil:

so to prevent this you need to take off the lid from time to time and just stir them around. This process is called 'sweating'.

Blending and puréeing

There are several ways to purée a soup. First of all, a good old-fashioned sieve will serve you very well: the contents of a soup pan can be pressed through it in a few minutes, especially if you use a ladle to do the squashing. Sieves can be difficult to wash, though, and perhaps a more satisfactory method is to whizz the soup to a purée in an electric liquidiser (blender). If you are using one of these, do remember that liquidising is liable to reduce food to a velvet-smooth consistency. Nearly everyone who likes to cook seems to own a food processor nowadays (see page 17). They are ideal if you want not too uniform a texture; for a velvet-smooth soup they take much longer than blenders and you do need to check very carefully for errant lumps after blending.

Soups for health

Vegetables are the ideal food to provide lots to eat with less calories. I have found that it is perfectly possible to make delicious and satisfying vegetable soups that contain no fat, and are therefore particularly low on calories. Simply combine 1 lb (450 g) mixed vegetables with 1 pint (570 ml) vegetable stock, and barely simmer for as long as possible – 3 hours would be ideal. Whizz to a purée in a blender, then season to taste. This long, slow cooking really draws all the flavour out of the vegetables.

You can now buy packets of ready chopped root vegetables specifically for this purpose in supermarkets. Alternatively, a good combination is carrots, swede, leeks, onion and celery.

Rescue operations

Beware of over-seasoning a soup, especially (a) if you are using a stock that's already seasoned and (b) if you are reducing the stock or soup. A concentration of flavour will also mean a concentration of seasoning, and it's very easy to end up with a soup that's too salty. I recommend tasting and seasoning right at the end.

If for these or any other reasons you have *over-salted* a soup, you have two possibilities. One is to add more unsalted liquid to dilute the salty flavour, though this way you risk also diluting the overall flavour. The other is to add a couple of raw potatoes cut in half and allow these to cook gently in the soup. They will absorb quite a bit of saltiness which may put things right. Remember to remove the potatoes before serving.

If a soup is *too thin*, removing the lid and allowing it to simmer gently will reduce and thicken (as described on page 63). Or, if you're short of time, you can make up a paste by mashing together softened butter and flour (say 1 tablespoon of each), then use a balloon whisk to whisk the paste into the soup; when it comes up to simmering point the soup will have thickened. Alternatively you can use arrowroot. This thickens liquid without clouding it – so it is the best choice for thickening a clear soup (see the recipe for *Chinese mushroom soup*, page 84).

Another fast way to thicken anything, when you're in a hurry, is to add some ground rice. What is so good about this is that you can just plonk a couple of tablespoons of ground rice into the hot liquid (it won't go lumpy) and whisk with a balloon whisk till sufficiently thickened – and if not, add a bit more.

If on the other hand your soup is *too thick*, you can thin it down with milk or stock, or even plain water.

Having said all this, let me now reassure you that by following the recipes with care you should have none of these problems!

LEEK, ONION AND POTATO SOUP
♦

(Serves 4–6 people)

This has to be one of my own favourites. Because I think butter has an affinity with leeks, I have been quite generous here – but the amount I've used could be halved.

4 large leeks
2 medium potatoes, peeled and diced
1 medium onion, chopped small
2 oz butter (50 g)
1½ pints light chicken stock or water (850 ml)
10 fl oz milk (275 ml)
salt and freshly milled black pepper
To serve
1½ tablespoons snipped chives (or, if unavailable, chopped parsley)
2 tablespoons cream or top of the milk

Trim off the tops and roots of the leeks, discarding the tough outer layer. Now split them in half lengthways and slice them up quite finely, then wash them thoroughly in two or three changes of water. Drain well.

In a large thick-based saucepan gently melt the butter, then add the leeks, potatoes and onion, stirring them all around with a wooden spoon so they get a nice coating of butter. Season with salt and pepper, then cover and let the vegetables sweat over a very low heat for about 15 minutes.

After that add the stock and milk, bring to simmering point, put the lid back on and let the soup simmer very gently for a further 20 minutes or until the vegetables are soft – if you have the heat too high, the milk in it may cause it to boil over. Now you can either put the whole lot into a liquidiser and blend to a purée, or else press it all through a sieve.

Return the soup to the saucepan and reheat gently, tasting to check the seasoning, and stirring in the snipped chives and adding a swirl of cream just before serving.

Note The chilled version of this soup is called *Vichyssoise*.

CHILLED AVOCADO SOUP
♦

(Serves 6 people)

This makes a lovely first course at a dinner party at any time of the year. It looks very pretty served in glass bowls to show off its pale pistachio green colour.

2 medium, ripe avocado pears
1 clove garlic, crushed
1 tablespoon lemon juice
1 pint cold chicken stock (570 ml)
10 fl oz soured cream (275 ml) or half
Greek yoghurt and half soured cream
salt and freshly milled black pepper

First halve the avocado pears, remove the stones and scoop out all the flesh – it's very important that you take care to scrape out all the very greenest part next to the skins, because this is what makes the soup such a lovely colour. Now chop the flesh roughly, and put it into the goblet of the liquidiser with the garlic, lemon juice, half the chicken stock and some salt and pepper.

Blend at high speed for about 15 seconds, then empty the contents into a soup tureen or bowl. Now stir in the soured cream and the rest of the stock, then whisk it a bit to get it all blended evenly. Cover the soup and chill very thoroughly for several hours. Serve it with one or two cubes of ice stirred in at the last minute.

Note Only make this soup on the day you intend to eat it, because if it's kept too long it tends to discolour.

CHILLED BEETROOT CONSOMMÉ

— ◆ —

(Serves 6 people)

This summer soup requires no fat for cooking and is suitable for slimmers if low-fat yoghurt is used at the end. Be sure to use *raw* beetroot.

1½ lb raw beetroot (700 g), peeled and chopped
10 large spring onions, chopped
a sprig of thyme
1 clove garlic, crushed
a few parsley stalks
1 bay leaf
a 2 inch (5 cm) strip thin orange rind
2½ pints water (1.5 litres)
1 cucumber
1 tablespoon red wine vinegar
1 tablespoon lemon juice
salt and freshly milled black pepper
To garnish
5 fl oz natural yoghurt (150 ml)
2 tablespoons snipped chives

Put the prepared beetroot in a large saucepan with the chopped spring onions, the thyme, garlic, parsley, bay leaf and orange rind, then pour in the water. Bring to the boil and simmer gently, uncovered, for about 1 hour. At the end of this time the beetroot will have lost its redness and have a pale look. Now peel and dice the cucumber, add it to the soup and simmer for about 10 minutes.

Next, have ready a large sieve set over a suitable bowl: pour the soup through the sieve and leave it to drain through. You should now have a good clear soup. Season to taste and add the vinegar and lemon juice to sharpen the flavour. Chill well and serve with a marbling of yoghurt and a garnish of snipped chives.

MINESTRONE WITH MACARONI

— ◆ —

(Serves 4-6 people)

I think a good home-made minestrone, in spite of its peasant origins, is in the luxury class simply because of its rarity. Serve it with coarse Italian-type bread and lots of freshly grated Parmesan to sprinkle over and you will have a very filling, satisfying treat.

2 oz streaky bacon (50 g), de-rinded and finely chopped
1 medium onion, finely chopped
2 celery stalks, finely chopped
6 oz carrots (175 g), finely chopped
2 tomatoes, fresh or from a tin, chopped
1 clove garlic, crushed
8 oz leeks (225 g), washed and finely chopped
6 oz green cabbage (175 g), finely shredded
25 g (1 oz) butter
1 tablespoon olive oil
2½ pints any good home-made stock (1.5 litres)
1½ tablespoons chopped fresh or ½ teaspoon dried basil
3 oz shortcut macaroni (75 g)
1 dessertspoon tomato purée
2 tablespoons chopped parsley
salt and freshly milled black pepper

To serve
lots of grated Parmesan cheese

First heat up the butter and oil in a large saucepan, then add the bacon and cook this for a minute or two before adding the onion, followed by the celery and carrots and then the tomatoes. Now stir in the crushed garlic and some salt and pepper, then cover and cook very gently for 20 minutes or so to allow the vegetables to sweat – give it an occasional stir to prevent the vegetables sticking.

Then pour in the stock along with the basil. Continue to simmer gently (covered) for about 1 hour. After that add the leeks, cabbage and macaroni and cook for a further 30 minutes.

Finally stir in the tomato purée, cook for another 10 minutes and, just before serving, stir in the parsley. Serve in warmed soup bowls and sprinkle with Parmesan cheese.

Note In the autumn finely chopped courgettes – instead of the cabbage – make a nice change.

SOUPE À L'OIGNON GRATINÉE
◆

(Serves 6 people)

This is so French that I've kept its original title. It's very filling and warming but remember that only fireproof soup bowls can safely go under the grill. You can use either six individual bowls or a large fireproof tureen (provided it's not too tall to go under the grill!) (Illus. opposite p. 129.)

1½ lb onions (700 g), thinly sliced
2 cloves garlic, crushed
2 oz butter (50 g)
2 tablespoons oil
½ teaspoon granulated sugar
2 pints good beef stock (1.2 litres)
10 fl oz dry white wine (275 ml)
salt and freshly milled black pepper
1–2 tablespoons brandy (optional)
To serve
6 large croûtons French bread (see page 98)
butter
8 oz Gruyère cheese (225 g), grated

In a large thick-based saucepan heat the butter and oil together. Add the prepared onions, garlic and sugar and cook over a low heat, stirring occasionally, for approximately 30 minutes or until the bottom of the pan is covered with a nutty brown, caramelised film. (This browning process improves both the colour and flavour.)

Next add the stock and wine, bring to the boil and simmer, covered, over a low heat for about 1 hour. Season to taste and, if you feel in need of something extra specially warming, add 1–2 tablespoons of brandy.

When you're ready to serve the soup, bring it up to simmering point and ladle it into six individual fireproof soup bowls (or one big one). Then place a croûton in each bowl, where it will float. Smother the croûtons with the grated cheese and place the whole lot under the grill until the cheese is bubbly and golden. Serve immediately.

WATERCRESS CREAM SOUP
◆

(Serves 4–6 people)

This is excellent at a dinner party and can, if you prefer, be served well chilled.

2 bunches watercress, de-stalked and chopped (reserve 4 sprigs for garnishing)
the white parts of 3 large leeks – approx. 1 lb (450 g), washed and chopped
2 medium potatoes, peeled and chopped
2 oz butter (50 g)
1½ pints very light chicken stock or water (850 ml)
5 fl oz double cream (150 ml)
salt and freshly milled black pepper

Melt the butter in a thick-based saucepan, then add the prepared leeks, potatoes and watercress and stir them around so that they're coated with the melted butter. Add some salt, cover with a lid and let the vegetables sweat over a low heat for about 20 minutes, giving the mixture a stir about half-way through.

After that, add the stock (or water), bring to simmering point and simmer, covered, for a further 10–15 minutes or until the vegetables are quite tender. Remove from the heat and when cool liquidise the soup – but not too vigorously. Return the soup to the saucepan, stir in the cream, season to taste and reheat gently. When serving, garnish each bowl with a watercress sprig.

SCOTCH BROTH

◆

(Serves 6–8 people)

This soup really needs to be made a day in advance – so that the fat can be lifted off the surface easily when the soup is cold. Reheat and you'll have one of the best winter 'stomach warmers' I know.

2 lb neck of lamb (900 g), cut into even-sized pieces
3 pints cold water (1.75 litres)
2 oz pearl barley (50 g), rinsed
1 large carrot
1 medium turnip
1 medium onion
3 leeks
¹/₂ small white cabbage
salt and freshly milled black pepper
To garnish
chopped parsley

Place the meat in a deep saucepan together with the cold water. Bring to the boil and skim off any scum which appears on the surface, then add the rinsed barley together with a little seasoning. Put a lid on the pan but tilt the lid slightly so that some of the steam can escape, then simmer, very gently, for about 1 hour.

Meanwhile prepare the vegetables: peel the carrot, turnip and onion and cut into ¹/₄ inch (5 mm) dice. Now trim the leeks, cutting off the root and leaving about 2 inches (5 cm) of green at the top. Halve lengthways, cut into small pieces, wash thoroughly, then drain well. Slice the cabbage thinly and wash and drain that well too.

When the broth has been cooking for 1 hour, add the vegetables. Bring to the boil again, half cover the pan with a lid and simmer gently until the vegetables are tender (about 45–60 minutes). Then remove from the heat and set aside to cool slightly.

Using a draining spoon, take out the meat and place it on a plate. Now separate the flesh from the bones, discard any fat and gristle as well as the bones, and return the meat to the pan. Leave until the soup is cold and the fat has solidified on top; scrape off the fat.

When required, reheat the broth, season to taste and serve piping hot with a sprinkling of chopped parsley on top.

ELIZA ACTON'S VEGETABLE MULLIGATAWNY

◆

(Serves 4 people)

Eliza Acton is one of my very favourite cookery writers and this is a recipe I've adapted from her cookery book published in 1840.

3 large onions, chopped
4 oz butter (110 g)
1½ lb peeled marrow or unpeeled courgettes (700 g)
1 large potato
8 oz tomatoes (225 g), peeled and chopped
long-grain rice measured to the 3 fl oz (75 ml) level in a measuring jug
boiling water measured to the 6 fl oz (just over 150 ml) level in a measuring jug
15 fl oz stock or water (425 ml)
1 dessertspoon Worcestershire sauce
1 teaspoon Madras curry powder
salt and freshly milled black pepper
To serve
small croûtons

First melt the butter in a large saucepan, then add the chopped onions and cook until they're a golden-brown colour. Meanwhile cut up the marrow into 1 inch (2.5 cm) cubes and peel and dice the potato. Now add these to the onions together with the tomatoes. Season well, then let the vegetables cook (covered) over a low heat until soft – about 20–30 minutes.

In the meantime put the rice in another saucepan with some salt, pour on the measured boiling water, bring to the boil, cover and cook gently until all the liquid is absorbed and the rice is tender.

Next, when the vegetables are cooked, turn them into a liquidiser and reduce to a purée. Then pour the purée back into the saucepan and stir in the cooked rice together with the stock, Worcestershire sauce and curry powder. This soup should have quite a strong flavour, so season to taste and add more curry powder if you think it needs it.

Reheat gently, cook for about 5 minutes more, then serve with some crisp croûtons of bread sprinkled in each bowl.

PUNCHNEP SOUP
◆

(Serves 6–8 people)

Punchnep soup is derived from a Welsh dish of puréed potatoes combined with puréed swedes or turnips (see page 266). In this recipe I have adapted the mixture to a soup, and I like it best with turnips.

1½ lb turnips (700 g), peeled and weighed after peeling
the white parts of 2 leeks
1 large potato, peeled – approx. 8 oz (225 g) after peeling
2 oz butter (50 g)
1 pint hot water (570 ml)
1 pint milk (570 ml)
freshly grated nutmeg
salt and freshly milled black pepper
To serve
2–3 tablespoons double cream

First split the leeks in half lengthways and cut into pieces of about ¼ inch (5 mm), wash well in cold water and drain in a colander. Then cut the peeled turnips and potato into cubes.

Next melt the butter in a thick-based saucepan, add the vegetables and stir them around so that they're well coated with the butter. Season with a little salt and pepper, cover with a lid and, keeping the heat very low, cook gently for 15 minutes, stirring from time to time. Now pour in the hot water and milk, bring to simmering point and simmer, again gently, for approximately 15 minutes or so until the vegetables are absolutely tender.

Then liquidise the soup or rub it through a sieve placed over a large bowl. Rinse the saucepan, return the purée to the pan and reheat slowly. Season to taste with salt and freshly milled black pepper and some freshly grated nutmeg. Make sure the soup is piping hot, then stir in a swirl of cream just before serving.

GARDENER'S SOUP

◆

(Serves 6–8 people)

This is a soup for autumn when there's nearly always a glut of tomatoes and the over-ripe ones are sold cheaply; or, as the title suggests, it's helpful for the gardeners whose tomato and cucumber crops threaten to overwhelm them.

12 oz ripe tomatoes (350 g)
12 oz cucumber (350 g), peeled and chopped
1 oz (25 g) butter
1 tablespoon oil
1 small onion, finely chopped
1 clove garlic, crushed
the outside leaves of a lettuce, shredded
1 medium potato, peeled and chopped
1 dessertspoon lemon juice
1 teaspoon dried basil
1 pint hot water (570 ml), mixed with 1 teaspoon tomato purée
2 teaspoons chopped parsley
salt and freshly milled black pepper

First drop the tomatoes into boiling water, then, after one minute, slip the skins off and chop the flesh roughly. Now in a thick-based saucepan melt the butter with the oil and soften the onion in it for 5 minutes. Next add the garlic, lettuce, cucumber, tomatoes and potato. Stir everything around, add seasoning and lemon juice, then pop the lid on and, keeping the heat low, let the vegetables sweat for a good 15 minutes.

Then add the basil and the hot water mixed with tomato purée, bring it up to simmering point, cover and simmer gently for a further 20 minutes or until the vegetables are soft.

Now pour the soup into a liquidiser, but only liquidise it for 6–8 seconds (the vegetables should be in very fine bits). Then sprinkle with parsley and serve hot with some fresh, crusty bread.

SMOKED BACON AND LENTIL SOUP

◆

(Serves 4–6 people)

This is a very substantial soup, best made with whole lentils which are a greeny-brown colour and don't need any soaking.

6 rashers smoked, streaky bacon, de-rinded and finely chopped
6 oz whole green-brown lentils (175 g), washed and drained
1 tablespoon oil
2 carrots, chopped
2 medium onions, chopped
2 celery stalks, sliced
8 oz tin Italian tomatoes (225 g)
2 cloves garlic, crushed
3 pints home-made stock (1.75 litres)
8 oz cabbage (225 g), finely shredded
2 tablespoons chopped parsley
salt and freshly milled black pepper

Heat the oil in a large cooking pot and fry the bacon in it until the fat begins to run. Then stir in the prepared carrots, onions and celery and, with the heat fairly high, toss them around to brown them a little at the edges. Now stir in the washed, drained lentils plus the contents of the tin of tomatoes followed by the crushed garlic then the stock.

As soon as the soup comes to the boil, put a lid on and simmer, as gently as possible, for about 1 hour. About 15 minutes before the end add the cabbage. Taste and season. Just before serving stir in the chopped parsley.

CHILLED SPANISH GAZPACHO

◆

(Serves 6 people)

This is a truly beautiful soup for serving ice-cold during the summer and it's particularly refreshing if we're lucky enough to have hot weather. However, please don't attempt to make it in the winter as the flavourless imported salad vegetables will not do it justice.

1½ lb firm ripe tomatoes (700 g)
4 inch piece of cucumber (10 cm), peeled and chopped
2 or 3 spring onions, peeled and chopped
2 cloves garlic, crushed

½ large red or green pepper, de-seeded and chopped

1 heaped teaspoon chopped fresh basil, marjoram or thyme (depending on what's available)

4 tablespoons olive oil

1½ tablespoons wine vinegar

approx. 10 fl oz cold water (275 ml)

salt and freshly milled black pepper

For the garnish

½ large red or green pepper, de-seeded and very finely chopped

4 inch piece of cucumber (10 cm), peeled and finely chopped

2 spring onions, finely chopped

1 hard-boiled egg, finely chopped

1 heaped tablespoon chopped parsley

salt and freshly milled black pepper

To serve

4 ice cubes

small croûtons

Begin by placing the tomatoes in a bowl and pouring boiling water over them; after a minute or two the skins will loosen and you can slip them off very easily. Halve the tomatoes, scoop out and discard the seeds and roughly chop the flesh.

Now place the tomatoes, cucumber, spring onions, crushed garlic and chopped pepper in a liquidiser, adding a seasoning of salt and pepper, the herbs, oil and wine vinegar. Then blend everything at top speed until the soup is absolutely smooth. (If your liquidiser is very small combine all the ingredients first, then blend in two or three batches.) Taste to check the seasoning and pour the soup into a bowl. Stir in a little cold water to thin it slightly – anything from 5 to 10 fl oz (150 to 275 ml) – then cover the bowl with foil and chill thoroughly.

To make the garnish, simply combine all the ingredients together with a seasoning of salt and freshly milled black pepper, and hand them round at the table together with small croûtons of bread fried till crisp in olive oil, well drained and cooled. Serve the soup with four ice cubes floating in it.

FRESH TOMATO SOUP WITH BASIL

♦

(Serves 4 people)

When I first wrote on cookery a reader wrote to the Editor of my newspaper, complaining my recipe for tomato soup didn't work. Rather conscientiously the Editor took the recipe home to try. He wrote to me saying, 'I've made your tomato soup and – its delicious!'

1½ lb ripe tomatoes (700 g), quartered (leave the skins on)
1 medium onion, chopped small
1 medium potato, chopped small
1½ tablespoons olive oil (preferably good quality)
10 fl oz stock (275 ml)
1 clove garlic, crushed
2 teaspoons chopped fresh basil
salt and freshly milled black pepper

Gently heat the olive oil in a thick saucepan, add the onion and potato and soften them slowly without browning. This takes 10–15 minutes.

Now add the tomatoes, stir well and let them cook for a minute. Pour the stock over the tomatoes, stir, season with salt and pepper and add the garlic. Cover and allow to simmer for 25 minutes.

When the soup is ready, pass the whole lot through a sieve to extract the skins and pips. Taste to check the seasoning, add the basil, then re-heat and serve with crusty French bread. If the weather is hot, this soup is just as delicious served ice-cold.

Note If you cannot get fresh basil use 1 teaspoon of dried, adding it at the same time as the tomatoes.

CARROT AND ARTICHOKE SOUP

♦

(Serves 6–8 people)

This not only has a delicious, very creamy texture and flavour, but you also have an added bonus because of its beautifully rich saffron colour.

1½ lb Jerusalem artichokes (700 g)
1 lb carrots (450 g)
3 oz butter (75 g)
1 medium onion, chopped
3 celery stalks, chopped
2½ pints light stock (1.5 litres)
salt and freshly milled black pepper

Start by peeling and de-knobbling the artichokes and, as you peel them, slice them into a bowl of cold water to prevent them discolouring.

Scrape and slice the carrots. In a cooking pot melt the butter, soften the onion and celery in it for 5 minutes, then stir in the carrots and artichokes. Add some salt and, keeping the heat low, put the lid on and let the vegetables sweat for 10 minutes. Then pour in the stock, stir well, put the lid back on and simmer for a further 20 minutes or until the vegetables are soft.

Now either liquidise the soup or pass it through a sieve. Taste to check the seasoning, reheat and serve.

CREAM OF CELERY SOUP
◆

(Serves 4 people)

Since EC regulations took effect our delicious Fenland celery is not allowed to be called that, so my local greengrocer refers to it quite affectionately as 'dirty celery' which it is of course. But once washed it has the best flavour in the world.

12 oz trimmed celery stalks (350 g), leaves reserved
4 oz potatoes (110 g), peeled and cut into chunks
the white parts of 2 medium leeks, cleaned and sliced
1 oz butter (25 g)
1 pint chicken stock (570 ml)
¼ teaspoon celery seeds
5 fl oz single cream (150 ml)
5 fl oz milk (150 ml)
salt and freshly milled black pepper

In a largish pan melt the butter over a low heat. Then chop the celery and add it to the pan with the potatoes and drained leeks. Stir well, coating the vegetables with butter, cover and cook for about 15 minutes.

Then add the stock with the celery seeds and some salt. Bring to simmering point, cover once more and cook very gently for 20–25 minutes or until the vegetables are really tender. Purée the soup by liquidising or sieving, then return to the pan, stirring in the cream and milk.

Bring the soup back to the boil, check the seasoning, adding more salt and pepper if necessary. Then just before serving, chop the reserved celery leaves and stir them into the soup to give it extra colour.

GARLICKY FISH SOUP

◆

(Serves 3–4 people)

This is half soup and half chowder, which makes a very substantial lunch dish.

1 lb fish fillets – haddock, cod or whiting (450 g), skinned and cut into smallish cubes
1 quantity fish stock (see page 67)
2 tablespoons olive oil
2 medium potatoes, peeled and finely chopped
3 cloves garlic, crushed
1 lb fresh tomatoes (450 g), peeled, or 14 oz tin Italian tomatoes (400 g)
1 teaspoon chopped fresh or ½ teaspoon dried basil
1 tablespoon lemon juice
2 tablespoons chopped parsley
salt and freshly milled black pepper

In a large, heavy saucepan or flameproof casserole heat the oil and add the diced potatoes and garlic. Leave to cook for about 5 minutes before adding the fish stock, the cubes of fish and the fresh tomatoes, chopped, or the contents of the tin of tomatoes (also chopped). Then sprinkle in the basil, add a squeeze of lemon juice, and simmer the soup gently for 15 minutes. After that taste to check the seasoning, and sprinkle in the chopped parsley just before serving.

TOMATO, APPLE AND CELERY CREAM SOUP

♦

(Serves 4 people)

This is one of John Tovey's famous soups, as served at his hotel, the Miller Howe, in the English Lakes, and it demonstrates his own method of sweating vegetables for quite a long initial cooking, sealed with greaseproof paper. This really brings out all the flavour.

4 oz onions (110 g), finely chopped
5–6 oz tomatoes (150–175 g), quartered – use the stalks as well
5–6 oz celery (150–175 g), cut into 2 inch (5 cm) lengths, plus leaves
5–6 oz apples (150–175 g), quartered – use the cores as well
2 oz butter (50 g)
2½ fl oz dry sherry (60 ml)
freshly grated nutmeg
1 small pinch of ground ginger
1 pint chicken or turkey stock (570 ml)
¼ teaspoon salt
freshly milled black pepper
To garnish
apple slices and snipped fresh chives

First melt the butter in a large, heavy pan, then add the onions and cook gently until golden (about 10 minutes), taking care that they don't burn or catch on the bottom. Add the sherry, vegetables, fruit, spices and seasoning to the pan, place a double thickness of greaseproof paper (well dampened with cold water) over the ingredients, and cover the pan with a lid.

Simmer very gently for 1 hour, checking from time to time that nothing is sticking. After that, add the stock to the contents of the pan (first removing the paper!), and stir everything. Now transfer the soup – in two batches – to a liquidiser and blend, then press through a sieve (to remove pips and stalks), and return to a clean pan. Reheat, check the seasoning, ladle into warmed soup bowls, and garnish each serving with an apple slice and some snipped chives. Serve with croûtons.

CHINESE MUSHROOM SOUP
♦

(Serves 4–6 people)

This needs a really good well-flavoured chicken stock as a base, then it provides a lovely light soup without too many calories. If you can get hold of dried Chinese mushrooms, use 6 oz (175 g) of these, plus 6 oz (175 g) fresh. Pre-soak the dried ones in some of the stock for 30 minutes.

12 oz small flat mushrooms (350 g), finely chopped
2 medium onions, finely chopped
1 tablespoon oil
3 pints good chicken stock (1.75 litres)
2 tablespoons long-grain rice
2 dessertspoons arrowroot
2 dessertspoons cold water
4 spring onions, finely chopped
salt and freshly milled black pepper

Begin by heating the oil in a large saucepan, then add the chopped onions and fry gently for about 10 minutes. Next add the prepared mushrooms, stir them around in the oil and cook for a minute or two. Now pour in the chicken stock, sprinkle in the rice and bring to simmering point, stirring occasionally to prevent the rice from sticking. Simmer gently, uncovered, for approximately 25 minutes.

Meanwhile, in a small basin, blend the arrowroot (which will thicken the soup) with the water until smooth.

When the soup is ready, add the blended arrowroot together with the spring onions and, stirring continuously, bring back to simmering point and simmer for 1 minute. Season to taste and serve very hot.

SEE ALSO

Chilled yoghurt and cucumber soup
Italian bean and pasta soup
Scallop cream soup
Thick bean and bacon soup
Thick pea soup

PÂTÉS AND STARTERS

◆

The whole idea of a first course (or starter, as it's become more popularly known) is that it should encourage the appetite, rather than spoil it. There's nothing worse than having to first struggle through a huge slab of rich pâté (and the bread needed to get it down), and then have to cope with a main course! In fact my enjoyment of special occasions at multi-starred restaurants has often been marred, simply because I couldn't find a plain enough starter to really appreciate the skills lavished on the main course. For me the biggest problem comes when I am confronted with an hors-d'oeuvre trolley.

Hors-d'oeuvre means literally 'outside work', which reflects the attitude of most nineteenth-century French chefs, who preferred to sub-contract the tedious job of preparing it. Most countries have some kind of hors-d'oeuvre: the Scandinavians their *smørrebrød*, the Italians their *antipasti*, the Spaniards their *entremeses*; but it was in France that the hors-d'oeuvre reached epic proportions – and also in Russia, where a separate room was often set aside for it! We still find the legacy of this in some restaurants, where an awesome array of meats, fish dishes, salads, eggs, canapés and so on get trundled in while glazed looks come over the faces of the diners. It is very tempting to load the plate with a selection of everything, and finish up with a complete meal rather than a starter. That, of course, destroys the whole point of a first course, so perhaps it's just as well that it isn't very practical for us to go to such lengths at home.

Now I accept that not everybody will share my simple tastes in food, but I still think it is a safe general rule to have only one rich course in a meal. In fact I have deliberately made a distinction between pâtés and starters in the title of this chapter because I prefer, on the whole, to serve pâtés on their own for lunch or supper, with plenty of crusty bread, and some pickled gherkins and a side-salad to counteract the richness. However, provided a main course is not too rich, a small portion of pâté *can* serve as a first course. If you bake croûtons of slices cut from a French loaf (see page 98), that will save you the last-minute bother of having to make toast.

SIMPLE STARTERS

———————— ◆ ————————

The key factor in the 'simple' approach to food is what I would call shrewd marketing. If the ingredients you buy are really good, then simple can mean five-star. Take for instance a *tomato salad*: served in late summer when the tomatoes are red and ripened (and of a good variety) with some fresh basil leaves, good fruity olive oil, coarsely ground pepper and crushed rock salt, and accompanied by crusty bread and creamy butter, it is a feast for a king. English *asparagus* in season, *artichokes* or even *avocado* served with vinaigrette may sound commonplace, but they're not when bought at their seasonal best and served with a vinaigrette made from the finest ingredients (why do restaurants so rarely get it right?).

If you've encountered *egg mayonnaise* with rubbery eggs and bottled salad cream, you would quite rightly dismiss it as the dullest thing on earth. But, oh, the real thing! Eggs boiled not quite hard but still a little creamy, and a proper home-made mayonnaise flavoured with garlic and looking like thick glossy ointment – there's a rare luxury indeed. Serve the halved eggs, 1 or 1½ per person, on a bed of sliced pickled dill cucumber and garnish with thin strips of anchovy and small black olives.

If you are able to shop at an Italian or French delicatessen, then what the French call *charcuterie* can provide a brilliantly simple starter: thin slices of *prosciutto* (Parma ham) in summer with fragrant slices of melon, in autumn with fresh sun-ripened figs, or even in winter with slices of peeled fresh mango. Come to think of it, it's also excellent just on its own with good bread and Normandy butter.

Again, the French raw cured version, *Bayonne ham*, needs nothing other than chunks of French baguette and unsalted butter to go with it. *Italian salamis* come in any number of varieties: experiment with them and serve with thin slices of *Mortadella* (salted matured sausage up to 12 inches/30 cm in diameter), olives, Italian pimentos, pickles and (my own favourite) tiny artichoke hearts preserved in oil.

If you come across some good fresh *Mozzarella*, this soft white cheese is a perfect accompaniment to slices of ripe tomatoes: sprinkle with chopped basil leaves, crushed rock salt and coarsely ground pepper, then drizzle some really good green fruity olive oil over the lot. Even supermarkets are now stocking the finest quality olive oil, which is the most vital ingredient in simple cooking.

Crudités is the generic title for various arrangements of raw vegetables or salad ingredients which can make a most attractive starter. They are served with a sauce such as *Aïoli sauce* (see page 439) or *Avocado sauce* (see page 403). The different vegetables are cut into long strips, dipped into the sauce, and then eaten with the fingers. An alternative – and perhaps better – arrangement is to shred or grate the ingredients. Grated carrot, shredded raw cabbage, thin slivers of raw fennel, some slices of cucumber and thin strips of red or green pepper would make a beautiful combination. Prepare each ingredient in a separate bowl and sprinkle over a little (not too much) vinaigrette. Then arrange a selection of vegetables in a pretty pattern on each plate, spooning a small quantity of *Aïoli sauce* or *Avocado sauce* in the centre. Other simple starters can be assembled from the whole family of *smoked fish*, and these are covered in the Fish chapter, starting on p. 101.

And finally a word about melons. There are several types of melon which, if they are bought in good condition, can make a light and simple start to a meal. My complaint is that in some restaurants the melon is often served over-chilled – or, worse still, it has been kept uncovered in the refrigerator and has absorbed other flavours! So always store melons in sealed polythene bags, and remember to bring them out of the fridge in time to lose a little of the chill.

To test melons for ripeness, press the opposite end of the fruit from the stalk with your thumb – if it gives a bit, then the fruit is ripe. A ripe melon should smell fragrant too.

Although sugar and ginger are traditional accompaniments, in my opinion a good melon doesn't need anything at all to go with it. I once had a beautiful cantaloupe melon ruined by being drowned in port (all I could taste in the end was the port). However, a good summery starter would be a mixture of chopped melon and some halved, de-pipped grapes sprinkled with lots of chopped fresh mint and a dressing (made with one part cider vinegar to four parts oil). Served in glass goblets it does look most attractive.

The most popular varieties of melon are:

CANTALOUPE (MUSK MELON)

This is usually small and green, with a very rough skin. Inside the flesh is deep orange with a lovely perfumed flavour.

CHARENTAIS

This too is a small melon, with a yellow-green skin and a golden yellow flesh with a distinctive flavour.

OGEN

This is another small melon, easily distinguished by its yellow and green striped skin. Inside the flesh is green.

HONEYDEW

This is larger and more commonly available than the others. Sometimes honeydews sport a dark green skin, sometimes a bright yellow one. The flavour depends on their ripeness: a really ripe one will be juicy and fragrant, an under-ripe one watery and tasteless.

FRESH FRUIT AND MINT VINAIGRETTE

◆

(Serves 6 people)

This recipe was devised by the late and much missed Peter Langan, who served it in his original restaurant Odin's on warm summer evenings. It's unusual, but really sharpens the appetite.

2 dessert apples, cored and chopped in ¹/₂ inch (1 cm) chunks, with skins left on (one red and one green for preference)
2 medium pears, cored and cut in ¹/₂ inch (1 cm) chunks, with skins left on
juice of ¹/₂ lemon
4 oz grapes (110 g), halved and de-pipped
2 oranges, peeled, pith removed, then cut into chunks
1 tablespoon chopped fresh mint
For the dressing
1 level teaspoon salt
3 tablespoons wine vinegar
6 tablespoons olive oil
4 tablespoons double cream
To garnish
6 sprigs fresh mint

Dice the apples and pears straight into a bowl, and pour the lemon juice over them to prevent discolouring. Stir gently to coat all the pieces, then add the grapes and orange chunks, stir in the chopped mint, cover the bowl with cling film and chill in the fridge for a couple of hours.

To make the dressing, place the salt and wine vinegar in a bowl, leave for a few minutes for the salt to dissolve, then add the olive oil. Whisk well to blend, then gradually stir in the double cream.

When you're ready to serve, divide the fruit among six glasses, pour the dressing over and garnish each with a sprig of fresh mint.

AVOCADO VINAIGRETTE

◆

(Serves 6 people)

A ripe, buttery textured avocado pear served with a really good vinaigrette is simplicity itself. The way to tell if the avocados are ripe is to hold them in the palm of the hand and give them some gentle pressure: if ripe, you'll feel them 'give' slightly.

3 ripe avocados
1 quantity vinaigrette dressing (see page 437), made with 1 large clove garlic
6 crisp lettuce leaves
1 tablespoon snipped fresh chives

Ideally the avocados shouldn't be halved until just before serving, but if you're at all anxious as to whether they're sound or not then you can halve them and have a look about an hour before serving – but *don't* remove the stone. If they look sound, then just replace the halves together and wrap in cling film.

To serve, split the avocados in half and remove the stones. If at all possible, don't do this until *just* before serving because they do tend to discolour quickly. Serve each half on a crisp lettuce leaf (if it won't sit straight, make a depression on the under-side with your thumb, and this might help), spoon some of the vinaigrette into the hollows left by the stones and sprinkle with the chives. Have some extra dressing on the table along with some crusty bread and creamy butter.

AVOCADO MOUSSE WITH PRAWNS AND VINAIGRETTE

◆

(Serves 8 people)

The mousse is a lovely pale pistachio colour, which provides a beautiful contrast to some pink juicy prawns. If you buy the prawns in their shells, you can use the shells boiled in 10 fl oz (275 ml) of water for 20 minutes then strained, to make a prawn stock, which gives added flavour.

2 ripe avocados
5 fl oz hot stock (150 ml)
½ oz powdered gelatine (10 g)
juice of ½ lemon
1 clove garlic, finely chopped
5 fl oz soured cream or Greek yoghurt (150 ml)
5 fl oz mayonnaise (150 ml) (see page 438)
6 oz peeled prawns (175 g) or 12 oz large prawns in their shells (350 g)
1 quantity vinaigrette dressing (see page 437)
salt and freshly milled black pepper

8 × 2½ inch (6 cm) small ramekins, lightly-oiled.

Put 3 tablespoons of the stock and the gelatine in a bowl and stand it in a pan of simmering water. Stir until the gelatine is dissolved, then pour into the goblet of a liquidiser or food processor with the rest of the stock. Next skin and stone the avocados, chop the flesh roughly and add it to the liquidiser (include the darker green part that clings to the skin – this will help the colour). Now add the lemon juice and garlic, and blend until it's completely smooth.

Empty the mixture into a bowl and stir in the cream or yoghurt and the mayonnaise very thoroughly, then season with salt and pepper. Spoon the mixture into the lightly-oiled ramekins, cover them with cling film and pop them into the fridge to set.

When you're ready to serve, slide a palette knife around the edge of each ramekin and ease the mousse away from the sides. Turn the mousses out onto serving plates, top each one of them with some of the prawns, and sprinkle some vinaigrette over each serving. Have plenty of crusty bread ready to go with this.

AVOCADO AND FRESH CRAB SALAD

◆

(Serves 4 people)

This is a marvellous summer starter, which can be made with the fresh dressed crabmeat that comes in small crab shells.

2 ripe avocados
4 oz fresh crabmeat (110 g)
a few crisp lettuce leaves, shredded
1 quantity yoghurt seafood sauce (see page 489)
For the garnish
4 lemon wedges
cayenne pepper
4 sprigs watercress

First halve and peel the avocados, removing the stones, then chop the flesh into small 1/2 inch (1 cm) pieces. Now arrange some shredded lettuce in four stemmed glasses or bowls, and divide the chopped avocados equally between each one. Next sprinkle the crabmeat – equally – over the avocado, then spoon the sauce over. Serve each one with a wedge of lemon to squeeze over, a faint dusting of cayenne pepper, and a sprig of watercress for a garnish.

WHITE BEAN AND TUNA FISH SALAD

◆

(Serves 6 people)

This Italian dish (otherwise known as *Tonno e fagioli*) is one of my husband's favourite first courses, and this is his recipe.

8 oz long haricot beans (225 g)
1 onion, halved
1 carrot, cut into chunks
1 bay leaf
1 sprig fresh thyme
2 × 7 oz tins tuna fish in oil (2 × 200 g)
1 Spanish onion, sliced thinly and separated into rings
2 level tablespoons chopped parsley
salt and freshly milled black pepper
For the dressing
1 teaspoon salt
2 cloves garlic, crushed
1 teaspoon mustard powder
1 tablespoon lemon juice
1 teaspoon wine vinegar
freshly milled black pepper
5 tablespoons olive oil
To serve
crisp lettuce leaves

The beans should be soaked overnight, or else covered with plenty of cold water, brought to the boil, simmered for 5 minutes, then left to soak for 2 hours. After that add the onion halves, carrot, bay leaf and thyme (but don't add any salt) and simmer the beans again for about an hour – or until they're tender.

While they are cooking make the dressing: crush the salt and garlic together, then add the mustard powder, lemon juice, vinegar and pepper. Add the olive oil and shake all together in a screw-top jar. Then, as soon as the beans are cooked, drain them thoroughly in a colander, removing the onion, carrot and herbs, and tip them into a large salad bowl. Pour the dressing over them while they are still warm (so they can really soak up all the delicious flavours). Taste the beans to check if there's enough salt: if not add a little more.

Meanwhile drain the tuna fish and break it up into largish flakes. When the beans have cooled, and you're ready to serve, stir in the onion rings, tuna flakes and parsley. Taste and season with salt and pepper, then arrange on six plates lined with lettuce leaves, and sprinkle more parsley over each serving if you like.

MARINATED MUSHROOMS
◆

(Serves 4 people)

This is a recipe inspired by my friend Pam Neil who runs the idyllic Highbullen Hotel in Devon, where they still serve it with a bowl of pungent garlic mayonnaise to dunk the mushrooms in – wonderful!

8 oz dark-gilled mushrooms (225 g), wiped and sliced
4 tablespoons olive oil
6 rashers streaky bacon, de-rinded and chopped small
2 cloves garlic, very finely chopped
8 fl oz red wine (225 ml)
salt and freshly milled black pepper
To serve
6 lettuce leaves
2 tablespoons chopped fresh parsley
Aïoli sauce (see page 439)

Heat the olive oil in a large frying-pan, then add the chopped bacon and fry until the fat begins to run. Then add the sliced mushrooms along with the garlic, and cook for another couple of minutes – shaking the pan and stirring the mushrooms around all the time. Now pour in the red wine, turn the heat up high and let it all bubble for a minute or two and reduce a little.

Turn the heat down and cook for a further 4 minutes. Season to taste and transfer to a serving dish. Allow the mushrooms to cool before popping the dish into the refrigerator to chill. Serve on crisp lettuce leaves with some chopped fresh parsley sprinkled on top, and some garlicky Aïoli sauce – about a dessertspoon per person.

ASPARAGUS AND CHEESE TART
◆

(Serves 4–6 people)

For those who don't grow their own asparagus – and have to pay high prices in the market – here is a recipe for a first course that makes a little go a long way.

For the pastry
4 oz plain flour (110 g) – this could be half wholewheat
and half white
a pinch of salt

1½ oz Parmesan cheese (40 g), grated
2 oz butter or margarine (50 g)
cold water, to mix

For the filling
12 oz asparagus (350 g), approx. 15 medium stalks
1½ oz Cheddar cheese (40 g), grated
2 large fresh eggs
10 fl oz double cream (275 ml)
1 level tablespoon grated Parmesan cheese
salt and freshly milled black pepper

Pre-heat the oven to gas mark 4, 350°F (180°C), and pop a baking sheet in to pre-heat as well.

An 8 inch (20 cm) round flan tin, greased.

First of all make up the pastry, adding the cheese to the flour before rubbing the fat in (see page 497). Roll it out and line the flan tin with it. Prick the base all over with a fork and cook for 10 minutes, then take it out of the oven and turn the heat up to gas mark 5, 375°F (190°C).

The asparagus should be cut into 1½ inch (4 cm) lengths and then half-cooked in a steamer for 5 minutes. Arrange the asparagus evenly over the pastry base, then sprinkle on the Cheddar cheese. Now whisk the eggs until frothy, and beat them into the cream together with a good seasoning of salt and black pepper. Pour this cream mixture over the asparagus and cheese, and sprinkle the grated Parmesan on top.

Place the tart on the pre-heated baking sheet in the oven for 40–45 minutes, or until the centre is firm and the filling golden-brown and puffy. This tart is delicious eaten hot or cold.

TARAMASALATA

◆

(Serves 8 people)

Whatever happened to real taramasalata? Unfortunately it has been eclipsed by the counterfeit, pink-blancmange-coloured variety that is mass produced. There must be a whole generation who have never tasted the genuine article. Here it is – again courtesy of my friend Pam Neil.

8 oz smoked cod's roe (225 g)
juice of ½ lemon
5 fl oz olive oil (150 ml)
5 fl oz groundnut oil (150 ml)
a little boiling water
1 clove garlic, crushed
1 tablespoon chopped fresh parsley

Before you start, the cod's roe should be soaked in cold water for at least a couple of hours, then rinse and drain it thoroughly before peeling off the skin. Now put the roe in a mixing bowl and mash it first to a pulp using a fork, then, with an electric beater, whisk it at top speed, gradually pouring in the lemon juice.

Now start adding the oils a drop at a time (still whisking as you would when making mayonnaise) and keep adding oil until the mixture becomes solid and dry – forming lumps and working its way up the sides of the bowl. At this stage you can start to beat in a little boiling water, say 2 fl oz (55 ml) or just enough to turn the mixture into a soft mousse. (Don't add the water before the mixture has become solid or it will separate.) Finally add the crushed garlic and parsley, and serve with croûtons or warm pitta bread and Greek olives.

Note You can make this a day ahead: cover it with cling film and keep refrigerated.

SMOKED MACKEREL PÂTÉ

♦

(Serves 8–10 people)

This is another recipe that has suffered a decline because of mass production. Home-made it is *very* good. In this recipe, you only need two smoked mackerel to feed eight to ten people as a first course for a dinner party, and the pâté can be made well in advance, so there is no last minute preparation.

2 medium smoked mackerel
4 oz cottage cheese (110 g)
5 fl oz soured cream (150 ml) or Greek yoghurt
juice of ½ large lemon
salt, freshly milled black pepper and grated nutmeg

To garnish
1 large lemon, cut in wedges
1 bunch watercress
a couple of pinches of cayenne pepper

Eight 2½ inch (6 cm) ramekins.

First skin the mackerel, then carefully remove all the fish from the bones (if the mackerel are already filleted simply scrape the flesh from the skins). Now flake the fish, and place it in the goblet of a liquidiser, then add the cottage cheese, soured cream and lemon juice. Switch on and blend until completely smooth, stopping the motor and stirring the mixture half-way through if you need to.

Next, spoon the mixture into a bowl, taste and season with salt and freshly milled black pepper, a pinch of nutmeg, plus a spot more lemon juice if you think it needs it. Pack into individual dishes, cover and chill for several hours before serving.

To serve, sprinkle on a touch of cayenne pepper, garnish with watercress and lemon wedges and serve with freshly made wholemeal toast, and slices of pickled dill cucumber.

SMOKED FISH PÂTÉ
◆

(Serves 8–10 people)

You can use any combination of smoked fish for this which was always served as a starter in the restaurant where I first learned to cook. The chef, Leo Evans, served it in deep scallop shells garnished with watercress and lemon, and crisp baked croûtons.

1 medium smoked trout
1 medium smoked mackerel
4 oz smoked eel (110 g)
4 oz smoked salmon (110 g) – small, cheaper scraps are perfectly good for this recipe
1 heaped teaspoon very finely chopped raw onion (optional)
8 oz butter (225 g), at room temperature
juice of 1 small lemon
freshly grated nutmeg
salt and cayenne pepper
To garnish
watercress and lemon quarters

To make the pâté, skin all the fish and take all the flesh from the bones – this is much easier than it sounds, and you'll find the flesh comes away quite easily. Put the trout, mackerel and eel into a large mixing bowl, and then chop the smoked salmon very finely (in fact chop it in the same way as you would chop parsley – into minute pieces). Now add the salmon to the other fish and, with a large fork, mash thoroughly until you have a fairly smooth paste.

At this point I like to add 1 heaped teaspoon of very finely chopped raw onion, but you can leave it out if you don't like it. Next, using a fork, mash and blend the whole lot with the butter and lemon juice. Then add about a quarter of a whole nutmeg, freshly grated, taste the pâté and season with as much salt and cayenne pepper as you think it needs. It may also need a touch more lemon juice.

Now pack it into a dish or terrine, cover well and chill lightly for an hour or two.

SMOKED FISH CREAMS
◆

(Serves 8 people)

Serve these light, puffy little creams garnished with plenty of watercress and accompanied by some *Hollandaise sauce* (page 394). A delicious first course for a special occasion. If your budget is tight, you can make these without the smoked salmon lining.

10 oz smoked haddock fillets (275 g)
freshly grated nutmeg
2 eggs, lightly beaten
10 fl oz double cream (275 ml)
8 oz sliced smoked salmon (225 g)
salt and freshly milled black pepper

Eight 3 inch (7.5 cm) ramekin dishes, well-buttered.

Begin by carefully skinning the haddock (you should have about 8 oz/225 g of flesh after this). Cut into pieces about 1½ inches (4 cm) square and place them in a liquidiser or food processor, along with a little salt, pepper and some freshly grated nutmeg. Switch the machine on and blend until the fish has turned to a smooth, even pulp. Then blend in the lightly beaten eggs. Transfer the mixture to a bowl, cover with cling film and leave it in the fridge overnight, or for at least 6 hours.

When you're ready to cook the fish creams, pre-heat the oven to gas mark 5, 375°F (190°C). Fill a large roasting tin with about 1 inch (2.5 cm) of boiling water and put this on the centre shelf of the oven.

Next return the fish mixture to the liquidiser together with the cream, and blend them together thoroughly. Now line the base and sides of each ramekin with smoked salmon – don't worry about doing this in pieces and patches, it won't show when they're finally turned out. Fill each ramekin three-quarters full with the mixture, then place all the ramekins in the tin containing the hot water. Cook for exactly 30 minutes. Serve the creams immediately, either in the ramekins or turned out onto plates (do this by holding each ramekin with a cloth, sliding a small palette knife round the edge and tipping the creams upside down onto the palm of your hand, then straight onto a plate the right way up). Serve as soon as possible.

COUNTRY PÂTÉ

◆

(Serves 10–12 people)

This is a rough, coarse, well-flavoured pâté. If you like you can use 1½ lb (700 g) of pork and only 6 oz (175 g) of liver. If veal is not available, minced beef will do instead. (Illus. opposite p. 160.)

12 oz lean veal (350 g), minced
1 lb fat belly pork (450 g), minced
8 oz pig's liver (225 g), minced
10 oz lean bacon (275 g), chopped small
1 rounded teaspoon salt
¼ teaspoon ground mace
1 or 2 cloves garlic, crushed
20 black peppercorns
15 juniper berries
4 fl oz dry white wine (110 ml)
1 fl oz brandy (25 ml)

A 2 lb (900 g) loaf tin or terrine.

If you give your butcher plenty of notice, he'll probably mince your meats for you. If not, use the medium blade of a mincer or chop them in a food processor.

To make the pâté, place the meats and bacon in a large bowl and mix them all very thoroughly. Add the salt, mace and garlic. Crunch the peppercorns and juniper berries on a flat surface using the back of a tablespoon, then add to the meat.

Now pour the wine and brandy over, have another really good mix, then cover the bowl with a cloth and leave it in a cool place for a couple of hours.

Before cooking the pâté, pre-heat the oven to gas mark 2, 300°F (150°C). Then pack the mixture into a loaf tin and place that in a meat-roasting tin half-filled with hot water. Bake for about 1¾ hours. By the time it has cooked the pâté will have shrunk quite a bit. Remove it from the oven and allow to cool without draining off any of the juices (because, when cold, the surrounding fat will keep the pâté moist).

When the pâté is cold, place a double strip of foil across the top and put a few weights on to press it down for a few hours – this pressing isn't essential but it helps to make the pâté less crumbly if you want to serve it in slices. Serve with hot toast, crusty bread, or croûtons of French bread, which you make as follows.

LARGE CROÛTONS

◆

French bread, cut into diagonal slices 1 inch (2.5 cm) thick
1 tablespoon olive oil
1 or 2 cloves garlic, crushed

Pre-heat the oven to gas mark 4, 350°F (180°C).

Begin by drizzling the olive oil onto a large solid baking sheet, add the crushed garlic then, using either your hands or a piece of kitchen paper, spread the oil and garlic all over the baking sheet. Now place the bread slices on top of the oil, then turn each one over so that both sides have been lightly coated with the oil. Bake them in the oven for 20–25 minutes (but do use a timer because a few minutes too long and they will be over-done). You can make these a day ahead, and store in an airtight tin once they have cooled.

CHICKEN LIVER PÂTÉ

◆

(Serves 4–6 people)

This is a fine smooth velvety pâté, which will serve four people for lunch or six as a first course. (Illus. opposite p. 160.)

8 oz chicken livers (225 g)
8 oz butter (225 g), at room temperature
2 tablespoons brandy
2 level teaspoons mustard powder
¼ teaspoon ground mace
1 level teaspoon chopped fresh or ¼ teaspoon dried thyme
2 cloves garlic, crushed
salt and freshly milled black pepper

Take a good thick frying-pan, melt about 1 oz (25 g) of the butter in it, and fry the chicken livers over a medium heat for about 5 minutes. Keep them on the move, turning them over quite frequently. Then remove them from the pan, using a draining spoon, and transfer them to an electric blender, or press them through a nylon sieve.

Now melt 5 oz (150 g) of the butter and add this to the blender. Then pour the brandy onto the juices left in the frying-pan (this is to rinse it out), and pour that over the liver. Then add the mustard, mace, thyme and garlic, season well with salt and pepper, and blend till you have a smooth purée.

Next press the whole lot into an earthenware pot of about 15 fl oz (425 ml) capacity, or six individual pots. Melt the remaining 2 oz (50 g) of butter and pour over, then leave to get quite cold. Cover with foil or cling film and leave it in the bottom of the fridge for a day or two. This is nice served with hot toast, sprigs of watercress, and a few gherkins or pickled dill cucumbers.

RILLETTES DE TOURS (PORK PÂTÉ)

◆

(Serves 6–8 people)

This is famous around the Loire district of France and sold everywhere in charcuteries – sometimes in thick chunks from a large terrine or packed into little pots. I would recommend this for anyone who doesn't like liver pâtés. (Illus. opposite p. 160.)

2 lb piece lean belly pork (900 g) – ask the butcher to remove rind and bones for you
8 oz back pork fat (225 g)
1 dessertspoon chopped fresh or 1 rounded teaspoon dried thyme
½ teaspoon ground mace
1 heaped teaspoon salt
2 cloves garlic, crushed
10 black peppercorns
10 juniper berries
4 fl oz dry white wine (110 ml)

Pre-heat the oven to gas mark 1, 275°F (140°C).

A 2 pint (1.2 litre) earthenware terrine.

With your sharpest knife, cut the pork lengthways into long strips about 1 inch (2.5 cm) wide, then cut each strip across and across again into smaller strips, and place these in the earthenware terrine. Cut the fat into small pieces too, and mix these in (the excess fat will help to keep the pork properly moist during the cooking). Now add the thyme, mace, salt and garlic along with the peppercorns and juniper berries (the last two both crushed with the back of a tablespoon). Pour in the wine.

Mix everything around to distribute the flavours, cover the terrine, place it in the centre of the oven and leave it there for 4 hours. After that, taste a piece of pork and add more salt (and pepper) if necessary. Now empty everything into a large sieve standing over a bowl and let all the fat drip through (press the meat gently to extract the fat). Leave the drained fat to cool.

Next take a couple of forks, and pull the strips of meat into shreds (sometimes it is pounded instead, but personally, I think it's worth persevering with the fork method). Then pack the *rillettes* lightly into the terrine, and leave to get cold. After that, remove the jelly from the bowl of fat, melt it gently and pour it over the *rillettes*. Then spread a layer of fat over the top to keep it moist. Keep the *rillettes* in the refrigerator (covered with foil or cling film) till needed. Serve with hot toast, crusty bread or crisp baked croûtons.

SEE ALSO

Alpine eggs
Courgettes and tomatoes au gratin
Dressed crab
Eggs chapter
Eggs en cocotte with soured cream and asparagus
Fillets of sole gratinés
Globe artichokes
Goujons of sole
Guacamole
Hot crab soufflé
Hummus bi tahina
Mixed vegetables à la Grècque
Moules à la marinière
Mussels with garlic stuffing
Potted haddock with capers
Provençal vegetable stew
Risotto alla Milanese
Scallops in the shell
Soused herrings
Stocks and soups chapter
Turkish stuffed tomatoes
Whitebait

FISH

◆

Unfortunately one of the really essential ingredients in fish cookery is the one that so often is missing, namely a good fishmonger. In many parts of the country fishmongers of any description have become rather thin on the ground, and to find a really reliable one has grown increasingly difficult. This is partly offset by the ready and regular supply of commercially frozen fish (which is probably the root cause of our vanishing fishmongers in the first place). However, unlike other types of frozen food, frozen fish has much to commend it: only the best quality is frozen and sub-zero temperatures do not materially affect the flavour – indeed very often rather more fresh flavour is retained by freezing (since it is generally carried out immediately or soon after the fish is caught).

Having said that, though, there is nothing to compensate for a trustworthy and friendly fishmonger, who is willing to help and advise. There are two ways to tell a good one: firstly if his shop is busy and attracting a lot of regular custom, and secondly by how much fish there is left on the slab towards the end of the afternoon. If there is a lot then beware, because it's all going to be put away and brought out again the next day. (One of the best fishmongers I ever knew was virtually sold out by two o'clock every day.)

In spite of our proud fish 'n' chip shop tradition and the dreaded, breaded fish fingers, as a nation we don't eat nearly enough fish. I suspect this is because, unlike some other countries, we have always had an over-plentiful supply of meat. Yet fish contains as much protein as meat, is easier to digest, and has one crucial advantage; it can be cooked so quickly. If you don't have a lot of time for cooking, think of fish. It can be grilled, fried, poached or baked to provide a nutritious meal in hardly any time at all.

BUYING FRESH FISH

◆

There is no mistaking really fresh fish. It has a plumpness and firmness about it that proclaims it to be fresh straightaway. Scaled fish should have a sequin-like iridescence, and all fishes' eyes look sparkling, almost alert (and in the case of herrings, red). In general the thing to look for is overall brightness: stale fish, however often they are hosed down, look grey, dull and droopy with blurred eyes and flabby flesh.

101

PREPARING FISH

— ♦ —

All fish, with the exception of sprats and other tiny species, should be gutted by the fishmonger, and all fish, apart from herrings and mackerel (see pages 114 and 116), should be skinned and filleted – if that's what is needed – by him. Why struggle at home with diagrams and blunt filleting knives, when you can have the job done for you at no extra cost? In fact fish is now so expensive there's all the more reason to have it prepared for you.

If you want to cook fish on the bone, then just ask to have it gutted and, where appropriate, scaled (if the fishmonger doesn't make a proper job of this, you can do it yourself by simply scraping along the skin with the blunt side of a knife in the opposite direction to the way the scales are, i.e. from head to tail). If you are lucky enough to buy your fish straight off a boat or even catch it yourself, then gutting at home isn't too complicated. You can either remove the insides through the gill-slits (if the heads are to be left on) by squeezing and scraping with a teaspoon, or by making a slit along the belly, opening the fish out and then scraping. If you are cutting off the heads some of the entrails will come out attached to the gills (which are bright red flaps underneath openings on each side of the head, and should also be cut away before cooking). Always wash away any traces of blood and slime, and then dry the fish as thoroughly as possible with kitchen paper or a clean cloth.

STORING FISH

— ♦ —

Like anything else, fish that has been frozen should not be allowed to thaw out and then be re-frozen – so if you want to freeze some yourself, check that it is very fresh. The safest rule obviously is to eat fresh fish as soon as possible, though a day's storage in the refrigerator isn't going to hurt. Exceptions to this, however, are skate and Dover sole, which because of a chemical that develops after death actually improve in flavour a couple of days after they are caught. How kind of nature to give us at least some fish that can cope with the time taken up by its journey inland.

METHODS OF COOKING FISH

— ♦ —

SHALLOW-FRYING

To shallow-fry a whole fish, or part of one, to the best degree of crispness, use olive oil. If on the other hand you'd like to get a buttery flavour, then use half oil and half butter (on its own butter burns too easily and can spoil the flavour). Solid fat is not very good for fish – except perhaps bacon fat or pure lard for frying herrings. Have enough oil or fat in the pan to give a depth of ⅛ inch (3 mm) and make sure it is really hot before the fish goes in. I think it best to thaw frozen fish before frying, whatever it says on the packet: the coldness of the fish brings the temperature of the fat down dramatically (and that is what makes food oily). Times for shallow-frying fish are approximately the same as for grilling (see the table on page 104).

DEEP-FRYING

I prefer a groundnut oil for this – and it can be stored and used several times over, but be careful to label the jar 'fish oil'. Ideally a cooking thermometer should be used to check the correct temperature of the oil (370°F, 187.5°C for fillets, goujons and fish in batter; 375°F, 190.5°C for whitebait, croquettes and fish cakes), and always warm the thermometer in hot water first to prevent the glass cracking. If you have no cooking thermometer, the best way of testing if the oil is hot enough is to throw a small cube of bread into it and if it turns golden-brown in 1 minute you can go ahead. Do not, however, allow the oil to overheat or the flavour will be spoiled.

The pan needs to be only one-third full of oil – any more than that and there is a danger of it bubbling over when the food goes in. A frying basket isn't necessary – the fish or the batter has a habit of getting stuck in the mesh – just use a draining spoon with a long handle to get the fish in and out.

Fish destined for the deep-fryer ought to be at room temperature, and should also be coated in either batter, breadcrumbs or flour to give it protection against the extreme heat. Chilled or frozen fish lowers the oil heat and the food will taste soggy and oily (and in any event try, if you can, to raise the heat under the pan as you lower the fish in, then turn it down again). To tell if the fish is cooked, the batter or coating turning a golden-brown is a good indication. Small fish or pieces of fish rise to the surface when they are cooked. But if in doubt, the best way of all is to try a bit. Always drain fried fish either on crumpled greaseproof or absorbent kitchen paper before serving.

GRILLING

The first tip here is to line the grill pan or grid with foil before you start – this will prevent a fishy flavour lingering in the pan. Pre-heat the grill to high, before placing the fish under it. White fish need to be brushed generously with melted butter before grilling, and basted with the buttery juices when you turn them. For grilling times see page 104.

POACHING

For poaching you need some form of liquid, though not too much of it: a mixture of white wine (or dry cider) and water with a few herbs, a bay

Type and size of fish	Grilling time
Whole Dover sole and plaice	4–6 minutes each side
Fillets of sole or plaice	2–3 minutes each side
Fish steaks (salmon, halibut, cod, turbot, monkfish etc.) weighing approx. 6–8 oz (175–225 g)	Allow 5–6 minutes each side and have extra butter ready for basting during cooking to prevent dryness
Whole mackerel	Make three diagonal scores on each side and brush with melted butter. Grill for approx. 6–7 minutes each side for 8 oz (225 g) fish
Herring	For 6–8 oz (175–225 g) fish, score as above and allow 4–5 minutes' grilling on each side

leaf, peppercorns, sliced onion, sliced carrot and a piece of lemon peel is a very suitable poaching liquid. Or for some white fish a mixture of milk and water with flavourings is used. The operative word here is gentle – the liquid should barely simmer, in order not to overcook or break up the fish. Rolled-up fillets of sole or plaice will only need 4–5 minutes' poaching: larger whole fish or pieces weighing 1½–2 lb (700–900 g) will need 7–10 minutes. I have to admit that, on the whole, I think it preferable to cook fish in the oven in foil rather than poach it, as this retains more of the flavour.

BAKING

This way the fish is brushed with melted butter or with oil (maybe with a stuffing added) and then baked in the oven – sometimes open, sometimes lightly covered with a piece of buttered foil for protection. At other times a small quantity of poaching liquid is used, or extra butter for basting: methods of baking vary quite a lot, so see the instructions in individual recipes.

IN FOIL OR EN PAPILLOTE

This is an excellent way to cook fish, because all the essential flavour and juices are retained inside a sealed parcel (which when opened will give off a beautiful, fragrant and appetising aroma). For fish like salmon and salmon trout, which are sometimes served cold, the parcels can be left unopened until just before serving. If you are required to *steam* fish, say for someone on a special diet, it can be wrapped in a foil parcel and placed in a steamer over boiling water. It will take 10–15 minutes according to thickness. Various flavourings can be added: lemon juice, wine, butter, slivers of onion, garlic, fresh herbs. In Italy I have eaten sole cooked like this surrounded by fresh mint leaves. For timings, see individual recipes.

POPULAR VARIETIES OF FISH

In the British Isles there are five main groups of fish available to us: white fish, oily fish, freshwater fish, smoked fish and shellfish. These last two groups will be dealt with on pages 121–37. Let's look first at some of the most popular varieties of the group known as white fish.

WHITE FISH

SOLE

First – because it is said to have the finest flavour of all – is the *Dover sole*. This is a flat fish, weighing anything from 8 oz up to 2 lb (225–900 g), white on the under-side with its speckled grey camouflage on the upper-side, with a rounded not pointed head. Its flavour is best preserved by serving it simply grilled. Ask the fishmonger to skin it for you, then brush it with melted butter, and give it from about 4 to 6 minutes on each side under a hot grill, depending on thickness. It is nice served with some parsley butter and lemon juice. I also believe that any fish (like meat) benefits in taste from being cooked on the bone instead of filleted.

Lemon soles (and *witch soles*) are similar fish, but look rather more pointed. They are certainly cheaper but don't compare in flavour.

GOUJONS OF SOLE

(Serves 2 as a main course or 4 as a first course)

Goujons are small strips of fish coated in egg and breadcrumbs. To make this more economical you could use plaice fillets but, either way, ask the fishmonger to skin them.

8 small fillets sole or plaice
3 tablespoons well-seasoned flour
1 large egg, beaten
4 oz fresh white breadcrumbs (110 g)
oil for deep-frying
To garnish
chopped fresh parsley

First wipe the fillets and cut them into thinnish strips diagonally across the grain. Roll the strips in the seasoned flour, then dip them first in the beaten egg and then in the breadcrumbs. (Have the breadcrumbs on a flat working surface so that you can roll the strips under the palm of your hand to get them well and evenly coated.)

Next heat the oil in a deep pan to 350°F (180°C) – test the temperature either with a thermometer or drop in a small cube of bread and if it turns golden and crisp in 1 minute it's hot enough. Then deep-fry the fish for 2–3 minutes until golden-brown. You'll probably need to do the frying in two or three separate lots. When cooked, drain on crumpled greaseproof or kitchen paper. Serve garnished with chopped parsley.

SKATE

Swimming in the sea, a skate looks like a cross between Concorde and a space-craft, with its huge wings. The wings are what we buy at the fishmonger, triangular in shape with a pinky flesh: if they are from a small fish they weigh about 8 oz (225 g) each, if from a large fish they are bought cut into pieces. It is a delicious fish: the flesh parts conveniently from the soft bones, which themselves stay intact, so there is little likelihood of finding any unwelcome, spiky bits of bone. It is hard to beat just washed, well dried, given a light coating of flour, then shallow-fried in a mixture of butter and oil till crisp and golden; or else served with browned butter, as in the next recipe.

A group of white fish belonging to the skate family – and often referred to rather misleadingly as rock salmon – are the *dogfish, huss* or *flake*. In fact they have nothing at all in common with salmon, actually are rather dull (if cheap) and need to be jazzed up a bit with other ingredients.

SKATE WITH BLACK BUTTER

♦

(Serves 4 people)

The important thing to remember here is not to overcook the butter – a split second too much and it can be burnt rather than browned.

4 skate wings
3 tablespoons white wine vinegar
1 bay leaf
1 blade mace
a couple of sprigs parsley
3 oz butter (75 g)
1 tablespoon chopped capers, drained
salt and freshly milled black pepper
To garnish
lemon slices

First of all place the skate wings side by side in a wide pan or a roasting tin. Sprinkle with salt and pepper, then add 2 tablespoons of the wine vinegar, the bay leaf, mace and parsley sprigs. Add enough water to cover, bring slowly to the boil and simmer over a low heat for 10–15 minutes, but be sure not to overcook the fish.

Meantime, slowly melt the butter in a small saucepan, then pour the clear golden butter into another saucepan, leaving the white sediment behind. Heat the butter until it's a rich warm brown, then remove at once from the heat, stir in the remaining vinegar and the capers and season with salt and pepper. Drain the fish well – discard the herbs – and arrange it on a warmed serving dish. Finally pour the butter over and garnish with slices of lemon.

THE COD FAMILY

There are several branches to this family, varying amongst themselves more in size than in texture or flavour. *Cod* itself is a very firm, flaky fish that can weigh up to 14 lb (6.5 kg) (*codling* is simply a small cod, by the way), but sadly it loses much of its flavour if not eaten very fresh. It is available all through the year. So too is *hake* (except sometimes in the early autumn), which is a similar if elongated version of cod. *Haddock* is another relation, smaller and more finely textured, much of which goes to be smoked. *Coley* is a rather dull cousin, *whiting* a much more succulent one, and Norwegian *red fish* a somewhat ferocious-looking one that surprisingly tastes as good as cod and is in need of more promotion. All these fleshy, firm fish lend themselves to a wide spectrum of seasonings, flavourings and sauces.

TURBOT AND HALIBUT

These are usually large flat fish, although turbot can be as small as 2 or 3 lb (900 g–1.3 kg) when it can be cooked whole with a stuffing. Halibut can weigh up to 40 lb (18 kg). Both are available all through the year, have a fine flavour, are quite expensive, but are easy to grill, fry, poach or bake in long cutlets on the bone.

PLAICE

A fish that does need, I think, some extra flavourings. It is a flat white fish, easily recognisable by the bright orange spots on the upper-side. A whole plaice can weigh up to 5 lb (2.25 kg) or be as small as 8 oz (225 g). It is available in Britain all the year round. You can grill it like Dover sole, but you might consider a sauce or flavoured butter to go with it. Deep-fried in a light crisp batter (page 108), it goes well with *Sauce tartare* (page 439). Filleted, it can be used in any sole recipe and the smaller frozen fillets are very good. *Dabs* and *flounders* are smaller, less interesting, versions of plaice.

BASIC FISH BATTER

♦

(Makes enough for four 6–7 inch/15–18 cm pieces)

I have found this very simple flour-and-water batter the best of all for deep-frying fish: it turns out really crisp.

4 oz self-raising flour (110 g)
¹/₂ teaspoon salt
5 fl oz water (150 ml), plus 1 scant tablespoon

Just sift the flour and salt into a mixing bowl, then gradually add the water, whisking continuously until the batter is smooth and free from lumps.

ITALIAN BAKED FISH

♦

(Serves 4 people)

Four pieces of any white fish can be used for this dish though my own personal choice is cod cutlets on the bone. (Illus. opposite p. 161.)

4 thick pieces white fish
2 tablespoons olive oil
1 medium onion, finely chopped
1 fat clove garlic, crushed
1 lb ripe tomatoes (450 g), peeled and chopped, or 14 oz tin Italian tomatoes (400 g)
4 oz mushrooms (110 g), thinly sliced
1 tablespoon chopped fresh basil
1 tablespoon capers, chopped
juice of ¹/₂ lemon
12 black olives
salt and freshly milled black pepper

Pre-heat the oven to gas mark 5, 375°F (190°C).

Start by making a good thick tomato sauce. Heat the olive oil in a saucepan and fry the onion for about 5 minutes. Now add the garlic and tomatoes. Season with salt and pepper, then bring to simmering point and cook gently – uncovered – for 15 minutes, stirring occasionally. Next add the sliced mushrooms, making sure that they are well stirred in. Simmer for a further 10 minutes until it looks like a thick sauce. Lastly stir in the basil and chopped capers.

Now place the fish in a shallow baking dish or tin, season with salt and pepper and sprinkle a little lemon juice on each piece. Next spoon an equal quantity of the sauce onto each piece of fish and arrange a few olives on top. Cover the dish with foil and bake on a high shelf for about 25 minutes, depending on the thickness of the fish. Serve this with new potatoes or brown rice and a tossed green salad.

Note If you cannot get fresh basil, use 1 teaspoon of dried, adding it with the tomatoes when making the sauce.

FISH KEBABS
♦

(Serves 2 people)

This is an unusual and delicious way of serving fish – any white fish, like the thick end of a cod fillet or haddock.

1 lb white fish (450 g)
3 tablespoons olive oil
1½ tablespoons lemon juice
1 tablespoon dry white wine
2 tablespoons finely chopped parsley
1 medium onion, quartered
1 medium green pepper, de-seeded, and chopped in 1 inch (2.5 cm) squares
salt and freshly milled black pepper
To garnish
lemon quarters

First remove the skin from the fish and cut it into 1 inch (2.5 cm) cubes. Next, put in a bowl the olive oil, lemon juice, wine and chopped parsley and seasoning and mix well with a fork to amalgamate thoroughly, then plunge the cubes of fish into it. Now separate the layers of the onion quarters and arrange them evenly over the fish. Put aside in a cool place to marinate for at least an hour.

When you're ready to cook the fish, pre-heat the grill to high and line the grill pan with foil. Then thread the pieces of fish onto skewers, alternating with pieces of onion and green pepper. Place the skewers on the grill pan, brush with the marinade and grill for a minute or two under the high heat. Then turn the heat to medium and cook for a further 4–5 minutes on each side, brushing on more of the marinade before turning.

Serve with brown rice, the juices from the pan poured over, and lemon quarters.

FISHERMAN'S PIE
◆

(Serves 4–6 people)

Whatever white fish is available can be used for this delicious family recipe, cod, haddock or whiting.

1½ lb white fish (700 g)
1 pint milk (570 ml)
4 oz butter (110 g)
2 oz plain flour (50 g)
4 oz peeled prawns (110 g)
2 hard-boiled eggs, roughly chopped
1 tablespoon capers, drained
3 tablespoons chopped fresh parsley
1 tablespoon lemon juice
salt and freshly milled pepper
For the topping
2 lb freshly boiled potatoes (900 g)
2 oz butter (50 g)
4 tablespoons milk
a little freshly grated nutmeg
1 oz strong Cheddar cheese (25 g), grated

Pre-heat the oven to gas mark 6, 400°F (200°C).

Start by arranging the fish in a baking tin and seasoning it well with salt and pepper. Then pour over half of the milk, dot with 1 oz (25 g) of the butter in flecks, and bake in the oven for 15–20 minutes. Then pour off (and reserve) the cooking liquid, and remove the skin from the fish, flaking the flesh into fairly large pieces.

Now make the sauce: melt the remaining 3 oz (75 g) butter in a saucepan, then stir in the flour and gradually add the fish cooking liquid – stirring well after each addition. When all the liquid is in, finish off the sauce by slowly adding the remaining milk and seasoning with salt and pepper.

Next mix the fish into the sauce, along with the prawns, hard-boiled eggs, capers and parsley (taste at this stage to see if it needs any more salt and pepper) and stir in the lemon juice. Now pour the whole mixture into a well-buttered 2½ pint (1.5 litre) baking dish.

Next cream the cooked potatoes with the butter and milk, add some salt, pepper and freshly grated nutmeg, then spread the mixture evenly all over the fish. Smooth the surface of the potato, then (using the rounded blade of a knife) pattern it by making impressions ½ inch (1 cm) deep in rows. Finally sprinkle the cheese all over and bake on a high shelf (same temperature) for about 30–40 minutes, or until heated through and browned.

FLAKY FISH PIE
◆

(Serves 4 people)

This is a wonderful recipe that transforms the humble haddock, cod or whiting into something really special.

12 oz any white fish (350 g)
milk
1 oz butter (25 g)
2 tablespoons plain flour
1 tablespoon chopped capers, drained
4 small gherkins, chopped
2 tablespoons chopped parsley
2 hard-boiled eggs, chopped
1 tablespoon lemon juice
salt and freshly milled black pepper
For the pastry
1 quantity quick flaky pastry (see page 515)
To glaze
beaten egg

First place the fish in a medium-sized saucepan with just enough milk to cover, bring to the boil, put the lid on and simmer gently for about 5–10 minutes. Now strain off the milk into a measuring jug and, when the fish is cool enough to handle, flake it into large pieces (discarding all the bones, skin, etc.).

Next, melt the butter in the same saucepan and stir in the flour. Cook for about 2 minutes over a medium heat, then gradually add 10 fl oz (275 ml) of the milk the fish was cooked in, stirring all the time. Bring the sauce to the boil, simmer gently for 6 minutes, then take the pan off the heat and add the flaked fish, chopped capers, gherkins, parsley and eggs. Season with salt and pepper and lemon juice. Cover and leave until the mixture is quite cold.

When you're ready to cook the pie, pre-heat the oven to gas mark 7, 425°F (220°C). Roll out the pastry to a 12 inch (30 cm) square, trimming if necessary. Lift the square onto a greased baking sheet, then place the cold fish mixture in the centre. Glaze around the edge of the pastry with beaten egg, then pull the opposite corners of the pastry to the centre and pinch all the edges together firmly, so you have a square with pinched edges in the shape of a cross. Glaze all over with beaten egg and decorate with any pastry trimmings. Glaze these too and then bake the pie for about 30 minutes or until the pastry is well-risen and golden.

BAKED FISH FILLETS WITH MUSHROOM STUFFING

◆

(Serves 3–4 people)

For this you need two Dover soles, boned, skinned and cut into fillets, or plaice fillets if you want a less expensive dish.

4 large fillets sole, skinned
1 oz butter (25 g)
1 tablespoon oil
1 small onion, finely chopped
8 oz dark-gilled mushrooms (225 g), finely chopped
freshly grated nutmeg
1 tablespoon finely chopped parsley
5 fl oz dry white wine or cider (150 ml)
2 level tablespoons plain flour
5 fl oz milk (150 ml)
lemon juice
1 tablespoon double cream
salt and freshly milled black pepper
To garnish
watercress

Pre-heat the oven to gas mark 4, 350°F (180°C).

First of all melt half the butter and all the oil together in a pan and fry the onion gently until soft and golden. Add the mushrooms and cook until all the juices have evaporated and the remaining mixture is a dryish, spreadable paste – this will take about 20 minutes. Remove from the heat, season with salt, pepper and nutmeg, then transfer all but 2 tablespoons of the mixture to a basin and mix with the parsley.

Next cut the fish fillets in half lengthways and spread an equal quantity of the mushroom mixture on the skinned side of each piece. Roll up from the head to the tail end and place closely together in a baking dish. Pour in the wine or cider, place a piece of buttered greaseproof paper directly on top of the fish and bake in the oven for 20 minutes.

Meantime, melt the remaining butter in a saucepan, blend in the flour and cook for 2 minutes, stirring continuously. When the fish is ready transfer it to a warmed serving dish, using a draining spoon; cover and keep warm. Now add the cooking liquid to the butter and flour mixture, beating all the time to get a smooth sauce, and also blend in the milk. Then bring to boiling point, stirring all the time, add the remaining mushroom mixture, season with salt, pepper and a squeeze of lemon juice and stir in the cream. Pour over the fish and serve garnished with watercress.

BAKED FISH WITH SOURED CREAM AND CAPERS

―――――――――― ♦ ――――――――――

(Serves 2 people)

This would be suitable for some thick fish cutlets – cod, halibut or turbot – or some thick pieces of fresh haddock.

2 × 8 oz (225 g) fish cutlets or thick fillets
2 fl oz dry white wine or dry cider (55 ml)
1½ oz butter (40 g)
1 teaspoon chopped fresh tarragon or ½ teaspoon dried tarragon, soaked for 10 minutes in 1 teaspoon lemon juice
the white part of 1 leek, chopped
1 teaspoon plain flour
5 fl oz soured cream (150 ml)
2 teaspoons chopped capers, drained
1 tablespoon finely chopped watercress leaves
salt and freshly milled pepper
To garnish
sprigs of watercress and lemon quarters

Pre-heat the oven to gas mark 5, 375°F (190°C).

Place the pieces of fish in a well-buttered baking dish just large enough to accommodate them. Then add the wine or cider and dot with half the butter. Season with salt and pepper, sprinkle in the tarragon, then cover the dish with foil and bake near the top of the oven for 20 minutes.

Meantime, melt the rest of the butter in a saucepan, add the chopped leek and let it soften gently. Then sprinkle in the flour and, stirring all the time, cook over a low heat for a couple of minutes.

When the fish is ready, lift up a corner of the foil and pour out its cooking liquid into a jug. Now add this liquid, a little at a time, to the mixture in the saucepan, stirring after each addition. When it's all added, bring to boiling point and cook for at least a minute. Then turn the heat low and stir in the cream, capers and chopped watercress. When it's heated through, pour it over the fish and serve garnished with sprigs of watercress and lemon quarters.

HALIBUT WITH BACON
♦

(Serves 4 people)

This recipe can be adapted for cod steaks or even monkfish. It is good with creamy mashed potatoes made with soured cream and a little freshly grated nutmeg.

4 halibut steaks (each single-portion size)
4 rashers back bacon, de-rinded
2 carrots, very thinly sliced
4 oz mushrooms (110 g), thinly sliced
1 celery stalk, very thinly sliced
1 large onion, finely chopped
10 fl oz dry white wine (275 ml)
2 tablespoons chopped parsley
¹/₂ teaspoon chopped fresh or a pinch of dried thyme
4 slices lemon
2 oz butter (50 g)
salt and freshly milled black pepper

Pre-heat the oven to gas mark 7, 425°F (220°C).

Start by laying the bacon slices in a well-buttered baking dish large enough to take the fish steaks in a single layer. Then sprinkle over the prepared carrots, mushrooms, celery and onion followed by the wine. Cover tightly with foil and bake for 30 minutes.

Next, remove the dish from the oven and arrange the fish steaks on top of the vegetables. Then sprinkle with parsley, thyme, salt and freshly milled black pepper; place a lemon slice on each steak and dot with flecks of butter. Cover the dish again with foil and bake for a further 15–20 minutes, then serve.

OILY FISH
♦

Under this heading comes a group of fish which are rich in flavour, but because of their slight oiliness do need to be eaten fresh.

HERRINGS

A prince of fish, in my opinion, a true delicacy when freshly caught. Yet until recently herring were amongst the cheapest and most abundant of our native fish, and little thought of in consequence. The irony is that present-day intensive fishing (for animal-feed products among other things) has contrived to put the species in jeopardy. It has therefore become scarcer and more expensive – and probably, like the oyster, will become more highly regarded.

It is quite possible you might find yourself faced at some time or another with the prospect of having to bone a herring. It is actually quite easy – more formidable in the anticipation than in practice. First of all ask the fishmonger to clean, scale and trim the fish – that much he must do. Then, when you get home, take a pair of scissors and cut each fish along the tummy, open it out (flesh-side down) on a board, then bash the fish out (with a rolling-pin if you like) to flatten it completely. Now press hard with your fingers all along the backbone, to loosen it from the flesh. Then, turning the fish over, get hold of the backbone at the head end and ease it away – it will bring all the little bones with it. If it proves a bit stubborn, use a sharp knife to prompt it a little. Remove any reluctant small bones left behind – and you have now boned a herring.

SOUSED HERRINGS
◆

(Serves 6 people)

These are delicious served with buttered home-made wholewheat bread and something salady, but they do need to be made a couple of days in advance so that they can marinate and absorb all the flavours.

6 freshly filleted herrings (frozen ones are not so good)
1½ tablespoons salt
2 dill pickles
made-up mustard
1 Spanish onion, thinly sliced
For the marinade
1 pint white wine vinegar (570 ml)
1 teaspoon whole allspice berries
1 teaspoon whole coriander seeds
½ teaspoon mustard seeds
1 dried chilli pepper
2 bay leaves
1–2 teaspoons brown sugar
5 fl oz water (150 ml)

You'll need six cocktail sticks.

First of all make the marinade in a saucepan by combining the vinegar, spices, bay leaves and sugar with the water. Bring to boiling point, then simmer very gently for 5 minutes. Remove from the heat and leave until cold.

Next sprinkle the herrings with the salt and let them drain in a colander for about 3 hours. After that rinse off the salt and dry off any excess moisture with kitchen paper. Now cut each dill pickle in three lengthways, spread the filleted side of each fish thinly with mustard and place a piece of dill pickle and some slices of onion horizontally at what was the head end of each fillet. Then roll up the fillets from the head to the tail end – the skin being on the outside – and secure each roll with a cocktail stick. Pack them into an oval earthenware casserole and sprinkle the remaining onion on top. Pour over the marinade, cover with a lid, and put them in the lowest part of the refrigerator. Leave for at least 48 hours before serving; they will keep well for at least a week.

MACKEREL

An under-estimated fish if ever there was one. It has a bad reputation with older generations, who were suspicious of its career as a scavenger (it is all right for humans to eat the flesh of other creatures, but wrong apparently for the poor mackerel). It was sad a few years ago to read of Cornish fishermen having to dump mackerel catches back in the sea because nobody would buy them, for mackerel eaten fresh (which they usually are) are a treat. If they look floppy, grey and dull they should be avoided of course: a fresh mackerel will be stiff and rigid, with a sparkling, positively beautiful rainbow hue.

The smaller mackerel are the best size to buy – working out at one fish per person. Bone them in exactly the same way as herrings (see page 115). They are excellent plainly grilled: make diagonal cuts across the body, season on both sides with salt and pepper, and give them about 6–7 minutes under a high grill on each side. They are traditionally – and rightly – served with a sharp purée of gooseberries flavoured with a little nutmeg, or with a purée of rhubarb flavoured with a spot of ginger.

MARINATED MACKEREL
♦

(Serves 3 people)

If you can get your fishmonger to fillet the mackerel for you, so much the better. If not, follow the instructions for boning herring on page 115.

3 mackerel, filleted
2 tablespoons olive oil
1 carrot, thinly sliced
1 onion, thinly sliced
15 fl oz dry white wine (425 ml)
5 fl oz cold water (150 ml)

| 1 teaspoon brown sugar |
| salt |

| *To flavour the marinade* |
| celery leaves |
| 1 inch strip lemon zest (2.5 cm) |
| 1 bay leaf |
| a few parsley stalks |
| 2 sprigs thyme |
| 1 clove garlic, crushed |
| 10 black peppercorns |
| 1 chilli pepper, de-seeded |

Begin by heating the oil in a thick-based saucepan, then add the carrot and onion and stir around. Cover and cook gently for 10 minutes. Next add the white wine and water, together with the marinade flavouring ingredients. Bring to simmering point, cover and cook gently for approximately 30 minutes.

Towards the end of the cooking time arrange the mackerel fillets in a single layer, in a suitably-sized heatproof gratin dish or roasting tin, then empty the contents of the saucepan over the fish. Bring up to simmering point on top of the stove and simmer for a minute.

Next, using a draining spoon, transfer the fillets to an oval earthenware casserole or dish which accommodates them neatly. Return the pan to the heat and boil the juices for 2–3 minutes or until reduced sufficiently just to cover the fish. Season to taste with salt, add the sugar, then strain the liquid over the fillets, discarding all the flavouring ingredients.

Put them aside to cool, then cover and chill for at least 12 hours before serving. (They will keep quite well for 3–4 days, covered, in the refrigerator.)

WHITEBAIT

Whitebait are tiny baby herring, rarely more than 1 inch (2.5 cm) long. At one time – more than a hundred years ago – they were caught at the mouth of the Thames, and consumed by Members of Parliament at 'whitebait feasts' in Greenwich at the end of the parliamentary session. Alas, they are almost never sold fresh nowadays – at least I've never seen them – but it doesn't matter too much, because frozen whitebait are perfectly good. They are eaten whole, deep-fried and crisp enough to rustle as they're served on the plate. Let them de-frost first, dry them thoroughly, then coat them with a dusting of flour and deep-fry them for about 3 minutes.

SPRATS

Cousins to the herring, only smaller – yet larger than whitebait. Usually they are 2½–3 inches long (6–7.5 cm). They are delicious fried or baked, and always a bargain price-wise.

DEEP-FRIED SPRATS IN MUSTARD SAUCE

◆

(Serves 2 people)

Fresh silvery sprats are always an economical fish, and deep-fried and crisp they really are a delicacy.

1 lb sprats (450 g)
seasoned flour
groundnut oil for deep-frying
2 pinches of cayenne pepper, to garnish
For the mustard sauce
1 oz butter (25 g)
¹/₂ small onion, chopped
¹/₂ oz plain flour (10 g)
2 teaspoons mustard powder
10 fl oz milk (275 ml)
2 teaspoons lemon juice
a generous pinch of sugar
salt and freshly milled black pepper

Make the mustard sauce first. Melt the butter in a saucepan and gently soften the onion in it for about 10 minutes. Now blend in the flour and cook very gently for a minute or two before adding the mustard powder. Now add the milk a little at a time, stirring after each addition, and, when it's all added, bring the sauce to boiling point and let it simmer very gently for about 3 minutes. Season to taste with salt, pepper, lemon juice and sugar, then keep the sauce warm while you prepare the sprats.

First make a small incision behind a gill of each fish and gently squeeze the belly up towards the head to eject the gut, but try to keep the head intact. Rinse the fish well and dry off any excess moisture with kitchen paper before tossing in the seasoned flour. Heat the oil in a deep pan to 350°F (180°C) – to test, either use a thermometer or throw in a small cube of bread and if it turns golden in about a minute the oil is hot enough. Now deep-fry the sprats for about 3 minutes – you'll probably need to do them in two or three separate lots. When cooked, drain on crumpled greaseproof or absorbent kitchen paper, keep hot and serve as soon as possible sprinkled with a little cayenne pepper and with the mustard sauce poured over.

FRESHWATER FISH
— ♦ —

TROUT

There are two kinds of trout, the *brown* and the *rainbow trout*: the latter has now become more widely available and less expensive because of notable success up and down the country with commercial fish-farming. These farming methods can produce small trout weighing 6–10 oz (175–275 g), which from frozen will poach in about 10 minutes (6 minutes if fresh). Put some parsley, lemon slices, a bay leaf, peppercorns, onion rings and a few herbs in the poaching water, along with a glass of white wine. When cooked, drain the fish and serve with parsley butter (see page 405). Alternatively they can be fried, dipped first in flour, and with a few capers and lemon juice or white wine added to the pan at the end. Trout also bakes and grills well: it is in fact an excellent all-round fish.

Note It is normal to leave the heads on, though the gills should be removed as usual.

TROUT WITH CAPER SAUCE
— ♦ —

(Serves 2 people)

A couple of frozen trout would be all right for this – only let them thaw first.

2 trout, gutted
5 tablespoons olive oil
1 large clove garlic, crushed
juice of 1 large lemon
4 oz capers (110 g), drained and coarsely crushed
salt and freshly milled black pepper

A few hours before cooking time, put the oil in a bowl with the crushed garlic and beat in the lemon juice followed by the capers and some salt and pepper. Then leave it aside for the flavour to develop.

When you're ready to cook the fish, remove the grill rack and line the grill pan with foil. Pre-heat the grill and arrange the fish over the foil, after gashing each side of the fish twice in the thickest part of their bodies, and brushing a little oil on both sides. Sprinkle with salt and pepper and pour on the caper sauce. Grill under a high heat so that the skins turn crisply brown – they will need 3–4 minutes on each side. Then serve with all the pan juices poured over and you'll need lots of crusty bread to mop up the liquid.

SALMON

The salmon has a fascinating career. Once matured – anything between two and seven years old – it will always return to the same river to spawn, sometimes to the exact spot where it was itself hatched. Unfortunately once a salmon enters the river it stops feeding and starts to deteriorate in quality. So commercially sold salmon are always caught in the estuary just as they leave the sea. Their season starts in February and goes on till mid-September: prices (never cheap, regrettably) begin to descend from June when there are more salmon available. One can never afford to buy any but the freshest, and these will have a bright silvery belly and flank, an iridescent purple-black back, with peach-coloured flesh that's firm to the touch.

Salmon is now also widely farmed; but I have to confess to a firm preference for what is called 'wild' salmon. True, farmed salmon is less costly but it's *still* expensive and I would rather buy less salmon and enjoy the incomparable flavour of the real thing.

The very best way to cook it is wrapped in buttered foil in the oven. If you are serving it cold, it can stay in the foil to cool and the skin can be taken off just before serving. A whole, 8 lb (3.5 kg) salmon can feed an entire party, but for a smaller number ask the fishmonger for a middle cut.

FOIL-BAKED FRESH SALMON

◆

(Serves 4 people)

1½ lb middle-cut salmon (700 g)
at least 2 oz butter (50 g)
2 bay leaves
salt and freshly milled black pepper

Pre-heat the oven to gas mark ½, 250°F (130°C).

Start by wiping the fish with some damp kitchen paper, then place it in the centre of a large double sheet of foil, generously buttered. Half the butter and both bay leaves should be placed in the centre cavity of the fish, and the rest of the butter smeared on top. Season well with salt and pepper, then wrap the foil over the salmon to make a loose but tightly sealed parcel. Put the foil parcel on a heatproof plate and bake in the oven for 1 hour, 10 minutes. The skin will come off very easily once the fish is cooked.

For larger pieces of salmon the cooking times are: 2 lb (900 g), 1½ hours; for 3 lb (1.3 kg), 2 hours; for 4 lb (1.8 kg), 2½ hours; for 5 lb (2.25 kg), 3 hours. Salmon steaks are not really suitable for this slow oven treatment. They are best wrapped in buttered foil and placed under the grill at a distance of about 4 inches (10 cm) from the heat. 6–8 oz (175–225 g) steaks will take about 20 minutes.

SALMON TROUT

Also called sea trout, though it is not exactly salmon, trout or sea-going. With its firm but delicate pink flesh, it is said to combine all the virtues of trout and salmon. It weighs anything from 1½–4 lb (700 g–1.8 kg), and can be cooked in exactly the same way as salmon (see above).

SMOKED FISH

One thing at which the British really excel is smoking fish. Nowhere else in the world can you get juicy kippers, smoked Finnan haddies, or sides of smoked salmon comparable to our own. It is an ancient art but, unlike so many that have died out, this one thrives and many traditional smokehouses have survived to supply a constant demand. Smoking was one of the earliest methods developed by man to preserve the surplus of summer for the lean winter, and it was quite logical really: cooking needed fire, and fire provided smoke. The carbon in the smoke reacted with the oils in the food to create a coating which not only had a preservative effect on the fish (or ham or whatever), but also imparted an interesting smoky flavour. Sometimes resinous woods were thrown on the fire at the end of the process to give the food a final tarry layer – which helped ward off flies.

Smoking is in fact the last stage in the preserving process. First comes the salting or brining, which starts to extract moisture from the fish; then comes air-drying or dripping which continues to dry the fish; then smoking which completes the drying and at the same time provides that 'antiseptic' coating. Smoking is only really effective for foods containing plenty of oil, and once again nature has done her bit by supplying just such rich, oily fish as herrings, mackerel and salmon.

Before the days of refrigeration and fast transport fish was much more heavily smoked: nowadays it is only lightly smoked to create flavour rather than to improve the keeping qualities. Lighter smoking also means less natural colour; dyes are often used now to make up for this and help the fish look more like the original heavily smoked product. There are two types of smoking. In cold smoking – at under 85°F (29°C) – care is taken not to cook the flesh, and this is used for haddock, salmon, bloaters and herring (kippers). With hot smoking the temperature reaches 90°F (32°C) and the fish is then lightly cooked at 180°F (82°C) and the results – like Arbroath smokies, mackerel, or buckling – have a stronger, smokier flavour.

While large-scale factory curing and smoking has provided a slightly blander species of smoked fish, at the same time it has put them within the reach of anyone who wants them, and this has kept up a demand. Demand, in turn, has benefited the small traditional smokehouses throughout the country. I am lucky, in this respect, to live near the

Pinney family at Butley Creek in Suffolk, where people come in pilgrimage to a tiny restaurant and shop to sample their unique smoked fish. Mr Pinney's patent process uses whole oak logs rather than the conventional sawdust (modern electric saws, he claims, can leave traces of oil in sawdust which sometimes spoils the flavour of the fish). Oak logs, too, need less attention than sawdust fires which, if unattended, have a habit of going out. Anyway the two modest-looking wooden ovens provide some of the best smoked fish I've ever tasted.

SMOKED SALMON

To start with, the king of them all. The best salmon are said to come from the coldest waters, and Scotch and Irish salmon can well claim to be the best in the world. Once smoked, prime Scotch salmon has a firmer flesh than any other, and can be carved by an expert in complete slices from head to tail, to an almost wafer-like transparency. To enjoy it at its very best (and how else can we afford to at current prices?) it should be carved to order and not pre-sliced and left to dry and curl at the edges. If you're buying it to take home, do have it wrapped carefully and eat it as soon as possible. Smoked salmon experts tend to dismiss pepper mill and lemon wedges when sampling it and, judging from the rare occasions when I have had the opportunity to try really good smoked salmon, I rather agree.

SMOKED TROUT

Smoked trout are delicately flavoured and therefore best served by themselves. To keep them succulent, their skins (their 'mackintoshes' as Margaret Costa aptly describes them in her *Four Seasons Cookbook*) should be left on till just before eating. Serve smoked trout with lemon wedges, and a mixture of a little grated horseradish and whipped cream (not too much horseradish or you will mask the fish flavour, and certainly do not use the commercial sauces which contain turnip amongst other odd ingredients).

SMOKED EEL

A delicacy almost on a par with smoked salmon in my opinion. It's cheaper if bought unfilleted – and better that way because it stays moister. Skinning and filleting at home is very easy. Serve smoked eel in the same way as smoked trout.

SMOKED MACKEREL

Ever since herring fishing has had to be controlled, smoked mackerel has really taken off commercially. It now comes dyed orange and vacuum-packed from supermarkets or, sadly, half defrosted from fishmongers' slabs. The best smoked mackerel is unfrozen and still intact in its skin – worth hunting around for. At Pinneys (see above) they serve smoked mackerel with a sweet brown sauce which matches its richness perfectly.

At home I like to make it into one of my favourite smoked fish pâtés (see page 95).

SMOKED COD'S ROE

This is delicious made into the rich, pink paste which is an anglicised version of the Greek taramasalata (usually made in Greece with salted grey mullet roe). It may seem horrifyingly expensive, but a little of it goes a long way – see the *Taramasalata* recipe on page 93.

THE SMOKED HERRING FAMILY

Kippers

A kipper is a fat, juicy herring which has been split, gutted, salted and smoked. One of the sad things in the history of kippering (a curing process invented in the 1840s by a man called John Woodger) is that since the last war – when some foods were required by weight rather than number – most kippers have been under-cured, because curing removes moisture and therefore weight. Most kippers today are also dyed: this is done to compensate for what would otherwise be their anaemic undercured appearance. Some undyed kippers are still available from parts of Scotland and the Isle of Man, but they're mainly available only in the north-west.

Look for plumpness, oiliness, a silvery-golden colour and a good smoky smell in a kipper. As I've said before, all fish (and meat) tastes better cooked on the bone, and kippers are no exception. I also think grilling is the best way to cook them.

Grilled kippers

Pre-heat the grill, then line the grill pan with foil (which will stop any kippery smells haunting the pan) and brush the foil with melted butter. Remove the heads and tails from the kippers with scissors, then lay the fish on the foil, skin side uppermost. Grill them for 1 minute, turn them over (flesh side uppermost), brush the flesh with melted butter and grill for a further 4–5 minutes until the butter is sizzling. Serve immediately with lemon to squeeze over them and perhaps a dash of cayenne. If you have an aversion to bones, you can of course buy kipper fillets: treat them in just the same way.

Jugged kippers

This is a traditional, and sometimes preferred, way to prepare kippers. All you do is remove the heads, then fold the sides of the fish together and pack vertically in a tall warmed jug. Now pour in enough boiling water to cover the kippers, put a lid or plate on top of the jug, and leave them in a warm place for 6 minutes. Then drain and dry them with kitchen paper, and serve on hot plates with a knob of butter to melt over each fish.

Bloaters

These are very popular in East Anglia. Instead of being split like kippers, the herrings are cured and lightly smoked whole (with guts intact!). When I bought my first bloater I thought there had been some mistake but, no, the guts are meant to provide that 'gamy' flavour. So, to cook them, split them and remove the guts, wipe them with kitchen paper and grill them just like kippers. Alternatively you can make a delicious *Bloater paste*, by pounding the flesh together with butter, lemon juice and a pinch or two of cayenne; serve it spread on toast or in brown bread sandwiches.

Smoked buckling

These are hot-smoked herrings, which need no further cooking, and are nice and juicy. Serve and eat them in the same way as smoked trout, or else separate them out into fillets (easily done with all smoked fish) and serve with thinly sliced onion rings, chopped dill-pickled cucumbers and soured cream.

Smoked sprats

These are young baby herrings, cured and smoked. They're fiddly to deal with but inexpensive and delicious. Skinning and filleting them is time consuming but not difficult. They can be served plain, sprinkled with lemon juice and cayenne.

THE SMOKED HADDOCK FAMILY

Finnan haddock

Six miles south of Aberdeen there's a village called Findon, where east coast haddock were first smoked over peat (Finnan is a derivative of Findon). Much smoked haddock still comes from the Aberdeen area, but some is also smoked in London nowadays. If you want to know the difference: in an Aberdeen cure the fish is split from head to tail so the backbone lies on the right-hand side of the tail; with a London cure the backbone lies on the left and an extra cut is made so that the flesh stands away from the bone. Finnan haddock is best cooked in the oven with a little milk to provide steam, and a generous amount of butter dotted over.

Arbroath smokies

These are young haddock (or occasionally whiting) that have been beheaded and gutted but otherwise left whole. They are then smoked to a dark, almost bronze, colour and always sold in pairs. They're usually eaten hot, brushed with butter on the outside and placed in the oven with a good knob of butter pressed down inside.

Smoked fillets

Usually these *are* haddock, but they can be any white fish (like cod). No smoked fillets have such good flavour as fish smoked on the bone, but they're convenient if you're in a hurry or don't want to be bothered with bones. Good, I think, for poaching, buttering and popping a poached egg on top.

Golden cutlets

Also known as block fillets, these are small smoked fillets of haddock or whiting – too small really to be of much use, but again suitable for a poached egg topping.

SMOKED HADDOCK WITH CREAM AND EGG SAUCE

◆

(Serves 4 people)

Smoked haddock is often served simply with a poached egg, but this recipe with chopped hard-boiled egg in a cream sauce is a delicious alternative.

1½ lb smoked haddock (700 g)
1 bay leaf
10 fl oz milk (275 ml)
approx 2 oz butter (50 g)
1 small onion, finely chopped
1 oz plain flour (25 g)
1 hard-boiled egg, chopped
3 tablespoons double cream
salt and freshly milled black pepper

Pre-heat the oven to gas mark 4, 350°F (180°C).

First place the fish in a baking tin, season with freshly milled black pepper and a little salt, tuck in a bay leaf and add the milk. Dot with ½ oz (10 g) of the butter in flecks and bake, uncovered, for about 20 minutes.

Meanwhile, melt the remaining butter in a saucepan and sauté the onion very gently without colouring it. When the fish is cooked, remove it from the baking tin, keep it warm and pour the liquid in which it was cooked into a jug. Stir the flour into the butter and onion mixture, then add the fish liquid a little at a time and blend to a smooth sauce. Cook over a very low heat for approximately 6 minutes, then stir in the hard-boiled egg and the cream.

Serve the fish with the sauce poured over, perhaps with some mashed potatoes.

SMOKED FISH PIE
♦

(Serves 4 people)

This is a lovely creamy fish pie with a mashed potato topping and a golden crust of melted cheese. You can in fact use any combination of smoked fish – sometimes a couple of ounces of smoked salmon offcuts make an interesting addition. (Illus. opposite p. 192.)

1½ lb smoked haddock (700 g)
4 kipper fillets, weighing a total 4–6 oz (110–175 g)
1 pint milk (570 ml)
4 oz butter (110 g)
1 bay leaf
2 oz flour (50 g)
2 hard-boiled eggs, roughly chopped
3 tablespoons chopped fresh parsley
1 tablespoon capers (these can be left out if not available)
1 tablespoon lemon juice
salt and freshly milled black pepper
For the topping
2 lb freshly boiled potatoes (900 g)
2 oz butter (50 g)
4 tablespoons milk
a little freshly grated nutmeg
1 oz strong Cheddar cheese (25 g), grated

Pre-heat the oven to gas mark 6, 400°F (200°C).

Arrange the fish in a baking tin, pour half the milk over it, add a few flecks of the butter and the bay leaf, then bake in the oven for 15–20 minutes. Pour off and reserve the cooking liquid, then remove the skin from the fish and flake the flesh into largish pieces.

Next make the sauce by melting the remaining butter in a saucepan, then stirring in the flour and gradually adding the fish liquid bit by bit, stirring well after each addition. When all the liquid is in, finish the sauce by gradually adding the remaining milk, seasoning with salt and pepper and simmering for 3–4 minutes.

Now mix the fish into the sauce, together with the hard-boiled eggs, parsley and capers (if using), taste to see if it needs any more seasoning, and stir in the lemon juice. Pour the mixture into a buttered baking dish (about 2½ pints/1.5 litres capacity).

Next prepare the topping. Cream the potatoes, starting off with a large fork, then finishing with an electric beater if you have one, adding the butter and milk. Season the potatoes with salt and pepper and add some freshly grated nutmeg, spread evenly all over the fish, then sprinkle with the cheese. Bake on a high shelf in the oven – still at gas mark 6, 400°F (200°C) – for about 30 minutes, by which time the pie will be heated through and the top will be nicely tinged with brown.

KIPPER FISH CAKES

◆

(Serves 4 people)

Boned kipper fillets are best for these, as there are no fiddly bits to worry about!

approx. 1 lb kipper fillets (450 g)
1 lb potatoes (450 g), scrubbed
1 hard-boiled egg, chopped
2 teaspoons English mustard
2 teaspoons grated onion
1 tablespoon chopped capers, drained
2 tablespoons chopped parsley
1–2 tablespoons cream or top of the milk
a little grated nutmeg
salt and cayenne pepper
butter and oil for frying
To garnish
watercress and lemon quarters

First boil the potatoes in their jackets in salted water until tender, then cool and drain them and peel off the skins. Place the potatoes in a bowl with the egg, mustard, onion, capers, parsley and cream.

Jug the kippers (as described on page 123), then flake the fish, discarding any bones and skin, and add the flesh to the potato mixture. Beat with a fork until everything is well combined, then season to taste with nutmeg and cayenne.

Heat sufficient butter and oil to cover the base of a thick frying-pan. Press the mixture into about twelve small cake shapes, then fry for about

5 minutes on each side until they are a golden-brown colour. Drain them on absorbent kitchen paper.

To serve, garnish with sprigs of watercress and lemon quarters (for squeezing the juice over the fish cakes) and have more cayenne pepper available for those who like it.

POTTED HADDOCK WITH CAPERS
♦

(Serves 8 people)

This is good as a light lunch with some home-made wholemeal bread, or as a first course with triangles of brown toast.

1 lb smoked haddock fillets (450 g)
8 oz unsalted butter (225 g), melted
a good pinch of hot curry powder
2–3 tablespoons lemon juice
salt and freshly milled black pepper
To garnish and serve
4 tablespoons capers, drained
watercress or parsley
lemon quarters

Place the haddock fillets in a pan, cover with boiling water and poach them for about 5 minutes, then remove from the pan and drain thoroughly. Now skin the fish and flake the flesh into the goblet of a liquidiser. Add the melted butter and blend until smooth. Then empty the mixture into a bowl and season – but be sparing with the salt. Stir in the curry powder and lemon juice to taste and fill eight individual dishes with the mixture.

Chop the drained capers and scatter some on the top of each dish. Cover with foil or cling film and put the dishes in the refrigerator so that the fish mixture becomes firm before serving. Serve with lemon quarters and sprigs of parsley or watercress.

MARINATED KIPPER FILLETS
♦

(Serves 4 people)

This dish, if you leave it to marinate long enough, puts kipper fillets in the smoked salmon class.

Hot cross buns (see page 53)

8 kipper fillets, approx. 12 oz (350 g) in weight

For the marinade
1 medium onion, thinly sliced into rings
2 teaspoons coriander seeds, crushed
2 bay leaves
1 heaped teaspoon mustard powder
1 dessertspoon brown sugar
2 fl oz wine vinegar (55 ml)
6 fl oz mild olive oil (175 ml)
freshly milled black pepper

To garnish
lettuce leaves, lemon slices and watercress

Turn the kipper fillets upside down on a flat surface and, using a sharp knife to help you, take off the skins. Then in a 1½ pint (850 ml) oval dish, layer the fillets with slices of onion and a sprinkling of coriander and freshly milled black pepper, tucking the bay leaves here and there.

Now in a screw-top jar dissolve the mustard powder and brown sugar in the vinegar and olive oil, screw on the lid and shake vigorously, then pour the mixture over the fillets. Now cover the dish very carefully, with either a lid or a double sheet of foil or cling film. Then leave the kipper fillets to marinate in the lowest part of the refrigerator for a minimum of 4 days or up to a week.

To serve, place two fillets on a crisp lettuce leaf for each person. Garnish with lemon slices and watercress, and serve with thinly sliced brown bread and butter.

SHELLFISH

♦

MUSSELS

I love the appearance of mussels: a rich saffron colour and they sit so prettily in the blue, boat-shaped shells. To me their aroma and flavour are the very essence of the sea. Some people accuse them of being dangerous to eat, but in fact mussel poisoning (unpleasant though never dangerous) is positively rare. If you know how to buy mussels and how to deal with them the risk is negligible. I would point out, however, that all shellfish is highly perishable. So you should always eat mussels (and any other type of shellfish for that matter) on the day you buy them.

Mussels are at their best in cold weather, so their season is usually from October to March. When you see them in a fishmonger's, a sign of

Soupe à l'oignon gratinée (see page 72)   129

freshness is that most of them are tightly closed: if there are a lot of 'gapers' don't bother. When buying mussels you need to allow at least 1 pint (570 ml) per person for a first course, and 1¹/₂–2 pints (about 1 litre) for a main course. That may seem a lot, but some will have to be discarded and, once they have been shelled, mussels are very small and light.

The ritual of cleaning and preparing them *sounds* more bother than it actually is. When you get them home, dump the mussels straightaway into a sinkful of cold water. First of all throw out any that float to the top, then leave the cold tap running over them while you take a small knife and scrape off all the barnacles and pull off the little hairy beards. Discard any mussels that are broken, and any that are open and refuse to close tight when given a sharp tap with a knife.

After you've cleaned each one, place it straight in another bowl of clean water. When they're all in, swirl them around in three or four more changes of cold water to get rid of any lingering bits of grit or sand. Leave the cleaned mussels in cold water until you're ready to cook them. As an extra safety precaution, always check mussels again after cooking – this time discarding any whose shells haven't opened.

MOULES À LA MARINIÈRE

◆

(Serves 4 people as a first course)

This is the most popular of all mussel recipes and, for me, a real treat served with crusty French bread and some chilled white wine.

4 pints mussels (2.25 litres), cleaned
2 oz butter (50 g)
1 clove garlic, chopped
1 onion, finely chopped
5 fl oz dry white wine (150 ml)
3 tablespoons double cream
salt and freshly milled black pepper
To serve
1 tablespoon freshly chopped parsley

In a wide-bottomed pan melt half the butter and, over a low heat, gently soften the garlic and onion. Then pour in the white wine and, when it comes to the boil, tip in the mussels – which should have been drained and dried a little first. Cover with a lid and leave on a high heat for 4–5 minutes. Then remove the lid and start lifting out the mussels as they open and place them on a warm dish – a draining spoon is best for this. Keep them warm in a very low heated oven. Throw away the empty half shells, and any mussels that have not opened up their shells during cooking.

Have ready a sieve lined with fine muslin; strain the liquid in which the mussels were cooked through this (discarding the onion), then return it to the pan. Simmer to reduce by half, then add the cream and the rest of the butter. Season with freshly milled black pepper and, perhaps, a little salt. When the cream has heated and the butter has melted, pour the sauce over the mussels resting in their half shells, and sprinkle on the chopped parsley.

MUSSELS WITH GARLIC STUFFING
♦

(Serves 4 people)

You *have* to like your garlic for this one and, if you do, be sure to have lots of crusty fresh bread to mop up the delicious juices.

4 pints mussels (2.25 litres), cleaned
4 oz butter (110 g), at room temperature
1 tablespoon lemon juice
1 heaped tablespoon chopped parsley
3 cloves garlic, crushed
salt and freshly milled black pepper

Pre-heat the oven to gas mark 8, 450°F (230°C).

Place the prepared mussels in a wide dry saucepan, cover and cook over a low heat (there's no need to add any liquid) until they all open. Remove and discard the empty half shells and throw away any mussels that haven't opened. Arrange the remaining mussels in their half shells in four individual fireproof dishes.

Next, in a basin, combine the butter, lemon juice, parsley and garlic, season with salt and pepper and mix well. Place a small dab of the savoury butter on each mussel then put the dishes on the top shelf of the oven and cook for 5–10 minutes or until the mussels are sizzling noisily. Serve immediately, still sizzling and bubbling.

SCALLOPS

Scallops with their bright orange roes come in decorative shells. The fish itself sits on a flat fan-shaped shell and is enclosed by a similar concave one (the shell scallops are traditionally served in). This curved shell has become a religious and cultural symbol: the shrine of St James the apostle at Compostella in Spain has adopted the scallop shell as its emblem, and scallops themselves have been named after the saint – hence *Coquilles St Jacques*. Scallops are a great delicacy, and in fact some of the best scallops in the world come from British waters off the Isle of Man, and the Cornish and Irish coasts.

When you're buying scallops, as with other shellfish, it's obviously best to buy them as fresh as possible (i.e. live in the shell); if their shells are closed you can be sure they're fresh. Don't worry if you're nervous about these things, the fishmonger will open and clean them ready for you. Some shops sell scallops already prepared, in which case you'd do well to make sure they look plump, firm and upright. If scallops look at all sad and soggy, then they've probably been prepared rather too long ago. An acceptable alternative to fresh scallops are the frozen ones – not so good, of course, but better than none.

Scallops cook very quickly. The corals take just a matter of seconds, so they are usually added to the cooking pan only shortly before serving.

SCALLOP CREAM SOUP

◆

(Serves 4–6 people)

This is very easy and quick to prepare and cook, but tastes really luxurious.

4 very large scallops (when taken out of their shells the total weight should be approx. 12 oz or 350 g), cleaned
2 oz butter (50 g)
1 medium onion, finely chopped
1 lb potatoes (450 g), peeled and diced
1 pint fish stock (570 ml) (see page 67)
10 fl oz cold milk (275 ml)
2 egg yolks
3 fl oz double cream (75 ml)
salt and freshly milled black pepper

First gently melt the butter in a fairly large saucepan, add the onion and cook it *very* gently without colouring it at all (about 10 minutes). Next add the diced potatoes, mix them in with the butter and onions, and season with salt and pepper. Then, keeping the heat very low, put the lid on the pan and leave the mixture to sweat for another 10–15 minutes.

After that pour in the hot fish stock, give it a good stir, cover the pan again and leave to simmer gently for a further 10–15 minutes.

Meanwhile you can be preparing the scallops: wash and dry them thoroughly and cut off the coral-coloured bits – chop these and keep them on one side on a separate plate. The white parts should be diced roughly, put in a saucepan with the cold milk and a little salt and pepper, then poached *very* gently for 8–10 minutes.

When the vegetables are cooked, transfer them and their cooking liquid to a blender and whisk to a purée (or else press it all through a nylon sieve). Now combine the white parts of the scallops (and the milk they were cooked in) with the potato purée. At this point the pieces of coral roe can be added and the soup gently reheated.

Finally beat the egg yolks thoroughly with the cream, remove the soup pan from the heat, stir in the egg mixture and return the pan to a *gentle* heat. Cook, stirring, until the soup thickens slightly – but be very careful not to let it come anywhere near the boil or it will curdle.

To serve, pour the soup into a warm tureen and ladle it into warm soup bowls. This really is one of the most delicate and delicious soups.

Note If you want to make this soup in advance, prepare it up to the egg yolk and cream stage. This final stage should only be done at the last minute, just before serving.

SCALLOPS IN THE SHELL
◆

(Serves 4 people as a first course)

I think these look very pretty served in the natural, deep shells, brown and bubbly from the grill. If these are not easy to come by, you can get very attractive heatproof shell-shaped dishes which can be used for all sorts of fish starters.

8 small or 4 large scallops, cleaned
10 fl oz dry white wine (275 ml)
butter
½ onion, finely chopped
4 oz mushrooms (110 g), sliced
1½ oz plain flour (40 g)
5 fl oz double cream (150 ml)
2 tablespoons white breadcrumbs
1 tablespoon grated Parmesan cheese
salt and freshly milled black pepper

Start by slicing the white part of each scallop into rounds, putting the corals on one side for use later. Then poach the white slices very, very gently in white wine until tender – about 10 minutes. (It's always necessary to cook scallops gently or they can become tough.) When they're cooked, strain them, reserving the liquid.

Now melt 2 oz (50 g) butter in a saucepan, add the onion and mushrooms and cook over a low heat for about 15 minutes. Then sprinkle in the flour, and add the scallop liquid very gradually, stirring continuously to obtain a thick smooth sauce. Add seasoning and a little more butter and cook gently for about 6 minutes.

Then remove the saucepan from the heat and stir in the white slices and the coral pieces of scallop, plus the cream. Now heat the mixture through over a very gentle heat, taking great care not to let it boil. Combine the breadcrumbs and Parmesan cheese. Divide the scallop mixture between four buttered scallop shells, sprinkle with the breadcrumbs and cheese, add flecks of butter and brown under a pre-heated grill.

PRAWNS AND SHRIMPS

If I was ever an aspiring gourmet, time has tempered me. No longer can I be tempted to peel 2 pints of cooked brown shrimps (a job which used to take all afternoon) to make a tiny amount of shrimp paste – admittedly delicious but consumed, it seemed, in a few seconds. But fresh, fat and juicy native prawns, *yes*, I will willingly peel to serve unadulterated – with just some lettuce, a squeeze of lemon or perhaps some home-made mayonnaise. They have to be fresh, native prawns though. For 'prawns' covers a multitude of varieties, many of them from warm foreign waters where they grow fast and often large. Even when unfrozen these lack the firm texture and flavour of our own. If I *have* to buy frozen prawns for cooking, the best I've come across are the Norwegian prawns which the food departments of one quality chain-store sell.

Just to confuse matters, what we call prawns the Americans call shrimps. But our tiny shrimps are almost a national delicacy when potted in Lancashire with melted butter and spices. At one time these potted shrimps came in prettily glazed porcelain pots, but now plastic has penetrated here too. One authority suggests that for the flavour of potted shrimps to be appreciated, they should be gently warmed till the butter just begins to flow. I agree, and I've found that melting the shrimp butter in a saucepan with a couple of tablespoons of fresh cream makes a lovely 'instant' sauce to serve with plain grilled fish.

Scampi, by the way, is the Italian name for what we used to call Dublin Bay prawns. They are not in fact prawns but a tiny member of the lobster family (yet another name for this shellfish is Norway lobster). All the meat lies in the tail and scampi are always sold headless, usually already boiled and rubbery and frozen, destined to end up coated in horrid orange breadcrumbs as a basket meal. If you are ever in Ireland, the native real Dublin Bay prawns are a delight.

How to peel prawns
Holding the prawn's head with your left hand and its tail with your right hand, uncurl the prawn and straighten it out as much as possible. Now press the head and tail towards each other in a straight line, and then pull them apart again – the shell should come away in your right hand, leaving the head and body in your left hand. Simply separate the head from the body.

SPICED PRAWNS WITH TOMATOES

◆

(Serves 2–3 people)

I think fresh boiled and peeled prawns are so delicious all they need is lemon juice, seasoning and some wholemeal bread and butter. Frozen prawns, on the other hand, need an imaginative recipe like this one.

8 oz packet frozen prawns (225 g), de-frosted and well drained
1 lb tomatoes (450 g), peeled and chopped
1½ tablespoons groundnut oil
1 large onion, halved and sliced
2 cloves garlic, crushed
¾ teaspoon coriander seeds
½ teaspoon cumin seeds
1 cardamom pod
1 teaspoon grated fresh root ginger or ½ teaspoon ground ginger
1 rounded teaspoon ground turmeric
½ teaspoon chilli powder
salt and freshly milled black pepper

In a large frying-pan heat the oil, then add the onion slices and fry gently for approximately 10 minutes or until softened and golden.

In the meantime, place the whole spices in a dry frying-pan and roast them over a gentle heat for about 5 minutes to draw out their aroma, then crush them with a pestle and mortar (or this can be done in a small basin using the end of a rolling pin). Then add all the spices, together with the garlic, to the onion and stir until everything is well heated. Now add the prawns and stir them around too, so that they're evenly coated with the spice mixture, then add the prepared tomatoes and some salt and freshly milled pepper. Bring to simmering point and cook for about 20–25 minutes, uncovered, by which time a lot of the excess liquid will have evaporated and the tomatoes will have reduced to the consistency of a sauce.

Serve with *Spiced pilau rice* (see page 275) or some nutty-flavoured brown rice cooked with onion.

CRAB

If you're not squeamish you can buy fresh, live crab and cook it yourself. I'm afraid I am squeamish and I could no more drop a live crab into boiling water than I could stab it through the head. I'm perfectly happy to leave the boiling to the experts and to find a reliable fishmonger to choose me a good cooked crab.

A good crab full of meat should feel heavy for its size. I bought one recently which weighed just over 1 lb (450 g) and it yielded almost 7 oz (200 g) of meat. From a large 2 lb (900 g) crab you should get about 12 oz (350 g) of meat. Together with some home-made mayonnaise and a salad, 7–8 oz (200–225 g) of crabmeat is plenty for two people as a main course – or can stretch between four for a starter.

How to dress crab

The first thing you do is to choose and buy your cooked crab. The fishmonger will pull it slightly open so that you can see it's full of meat and not empty. Back in your kitchen you'll need a chopping board, two bowls (one for the white meat and one for the dark meat), a small sharp knife, a teaspoon, a metal skewer (preferably flat), and either a small hammer or a pair of nutcrackers.

Put the crab on its back on the chopping board, so that the claws and softer body shell face upwards, then simply twist off the legs and claws – they'll come away very easily – and put them on one side.

Now put your thumbs against the hard back shell close to the crab's tail, and push and prise the body section out and away from the hard back shell. From the body section you now remove and discard (i) the small greyish-white stomach sac, just behind the mouth and (ii) the long white pointed 'dead man's fingers'. These can be easily distinguished and it is a quick and easy job to remove them.

The body shell (and in particular the parts where the legs and claws joined the body) is a mass of tiny crevices, all harbouring delicious meat. Scrape and pick the meat out, dividing it between the bowls according to the colour of the meat. Remove the meat from the hard back shell in the same way.

Crack the claws and legs with your hammer or nutcracker then, with a skewer, poke out all the white meat into the appropriate bowl.

If you want to serve the crab in the hard back shell, break off the jagged, overlapping rim from all round the edge of the shell, then wash and dry it well, and smear it inside with oil.

Then season the white meat with salt, freshly milled pepper, cayenne and lemon juice (chopping or shredding the meat a little). Now season the brown meat in the same way. Place it down the centre of the shell, and place the white meat on either side. Finally decorate the crab with finely chopped parsley and serve with a fresh crisp salad and some home-made mayonnaise (see page 438).

HOT CRAB SOUFFLÉ

♦

(Serves 4–6 people as a first course)

Crabmeat makes one of the nicest of all hot savoury soufflés.

meat from a freshly cooked crab, weighing 1 lb (450 g), or 8 oz (225 g) frozen mixed brown and white crabmeat, thawed
1½ oz butter (40 g)
1½ oz flour (40 g)
5 fl oz single cream (150 ml)
5 fl oz milk (150 ml)
1 tablespoon grated onion
2 tablespoons grated Parmesan cheese
½ teaspoon mustard powder
3 tablespoons chopped parsley
1½ teaspoons anchovy essence
1–2 teaspoons lemon juice
5 egg yolks
6 egg whites
salt and cayenne pepper

Pre-heat the oven to gas mark 6, 400°F (200°C), and put in a baking sheet on the shelf below centre.

First grease a 4 pint (2.25 litre) baking or soufflé dish. Then melt the butter in a saucepan, stir in the flour and cook for 1–2 minutes. Then gradually add the cream and milk, a little at a time, stirring after each addition. Bring to the boil and – still stirring – allow it to simmer for a minute or two. Now remove the pan from the heat and stir in the rest of the ingredients, except for the crabmeat and egg whites.

Next, add the crabmeat and taste the mixture – it should have quite a strong flavour. If not add some more anchovy essence, salt, cayenne and lemon juice. Now whisk the egg whites until stiff but not dry and, using a metal spoon, fold them into the crab mixture, then pour the soufflé into the prepared baking dish. Put the dish on the pre-heated baking sheet in the oven and bake for 45–50 minutes. After about 30 minutes, check to see that the top of the soufflé is not getting too brown – if it is, cover with foil. Serve *immediately* it's cooked.

SEE ALSO

Anchoïade
Avocado mousse with prawns and vinaigrette
Avocado and fresh crab salad
Baked mackerel with herb stuffing
Brown rice and tuna fish salad
Buttery kedgeree
Fillets of sole gratinés
Fish cakes
Garlicky fish soup

Kipper quiche
Poached trout with herbs
Salade Niçoise
Smoked fish creams
Smoked fish pâté
Smoked mackerel pâté
Taramasalata
Trout with butter, cream and chives
White bean and tuna fish salad

MEAT:
ROASTING AND POT-ROASTING

◆

When it comes to meat in this country, we are confronted with a paradox. On the one hand we are told we eat too much meat and that is not healthy for us; on the other hand more and more sophisticated forms of intensive rearing are developed to encourage us to eat more meat. The result of this rearing is to produce meat that is a pale shadow of what meat should – indeed used to – look like and taste like.

The irony is that this country has an abundance of hill pasture where no arable crops can grow, but where animals *can* graze naturally, ranging free as it were. The flavour of Welsh mountain sheep, Highland beef, or pork that has the run of fields or orchards is unsurpassed. Yet there is a way we could all resolve this paradox, and that is to eat *less* meat and stop intensive rearing, which does not allow for proper growth and the maturity that brings quality and flavour, and which can subject us to the kind of health scares we have experienced recently.

Of course our meat would be more expensive, but that would encourage us to eat it less and the health lobby would be happier. But to compensate for that, when we *do* eat it, it would be of infinitely better quality and flavour.

OVEN-ROASTING

◆

Strictly speaking, roasting means exposing a piece of meat to an open fire, turning it (usually on a spit) so the air circulates around it and each part comes near to the source of the heat and the whole is cooked evenly. True roasting in fact is more like grilling as we know it: the nearest equivalent is the modern spit-roast, which is fitted to some domestic ovens or sold as a separate unit. Still, for most of us, in practical terms roasting means cooking a joint inside an ordinary oven.

It is best to begin roasting with a very high oven setting (gas mark 9, 475°F, 240°C) and then lower the heat to continue cooking. This blast of heat at the beginning produces a more attractive-looking joint with a tasty outside crust. In order to approximate some circulation of air in an enclosed oven, setting the joint on a roasting rack is often advised. It doesn't make a great deal of difference, though, unless you object to the very crusty, well-cooked bit of the meat that sits on the base of the roasting tin. With something like a piece of sirloin or a rib joint on the bone, the bone itself provides a form of built-in rack.

POT-ROASTING

———— ◆ ————

The trouble with a straightforward roast, quite apart from requiring the more expensive cuts of meat, is that the meal as a whole (including Yorkshire pudding and roast potatoes) can take up a great deal of your time and attention. Pot roasts on the other hand leave you in peace. You still get a reasonably-sized joint to carve and at a cheaper price.

The principle of pot-roasting is long, slow cooking of the meat in a fairly heavy cooking-pot (with a tight-fitting lid) in a small amount of liquid which can be stock, wine or cider. This creates a steamy atmosphere inside the closed pot, which keeps the joint moist as it cooks. Herbs and vegetables may be added too, and sometimes the meat is marinated first. The finished dish should be very tender and succulent.

BEEF

———— ◆ ————

Scotch beef, bred in the Highlands, grass-fed, mature and well hung, is the best in the world, and in the last couple of years I have also had some very good Irish beef, but I cannot reconcile myself to the immature barley-fed variety (which is widely sold in my neighbourhood at any rate): an insipid imitation of what good beef should be, it seems to me. I really feel it would be better to have less meat – make a really good piece of beef a treat – so that we would not have to rear it so intensively.

I have heard breeders say that this mass-produced beef is what the housewife wants; that is, lots of it, tender and almost fatless. But what people so often fail to realise is that fat means flavour: tender lean meat that is lacking the one essential, flavour, is no pleasure at all. Nature has so arranged things that when a good piece of meat with its proper percentage of fat is placed near a fire or in an oven, the heat draws out some of the juices while the fat melts and bastes the meat within as well as outside, keeping the meat succulent (which is why wise old cooks, and wise new ones too, take care to baste the meat as it is roasting). If you can't eat the fat at the end, that doesn't matter; its presence during cooking is the essential thing.

CUTS FOR OVEN-ROASTING

The cardinal rule here is to buy the right cut in the first place. It's no wonder that letters pour in from people who are unsuccessful in roasting beef when you consider some of the so-called roasting joints on offer – all manner of things get tied up with string and labelled 'roasting'. My advice is to buy an unequivocal, decent-sized piece of *sirloin* for a special occasion, and otherwise a *double rib joint* (which as it happens is next door, anatomically).

Do buy and cook your joint *on the bone*. You won't be paying any extra, since meat bought on the bone costs less per pound. The bone provides a good conductor of heat inside the joint, thus cooking the meat more evenly with less loss of juices; it also helps to stop the meat disintegrating, which you will appreciate when you come to carve. If you are worried that your family is too small to cope with a large joint, bear in mind that good roast beef is delicious cold with chutney and jacket potatoes, and minced it makes lovely rissoles and cottage pie. However, if you prefer it, both the above joints can be boned and rolled. When you buy a piece of sirloin, make sure it contains the 'eye' or undercut, which some butchers take out and sell as fillet steak (which it is). A decent joint of sirloin on the bone will weigh 4–5 lb (1.8–2.5 kg). If you choose a wing rib for roasting, then ask for a 'double rib' as a single one is too thin – it looks the same as a sirloin but without the undercut. A more economical roasting joint – which unhappily is not always available unless you order it – is a cut called the *aitchbone*. A whole one is very large, but some butchers will sell part of one. It comes from the pelvic region of the animal, just behind the rump, and as it needs slower roasting it isn't really suitable for eating rare, but its flavour is excellent.

CUTS FOR POT-ROASTING

The medium-priced and cheaper cuts are usually the most suitable for pot roasts: *silverside* and *top rump* are both good, and so is *chuck* and *blade*, boned and rolled. My favourite is *brisket* (economical and with lots of flavour), but you need a reliable butcher to roll it for you, because a lot of excess fat and gristle can be lurking unseen inside.

ROASTING BEEF

Dust the fat-surface with a mixture of flour and dry mustard, and sprinkle with freshly milled pepper (but no salt, since this encourages the juices to escape). Start by giving it 20 minutes at gas mark 9, 475°F (245°C), then lower the heat to gas mark 5, 375°F (190°C), and cook for 15 minutes per pound (450 g) (for rare), plus 15 extra minutes (for medium-rare) or 30 minutes extra (for well-done), and baste the meat by spooning the pan juices over it from time to time during the cooking.

Try to plan the meal so that the joint is allowed to 'relax' for about 30 minutes before carving. Keep it in a warm place but don't worry that it will become cold – it will hold its heat for this time. Removing it from direct heat will firm up the texture, making it easier to carve. This will also permit you to increase the heat in the oven for the roast potatoes and Yorkshire pudding. As the meat relaxes, some of the juices will exude onto the plate: these should be added to the gravy. And while on the subject of carving, may I refer you to my comments on knives on page 14. Carving is only difficult and dangerous when the knife is blunt.

ACCOMPANIMENTS TO BEEF

Grating fresh *horseradish* is a tiresome job: the fumes cause tears and discomfort. It is possible, though, to buy preserved grated horseradish, which you can combine with cream to make your own sauce – or else stir a little grated horseradish into some commercially bottled horseradish sauce to give it an extra kick. Whether it is on its own or mixed with cream, grated horseradish is very strong – so be warned. *Mustard* is the other traditional accompaniment, and should be freshly made up 10 minutes, at least, before it is needed. *Yorkshire pudding* was originally served as a first course, to temper the appetite and make the meat go further. But crisply-made Yorkshire pud is now – and with every reason – something of a delicacy. There are just a few rules: for a successful pudding you must (i) have the oven very hot, (ii) use a flameproof metal container, and (iii) always use plain flour rather than self-raising.

YORKSHIRE PUDDING

◆

(Serves 4 people)

The best container I've come across for Yorkshire pudding is a cast-iron enamelled gratin dish which fits this recipe perfectly, or if I want to feed eight people I make double the mixture and use two dishes. Alternatively an 11 × 7 inch (28 × 18 cm) solid roasting tin will do.

3 oz plain flour (75 g)
1 egg
3 fl oz milk (75 ml)
2 fl oz water (55 ml)
salt and freshly milled pepper
2 tablespoons beef dripping (for the roasting tin)

First read the notes on Yorkshire pudding above!

To make the batter, sift the flour into a bowl, make a well in the centre, break an egg into it and beat it, gradually incorporating the flour, milk, water, and seasoning (an electric hand-whisk will do this in seconds). You don't have to leave batter to stand, so make it when you're ready.

About 15 minutes before the beef is due to come out of the oven, increase the heat to gas mark 7, 425°F (220°C), and place the gratin dish or roasting tin on a baking sheet on a free shelf, adding the dripping. After 15 minutes remove the meat and leave on one side to rest, then place the pudding tin over direct heat while you pour the batter into the sizzling hot fat. Then return the tin to the baking sheet on the highest shelf (or second highest, if you have roast potatoes on that one). The pudding will take about 25–30 minutes to rise and become crisp and golden. Serve as soon as possible, as it loses its crunchiness if it has to wait around too long.

BŒUF EN DAUBE

◆

(Serves 6 people)

3–3½ lb top rump of beef (1.3–1.6 kg), tightly rolled and tied
2 oz dripping (50 g)
1 tablespoon plain flour
10 fl oz stock (275 ml)
4 tomatoes, peeled and quartered
2 oz dark-gilled mushrooms (50 g), sliced
1 tablespoon flour and 1 oz (25 g) butter, worked to a paste
freshly milled black pepper
For the marinade
10 fl oz red wine (275 ml)
2 tablespoons olive oil
2 tablespoons red wine vinegar
2 onions, halved and sliced
2 carrots, sliced in rounds
1 bay leaf
2 inch strip orange rind (5 cm)
½ teaspoon whole black peppercorns
6 allspice berries
2 cloves garlic, chopped
1 sprig fresh thyme
2 teaspoons salt

First prepare the marinade by combining all the ingredients in a bowl, then put in the meat. Cover with a cloth, then put in a cold place for at least 12 hours, and during that time, turn the meat over occasionally.

When you wish to begin cooking, pre-heat the oven to gas mark 1, 275°F (140°C). Remove the meat from the marinade and dry it thoroughly on kitchen paper.

Now heat the dripping in a thick cooking pot which will take the meat neatly and, when the fat is hot, add the meat and sear it all over – it should be a nutty-brown colour. Then transfer to a plate, and pour off all but about 1 tablespoon of the fat from the pan.

Next, remove the carrot and onion from the marinade with a draining spoon, reserving the liquid. Dry them on kitchen paper, then tip them into the cooking pot and fry them until they are lightly browned. Then stir in the flour and brown this slowly, but be careful it doesn't burn. Now stir in the reserved marinade liquid and flavourings, stock, tomatoes and mushrooms, add the meat and season with freshly milled black pepper.

Bring to simmering point, cover with a piece of foil and a tight-fitting lid, then place the pot in the centre of the oven and let the beef cook slowly for about 3 hours. The meat is fully cooked when a skewer can be inserted easily.

When ready, remove the meat and keep warm. Tip the contents of the pot into a sieve placed over a bowl and press the vegetables against the side of the sieve to extract all the juices, then discard all the debris in the sieve. Return the liquid to the pan and boil quickly to reduce and concentrate the flavour. Now add the butter-and-flour paste and whisk, with a balloon whisk, until the sauce thickens.

Season to taste with salt and pepper. Carve the meat, pour over some of the sauce and pour the rest into a warmed sauce-boat. I would serve this with plain boiled or roast potatoes, and something green and leafy like Brussels sprouts or spring cabbage.

ENGLISH POT-ROAST

◆

(Serves 4–6 people)

You *could* use topside or silverside for this, but rolled brisket has the best flavour of all.

2¹/₂ lb rolled brisket (1.25 kg)
6 small whole onions, peeled
6 smallish carrots, peeled
4 celery stalks, cut in three
¹/₂ large swede, peeled and cut in chunks
beef dripping
4 oz dark-gilled mushrooms (110 g)
10 fl oz hot stock (or hot water enriched with ¹/₂ teaspoon Worcestershire sauce and 2 teaspoons mushroom ketchup) (275 ml)
1 bay leaf
1 sprig thyme
1 tablespoon flour and 1 oz (25 g) butter worked to a paste
salt and freshly milled black pepper

Pre-heat the oven to gas mark 1, 275°F (140°C).

First melt the dripping in a thick cooking pot and, when it's hot, put in the meat and sear and brown it all over, then transfer it to a plate.

Next lightly brown the onions, carrots, celery and swede, then remove them temporarily to the plate too.

Next, empty all the fat from the pot, then replace the brisket and arrange the browned vegetables and mushrooms around the meat. Add the hot stock, bay leaf and thyme and a little salt and pepper. Cover with foil and a tightly fitting lid and as soon as you hear simmering, place in the centre of the oven and leave for about 3 hours.

When ready, place the meat and vegetables on a warmed serving dish, then bring the liquid to the boil and boil briskly until reduced slightly. Add the butter-and-flour paste and whisk until the sauce thickens. Serve the sauce with the meat and vegetables and some sharp English mustard or horseradish. A green vegetable would be a good accompaniment.

BOILED BEEF AND DUMPLINGS

◆

(Serves 6–8 people)

Salted silverside would do for this, but salted brisket is even better.

3 lb joint boned and rolled salted brisket (1.3 kg) (ask your butcher if it needs soaking or not)
1 sprig thyme
1 bay leaf
a few parsley stalks
6–8 medium carrots
6–8 small onions
2 turnips, quartered
2–3 celery stalks, cut into 1 inch (2.5 cm) lengths
salt and freshly milled black pepper
For the dumplings
4 oz self-raising flour (110g)
2 oz shredded suet (50 g)
¼ teaspoon dried mixed herbs

Place the meat in a deep saucepan and cover it with cold water. Add the herbs, some salt and pepper, and bring slowly to the boil. Cover and simmer for about an hour, skimming the surface to remove any scum half-way through. Then add the vegetables, cover and simmer gently for another hour or until tender.

To make the dumplings, mix the flour, ¼ teaspoon salt and some pepper in a bowl. Stir in the suet and herbs and add just enough water to make a soft but not too sticky dough. Shape it into eight small dumplings.

Next remove the meat from the pan and keep warm. Pop the

dumplings into the pan, cover and cook for 20–25 minutes. Slice the beef and serve it surrounded by the vegetables and dumplings with a little of the broth as a gravy, and plenty of mustard.

PORK

The pig has long played an honourable part in the British diet. Every part of him can be consumed: even his skin translates into crisp, crunchy crackling and his fat is rendered down into pure lard. Before the Enclosure Acts and the industrial revolution, almost every cottage kept its pig which was consumed by the family in the seasons when there was an R in the month (this was before the days of refrigeration). Winter sealed the fate of the cottage pig; the dressed boar's head was a festive Christmas dish, and the salting, lard-making and preserving of the pork were all done in the coldest weather. Even the pig-sty was cleansed by the sharp January frosts, ready for the young porker to be moved in in the spring and be fattened up for the next winter. By a happy coincidence a cottage would often have a small orchard attached, where in autumn the windfall apples provided a succulent addition to the pig's diet (so apple sauce became a natural environmental accompaniment for him when he got served up on the plate).

Today pork is reared fairly intensively. Again our modern preoccupation with leanness has taken its toll on character and flavour. For good, well-flavoured pork it is essential to shop around for a reliable butcher who buys in turn from a reliable farmer.

CUTS FOR ROASTING

Leg of pork
This is the most popular roasting joint, but because of its size it mostly has to be sold in two pieces or else boned and rolled without the knuckle. This cut promises the most lean meat but not, I think, such a sweet flavour as others.

Loin of pork
This is also a prime roasting joint (and the best one for lots of crackling), equivalent in the anatomy of the animal to the sirloin and ribs of beef. It is best bought on the bone, but the butcher *must* chine it for you – that is, loosen the bone yet leave it attached so it can easily be cut away before carving.

Blade bone

This comes at the top of the foreleg, so could be more accurately described as a piece of the shoulder – in fact it does often come boned and rolled with crackling tied round it, and called shoulder of pork. The meat has an excellent flavour when cooked on the bone. Alternatively it can be boned for you and stuffed before roasting.

Spare rib

Like loin, this is sometimes sold as individual chops. It is actually the collar of the animal and, when roasted, full of flavour.

Hand and spring

This is the curious name for the upper part of the foreleg of the pig, which happens to be well endowed with crackling and can be boned, stuffed and then roasted.

Belly of pork

Sometimes sold in rashers as streaky pork, but the thick end (i.e. the leanest end) can be bought as a roasting joint. It has much to recommend it, good crackling, a sweet flavour, and not least it is the most economical joint.

Fillet and tenderloin

These on the other hand are amongst the most expensive, but they are lean cuts without any wastage. In my opinion they need other flavours and ingredients with them to create interest.

ROASTING PORK

If you want to serve genuinely crisp crackling (see pages 150–1), ask the butcher to score the skin well. (If you have to do it yourself, use the tip of a sharp knife and cut down the skin with quick, jerky movements.) You won't get crunchy crackling if there is insufficient scoring, nor if the skin is not dry. If the pork has been wrapped, take the wrapping off as soon as you get it home, dry thoroughly and leave uncovered in the fridge. Then sprinkle the scored surface quite generously with salt to give it a thin coating but only at the last minute, as salt draws out moisture. On no account put any fat near the crackling.

For a touch of extra flavour, insert a few slivers of garlic into the flesh (make a small incision first) and sprinkle some fresh thyme or rosemary over the joint. Place it on its own in a roasting tin – there is fat enough in the meat to lubricate it while it's cooking – and give it 20 minutes in the oven at gas mark 9, 475°F (245°C), then lower the heat to gas mark

5, 375°F (190°C), and continue roasting for 35 minutes to the pound (450 g) for leg or loin of pork. For other joints mentioned above lower the heat to gas mark 4, 350°F (180°C), and allow 45 minutes per pound (450 g).

What goes wrong with crackling

Several things can turn the skin into tough old leather instead of crackling. One is using too deep a roasting tin, where that part of the crackling inside does not get proper exposure to the heat. Another reason could be that the skin was wet and soggy (especially if the meat has been frozen): to get good crackling it has to be dried thoroughly before salting and cooking. Another mistake is to plaster fat on the surface before cooking.

ACCOMPANIMENTS TO PORK

Apples have traditionally been associated with pork – either as a simple apple sauce (see the recipe below) or in *Spiced apple and onion sauce* (page 398). For a special occasion, try a little idea from across the Channel, *Prunes in Armagnac* (page 202).

CLASSIC APPLE SAUCE

◆

(Serves 4–6 people)

This is a very British sauce – possibly because Bramley Seedling and Cox's apples are only to be found here. Together they make the very best combination.

8 oz Bramley apples (225 g)
8 oz Cox's apples (225 g)
¾ oz caster sugar (20 g)
2 tablespoons water

Peel, core and slice the apples as thinly as possible, straight into a good solid saucepan. Then sprinkle in the sugar, add the water and put a tight-fitting lid on. Stew the apples for about 15 minutes over a very gentle heat or until they are soft and fluffy (the Cox's take the longer time). Stir them once or twice during the cooking, and when they are ready beat to a purée with a large fork, then pour into a warmed sauce boat. This is also excellent with roast duck and lightly smoked cured pork.

STUFFED PORK TENDERLOIN
◆

(Serves 4 people)

This is a good recipe for a dinner party, as it's easy to carve and serve. To serve eight just double the ingredients and use two tenderloins.

1 pork tenderloin, approx. 1 lb (450 g) in weight
¹/₂–³/₄ oz butter (10–20 g), softened
3–4 rashers streaky bacon, de-rinded
salt and freshly milled black pepper
For the stuffing
1 oz butter (25 g)
1 medium onion, finely chopped
¹/₄ teaspoon dried thyme
¹/₄ teaspoon dried sage
3 oz mushrooms (75 g), finely chopped
4 oz fresh breadcrumbs (110 g)
4 tablespoons chopped fresh parsley
grated rind of 1 lemon
2 teaspoons lemon juice
1 egg, beaten with 2 tablespoons cream or top of the milk
For the gravy
1 tablespoon flour
approx. 10 fl oz dry white wine or dry cider (275 ml)

Pre-heat the oven to gas mark 4, 350°F (180°C).

Leave the fat on the tenderloin, as this will help to keep it moist. With a sharp knife, split it in half lengthways and, using a rolling-pin, batter the two halves to flatten and widen them slightly. Season with salt and freshly milled black pepper.

To make the stuffing, melt the butter in a pan and fry the onion and herbs gently for about 10 minutes, then add the mushrooms and raise the heat slightly. Cook for a further 3–4 minutes or until the juices from the mushrooms have almost evaporated, then empty the contents of the pan into a bowl and add the rest of the stuffing ingredients. Fork the mixture together lightly, then season to taste.

Next spoon the stuffing into one half of the tenderloin, patting it down to firm it slightly, then place the other half on top. Smear with some butter and season with freshly milled black pepper. Cover the top of the fillet with the de-rinded bacon and tie with string at about 2 inch (5 cm) intervals to keep it neat and tidy, then transfer, carefully, to a buttered roasting tin. Bake near the top of the oven for 1 hour, then place on a serving dish and keep warm.

To make the gravy, stir the flour into the pan juices, add the wine and some seasoning and let it bubble until syrupy.

To serve, carve the meat into thick slices and pour over the gravy. A garnish of fried apple rings (see *Loin of pork Dijonnaise*, page 150) would go well with it.

ROAST PORK WITH GREEN BUTTER

♦

(Serves 8 people)

Ask the butcher – giving him a bit of notice – to bone out a hand and spring of pork for this recipe.

5–5¹/₂ lb hand and spring of pork (2.25–2.5 kg), boned but not rolled
salt
white wine
For the butter
1 teaspoon rock salt
1 teaspoon black peppercorns
1 teaspoon juniper berries
1 clove garlic
1¹/₂ oz butter (40 g)
juice of ¹/₂ lemon
grated rind of 1 lemon
1 tablespoon chopped parsley
1 tablespoon chopped watercress

Pre-heat the oven to gas mark 8, 450°F (230°C).

First of all, using a pestle and mortar or a bowl and the end of a rolling-pin, grind down the rock salt, peppercorns, juniper berries and garlic. Then add them to the butter with the lemon juice and rind, the chopped parsley and watercress, and mix thoroughly.

Next, lay the boned joint, rind side down, on a flat working surface, wipe it with kitchen paper, then spread the butter mixture carefully all over it. Now tie it with string in several places so that it has the appearance of a long, roundish sausage, transfer it to a roasting tin and sprinkle with salt.

Roast the joint for 25 minutes, then turn the heat down to gas mark 5, 375°F (190°C), and roast for a further 2 hours. To make sure that the meat is cooked, test with a skewer – the juices should be yellowy without any trace of pinkness. Remove the string before carving and use the pan juices and a dash of white wine to make a gravy to serve with it.

LOIN OF PORK DIJONNAISE

◆

(Serves 6–8 people)

This has a lovely golden crust and the crackling is cooked separately to go with it. (Illus. opposite p. 193.)

1 piece loin of pork with crackling, approx. 3 lb (1.3 kg) in weight
3 level tablespoons fresh breadcrumbs
1 heaped teaspoon whole peppercorns
1 heaped teaspoon dried sage
3 level teaspoons Dijon mustard
salt
For the gravy
a little plain flour
10 fl oz dry cider (275 ml)
For the garnish
3 small Cox's apples
1 oz butter (25 g)

Pre-heat the oven to gas mark 7, 425°F (220°C).

Start by scoring the skin of the pork with the tip of a sharp knife. Then take off the skin, together with about half the layer of fat underneath – in one piece if possible. Place this on a shallow baking tray, sprinkle generously with salt, then put it on the highest shelf of the oven for 15–20 minutes or until it is a very crisp and crunchy piece of crackling to accompany the meat. When you remove it from the oven, pour the fat into a bowl to use later for frying, etc.

Meantime, place the breadcrumbs in a mixing bowl, crush the peppercorns with a pestle and mortar or using the back of a tablespoon, and add them to the breadcrumbs together with the sage and about ½ teaspoon salt.

Next spread the mustard all over the layer of fat left on the pork, then press the breadcrumb mixture firmly all over, making sure that it is well coated. Transfer the joint to a roasting tin and place a square of foil lightly on top. Place the meat on a high shelf in the oven, reduce the heat to gas mark 5, 375°F (190°C), and roast the pork for about 2 hours, basting occasionally, and removing the foil for the last 30 minutes.

When the pork is cooked, leave it in a warm place to relax, then spoon off the fat from the roasting tin. Sprinkle a little flour into the juices and make some gravy with the cider.

For the garnish, core the apples and cut into rings – but do not peel – and fry gently in butter till tender. Serve the pork cut in slices with the gravy and some crackling, garnished with the fried apple rings. New potatoes and a green vegetable would be good with this in summer, and in winter roast potatoes and braised red cabbage.

HAM, GAMMON AND BACON

Each of these is a term used to describe meat from the pig that has been cured, i.e. preserved and flavoured, in several different ways, either by salting, smoking or steeping in brine (or molasses or honey). There are hundreds of refinements of the curing process used throughout the world: the wafer-thin Parma ham or *prosciutto* is a great delicacy in Italy, and in France the raw ham from the Bayonne district in the Pyrenees is smoked with aromatic herbs. In this country we have our own specialities. *York ham* is the most famous. It is dry salt-cured and lightly smoked with a mild flavour. A similarly mild cure is the *Wiltshire cured ham*. For those who like a stronger, smokier flavour there is the *Suffolk cure*, which is prepared in molasses which adds a sweetness to the flavour. *Bradenham ham*, very expensive, is also steeped in molasses, which turns the skin completely black.

SOAKING

Whole hams need long soaking, not just to remove the saltiness from them but also to replace some of the moisture lost during the curing. Whole hams should always carry the specific curer's soaking and cooking instructions. For smaller gammon and bacon joints the modern curing methods are far less salty than they used to be, and soaking is not so essential. The ideal would be to cover them with water overnight, but, failing that, a joint can be immersed in cold water and brought up to the boil. This water should then be thrown out and the cooking started with fresh water.

CUTS

The best cuts for boiling or roasting are *middle-cut gammon* (the leanest and best), *bacon collars*, *corner gammon* or *gammon slipper*. If you want to eat a joint of boiled gammon or bacon cold, it is a good idea to give it 15 minutes less cooking time and leave it to cool in its cooking water, which will keep it extra moist. In general the cooking time for joints is 25 minutes per pound (450 g), and for whole hams 15–20 minutes per pound (450 g).

SMOKED CURED PORK LOIN

This is a delicious variation, something in between gammon and pork. The tenderloin is cured and lightly smoked, then wrapped in a sort of netting to make a neat lean joint, compact and very easy to carve. It is usually sold pre-packed with cooking instructions on the packet recom-

151

mending roasting at gas mark 3, 325°F (170°C), for 45 minutes per pound, plus an extra 20 minutes. I like to wrap it in foil, then unwrap the foil 30 minutes before the end of the cooking time. That way it stays juicy but might need an extra 20 minutes' cooking. Serve it with *Parsley sauce* (page 393) or *Buttery onion sauce* (page 396), or if cold with *Cumberland sauce* (page 399) or pickles and chutney.

BAKED GAMMON

I have now adopted the foil-wrapped baking method. If I cook a whole gammon, I soak it in a plastic bucket of cold water for 2 days, changing the water twice. If it's a cut of gammon I simply cover it with cold water in a large saucepan, bring it to the boil, then throw the water out and proceed to bake as on page 153.

BACON POT-ROAST

◆

(Serves 6–8 people)

In this recipe the bacon is half simmered, then finished off as a pot-roast on a bed of vegetables.

3 lb collar of bacon (1.3 kg)
1 small potato, peeled
1 small onion, stuck with a few cloves
1 bay leaf
6 black peppercorns
10 fl oz dry cider (275 ml)
For the pot-roasting
1 small swede, cut into chunks
2 carrots, sliced
1 onion, sliced
3 celery stalks, cut into chunks
2 oz butter (50 g)
freshly milled black pepper

Begin by placing the joint in a suitably-sized saucepan along with the potato (to take care of any saltiness), the onion, bay leaf and peppercorns. Pour in the cider and top up with enough cold water just to cover the bacon. Then cover with a lid and simmer the joint for 45 minutes. Towards the end of that cooking time, pre-heat the oven to gas mark 4, 350°F (180°C).

Meanwhile fry the prepared pot-roasting vegetables in the butter to tinge them with colour, then arrange them in the bottom of a suitably-sized casserole. Season with some pepper, and when the 45 minutes are up, remove the bacon from its liquid, cut off the skin with a sharp knife, and place the joint on top of the vegetables in the casserole. Pour in enough of the cooking liquid just to cover the vegetables, season only with pepper, put a lid on and place the casserole in the oven for a further 45 minutes. Serve the bacon cut in slices, with the vegetables and some of the juice spooned over.

BAKED SUGAR-GLAZED WHOLE GAMMON
◆

(Serves 20–25 people)

1 whole gammon, approx. 12–14 lb (5.4–6.3 kg) in weight
2 tablespoons made-up mustard
2 heaped tablespoons demerara sugar
approx. 24 whole cloves

Pre-heat the oven to gas mark 3, 325°F (160°C).

You will need extra-wide baking foil.

Soak the gammon as described on page 152, or according to the supplier's instructions. Then tear off two very large pieces of foil and arrange one lengthways and the other widthways over your largest roasting tin. Place the gammon in the centre and bring the widthways piece of foil up first and seal the two ends together by folding over to form a kind of pleat. This should be done loosely so there is room for air to circulate around the gammon. Now bring the lengthways pieces up at each end and tuck these all round to seal what is now a parcel.

Place the parcel (in the tin) in the oven and let it bake for 20 minutes per pound (450 g) – that is 4 hours for a 12 lb (5.4 kg) piece or 4 hours, 40 minutes for a 14 lb (6.3 kg) piece. About 30 minutes before the end of the cooking time, remove the gammon and increase the heat to gas mark 7, 425°F (220°C). Open up the foil and transfer the gammon to a work surface (with help!). Now drain off all the juices (and reserve these in a bowl: the bacon fat will solidify and can be used for frying and the jelly for enriching lentil or pea soups). Next peel off all the skin – make a couple of horizontal incisions and you should be able to peel it off in strips, using a cloth to protect your hands from the heat.

Now score the fat with criss-cross cuts, making a diamond pattern. Stud a clove into the centre of each diamond shape, then smother the mustard all over, using a palette knife to spread it evenly. Finally sprinkle the sugar all over and press it in with your hands. Return the gammon to the tin and bake for a further 30 minutes or until it is a glazed, golden-mahogany colour.

If it's to be served hot, leave it to rest for about 45 minutes before carving. If cold, leave it to cool slowly overnight. Hot or cold, *Cumberland sauce* (see page 399) is the very nicest accompaniment.

For a smaller joint of boned gammon, such as a middle cut of, say, 5–6 lb (2.25–2.75 kg), pre-soak as explained and cook in exactly the same way, using half the quantity of glazing ingredients. Calculate the cooking time based on 20 minutes per pound (450 g) and glaze during the last 30 minutes.

LAMB

◆

If Scotland has the finest beef, then I think Wales or the Lake District has the best lamb – even the sheep in the hills seem to look more attractive, whiter and woollier than elsewhere. Even so, most lamb in Britain is extremely good, since it has the advantage of living happily in its natural habitat – in other words a large percentage being completely free-range. It therefore has a natural seasonal cycle, which is at its peak in June, July and August (in fact it progresses from West Country lamb which is available by April to Scottish lamb which reaches the shops in August). New Zealand lamb starts to arrive in December. There is nothing to beat fresh lamb in June after it has had all the benefit of grazing on the lush green spring grass. And what a happy coincidence that all the young spring vegetables are in season too: tiny melt-in-the-mouth peas, baby carrots tossed in herb butter and fresh Jersey potatoes.

CUTS FOR ROASTING

Leg and shoulder of lamb
These are the commonest, most popular cuts. Shoulder is more economical and has the sweetest meat of the two, because it is interlaced with layers of fat which melt and keep it moist during the cooking. Some people are averse to shoulder because they think it is hard to carve, though I feel a really sharp knife solves most problems.

Best end of neck
This is another joint that can be roasted. But it is extremely fatty and as the inside should conventionally be slightly pink and underdone, the result is that the layers of fat don't have time to melt. So often have I eaten this in a restaurant where it has arrived surrounded by an unappetising layer of undercooked fat. My own preference is to slice it into cutlets and grill them to crisp up the fat.

Breast of lamb
When rolled and stuffed this makes an economical roast, and has the sweetest meat.

ROASTING LAMB

To roast a shoulder or leg of lamb, pre-heat the oven to gas mark 8, 450°F (230°C), give it 30 minutes, then turn down the heat to gas mark 4, 350°F (180°C), and time it for 30 minutes to the pound (450 g) thereafter. (If you like the flavour of garlic, a few slivers inserted here and there won't go amiss.)

ACCOMPANIMENTS TO LAMB

In the summer *mint sauce* is a favourite accompaniment, but be careful – strong malt vinegar can mask all the flavour of the meat. Better, I think, to use a milder wine vinegar and even dilute it with water. Use 3 tablespoons of chopped mint, 1 tablespoon of wine vinegar and about 3 tablespoons of water. Some very finely shredded lettuce and a spring onion, also very finely chopped, are nice additions.

Redcurrant jelly goes equally well with lamb. But do make sure it's a really authentic one that is actually based on redcurrants. My own favourite accompaniment, however, is a combination of both these: *Redcurrant, orange and mint sauce* (see page 400).

STUFFED BREAST OF LAMB

♦

(Serves 2 people)

This needs a large breast of lamb. Ask the butcher to remove the bones for you, but if you don't have this done by him, you'll find them quite easy to remove provided you have a sharp knife.

1 large breast of lamb
For the stuffing
2 oz fresh breadcrumbs (50 g)
1 medium onion, very finely chopped
1 tablespoon chopped fresh parsley
1 tablespoon chopped fresh mint
¼ whole nutmeg, grated
1 teaspoon finely crushed rosemary
grated rind of ½ lemon
1 small egg, beaten
salt and freshly milled black pepper

Pre-heat the oven to gas mark 4, 350°F (180°C).

First of all, in a mixing bowl put the breadcrumbs, onion, parsley, mint, grated nutmeg, rosemary and lemon rind, and season well with pepper and salt. Mix thoroughly, then stir in the beaten egg to bind the mixture together.

Now spread the stuffing evenly over the breast of lamb. Roll it up gently but not too tightly, tuck the flap end over, then tie securely with string in three places – again not too tightly. Tuck in any bits of stuffing that fall out. Wrap the meat in foil, set in a roasting tin and cook for 1½ hours. At the end of this time unwrap the foil, baste with the juices and let it brown for a further 30 minutes.

Serve the meat cut into thick slices with a thin gravy made with the pan juices and some redcurrant jelly.

SHOULDER OF LAMB WITH RICE AND KIDNEY STUFFING

♦

(Serves 4–6 people)

This, again, is an excellent dinner-party recipe. It's easy to carve and serve, doesn't mind waiting around and tastes absolutely delicious.

3½–4 lb shoulder of lamb (1.6–1.8 kg), boned but not rolled
½–1 oz butter (10–25 g), softened
salt and freshly milled black pepper
For the stuffing
2 oz butter (50 g)
1 onion, finely chopped
1 clove garlic, crushed
2 oz long-grain rice (50 g)
1 teaspoon chopped fresh or ½ teaspoon dried thyme
5 fl oz stock (150 ml)
4 lambs' kidneys, cored and skinned

First prepare the stuffing. Heat 1 oz (25 g) of the butter in a small saucepan and gently fry the onion in it until softened and golden. Then stir in the garlic, the rice and thyme and cook for a further 2 minutes before pouring in the stock. Now bring it all up to simmering point, cover and cook gently for about 15–20 minutes (by which time the rice should have absorbed all the liquid and be just tender). Pre-heat the oven to gas mark 5, 375°F (190°C).

Meanwhile, heat the rest of the butter in another saucepan. Slice the kidneys and toss them in the hot fat for a minute over a fairly high heat, then stir the kidneys into the cooked rice. Now lay the meat, skin-side down, on a board and pack the stuffing into all the pockets and crevices left after boning. Roll the joint up and tie it into a neat shape with string. Place it in a meat-roasting tin, smear it with softened butter and season with salt and pepper, then bake in the oven for 1½–2 hours.

Make a thick gravy from the pan juices and some white wine to go with the lamb. Young carrots and fresh shelled peas would be perfect with this.

BAKED LAMB WITH CORIANDER

♦

(Serves 4 people)

If you don't want to spend too much time but would like to cook lamb a little differently, then this is a good recipe. Double the quantities if you are cooking a whole leg or shoulder. Personal taste will dictate the amount of garlic you use – I suggest either 1 large clove or 2 small ones.

¹/₂ **leg of lamb – fillet end (weigh it before you start)**
1–2 cloves garlic, cut into slivers
1 heaped tablespoon coriander seeds, crushed
1 oz butter (25 g)
10 fl oz red wine (275 ml)

Pre-heat the oven to gas mark 5, 375°F (190°C).

First, with the point of a sharp knife, make six to eight evenly placed incisions in the meat, and put slivers of garlic and the crushed coriander seeds in these cuts. (If you haven't a pestle and mortar to crush the seeds, use the back of a tablespoon.)

Smear the butter over the surface of the lamb, then place the meat in a roasting tin and cook in the pre-heated oven for 30 minutes to the pound (450 g), or less if you like it really pink. When the lamb is cooked, transfer to a warmed serving dish, tip off the fat from the roasting tin and add the wine. Boil briskly over direct heat for about 5 minutes until the wine has reduced.

To serve, carve the lamb in thick slices. Redcurrant jelly goes well with it.

SEE ALSO

American hamburgers
Beefsteak and kidney pie
Beefsteak and kidney pudding
Bœuf en croûte
Cevapcici (Yugoslav kebabs)
Country pâté
Gratinée of ham and eggs
Indian kebabs
Lamb kebabs
Leg of lamb baked with butter and herbs
Meat loaf

Mustard-glazed lamb cutlets
Old English rabbit pie
Pork chops with cream and mushrooms
Pork chops with sage and apples
Pork spare ribs in barbecue sauce
Rillettes de Tours
Rissoles
Special cottage pie
Steak au poivre
Turkish stuffed peppers

MEAT:
CASSEROLES AND BRAISED DISHES

◆

Stews, casseroles, ragoûts, hotpots, carbonnades, navarins . . . there are any number of names for what is essentially the same method of cooking meat. All of them spring from that momentous (though unrecorded) moment in history when someone discovered that they could protect their meat from the fierce direct heat of a fire by insulating it in a clay pot. The advantages were soon obvious, I'm sure: the pot could also contain liquid and vegetables and flavouring which the meat could absorb, and the longer, slower cooking made the meat more tender, no matter what part of the animal it came from. Nothing has really changed today, except perhaps for the clay pot, now replaced by decorative oven-to-table casseroles.

We tend to lump together all recipes that are cooked in a pot and call them casseroles. But, strictly speaking, there is a difference. *Stewing* is done on the top of a cooker with heat being applied directly to the underneath of the pot; while *casseroling* takes place inside the oven with heat circulating all around the pot. In both cases the meat is cut up fairly small and cooked in a liquid (stock, wine, water, cider or whatever).

Braising, like casseroling, is done in the oven, but the meat is cooked in much larger pieces and only a minimum of liquid is added, so that the meat actually cooks in the steam for the most part.

The numerous other names given to meat cooked in a pot refer to specific recipes, or types of recipe (e.g. the hallmark of a good hotpot is a layer of crunchy golden potatoes over the top).

But whatever names we choose to give it, I now feel that the casserole has become one of the cornerstones of British family cooking. With more and more women devoting their time to careers, feeding families of four or more with expensive steaks or chops is not a very practical proposition. Casseroles on the other hand can be prepared (even cooked) ahead. They can be left to simmer slowly without attention from the cook, and costs can be kept down quite a lot by stretching the meat with the addition of vegetables and pulses. Most casseroles freeze well too, so one batch of cooking can make several meals.

It is for these reasons that it's helpful to have a good collection of casserole recipes that range from the everyday to those suitable for entertaining. Here is a selection of my own tried and trusted favourites, showing, I hope, how with a little bit of imagination a couple of pounds of stewing meat can be transformed into something really delicious and special.

This chapter, incidentally, covers all kinds of meat except poultry, which is dealt with in the following chapter.

CHOOSING THE RIGHT CUTS

It is the forequarter meat on an animal that's usually the most suitable for stewing and braising – everything from the waist up. Without becoming too technical, it is the front portion that initiates the movements of the animal and therefore works harder than the back portion. This means there is more muscle there, and more of something called connective tissue, a gelatinous substance which builds up as the animal matures. Conveniently, there is also rather more fat marbling the forequarter meat, so that during the longer, slower cooking that's needed for these cuts, there is a gradual rendering-down of the connective tissue (which provides flavour and body to the sauce), and at the same time an internal basting of the meat fibres by the marbling of fat. This does a splendid job of keeping the meat succulent, and (because there's a good deal of flavour in the fat itself) is the reason why forequarter meat *develops* flavour as it cooks.

In short, these factors perhaps explain why so often the cheaper cuts of, say, leg and shin beef, given longer cooking, have a beefier flavour than the more expensive hind-quarter cuts: a very slow-cooked piece of shin actually has more beef flavour than a grilled fillet steak.

I find certain cuts of so-called stewing steak better for some dishes than for others, so that in all my recipes I name the cut – and suggest you always ask for it by name too. Unidentified stewing, or braising, steak can often be a mixture and can cook unevenly, I've found. Below is a list of the cuts that are suitable for braising and stewing; these cuts are always from the same part of the animal's anatomy but, confusingly, the *way* they're cut varies from region to region. The names vary even more – in fact one cut (I call it *thick flank*) has some 27 different names up and down the country!

BRAISING BEEF

My own favourite cut for braising is called *chuck* and *blade steak* where I live in East Anglia. In other regions it can be called *shoulder*, which is exactly where it is.

If you want large pieces of meat rather than cubes, *thick flank* is suitable: actually from the hind-quarters and called *round* or *flesh end* in Scotland or *bedpiece* elsewhere.

Beef skirt comes from below the diaphragm of the animal. It is an excellent cut for braising and one end can even be grilled if scored across the grain and tenderised by marinating before cooking.

STEWING BEEF

Next come stewing cuts from the *neck* and *clod*. These are accorded some undignified titles such as *sticking*, or in Scotland *gullet*, or in the North *vein* or *sloat*! Also suitable for stewing is *thin flank*, sometimes just called *flank*.

Both the *leg* and the *shin* provide excellent stewing meat, with an exceptionally good flavour. But because of the extra amount of connective tissue these cuts need much longer stewing than any of the other cuts of beef I have mentioned, and they are not suitable for braising.

LAMB

For stewing, *middle neck* or *scrag end of neck* are generally used as the bones impart delicious juices to the liquid. Also *best end of neck chops* are ideal for braising (as in *Lancashire hotpot*). In Scotland these are called *single loin chops* and in the Midlands simply *cutlets*. Both these shoulder cuts will also roast (see page 154).

PORK

Pork for braising usually comes from the region of the shoulder. The upper part is called either *shoulder* or *spare rib*. The lower part of the shoulder is known as *hand and spring*.

THE PRINCIPLES OF CASSEROLE COOKERY

TRIMMING AND SIZE OF MEAT PIECES

One thing that's often disappointing with cuts of braising steak (and this is especially true of the packaged meat found in supermarkets) is that they are sliced too thinly. For braising in whole slices, cuts of 1/4–3/4 inch (5 mm–2 cm) thick are all right, but for many casseroles the ideal sized pieces are 1 1/2 inches (4 cm) square and 1 1/4 inches (3 cm) deep. Therefore it is preferable to buy a piece and cut it up yourself. Trim off *excess* fat and gristle before using, but remember that some connective tissue and marbling add richness to the finished dish.

HOW MUCH PER PERSON?

This depends on many things – how much the meat needs to be trimmed, what extra ingredients go into the casserole, what other dishes you plan to serve at the same meal and so on – but I find that 6–8 oz (175–225 g) of meat per person is needed if someone has a large appetite. For a normal appetite 6 oz (175 g) per person is usually adequate. Moreover in all meat recipes I have allowed a certain latitude, indicating they could serve two to three or four to six etc., so that you can choose for yourself.

160

Left: **Rillettes de Tours** (see page 99); *top:* **Country pâté** (see page 97); *right:* **Chicken liver pâté** (see page 98)

BROWNING THE MEAT

Most, though not all, meat benefits from being seared in hot fat before the liquid is added. I have found that searing meat at a *high* temperature, as compared with browning it over a *medium* heat, results in far less visible loss of juices. Meat fibres contract when heat is applied, squeezing out juices from inside: but if the heat is high enough these juices will be burnt into a crust on the meat instead of being lost in the cooking fat. I would also add that this dark, mahogany-coloured crust on the outside of the pieces of meat gives a richer, better flavour to a casserole.

One important point, if you're browning meat in batches and removing it to a plate, is to make sure that whatever juices do run out are re-incorporated into the casserole and not lost. And one final point: *never overcrowd* the pan during the browning. If you do, there will be too much steam rushing out and the meat will never brown because it will have become damp. So remember, brown only a few pieces at a time.

LIQUID FOR CASSEROLES

The liquid in a casserole, mingling with the meat juices that do escape, provides the finished sauce. *Bone stock* is good for beef casseroles, but failing that plain hot water enriched with a few drops of Worcestershire sauce and mushroom ketchup makes a handy instant stock. Red or white *wine* will add extra flavour of its own, and its acidity will actually help to tenderise the meat as it cooks. *Beer* (pale or brown ale, or stout) makes a deliciously rich sauce: the long, slow cooking transforms it completely, leaving no trace of its original bitterness. *Tomatoes* – fresh peeled or tinned Italian plum tomatoes – also give body and flavour to certain casseroles, like *Hungarian goulash* (see page 166). A good alternative is hot water enriched with tomato purée. *Cider* is also delicious in casseroles – but it must be dry cider.

Thickening casseroles
Some casserole recipes call for the liquid to be thickened, and this can be done in various ways. The most popular way is to add some flour to the casserole after the meat has been browned (so that it can mingle with the juices and fat in the pan) and before the liquid is added. It is exactly the same principle as for the thickening of a white sauce (described on page 387). Another way to thicken a casserole is to toss the meat in seasoned flour before browning it (see recipe for *Braised steak and onions in stout*, page 168). Alternatively, when the casserole has completed cooking, the liquid can be strained off and simmered until slightly reduced and thickened. Or a flour and butter paste can be whisked into the liquid at the end of cooking time: 1 oz (25 g) butter worked into 1 oz (25 g) flour should thicken 1 pint (570 ml) liquid. This butter-flour paste, called *beurre manié* in classic cooking, can be frozen in blocks in ice-cube trays – but it doesn't take a minute to make as and when you need it. Add it to the liquid in little flecks, and use a balloon whisk to whisk it in.

Italian baked fish (see page 108)

VEGETABLES

If vegetables are to be included along with the meat in a casserole, the main consideration is not to cut them too small. This is a common mistake and results in the vegetables disintegrating under the strain of the long cooking. This applies particularly to onions, which if sliced too small can collapse altogether. It's far nicer, I think, to be able to discern slices of onions that have retained their shape. Vegetables that cook quite quickly (such as green peppers and mushrooms) are usually added to a casserole half-way through or towards the end of cooking time.

COOKING TEMPERATURES AND TIMES

Slowly, slowly is the word that needs to be emphasised here. It is said that the correct simmering temperature is reached when the liquid shows the barest shimmer of movement and an occasional bubble breaks the surface. I have found that, using a heavy flameproof casserole, the ingredients for a beef casserole can be brought slowly up to simmering point on top of the stove, then transferred to the middle or low shelf of a pre-heated oven. Gas mark 1, 275°F (140°C), is gentle enough to produce the very best results. But ovens vary and different types of cooking pots will affect temperatures too, so you may have to adjust the oven temperature accordingly.

The time a casserole takes to cook will vary from 2–2$\frac{1}{2}$ hours for chuck, blade and thick flank, up to 4 hours for shin, leg and neck. Pork cuts for braising and casseroling normally take 1$\frac{1}{2}$ hours, and lamb much the same.

SKIMMING

If a fair amount of fat has come out of the meat during the cooking, it will settle on the surface and can be removed by tilting the casserole slightly and spooning off with a large kitchen spoon. And if there's still some left, another tip is to float two or three pieces of absorbent kitchen paper on the surface – this should soak up any fat remaining. Of course, if you've had time to make the casserole in advance, the fat on the surface will solidify as it cools and can then just be lifted off. Which brings me to:

REHEATING

Many casseroles seem to improve in flavour if kept overnight (cool them quickly and keep them in a refrigerator, by the way, once they're cold). This means it's quite possible to make two casseroles while the oven is in full swing, and keep one for the next day. The reheating must be done very thoroughly, though, either on top of the stove over a very low heat or in an oven heated to gas mark 3, 325°F (170°C). Either way, the food must come up to a gentle simmer and maintain that temperature for 30 minutes to kill off any harmful bacteria. So it will take 45 minutes in all.

NOTES ON EQUIPMENT

◆

COOKING POTS AND CASSEROLES

I've found the most useful type of casserole is the heavy cast-iron kind with enamelled lining. It isn't the cheapest *but* it does conduct the heat evenly and has the advantage of being suitable for cooking on top of the stove and inside the oven. It is also attractive enough to take to the table. If you're buying saucepans it is useful to get the double-handled variety that can also serve as casseroles.

A 4½ pint (2.5 litre) capacity casserole is the average family size, but you might also find a smaller size (3 pint or 1.75 litre) useful at times and a larger one (6½ pint or 4 litre) for entertaining. What one's aiming for is a pot that contains the ingredients comfortably without leaving masses of empty space. Well-fitting lids are *very* important, because they minimise the loss of liquid by evaporation during the cooking. If you happen to have a lid that doesn't fit too well, cover the casserole with foil first to make it fit more snugly. And it follows that you should leave it be: too many peeps and stirs will let some of the flavour out as effectively as an ill-fitting lid.

ELECTRIC SLOW COOKERS

These are self-contained cooking pots which are sometimes called crockpots, with their own electric element which is geared to producing the slow continuous heat needed for casseroles. They use very little electricity, and are useful for those who are out at work all day since they can be left unattended quite safely. On a high setting a casserole will take around 5 hours; on a low one it will take an average of 8 hours, and won't come to any harm if left for 10!

If you're not at home all day, to use one of these effectively you must of course prepare everything before you go and allow 20 minutes or so for the casserole to pre-heat. If you're considering buying one, ask yourself if you are the sort of person who is organised enough to see to all this before you go out.

PRESSURE COOKERS

Pressure cooking can cut down the time needed for casseroles to about one-third of normal. So speed, and the consequent saving in fuel costs, are the self-evident advantages of this method. It has also been pointed out that because everything is locked away from the air, and cooked for a shorter time, losses of vitamins and minerals are reduced to a minimum. Pressure cookers can be transported easily and used on any sort of cooker, so they're ideal to take on self-catering or camping holidays.

Those are the pluses, but there are also disadvantages: (i) as I have explained, the flavour of the cheaper cuts develops with long, slow cooking – so a certain amount can be lost with speedier cooking under pressure; (ii) the liquid content in pressure cookers has to be a minimum of 15 fl oz (425 ml), and I often find I want to use less than this. Also no thickening can be added till after the pressure cooking, so this has to be a separate process at the end.

In my experience many busy people swear by their pressure cookers and use them whenever possible: others (like myself) use them very rarely. In the end it's a matter of personal preference, so if you are wondering whether or not to invest in one yourself, do get a book on pressure cooking from the library and study the facts for yourself first.

BEEF IN BEER
◆

(Serves 4–6 people)

This is an old Flemish recipe often known by its original name *Carbonnade de bœuf à la flamande*. Sometimes large baked croûtons sprinkled with grated cheese are arranged on the top of the cooked beef and the dish is then popped under the grill until the cheese is bubbling. Whether you do this or not, this recipe has a beautiful rich sauce and is one of my firm favourites.

2 lb chuck steak (900 g), cut into 2 inch (5 cm) squares
1 tablespoon olive oil
12 oz onions (350 g), quartered then separated into layers
1 well heaped tablespoon plain flour
15 fl oz light ale (425 ml)
1 sprig fresh thyme or ¹/₂ teaspoon dried thyme
1 bay leaf
1 fat clove garlic, crushed
salt and freshly milled black pepper

Pre-heat the oven to gas mark 1, 275°F (140°C).

Heat the oil in a large flameproof casserole until sizzling hot then sear the meat in it – just a few pieces at a time – till they become a dark mahogany brown all over. As the pieces brown, remove them to a plate, then add the onions to the casserole and, with the heat still high, toss them around until brown at the edges. Now return the meat to the casserole together with any juices. Add the flour, turn the heat down, and using a wooden spoon stir it around to soak up all the juices. It will look rather stodgy and unattractive at this stage but that's quite normal.

Next gradually stir in the light ale and, while everything *slowly* comes up to simmering point, add the thyme, bay leaf, crushed garlic, and some salt and freshly milled black pepper.

As soon as it begins to simmer, stir thoroughly, put on a tight-fitting lid and transfer the casserole to the middle shelf of the oven.

Cook at a gentle simmer for 2¹/₂ hours. Don't take the lid off and have a taste half-way through because, early on, the beer hasn't had time to develop into a delicious sauce; the beautiful aroma will make you very hungry, but please leave it alone!

Note If you want to serve this in the traditional Flemish way, follow the instructions for the baked croûtons with cheese in the onion soup recipe (see page 72). Just place these on top of the meat and brown the cheese under the grill. Mashed potatoes and red cabbage are good with this.

SIMPLE STROGANOFF
♦

(Serves 3–4 people)

The classic recipe for Stroganoff is made with thin strips of fillet steak, cooked and served very quickly; it needs rather exact timing. This version, however, is made with strips of chuck steak, which costs less, has more flavour, and can be cooked slowly on top of the stove demanding no particular skill.

1¹/₂ lb lean chuck steak (700 g)
2 large onions
2 oz butter (50 g)
10 fl oz dry white wine or dry cider (275 ml)
1 lb mushrooms (450 g), sliced
10 fl oz soured cream (275 ml)
freshly grated nutmeg
salt and freshly milled black pepper

First trim the meat and cut it into thin strips, about ¹/₄ inch (5 mm) wide and no more than 2¹/₂ inches (6 cm) long. The onions should be peeled, cut in half, then each half sliced and the layers separated out into half-moon shapes.

Now melt the butter in a thick-based saucepan or flameproof casserole and gently soften the onions for 5 minutes or until they have turned pale gold. Then, with a slotted spoon, remove them to a plate.

Next, turn the heat up high, add the pieces of meat to the casserole (a few at a time) and brown them. Then reduce the heat, return the onion and all the meat to the pan, season with salt and pepper and pour in the wine or cider. Bring to simmering point, cover and let it cook very gently on top of the stove for 1¹/₂ hours – stirring it just now and then.

When the time is up stir in the mushrooms (which will add a lot of juice in case you think it seems a little dry), put the lid back on and leave to cook very gently for a further 30 minutes or until the meat is tender.

Then taste to check the seasoning, and stir in the soured cream with a good grating of fresh nutmeg. Let the cream heat through (but not boil) and serve the Stroganoff with plain boiled rice and a green salad.

HUNGARIAN GOULASH
◆

(Serves 4 people)

This makes a fairly economical dinner party dish: it is very easy to prepare and won't mind hanging around if your guests are late. It also goes very well with braised red cabbage (see recipe on page 236).

1½ lb chuck steak (700 g), trimmed and cut into 1½ inch (4 cm) cubes (some supermarkets sell this ready trimmed)
1 tablespoon olive oil
2 large onions, roughly chopped
1 clove garlic, crushed
1 rounded tablespoon plain flour
1 rounded tablespoon Hungarian paprika
14 oz tin Italian tomatoes (400 g)
1 medium green or red pepper
5 fl oz soured cream (150 ml)
salt and freshly milled black pepper

Pre-heat the oven to gas mark 1, 275°F (140°C).

Begin by heating the oil in a flameproof casserole till sizzling hot. Then brown the cubes of beef on all sides, cooking a few at a time and transferring them to a plate with a slotted spoon as they brown.

Now, with the heat turned to medium, stir in the onions and cook them for about 5 minutes or until they turn a pale golden colour. Then add the crushed garlic and return the meat to the casserole. Sprinkle in the flour and paprika and stir to soak up the juices. Next, add the contents of the tin of tomatoes, season with salt and pepper and bring everything slowly up to simmering point before covering with a tight-fitting lid and transferring the casserole to the middle shelf of the oven. Cook for 2 hours.

Prepare the pepper by halving it, removing the seeds and cutting the flesh into 2 inch (5 cm) strips. Then, when the 2 hours are up, stir the chopped pepper into the goulash, replace the lid and cook for a further 30 minutes.

Just before serving, stir in the soured cream to give a marbled creamy effect, then sprinkle a little more paprika over and serve straight from the casserole, with some rice (or vegetables).

BŒUF BOURGUIGNONNE

◆

(Serves 6 people)

This is my adaptation of the famous French classic: beef braised in Burgundy, garnished with cubes of bacon, button onions and mushrooms. If you want to cut the cost then try using dry cider, which gives different results but is every bit as good.

2 lb chuck steak (900 g), cut into 2 inch (5 cm) squares
3 tablespoons olive oil
1 medium onion, sliced
1 heaped tablespoon plain flour
15 fl oz red Burgundy (425 ml)
2 cloves garlic, chopped
2 sprigs fresh thyme or ½ teaspoon dried thyme
1 bay leaf
12 oz small onions (350 g)
8 oz smoked or green streaky bacon (225 g), bought in one piece then cut into cubes
4 oz dark-gilled mushrooms (110 g), sliced
salt and freshly milled black pepper

Pre-heat the oven to gas mark 1, 275°F (140°C).

Heat 2 tablespoons of the oil to sizzling point in a large flameproof casserole and sear the chunks of beef – a few pieces at a time – to a rich, dark brown on all sides. Using a slotted spoon, remove the meat as it browns to a plate. Next add the sliced onion to the casserole and brown that a little too. Now return the meat to the casserole, sprinkle in the flour, stirring it around to soak up all the juices, then gradually pour in the Burgundy –stirring all the time. Add the chopped garlic and herbs, season with salt and pepper, put the lid on and cook in the oven for 2 hours.

Then, using a bit more oil, fry the button onions and cubes of bacon in a small frying pan to colour them lightly, and add them to the casserole together with the sliced mushrooms. Put the lid back on and cook for a further hour. The French accompaniment of potatoes boulangère and green salad would be good with this, or else tiny new potatoes and ratatouille.

BRAISED STEAK AND ONIONS IN STOUT

◆

(Serves 2–3 people)

For this recipe you'll need four pieces of braising steak – chuck or blade.

1 lb braising steak (450 g), cut into four pieces
1 tablespoon oil
seasoned flour
2 largish onions, halved and sliced
5 fl oz stout (150 ml)
1/2 teaspoon Worcestershire sauce
salt and freshly milled black pepper

Pre-heat the oven to gas mark 1, 275°F (140°C).

Melt the oil in a flameproof casserole and, when it's sizzling hot, coat the meat in seasoned flour and brown the pieces on both sides till they're a good rich brown colour. Lift them out of the casserole and reserve on a plate.

Now fry the onions to brown them well at the edges, then arrange the meat on top (plus any juices that are on the plate) and season with salt and pepper. Next pour in the stout and Worcestershire sauce. Then put the lid on and transfer the casserole to the oven. Cook for approximately 2½ hours or until the meat is tender.

Note If you like you could braise the steak on top of the stove using a very low heat but, because this method seems to cause a bit more evaporation, add 1 extra fl oz (25 ml) of stout.

STEWED SHIN OF BEEF WITH MUSHROOM DUMPLINGS

◆

(Serves 4–6 people)

For years I never bought shin of beef because it looked so unappealing, but I missed out because those sections of connective tissue melt down during the long, slow cooking and provide extra flavour and enrichment to the sauce. Now, for an old-fashioned brown stew, I wouldn't use anything else.

2 lb shin of beef (900 g), cut in bite-sized cubes
1 oz beef dripping (25 g)
12 oz onions (350 g), quartered
2 large carrots, scraped and cut into large chunks

1 heaped tablespoon flour
15 fl oz hot beef bone stock (425 ml) or hot water
enriched with 1 teaspoon Worcestershire sauce
2 teaspoons mushroom ketchup
1 sprig fresh thyme or ¹/₂ teaspoon dried thyme
1 bay leaf
salt and freshly milled black pepper
For the dumplings
4 oz self-raising flour (110 g)
2 oz shredded suet (50 g)
2 oz mushrooms (50 g), very finely chopped
1 onion, finely grated

Pre-heat the oven to gas mark 1, 275°F (140°C).

In a flameproof casserole melt the beef dripping and, when it's smoking hot, brown the pieces of beef – a few at a time – to a really dark rich brown colour. As the pieces brown remove them to a plate using a slotted spoon. Next fry the onions and carrots so that they turn dark at the edges. Now spoon off any excess fat, turn the heat down, return everything to the casserole, and sprinkle in the flour, stirring it in well to soak up the juices. Next, gradually stir in the hot stock and the mushroom ketchup, add the thyme, bay leaf and seasoning and bring everything slowly up to simmering point. Then put on a very well-fitting lid, using foil if you need to. Now transfer the casserole to the lowest shelf of the oven and cook for 3 hours or until the meat is tender.

Towards the end of the cooking time, make the dumplings. Sift the flour into a mixing bowl, add some pepper and a pinch of salt, then stir in the suet, the chopped mushrooms and the grated onion. Add enough cold water to bring it all together to make a fairly stiff but elastic dough that leaves the bowl cleanly. Divide the dough into eight pieces and roll each portion into a dumpling shape.

When the stew is ready, take out all the meat and vegetables using a draining spoon and put them on a large warm serving dish. Cover with foil and keep warm in the bottom of the oven.

Season the liquid to taste, then bring it up to a very fast boil. Put the dumplings into the bubbling liquid, cover and cook for 20–25 minutes, making sure they don't come off the boil. When the dumplings are ready put them all round the meat and vegetables, pour over some of the gravy and serve the rest in a sauce-boat.

TRADITIONAL LANCASHIRE HOTPOT

♦

(Serves 4 people)

This has acquired its name from the time when it was baked at home, then wrapped in blankets to keep hot and provide lunch for a day at the races.

2 lb best end and middle neck of lamb (900 g), cut into chop-sized pieces
4 lambs' kidneys, cored, skinned and chopped fairly small
dripping
12 oz onions (350 g), roughly chopped
a little butter
1 tablespoon flour
1 pint hot water (570 ml), mixed with ½ teaspoon Worcestershire sauce
1 bay leaf
2 sprigs fresh thyme or ½ teaspoon dried thyme
2 lb potatoes (900 g), cut into ¾ inch (2 cm) slices
salt and freshly milled black pepper

Pre-heat the oven to gas mark 3, 325°F (170°C).

First trim the meat of any excess fat. In a large frying-pan heat some dripping until it is smoking hot, then brown the pieces of meat two or three at a time until they all have a good brown crust. As they cook, remove them to a wide casserole. Brown the pieces of kidney too, and tuck these in amongst the meat.

Next fry the onions – add a little butter to the pan if you need any extra fat – cooking them for about 10 minutes till they turn brown at the edges. Now stir in the flour to soak up the juices, then gradually add the hot water and Worcestershire sauce, stirring or whisking until flour and liquid are smoothly blended. Season with salt and pepper and bring it up to simmering point, then pour it over the meat in the casserole. Add the bay leaf and thyme, then arrange the potato slices on top, in an overlapping pattern like slates on a roof. Season the potatoes and add a few flecks of butter here and there. Cover with a tight-fitting lid and cook near the top of the oven for 1½ hours, then remove the lid and cook for a further 50 minutes.

I sometimes finish off the hotpot under the grill. If you brush the potatoes with a little more butter and place the casserole under a hot grill they crisp up and brown beautifully. Alternatively, if you think they're not browning enough during cooking, you can turn the heat in the oven right up during the last 15 minutes.

IRISH STEW WITH PARSLEY DUMPLINGS
◆

(Serves 4 people)

I don't make any claims about this so far as its Irish authenticity is concerned, but it does taste very good.

2¹/₂ lb lean middle neck and scrag of mutton or lamb (1.25 kg)
2 tablespoons seasoned flour
12 oz onions (350 g), sliced
8 oz carrots (225 g), sliced
2 medium leeks, washed and sliced
1 large potato, peeled and sliced
1 tablespoon pearl barley
hot water
salt and freshly milled black pepper
For the dumplings
4 oz self-raising flour (110 g)
1 tablespoon chopped fresh parsley (if fresh is not available make plain dumplings)
2 oz shredded suet (50 g)

First wipe the pieces of meat and cut away excess fat, then dip them in the seasoned flour. Now put a layer of meat in the bottom of a large saucepan, followed by some onion, carrot, leek and potato and season with salt and pepper. Then put in some more meat and continue layering the ingredients until everything is in.

Now sprinkle in the pearl barley followed by approximately 2 pints (1.2 litres) hot water and bring to simmering point. Spoon off any scum that rises to the surface, then cover the pan with a well-fitting lid and leave to simmer over a low heat for about 2 hours.

About 15 minutes before the end of the cooking time, make the dumplings. Mix the flour, some salt and pepper and the parsley in a bowl. Then mix in the suet – but it mustn't be rubbed in. Add just sufficient cold water to make a fairly stiff but elastic dough that leaves the bowl cleanly. Shape it into eight dumplings.

When the stew is ready, remove the meat and vegetables with a slotted spoon onto a large warm serving dish. Cover with foil and keep warm.

Season the liquid to taste, then bring to a brisk boil. Put the dumplings in, cover and cook them for 20–25 minutes, making sure that they don't come off the boil.

Serve the meat surrounded by the vegetables and dumplings, with some of the liquid poured over and some in a gravy boat.

RAGOÛT OF LAMB
◆

(Serves 2–3 people)

Neck of lamb isn't cheap any more but it is less expensive than many other cuts and, because of the bones, always gives the maximum amount of flavour. This, I think, is an excellent summer casserole.

2 lb neck of lamb, either middle neck or scrag end or a mixture of both (900 g)
1 tablespoon oil
2 medium onions, roughly chopped
2 cloves garlic, crushed
1 heaped tablespoon flour
1 pint boiling water (570 ml)
1 sprig fresh thyme or ½ teaspoon dried thyme
1 bay leaf
12 oz new potatoes (350 g), scraped
4 medium tomatoes, peeled
salt and freshly milled black pepper

Pre-heat the oven to gas mark 1, 275°F (140°C).

First trim any excess fat from the meat, wipe each piece and season it with salt and freshly milled pepper. Then heat the oil in a largish flameproof casserole, and brown the meat a few pieces at a time. When they're nicely brown transfer them to a plate, using a draining spoon.

Now gently fry the onions in the fat left in the pan – this will take about 10 minutes or so. Then, when the onions are softened and browned a little bit round the edges, add the garlic. Next stir in the flour, to soak up the juices, and gradually pour in the hot water, stirring to make a sort of gravy.

When simmering point is reached, return the pieces of meat to the casserole and add the thyme, bay leaf and more seasoning – it won't look much at this point, but not to worry.

As soon as it comes back to simmering point, put the lid on and transfer the casserole to the oven. Cook it for about 1 hour, then tilt the casserole and spoon off any visible fat (or mop it up with absorbent kitchen paper) before adding the scraped potatoes and peeled tomatoes. Put the lid back on and return to the oven to cook for a further 45 minutes, or until the potatoes are cooked.

NORMANDY PORK WITH CREAM AND APPLES

◆

(Serves 4 people)

This is quite rich and special. It needs a lightly cooked green vegetable or a crisp green side-salad to go with it.

4 medium pork spare rib chops or loin chops, with any excess fat trimmed away
2 oz butter (50 g)
1 teaspoon chopped fresh or ½ teaspoon dried thyme
1 large onion, cut into thin rings
1 clove garlic, crushed
1 medium cooking apple
1 large Cox's apple
sugar
10 fl oz dry cider (275 ml)
3 tablespoons double cream
salt and freshly milled black pepper

Pre-heat the oven to gas mark 5, 375°F (190°C).

Begin by melting half the butter in a thick frying-pan and frying the pork chops on both sides to a nice crusty golden colour. Then, using a draining spoon, transfer them to a suitably-sized casserole and sprinkle with thyme.

Now add the remaining butter to the pan and fry the onion and garlic for 5 minutes to soften. Meanwhile, core the apples and cut them into thick rings, leaving the peel on as this gives extra flavour. Next transfer the softened onion and garlic to the casserole, then fry the apple rings in the same fat just for a few seconds on each side and transfer them to the casserole as well, sprinkling on about a teaspoon of sugar.

Next, spoon off any fat still left in the pan and then pour in the cider. Bring it up to simmering point, pour it into the casserole and season with salt and freshly milled black pepper. Now put a lid on and then place the casserole into the oven, and cook for about 30–40 minutes or until the chops are cooked. Then, to finish off, pour in the cream, stir it into the juices and serve immediately.

BRAISED PORK WITH APPLES AND CIDER

◆

(Serves 4 people)

This is a hearty winter dish that can be left on its own for 3 hours if you plan to be out. You could also leave some red cabbage to braise in the oven with it and return to a complete meal.

173

4 thick lean belly pork strips or spare rib chops
1 tablespoon olive oil
6 rashers unsmoked streaky bacon, de-rinded
6 juniper berries, crushed with the back of a spoon
2 cloves garlic, finely chopped
1 large cooking apple, peeled, cored and sliced
2 medium onions, chopped small
5 fl oz dry cider (150 ml)
1½ lb potatoes (700 g), peeled and thickly sliced
a little butter
salt and freshly milled black pepper

Pre-heat the oven to gas mark 1, 275°F (140°C).

If the pork is very fatty, trim away the excess. Heat some oil in a frying-pan and brown the pork on both sides, then transfer to a wide shallow casserole. Next, in the same pan, fry the bacon rashers a little until the fat starts to run. Then, using a draining spoon, place the bacon on top of the pork and season, but be careful with the salt as there'll be some in the bacon.

Now sprinkle over the juniper berries and garlic, then spread the slices of apple and onion on top. Add the cider and cover with a layer of overlapping potatoes. Finally, put a few dabs of butter on top, cover the dish first with greaseproof paper or foil, and then with a close-fitting lid. Transfer to the oven and cook for 3 hours.

Toward the end of the cooking time, pre-heat the grill to its highest setting. When the oven time is completed, place the dish, uncovered, under the grill so the potatoes become brown and crispy.

SPANISH PORK WITH OLIVES

♦

(Serves 4–6 people)

This casserole has what I'd call a rich Mediterranean flavour. Nice served with *Saffron rice* (page 276).

2 lb shoulder of pork (900 g), trimmed and cut into bite-sized cubes
2 tablespoons olive oil
2 medium onions, sliced
1 rounded tablespoon plain flour
1 lb tomatoes (450 g), peeled and chopped, or 14 oz tin tomatoes (400 g), chopped
6 fl oz red wine (175 ml)
2 cloves garlic, crushed
1 teaspoon dried or 1 tablespoon fresh basil

1 green pepper, de-seeded and chopped
2 oz Spanish pimento-stuffed green olives (50 g), sliced
salt and freshly milled black pepper

Pre-heat the oven to gas mark 1, 275°F (140°C).

Begin by heating the oil in a large flameproof casserole, then add the cubes of pork and brown them on all sides. Cook only a few cubes at a time and remove them to a plate as they're done. Then add the onions to the casserole and brown them for a few minutes before returning the meat to the pan and sprinkling in the flour.

Stir everything well and add the chopped tomatoes – pour boiling water over fresh tomatoes first to help get the skins off. Pour in the wine, add the garlic, basil and a seasoning of salt and pepper. Stir, bring slowly to simmering point, then cover with a tight-fitting lid.

Transfer the casserole to the centre shelf of the oven and cook for 1½ hours. Add the chopped pepper and sliced olives, cover again, then cook for a further 30 minutes.

OSSOBUCO

◆

(Serves 4 people)

This is a famous Italian casserole: shin of veal cooked in white wine with tomatoes. Try to buy the pieces of shin about 2 inches (5 cm) thick.

4 large pieces shin of veal
1 medium onion, roughly chopped
1 clove garlic, crushed
2 oz butter (50 g)
10 fl oz dry white wine (275 ml)
12 oz tomatoes (350 g), peeled and chopped
1 tablespoon tomato purée
salt and freshly milled black pepper
For the garnish
1 large clove garlic, finely chopped
2 heaped tablespoons chopped fresh parsley
grated rind of 1 small lemon

You'll need a wide, shallow, flameproof casserole that can hold the pieces of veal in one layer.

In the casserole melt 1 oz (25 g) of the butter and fry the onion and garlic till pale gold – about 10 minutes. Then remove them to a plate with a slotted spoon. Now add the rest of the butter and fry the pieces of veal, to brown them lightly on both sides. Then pour over the wine, let it bubble and reduce a little before adding the onion, garlic, tomatoes, tomato purée and a seasoning of salt and freshly milled black pepper.

Then cover the casserole and leave it to cook gently on top of the stove for about 1 hour. After that, take off the lid and let it cook for another 30 minutes or so or until the meat is tender and the sauce reduced.

Before serving, mix together the garnish ingredients, then sprinkle all over the meat. Serve this with rice (preferably *Risotto alla Milanese*, see page 277) – and don't forget to dig out the marrow from the centre of the bone: it's the best bit.

BRAISED MEATBALLS WITH PEPPERS AND TOMATOES

◆

(Serves 4–6 people)

This is another economical but really delicious recipe, probably best made in the autumn when there's a glut of tomatoes and green peppers.

1 lb best quality lean minced beef (450 g)
8 oz good pork sausagemeat (225 g)
2 slices bread
½ green pepper, de-seeded and finely chopped
1 egg, beaten
1 medium onion, minced or very finely chopped
1 large clove garlic, crushed
1 dessertspoon fresh or ¾ teaspoon dried oregano
1 tablespoon chopped fresh parsley
1 dessertspoon tomato purée
salt and freshly milled black pepper
flour, for coating the meatballs
oil, for frying the meatballs
For the sauce
1 small onion, chopped
½ green pepper, de-seeded and chopped
14 oz tin Italian tomatoes (400 g) or 1 lb ripe tomatoes (450 g), peeled and chopped
1 clove garlic, crushed
1 tablespoon chopped fresh or 1 teaspoon dried basil

Begin by making the meatballs. Cut the crusts off the bread and mash it to crumbs with a fork; then, in a large mixing bowl, mix it together very thoroughly with the rest of the meatball ingredients and salt and pepper, using your hands.

Now take the pieces of the mixture – about a tablespoon at a time –

and roll each into a small round. You should get about sixteen to eighteen altogether. Coat each one lightly with flour, then brown them in the oil in a large frying-pan. Meanwhile pre-heat the oven to gas mark 5, 375°F (190°C).

When the meatballs are browned transfer them to a casserole and, in the juices remaining in the frying-pan, prepare the sauce by softening the onion and green pepper for 5 minutes before adding the tomatoes, garlic and basil, then simmer for a couple of minutes. Taste and season, then pour the sauce over the meatballs in the casserole and cook, with a lid on, in the oven for 45 minutes. After that take off the lid and cook for a further 15–20 minutes.

This is nice served on a bed of buttered noodles, with a crisp green salad.

BRAISED BEEF IN GUINNESS WITH PICKLED WALNUTS

◆

(Serves 6–8 people)

I like to use cubes of lean brisket for this particular casserole and serve creamy mashed potato with it to absorb some of the beautiful black, velvety sauce. Spiced red cabbage is also a very good accompaniment.

3 lb brisket of beef (1.3 kg), cut into 2 inch (5 cm) cubes
2 tablespoons olive oil
8 oz onions (225 g), quartered then separated into layers
1 well heaped tablespoon plain flour
1 pint Guinness (570 ml)
1 sprig fresh thyme
1 bay leaf
1 large clove garlic, crushed
12 pickled walnuts (the contents of a 14 oz/390 g jar), halved
salt and freshly milled black pepper

Pre-heat the oven to gas mark 1, 275°F (140°C).

Start by heating the oil in a large flameproof casserole and, when it's hot, add the meat, a few pieces at a time, and sear them until they're nice and brown. As they brown remove them to a plate. Then add the onions and cook until brown at the edges. Lower the heat and return the meat to the casserole (together with any juices on the plate), then stir in the flour using a wooden spoon.

Now stir in the Guinness and add the thyme, bay leaf, garlic and pickled walnuts. Season with salt and pepper and bring the whole lot slowly up to simmering point. Cover the casserole and transfer to the centre of the oven. Cook for 3 hours – and don't be tempted to try it half-way through because the beer needs time to transform itself into a delicious sauce.

SAUSAGES BRAISED IN RED WINE
♦

(Serves 4 people)

This is best made with very good quality pork sausages, preferably the spicy herby sort that some butchers make themselves.

1 lb pork sausages (450 g)
8 oz lean streaky bacon in one piece (225 g), cut into cubes
8 oz small button onions (225 g)
olive oil
1 heaped teaspoon plain flour
10 fl oz red wine (275 ml)
1 clove garlic, crushed
1 bay leaf
1 teaspoon chopped fresh or ¹/₂ teaspoon dried thyme
6 oz mushrooms (175 g), sliced if large
salt and freshly milled black pepper

Take a large flameproof casserole, heat a little oil in it and brown the sausages all over. Then, using a slotted spoon, remove them to a plate while you lightly brown the bacon cubes and onions. When they're done, sprinkle in the flour to soak up the juices, then gradually stir in the wine. Now pop the sausages back in, plus the garlic, bay leaf, thyme and a little seasoning. Put the lid on when simmering point is reached, turn the heat as low as possible and simmer very gently for 30 minutes.

After that add the mushrooms, stirring them in well, then leave everything to cook for a further 20 minutes – this time without a lid. Serve with what else but a pile of creamy mashed potato.

SEE ALSO

Beef curry with whole spices
Braised steak with green peppercorn sauce
Cassoulet
Chilli con carne
Marinated pork with coriander
Moussaka

POULTRY

◆

CHICKEN

◆

Once upon a time chicken was a luxury, an expensive family treat for a special occasion. Now we have moved to the other extreme: chickens are available absolutely everywhere. They are threaded onto rotisseries in shop windows in every high street, there are chains of take-away chicken shops, freezer centres are full of them. Any part or portion of a chicken can be bought separately. It is a credit to our farmers that they have put chicken within the reach of everyone at what, in these days, is a very reasonable price.

At the same time a question remains, one which in our passion for progress I hope we won't overlook. The question of flavour – a word which I fear is too rarely mentioned in our modern chicken production industry. Loss of flavour is the price we seem to have paid for our abundance of chickens. So what's happened and where has the flavour gone? Let's consider our chickens' progress to the table from scratch, as it were.

REARING

To produce today's enormous quantity of chicken, speed is the one thing that's necessary. And what farmers have done is to speed up growth and development so that the ubiquitous broiler of 1½–3 lb (700 g–1.3 kg) in weight is ready for cooking in eight weeks or so. Such a chicken is already at a disadvantage, as lack of maturity also means lack of flavour. To speed up growth sufficiently, first-class protein of animal and vegetable origin has to be used for part of the feeding. In some cases where this type of feed is not correctly controlled it is sometimes possible for the chicken's flesh to be impregnated with a foreign flavour or worse still, as we have seen in recent times, to be infected.

PRODUCTION

When a chicken destined for freezing is killed in a factory it is immediately eviscerated and very quickly moves on to the next stage, the cooling. Now the fastest cooling process is by water, which is fine for a quick turnover but, from the point of view of the consumer, means that the cooling chickens can – and do – absorb quite a bit of water. Up to

179

7.4 per cent of its weight is the permitted level, but in some chickens it is even more. In some instances the birds are injected with a chemical called polyphosphate, which encourages water absorption. Producers claim this makes the flesh moist. I would claim it makes it watery. (You do have a choice here – polyphosphate-injected chickens have to be labelled as such.) Our water-logged chickens then move along in sub-zero temperatures to be deep-frozen.

WHAT'S WRONG WITH FREEZING?

Not a lot, provided (a) the chicken has not absorbed nearly 10 per cent of its weight in water, (b) the process of rigor mortis has been completed, and (c) some maturation has been allowed to take place before freezing so that flavour has a chance to develop (as it does naturally if a bird is hung). The trouble with the freezing of most chickens is that none of the above happens and – quite apart from flavour – if a bird is frozen within 6 or 8 hours of killing and rigor mortis is not complete, the flesh becomes tough and chewy. Equally, when the birds are frozen the process must be done quickly or else large ice crystals can form which penetrate the flesh and cause the texture to be stringy.

ALTERNATIVE CHICKEN

Free-range
This is one alternative to frozen chicken, but it's only fair to point out here that the free farmyard type of chicken is not necessarily always better: hens scratch about and can eat all sorts of undesirable things which could taint the flesh. Also it is simply unrealistic to supply our size of population with free-range chickens. However, it's not all gloom:

Chill-fresh
One quality chain store with branches throughout the country pioneered a method of chicken production which, although the cost is higher, has now been adopted quite widely. These fresh chickens are reared on selected farms where they can feed and take water ad lib, and stress and crowding are avoided (a good-tasting chicken, it seems, has to be contented!). After they're killed these birds are cooled by air; rigor mortis occurs naturally and, by enzyme action, there is a certain amount of maturation and flavour development under correct temperature control.

New York-dressed
This is the name given to fresh chicken which is hung, so that flavour matures. In this case the bird is eviscerated only at the point of purchase.

CHOOSING YOUR CHICKEN
We can choose the quality of chicken we want to eat. First, from a

reliable poulterer, who knows his source of supply is of high quality and whose poultry is eviscerated only at the point of purchase. Secondly we can choose a fresh, chilled chicken that has not been subjected to water-cooling (water-cooled chicken looks very pale and white, air-cooled chicken has a healthy, pinkish tone). Or we can choose frozen chicken from a good supplier. I have outlined the hazards of freezing broilers above, but with correct and careful freezing quality *can* be achieved. My suggestion is to use frozen chickens for casserole cooking (because the water content can cause them to steam rather than roast).

Chickens are sold in various categories of size and weight and, obviously, you need to select the right chicken for the right recipe. There are four principal ways of cooking: (i) roasting; (ii) pot-roasting and casseroling; (iii) shallow and deep-frying; (iv) grilling and barbecuing. Here is the range of chickens and how to cook them.

Poussins and double poussins
These are baby chickens weighing up to 2 lb (about 1 kg) each, with not a lot of flavour to them. But split in half and marinated overnight they make very good barbecue food.

Broilers
These are the uniform immature birds which weigh in at $2^1/_2$–$3^1/_2$ lb (1.25–1.6 kg). If good quality, what they lack in flavour is made up for in tenderness. So, jointed, they're suitable for any recipe that calls for chicken to be grilled or fried.

Roasting chickens
These are the 4–5 lb birds (1.8–2.25 kg). Their extra age and development means more chicken flavour, and they can take the longer cooking time needed for roasting. These are the best for casseroles too. It is now possible to buy larger birds for the table weighing up to 8 lb (3.6 kg).

Large roasters
These have the best flavour of all and are ideal for a large family meal like Sunday lunch. You can either follow the instructions for cooking a small turkey (on page 200) or use the timings given on pages 184–5.

Boiling fowl
These are the tough old birds! They're not suitable for roasting, but can certainly be given long, slow cooking in a casserole or else used for stock-making.

STORING FRESH CHICKEN

If you buy a fresh chicken, try to get it home as soon as possible. Then remove the wrapping and, most important, the giblets if they are tucked inside. Place it on a plate, cover loosely and put it in the lowest part of the fridge: it will keep for 3 days.

STORING AND THAWING FROZEN CHICKEN

If you're tackling a frozen chicken, the most important rule is that the bird must be completely and thoroughly de-frosted before it is cooked. Food poisoning can occur if you begin to cook the bird while it is still partly frozen, because this creates the semi-warm conditions in which food bugs thrive and multiply. The thawing times below are produced by the Poultry Information Service.

Size of Bird	THAWED AT ROOM TEMPERATURE 65°F (16°C)	THAWED IN A REFRIGERATOR 40°F (4°C)
2 lb (900 g)	8 hours	28 hours
3 lb (1.3 kg)	9	32
4 lb (1.8 kg)	10	38
5 lb (2.25 kg)	12	44
6 lb (2.75 kg)	14	50
7 lb (3 kg)	16	56

Frozen chicken can be stored in the freezer for up to 9 months, or up to 1 month in the frozen food compartment of a refrigerator (depending on the star rating), but once thawed should not be re-frozen.

JOINTING A CHICKEN

This is nothing to be afraid of. First of all, if you're buying chicken from a butcher or poulterer, you can ask him to joint it for you (everything costs so much these days, we should get all the value we can). If you need to do it yourself at home, there are really only two requirements: a really sharp knife and perhaps a pair of good kitchen scissors (or poultry shears). Follow the instructions, and don't worry too much if the joints aren't perfectly neat. Once the chicken is cooked no-one will know.

First, cut through the parson's nose, then stand the chicken in a vertical position (neck end down). Insert the knife into the cut you've already made, and cut straight down the back of the chicken. Place it skin-side down, open it out flat, and cut right through the breastbone. Now turn the two halves of the chicken skin-side up, stretch out the leg as far as you can, then cut through the natural line dividing the leg from the breast. For six portions turn the legs over, find the thin white line at the centre of the joint, and cut through it. For eight portions, cut the breast portion in half.

BONING A CHICKEN

I'm afraid this is something that goes against the grain with me. I was brought up to believe that bones in the meat during cooking enhance flavour (you can test this yourself: eat that little piece of chicken that adheres to the wing bone, and you can really taste the concentrated chicken). Boning a chicken may indeed make it easier to carve – but what about the trouble of boning it in the first place! I can't help thinking that sheer theatrical effect is the reason for some people producing something resembling a stuffed rugby ball in the name of chicken.

STUFFING FOR CHICKEN

Stuffing was invented for a very good reason. In the case of roasting chicken, where the flesh is very lean and could easily dry out if the fire was fierce, the stuffing provided lubrication – a sort of internal basting to give extra juiciness, particularly to a large bird needing long cooking. A chicken stuffing should have a fair amount of juicy ingredients, like minced pork sausagemeat or a generous quantity of butter.

TRUSSING CHICKEN

I am happy to say we can all abandon our needles and thread. In all the research I've done over the years I can find no reason for trussing other than the neat appearance it gives a bird, and the supposed ease of carving. A well-cooked bird which has not been trussed is, in fact, quite simple to carve, and neat appearances don't matter if you are going to carve in the kitchen – which is the most suitable place to carve in any case.

CARVING CHICKEN

As always, the cardinal requirement is a sharp knife, then it's easy. And the same rule applies to chicken as to other roast meats and poultry, and that's to allow a good 10–15 minutes between completion of cooking and carving. This lets the juices which have welled up to the surface during cooking seep back into the flesh to keep it succulent. It also makes carving neat slices much easier.

Secure the chicken with a fork, insert knife between leg and body and remove thigh and drumstick in one piece. Remove the wing on the same side, then slice the breast. Repeat this on the other side of the bird. Lastly, divide the thigh and drumstick, cutting through the joint to obtain two leg portions.

TRADITIONAL ROAST CHICKEN WITH STUFFING

◆

(Serves 6–8 people)

As you've probably gathered, I'm a traditionalist and one of the pleasures of the table for me is the aroma of a carefully roasted chicken with crisp brown skin and sizzling juices underneath. Perfect accompaniments would be a stuffing of pork flavoured with sage and onion, a few crisp pieces of bacon (which protected the breast during roasting), a jug of creamy bread sauce, and a gravy made with chicken juices and giblet stock. In this age of fast, convenience living it can be a real therapy to lavish care and thought on cooking something simple really well.

5–6 lb roasting chicken, including neck and giblets (2.25–2.75 kg)
3 oz butter (75 g)
6 rashers fat streaky bacon
salt and freshly milled black pepper
For the stuffing
8 oz minced pork or good quality pork sausagemeat (225 g)
2 oz fresh breadcrumbs (50 g)
1 smallish onion, very finely chopped or grated
1 dessertspoon dried sage
For the gravy
giblet stock (see page 65)
a little plain flour

Pre-heat the oven to gas mark 5, 375°F (190°C).

In advance make up a strong, reduced giblet stock according to the instructions on page 65. Then, to prepare the chicken for the oven, make the stuffing.

The stuffing

Here I part company with many other cooks and follow my mother's advice, which is to place some stuffing inside the body cavity as well as the breast (which provides moisture and flavour to permeate the inside of the whole bird during cooking). It also means there's some stuffing left over to go with the cold chicken the next day! You can of course make a smaller quantity of stuffing and just use it for the breast if you prefer. For variation you could add a small chopped apple and the chicken liver, finely chopped.

The stuffing is made simply by combining all the ingredients thoroughly in a bowl, and seasoning well with salt and pepper. To stuff the breast: at the neck end you'll find a flap of loose skin, and if you gently loosen this you'll eventually be able to make a triangular pocket between the breast and the skin. Pack about one-third of the stuffing in as far as you can, but not too tightly (or it might swell and burst during cooking) then pat it down to make a nice rounded shape. Now tuck the neck flap under the bird's back and secure it in place with a small skewer. Then place the rest of the stuffing inside the body cavity.

The chicken

Next smear the butter generously over the bird (if the skin is at all damp, dry it first) and tuck an extra lump of butter at the points where the thighs join the body. Season with salt and pepper, then place the bacon strips in a row – slightly overlapping each other – all along the breast.

Lay the chicken on its back in a roasting tin on a highish shelf in the oven, then calculate the cooking time which will be 20 minutes to the pound (450 g) and *sometimes* 20 minutes over. It is this final 20 minutes that has to be flexible because larger birds don't take as long as might be expected, and also because ovens vary.

Every 20 minutes or so during roasting baste the bird thoroughly with the buttery juices to keep it moist, and after 1 hour remove the now-crisp bacon slices and reserve them in a warm place for serving; 20 minutes before the end of the cooking time increase the heat to gas mark 7, 425°F (220°C), just to give the skin a final crisping.

Is it cooked?

The all-important question. There are three tests I use. (1) If you pierce the thickest part of the thigh with a thin skewer, the juices running out should be golden and clear. If they're pink it is not ready. (2) If the juices were golden and clear, then test the leg by tugging it gently away from the body. If you feel it give, it is ready. (3) (This is if a chicken is not stuffed.) Tip the chicken up and examine the juices running out of the body cavity – they should be golden and clear, and not at all pink.

To serve

When it's cooked, set the chicken on a hot dish in a warm place and leave it to 'relax' for 10–15 minutes. Meanwhile spoon or pour off any excess fat from the corner of the tin, stir a little flour into the juices and make gravy with the giblet stock, simmering to reduce and concentrate the flavour. Carve the chicken, and serve with the stuffing, bacon pieces, gravy and creamy bread sauce (page 398).

CREAMED CHICKEN WITH AVOCADO

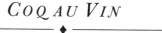

(Serves 4 people)

This recipe is a delicious way to use left-over cooked chicken or, if you have to work all day and prepare supper when you get home, it's a quick and easy way to jazz up some ready-cooked chicken from a quality chain store.

1 lb cold cooked chicken meat (450 g), cut into small strips
2 oz butter (50 g)
2 oz plain flour (50 g)
10 fl oz milk (275 ml)
5 fl oz chicken stock (150 ml)
5 fl oz single cream (150 ml)
1 tablespoon dry sherry
lemon juice
2 ripe avocados
1 oz mild cheese (25 g), grated
salt and freshly milled black pepper

Pre-heat the oven to gas mark 6, 400°F (200°C).
2¹/₂ pint (1.5 litre) ovenproof baking dish.

Begin by melting the butter in a medium-sized saucepan, add the flour and blend to a smooth paste. Cook for 2 minutes, then gradually stir in the milk, stock and cream and, stirring all the time, bring to simmering point and cook very gently for 2 or 3 minutes. Then remove the pan from the heat and add the chicken pieces, sherry, salt, pepper and lemon juice to taste.

Now halve and quarter the avocados and, having removed the stone and skins, slice the flesh thinly and cover the base of the gratin dish with the slices. Sprinkle over a little lemon juice, spoon the chicken mixture on top and, finally, add the grated cheese. Transfer to the pre-heated oven and bake for 20–25 minutes or until the sides start to bubble. A crisp, green salad is a nice accompaniment.

COQ AU VIN

(Serves 6–8 people)

A truly authentic *Coq au vin* is made, obviously, with a cock bird, and some of the blood goes into the sauce which, by the time it reaches the table, is a rich, almost black colour. In Britain we make a less authentic adaptation, but it makes a splendid dinner party dish.

5 lb chicken (2.25 kg), cut into 8 joints (see pp. 182–3)
1 oz butter (25 g)
1 tablespoon oil
8 oz unsmoked streaky bacon in one piece (225 g)
16 button onions
2 cloves garlic, crushed
2 sprigs fresh thyme
2 bay leaves
1¼ pints red wine (725 ml)
8 oz dark-gilled mushrooms (225 g)
1 tablespoon plain flour and 1 rounded tablespoon softened butter, worked to a paste
chopped parsley, to garnish (optional)
salt and freshly milled black pepper

A large flameproof pot, wide and shallow to take the joints in one layer.

Melt the butter with the oil in a frying-pan, and fry the chicken joints, skin side down, until they are nicely golden; then turn them and colour the other side. You may have to do this in three or four batches – don't overcrowd the pan. Remove the joints from the pan with a draining spoon, and place them in a large cooking pot. The pot should be large enough for the joints to be arranged in one layer yet deep enough so that they can be completely covered with liquid later. The pot must also be flameproof.

Now de-rind the bacon and cut it into fairly small cubes, brown them also in the frying-pan and add them to the chicken, then finally brown the onions a little and add them too. Next place the crushed cloves of garlic and the sprigs of thyme among the chicken pieces, season with freshly milled pepper and just a little salt, and pop in a couple of bay leaves.

Pour in the wine, put a lid on the pot and simmer gently for 45–60 minutes or until the chicken is tender. During the last 15 minutes of the cooking, add the mushrooms and stir them into the liquid.

Remove the chicken, bacon, onions and mushrooms, place them on a warmed serving dish and keep warm. (Discard the bay leaves and thyme at this stage.)

Now bring the liquid to a fast boil and reduce it by about one-third. Next, add the butter and flour paste to the liquid. Bring it to the boil, whisking all the time until the sauce has thickened, then serve the chicken with the sauce poured over. If you like, sprinkle some chopped parsley over the chicken and make it look pretty.

Note The results are different but every bit as delicious if you use cider instead of wine, but it must be *dry* cider. I also like now to give this half its cooking time the day before, let it cool, then refrigerate and give it the other half of the cooking time before serving. At the half-cooked stage, turn the chicken pieces over so that they can absorb all the lovely flavours overnight.

CHICKEN IN THE POT

◆

(Serves 4 people)

This is the *poule au pot* associated with Henri IV of France, whose ambition was that every family in his kingdom might be able to afford to eat this dish every Sunday.

3½ lb freshly drawn chicken with giblets (1.6 kg)
8 oz unsmoked streaky bacon in one piece (225 g)
3 tablespoons olive oil
12 button onions
4 medium carrots, cut in 1 inch (2.5 cm) chunks
4 small turnips, quartered
1 clove garlic, crushed
10 fl oz dry white wine (275 ml)
15 fl oz chicken stock (425 ml), made with the giblets (see page 65)
1 small bunch parsley stalks
a few celery leaves (optional)
2 sprigs fresh thyme or ¾ teaspoon dried thyme
1 bay leaf
8 oz mushrooms (225 g), sliced
1 tablespoon plain flour and 1 rounded tablespoon softened butter, worked to a paste
salt and freshly milled black pepper

Pre-heat the oven to gas mark 6, 400°F (200°C).

First heat the oil in a large flameproof casserole, then cut the bacon into chunks and fry it a little with the peeled button onions. When the bacon and onions have coloured slightly, remove them with a slotted spoon and keep them on one side.

Now, with the oil fairly hot, fry the chicken whole (as you would a piece of meat for a pot-roast), turning it several times to brown evenly all over, then remove it from the casserole. Next fry the carrots, turnips and crushed garlic for about 5 minutes, stirring them all around so that they brown slightly. Now put the bacon and onion back in the pan. Push everything to the sides and sit the chicken in the centre. Next pour in the wine and stock, add the parsley and celery leaves (if using) tied in a bundle, plus the thyme, bay leaf and salt and pepper. Bring to simmering point, then transfer the casserole to the oven (the casserole should be without a lid, but place a piece of foil over the chicken breast) and let it cook for 30 minutes, uncovering and basting the chicken breast now and then with the surrounding stock.

After 30 minutes remove the foil, add the sliced mushrooms, then cook for another 30 minutes, again basting fairly often with the juices. When the chicken is cooked, take the casserole from the oven, remove the chicken, drain it well and put it on a warmed serving dish. Surround it with the well-drained vegetables and bacon, and discard the bay leaf and herbs.

Now place the casserole over a direct heat and boil the liquid fiercely to reduce it by about a third. Then whisk in the flour and butter paste, and bring back to the boil, whisking continuously until the sauce thickens. Now taste to check the seasoning, then carve and serve the chicken and vegetables with the sauce poured over them.

CHICKEN WITH LEMON SAUCE

◆

(Serves 4 people)

This is a light, summery recipe with a sharp lemon sauce.

4 lb chicken with giblets (1.8 kg)
3 oz softened butter (75 g)
1 dessertspoon lemon juice
1 teaspoon chopped fresh tarragon
1 lemon
salt and freshly milled black pepper
For the sauce
5 fl oz stock (150 ml), made with the giblets (see below)
2 oz butter (50 g)
1 tablespoon flour
grated rind of ½ lemon
1 tablespoon lemon juice
5 fl oz double cream (150 ml)

Pre-heat the oven to gas mark 6, 400°F (200°C).

Make the giblet stock as described on page 65 using 15 fl oz (425 ml) water, then reduce it down to 5 fl oz (150 ml) to give a concentrated flavour. This should be done in a wide saucepan without a lid, boiling vigorously.

Prepare the chicken for roasting by mixing the butter with ¼ teaspoon of salt, some freshly milled pepper and the lemon juice. Add the tarragon, then spread this mixture evenly all over the chicken. Now cut the lemon into quarters and place these inside the chicken. Next place the chicken in a roasting tin and cover the breast with buttered foil. Roast for 1¼–1½ hours, basting the chicken quite often with the buttery juices. Remove the foil from the breast during the last 30 minutes.

While the cooked chicken is 'relaxing' in a warm place, make the sauce. Melt the butter in a small saucepan, blend in the flour, then gradually stir in the giblet stock, lemon rind and juice. Bring to the boil, stirring all the time, simmer for 2–3 minutes, then add the cream and some of the juices from the roasting tin. Carve the chicken and serve on a bed of rice with the sauce poured over.

CHICKEN IN BARBECUE SAUCE
♦

(Serves 4 people)

If you can, buy fresh chicken drumsticks or thigh joints. Alternatively you could use chicken breasts, either whole or cut in half. This is one of the easiest supper dishes I know.

8 small chicken joints
olive oil
freshly milled black pepper
1 medium onion, chopped small
For the sauce
5 tablespoons dry cider (or wine)
5 tablespoons soy sauce
1 heaped tablespoon tomato purée
1 heaped teaspoon ground ginger
1 heaped teaspoon mustard powder
1 fat clove garlic, crushed
1 tablespoon soft brown sugar

Pre-heat the oven to gas mark 6, 400°F (200°C).

First of all, make sure the chicken joints are absolutely dry by patting them with kitchen paper. Then rub each joint all over with olive oil and season with freshly milled pepper (but no salt because of the sauce). Now pop them into a shallow roasting tin, tucking the chopped onion in amongst them and sprinkling them with a few drops of oil. Place the tin on the highest shelf in the oven and let them cook for about 30 minutes. Meanwhile make up the barbecue sauce simply by whisking all the sauce ingredients together with a fork until blended thoroughly.

When the chicken has been cooking for 30 minutes, pour off any excess oil from the roasting tin, then pour the barbecue sauce over the chicken and cook for a further 25 minutes, basting frequently.

This is nice served with brown pilau rice and a salad.

CHICKEN WITH WHOLE SPICES

◆

(Serves 4 people)

This tastes authentically Indian, but with an added 'home-made' fresh-ness that is so often lacking in Indian restaurants.

4 lb chicken (1.8 kg), cut in 8 pieces
2 cloves garlic, crushed
1 heaped teaspoon ground ginger or 1 dessertspoon grated fresh root ginger
2 teaspoons ground turmeric
1½ tablespoons groundnut oil
salt and freshly milled black pepper
For the spice sauce
¾ teaspoon whole cumin seeds
1 teaspoon whole coriander seeds
8 whole cardamom pods
1 oz butter (25 g)
½ tablespoon groundnut oil
2 onions, very finely chopped or minced
1 medium green pepper, de-seeded and finely chopped
2 dried red chilli peppers, de-seeded and very finely chopped
1 bay leaf, crumbled
5 oz natural yoghurt (150 g), mixed with 2 fl oz hot water (55 ml)

Prepare the chicken a few hours before cooking. Arrange the pieces in an oblong meat-roasting tin. In a small bowl mix together the crushed garlic, ground ginger and turmeric with the groundnut oil. Now, with a sharp knife, make several incisions in the chicken pieces, season with salt and pepper, then coat them as evenly as possible with the oil and spice mixture. Leave in a cool place (but not in the fridge) so that the flavour penetrates.

When you're ready to cook the chicken, pre-heat the oven to gas mark 6, 400°F (200°C). Place the tin on the highest shelf, uncovered, and cook for about 20 minutes or until the chicken pieces are a nice golden colour.

Meanwhile, prepare the whole spices. First of all place them in a thick-based frying-pan over a medium heat for about 1–2 minutes until they turn one shade darker, tossing them to keep them on the move. This warming of the spices helps to draw out all the flavour. Next grind them and crush finely, either with a pestle and mortar or in a basin using the end of a rolling pin. Next, melt the butter and oil in a frying-pan. Add the onions and green pepper, and cook for 5 minutes. Now

191

add the crushed spices, chillies and crumbled bay leaf, stir and cook for a further 5 minutes. Take the pan off the heat, stir in the yoghurt and water and add a little salt.

Now pour this mixture all over the chicken pieces, cover the tin with a double sheet of foil and bake for 30 minutes with the heat reduced to gas mark 4, 350°F (180°C). Then remove the foil and let the chicken cook for approximately a further 10 minutes.

Serve with *Spiced pilau rice* (see page 275) and mango chutney.

COLD CHICKEN PIE

◆

(Serves 8 people)

This is a delicious centrepiece for a picnic, or any sort of lunch out of doors.

For the pastry
2 oz lard (50 g), at room temperature
2 oz butter (50 g), at room temperature
8 oz plain flour (225 g), sifted
cold water, to mix
beaten egg, to glaze

For the filling
2 or 3 skinned chicken breasts, approx. 1¹/₂ lb (700 g) in weight
1 teaspoon ground mace
1 lb pork sausagemeat (450 g)
6 spring onions, finely chopped
1 teaspoon chopped fresh or ¹/₂ teaspoon dried thyme
1 tablespoon chopped fresh or ¹/₂ tablespoon dried sage
rind and juice of ¹/₂ lemon
2 tablespoons double cream
salt and freshly milled black pepper

Pre-heat the oven to gas mark 6, 400°F, (200°C).

A round, 8 inch (20 cm) diameter pie-tin with rim and sloping sides which is 2 inches (5 cm) deep.

First make up the pastry by rubbing the fats into the sifted flour till the mixture resembles fine breadcrumbs, then adding just enough water to make a dough that leaves the bowl clean. Rest the dough in a polythene bag in the fridge for 30 minutes, then use half of it to line the pie-tin.

Next, cut the chicken into ¹/₂ inch (1 cm) pieces, place them in a bowl, add the mace and season with salt and pepper.

Smoked fish pie (see page 126)

· Now, in a separate bowl, combine the sausagemeat with the spring onions, the thyme and sage, the lemon rind and 2 teaspoons of the lemon juice. Pour in the cream and mix everything together well to make a soft mixture (rather like a cake mix) – if necessary, add a little more cream. Next put one-third of the sausagemeat mixture in the bottom of the pastry-lined tin and spread it flat. Now put half the chicken pieces on top and sprinkle in any remaining lemon juice, then add another layer of one-third of the sausagemeat, followed by the rest of the chicken and a final layer of sausagemeat.

Roll out the rest of the pastry and use it to cover the pie – which will be well piled up, dome-like, by now. Seal the edges well, glaze with some beaten egg and bake on a baking sheet in the oven for 30 minutes. Then reduce the heat to gas mark 4, 350°F (180°C), and cook for a further 1¼ hours.

CHICKEN WITH GRAPE STUFFING

◆

(Serves 4 people)

Here's a nice recipe for serving in summer, when the seedless grapes are in season.

| 4 lb roasting chicken with giblets (1.8 kg) |
| 2 oz butter (50 g), at room temperature |
| salt and freshly milled black pepper |
| |
| *For the stuffing* |
| 3½ oz butter (85 g) |
| 1 medium onion, finely chopped |
| 4 oz fresh breadcrumbs (110 g) |
| 4 cloves garlic, crushed |
| 1 tablespoon chopped fresh parsley |
| 1 teaspoon chopped fresh or ½ teaspoon dried tarragon |
| 6 oz seedless grapes, or halved and de-seeded grapes (175 g) |
| |
| *For the gravy* |
| giblet stock (see page 65) |
| a little plain flour |
| 4 tablespoons dry white wine |

Pre-heat the oven to gas mark 5, 375°F (190°C).

First make the stuffing. Melt ½ oz (10 g) of the butter in a small saucepan and cook the finely chopped onion for about 6 minutes or until softened, then add the remaining butter and allow it to melt. Now

Loin of pork Dijonnaise (see page 150)

transfer the onion and the buttery juices to a bowl, add the breadcrumbs, then stir in the crushed garlic, chopped parsley, tarragon and grapes. Taste and season with salt and pepper.

Next loosen the breast skin of the chicken a little to make a pocket for the stuffing. Place the stuffing in the pocket but don't overfill – if you do, the skin will burst when cooking. Secure the skin flap underneath with a small skewer. Season the chicken all over with lots of salt and pepper, then rub it all over with the softened butter, and cover the breast with buttered foil.

Place the chicken in a roasting tin and cook for approximately 1 hour, 20 minutes, basting the meat with the buttery juices every 20 minutes or so. Remove the foil 30 minutes before the end of the cooking time to brown the breast.

Meanwhile make some giblet stock (see page 65), then boil it, without a lid, to reduce it and concentrate the flavour. To test if the chicken is cooked, pierce the thickest part of the thigh with a thin skewer: if cooked, the juices will run golden and clear. Drain the chicken thoroughly and keep warm while you make the gravy.

Carefully tilt the roasting tin and pour off some of the excess fat. Then put the tin over direct low heat and blend in a little flour. Keep stirring and allow the flour to brown before gradually adding the wine and sufficient strained giblet stock to make a thin gravy. Taste and season with salt and pepper. Carve the chicken and serve, passing the gravy round separately.

FRIED MUSTARD-AND-HERB-COATED CHICKEN

—— ♦ ——

(Serves 4 people)

This is a very good recipe for jazzing up the mass-produced chicken drumsticks or thighs that come in packets. They also make excellent picnic food.

8 small chicken joints
1 tablespoon authentic Dijon mustard
2 tablespoons made-up English mustard
2 egg yolks
2 tablespoons double cream
5 oz breadcrumbs (150 g), mixed with 2 teaspoons chopped fresh or 1 teaspoon dried mixed herbs
plain flour
salt and freshly milled black pepper
groundnut or olive oil, for frying

First remove the skin from the chicken joints. (If you make an incision first with a sharp knife the skin will pull off very easily.) Then in a small basin mix the two mustards, egg yolks and cream until well blended and smooth. Then place the breadcrumb and herb mixture on a square of greaseproof paper and some flour on another piece. Season each chicken joint with salt and pepper and dust with flour, then dip in the mustard mixture to coat it evenly, and finally roll the joint in the breadcrumbs and pat the coating on firmly. Chill the joints for 3–4 hours so that the mustard flavour can develop and the coating become firm.

Then in a very large frying-pan (or two smaller ones) heat about an inch (2.5 cm) of oil to the point where a small cube of bread froths on contact. Then fry the chicken joints over a medium heat, turning them from time to time, until they're crisp and golden – about 20 minutes. Drain the chicken joints on crumpled kitchen paper and serve hot.

DUCK

♦

Whatever mass-produced chicken lacks in character and flavour, our duck makes up for, I think. Perhaps that's because we eat relatively little duck in this country: if demand increased no doubt we'd have another plentiful but uniform bird. In the meantime duck, though comparatively expensive, makes a superb choice for a dinner party. In the first place you'll be serving something special; secondly duck has the advantage of needing almost no attention while it's cooking; and thirdly, if your guests happen to be late, your duck will happily wait for them without being spoiled.

BUYING DUCK

If possible, try to get a fresh duck. If you can't a frozen one will do, so long as you bear in mind one important point: ducks are very fatty birds and sub-zero temperatures do not prevent rancidity developing. So while a duck that's been frozen for 3 months will be perfectly good, after that it will begin to deteriorate. A duck frozen for a year will not be very good at all. It is of course essential that frozen duck is completely de-frosted before cooking.

The weight of a duck is very important, because to get a crisp, fat-free finish it needs long, slowish cooking – and that means the weight of the bird will be considerably reduced by the end of the cooking time. So to serve four people, buy a 5 lb or preferably a 6 lb bird (2.25 or 2.75 kg); to serve six or eight people you'll need two ducks of this size.

It is now possible to buy duck portions, and those on the bone can be roasted till crisp and golden. But I'm not a fan of the ready-skinned and boned breast portions, where all that's best about a duck has been discarded.

DRYING DUCK

To cook a duck to a lovely crisp finish, it has to be fairly dry before it goes into the oven. If it has been frozen (or even if it's a fresh duck which came wrapped in a polythene bag) and the skin looks damp, dry it thoroughly with a clean tea cloth or some absorbent kitchen paper. It is also a good idea to check that the inside of the duck is dry too. Then leave the bird in a cool dry place for several hours for the air to dry it as well. The Chinese hang theirs up on lines in a draughty place and one typical 'colour supplement' article once recommended drying a duck with a hair-drier! I can assure you, you don't need to resort to such measures to get a crisply cooked duck.

STUFFING DUCK

Personally I never put stuffing inside a duck, because (i) duck meat doesn't need lubricating, and (ii) the stuffing tends to absorb too much of the duck fat. But if you like you can prepare some *Pork, sage and onion stuffing* (see the recipe on page 198), roll the mixture into little balls, flour them and fry them to serve with the finished duck. That's especially nice if the duck is also served with an apple sauce. Alternatively it is excellent with *Prunes in Armagnac* (see page 202).

COOKING TIMES FOR DUCK

In France duck is often served pink and under-done, or sometimes the skin and bones are removed and only the breast is cooked. Pressed duck is also considered a delicacy, though it's not to my taste. In England we tend to prefer our duck cooked whole and for quite a long time, so that the high proportion of fat can be rendered down and run out, leaving moist flesh and a mahogany-coloured crisp skin (rather like crackling); 30 minutes per pound (450 g) is a general guideline. This longer style of cooking does mean that the wings and part of the legs are frazzled but, believe me, the rest is so good that it's worth the small loss. If you've ever had duck cooked in the Chinese way, this is almost that crunchy but with some soft flesh as well. However, if you prefer duck in the French manner, you can cut down the cooking time.

ROAST DUCK

◆

(Serves 4 people)

6 lb duck (2.75 kg)
salt and freshly milled black pepper
1 bunch watercress, to garnish

Pre-heat the oven to gas mark 7, 425°F (220°C).

The golden rule is never to put any sort of fat near duck, because it has more than enough of its own. Just place the bird in a roasting tin, then prick the duck skin all over – going deep into the flesh – with a skewer (to leave little escape routes for the fat to run out). Season the duck quite liberally with salt and pepper, then place the tin on a highish shelf in the oven (see note at end).

After 20 minutes turn the heat down to gas mark 4, 350°F (180°C), then basically all you have to do is leave it alone for 3 hours – just once or twice pouring off the fat that has collected in the roasting tin. Pour the fat into a bowl – don't throw it away; it is lovely for roasting or sautéing potatoes.

When the cooking time is up, remove the duck from the tin, first tipping it up to let excess fat drain out of the body cavity, and place it on a carving board. Leave it to 'relax' for 5 minutes, then divide it into portions: all you need do is cut the bird in half lengthways (i.e. along the length of the breast and through the backbone) with a sharp knife, then cut the halves into quarters – you may need the help of some kitchen scissors here. Leaving any escaped pieces of bone behind, sit the quarters up together on a warm serving dish and garnish with watercress.

Note It is best to place the duck on a rack in the roasting tin. If the rack from your grill pan will fit into the oven, you can use that. Failing that, a crumpled wedge of foil would do as well.

SAUCES FOR DUCK

To make a gravy, simmer up some stock with the duck giblets (as for *Chicken giblet stock*, page 65). Pour off the fat from the roasting tin and, over direct heat, add some flour to the juices that are left and stir it around. Now blend in the giblet stock (plus some wine if you feel like it) and simmer gently to thicken slightly.

Alternatively you can serve it with *Bitter orange sauce* or *Morello cherry sauce* (pages 400–1), which are my own favourites.

TURKEY

———— ♦ ————

I come from a long line of turkey cooks and, throughout my life once a year, I have enjoyed the annual ritual of feasting not just on turkey but also on all the favourites that traditionally go with it.

Fashions in cooking turkey have come and gone, but ever since kitchen foil was introduced I have stood firm and stuck to the method which, in our family, has always been a hundred per cent successful (which is to say, cooking in foil). I can honestly say we've never had a turkey that's too dry, so we've never become bored with it cold. On the contrary, our enthusiasm for turkey lasts down to the jelly and dripping – delicious on toast for breakfast – and to the beautiful soup you can make from the carcass. I offer you here the family recipe for roast turkey with all the trimmings, but first a few words about buying a turkey.

BUYING TURKEY

Try if possible to get a fresh bird, and remember to order it in plenty of time. If you can only buy a frozen bird, or it's more convenient, try to buy one that has been frozen without added water, then don't forget to allow plenty of time for it to de-frost slowly and *completely*. Always remove the giblets as soon as you can – with a fresh bird immediately you get home, with a frozen one as soon as it has thawed.

PREPARING TURKEY

Let the bird come to cool room temperature before you cook it (i.e. remove it from the refrigerator, cold garage, shed or wherever the night before if you plan to eat your turkey dinner in the middle of the day). Also make the stuffing the night before, but *don't* yet stuff the turkey – it is important to let the air circulate round the inside of the bird. Stuffing made in advance also needs to be taken from the fridge the night before. The point is that if everything is chilled when it goes into the oven, it upsets the cooking times. Also remove and discard the trussing strings if there are any – they are not needed. The stuffing for the turkey and the giblet stock can be prepared the day before.

LEFT-OVER TURKEY

Use turkey left-overs as you would chicken – in *Creamed chicken with avocado* (page 186) or *Creamy chicken curry* (page 630).

PORK, SAGE AND ONION STUFFING
◆

(For a 12–14 lb/about 5.4–6.3 kg turkey)

As I said earlier in connection with chicken, I believe a stuffing is a good means of providing some lubrication and juiciness inside a lean-meated bird while it's cooking. Minced pork or good pork sausagemeat used as a base to a stuffing provides this lubrication.

4 heaped tablespoons white breadcrumbs
1 large onion, grated or very finely chopped
1 heaped dessertspoon dried sage
2 lb pork sausagemeat (900 g)
1 egg, beaten (optional)
salt and freshly milled black pepper

First combine the breadcrumbs with the onion and sage in a large mixing bowl, then stir in a little boiling water and mix thoroughly. Next work the sausagemeat into this mixture and season with salt and pepper. If (like me) you prefer your stuffing crumbly when it's cooked, leave it as it is. If you like to carve it in slices, then add a beaten egg to bind it all together.

CHESTNUT AND APPLE STUFFING

◆

(For a 12–14 lb/about 5.4–6.3 kg turkey)

This stuffing is also delicious but Christmas, with all the extra work involved, is not the time to be peeling and skinning chestnuts – a beastly job at the best of times. As they are going to be mashed anyway, I really think a tin of whole or puréed natural chestnuts (unsweetened) will do fine.

1 lb tin natural chestnuts (450 g)
1¹/₂ lb pork sausagemeat (700 g)
1 lb cooking apples (450 g), peeled, cored and finely chopped
1 medium onion, finely chopped
1 egg, beaten
salt and freshly milled black pepper

Drain the chestnuts into a large bowl, and mash them almost to a pulp with a fork. Combine them with the rest of the ingredients (except the egg) and mix thoroughly. Then add the beaten egg to bind everything together.

TURKEY SIZES AND TIMINGS

A good size of turkey for the average family is 12–14 lb (about 5.4–6.3 kg). This is oven-ready weight – which is equivalent to 14–16 lb (6.3–7.2 kg) New York-dressed weight. But on page 200 you'll find cooking times for varying sizes of turkey.

It might be helpful to beginners if I give you an account of the exact timings of a recent turkey of mine. The turkey (14 lb/6.3 kg oven-ready weight) went into the oven, pre-heated to gas mark 7, 425°F (220°C), at 8.15 am. The heat was lowered to gas mark 3, 325°F (170°C), at 8.55. The foil came off and the heat was turned up to gas mark 6, 400°F (200°C), at 12.30. Then with lots of basting it was cooked by 1.15 and served by 1.45.

Cooking times for other sizes of turkey

8–10 lb turkey (3.6–4.5 kg):
30 minutes at the high temperature, then 2¹/₂–3 hours at the lower temperature, then a final 30 minutes (uncovered) at gas mark 6, 400°F (200°C).

15–20 lb turkey (6.75–9 kg):
45 minutes at the high temperature, then 4–5 hours at the lower temperature, then a final 30 minutes (uncovered) at gas mark 6, 400°F (200°C).

Please bear in mind that ovens, and turkeys themselves, vary and the only sure way of knowing if a bird is ready is by using the tests described in the recipe.

TRADITIONAL ROAST TURKEY
◆

Cooking a turkey for the first time at Christmas, when in-laws and other guests are probably milling around, can be quite a traumatic experience. I think the secret of success is to give the turkey a good blast of heat to begin with, and once you've got it going (i.e. the heat has penetrated right through) you can then turn the oven down and let the turkey cook through more gently. It is also a good precaution to calculate your starting time so that the bird should complete cooking at least 30 minutes before you plan to sit down to eat. That way it has a chance to 'relax' so that the flesh can re-absorb the juices that have bubbled to the surface; it also allows sufficient time to give the turkey another 10 minutes' or so cooking time if it needs it.

12–14 lb oven-ready turkey (5.4–6.3 kg)
6 oz softened butter (175 g)
8 oz very fat streaky bacon (225 g)
salt and freshly milled black pepper
1 quantity pork, sage and onion stuffing or chestnut and apple stuffing (see pages 198–9)
For the gravy
about 2 tablespoons plain flour
giblet stock (see page 66)

Pre-heat the oven to gas mark 7, 425°F (220°C).
1 packet extra-wide baking foil.
Begin, on the morning of cooking, by stuffing the turkey. Loosen the skin with your hands and pack the stuffing into the neck end, pushing it up between the flesh and the skin towards the breast (though not too tightly because it will expand during the cooking). Press it in gently to make a nice rounded end, then tuck the neck flap under the bird's back

and secure with a small skewer. Don't expect to get all the stuffing in this end – put the rest into the body cavity.

Now arrange two large sheets of foil across your baking tin – one of them widthways, the other lengthways (no need to butter them). Lay the turkey on its back in the centre, then rub it generously all over with the butter, making sure the thigh bones are particularly well covered. Next season the bird all over with salt and pepper, and lay the bacon over the breast with the rashers overlapping each other.

The idea now is to wrap the turkey in the foil. The parcel must be firmly sealed but roomy enough inside to provide an air space around most of the upper part of the turkey. So bring one piece of foil up and fold both ends over to make a pleat along the length of the breast-bone – but well above the breast. Then bring the other piece up at both ends, and crimp and fold to make a neat parcel.

Place the roasting tin on a low shelf in the oven and cook at the initial high temperature for 40 minutes.

After that lower the heat to gas mark 3, 325°F (170°C), and cook for a further 3 hours for a 12 lb (around 5.4 kg), or 3½ hours for a 14 lb (around 6.3 kg) bird. Then tear the foil away from the top and sides of the bird and remove the bacon slices to allow the skin to brown and crisp. Turn the heat up to gas mark 6, 400°F (200°C), and cook the turkey for a further 30 minutes. The turkey will need frequent basting during this time, so the whole operation will probably take nearer 40–45 minutes.

To test if the bird is cooked, pierce the thickest part of the leg with a thin skewer: the juices running out of it should be golden and clear. And the same applies to any part of the bird tested – there should be no trace of pinkness in the juices. You can also give the leg a little tug, to make sure there is some give in it.

Then remove it from the roasting tin (using a carving fork and fish slice) and transfer it to a warm carving dish. If you can engage someone's help while lifting it, it's a good idea to tip the turkey to let the excess juice run out. Leave the turkey in a warmish place for 30–60 minutes to 'relax' before carving: provided it's not in a draught it will stay hot for that length of time, and it will give you a chance to turn the heat up in the oven to crisp the roast potatoes (you'll find my recipe for *Roast potatoes* on page 252).

Meanwhile, to make the gravy, tip all the fat and juices out of the foil into the roasting tin. Spoon off all the fat from the juice in a corner of the tin, then work about 2 tablespoons of flour into the remaining juices over a low heat. Now, using a balloon whisk, whisk in the giblet stock (see page 66) bit by bit, until you have a smooth gravy. Let it bubble and reduce a little to concentrate the flavour, and taste and season with salt and pepper. (And when you have carved the turkey, pour any escaped juices into the gravy.)

CRANBERRY AND ORANGE RELISH

◆

(Serves 8 people)

This cranberry sauce is an excellent accompaniment to the Christmas turkey, but there is no need to confine it to that: it goes just as well with many poultry, pork or ham dishes too.

1 lb fresh cranberries (450 g)
rind and juice of 1 orange
a piece of cinnamon stick
4 cloves
½ teaspoon ground ginger
3 oz sugar (75 g)
2 tablespoons port

Begin by mincing the cranberries finely, then put them into a saucepan. Remove the very thin outer rind of the orange (with a potato peeler if you like) and cut into very thin strips. Now add these strips together with the juice of the orange to the minced cranberries, followed by the cinnamon stick, cloves, ginger and the sugar. Bring the whole lot to boiling point, put a lid on and cook gently for about 5 minutes. Then take the pan off the heat and stir in the port. Pour everything into a serving bowl, cover it and leave in the refrigerator until required (remembering to remove the cinnamon and cloves before serving).

GOOSE

◆

Try to get a fresh goose, but if you can only get hold of a frozen one, remember to de-frost it very thoroughly and dry well.

ROASTED STUFFED GOOSE WITH PRUNES IN ARMAGNAC

◆

(Serves 8 people)

There was a time when goose, rather than turkey, was the traditional family treat at Christmas. If you recall it was the centrepiece of the famous lunch in Dickens' *A Christmas Carol*:

A breathless pause as Mrs Cratchit, looking slowly all along the carving-knife, prepared to plunge it in the breast; but when she did, and when the long-expected gush of stuffing issued forth, one murmur of delight arose all round the board, and even Tiny Tim beat on the table with the handle of his knife and feebly cried, 'Hurrah!' There never was such a goose.

When turkey began to be extensively farmed, the poor old goose was somewhat eclipsed. But in the past few years it has come back to its own and supplies are now plentiful during the Christmas period. In this recipe it is served with apples and a delicious French accompaniment of juicy prunes plumped up in Armagnac.

10–12 lb young goose with giblets (4.5–5.4 kg)

For the apple stuffing
1¹/₂ lb Bramley apples (700 g), cut roughly into ¹/₂ inch (1 cm) slices
¹/₂ lb prunes (225 g), soaked, stoned and chopped
1 large onion, roughly chopped
2 tablespoons Armagnac
¹/₈ teaspoon ground cloves
¹/₄ teaspoon ground mace
salt and freshly milled black pepper

For the forcemeat stuffing
the goose liver, finely chopped
1 Cox's apple, finely chopped
10 oz minced pork or good pork sausagemeat (275 g)
1 medium onion, finely chopped
2 oz breadcrumbs (50 g)
2 level teaspoons dried sage
salt and freshly milled black pepper

For the prunes in Armagnac
12 oz dried prunes (350 g)
1 pint cold tea (570 ml)
2 oz granulated sugar (50 g)
5 fl oz Armagnac (150 ml)

Make the apple stuffing by mixing all the ingredients together.

Make the forcemeat stuffing by mixing all the ingredients together.

You can prepare the prunes several days in advance. Soak them overnight in the cold tea, then drain them, barely cover with water, add the sugar and simmer for 15 minutes. Drain, sprinkle over the Armagnac, cover and leave in the fridge.

Pre-heat the oven to gas mark 7, 425°F (220°C). Then begin by placing the forcemeat stuffing into the neck flap end of the goose, pressing it in as far as you can, tucking the neck flap all round it, then patting it with your hands to make a rounded shape. Secure the flap underneath with a small skewer. Next, place the apple stuffing in the body cavity as it is – although it looks raw and chunky, after cooking it will collapse to a fluffy mass.

Season the goose well with salt and pepper, lay it on a rack in a roasting tin, then place it in the centre of the pre-heated oven. Give it 30 minutes' initial cooking, then reduce the temperature to gas mark 4, 350°F (180°C), and give it another 3 hours. That is for an 11 lb (5 kg) goose plus stuffing: roast a 10 lb (4.5 kg) bird for 15 minutes less; a 12 lb (5.4 kg) bird for 15 minutes more.

Make a stock with the giblets as for chicken giblet stock on page 65.

When the goose is cooked the juices will run clear if you pierce the thickest part of the leg with a skewer. Remove the bird to a serving dish, snap off the wing tips and allow to rest for 20 minutes before serving.

Drain off the fat from the tin and make a light gravy with the giblet stock and a little wine. Heat the prunes gently in a frying-pan, and stand in a warmed dish. Give each person a little of each of the stuffings, and serve the gravy and sauce separately. The nicest vegetable accompaniments would be some crisp roast potatoes and spicy baked red cabbage.

ANTHONY'S CHOPSTICK CHICKEN
◆

(Serves 4 people)

Fourteen-year-old Anthony Harold is a very talented young cook, who for most of his life has cheerfully and bravely been fighting a rare blood disease. Through his interest in cooking he and I have long been in contact – most recently during the filming of a programme about Anthony in the BBC tv series called *The Visit*. In that programme he 'took over' the kitchen of the Auberge de Provence in London to cook a complete meal for me! In return I invited him to provide a recipe for this new edition. This is it, and I can promise it is extremely good.

2 large chicken breasts, cut into strips ¼ inch (5 mm) thick
2 tablespoons groundnut oil
2 small cloves garlic, finely chopped
1 inch (2.5 cm) piece of fresh root ginger, finely chopped
2 small leeks, cleaned and cut into 1½ inch (4 cm) strips
2 small carrots, scrubbed and cut into 1½ inch (4 cm) strips
4 oz mange tout (110 g), topped and tailed
1 tablespoon yellow bean sauce or light soy sauce

Begin by heating a large frying-pan and adding the oil. After a minute put in the garlic and ginger, stir-frying until they start to colour. Keeping the heat at medium, add the chicken strips and continue stirring them until they start to colour. Next add the leeks and carrots, stir-fry them for another minute, then turn the heat down, put a lid on the pan and cook for just 2 minutes.

Now remove the lid and add the mange tout and yellow bean or soy sauce. Stir well over a medium heat for another minute, then serve immediately. This dish is nice on its own or with plain fried rice. Don't forget to try eating it with chopsticks: it's much more fun!

SEE ALSO

Chicken liver pâté
Chicken paprika
Chicken salad with tarragon and grapes
Creamy chicken curry
Pheasant with cream and apples
Spiced chicken

OFFAL

◆

One of my favourite cookery writers, Margaret Costa, once called a chapter on offal 'awful offal'. Not that offal is awful, she explains, but the *name* sounds awful. I agree with her, but find the various alternatives (like 'spare parts') equally off-putting. In fact the whole subject can be discouraging to some people not just because of its anatomical origins – the word itself is derived from those parts that 'fall off' or are rejected when a carcass is dressed – but because so often the meat has been neither sensitively nor imaginatively cooked. Lumps of semi-boiled watery kidney in a steak-and-kidney pie, or unevenly cut paving-slabs of over-cooked liver, these are the real culprits. In working on, and testing for, this chapter I have actually converted several people to offal who would otherwise never have considered eating it!

Offal really has an important place in our diet. Not only can it supply a generous amount of essential nutrients, but it does so at a very economical price. Being rich and concentrated in flavour means a little goes a long way, and items such as ox kidneys and liver, or pork kidneys, provide relatively cheap and quite delicious meals, as I hope the recipes in this chapter will show. But first let's consider some of the items in question.

LIVER

◆

Rich in iron and many vitamins, so most nutritionists would have us all eat liver at least once a week. In cooking it there are two important considerations. One is to try to persuade an obliging butcher to slice the liver *thinly* and *evenly* for you. And having achieved that, your next objective is to cook it carefully and, if frying or grilling it, quickly. If you cook it too long, it will be tough and dry.

CALVES' LIVER

This is the most expensive and said to be the finest flavoured. Serve it thinly sliced and lightly fried (so that it's still slightly pink) in butter, with some crisp fried bacon to go with it.

OX LIVER

This is the cheapest, but excellent braised with lots of onion and a thick gravy. With its rather coarser texture it isn't suitable for frying or grilling.

LAMBS' LIVER

My own favourite. Properly cooked it can be meltingly tender with a delicious flavour. If you're unable to buy it thinly sliced, try cutting it up into evenly-sized strips, as in *Liver in yoghurt and juniper sauce* (page 213).

PIGS' LIVER

This is extremely strong-flavoured and, in my opinion, not suitable for grilling, frying, or even casseroling. However, it is just the thing for pâtés and terrines and the recipe for *Faggots and peas* (page 212).

PREPARATION OF LIVER

All that needs to be done is to pull off any skin and snip out any odd bits of fat or tubes with kitchen scissors. Always slice the liver as thinly as possible for grilling or frying.

NOTES ON FRYING AND GRILLING LIVER

Always wipe the liver as dry as possible with kitchen paper first. Only calves' and lambs' liver are suitable for grilling or frying.

To fry
Lightly dust the pieces with seasoned flour and fry in hot butter or oil over a medium heat. It's important to get a good brown crust on the meat, and then only turn once after 3–4 minutes (or when you can see tiny droplets of blood beginning to form on the uncooked surface). Cook for a further 3–4 minutes.

To grill
Brush the liver with oil or butter and give it a minute longer on both sides than for frying.

KIDNEYS
—————— ♦ ——————

These too are packed full of nutrients. All types of kidneys are excellent for cooking, given the appropriate treatment for the right recipe. One point to remember is that kidneys do not have such a good flavour if stored too long. It's best to cook them really fresh, preferably on the day of purchase. If that's not possible, keep them until the next day but no longer.

VEAL KIDNEYS

These are very expensive and, outside large cities, not easy to come by. They need gentle cooking and are usually served plain or with a light sauce.

OX KIDNEY

This is an essential ingredient for steak and kidney pie or pudding (see pages 512 and 513) – no other type of kidney will give the proper, traditional flavour. Ox kidney is cheap and, though it is not recommended for grilling or frying, it is excellent stewed, braised, or especially curried (see page 218). Should you want to grate your own suet, by the way, the fat around an ox kidney is the best for this.

LAMBS' KIDNEYS

I'm particularly fond of plump, juicy lambs' kidneys which are available through the spring and summer months, when home-grown lamb is in its peak season. Frozen or imported, they are never quite as good, so if you buy these in the winter, they do need a good-flavoured sauce to go with them. If you can, buy lambs' kidneys still encased in their own fat, which seems to keep them fresher. It peels off easily, and if you place the fat in a meat-roasting tin in a low oven, it will render down to a bowlful of the most delicious cooking fat (which will have cost you nothing).

PORK KIDNEYS

In the past cooks have tended to subject pork kidneys to various periods of pre-soaking and blanching, to tone down what used to be a rather strong flavour. Nowadays, with more intensive meat production, we're eating blander, younger pork and I think this is the reason why the kidneys are milder, tender and quite delicious. They can therefore be cooked without any special treatment and, if you like their flavour, it may be useful to know that pork kidneys can be sliced and used as an alternative in any of the lambs' kidney recipes in this chapter.

PREPARATION OF KIDNEYS

To prepare lambs' or pork kidneys, first remove the skins, then slice the kidneys in half lengthways. Now use a pair of kitchen scissors to snip out the cores (which look like solid fatty lumps) – simply pinch the cores between your fingers and snip all around them with the scissors. With ox or calves' kidneys the process is just reversed: instead of cutting the core away from the kidney, you snip the lobes of kidney away from the core. (If I'm making a steak and kidney pudding, I sometimes pop the cores plus any little piece of kidney still attached into a pan with an onion, carrot and herbs and boil up some stock, which after skimming makes a delicious gravy for serving with the pudding.)

TONGUE

OX TONGUE

Salting improves the flavour of an ox tongue and so (especially around Christmas or party-time when there's a house full of people to feed) a salted tongue is the best kind to buy. Cooked and pressed and served cold, it goes well with *Cumberland sauce* (page 399) or *Spiced plum chutney* (page 606). For its preparation and cooking details see page 221.

LAMBS' TONGUES

These are nicest braised until the skins slip off easily (which is done by slitting the under-side of each tongue and then carefully peeling away the skin), then sliced, reheated gently and served with a hot *Parsley sauce* (page 393) or in a casserole (see page 220).

OXTAIL

There is something about the flavour and aroma of an oxtail braising in the oven that's very comforting on a bitter cold winter's day. Choose an oxtail that clearly has plenty of flesh around the bone: one complete oxtail will serve three to four people. It is particularly good with haricot beans (see the recipe on page 222), which seem to absorb so much of the flavour.

HEART

Invariably when I attempt to write about cooking heart, I find the description and detail end up sounding comical. Facts like 'a heart is heavy in proportion to its size' or 'long, slow cooking makes a heart tender' almost seem like something out of a romantic novel! Anyway lambs' hearts, in my opinion, are the nicest. Allow one per person, wash in cold water, then use a pair of kitchen scissors to cut out all the tubes and the dividing wall in the centre. You then have a convenient cavity for a stuffing (which I think is really essential).

SWEETBREADS

———————— ♦ ————————

I am often asked what exactly *are* sweetbreads? In fact they're glands, more specifically the thymus and pancreas glands of the animal. They are – rightly – considered to be a great delicacy and are not readily available without pre-ordering. Ox sweetbreads are fairly tough and they need long, slow cooking; calves' sweetbreads are rare and much more tender; but best of all are lambs' sweetbreads. For the last two the preparation is the same. Pre-soak the sweetbreads in cold water for 1–2 hours, then boil in fresh water: 5 minutes for lambs', 10 minutes for calves'. Cool them in a colander under cold running water then, using a sharp knife, remove any gristle, skin and veins.

TRIPE

———————— ♦ ————————

Tripe is the stomach of an ox. It has to be treated by blanching and pre-soaking, and this is done by the supplier or the butcher. It's this initial treatment that gives tripe its bleached white appearance. Honeycomb tripe – which a friend of mine describes as having the feel and texture of slithery knitting! – is very good when cooked with love and, judging by its regular appearance in supermarkets, is still popular. Normally it needs about an hour's further cooking at home, but this can vary so check cooking times with your supplier. If it is over-done it becomes limp, when ideally it should still have some 'bite' to it.

PEPPERED LIVER

———————— ♦ ————————

(Serves 2 people)

This is more or less the same as *Steak au poivre* but quite a bit cheaper and – if you like liver – every bit as good.

12 oz lambs' liver (350 g) – ask the butcher to cut it into the thinnest slices possible
2 teaspoons whole black peppercorns
1 tablespoon flour
1 level teaspoon salt
1 tablespoon olive oil
1 teaspoon butter
5 fl oz red or white wine (150 ml)

You'll need to crush the peppercorns first, and this can present one or two problems. If you've got a pestle and mortar you're home and dry; if you haven't, then the best way to crush them is by exerting a lot of pressure on the back of a tablespoon with the peppercorns underneath it. This last method can often result in one or two peppercorns escaping and rolling off onto the floor, if you're not careful. So be warned.

When you've got the peppercorns coarsely crushed, add them to the flour with the salt. Then dip the pieces of liver in it, pressing the pepper in a bit on both sides. Now in a large heavy-based frying-pan heat the oil and butter to the foamy stage, then put the liver slices in and cook them gently for a minute or two. As soon as the blood starts to run, turn them over, and gently cook them on the other side for slightly less time.

Whatever you do, don't overcook the liver or it will be dry and tough. Transfer the slices onto a warm serving dish, add the wine to the pan, let it bubble and reduce, then pour it over the liver and serve immediately.

PAPRIKA LIVER
◆

(Serves 3–4 people)

This is one of my favourite liver recipes – quick, simple and very good.

1 lb lambs' liver (450 g), cut into narrow strips about 2¹/₂ inches (6 cm) long
3 oz butter (75 g)
1 large onion, very finely chopped
1 green pepper, de-seeded and cut into narrow strips about 1¹/₂ inches (4 cm) long
1 level tablespoon Hungarian paprika
5 fl oz red wine (150 ml)
5 fl oz soured cream (150 ml)
salt and freshly milled black pepper

First melt 2 oz (50 g) of the butter in your largest frying-pan, add the onion and green pepper and soften them over a gentle heat for about 7 or 8 minutes. Transfer the vegetables to a plate using a draining spoon.

Now, with the heat fairly high, melt the extra butter and add the strips of liver. Let them cook and brown, and when the blood starts to run turn them over and cook them for just another minute or so before adding a seasoning of salt and pepper, the paprika and the vegetables. Then pour in the wine and let it bubble and reduce slightly (for about 2 minutes). Then – off the heat – stir in the soured cream until you have a nice smooth sauce.

Serve the liver straight from the pan onto pre-heated plates, with the onion, pepper and sauce spooned over it. This is delicious served with brown rice and some fried shredded cabbage.

FAGGOTS AND PEAS
———————— ◆ ————————

(Serves 4 people)

Faggots are a real old-fashioned treat – traditionally served with 'mushy' peas. You can, if you prefer, reduce the quantity of liver and increase the pork and bacon.

4 oz unsmoked bacon (110 g), bought in one piece, then cut into 1 inch (2.5 cm) cubes
1 lb pigs' liver (450 g), cut into 1 inch (2.5 cm) cubes
6 oz fat belly pork (175 g), cut into 1 inch (2.5 cm) cubes
2 medium onions, quartered
15 fl oz stock (425 ml)
2 oz fresh white breadcrumbs (50 g)
1 teaspoon chopped fresh thyme
³/₄ teaspoon dried sage
¹/₄ teaspoon ground mace
salt and freshly milled black pepper
For the mushy peas
12 oz green split peas (350 g)
1 teaspoon tomato purée
1 teaspoon Worcestershire sauce
1 dessertspoon mushroom ketchup
1¹/₄ pints water (725 ml)
1 onion, quartered
2 oz butter (50 g)

Pre-heat the oven to gas mark 5, 375°F (190°C).

First of all, place the cubes of bacon, liver and pork in a casserole along with the quartered onions, then pour in the stock. Cover the casserole and cook in the centre of the oven for 45 minutes, then drain the meat and onions in a sieve (reserving the liquid). Next, using the fine blade of a mincer, mince the meat and onions into a mixing bowl, then add the breadcrumbs, herbs and spice. Season with salt and pepper, and mix to combine everything thoroughly. Next use your hands to shape the mixture into eight good-sized balls.

Grease a shallow baking dish, and arrange the faggots in a single layer in it. Pour over 10 fl oz (275 ml) of the reserved liquid, and bake (uncovered) on a high shelf of the oven for 45 minutes.

To cook the peas, mix the tomato purée, Worcestershire sauce and ketchup with the water, and pour this into a pan, adding the onion quarters. Bring to the boil, then add the split peas and bring back to the boil. Now turn the heat down, cover the pan and simmer gently for 45–60 minutes, or until the peas are absolutely tender. After that, mash the butter into them, along with a seasoning of salt and pepper. If they seem a bit on the dry side, you can mix them with a bit of the stock left over from the faggots. Serve the peas with the faggots, and the juices poured over.

LIVER IN YOGHURT AND JUNIPER SAUCE

◆

(Serves 4 people)

1 lb lambs' liver (450 g) – ask the butcher to slice it very thinly
1 largish onion
2 oz butter (50 g)
1 teaspoon olive oil
1 heaped teaspoon juniper berries, crushed
1 clove garlic, crushed
5 oz natural yoghurt (150 g)
salt and freshly milled black pepper

First prepare the liver by cutting it into very thin strips, about 1½ inches (4 cm) long. The onion should be peeled, cut in half and then sliced thinly and the slices separated into little half-moon shapes.

Now take a thick frying-pan, melt the butter and oil together over a low heat until foaming, then add the onion, juniper and crushed garlic. Cook them gently, without browning, for about 10 minutes. Now add the pieces of liver, increasing the heat, and brown them quickly and evenly by turning them – be careful not to overcook them. When they're browned, turn the heat right down again, take the pan off the heat and add the yoghurt – stirring it down into the pan juices – then return to the gentle heat and let it all simmer very, very gently for about 5 minutes. Taste, season with salt and freshly milled black pepper, then serve the liver and sauce with rice and a side-salad.

Note The cooked yoghurt sometimes takes on a slightly separated appearance but this is normal and in no way affects the flavour.

OX LIVER AND BACON HOTPOT

◆

(Serves 4 people)

This is another economical family supper dish – just 1 lb (450 g) of ox liver will be plenty for four people.

213

1 lb ox liver (450 g), cut into slices no more than ¼ inch (5 mm) thick
4 oz streaky bacon (110 g), de-rinded and cut into small pieces
1 heaped tablespoon seasoned flour
3 fairly large onions, sliced
1 medium carrot, cut into chunks
1 celery stalk, cut into chunks
2 oz swede (50 g), cut into chunks
1 level teaspoon dried sage
stock or water
1 teaspoon Worcestershire sauce
2 lb potatoes (900 g), peeled and cut into fairly thick slices
a little beef dripping or butter
salt and freshly milled black pepper

Pre-heat the oven to gas mark 3, 325°F (170°C).

First of all, toss the slices of liver in the seasoned flour to coat them well, then arrange them in a good-sized casserole and sprinkle in any left-over flour. Then add the bacon and sliced onion, together with the chunks of carrot, celery and swede. Add the sage and a good seasoning of salt and pepper. Next pour in just enough stock or water barely to cover the ingredients in the pot – probably about 1 pint (570 ml) – then add the Worcestershire sauce. Finally, cover the top with a thick layer of potatoes, overlapping each other, then season again with salt and pepper. Cover the casserole and cook in the oven for 2 hours. After that, take the lid off and cook for a further 30 minutes.

When the time's up, brush the potatoes with a little melted beef dripping or butter and pop the casserole under a pre-heated hot grill to get a nice crusty top to the potatoes.

LAMBS' KIDNEYS IN RED WINE

◆

(Serves 2 people)

This goes very well with some brown basmati rice cooked with onion, or else with some very creamy mashed potato (see page 252). (Illus. opposite p. 224.)

6 small lambs' kidneys
2 oz butter or dripping (50 g)
1 large onion, chopped
1 clove garlic, crushed
4 rashers unsmoked bacon, de-rinded and chopped
12 oz dark-gilled mushrooms (350 g)

1 level tablespoon flour
1/2 teaspoon chopped fresh or 1/4 teaspoon dried thyme
10 fl oz red wine (275 ml)
salt and freshly milled black pepper

Begin by melting the fat in a pan and softening the onion and garlic in it for 5 minutes. After that add the chopped bacon and the mushrooms, and cook for a further 10 minutes. Meanwhile prepare the kidneys: cut them in half and remove the skins, then snip out the cores with a pair of kitchen scissors.

Now add the halved kidneys to the pan and cook them to colour a little, stirring them around the pan. Next sprinkle in the flour and stir it to soak up the juices, then add the thyme and pour in the red wine. Bring the whole lot to simmering point; season with salt (not too much, because of the bacon) and pepper. Then cover the pan and simmer gently for 15 minutes. Then remove the lid and simmer for a further 10 minutes.

KIDNEYS IN FRESH TOMATO SAUCE
◆

(Serves 2 people)

I first had these served al fresco on a flowery terrace in Tuscany on a warm summer evening. They are simplicity itself, yet really fresh tasting. Lovely with a pile of lightly buttered fresh noodles and a salad.

6 lambs' kidneys
1 medium onion, chopped
1 1/2 tablespoons olive oil
12 oz ripe tomatoes (350 g)
1 level dessertspoon plain flour
1 level tablespoon tomato purée
1 clove garlic, crushed
1 1/2 teaspoons chopped fresh or 3/4 teaspoon dried basil
salt and freshly milled black pepper

Prepare the kidneys by peeling off the skins, cutting them in half and snipping out the white cores with some scissors. It's important to take out the cores – if you don't, the kidneys will be tough.

In a medium-sized saucepan, cook the onion gently in the olive oil for 6 minutes or so. Meanwhile pour boiling water over the tomatoes, slip the skins off and chop up the flesh roughly. Now add the kidneys to the onion, turn up the heat a little and let the kidneys brown, stirring them and turning them around. Next sprinkle in the flour and cook it for a minute or two, then add the chopped tomatoes, tomato purée and garlic. If you are using dried basil add it now, but if it's fresh keep it on one side. Have another good stir, season with salt and pepper, and simmer (uncovered) over a gentle heat for about 20 minutes. If using fresh basil, stir it in just before serving.

PORK KIDNEYS IN MUSHROOM AND ONION SAUCE

♦

(Serves 4–6 people)

1 lb (450 g) pork kidneys will serve four to six very economically, especially in this recipe which has lots of delicious sauce.

1 lb pork kidneys (450 g) – 4–6 kidneys depending on size
6 rashers streaky bacon, de-rinded and chopped
a little oil for frying
For the sauce
3 oz butter (75 g)
2 onions, very finely chopped
8 oz mushrooms (225 g), very finely chopped
1 oz plain flour (25 g)
15 fl oz cold milk (425 ml)
freshly grated nutmeg
salt and freshly milled black pepper

Start by making the sauce. Melt half the butter in a saucepan, then add the chopped onion and cook for 5 minutes to soften. Next add the chopped mushrooms, stir them in and cook – gently – for about 30 minutes without a lid or until the mixture is reduced to a pulp (give it an occasional stir to prevent it sticking).

Meanwhile make a white sauce by combining the remaining butter with the flour, milk, and some salt and pepper in a saucepan and whisking it over a medium heat until it starts to bubble and thicken. Stir it (with a wooden spoon to get right into the corners), whisk again very thoroughly, then turn the heat down as low as possible and cook the sauce gently for 6 minutes.

When the mushroom mixture is ready, gradually stir the white sauce into it. Check the seasoning, add a good grating of whole nutmeg, then leave it on one side while you prepare the kidneys.

First halve them, then using a pair of scissors snip out the cores and slice the kidneys across into bite-sized pieces. Now heat a little oil in a frying-pan and add the chopped bacon and kidneys. Fry them over a medium heat until the kidneys are lightly browned (don't overcook them or they will get tough – there should be just a hint of pink in the centre). Then stir the bacon and kidneys into the mushroom sauce. Reheat gently, check the seasoning and serve with brown rice and a green vegetable.

CURRIED LAMBS' KIDNEYS

♦

(Serves 2 people)

This can be made with two pork kidneys, chopped, instead of lambs' kidneys.

6 lambs' kidneys
1 clove garlic, crushed
1 level teaspoon ground ginger
¹/₂ teaspoon chilli powder
1 level teaspoon ground turmeric
1 level teaspoon ground cumin
1 level teaspoon ground coriander
1¹/₂ tablespoons groundnut oil
1 large onion, very finely chopped
1 dessertspoon tomato purée
5 fl oz water (150 ml)
2 rounded tablespoons natural yoghurt
salt and freshly milled black pepper

Begin by snipping the skin off the kidneys, then halve them lengthways and cut out the white cores using some kitchen scissors. Now cut each kidney half into three or four pieces. Then, in a bowl, mix the garlic and all the spices together, add the kidney pieces and stir to coat them well. Cover the bowl with foil and leave to stand for an hour or so at room temperature.

After that, heat the oil in a wide, solid-based saucepan and soften the onion in it until it just begins to brown; then turn the heat right up, add the kidney pieces with all the spices and toss them around to brown quickly. Next mix the tomato purée with the water and gradually stir this into the kidney mixture. Then season with salt and pepper, cover the pan and simmer very gently for 30 minutes, stirring once or twice. When the cooking time is up, taste to check the seasoning. Beat the yoghurt until smooth, and stir it into the kidney mixture over a gentle heat. Leave on the heat just long enough to heat the yoghurt through, then serve with *Spiced pilau rice* (see page 275) and chutney.

KIDNEYS IN JACKET POTATOES
———————————— ♦ ————————————

(Serves 4 people)

This is a lovely combination of kidney and bacon juices soaked into the potato.

4 large potatoes
4 lambs' kidneys, skinned and cored
oil
2 oz butter (50 g)
8 rashers streaky bacon
a little made-up English or Dijon mustard
salt and freshly milled black pepper

Pre-heat the oven to gas mark 5, 375°F (190°C).

Clean the potatoes by wiping them with a damp cloth – or if they're very dirty by scrubbing them. Then dry them as well as possible (if you wash them sufficiently early, you can leave them to dry for an hour or two). Rub the lightest film of oil into the skins of the potatoes (this makes them crisp), then bake them in the oven for 1–1¹/₂ hours, depending on their size. Test with a skewer to see if they're cooked.

When the potatoes are cooked, remove them from the oven and turn up the heat to gas mark 6, 400°F (200°C). Holding them in a cloth (they're very hot!) make an incision with a knife lengthways and crossways, and lift the four corners of skin up and pull them back a bit. Now make a depression in the centre of each potato, using a tablespoon. Season well with salt and pepper and add a knob of butter to each one. Then spread the rashers of bacon with mustard and wrap two round each kidney. Lay a wrapped kidney in each potato and return to the oven for 30 minutes. Serve immediately, with a green salad on the side.

CURRIED OX KIDNEYS
———————————— ♦ ————————————

(Serves 6 people)

Another very economical, yet rather special, curry.

2 lb ox kidneys (900 g)
2 large onions
2–3 tablespoons groundnut oil
1 dessertspoon ground coriander
1 teaspoon ground turmeric
1 teaspoon whole cumin seeds

5 oz natural yoghurt (150 g)
1 tablespoon tomato purée
10 fl oz water (275 ml)
2 fat cloves garlic, crushed
about ¹/₂ teaspoon crumbled dried chilli pepper, de-seeded
salt

Begin by cutting the kidneys into pieces about 1 inch (2.5 cm) square, removing all the fat and cores as you do so. Then halve and thinly slice the onions (although this may look an awful lot of onion, it reduces to about half its initial volume).

Now heat the oil in a largish pan and, when it's sizzling hot, brown the kidneys, removing them to a plate afterwards with a slotted spoon. Stir in the onions and cook until they are golden brown, adding a little more oil if necessary. Now add the coriander, turmeric and cumin seeds and cook for a minute or two before stirring in the yoghurt and tomato purée, water and crushed garlic. Finally add the chillies and the kidneys. Season with salt, bring to simmering point, then cover and simmer gently for about an hour. Then take the lid off and continue to cook gently for a further 30 minutes or until the kidney is tender and the sauce thickened. Then serve on a bed of *Spiced pilau rice* (see page 275).

PORK KIDNEYS IN CHILLI SAUCE

◆

(Serves 4 people)

The robust flavour of pork kidneys is well suited to a spicy sauce, like the one in this recipe.

6 pork kidneys
3–4 tablespoons olive oil
2 medium onions, roughly chopped
1 large green pepper, de-seeded and chopped
1 clove garlic, crushed
¹/₂ teaspoon crumbled dried chilli pepper, de-seeded
1 dessertspoon flour
14 oz tin Italian tomatoes (400 g)
1 tablespoon tomato purée
salt and freshly milled black pepper

First prepare the kidneys by skinning them, halving them lengthways and removing the core, then slicing them across into pieces about ¹/₄ inch (5 mm) thick.

Now heat 3 tablespoons of olive oil in a good-sized flameproof casserole and brown the kidneys quickly over a high heat, then remove them to a plate. Next add the onion and green pepper to the oil left in the pan (you can add a little more oil if needed), and soften them for 5 minutes or so. Then stir in the garlic and the crumbled chilli and cook for a minute or two before returning the pieces of kidney to the pan.

Stir in the flour to soak up the juices, then pour in the contents of the tin of tomatoes, and add the tomato purée. Season well with salt and pepper, then simmer gently over a low heat for about 20–25 minutes without a lid. This is nice served with some rice and a salad.

LAMBS' TONGUE CASSEROLE
♦

(Serves 6 people)

Lambs' tongues make an excellent family casserole.

2 lb lambs' tongues (900 g)
For the stock
1 medium carrot
1 medium onion
1 celery stalk
1 bay leaf
1 bunch parsley stalks
6 whole black peppercorns
salt
For the casserole
10 fl oz stock (275 ml) – see method
10 fl oz dry cider (275 ml)
1 oz lard (25 g)
8 carrots, halved across
10 button onions, peeled but left whole
2 rashers streaky bacon, de-rinded and chopped
4 oz mushrooms (110 g), halved if large
1 oz plain flour (25 g)
salt and freshly milled black pepper
To garnish
4 tablespoons chopped fresh parsley

First of all, rinse the lambs' tongues in cold water, then place them in a large saucepan together with the vegetables and herbs for the stock (see ingredients). Season with just a little salt and pour over enough cold water to cover. Bring to the boil, cover the pan, then simmer gently for 1½ hours. After that time, remove the lambs' tongues from the pan and continue to boil the stock — without a lid so that it can reduce. When the tongues are cool enough to handle, strip the skins from them and trim the bases (the discarded bits can go back into the pan while the liquid is reducing).

At this stage, pre-heat the oven to gas mark 3, 325°F (170°C). When the liquor has reduced to about 10 fl oz (275 ml), strain it into a measuring jug and make it up to 1 pint (570 ml) with cider.

Now heat the lard in a flameproof casserole, cut the tongues into slices about ¼ inch (5 mm) thick and fry these in the lard until browned — then remove them to a plate with a draining spoon. Stir the halved carrots and button onions into the fat remaining in the pan and let these brown before adding the bacon and mushrooms. Cook them a little and return the slices of tongue to the pan.

Sprinkle in the flour, give it a good stir and cook for another couple of minutes before adding the stock and cider mixture. Bring it all up to simmering point, put a lid on the casserole and then cook in the oven for 1 hour. Taste and season if necessary, and just before serving sprinkle in the chopped parsley.

COLD PRESSED OX TONGUE
♦

(Serves 10–12 people)

To press a pickled ox tongue yourself may sound a bit daunting but it's much easier than it sounds.

4–4½ lb pickled ox tongue (1.8–2 kg)
1 large onion, quartered
2 leeks, split and washed
2 carrots, cut into chunks
1 clove garlic, peeled
a few parsley stalks
1 bay leaf
6 whole black peppercorns
2 teaspoons powdered gelatine
2 tablespoons port

A 5–6 inch (13–15 cm) deep cake tin or soufflé dish.

When you get the tongue home, scrub it well with a stiff brush, then soak it for about half a day in cold water. Throw the water away and place the tongue in a deep pot, cover with 6–7 pints (3.5–4 litres) of fresh cold water and bring it to the boil. Now skim away all surface scum before adding the prepared vegetables, garlic, herbs and peppercorns. Simmer very gently for about 3½ hours.

The tongue will be ready when the skin along the surface is blistered and the 'T'-shaped bone at the root of the tongue comes away easily when pulled. Take the tongue out of the pot, then douse it with cold water and strip away all the skin. Trim the ragged and gristly bits of the meat at the root and underneath the tongue to neaten it, then curl the tongue round and fit it into the tin or dish.

Now boil the cooking liquor briskly, to reduce it and concentrate the flavour a bit. Then sprinkle the gelatine into a little cold water in an old cup and melt it over simmering water until absolutely clear before straining it into 10 fl oz (275 ml) of the cooking liquor. Add the port and pour the mixture over the tongue. Put a saucer on top, weight it heavily, then leave for several hours or overnight until cold and set. Serve the tongue with some chopped jelly as a garnish. This is delicious with an assortment of pickles and chutneys (see the Preserving chapter) or *Cumberland sauce* (page 399).

OXTAIL WITH HARICOT BEANS

◆

(Serves 4 people)

This is, I think, one of the best ways of cooking an oxtail as the floury texture of the beans absorbs all the delicious flavour. Start preparing the beans well in advance.

8 oz haricot beans (225 g) – the long type
1 large oxtail, cut into joints
2–3 oz beef dripping (50–75 g)
plain flour
2 medium carrots, cut in chunks
2 medium onions, sliced
1 medium turnip, cut into longish chunks
2 large celery stalks, chopped
3/4 teaspoon dried thyme or 1 sprig fresh thyme
15 fl oz hot stock (425 ml)
15 fl oz red wine (425 ml)
salt and freshly milled black pepper

Pre-heat the oven to gas mark 2, 300°F (150°C).

The beans should be either soaked overnight or covered with plenty of water, brought to the boil, simmered for 5 minutes then left to soak for 2–3 hours.

Melt the dripping in a large frying-pan until sizzling hot. Coat each piece of oxtail with some flour seasoned with salt and pepper and fry them to a really good nutty-brown colour – then place them in a casserole. Next, fry the vegetables – adding more dripping to the pan if you need to – until they're nicely tinged with brown at the edges. Now add the vegetables to the oxtail along with the drained beans, stirring everything round a bit and adding the thyme.

Stir 1 rounded tablespoon of flour into the juices left in the frying-pan and gradually add the stock a little at a time, followed by the wine (stirring constantly to prevent lumps). Season the sauce with freshly milled pepper, but no salt as it can toughen the beans. Pour the sauce over the rest of the ingredients, put on a close-fitting lid and cook in the oven for 3 hours.

Before serving, spoon off any surface fat and season with salt, tasting as you do so. This is very good with braised red cabbage (see page 236).

SWEETBREADS WITH SOURED CREAM AND ONION SAUCE

♦

(Serves 4–6 people)

These I like to serve with plain boiled basmati rice and a green leafy vegetable such as spinach.

2 lb calves' sweetbreads (900 g)
1 tablespoon lemon juice
¹/₂ teaspoon salt
For the sauce
2 oz butter (50 g)
2 large onions, very thinly sliced
³/₄ oz plain flour (20 g)
¹/₂ teaspoon mustard powder
10 fl oz light stock (275 ml)
5 fl oz soured cream (150 ml)
a squeeze of lemon juice
salt and freshly milled black pepper
To garnish
fried croûtons and chopped parsley

First, soak the sweetbreads in cold water for about 2 hours, changing the water fairly frequently. Then drain and place them in a saucepan with a further 2 pints (1.2 litres) of fresh cold water, and add some lemon juice and salt. Bring to the boil, reduce the heat to give a gentle simmer and cook for about 15 minutes. Drain the sweetbreads and douse with cold water. Now split them into pieces, removing any bits of tubes and tough outer membrane that you may come across. Then cover them and put them on one side.

Now, to make the sauce, melt the butter in a large saucepan. When it is frothy, stir in the sliced onions and cook them over a very low heat for about 15 minutes until the onions are soft without being coloured. Then stir in the flour and mustard and cook for about 2 minutes before stirring in (gradually) the stock. Bring to the boil, still stirring, then cover and simmer gently for 15 minutes.

Rub the contents of the pan through a sieve (or liquidise). Now return the sauce to the rinsed-out pan, and stir in the cream. Return the sweetbreads to the pan and reheat – very gently or the cream will separate. Taste and season with salt, pepper and lemon juice. Pour into a warmed serving dish, surround with croûtons and garnish with chopped parsley.

TRIPE AND ONIONS

◆

(Serves 2–3 people)

For some this is a great delicacy. For others something they would rather not think about! This recipe comes from Yorkshire where the older generation have always held it in high regard.

2 lb tripe (900 g)
approx. 2 pints light stock or water (1.2 litres)
1 large carrot, cut into chunks
1 whole onion, peeled and stuck with a clove
2 celery stalks, cut into chunks
1 bay leaf
1 sprig thyme
6 whole black peppercorns
1½ lb Spanish onions (700 g), thinly sliced
2 oz butter (50 g)
1 tablespoon oil
1–2 tablespoons cider vinegar
chopped parsley, to garnish

First place the tripe in a large saucepan and pour in enough stock (or water) to cover, then add the carrot, whole onion, celery stalks, the bay leaf, thyme and whole peppercorns, bring up to boiling point, then cover and simmer for 30 minutes to an hour (this depends on how much blanching the tripe has had – your butcher should be able to tell you; it should still be a bit chewy after it has been simmered). Meanwhile cook the sliced onions in 1 oz (25 g) of the butter and 1 tablespoon of oil in a large frying-pan until golden but still slightly crisp. Scrape into a warmed serving dish and keep hot.

Next drain the cooked tripe, dry it as much as possible, then cut it into roughly 1 inch (2.5 cm) squares. Discard the vegetables, bay leaf

Lambs' kidneys in red wine (see page 214)

etc. Heat the remaining butter and fry the tripe until golden and lightly crisped. Cover the onions with the tripe, then pour the vinegar into the frying-pan and swirl it round, scraping the base and sides of the pan – then pour the vinegar over the tripe. Sprinkle with the parsley and have extra vinegar on the table.

SEE ALSO

Beefsteak and kidney pie
Beefsteak and kidney pudding
Chicken liver pâté
Risotto with chicken livers and mushrooms
Shoulder of lamb with rice and kidney stuffing

Fried cabbage with bacon (see page 235)

VEGETABLES

◆

In this country meat-eating has been virtually part of our heritage: apart from periodic shortages during wars or depressions the British have been renowned for their huge consumption of meat and game. And as a nation entirely surrounded by sea, our fish intake has been pretty high too. It's not surprising then that vegetables have not featured largely in the history of our cooking – their role has been to help the meat go down, rather than as things to be enjoyed in their own right.

Now something approaching a revolution has occurred. First, a new era of health consciousness has prompted an enormous swing not just to vegetarianism but towards the virtues of vegetables in general. Secondly we have now entered an age of what I would call global marketing where practically every variety of vegetable is available to us most of the time from some part of the world or other.

This *can* make for a more interesting diet of vegetables but, equally alas, it can have the opposite effect. We can so easily lose sight of the perfectly varied diet provided by the changing seasons. Take for example the broccoli family. Oh the joy of those first sprigs of fresh young broccoli in the early spring after the winter surfeit of Brussels sprouts or cabbage! But now imported supplies of its cousin, calabrese, have become a permanent fixture on the supermarket shelf, and the old saying that familiarity breeds contempt can never have been truer than in the dining room.

Not all the joys of anticipation have been removed, however. No foreign imports can usurp the native delights of British runner beans, or potatoes like Jersey Royals or the better varieties of English tomatoes. Where we can be grateful to 'progress' is in the fact that those vegetables that *do* grow better in other soils and climates are now jetted to us with minimum delay.

In the end the real pleasure of vegetables must be in their flavour. One head of Fenland celery after a November frost is worth a dozen imported specimens. The first tiny green Brussels sprouts, their flavour sharpened too by the autumn frosts, are in a different league from the insipid early August arrivals. The first young shelled peas of mid-June are a delicacy almost as exclusive as truffles, not least I'm afraid because of the extraordinary back-to-front policy of freezing the majority as soon as they're ready!

Finally a word about designer vegetables. In spite of what they say, small is not always beautiful. Lilliput veg may be up-market, but that's all. If you really value flavour forget baby sweetcorn, ignore minuscule carrots and anything else that looks unusually stunted. 'Young' means tender and succulent, 'baby' too often means tasteless.

In the notes which follow I have recommended some varieties of different vegetables. These suggestions are largely for the benefit of the home-grower. Unfortunately, they may not all be readily available in the market at present. Once again this is something that only we, the consumers, can do anything about, by insisting that we want the vegetables that *taste* best.

Vegetables, like most fresh foods, are best eaten when they are in season. Here is a quick checklist of what it makes sense to buy when.

Summer

Asparagus	Fennel
Beans: broad,	Globe artichokes
dwarf, runner	Mange tout
Cabbage	Marrow
Carrots	Mushrooms
Cauliflower	New potatoes
Celery	Peas
Corn-on-the-cob	Spinach
Courgettes	Tomatoes

Winter

Aubergines	Jerusalem artichokes
Broccoli	Leeks
Brussels sprouts	Onions and shallots
Cabbage	Parsnips
Red cabbage	Potatoes
Carrots	Swedes
Cauliflower	Turnips

A final note before going on to the preparation of vegetables: an important part of your kitchen equipment is – a plain thin skewer. Sliding a skewer into a potato or Brussels sprout to test for tenderness is still the easiest way to see if vegetables are cooked.

ASPARAGUS

Asparagus (or 'grass' as it's known in the trade) is a very regal vegetable. While the carefully graded bunches of matching spears might sometimes seem an expensive luxury, the loose ungraded asparagus can be reasonable at the height of the (short) season. These are also the very thin stalks called sprue, which are cheapest of all and are excellent for soups or quiches. I'm no gardener, but some time ago I planted some 2-year-old crowns and now asparagus obligingly appears in profusion during May and June all by itself. Those few stalks that are really too thin to be picked up with the fingers can be used in a quiche or with *Eggs en cocotte with soured cream and asparagus* (see page 474).

TO COOK ASPARAGUS

Steaming is the only way to cook asparagus – its flavour is so delicate I'm absolutely against ever putting it into water. You can buy specially shaped asparagus steamers, but I find it hard to justify the expense. An ordinary steamer (as used for steamed puddings) or a vegetable steamer (as described on page 11) will do very well. Trim the stalks down to a reasonable length, 8–9 inches (20–23 cm), which will get rid of most of the 'woody' part, fit them inside the steamer and sprinkle them with salt. Place the steamer over a saucepan of boiling water and let the asparagus cook for 8–12 minutes, depending on the thickness of the stalks. Meanwhile heat up some butter in a pan to the frothy stage, and when the asparagus is ready serve it on hot plates with the butter poured over (and some crusty bread to mop up the juices afterwards). Alternatively you can serve it with *Hollandaise sauce* (see page 394), which will keep warm in a bowl over a pan of not quite simmering water. Don't forget the napkins and finger bowls.

Note 2 lb (900 g) of asparagus is a generous serving for four people.

AUBERGINES

♦

Aubergines are extremely beautiful vegetables, dark, shiny, rich maroon. Some are long – rounded at one end and thinner at the other – with a cap of green leaves and a stalk. Others are round and squat-looking. Inside they are all cream-coloured, with a flavour quite unlike that of any other vegetable (the peel itself has a lot of flavour). Because they contain a great deal of water it is always best to sprinkle the insides or the cut slices with salt – which will draw some of the excess water out. Place the salted aubergines in a colander, put a plate on top and weight it down, and in half an hour or so a lot of the surplus moisture will drain out and you can squeeze out more by pressing down on them at the end. Then dry them in a cloth and they're ready to be cooked. (There is no need to wash off the salt as they'll need it in the cooking).

BAKED AUBERGINES WITH TOMATOES

◆

(Serves 4 people)

Cooked like this aubergines can make a good accompaniment to lamb, or even be eaten as a lunch dish on their own.

4 aubergines, approx. 1¾ lb (800 g) in weight
4 tablespoons oil
1 large onion, finely chopped
6 largish tomatoes, peeled and chopped
2 cloves garlic, crushed
2 tablespoons finely chopped parsley
a good pinch each of ground allspice, cinnamon and caster sugar
salt and freshly milled black pepper
For the topping
2–3 tablespoons dry white breadcrumbs
1 tablespoon grated Cheddar cheese
1 oz butter (25 g)

First prepare the aubergines: cut each one into smallish pieces, pile them all in a colander, sprinkle with salt (2 heaped teaspoons), then place a plate on top of them. Weight it down with a scale-weight and leave to drain for 1 hour.

When you're ready to cook, pre-heat the oven to gas mark 5, 375°F (190°C), and butter a shallow baking dish generously. Drain the aubergines and dry them thoroughly on kitchen paper, then heat the oil in a frying-pan. Add the aubergines to the pan and fry to a pale-golden colour, then add the chopped onion and carry on cooking until that has softened a bit.

Next add the tomatoes, garlic and parsley, the spices and sugar, and season with salt and pepper. Let everything simmer gently for about 5 minutes, stirring occasionally. Then transfer the mixture to the baking dish, sprinkle the top with a mixture of the cheese and breadcrumbs, and dot the surface with flecks of butter.

Bake near the top of the oven for about 30 minutes, or until browned.

BEANS

◆

BROAD BEANS

These are the first beans of spring and are at their best, I think, when they're young and tender. So many people claim not to like them because they have only tasted the old (probably over-boiled) toughies. My friend John Tovey makes a delicious salad of broad beans filleted, that is removing all the skins and using only the bright green centres. I would never have the patience to do that, but for those who grow their own I would recommend that they harvest some of the immature pods (not more than finger-thick) and try cooking them whole – see the recipe below. Shelled broad beans need very light cooking, just 4–6 minutes in a steamer, and are delicious served tossed in *Herb butter* (page 405) or else in a salad with bacon (see page 453).

DWARF BEANS

These are sometimes called *haricots verts* (tiny flat baby beans) or Bobby beans (which are actually rounder and larger). Our home-grown varieties in summer are good, but some of the year-round imported ones can be quite tasteless. To cook them, top and tail them with scissors, and steam or cook in boiling salted water for about 4–6 minutes if they're really tiny, 8–12 minutes if larger. I like to drain them, put them back in the pan and toss with olive oil, a little crushed garlic and pepper and salt before serving.

RUNNER BEANS

Is there anyone who doesn't love these? They are, in my opinion, superior in flavour to any of the other beans, and for that reason I would supplement them with nothing more than salt and pepper, and perhaps a little butter. To prepare them, use a sharp paring knife to top and tail them, and pare away the stringy edge along the seams of each bean. Slice them thinly, diagonally (an operation which, I've come to the conclusion, is really done best with a bean slicer – the kind with a handle). Boil them in salted water for 5 minutes or so, depending on their age.

BABY BROAD BEANS IN PARSLEY SAUCE

♦

(Serves 4 people)

This recipe is for gardeners who can pick their broad beans very young – no more than finger thick – and cook them, chopped, in their pods.

1 lb young broad beans (450 g)
2¹/₂ oz butter (60 g)
1¹/₂ oz plain flour (40 g)
10 fl oz milk (275 ml)
1 teaspoon lemon juice
4 tablespoons chopped fresh parsley
salt and freshly milled black pepper

First wash, top and tail the beans, then cut them into ½ inch (1 cm) lengths. Place them in a saucepan, pour in enough boiling water just to cover, and add some salt. Cover, and when they come to the boil, simmer them for about 10 minutes.

Meanwhile start to make the sauce by melting 2 oz (50 g) of the butter in a small saucepan, add the flour and beat until smooth. Then gradually add the milk, beating until smooth after each addition. Allow the mixture to cook for a few minutes over a gentle heat. Now when the beans are cooked, strain the cooking liquid into a jug. Drain the beans well and place them in a warm serving dish.

Then quickly beat 5 fl oz (150 ml) of the cooking liquid into the sauce – again gradually. Season to taste with salt, pepper and lemon juice, then throw in the parsley and stir in the remaining butter. Serve the beans with the sauce poured over.

PURÉE OF BROAD BEANS

◆

(Serves 2–3 people)

This light, fluffy, green purée would be an excellent accompaniment to any pork or bacon dish, and is a lovely partner to some good pork sausages.

2 lb broad beans (900 g), shelled
1 oz butter (25 g)
2½ fl oz single cream or top of the milk (60 ml)
freshly grated nutmeg
salt and freshly milled black pepper
To garnish
a few snipped chives

Place the beans in a steamer sprinkled with salt, or else in lightly salted water, and cook for 4–6 minutes or until tender. Then drain them well and transfer them to the goblet of a liquidiser or food processor together with the butter, cream, some freshly grated nutmeg and a seasoning of salt and pepper. Whizz them to a purée, taste to check the seasoning, then serve with a few snipped chives sprinkled over.

BROCCOLI

◆

Sprouting broccoli – purple or white – and calabrese, which is the wider curly-headed variety, can be used in precisely the same way as cauliflower (see, for instance, *Sautéed cauliflower with coriander*, page 383). The leafy sprouting heads can be either boiled or steamed briefly, then finished off by tossing in butter with salt and pepper. For a light, wafer-crispness, try deep-frying the small heads – as in one of the following recipes. If you find you have a lot of broccoli stalks, you can chop them finely and add to a soup such as *Minestrone* (page 71), or else slice them thinly into diagonal slices and use them in a stir-fried vegetable dish as in the following recipe.

CHINESE STIR-FRIED GREEN VEGETABLES
◆

(Serves 2 people)

The principle of stir-frying involves speed of cooking with a high heat. As the vegetables come into contact with the hot surface of the pan or wok, the heat seals in the flavour and all the nutrients are retained. It's not essential to have a wok, but you do need a large roomy frying-pan so that the vegetables are not overcrowded.

4 oz broccoli or calabrese (110 g)
4 oz Chinese leaves or other cabbage (110 g)
1 large leek
2 tablespoons groundnut oil
1 heaped teaspoon grated fresh root ginger
1 large clove garlic, sliced
2 spring onions, finely chopped
2 tablespoons dry sherry mixed with 2 teaspoons soy sauce and 2 tablespoons water

Begin by preparing the vegetables. Cut off the flowery heads of the broccoli and separate them into smallish pieces, then slice the stalks diagonally into quite thin slices. Slice the Chinese leaves across into 1 inch (2.5 cm) rounds, then slice these, dividing them into two. Now remove any dirt from the leek by slicing it vertically almost through and fanning it out under a cold running tap. Then dry it, finish off cutting it in half lengthways, then cut it across into 1 inch (2.5 cm) rounds, which will separate out into little squares.

When you're ready to cook the vegetables, heat the oil in a wok or large frying-pan until it is very hot, then add the ginger and garlic and cook these for about half a minute – stirring them around all the time – before adding the broccoli. Stir this around the pan for another minute, then add the Chinese leaves and leek. Keep everything on the move around the pan for another minute, making sure everything comes into contact with the very hot base of the pan.

Finally add the spring onions and then the sherry-and-soy mixture, and let the whole lot go on cooking for a further 4–5 minutes (depending on how crisp you like your vegetables). Then serve straightaway.

BROCCOLI FRITTERS
———————— ♦ ————————

(Serves 2–3 people)

This recipe can also be adapted for leeks, carefully cleaned, dried and then sliced into rings approximately 1/4 inch (5 mm) thick.

8 oz small broccoli sprigs (225 g) – if you buy 1 lb (450 g) you should be able to pick off the correct weight of sprigs
2 egg whites
2 level tablespoons plain flour
groundnut oil for deep-frying
To serve
1 teaspoon crushed sea salt and coarsely milled black pepper

Fill a deep-fryer or else a largish saucepan to one-third of its capacity with oil, and start to heat it up to 360°F (185°C) – or until a cube of bread turns golden in 60 seconds. Meanwhile crumple some greaseproof paper and lay it in a serving dish, and keep this warm.

Now whisk the egg whites to the stiff peak stage, then coat the broccoli sprigs, first in the flour, then in the beaten egg white. Deep-fry them – in two batches – shaking the pan gently and using a knife to stir the sprigs around and separate them; 2–3 minutes for each batch should be enough, so the whole operation is fairly quick. Then drain them on the crumpled greaseproof paper, sprinkle with crushed sea salt and coarse pepper and serve immediately or they'll lose their crispness.

BRUSSELS SPROUTS
———————— ♦ ————————

My advice is to ignore totally those pale (and highly expensive) sprouts that turn up at the end of August in the shops. More than any other vegetable, Brussels sprouts need a sharp frost on them to heighten the flavour (and what need of sprouts have we in August, with so many other vegetables and salads in season?). The best-quality Brussels are like tight round buttons: take off the damaged outer leaves, make a cross-wise incision at the stalk end (to enable it to cook as evenly and quickly as the leaves), then preferably steam them, or else pour just enough boiling salted water over to cover and simmer gently for 5–8 minutes, depending on their size. Test them with a skewer, and try not to overcook them – they should be still firm and bright green. Then drain, season and serve in butter. Even better, boil them for a little less time, have some melted butter ready in a frying-pan, quite hot and frothy (or bacon fat), and toss them quickly in that over a gentle heat.

CABBAGE

◆

Cabbage is certainly treated with more respect now than it used to be. I still remember school cabbage – too much stalk, too much water and much too much cooking. Nowadays its versatility is more widely recognised: it can be stir-fried or steamed or finely shredded and eaten raw in a salad. We are also able to enjoy quite a wide variety. There is January King which has slightly pink outer leaves, and cabbage greens (sometimes called spring greens), Savoys with their very green crinkly outer leaves and also a summer cabbage called Hispi, which is like a tall tight bud, firmly leafed and with a delicate flavour. The white cabbage, sometimes called Drumhead, is better for salads or *Fried cabbage with bacon* (see page 235) as it tends to look insipid after steaming or boiling.

Cabbage should always be eaten as fresh as possible – it loses nutrients if stored for too long. An unwrapped fresh cabbage should *look* bright and crisp with its outer leaves intact (often if it's had its outer leaves removed, it was because they were limp which is not a good sign!). The heart should feel firm and the leaves should squeak as you pull them apart.

When cooking discard any really tough outer leaves and cut the cabbage in quarters. Slice away the core from the inside of each quarter and cut away the outer ribs, then shred each quarter horizontally. Place the cabbage in a steamer, sprinkle with salt and set over simmering water to steam till it is tender but still retains some bite (about 4–6 minutes). Lightly boiled cabbage is not to be despised if it is done carefully. Pack it in a saucepan with a well-fitting lid, add salt and enough boiling water to come about half-way up. Boil for 5–6 minutes, pressing it down and turning it over half-way through. Again, cook till tender yet still retaining some bite. Drain in a colander, then place a plate and a weight on top for a couple of minutes to press all the excess water out. Finally add some freshly milled black pepper and chop the cabbage up a little.

FRIED CABBAGE WITH BACON

◆

(Serves 2 or 3 people)

This is good enough for a meal on its own, and excellent with sausages and jacket potatoes. (Illus. opposite p. 225.)

1 lb cabbage (450 g), any variety, prepared and shredded
1 medium onion, chopped small
2 oz bacon (50 g), de-rinded and cut into lardons (tiny cubes), or streaky bacon, chopped small
2 tablespoons olive oil
1 clove garlic, crushed
salt and freshly milled black pepper

Take a large frying-pan and begin by frying the onion and bacon together in olive oil for about 5 minutes. Then add the crushed garlic and cook for another 2 or 3 minutes. Now stir in the shredded cabbage (which will seem rather bulky at first, but as the heat gets to it it will start to collapse) and keep stirring it now and then so it cooks evenly. Season with freshly milled pepper, but taste before adding salt because of the bacon. The cabbage should cook in about 10 minutes and still retain its crispness, but if you prefer it softer put a lid on the frying-pan – which will give it some steam.

CABBAGE WITH GARLIC AND JUNIPER

◆

(Serves 2–3 people)

This recipe, gleaned from the famous Miller Howe hotel in the English Lakes, is one of my favourite vegetable dishes.

1 lb cabbage (450 g), any variety, prepared and shredded
2 tablespoons olive oil
1/2 medium onion, finely chopped
6 juniper berries
1 clove garlic, crushed
salt and freshly milled black pepper

In a good solid saucepan or flameproof casserole, gently heat the olive oil and soften the onion in it for 5 minutes. Meanwhile crush the juniper berries (either with a pestle and mortar, or by placing them on a flat surface and crushing them with the back of a tablespoon). Then add these to the onion along with the crushed garlic. Fry for about 1 minute longer, then add the shredded cabbage. Stir until it's all glistening with oil, season with salt and pepper, put a lid on and let it cook in its own juice for 10 minutes – stirring once or twice so that it cooks evenly.

RED CABBAGE

◆

There was a time when red cabbage was confined to a lethal dose of malt vinegar inside a pickle jar. But now it's becoming much more popular as a delicious vegetable. Braised slowly in the oven with apples and spices, it is the perfect accompaniment to roast pork or pork sausages and is very good served with *Cassoulet* (see page 314). When choosing red cabbage look for tight heads with a 'bloom' on the outer leaves.

BRAISED RED CABBAGE WITH APPLES

◆

(Serves 4 people)

2 lb red cabbage (900 g)
1 lb onions (450 g), chopped small
1 lb cooking apples (450 g), peeled, cored and chopped small
1 clove garlic, chopped very small
1/4 whole nutmeg, freshly grated
1/4 level teaspoon ground cinnamon
1/4 level teaspoon ground cloves
3 tablespoons brown sugar
3 tablespoons wine vinegar
1/2 oz butter (10 g)
salt and freshly milled black pepper

Pre-heat the oven to gas mark 2, 300°F (150°C).

Discard the tough outer leaves of the cabbage, cut it into quarters and remove the hard stalk, then shred the cabbage finely.

In a fairly large casserole, arrange a layer of shredded cabbage seasoned with salt and pepper, then a layer of chopped onions and apples with a sprinkling of garlic, spices and sugar. Continue with these alternate layers until everything is in.

Now pour in the wine vinegar, add the butter, put a lid on the casserole and let it cook very slowly in the oven for about 1 1/2–2 hours, stirring everything around once or twice during the cooking. Red cabbage, once cooked, will keep warm without coming to any harm. It will also gently reheat very successfully.

CARROTS

———————————— ◆ ————————————

The young carrots of spring and early summer, sold still in bunches, are sweet, tender and delicious. We grow a variety called Early Nantes, which have the sweetest flavour and fragrance. When you're buying 'bunch' carrots your supplier may offer to cut off the tops, but I think these are better left on until you're ready to cook them (somehow this seems to keep them fresher). Don't scrape new carrots – just rinse each one under a cold tap – and when you're cooking them either steam them, or place them in a saucepan, pour boiling water over (but not too much), add some salt, then simmer gently, watching them like a hawk, for 10–15 minutes, depending on their thickness. Test them with a skewer – they should be tender but under no circumstances soggy. I like to toss them in a little *Herb butter* (page 405) or use the recipe below.

Maincrop carrots, I have found, taste better if you manage to buy them with the earth still clinging to them – scrubbing and packing them in polythene bags may be convenient but not the best thing for them. Scrub and scrape the skins (even older carrots don't need peeling), and if they are large, tough and woody then cut them in quarters vertically and excise the centre core if it's hard. Cook them in very little boiling salted water (just enough to cover) with 1/4 teaspoon of sugar added. They will take from 8 to 10 minutes to cook, depending on size. Then drain them and toss in butter or bacon fat before serving.

What my Welsh grandmother used to do after draining was to chop the carrots finely, adding some freshly milled black pepper and a knob of butter. That makes a nice change when cooking winter carrots.

YOUNG CARROTS WITH TARRAGON BUTTER

———————————— ◆ ————————————

(Serves 4 people)

1 lb young small carrots (450 g), washed but left whole
1 oz butter (25 g)
1 teaspoon chopped fresh tarragon leaves
salt and freshly milled black pepper

Place the carrots in a steamer fitted over a saucepan of simmering water. Sprinkle them with salt, then steam them until tender – about 10–15 minutes depending on their thickness and how crunchy you like them. Meanwhile mix the butter with the tarragon and some freshly milled black pepper, then when the carrots are ready toss them in the tarragon mixture so that each one gets a light glistening of butter.

Note Instead of tarragon butter, a mixture of 3 finely chopped spring onions and 1 tablespoon of cream can be tossed in at the end of the cooking time.

CAULIFLOWER

——————— ♦ ———————

Whatever did cauliflowers do to deserve their over-boiled, watery-white-sauce image? They have far more potential than that, as I hope the recipes here show. Since I've been growing them in my garden I've come to the conclusion that bleached whiteness is not necessarily the hallmark of a good cauliflower: my home-grown caulis have all been creamy-yellow and quite delicious. Tightness and fresh-looking leaves are what to look for when buying.

One of the nicest ways to cook cauliflower is to separate it first into largish florets, then pack them upright (i.e. stalk downward) in a large, wide saucepan. Tuck in a bay leaf, season with salt and pepper and a little freshly grated nutmeg, then pour in just about 1½ inches (4 cm) of boiling water. Cover with a lid and simmer for about 5–6 minutes – this way the stalks will cook in the water, and the florets in the steam. Afterwards drain them and toss them in butter before serving. Alternatively they can be separated out into florets and cooked completely in a steamer.

For a spicier recipe see *Sautéed cauliflower with coriander* (page 383).

CAULIFLOWER WITH GARLIC AND BACON

——————— ♦ ———————

(Serves 3–4 people)

In this recipe the sprigs of cauliflower are first blanched and then finished off in the oven.

1 medium cauliflower
2 oz butter (50 g)
2 tablespoons olive oil
1 small onion, finely chopped
1 clove garlic, crushed
2 rashers streaky bacon, de-rinded and chopped
2 tablespoons fresh breadcrumbs
1 tablespoon chopped fresh parsley
salt and freshly milled black pepper

Pre-heat the oven to gas mark 5, 375°F (190°C).

Begin by dividing the cauliflower into walnut-sized florets; place them in a saucepan and just cover them with boiling water. Add some salt, bring up to the boil, simmer for 2 minutes, then drain well in a colander.

Next, using the same saucepan, melt half the butter together with the oil and cook the onion and garlic for about 5 minutes to soften them, then add the bacon and cook for another 5 minutes. Now add the rest of the butter and, when it's melted, stir in the breadcrumbs and parsley and cook for a further minute or two. Then place the drained cauliflower either in a meat-roasting tin or a gratin dish and spoon the breadcrumb mixture evenly on top.

Bake in the oven for 10–15 minutes and, after about 5 minutes of the cooking time, baste with the buttery juices. When ready the cauliflower should be tender but still firm. Before serving, sprinkle on some freshly milled black pepper.

This recipe is essentially a side vegetable dish but you could, if you like, cover the cauliflower with a cheese sauce before it goes into the oven, sprinkling some cheese on top. Then serve with brown rice as a more substantial supper dish.

CELERY

I never buy imported celery out of season because it never tastes anywhere near the same as our own. I think it's at its best after a good November frost, and Fenland celery is particularly delicious when the black earth still clings to it and the stalks are white all the way up to the leaves.

If you scrub the stalks under cold running water and dry them with a cloth they'll stay crisp stored in a plastic bag in the lowest part of the fridge for several days, but remember to seal the bag well. Home-made bread, good cheese and crisp celery are one of the nicest instant meals I know. However, it's just as delicious cooked, as in the following recipe, which also explains how to clean and prepare it.

BRAISED CELERY WITH CHEESE AND ONION SAUCE

———— ♦ ————

(Serves 4 people)

1 large or 2 small heads of celery
1 oz butter (25 g)
1 tablespoon oil
1 carrot, thinly sliced
1 onion, thinly sliced
¼ teaspoon celery seeds
salt and freshly milled black pepper
For the sauce
milk
1 oz butter (25 g)
1 smallish onion, finely chopped
½ oz flour (10 g)
3 oz Cheddar cheese (75 g), grated
1 egg yolk
1 tablespoon grated Parmesan cheese

Pre-heat the oven to gas mark 4, 350°F (180°C).

For this you'll need a large flameproof casserole.

Prepare the celery by breaking off the outer stalks and then separate the stalks, leaving the inner ones attached to the root. Peel off the outer root, then cut it vertically so that the inner stalks still have some of the delicious root clinging to them. Now cut all the stalks in half horizontally. Then use a bristle brush to clean each one under cold running water.

Next blanch the celery by putting it in boiling salted water for about 5 minutes. Drain well, reserving the cooking water.

Now in a flameproof casserole, heat the butter and oil, add the prepared carrot and onion and cook for about 5 minutes. Add the drained celery and 5 fl oz (150 ml) of the cooking water. Sprinkle with the celery seeds and season with a little salt and pepper. Place the casserole in the oven and bake, covered, for 30 minutes or until the celery is tender.

When ready transfer the vegetables to a serving dish, using a slotted spoon. Empty the cooking liquid into a measuring jug and make it up to 10 fl oz (275 ml) with milk.

To make the sauce, heat the butter in a saucepan and fry the finely chopped onion until golden, then blend in the flour and cook for a couple of minutes before adding the milk mixture a little at a time, stirring well after each addition. Bring to simmering point, still stirring, and simmer gently for a minute or two, then remove from the heat and beat in the cheese and egg yolk. Pour the sauce over the vegetables, sprinkle on the Parmesan cheese, and bake in the oven for a further 20 minutes or until you're sure it's all piping hot. Served with brown rice this makes a complete and delicious vegetarian meal for two.

Corn-on-the-cob

This is something I've never grown myself, but a more green-fingered neighbour always lets me have some of his surplus cobs, and once a year we have a feast (on our own, getting faces and fingers smothered in butter and sharing a damp tea towel). On the streets of Istanbul, I recall, every corner seemed to have corn-on-the-cobs being grilled over open charcoal fires, and groups of people standing round munching their way through them!

At home we boil the cobs. First remove the husks and fibrous bits, then wash the cobs and plunge them into boiling water (10 minutes is usually sufficient). Test the kernels for tenderness with a skewer, then drain well and have some hot melted butter and hot plates handy. Pour some butter over each cob, and season well with salt and coarsely ground black pepper. They are easiest to eat if you stick small skewers or forks into each end, and use these to hold them. And if you want to be more refined than us, have some finger-bowls and linen napkins on the table.

Courgettes

Courgettes (or zucchini) are the easiest vegetables in the world to grow – and perhaps the hardest to stop growing! If you don't inspect them every day during their season you will end up with mature marrows, rather than baby ones (which is what courgettes really are). Like their elders, they do contain a fair amount of water and sometimes this can be bitter. So if you have the time, prepare them by slicing them thinly into rounds (always leaving the skin on), then layer them in a colander, sprinkling each layer with salt, and place a suitably-sized plate on top. Weight this down with a heavy object (like scale-weights), and after 30 minutes quite a bit of water will have been drawn out. Dry them really thoroughly in a clean cloth, and then they're ready to cook. I prefer not to put any water near them – just fry them in a mixture of butter and olive oil for about 7 minutes (like sautéed potatoes), so the edges turn crisp and golden.

COURGETTE FRITTERS

For these, cut the courgettes into 2 inch (5 cm) lengths (skins on), then cut each length in half horizontally, and cut each half into chip-like lengths. Salt and drain these as above, dry well, then cook in exactly the same way as *Broccoli fritters* (see page 233).

COURGETTES AND TOMATOES AU GRATIN

◆

(Serves 2–4 people)

This is a very quick and easy vegetarian supper dish for two people, especially good if you grow your own tomatoes and courgettes and have a glut to use up. You could also serve it as a starter for four people.

4 medium courgettes, sliced but *not* peeled
2 tablespoons olive oil
1 large clove garlic, crushed
4 oz Italian Mozzarella (or Cheddar) cheese (110 g), sliced
4 large tomatoes, peeled and sliced
4 level tablespoons grated Parmesan cheese
1 tablespoon chopped fresh basil, or 1 teaspoon dried oregano
salt and freshly milled black pepper

Pre-heat the oven to gas mark 5, 375°F (190°C).

If you have the time salt, drain and dry the sliced courgettes as described earlier. Heat the oil in a frying-pan large enough to hold the courgettes in one layer (otherwise do them in two batches), add the crushed garlic and sauté the courgette slices to a nice golden colour on each side. Next arrange layers of courgettes, cheese slices and sliced tomatoes in a heatproof gratin dish so that they overlap each other slightly like slates on a roof. Finally sprinkle on the grated Parmesan, basil or oregano and salt and freshly milled pepper. Then bake on a high shelf in the oven for 30 minutes. Serve this with lots of crusty bread and a green salad with a sharp lemony dressing.

FENNEL

◆

This is dealt with primarily in the chapter on Salads (see page 435), but it is also extremely good served as a vegetable. When cooked the aniseed flavour is definitely less pronounced.

BRAISED FENNEL

♦

(Serves 4 people)

In the eighteenth century fennel was used quite a lot in English cooking, so let's hope it will become more popular here again.

4 bulbs fennel, uniform size if possible
2 rashers streaky bacon, de-rinded
1 oz butter (25 g)
1 carrot, sliced
¹/₂ onion, sliced
chopped parsley
salt and freshly milled black pepper

First trim the green shoots from the tops of the fennel bulbs and shave off the bases. Then peel off any outer layers if they seem brownish, and halve the bulbs across their widest part. Put them into a large saucepan of boiling water, bring to the boil again and blanch for 3–4 minutes. Then drain them – reserving 5 fl oz (150 ml) of the water.

Now fry the bacon in the butter in a large saucepan or casserole, stir in the sliced carrot and onion and cook for a few minutes before pouring in the reserved water and adding some salt and freshly milled black pepper. Arrange the fennel in the base of the pan, bring to simmering point, cover and cook gently for about 45 minutes, turning the fennel occasionally.

When cooked, transfer to a serving dish along with the vegetables, bacon and some of the juices. Sprinkle with parsley and serve.

GLOBE ARTICHOKES

♦

It would be hard to find a prettier vegetable than this: its aesthetic presence animates any table display. Although globe artichokes were once very popular in Britain, the biggest crop now comes from Brittany in the late spring. It may be, with the waning of their popularity, that people do not know how to prepare and eat them. So first let me explain that globe artichokes are – as indeed they look – large members of the thistle family, and have three distinct parts. There are the leaves (the bottom parts of which are edible), the choke (inedible) and the heart which is very edible.

HOW TO PREPARE AND COOK ARTICHOKES

First remove about four of the toughest outer leaves, then place the artichoke at the edge of a table so that the stalk overlaps the edge. Grasp the stalk and snap away the stem, removing also some of the tough fibres running up into the base. Now remove the inedible choke: carefully spread the leaves apart until you come to the central cone of thinner, lightly-coloured leaves. Then pull this cone out in one piece and underneath it you'll find the hairy 'choke' – scrape this all out of the heart with a teaspoon, and add a little lemon juice to stop the inside discolouring. Now rinse out the artichokes and leave them upside down in some cold water to which some more lemon juice has been added (about 1 tablespoon to 2 pints/1.2 litres of water), until you are ready to cook them.

Don't boil artichokes in iron or aluminium pans, as this can discolour them. Have your chosen pan ready filled with salted boiling water with a tablespoon of lemon juice (or white wine vinegar) added. Gently boil the artichokes, uncovered, for about 30–40 minutes or until one of the outer leaves pulls away easily and the bases feel tender when tested with a skewer. Then drain the artichokes upside down in a colander, shaking them to get rid of the excess water.

HOW TO EAT ARTICHOKES

This does have its comic side, with ever-mounting piles of discarded leaves scarred with rabbit-toothed marks! Artichokes can be served cold or, perhaps better, just tepid. Tear off one leaf at a time, dip it into the sauce (see below), and eat the tender rounded part at the base. When you arrive at the heart, cut it into sections with a knife and fork and eat with the rest of the sauce. Don't forget to have plenty of napkins, some finger-bowls, and a large plate for the discarded leaves.

SAUCES FOR ARTICHOKES

To serve warm, I would recommend *Quick hollandaise* (page 34) or *Hot lemon butter* (page 406) – pour the latter immediately into the cavity of each artichoke. For serving cold, I suggest either *Vinaigrette* (page 437) or some *Home-made mayonnaise* with garlic (page 438).

JERUSALEM ARTICHOKES
◆

These are vegetables with a distinctive flavour and are another neglected delicacy. Although they're cheap and couldn't be easier to grow, they are largely ignored. My guess is that this is because of their ugliness: the tubers do look most misshapen, covered with daunting knobbly bits. There's no need to be daunted. If you're prepared to buy slightly more than you actually need, you can soon cut off (and discard) the knobbles, which makes life a lot easier. They are then easy to peel, but as they discolour quickly pop them straight into cold water as you peel. As a vegetable they can be roasted like potatoes or sautéed, or cooked as in

Potatoes boulangère (page 255) with leeks substituted for the onions, or made into a cream purée. Best of all, I think, they make a really delicious soup with a truly creamy texture (*Carrot and artichoke soup*, page 80).

LEEKS

There is a period, from about the end of January to the end of March, when fresh vegetables seem a bit thin on the ground. But nature hasn't let us down: it provides an abundance of leeks throughout the winter and these two months are the time to make the most of them. Having said that, though, leeks are best served in the simplest possible manner – no water, no white sauce, just a little seasoning.

Sometimes leeks can arrive rather dusty, so care is needed when preparing and cleaning them. The best way is to cut off all but about 1¹/₂ inch (4 cm) of the green part, and trim off the root end. Then, using a small sharp knife, make a vertical slit down two-thirds of each leek. Now you can hold each leek under a cold running tap, spreading the layers out in a fan shape to wash out any hidden dirt.

BUTTERED LEEKS

(Serves 4 people)

1¹/₂ lb leeks (700 g), trimmed and washed
2 oz butter (50 g)
salt and freshly milled black pepper

Chop the cleaned leeks into roughly 1¹/₂ inch (4 cm) pieces. Then melt the butter in a thick-based saucepan, and add the slivers of leek, stirring them around thoroughly. Season with salt and freshly milled pepper, and let them sweat in their own juices for 5–6 minutes. If you stir them now and then there is no need to cover the saucepan.

MANGE TOUT

These are tiny under-developed peas that are cooked and served in their pods. Unfortunately they are now suffering from a degree of over-exposure, as the imported ones are available all the year round. In cooking them there are two important points to bear in mind: on no account should they be overcooked – the end results should be really crunchy – and they should not be allowed even a sniff of water. Top and tail the pods. Melt 2 oz (50 g) of butter in a wide, shallow saucepan (or a frying-pan), stir in 1 lb (450 g) of mange tout gently to get each one coated in the butter, add some salt, and then just toss them around over a medium heat. They cook very quickly, in just 1–2 minutes.

STIR-FRIED MANGE TOUT
◆

(Serves 2 people)

6 oz mange tout (175 g), topped and tailed
1 tablespoon oil
1 teaspoon grated fresh root ginger
1 teaspoon soy sauce
1 tablespoon dry sherry
1 tablespoon water

Start by heating the oil and ginger in a frying-pan over a low heat for about 10 minutes so that the ginger flavour really permeates the oil. Then turn the heat up high and add the prepared mange tout, stirring them around in the hot oil and keeping them on the move until they are paler in colour and begin to cook – about 1 minute.

Then mix the soy sauce, sherry and water together and pour the mixture over the mange tout, still stirring everything around. Next put a lid on the pan and leave them to cook for about 5 more minutes – but be careful not to overcook them, they do need to be quite crunchy.

MARROW
◆

If you grow courgettes then you're bound to find that some have remained hidden from view under the large flat leaves – and before you know it you have a young marrow on your hands. If so, then pick it immediately because the older monsters aren't much good for anything. If you are buying a marrow the same rule applies: small is beautiful, not more than 1½–2 lb (700–900 g). The way to tell a young marrow – apart from its size – is to look for a shiny skin, and when you press along one of the ridges with your thumb, it should leave an impression.

Young marrows should be cut up into large 1½ inch (4 cm) cubes (with the skin left on) and cooked, sprinkled with salt, in a steamer over simmering water until tender. Serve with a *Herb butter* (see page 405) or try the following recipe which transforms marrow into something special.

Baked Marrow with Tomatoes and Coriander

◆

(Serves 4 people)

If, like me, you've sometimes suffered from rather too many home-grown marrows, do try this way of cooking them – which also takes care of any tomatoes that are too ripe for a salad.

1½ lb young marrow (700 g)
8 oz ripe tomatoes 225 g – approx. 4 medium ones, peeled and chopped
1 tablespoon oil
½ medium onion, chopped
1 clove garlic, crushed
½ teaspoon whole coriander seeds, crushed in a pestle and mortar or with the back of a tablespoon
1 dessertspoon chopped fresh or 1 level teaspoon dried basil
salt and freshly milled black pepper

Pre-heat the oven to gas mark 3, 325°F (170°C).

Melt the oil in a flameproof casserole, add the onion and garlic, and soften them over a gentle heat for 5 minutes. Stir in the chopped tomatoes and cook for a further 5 minutes.

If the marrow is young and fresh it won't need peeling: just cut it into approximately 1½ inch (4 cm) chunks. Add them to the tomatoes and onions along with the crushed coriander seeds. Then add the basil if it's dried (if you're using fresh basil, add it at the end), and season with salt and pepper. Stir everything around well, put a lid on, and place the casserole in the oven to cook for 1 hour or until the marrow is tender. About 10 minutes before the end of the cooking time, put the casserole back on the top of the stove and simmer without a lid to reduce some of the liquid.

Note This is equally good served cold – or reheated the next day.

Mushrooms

◆

The best mushrooms I've ever tasted were those I gathered on early-morning walks through the mountains of Wales, as a small child. My grandfather seemed able to spot a field mushroom from dozens of yards away, and I would run and pick them – some small, round and delicate with pink gills, others large and flat and velvet-brown. Back at home they would sizzle in bacon fat for breakfast, with plenty of bread to mop up the last traces of juice.

Field mushrooms are still a delicious, if rare, treat. Cultivated mushrooms are not quite the same, but at least they are plentiful, always available and not too expensive. I rarely use the 'button' variety, which I find rather tasteless. I much prefer the fully-opened caps with pink or brown gills. One of the nicest mushroom-flavoured recipes is *Marinated mushrooms* (see page 92), which makes a very good first course. For a really concentrated mushroom flavour – for sauces, stuffing or quiches – make what the French call *Duxelles* (see, for instance, *Boeuf en croûte* on page 516 and *Cheese tartlets with mushroom pâté* on page 427).

DUXELLES

◆

8 oz mushrooms (225 g), very finely chopped
1 oz butter (25 g)
1 medium onion, very finely chopped
freshly grated nutmeg
salt and freshly milled black pepper

First heat the butter in a saucepan, then stir in the onion and cook it for 5 minutes before adding the mushrooms to the pan. Continue to cook gently for 30 minutes (uncovered) so that all the liquid evaporates and the mixture becomes a thick paste. Season the mixture with salt, pepper and a grating of nutmeg.

MUSHROOMS IN HOT GARLIC BUTTER

◆

(Serves 4 people)

This recipe is for people who, like me, love the sizzling garlic butter that goes with snails but cannot eat the snails.

1 lb mushrooms (450 g)
2–3 large cloves garlic, crushed
6 oz butter (175 g), at room temperature
1–2 tablespoons chopped fresh parsley
1 tablespoon lemon juice
salt and freshly milled black pepper

Pre-heat the oven to gas mark 7, 425°F (220°C).

Begin by preparing the mushrooms simply by wiping them with kitchen paper, then pull off the stalks – but don't discard them. Now, in a small basin, combine the crushed garlic with the butter, and stir in the parsley and lemon juice. Season the mixture with salt and black pepper.

Next arrange the mushroom caps, skin side down, in a gratin dish or roasting tin, with the stalks arranged amongst them. Place a little of the garlic butter mixture into each cap, and spread whatever remains over the stalks as well.

Now place the dish on the top shelf of the pre-heated oven and cook for 10–15 minutes or until the butter is sizzling away and the mushrooms look slightly toasted. Serve straight from the oven with lashings of crusty bread to mop up the garlicky juices.

ONIONS (AND SHALLOTS)

On the subject of preparing onions, I would like to say that in my many years of cooking I have been regaled with countless theories on how not to cry. None of them have worked! I do now own a food processor, which chops onions finely, so perhaps I don't weep as much as I used to. The mildest onions are the large Spanish type, and these are good for slicing and eating raw in salads. It is the medium-sized home-grown variety that are the real tear-jerkers.

Shallots – I grow the purple shallots – keep very well through the winter if stored correctly. Usually they are mild-flavoured, and especially good for cooking whole in a number of recipes. I make a habit of pickling some shallots for Christmas – and the recipe for that is on page 612.

CRISP-FRIED ONION RINGS

First you need to heat some oil in a deep-fryer to 350°F (180°C). Cut 2 onions into thinnish slices and separate out the rings. Beat up 1 large egg white to the stiff peak stage, then dip the rings first into seasoned plain flour, then into the egg white. Deep-fry them a few at a time until crisp and golden (1–2 minutes). Drain on some crumpled greaseproof paper, and serve as soon as possible. These are lovely served with steak or liver.

PARSNIPS

This is another vegetable that needs a good sharp frost to really sharpen up its flavour; and since there are so many other vegetables about in the autumn, it is best to wait till the end of October or into November if you want to eat them at their best. Peel them thinly, quarter them lengthways, and cut out the woody core before cooking. Steam or, even better, bake them.

BAKED PARSNIPS

◆

(Serves 4 people)

These are the perfect accompaniment to a Sunday roast – especially as the oven is already on.

1 lb parsnips (450 g), prepared (see page 249)
1 oz butter (25 g)
1 dessertspoon groundnut oil
salt

Pre-heat the oven to gas mark 6, 400°F (200°C).

Put the butter and oil in a good solid roasting tin, or cast-iron gratin dish, then transfer to the oven to heat through. Meanwhile blanch the prepared parsnips in boiling salted water for 3 minutes, then drain well and shake off all the excess moisture.

As soon as the fat is sizzling, remove the tin or gratin dish from the oven and place it on direct heat to keep it sizzling. Add the parsnips, using tongs, then as each one hits the fat turn it over so the surface of each parsnip is coated. Now replace the tin on the lowest shelf of the oven. Bake them for about 40 minutes, turning them over once during that time. They should be a lovely golden-brown colour. Drain on kitchen paper and serve straightaway.

CREAMED PARSNIPS

◆

(Serves 4 people)

Even people who think they don't like parsnips usually admit that they like this.

1 lb parsnips (450 g)
5 fl oz single cream (150 ml)
freshly grated nutmeg
salt and freshly milled black pepper

Peel the parsnips and cut out the woody centre bits, then cut them up into small cubes. Then place them in a steamer over some simmering water, sprinkle with salt, and steam – covered – for approximately 10 minutes or until tender when tested with a skewer.

Now, either purée them with the cream in a liquidiser or sieve them and beat in the cream a little at a time with a fork. Taste and season with freshly grated nutmeg, salt and pepper and, if you think the mixture is too dry, mix in 1 or 2 tablespoons of the steaming water.

POTATOES

———— ♦ ————

Potatoes are the most important source of Vitamin C in our diet – it was only when potatoes became one of our staple foods in the eighteenth century (we now eat approximately 6 oz/175 g per head a day) that diseases like scurvy began to die out. The protein value of potatoes is higher than in most other plant foods. Per ounce, of course, an orange will give you more Vitamin C, but whereas we don't all eat an orange a day most of us do eat potatoes. Having said that, it is also a fact that careless preparation and cooking can destroy much of their goodness as well as flavour – I'd go so far as to say that learning to cook potatoes so that they really taste like potatoes is one of the most important lessons in cooking.

PREPARATION

That part of the potato directly beneath the skin is richest in nutrients, so peeling needs to be done with a certain amount of care. Ideally they should not be peeled at all. New potatoes taste better with their skins left on, and maincrop potatoes too are better just scrubbed, then boiled or steamed with the skins on, and peeled afterwards. When the actual skins are eaten (as with jacket potatoes) they provide fibre, another valuable item conspicuously lacking in our modern diet. Where a potato obviously has to be peeled, to preserve the best part beneath the skin it is preferable to use a good potato peeler that pares off the thinnest amount of peel.

BOILING OR STEAMING

First, new potatoes. Here opinion is unanimous that they should be started off in boiling water – so they can be cooked in as short a time as possible and so retain most of their flavour. With maincrop potatoes it is said that putting them in cold water and bringing them up to the boil helps them absorb some of the water and become juicier (new potatoes contain more water and have no need of this), and that it also helps prevent them breaking up.

My own opinion is based on the idea that in general water is the enemy of flavour (with potatoes as with all root vegetables): so I prefer to add boiling water to maincrop also, so they spend less time in contact with the water, and breaking is never a problem with a good quality variety like red Desirée. At all events the heat, once they have returned to the boil, should be gentle; and to stop the water evaporating too fast a well-fitting lid is essential.

To steam potatoes – which is the best way of preserving nutrients and flavour – place them in a steamer over a saucepanful of boiling water, sprinkle them with salt, cover the steamer with a lid and steam until tender. How much salt? This really depends on who is going to eat them, but a rough guide is 1 rounded teaspoon to each pound (450 g) of potatoes. To serve: once the boiled potatoes have been drained, place a clean cloth over the saucepan instead of the lid. This will absorb some steam and give them a floury edge.

MASHED OR CREAMED POTATOES

How you mash or cream potatoes can be a personal thing: my mother won't use anything but a large kitchen fork, while several friends of mine swear by their potato mashers. Inclined to laziness myself, I use my electric hand whisk. But whichever implement you use, make sure your saucepan is big enough to give you plenty of mashing room. Drain the potatoes first, add a little salt and freshly milled pepper, a good knob of butter – 1 oz (25 g) per pound (450 g) of potatoes – and preferably cream or top of the milk (2 tablespoons per pound); failing that, milk will do. Then whisk, beat or mash until the potatoes are soft, creamy and free from lumps. Here are a few variations:

Creamed potatoes with soured cream and chives

Soured cream is delicious with potatoes – a 5 fl oz (150 ml) carton for 2–3 lb (1–1.3 kg) of potatoes. Whisk it in with the butter, along with 3 tablespoons of snipped chives or finely chopped spring onions.

Creamed potatoes with nutmeg

Again use soured cream or fresh natural yoghurt (if it's not *fresh*, yoghurt will be too acid for this) to whisk into the potatoes, then finish off with about ¼ nutmeg, freshly grated.

CRUNCHY ROAST POTATOES

I've deliberately added the word 'crunchy' because I believe properly cooked roast potatoes are a rare delicacy, and it is crunchiness that is so often missing. The first essential ingredient is a cast-iron gratin dish or, failing that, a good, solid roasting tin with a really sound base – the cheap, tinny ones that buckle in a hot oven are useless. For the sake of flavour the best sort of fat to use is the same as the meat with which the potatoes will be served (i.e. beef dripping for beef, lamb dripping for lamb, lard for pork), and if you're roasting the joint in the oven you can probably spoon off enough fat from that for the potatoes; the best alternative to these is pure lard.

Because the fat for roasting needs to be *really* hot, it is not a good idea to roast the potatoes around the meat (besides, if you have a large family, there simply won't be room). The oven temperature should be gas mark 7, 425°F (220°C). If the joint is still roasting, remove it to a lower shelf; if it is cooked, take it out of the oven (a joint will hold the heat for about 40 minutes, in a warm place, and, as I have said elsewhere, is all the better for 'relaxing' before it is carved).

Place the roasting tin to pre-heat with about 2 oz (50 g) of fat per pound (450 g) of potatoes. Then peel and cut the potatoes into even sizes, pour boiling water over them, add some salt, and simmer for 10 minutes – then drain (reserving the water for gravy). Now put the lid back on the saucepan and shake it vigorously up and down: what this does is roughen the edges of the potatoes and make them floury, giving a crispier surface.

Make sure the fat in the roasting tin is really hot when the potatoes reach it: if it is, the outsides of the potatoes will be immediately sealed; if it isn't, they will stick or become greasy. As you add the potatoes to the tin, the temperature of the fat will come down – so what you do is remove the tin from the oven (closing the door to keep the heat in) and place it over direct heat: medium should be enough to keep the fat sizzling. Then spoon in the potatoes, tilt the pan (holding it with a thick oven glove) and baste each one with a complete covering of hot fat. Now transfer them to the highest shelf of the oven, and roast for 45–55 minutes. Turn them over at half-time.

Note Roast potatoes don't take kindly to being kept warm, so serve them as soon as possible.

CHIPS

A perfect chip should be (i) crisp on the outside, (ii) soft, almost melting, in the middle, and (iii) dry, which is to say not greasy, oily or soggy. It is relatively easy to cook soggy chips, but far more difficult to produce a beautifully dry, crisp and melting chip.

To start with you need the right kind of potato. New potatoes – apart from being too small to chip – ought only to be cooked in their skins. Of the maincrop potatoes the best are the mealy-textured varieties like King Edward, Desirée and Romano which are reds, or Majestic and Maris Piper (whites). Once the potatoes are peeled you could slice them up with a chip-cutter, though that always seems to require a great deal of strength. I prefer to use a small sharp knife, slicing the potatoes first across, at intervals of just less than ½ inch (1 cm), then slice into chips the size of my little finger.

If you have time at this stage to soak the chips for half an hour – to reduce their starch content and swell them with water – all well and good: if not, make sure you rinse them well under cold water. Most important of all, dry them *thoroughly* in a clean tea towel.

To fry them you can use either lard or oil, but if it is oil I do advise a good quality groundnut oil (because there are so many nasty cooking oils on the market which will impregnate your chips with their unwelcome flavour). Fill the chip-pan, or at least a wide, thick-based saucepan, only one-third full of oil or lard – any more than that and it will very likely bubble over the top when the chips go in. The temperature of the oil/lard is all-important. It should have reached 375°F (190°C) before the chips go in, and the only accurate way to tell is by using a cooking thermometer (and place it in the pan at the beginning, to eliminate any danger of it cracking in the hot fat). In the absence of a thermometer you can test the temperature by frying a cube of bread: if it browns within 1 minute, the chips can go in.

The safest way to lower the chips in gently is to use a chip-basket, and be ready to pull it out if the fat erupts too violently (which probably means the chips were not dry enough). Fry the batch for 4–5 minutes and then remove them – you can hang the basket on the lip of the pan in fact. The temperature of the fat will now have dropped dramatically, and it must be reheated to 390°F (195°C) for the final browning – which will take just 1 or at the most 2 minutes. Watch the chips very carefully at this stage and lift them out as soon as they are golden-brown – any longer and they will turn hard.

Now transfer the chips to a warmed serving dish lined with either some crumpled greaseproof paper or kitchen paper, to remove any vestiges of fat. Then remove the paper, crush some flaky sea salt and some coarsely ground pepper over them and take them straight to the table. Chips *cannot* be kept hanging round or even kept warm successfully: within no time they will start to go soggy, no matter how crisp they were when they came out of the pan.

JACKET POTATOES

One of the nicest and most nutritious ways of eating potatoes (I love the crisp skins dipped in home-made chutney!). Cara, Maris Piper, King Edward are all good for serving in their jackets, but my favourite is Desirée. If you can, scrub and thoroughly dry them in a cloth well in advance as this will help to crisp the skins. Before baking, pre-heat the oven to gas mark 7, 425°F (220°C), prick the potato skins in several places (to prevent splitting), then rub the skins with a smear of olive oil all over and a little bit of salt as well. Large potatoes will take about 1–1½ hours to bake through. To speed up the cooking time, you can insert metal skewers through the potatoes, but in fact a lower temperature (gas mark 5, 375°F, 190°C) and longer cooking will give you a tougher, more crunchy skin. To test if they are done, push a skewer into the thickest part of the flesh; then slit them open and serve with a generous knob of butter and some seasoning. And here are a few alternative fillings:

Jacket potatoes with soured cream and chives
For 3–4 potatoes, mix 5 fl oz (150 ml) of soured cream with a bunch of freshly snipped chives and a seasoning of salt and freshly milled pepper. When the potatoes are cooked, hold them with a cloth and make a slit lengthways across the top and then widthways: then lift up the four flaps of skin and make a depression in the potato. Add a knob of butter to each one, and pour in the cream-and-chive mixture.

JACKET POTATOES STUFFED WITH GARLIC AND HERBS

◆

(Serves 3 or 6 people)

If the potatoes are large one half potato per person will be sufficient as an accompaniment. Or two halves per person will make a good vegetarian supper dish with a salad.

3 large jacket potatoes, prepared and cooked as above
For the filling
5 oz cream cheese containing garlic and herbs (150 g) or plain cream cheese or, for less calories, cottage cheese
1 oz butter (25 g) or low-fat spread
2 cloves garlic, crushed
2 tablespoons chopped fresh parsley
2 tablespoons snipped fresh chives
2 oz Cheddar cheese (50 g), grated
salt and freshly milled pepper

Pre-heat the grill.

When the potatoes are cooked, slice them in half then, holding each half with a cloth, scoop out the cooked potato into a bowl. Then combine the potato with the cream cheese (or cottage cheese), butter, garlic and herbs, and season to taste with salt and pepper. Pile the mixture back into the empty potato shells, sprinkle each half with the grated Cheddar, and pop them under the grill until they're brown and bubbling.

POTATOES BOULANGÈRE

◆

(Serves 4–6 people)

This French method of cooking potatoes gets its name from the bakeries where villagers, short of fire fuel, would take their pots of potatoes along to cook in the bread ovens. This is a particularly good dish to serve at a dinner party as it needs no last-minute attention and will wait quite happily if you're running late.

2 lb potatoes (900 g)
1 largish onion
5 fl oz hot stock (150 ml)
5 fl oz milk (150 ml)
1 oz butter (25 g)
salt and freshly milled black pepper

Pre-heat the oven to gas mark 4, 350°F (180°C).

The best cooking utensil for this recipe is either an oblong meat-roasting tin or a large, shallow flameproof gratin dish. Butter it generously (all over the sides as well), then peel the potatoes and cut them into thinnish slices. Peel the onion and chop it finely.

Now arrange a layer of potatoes over the base of the tin, followed by a sprinkling of onion and a seasoning of salt and freshly milled black pepper. Continue with another layer of potatoes, and so on until everything is in and you finish up with a layer of potatoes (seasoned) at the top. Pour in the stock and milk, and fleck the surface all over with dots of butter.

Place the tin on the highest shelf of the oven, and leave it there for about 45 minutes or until the potatoes are cooked and the top layer is nicely golden-brown.

Note For a change, use a chopped leek instead of an onion.

GRATIN DAUPHINOIS

♦

(Serves 3–4 people)

This is so often served in restaurants as a gooey sludge that seems to have hung around too long. But home-made, straight from the oven, it is truly one of the great classics. I know it does seem extravagant to use 5 fl oz (150 ml) cream for 1 lb (450 g) potatoes, but I would forego a pudding with cream once in a while in order to justify it.

1 lb good quality potatoes (450 g) – King Edward or Desirée
1 small clove garlic, crushed
5 fl oz double cream (150 ml)
5 fl oz milk (150 ml)
freshly grated nutmeg
1 oz butter (25 g)
salt and freshly milled black pepper

Pre-heat the oven to gas mark 2, 300°F (150°C).

An 8½ inch (21 cm) oval, shallow gratin dish, well-buttered.

First, peel the potatoes and slice them very, very thinly (a wooden

Buttered new potatoes with parsley, mint and chives (see page 258)

mandoline is excellent for this operation, if you have one), then plunge the potato slices into a bowl of cold water and swill them round and round to get rid of some of the starch. Now dry them very thoroughly in a clean tea cloth. Then in the gratin dish arrange a layer of potato slices, a sprinkling of crushed garlic, pepper and salt and then another layer of potatoes and seasoning.

Now mix the cream and milk together, pour it over the potatoes, sprinkle with a little freshly grated whole nutmeg, then add the butter in flecks over the surface, and bake on the highest shelf in the oven for 1½ hours.

Note Sometimes cheese is added to this, but I think it masks the potato flavour too much.

SAUTÉ POTATOES LYONNAISE

◆

(Serves 2 people)

This is the basic method for making sauté potatoes, but if you prefer them plain, simply leave the onion out. The secret of really crisp sauté potatoes is, first of all, to use olive oil if at all possible and, secondly, to use two or three frying-pans so that the potatoes can cook in a single layer and not overlap each other.

2 lb Desirée potatoes (900 g)
4–5 tablespoons olive oil
1 small onion, finely chopped
coarse rock salt and freshly milled black pepper

Have ready a warm serving dish with some crumpled greaseproof paper or kitchen paper placed in it.

First thinly peel the potatoes and cut them into evenly-sized pieces – but not too small. Put them in a saucepan, cover them with boiling water, add some salt, bring to simmering point and cook for 15 minutes. Then drain them, arrange them on a wooden board and slice them thinly and evenly.

For the next stage you need two medium frying-pans and a small saucepan. Heat a tablespoon of olive oil in the saucepan, add the onion and fry gently. Now heat 2 tablespoons of oil in each frying-pan and when it begins to sizzle add the potatoes, dividing them between the pans so that they don't overlap. Fry them over a high heat, turning them after 5–7 minutes to cook on the other side until they are golden-brown and crisp all over. Then, using a slotted spoon, transfer them to the crumpled paper to drain and scatter on the fried onion. Loosen the top of the pepper mill a little to get a really coarse grind and sprinkle over the potatoes; crush some rock salt between your finger and thumb and sprinkle on.

Risotto alla Milanese (see page 277)

Lastly pull out the paper from underneath and serve at once – if you delay the potatoes will go soggy.

For *Sauté potatoes Niçoise* cook half a green or red pepper finely chopped and a crushed clove of garlic with the onion. Add approximately 6 stoned and chopped black olives, then stir the mixture into the potatoes and sprinkle with freshly chopped herbs or parsley before serving.

NEW POTATOES

Around April we begin to get the first imported new potatoes, by which time the old ones are looking decidedly wrinkled and sprouty. However these very early imported potatoes are often disappointing in flavour, and it's only when our home-grown varieties start to make an appearance that their true delicacy can be appreciated – and that goes especially for the Jersey Royals.

Freshness is the key to buying new potatoes. Pick one up before you buy and rub your thumb along it – if the skin slips away with your thumb, you can be sure the potatoes are really fresh.

To prepare them, all you actually need to do is to rinse them clean under a cold tap. Don't scrape or peel them, because the skins are full of flavour and nutrients.

New potatoes also deserve careful cooking: either steam them sprinkled with salt and a few sprigs of mint, or place the largest ones on the base of the pan, with the smaller ones on top. Add some salt and mint, and pour in enough boiling water to come not more than three-quarters of the way up (so that, in effect, the smallest potatoes are cooked in the steam and will be ready at about the same time as the larger ones). Use a tight-fitting lid, and test with a skewer to see if they are cooked after about 20 minutes.

BUTTERED NEW POTATOES WITH PARSLEY, MINT AND CHIVES

◆

(Serves 4 people)

Made with the first young Jersey potatoes, or some well-flavoured mainland variety, these are so good you could eat a plateful all by themselves! (Illus. opposite p. 256.)

| 2 lb Jersey or mainland new potatoes (900 g) |
| 1 sprig fresh mint |
| 1½ oz butter (40g) |
| 1 tablespoon chopped fresh parsley |
| 2 tablespoons chopped fresh mint |
| 1 tablespoon snipped fresh chives |
| salt (ideally rock salt) and freshly milled black pepper |

Wash but don't scrape the potatoes as there are a lot of nutrients as well as flavour in the skins. Place the larger ones over the base of the saucepan and pop the smaller ones on top. Pour in enough boiling water to not quite cover, add some salt and the sprig of mint. Cover with a tight-fitting lid, and simmer gently for about 20 minutes. Test them with a skewer, and remember they must be tender but still firm – overcooking really does spoil them. Alternatively steam them, sprinkling them with salt and tucking the mint in amongst them.

Meanwhile mix the butter and herbs thoroughly together with some pepper. Then drain the cooked potatoes, add the herb butter, put the lid back on and swirl the pan around to get each one thoroughly coated. Remove the lid and just savour the delicious aroma for a couple of seconds before you dish them out!

PEAS

♦

I hear some people now saying they actually prefer frozen peas to fresh peas, because those bought in the pods from supermarkets are so often hard and old. It's quite true that growers – and I live amongst many of them – have found the demand from freezing companies more lucrative, and growing peas to sell fresh has become uneconomical. But nothing will convince me that the uniform frozen peas can ever compare with those freshly picked, mouthwateringly tender and sweet. The answer, as always, is for us to keep asking for fresh peas, and then they will come back.

The best way to cook them is briefly. Pour boiling water into the pan to reach half-way up the peas, add some salt, cook and in just a couple of minutes, your peas will be ready. I don't find it necessary to add mint or butter, or anything to add to their flavour. If the peas you have grown, or bought, happen to be getting on a bit, the following recipe is good for braising them into tenderness.

BRAISED PEAS WITH LETTUCE AND SPRING ONIONS

———————— ♦ ————————

(Serves 4 people)

This is a very good recipe for using fresh shelled peas that are not so young. Although they're not so tender, they do have a delicious flavour, and I quite like the firmer, more mealy texture.

2 lb peas (900 g), freshly shelled (weight before shelling)
8 spring onions
6 lettuce leaves
1 oz butter (25 g)
4 tablespoons water
a pinch of sugar
1 level teaspoon salt

Trim the onions – you only need the bulbous white part – and break the lettuce leaves into wide strips. Then melt the butter in a thick-based saucepan and add the onions, lettuce and peas. Stir well, then add the water, sugar and salt. Bring to simmering point, then cover the saucepan and let it cook over a very, very gentle heat for about 20–25 minutes (keeping an eye on the pan, and shaking it now and then to prevent the vegetables sticking). Add just a little more water if you think it needs it.

SPINACH

———————— ♦ ————————

A very versatile vegetable, spinach – and there's something very wholesome about it when the leaves are young, fresh and squeaky. Fresh spinach can be rather dusty or muddy: the best way to deal with this is to fill the sink with cold water, pick out any damaged or brown leaves and remove any tough stalks, then plunge the rest in the water and swirl them around. Do this in two to three changes of water, then let it all drain in a colander, shaking it well over the sink. Young spinach leaves can be wiped and used raw in a delicious salad (see page 445). When cooked, spinach loses roughly half its weight – so 1 lb (450 g) of spinach is only enough for two people.

Spinach has plenty of moisture in it, so it needs no water at all for cooking. For 1 lb (450 g) of spinach leaves, melt 1 oz (25 g) butter in a thick-based saucepan, then, keeping the heat at medium, pack the spinach leaves in. Add some salt, put on a tight-fitting lid, and let it cook for about 30 seconds. Then take the lid off and you'll find the spinach has collapsed down into the butter. Give it a stir so that the top leaves get pushed down to the base of the pan, replace the lid and give it another 30 seconds or so, shaking the pan a couple of times – I find the whole operation takes less than 2 minutes. Next drain the spinach in a colander, pressing it well with a saucer to get rid of any excess water. You can now return it to the pan, and season with freshly milled pepper and – best of all – nutmeg. Add a bit more butter or, if you like, a tablespoon of fresh cream.

For a delicious sauce to accompany fish or rice dishes see *Spinach and cheese sauce* (page 393).

BAKED SPINACH WITH BROWN RICE AND CHEESE

◆

(Serves 2–3 people)

For this meatless supper dish you can use either fresh or frozen spinach.

1 lb fresh spinach leaves (450 g), washed and chopped, or 8 oz frozen spinach (225 g), thawed
brown rice measured to the 8 fl oz (225 ml) level in a measuring jug
1 teaspoon butter
1 tablespoon oil
1 onion, finely chopped
16 fl oz hot water (450 ml)
4 oz Cheddar cheese (110 g), grated
2 large eggs, beaten
2 tablespoons chopped parsley
freshly grated nutmeg
salt and freshly milled black pepper
For the topping
2 tablespoons wholewheat breadcrumbs
1 tablespoon melted butter
a couple of pinches of cayenne pepper

Pre-heat the oven to gas mark 4, 350°F (180°C).

Melt the butter and oil in a saucepan and soften the onion in it, then stir in the rice to get it nicely coated with oil. Add the hot water, stir once, and simmer gently with a lid on for 40 minutes or until the liquid has been absorbed and the grains are tender.

As soon as the rice is cooked, cool it in a bowl, then combine it with the grated cheese, and stir in the eggs and parsley followed by the chopped spinach. Season well and add a good grating of nutmeg.

Now place the mixture into a large oiled pie dish, mix the breadcrumbs with the melted butter and cayenne and sprinkle that over the top. Bake in the oven for about 35 minutes.

EGGS FLORENTINE

♦

(Serves 2 people)

This is a very quick supper or lunch dish for two people. Some recipes call for hard-boiled eggs but I think they taste far nicer baked in with the spinach.

1 lb fresh spinach (450 g), cooked, or 8 oz frozen spinach (225 g), thawed – either should be well drained
4 large fresh eggs
1 tablespoon double cream
freshly grated nutmeg
salt and freshly milled pepper
For the sauce
1½ oz butter (40 g)
10 fl oz milk (275 ml)
1 oz plain flour (25 g)
3 oz Lancashire cheese (75 g), grated
1 tablespoon double cream
For the topping
1 oz Parmesan cheese (25 g), grated
a little extra butter

Pre-heat the oven to gas mark 5, 375°F (190°C).

First butter a large shallow baking dish generously, arrange the cooked spinach over the base, season with pepper, a little salt and freshly grated nutmeg. Then sprinkle the tablespoon of cream over and pop the dish in the lower part of the oven to heat through.

Now, for the sauce, place the butter, milk and flour in a saucepan and whisk over heat to make a smooth white sauce. Then stir in the grated Lancashire cheese and cook the sauce for 3 minutes over a very gentle heat – stirring now and then.

Now take the baking dish out of the oven, make four depressions in the spinach and gently break the eggs into each one (I like to sprinkle just a little salt and pepper onto the yolks.) Stir the tablespoon of cream into the cheese sauce and pour it over the eggs to cover everything completely. Sprinkle with Parmesan, add a few flecks of butter here and there and bake on a high shelf in the oven for 15–20 minutes.

Swedes

———— ◆ ————

Like all root vegetables, swedes store well and are perfect for long, slow cooking in stews and casseroles, where they can extend the meat considerably as well as add character of their own. I like them steamed and chopped with an equal quantity of carrots and a knob of butter. They are also good cut in longish chunks and baked in the same way as parsnips (see page 250).

Mashed Swedes with Crispy Bacon

———— ◆ ————

(Serves 4–6 people)

2 lb swedes (900 g)
6 rashers bacon, de-rinded and chopped small
1¹/₂ oz butter (40 g)
2 tablespoons single cream
salt and freshly milled black pepper

Start by peeling the swedes and cutting them into smallish cubes. Put them in a saucepan and just cover them with water. Add salt, bring to simmering point and cook gently for 15–20 minutes or until tender when tested with a skewer. (You could also steam them for approximately the same length of time.) Then tip them into a colander to drain thoroughly.

Return the saucepan to the heat, add half the butter and fry the chopped bacon until it begins to crisp. Now return the swedes to the saucepan, add the remainder of the butter and the cream and mash well to a creamy consistency. Taste and season with freshly milled black pepper and pile onto a warmed dish to serve.

Tomatoes

———— ◆ ————

Here I would like to make a personal plea to tomato-growers. Please could we have some choice of variety? And – just as potatoes now have to be labelled according to variety – could not tomatoes be identified also? The growers have always claimed that the average consumer, whoever that is, wants a uniform size (i.e. eight toms to the pound); and since boring old Moneymaker and similar varieties obligingly conform to this, that's what we get. In fact I can hardly believe this premise to be true – after all what is the difference between two large tomatoes cut into quarters and four small ones halved?

There's another problem too. Most commercial tomatoes are harvested before they have fully ripened, and therefore tend to become pithy and woolly inside. It's no wonder that people who travel to the continent take on a wistful look when speaking about French or Italian tomatoes. (Mind you, I would point out that just because a tomato is large and misshapen, it is not automatically better: it depends on the variety and the soil in which it is grown.)

At home we have grown a small outdoor bush variety called Little Pixie, which produces very sweet tomatoes (and you don't have to pinch out the leaves). I have even seen these grown in window boxes and grow bags. For more experienced home tomato-growers, there once was a variety called Ware Cross (which my grandfather used to grow) – lovely deep red fruits with sweet green centres – but sadly it is not available now. There is, though, a small sweet tomato called Gardener's Delight – which is best for flavour, coming out top in a tomato-tasting by growers – and at the other end of the spectrum we can get the larger tomatoes (more like the continental varieties) which are firmer for slicing. These are called 'beef' tomatoes but there is not as yet a choice of varieties.

For most of the standard varieties you need a well-flavoured salad dressing (see *Tomato salad*, page 444) or when cooking them a gutsy, well-seasoned recipe.

Note If you have a lot of green tomatoes at the end of the season, see *Spiced green tomato sauce* (page 401) and *Green tomato chutney* (page 608).

TO SKIN TOMATOES

Pour boiling water over them, leave for 5 minutes, then drain and cover with cold water to make them cool enough to handle. The skins will slip off very easily.

TURKISH STUFFED TOMATOES
♦

(Serves 4 or 8 people)

These are good for a light lunchtime dish with salad for four people, or this quantity will also serve eight people as a 'starter'.

8 really large ripe tomatoes
Italian rice measured to the 5 fl oz (150 ml) level in a measuring jug
1 small onion, finely chopped
olive oil
1 clove garlic, crushed
1 teaspoon ground cinnamon
1 tablespoon pine nuts (available at Greek or health-food shops)

| 1 tablespoon currants |
| 10 fl oz hot stock or water (275 ml) |
| 1 teaspoon fresh chopped thyme |
| sugar |
| salt and freshly milled black pepper |

Pre-heat the oven to gas mark 4, 350°F (180°C).

Begin by cooking the rice. Fry the onion in a tablespoon of olive oil in a saucepan until softened, then add the crushed garlic and pour in the rice. Add the cinnamon, pine nuts and the currants and give everything a good stir to get it well coated. Then season with some salt and pepper and pour in the hot stock. Stir just once, cover with a lid and let it simmer gently for 15–20 minutes or until all the liquid has been absorbed and the grains of rice are tender. Then remove the rice from the heat, add the thyme and fluff it with a skewer.

Prepare the tomatoes by slicing off a little of the round end and scooping out all the core and seeds – trying to leave as much of the actual flesh as possible. Put a pinch of sugar into each hollowed-out tomato, then pack each one with the rice mixture and replace the lids. Place the tomatoes in a meat-roasting tin with a little water in the bottom, drizzle a few drops of olive oil over each one and bake for 25–30 minutes. They are lovely eaten hot or cold.

TURNIPS

♦

I think turnips are much under-estimated – probably because they have been too often badly cooked in the past, boiled to death and waterlogged. However the first, tiny creamy-purple tinged turnips arrive in June and are a real delicacy if properly cooked. The larger winter variety, just cut into chunks, browned in dripping and added to stews and casseroles, are marvellous, or they can be sliced in a *Cornish pasty pie* (page 506). A more sophisticated way to serve them would be *Turnips and leeks boulangère*. Follow the recipe on page 255 for *Potatoes boulangère*, but using instead of potatoes and onions the equivalent quantities of turnips and leeks.

In Scotland turnips are whipped to a purée – bashed neeps – and in Wales they serve punchnep, a delicious combination of creamed potatoes and turnips whipped to a smooth purée, which Dorothy Hartley in her excellent book *Food in England* describes as looking like 'hot alabaster'. To prepare turnips, peel them as thinly as possible and keep them in cold water till ready to cook, to prevent them browning.

BUTTERED TURNIPS

Peel 1 lb (450 g) turnips and dice them into fairly small cubes. Now blanch them in boiling water for 3 minutes, drain well, then finish off by tossing them in 3 oz (75 g) melted butter in a large frying-pan – keeping the heat fairly gentle so they don't brown (5 minutes should be long enough). Serve them sprinkled with snipped chives or chopped parsley.

PUNCHNEP

(Serves 4 people)

Although it might seem unnecessary, the secret of this to get the right flavour is to boil the vegetables separately.

1 lb potatoes (450 g), peeled and cut into chunks
1 lb turnips (450 g), peeled and cut into chunks
3 fl oz single cream (75 ml)
1 oz butter (25 g)
salt and freshly milled black pepper

Put the potatoes in one saucepan and the turnips in another and cover both with boiling water. Season with salt and simmer – covered – until the vegetables are tender. (You'll find the potatoes will be ready about 5 minutes before the turnips.)

Meanwhile warm a shallow oval serving dish and, when the vegetables are ready, drain off the water, then combine them in one saucepan. Next pour the cream into the empty saucepan and warm it over a gentle heat. Add the butter to the vegetables, season well and mash thoroughly. Now empty the mixture into the warmed dish, then, using a skewer or similar implement and a circular movement, make several holes in the vegetables and pour the hot cream into the holes. Serve immediately.

GLAZED BABY TURNIPS

(Serves 4 people)

Baby turnips about the size of golf balls are creamy-white with leafy green tops, and usually sold in bunches in the summer, when they are in season.

2 lb young turnips (900 g)
light stock
1 teaspoon Dijon mustard
2 tablespoons dry white wine or dry cider
1 level teaspoon sugar
chopped parsley
salt and freshly milled black pepper

First of all prepare the turnips by peeling them carefully and thinly with a potato peeler, then put them into a saucepan of boiling water and boil for 3 minutes. Next drain in a colander and then return them to the saucepan. Now add just enough stock to cover the turnips, bring this to the boil and simmer (uncovered) for about 10 minutes, or until the turnips are tender. Use a draining spoon to remove the turnips, place them in a warmed serving dish and keep hot while you make the glaze.

Next blend the mustard with a little of the white wine and add to the stock in the saucepan with the remainder of the wine and the sugar. Reheat and simmer rapidly (without a lid) until the liquid has reduced to a syrupy consistency. Taste and season with salt and freshly milled pepper, then pour the syrup over the turnips, sprinkle with plenty of chopped parsley and serve.

SEE ALSO

A risotto for spring
Asparagus and cheese tart
Baked stuffed courgettes
Broccoli cheese soufflé
Brown rice, lentil and mushroom salad
Brown rice and vegetable gratin
Bubble and squeak
Buckwheat and vegetable pie
Cabbage leaves stuffed with rice
Courgette and cheese quiche
Cucumber with soured cream and dill
Dolmades (stuffed vine leaves)
Hazelnut and vegetable burgers
Italian stuffed aubergines
Kidneys in jacket potatoes
Lentil and vegetable moussaka
Marinated mushrooms

Mushroom and onion quiche
Non-meat loaf
Onion rice
Pipérade
Provençal vegetable stew
Rice with mushrooms
Rice with peppers
Risotto with chicken livers and mushrooms
Sautéed cauliflower with coriander
Sautéed mixed vegetables
Spinach and cream cheese quiche
Spinach pasties
Thick onion tart
Turkish stuffed peppers
Vegetarian goulash
Vegetarian shepherd's pie

RICE AND OTHER GRAINS

$\blacklozenge$

Without cereals (which for our purposes means rice, wheat, oats, maize, rye, barley, buckwheat and millet) man would not have got very far on this planet. Their cultivation goes back at least to the Stone Age, and every great civilisation since then has relied on one or other of them. Even today, rice is still the staple food for half the world's population, and very efficient it is too, being a good source of the proteins and vitamins essential to health – at least in its natural form. For here is a certain irony: for a long time all our energy and ingenuity has been directed towards transforming our cereals into forms far removed from their natural state – refining and whitening our wheat flour, polishing our rice grains, creating new breakfast cereals. The result of course was a loss in nutrients, and flavour. I touched on the problem – in so far as it concerned wheat – in the chapter on Bread, but the situation has been much the same for most of our grain products, particularly rice.

Now, however, the wholefood movement has at last created a demand for natural grains and cereals, to the extent that even the modern equivalent of the open-all-hours corner shop has a selection of whole grains alongside the refined varieties. Here at least we have a choice. I hope this section will offer a few ideas on how to make the most of this choice, but first let's look at the most adaptable of all the grains, rice, and see what happens to it in its preparation.

RICE

$\blacklozenge$

If you were able to magnify a rice grain, when it's first harvested and cleaned of mud, leaves and stem, what you would see is something rather like a nut with an outer inedible shell, which has to be removed and discarded. Inside that would be the outer casings (again just like a nut – think of an unblanched almond): these are bran layers, a brown outer layer and a whiter inner one. Beyond these is the starchy centre (endosperm) which also contains the embryo (or germ). It so happens that this starchy kernel is one of the most easily-digested of all available foods, taking about half the time to be digested that most other foods require.

HOW RICE IS TREATED

In poorer countries rice is still pounded by hand, either with pestle and mortar or between grinding stones, to remove the inedible husk. In industrialised countries (like America where much of our rice now comes from) this is done in large, modern rice mills where the grain is not only cleaned and hulled by machine, but also 'polished' to remove the bran layers and germ and to scour the grain down to a translucent white, refined, purified endosperm – in other words the end product is depleted of a lot of its original vitamins and minerals.

GRADES OF RICE

Rice is produced, in most major growing countries, in three sizes of grain, each one suitable for different kinds of dish:

Short-grain
Often simply called pudding rice in Britain, this is a quick-growing rice (which is why it is the cheapest). The grains are fat and almost round, with barely more length than width. They are also rather chalky, which makes them sticky when cooked, and are therefore best suited to rice puddings – they cook to a lovely creamy consistency in the milk.

Medium-grain
A sort of half-way rice, neither as sticky when cooked as short-grain nor as cleanly separate as long-grain. It isn't widely available in this country, but when it is, it should be used for croquettes, rice moulds or some risottos.

Long-grain
These grains are four or five times as long as they are wide, with scarcely any chalkiness (which means they are fluffy and separate when cooked). To buy good quality long-grain you should look for really fine, needle-pointed ends and, with white rice, a certain translucence.

PREPARED RICE

Then, apart from the shape of the grain, rice also reaches the shops in different degrees of preparation, which affect both the cooking and the taste:

Brown rice
This is the whole natural rice grain, with only the inedible outer husk removed: the bran layers and germ are left intact. It comes in the three sizes mentioned above, and is a rather appealing mixture of green and

brown in colour. Personally I think long-grain brown rice (in particular Patna, see below) is the nicest of all rices, and for two reasons: (i) it contains the highest percentage of fibre, natural vitamins and minerals, and (ii) it has most flavour and 'bite' to it after it's cooked. It takes longer to cook than white rice and, paradoxically, it is more expensive to buy (considering it has gone through fewer processes). But it stores well and can safely be bought in bulk.

White (polished) rice

This is the refined one that has had all but the starchy endosperm removed. It is pearly white and comes in all three grain sizes, the long-grain type being the most commonly available rice in shops and supermarkets.

Easy-cook rice

This white rice is so-called because it has been treated by a special steaming process (rather like pressure cooking) *before* milling. It is claimed by the manufacturers that this processing helps the grain to retain much of its nutritional content, and hardens it so it becomes less starchy and remains separate in the cooking – although it needs a little more cooking time than ordinary polished white rice. (However, I tested a batch of easy-cook rice alongside some ordinary long-grain white rice, both of them American, and found that using the *Perfect rice* method given on page 274, the ordinary long-grain was every bit as easy – and 25 per cent cheaper! Still, if you feel safer using easy-cook then just allow 10 minutes' extra cooking.)

Pre-cooked rice

This is sometimes described as pre-digested! It is polished white rice which is cooked or half-cooked after milling, then dried so all it needs is to re-absorb the water it lost in the drying. My own opinion of it is – that it's like sliced white bread: blotting paper!

Wild rice

This is not strictly a rice grain but a form of grass seed, harvested exclusively in America. It is quite expensive but has a deliciously nutty, almost smoky, flavour. It can be served on its own – boil for 30 minutes, but check on it after 20 (it should be just tender but not mushy) – or you can supplement it by mixing it with other rice, which has been cooked separately.

SOME REGIONAL VARIETIES

Finally, rice is sometimes described by names which refer to the countries or regions where it was grown. Here are some of them:

Patna rice

A generic term used to describe the long-grain rice grown all round the world. The name derives from the days when it was first grown in Patna (an area of north-east India) and exported to Europe. Since most of our long-grain rice now comes from America, the Americans are slightly puzzled as to why we should still refer to their rice as 'Patna'!

Basmati rice

This is a very fine quality rice with a superb flavour, and does in fact come from India. In my opinion it is the best sort to serve with a curry. I used to find it quite tricky to cook till I used Elizabeth David's method, given in her book *Salts, Spices and Aromatics*, and have never had a failure since. Brown basmati is now widely available too, and that has the best flavour of all.

Carolina rice

A general name for rice, referring to the region in America where rice was first planted in 1694. In actual fact most rice production in America has now shifted to other states.

Arborio (Italian) rice

This is the rice that's grown in northern Italy. Its quality is superb: the grains are rounder and much plumper than long-grain, and if you rub a grain of it between your fingers, you can see clearly an outer translucent edge and a white core in the centre. To make a true risotto you need arborio rice – it takes longer and in this case it's not meant to be fluffy and separate, but because it's stirred quite frequently it cooks to a rather creamy consistency (see recipes for *Risotto alla Milanese* and *Risotto with chicken livers and mushrooms*, pages 277–8).

There are two types available: one is very white and the grains look chalky. The other is browny-yellow and has a more polished look. This latter kind is treated to make the grains firmer and more separate (presumably because that is what the export market wants).

The so-called 'easy-cook' Italian is good as an all-purpose rice. It does have a better flavour and texture, I think, than ordinary long-grain white rice. It can be cooked exactly as in the *Perfect rice* recipe. But don't confuse this with the true risotto rice – that should always be the best arborio.

271

OTHER RICE PRODUCTS

When rice is milled, some of the grains are broken and these are used to make *rice flakes*, which are used for puddings, and *rice flour* which is used for confectionery and cooking, and makes a good thickening agent. One tablespoon of rice flour per 10 fl oz (275 ml) of liquid will thicken a soup or stew beautifully: just whisk it into the liquid and bring to simmering point. This has a great advantage for slimmers, because it enables you to thicken a sauce without fat and flour; and a little stirred into yoghurt used in cooking stops it separating.

DO NOT BE AFRAID!

So many people have told me they can't cook rice, and yet (rather like omelette-making) there's nothing intrinsically difficult about it: once it has been explained, you should be well away. So if you're one of those people who live in fear of cooking rice, here is a complete guide to trouble-free rice cookery. The following points apply to long-grain white and brown rice but not to Italian rice – for which guidelines are given in the recipe for *Risotto alla Milanese*.

(1) First of all buy good quality long-grain rice. The better supermarket chains stock both brown and white basmati, and many wholefood stores will sell it in bulk to cut the cost.

(2) Don't wash rice because it is thoroughly cleaned at the milling stage, and washing it later removes some of the nutrients (anyway the high temperature of the cooking will purify it).

(3) Always measure rice and liquid by *volume* and not by weight. Cups and mugs are often recommended, but I find they vary so much it's impossible to gauge whether a certain cup will be enough for such and such a number of people. So I now always measure both rice and cooking liquid in a glass measuring jug. I find that filling the jug with rice up to the 5 fl oz (150 ml) level gives enough for two people (up to the 10 fl oz/275 ml level for four people and so on) and this provides fairly generous portions. Then I empty the rice out of the jug and measure into it exactly *twice* that amount of liquid (i.e. up to the 10 fl oz/275 ml level for two people, up to the 1 pint/570 ml level for four people and so on).

(4) Please leave rice alone while it's cooking! Lack of confidence in the kitchen always manifests itself in over-handling, and it is the nervous cooks who are forever peeping, prodding and stirring and that, so far as rice is concerned, is a disaster. Why? Because rice grains are delicate and easily broken: if you start to stir them while they're cooking, they break, releasing the starch inside and turning them sticky.

(5) Use a wide, shallow saucepan or flameproof casserole or, if you are cooking rice for a lot of people, the best utensil is a large frying-pan with

a lid. Be gentle: once boiling point has been reached turn the heat down to the barest simmer. Try not to lift the lid: I think rice should be cooked as briefly as possible, and each time the lid is lifted steam and heat escape and the cooking time is unnecessarily prolonged.

(6) Timing *is* important and it remains the same regardless of the quantity of rice you are cooking. For long-grain white rice I find 15 minutes is just enough. When the time is up, tip the pan to one side and check there is no liquid left unabsorbed – if there is, give the rice a couple of minutes more.

(7) The way to test rice is to bite a couple of grains: they should be tender but firm. Then either leave the rice in the pan and cover with a tea cloth to absorb the steam for 5–10 minutes, or tip it out into a warmed shallow serving dish, and cover with a cloth for the same length of time. Just before serving separate the grains and fluff them with a skewer (which works better, I find, than a fork).

(8) It is inadvisable to keep rice warm for long but it will keep for 20 minutes without coming to harm if you put it in a bowl placed over a saucepan of barely simmering water or place it in the warming compartment of the oven. Cover the bowl with a clean tea towel but don't put a lid on top.

(9) Cooked rice keeps well (even up to a week) in a bowl covered with cling film in the refrigerator. To reheat it, just place it in a thick-based saucepan with a couple of tablespoons of water, cover and warm it gently, shaking the pan from time to time. It will only take a couple of minutes.

(10) All the above information applies also to the cooking of brown rice, except that this takes 40–45 minutes to cook instead of 15 (extra time that's easily warranted by the character and flavour of brown rice).

LIQUID FOR COOKING RICE

Plain salted water is fine for cooking savoury rice. The liquid should be boiling (to save time I always pour it into the measuring jug straight from a boiling kettle). Stock is an excellent alternative, particularly if the rice is to be served with chicken (use chicken stock) or beef (use beef stock), and for fish a fish stock is especially good. I don't recommend stock cubes, as I find them too strong, masking the delicate flavour of the rice.

PERFECT RICE

---◆---

(Serves 2 people)

A friend of mine swore she'd *never* be able to cook rice: she had tried – she said – every sort of rice and every kind of method, only to be teased so much by her family that she gave up completely. Now I'm happy to report she has been persuaded to follow the method below and has had perfect rice every time. What is perfect rice? Simply this, that when it's cool enough to handle you can pick up a handful that will run through your hands in a stream of perfectly separate grains. You will need:

long-grain white or brown rice measured to the 5 fl oz (150 ml) level in a measuring jug
boiling water or stock measured to the 10 fl oz (275 ml) level in a measuring jug
1 dessertspoon oil or ½ oz butter (10 g)
salt

One small, solid-based saucepan or flameproof casserole, and a shallow serving dish, warmed.

Begin by heating the oil or butter gently, just to the melting stage, then add the rice and, using a wooden spoon, stir the grains to get them all thoroughly coated and glistening with fat.

Now add the boiling water or stock and salt, stir just once as the liquid comes up to simmering point, then put on a tight-fitting lid. Turn the heat down to keep the gentlest simmer – then go away and leave it completely alone. Don't take the lid off and, above all, don't stir it. After exactly 15 minutes, if the rice is white (40 if it's brown), I give you permission to have a look and test a few grains. If they're tender, and, when you tilt the pan almost on its side, you can see no trace of liquid left, the rice is cooked.

Now tip it out into a warmed serving dish, using a rubber spatula to dislodge any grains that refuse to leave the base. Lightly fluff the grains with a skewer. Serve immediately. Or if you need to keep it warm – say for up to 20 minutes – cover the bowl with a tea cloth (which will absorb the steam and help to keep the grains separate) and place it over a pan of hot but not boiling water.

Note I find a wide, shallow serving dish makes it easier to fluff the grains, as they can be spread out more easily.

This method of cooking rice can be used with all kinds of flavourings. Here are some suggestions. The quantities given will be sufficient to flavour rice for four people.

Onion rice
Cook 1 finely chopped medium onion in the oil or butter for 5 minutes before stirring in the rice. Then proceed as above.

Rice with peppers
Cook ¹/₂ chopped onion and ¹/₂ chopped green or red pepper in the oil or butter before stirring in the rice.

Rice with mushrooms
Cook ¹/₂ chopped onion and 4 oz (110g) chopped mushrooms in the oil or butter before stirring in the rice.

Rice with herb butter
When the rice is cooked, add a knob of *Herb butter* (see page 405) so it melts into the rice as you fluff it.

SPICED PILAU RICE
♦

(Serves 4 people)

This fragrant rice is lovely to serve with curries and spiced dishes.

long-grain white rice measured up to the 10 fl oz (275 ml) level in a measuring jug (basmati for preference)
boiling water measured up to the 1 pint (570 ml) level in a measuring jug
1 tablespoon groundnut oil
1 small onion, finely chopped
1 inch cinnamon stick (2.5 cm)
³/₄ teaspoon cumin seeds, crushed
2 cardamom pods, crushed
1 dessertspoon ground turmeric
1 bay leaf
salt

Heat the oil in a thick-based saucepan and soften the onion in it for about 3 minutes. Then stir in the spices, bay leaf and salt and allow a minute or two while the heat draws out their fragrance. Next stir in the measured rice, and when it's well coated with oil and spices, pour in the boiling water. Stir once, put on a tight-fitting lid, and simmer gently for 15 minutes or until the rice is tender. Tip into a serving dish straightaway, cover with a tea towel for 5 minutes, then fluff with a skewer and remove the cinnamon stick, bay leaf and cardamom pods before serving.

SAFFRON RICE

◆

(Serves 4 people)

I buy saffron from a large chain-store chemist and crush the strands with a pestle and mortar.

long-grain white rice measured up to the 10 fl oz (275 ml) level in a measuring jug
boiling water or chicken stock measured up to the 1 pint (570 ml) level in a measuring jug
1 small onion, finely chopped
1 tablespoon olive oil
1 oz butter (25 g)
½ teaspoon powdered saffron
salt

Begin by softening the onion in the oil and butter for 5 minutes, then stir in the saffron and allow 1 minute for the heat to draw out the flavour before adding the rice. Stir to get the rice nicely coated with the oil and butter, then add the boiling water or stock. Stir again once and add salt.

Then, when it comes to the boil, cover with a lid and leave it to simmer very gently for 15 minutes or until all the liquid has been absorbed. Don't stir it or peek, but leave it alone until the 15 minutes are up. Then taste a grain without stirring the rice and tilt the pan a little to check that the liquid has been absorbed.

When the rice is cooked tip it onto a warm, shallow serving dish and fluff with a skewer before serving.

RISOTTO ALLA MILANESE

◆

(Serves 4 people as a main course)

This recipe (and the following one) is only suitable for Italian rice, which needs quite different treatment from long-grain rice. A high proportion of liquid is used, the rice is cooked in an uncovered pan, and a good deal of stirring is necessary – particularly towards the end of cooking. It's a relatively simple dish but absolutely beautiful if made properly. You can either serve it on its own as a first course or it's very good served as an accompaniment to *Ossobuco* (page 175). (Illus. opposite p. 257.)

Italian rice measured to the 12 fl oz (350 ml) level in a measuring jug
5 tablespoons dry white wine
approx. 2 pints boiling chicken stock (1.2 litres)
4 oz butter (110 g)
¹/₂ teaspoon powdered saffron
1 medium onion, chopped
2 tablespoons bone marrow (from an obliging butcher)
4 tablespoons freshly grated Parmesan cheese
salt and freshly milled black paper

Begin by melting half the butter in a heavy-based saucepan, add the saffron and allow 1 minute for the heat to draw out the flavour. Then add the chopped onion and bone marrow and cook, over a low heat, for about 10 minutes until softened.

Stir in the rice and cook for a minute or two before adding the wine and some salt. Stir gently once, then simmer over a low heat, without a lid, until the liquid has been absorbed (about 10–15 minutes). Now put in a ladleful of the boiling stock and again let it simmer until the stock has nearly all been absorbed but the rice is still moist. Continue adding the boiling stock a ladleful at a time until the rice is tender but still creamy. There should still be a very little liquid visible – a risotto should be soupy rather than mushy (see page 271). Stir as necessary to prevent the rice from sticking to the bottom of the pan – particularly towards the end.

When the rice is cooked, remove the pan from the heat, stir in the remaining butter and Parmesan cheese. Cover and leave to stand, off the heat, for 5 minutes before serving. Season to taste, then serve with lots more freshly grated Parmesan cheese on the table.

RISOTTO WITH CHICKEN LIVERS AND MUSHROOMS

◆

(Serves 2–3 people)

If you're using frozen chicken livers – the sort that come in 8 oz (225 g) cartons – do make sure they are thoroughly de-frosted before you start.

For the sauce
1½ oz butter (40 g)
1 medium onion, thinly sliced
2 oz streaky bacon (50 g), de-rinded and chopped
8 oz chicken livers (225 g), cut into lobes
8 oz mushrooms (225 g), sliced
5 fl oz boiling chicken stock (150 ml)
1 bay leaf
1 heaped tablespoon tomato purée
1 teaspoon dried basil
salt and freshly milled black pepper
For the risotto
1½ oz butter (40 g)
1 medium onion, chopped
Italian rice measured to the 8 fl oz (225 ml) level in a measuring jug
5 fl oz dry white wine (150 ml)
1¼ pints boiling chicken stock (725 ml)
To garnish
1 oz Parmesan cheese (25 g), grated

The risotto and sauce are made in separate saucepans, but need to be cooked at the same time. For the sauce, put the butter in a fairly large saucepan and sauté the sliced onion until soft and golden. Add the bacon and cook for a further 2 or 3 minutes.

Now, for the risotto, melt the butter in a bigger saucepan and cook the chopped onion until softened. Stir in the rice and cook until slightly browned. Next add the wine and continue to cook, uncovered, over low heat until it has all but evaporated. Then add a generous 10 fl oz (275 ml) of the boiling chicken stock. Cover and cook over a gentle heat for approximately 20 minutes. Then add a ladleful of stock and when that is absorbed continue to add a ladleful at a time, as and when the rice requires it – it will probably take 1¼ pints (725 ml) in all.

While the rice is cooking you can go back to the sauce: turn the heat up high under the pan and add the chicken livers and, when they've turned a rich brown, stir in the mushrooms. Let them cook for 2 or 3

278

minutes before adding the chicken stock, the bay leaf, tomato purée and basil. Season and cook gently for 10 minutes until the mixture is reduced to a good sauce consistency.

Keep the sauce warm and, when the rice is ready, serve the risotto with the sauce spooned on top and sprinkle with freshly grated Parmesan cheese.

A RISOTTO FOR SPRING

♦

(Serves 4–6 people)

This is not an Italian risotto, but simply an attractive lunch dish of brown rice, cheese and lightly sautéed green vegetables.

long-grain brown rice measured to the 15 fl oz (425 ml) level in a measuring jug
1½ pints boiling vegetable stock or water (850 ml)
1½ tablespoons olive oil
1 small onion, chopped
4 oz strong Cheddar cheese (110 g), grated
2 tablespoons freshly grated Parmesan cheese
salt, cayenne and freshly milled black pepper
For the sauce
2 tablespoons olive oil
1 oz butter (25 g)
1 small cauliflower, divided up into thumbnail-sized florets
1 lb broccoli (450 g) – pick off and use the heads only
2 leeks, cleaned and chopped into ½ inch (1 cm) pieces
8 oz fresh spinach (225 g), washed, dried and shredded
To garnish
4 spring onions, very finely chopped, including the green part

Begin the rice by heating the olive oil in a medium-sized, thick-based saucepan and frying the onion for 5 minutes. Next, add the rice and stir it around so that the grains are well coated with oil. Now add the boiling stock or water and some salt, stir once, then bring to simmering point. Cover and let the rice simmer very gently for 40 minutes or until the grains are tender.

About half-way through the rice cooking time, begin the sauce. Melt the 2 tablespoons oil with the butter in a very large frying-pan (or divide between two medium-sized pans); add the cauliflower, broccoli, leeks and some seasoning. Then, over a medium heat, move the vegetables around until they have browned a little but still retain their crispness – say for about 8 minutes. Now add the spinach; it will appear somewhat bulky to begin with but will soon collapse. Cook, stirring occasionally, for about 5 minutes. Meanwhile turn the grill on to high.

When the rice is cooked put it into a shallow heatproof serving dish and fluff it. Add half the Cheddar cheese and half the Parmesan and stir them in. Add the vegetables and stir again. Then sprinkle the remaining Cheddar and Parmesan on top, together with a pinch or two of cayenne.

Now place the dish under the grill and let the cheese topping melt and brown. Garnish with the spring onions.

BUTTERY KEDGEREE

◆

(Serves 4 people)

This was a typical breakfast dish in the days when grand Victorian breakfast dishes were spread out on handsome Victorian sideboards. Nowadays it is a very good lunch or late supper dish.

long-grain white rice measured to the 8 fl oz (225 ml) level in a measuring jug
boiling liquid measured to the 16 fl oz (450 ml) level in a measuring jug (see method)
1¹/₂ lb thick smoked haddock fillets (700 g)
4 oz butter (110 g)
1 onion, chopped
³/₄ teaspoon hot curry powder (Madras)
3 hard-boiled eggs, peeled and chopped
3 heaped tablespoons chopped fresh parsley
1 tablespoon lemon juice
salt and freshly milled black pepper

First place the haddock fillets in a saucepan and cover them with 1 pint (570 ml) cold water. Bring to the boil, put on a lid, and simmer gently for about 8 minutes. Then drain off the water into a measuring jug. Transfer the haddock to a dish, cover with foil and keep it warm.

Now, using the same saucepan, melt 2 oz (50 g) of the butter and soften the onion in it for 5 minutes. Next stir in the curry powder, cook for half a minute, then stir in the measured rice and add 16 fl oz (450 ml) of the haddock cooking water. Stir once then, when it comes up to simmering point, cover with a tight-fitting lid and cook, very gently, for 15 minutes or until the rice grains are tender.

When the rice has been cooking for 10 minutes, remove the skin from the fish and flake it. Then, when the rice is ready, remove it from the heat and fork in the flaked fish, hard-boiled eggs, parsley, lemon juice and the remaining 2 oz (50 g) of butter.

Now cover the pan with a folded tea towel and replace it on very gentle heat for 5 minutes. Then tip the kedgeree quickly onto a hot serving dish, season to taste and serve.

BROWN RICE, LENTIL AND MUSHROOM SALAD

◆

(Serves 4 or 8 people)

This recipe is enough for four people as a main course or for eight as a side-salad.

brown rice (basmati for preference) measured to the 8 fl oz (225 ml) level in a measuring jug
boiling water measured to the 16 fl oz (450 ml) level in a measuring jug
8 oz whole green-brown lentils (225 g)
¹/₂ oz butter (10 g)
salt
4 oz mushrooms (110 g), thinly sliced
8 spring onions, thinly sliced – green tops as well
¹/₂ large green pepper, de-seeded and finely chopped
1 tablespoon finely chopped walnuts
6 inch (15 cm) piece unpeeled cucumber, chopped
For the dressing
5 dessertspoons oil
1 dessertspoon wine vinegar
1 rounded teaspoon mustard powder
1 clove garlic, crushed
salt and freshly milled black pepper
To garnish
a few crisp lettuce leaves
sliced tomatoes
2 heaped tablespoons chopped parsley

Begin by cooking the lentils in plenty of (unsalted) boiling water for about 30–40 minutes or until they're *just* soft but not mushy. Meanwhile, in another saucepan melt the butter, stir in the rice to get it nicely coated, then pour in the boiling water. Stir once, cover and simmer very gently for 40–45 minutes until the rice is tender and has absorbed the liquid.

While the lentils and rice are cooking, prepare the dressing by mixing together in a bowl the oil, vinegar, mustard, garlic, salt and some freshly milled pepper.

Then drain the lentils, combine them with the cooked rice in a salad bowl, and while they're still warm pour on the dressing. Mix well and leave to cool. Then stir in the rest of the ingredients and serve on a bed of crisp lettuce leaves. Finally garnish with sliced tomatoes and chopped fresh parsley.

TURKISH STUFFED PEPPERS

◆

(Serves 4 people)

This is one of the nicest recipes for using left-over cooked lamb and making it into something really special. Beef could be used but is not quite as good as lamb.

long-grain white rice measured to the 8 fl oz (225 ml) level in a measuring jug
boiling water measured to the 16 fl oz (450 ml) level in a measuring jug
4 medium green or red peppers
olive oil
2 medium onions, chopped
2 cloves garlic, finely chopped
approx. 12 oz cooked lamb (350 g), cut into very small pieces
2 tablespoons currants
2 dessertspoons pine nuts
1/2 teaspoon ground cinnamon
1/2 teaspoon dried oregano
14 oz tin Italian tomatoes (400 g)
4 teaspoons tomato purée
salt and freshly milled black pepper

Pre-heat the oven to gas mark 5, 375°F (190°C).

Begin by melting some oil in a saucepan, then stir in the rice. When it is well coated with oil, pour in the boiling water and add a sprinkling of salt. Put a lid on and simmer for approximately 15 minutes, or until all the liquid has been absorbed.

Meanwhile fry the onions and garlic in a little more oil for a couple of minutes, then add the meat together with the currants and pine nuts. Season well with salt and pepper, stir in the cinnamon, oregano and two of the tomatoes plus a tablespoon of juice from the contents of the tin, then turn the heat very low and leave to simmer very gently.

Now prepare the peppers by slicing off the stalk ends and pulling out the core and the seeds. Run each one under cold water to make sure all the seeds are gone, then sit them upright in a small casserole (just so there's not too much room for them to keel over). When the rice is cooked, add it to the pan containing the meat and stir well to combine everything. Taste to check the seasoning at this point.

Now spoon the mixture into each of the peppers: pack it down well to get as much in as you can, and put the rest all around the base of the peppers. Finally, put a teaspoon of tomato purée on top of each pepper and pour the rest of the tin of tomatoes all around the peppers.

Cover the casserole, and cook in the oven for 45–50 minutes or until the peppers are tender when tested with a skewer.

BROWN RICE PUDDING WITH PRUNES AND APRICOTS

◆

(Serves 4–6 people)

This is a pudding for wholefood-minded people, deliciously different from the traditional rice pudding.

brown rice measured to the 10 fl oz (275 ml) level in a measuring jug
milk measured to the 1 pint (570 ml) level in a measuring jug
4 tablespoons dark brown sugar
1 egg, beaten
½ teaspoon ground cinnamon
¼ nutmeg, grated
4 oz dried apricots (110 g) and 6 oz prunes (175 g), both soaked overnight then drained and chopped
5 oz natural yoghurt (150 g)

In a thick-based saucepan bring the milk to the boil and sprinkle in the rice. Stir, then cover and cook over a very low heat for about 50 minutes or until the rice is tender. Keep an eye on it or the milk may boil over and, towards the end of the cooking time, have a peep as you might need to add a drop more milk. Then take it off the heat and stir in 3 tablespoons of the sugar, the beaten egg, cinnamon and nutmeg.

Next, butter a 4 pint (2.25 litre) casserole, spread half the rice mixture in it and top this with half the fruit. Spread the rest of the rice on top and cover this with the remaining fruit. Cover the casserole with a lid and bake in a pre-heated oven for 30 minutes at gas mark 4, 350°F (180°C).

At the end of the cooking time, remove the pudding from the oven, spread the yoghurt over the top and sprinkle with the remaining tablespoon of sugar.

Note This is just as delicious served cold, if you have any left over.

OTHER CEREAL GRAINS

There are two kinds of cereal available: whole natural cereals and refined cereals. Although we have in the past eaten far more of the latter – millions of pounds' worth of advertising has persuaded us to do so – now we can choose for ourselves. The supermarket shelves present a dazzling array of breakfast cereals which are made from 100 per cent wholewheat, and say so on the packet. My advice is to choose these: they contain the whole grain, fibre and all, and have no need of added vitamins.

WHOLE GRAIN CEREALS

Packaged breakfast foods are by no means the only way to consume cereals. A whole variety of grains come to us (as rice does) in several guises. The uses of some may be unfamiliar; but if they are natural whole grains as opposed to refined ones, what they all have in common is real nutrition and flavour.

To be sure that the grains you buy are whole grains, it makes sense to go to a wholefood shop – because the grains sold in grocers and supermarkets are often refined.

Barley

A great deal of our barley, of course, finds its way into beer, but the grain is also sold – most often as *pearl barley*, which is the refined variety, or as *pot barley*, which is the whole grain with only the inedible husk removed, and is found in health-food shops. Both these are good additions to stews or soups (see the recipes for *Irish stew*, page 171, and for *Scotch broth*, page 74). *Barley flakes* are the grains mechanically rolled into flakes, and an excellent use for these is in *Muesli* (see page 286).

Rye

This is more commonly milled into various grades of flour for bread-making – *coarsely milled rye*, for instance, is used in the production of pumpernickel bread; and *rye flour* (because of its quick fermentation) is often added to wheat flour to give bread a slightly 'sour' flavour. Like other grains, *flaked rye* can be bought in health-food shops.

Wheat

We've already examined all the different varieties of wheat flour in the chapter on Bread, but the grain itself – or parts of it – has many other applications. *Wholewheat grains* can be soaked for a few hours, then cooked in the same way as rice (but take longer): the result is chewier, and some people prefer to combine the wholewheat grains with some rice

284

or beans. *Wholewheat flakes* are good in *Muesli* (see page 286). *Cracked wheat* (which is simply the whole grain lightly crushed) is sometimes sprinkled on bread before baking, or included, as in malted grain loaves, in the dough itself. *Wheatgerm* is the embryo of the grain, and contains a very high proportion of vitamins, minerals and oils: it is sold separately and a few teaspoons sprinkled on your yoghurt, porridge or fruit salad is a good way of upping your vitamin intake for the day! *Wheat bran* is the layer that lies just below the inedible outer husk of the wheat grain. If you're living on a diet that contains about five slices of wholewheat bread a day plus fresh fruit and other wholefoods, you'll probably be getting enough dietary fibre. On the other hand if you prefer white bread and other refined foods, it might be a good idea to incorporate some wheat bran into your diet. The best way to do this, I think, is to sprinkle it onto ordinary breakfast cereals and pour on some milk so that it slips down almost unnoticed. *Semolina* is also made from wheat grain: basically it's the starchy part of hard wheat in granular form, before it has been finely milled. See the delicious recipe for *Roman gnocchi* on page 421.

Oats

Much used in biscuit-making – see the Scones and Biscuits chapter for the different grades of *oatmeal* (milled oats) and varieties of *oat flakes*. In F. Marian MacNeill's charming book *The Scots Kitchen*, oats are referred to as 'the flower of the Scottish soil', so it's not surprising that some of the best recipes for using oats come from Scotland and the pride of them all is *Porridge* (see the recipe on page 286).

It is now possible to buy oat germ and bran (they are not separated as with wheat). This is said to help reduce cholesterol levels in the blood and is therefore good for sprinkling into muesli and other breakfast cereals.

Buckwheat

This is strictly speaking not a grain, but its use and preparation are much the same. *Buckwheat flour* is traditionally used for the Russian type of pancakes known as blinis, and for the Breton version known as *galettes* (see the Pasta and Pancakes chapter). The *whole buckwheat* seeds can be bought roasted – in which case they're sometimes called *kasha* – or in their natural state. They have a delicious and distinctive grainy flavour, cook very much like rice, and combine beautifully with vegetables for a savoury dish like the one on page 322.

HOME-MADE MUESLI

My quarrel with some of the branded mueslis is that they usually contain rather a lot of dried milk powder (which is not really something I want to eat in spoonfuls) plus the inevitable sugar, making most of them too sweet. If you have a wholefood shop within easy distance you can probably buy an unsweetened muesli base, or you can buy the grains and other ingredients and make it at home. This is only a guide: you can add or subtract as you like.

8 oz wholewheat flakes (225 g)
8 oz rye flakes (225 g)
8 oz whole oat flakes (225 g)
8 oz barley flakes (225 g)
12 oz unsalted roasted peanuts (350 g)
6 oz sunflower seeds (175 g)
1 lb sultanas (450 g)
8 oz raisins (225 g)

This is a basic mixture, but there are 101 variations — the nuts for instance could be roasted hazelnuts, brazils, walnuts, or, if you're feeling rich, slivered roast almonds with the skins left on. The fruit too can be varied: chopped dates, dried apricots or figs, or chopped dried apple rings. Personally I think the proportions of fruit here make the addition of sugar unnecessary, but if it isn't sweet enough for you add some more dried fruit. When serving muesli you can sprinkle in some wheat bran, which will slip down unnoticed amongst all the other good things. Wheatgerm, oatgerm and oat bran can be added too and fresh fruits in season. Other optional items might be dried banana flakes or chopped dried prunes. Milk is always poured over and, if you're trying to cut down on fats, semi-skimmed milk is better.

TRADITIONAL OATMEAL PORRIDGE

(Serves 2 people)

Traditions surrounding porridge-making are legion: sometimes the oats were added in batches, some at the beginning, some half-way through, and some at the end — the undercooked ones giving a contrast in texture and a nuttier flavour. Salt wasn't added till half-way through, in case it should toughen the grains before they cooked: today the Scots still make their porridge well salted.

1 pint water (570 ml)
2¹/₂ oz medium oatmeal (60 g)
1 teaspoon salt

To serve
dark brown sugar (optional)
5 fl oz single cream (150 ml)

In a medium saucepan, bring the water up to a fast boil, then sprinkle in the oatmeal slowly, whisking it in with a balloon whisk. Carry on whisking until the mixture returns to the boil, then reduce the heat, cover the pan and let the porridge cook very gently for 10 minutes. After that add the salt, whisk it in, cover again and cook gently for a further 15 minutes or so.

The traditional way to eat porridge is without sugar, and with an individual bowl of cream. But if you have a sweet tooth, sprinkle dark brown sugar over the porridge, let it melt a little, then pour in the cream so that it mingles with the sugar and marbles the surface. Wonderful on a cold, frosty day!

SEE ALSO

Aduki bean and brown rice salad
Baked spinach with brown rice and cheese
Brown rice and tuna fish salad
Buckwheat and vegetable pie
Cabbage leaves stuffed with rice
Cider baked apples with toasted muesli
Dolmades (stuffed vine leaves)
Eliza Acton's rich rice pudding
Green herb and rice salad
Ham, egg and cheese risotto
Rice salad
Shoulder of lamb with rice and kidney stuffing
Turkish stuffed tomatoes

VEGETARIAN COOKING

♦

Vegetarian food is now right where it should be – firmly in the mainstream of everyday eating, rather than regarded as some remote and cranky tributary. It is a triumphant reflection of this that even multi-starred restaurants now offer vegetarian gourmet menus created with the flair and imagination that goes into the rest. I have no personal inclination to be a vegetarian, but what does inspire me is the freshness and variety – and potential – of a good deal of vegetarian cooking. Through travel, and articles and television programmes, we are now much more familiar with other countries' cuisines in many of which vegetarian cooking has a central place. At the same time a demand has been created for a whole new range of ingredients and we are fortunate to live in an age when we can shop globally, as it were, in most high streets.

All this presents us with a challenge – and at a time when we are being urged to eat less meat for our own good as well. For those of us who really enjoy good meat it is no great sacrifice to give up polyphosphate-injected chicken, barley-fed beef or chemically-cured bacon. The positive aspect is the pleasure of discovering how *satisfying* (not to mention economical) it is to produce a really delicious meal without any meat.

VEGETARIAN MYTHS

♦

Vegetarians themselves have been known to make rash claims, such as that vegetarians are slimmer, healthier, and less aggressive than carnivores. Rubbish. I know a number of rather plump vegetarians who are subject to the same bouts of 'flu or rheumatism as the rest of us (for that matter I also know slim meat-eaters who seemingly never have a day's illness!). The facile connection between eating meat and aggression (a theory derived, I believe, from a comparison between the fierce meat-killing lions and tigers and the peace-loving, plant-eating elephants) does seem to crumble when you consider that the most aggressively-minded man of recent history, Hitler, was – guess what – a vegetarian.

Thick onion tart (see page 293)

THE PROTEIN QUESTION

———————— ◆ ————————

The proteins in our food are essential for health, though to judge from some current advertising campaigns, which glorify products as being 'rich in protein' or 'high-protein', you might be forgiven for thinking that we need all the body-building ingredients that we can possibly push down our throats. The truth is that an average adult has a minimum protein requirement of 45 grams a day, and can do very nicely on 75 grams. This is a target that non-meat eaters can reach comfortably, with the only reservation being that they must find a *balance* of foods in their diet.

FIRST- AND SECOND-CLASS PROTEINS

Without getting over-scientific, proteins themselves are made up of what are called 'amino acids', eight of which are essential to our health. First-class proteins contain all eight essential amino acids, and these are found in meat and fish, poultry, eggs, cheese, milk and so on. But (as some meat-eaters point out) nuts and beans are second-class proteins, which is to say they are deficient in at least one of these amino acids.

That is not to say that eating only second-class protein foods cannot provide a balanced diet, however. Nature, as she usually does, has arranged things perfectly adequately by ensuring that the amino acid lacking in one plant food is supplied by another. A good example of plant foods complementing each other to provide the eight essential amino acids is beans on toast!

Should you wish to embark, full-time or part-time, on a non-meat diet, what you require to eat is a balanced selection of cheese, milk, cream, butter, eggs, pulses, nuts, wholewheat bread, grains, fresh vegetables and fresh or dried fruit.

One of the positive aspects of a vegetarian diet is that it actually provides plenty of variety, whereas meat-eaters can be inclined to stick endlessly to a meat-and-two-veg routine. A typical day's meals which provide all the necessary nutrients (and amino-acids) for a vegetarian could be: breakfast of muesli with milk, wholewheat toast and coffee. Lunch of something like cheeses, salad and wholemeal bread with fresh fruit to follow. And for dinner perhaps curried nut roast with vegetables, and yoghurt to follow. To me that sounds as delicious and appetising as any meat-centred diet.

But it is not the purpose of this chapter to convert anyone to vegetarianism, nor indeed to perpetuate the unnecessary distinctions between 'us' and 'them'. It is intended to offer a collection of delicious meatless main courses, which are both interesting and easy on the pocket.

Macaroni with leeks and bacon (see page 335)   289

SPINACH PASTIES

♦

(Makes 6)

These are very easy to make and you can use either a packet of frozen puff or filo (see page 291) pastry or the *Quick flaky pastry* given on page 515.

---

8 oz ready-made puff pastry (225 g) or quick flaky pastry made with 6 oz (175 g) flour and 4 oz (110 g) margarine (see page 515)

1 egg, beaten, to glaze

For the filling

8 oz cooked spinach, fresh or frozen (225 g) – if you use fresh you'll need 1 lb (450 g) to make 8 oz (225 g) cooked weight

1 oz butter (25 g)

2 oz cottage cheese (50 g) or fromage frais or quark

1½ oz Parmesan cheese (40 g), freshly grated

1 small clove garlic, finely crushed

¼ teaspoon dried dillweed

freshly grated nutmeg

lemon juice to taste

salt and freshly milled black pepper

Heat the oven to gas mark 7, 425°F (220°C).

A baking sheet, lightly-greased.

Begin by placing the fresh spinach in a thick-based saucepan with a little salt. Put a lid on and cook over a gentle heat until it collapses down and becomes tender (you may need to turn it over once). It will need 3–5 minutes in all, then drain it well in a colander. If the spinach is frozen, cook it without a lid until most of the moisture has evaporated. After that beat in the butter, cheeses and the rest of the filling ingredients, season and leave to cool.

Roll out the pastry fairly thinly, then, using a small saucepan lid or saucer, cut out six rounds about 6 inches (15 cm) in diameter. It will be necessary to re-roll the pastry scraps to get six rounds. Then put about a tablespoon of the cooled spinach mixture on one half of each pastry circle.

Brush the pastry edges with beaten egg, then bring one half of a pastry circle over to cover the spinach filling on the other half, pressing the edges together to seal well and form the pasty. Repeat this with the other five circles. Glaze with beaten egg, then place the six pasties on the greased baking sheet.

Make a small ventilation hole in the centre of each one and bake on the second shelf from the top of the oven for about 15 minutes or until the pasties have risen nicely and are golden-brown.

SPINACH FILO PARCELS

◆

(Makes 6)

Using the same filling ingredients and quantities as opposite for the *Spinach pasties*, you can make these alternative and very easy 'parcels' of filo pastry, which can readily be bought frozen. Serve them with some fromage frais mixed with finely chopped cucumber or with a *Fresh tomato sauce* (see page 329). If you're not using the whole packet of filo pastry, it can safely be re-frozen because there's no fat in it.

1 quantity spinach filling (see page 290)
3 sheets filo pastry, thawed
oil
2 teaspoons sesame seeds
salt and freshly milled black pepper

Pre-heat the oven to gas mark 6, 400°F (200°C).

For the filling, follow the instructions in the previous recipe. For the filo pastry, cut each sheet of pastry in four lengthways, and brush one strip lightly with oil (cover the remaining pastry to keep it from drying out). Place 1 tablespoonful of the filling near one end of the strip, a little in from the edge. Now fold one corner of the short end over the filling to form a triangle. Keep folding the triangle over until you get to the end of the strip. Repeat this process with the five remaining strips (you will have two strips left over which can be re-frozen with the rest of the pastry).

Lightly oil a baking sheet, place the parcels on it and sprinkle them with sesame seeds. Bake in the oven for 12–15 minutes until they are golden-brown.

BROWN RICE AND VEGETABLE GRATIN

◆

(Serves 2 people)

This is a really delicious supper dish for two people. The different textures and flavours of the vegetables, coupled with the firm 'bite' of the rice moistened with a cheese sauce all add up to proof that economy and simplicity can still come up trumps!

long-grain brown rice measured to the 8 fl oz (225 ml) level in a measuring jug
boiling water measured to the 16 fl oz (450 ml) level in a measuring jug
¹/₂ oz butter (10 g)
1 tablespoon oil
1 medium onion, roughly chopped
1 carrot, cut into ¹/₄ inch (5 mm) chunks
1 large celery stalk, cut into ¹/₄ inch (5 mm) chunks
salt
For the cheese sauce
1 oz butter (25 g)
1 oz plain flour (25 g)
10 fl oz cold milk (275 ml)
¹/₂ teaspoon made-up mustard
2 pinches of cayenne pepper
1¹/₂ oz strong Cheddar cheese (40 g), grated
For the vegetables
1 tablespoon oil
4 oz broccoli or cauliflower (110 g), divided into 1 inch (2.5 cm) florets
4 oz Chinese leaves or white cabbage (110 g), shredded into wide strips
To finish
1¹/₂ oz strong Cheddar cheese (40 g), grated

Start off in a thick-based saucepan by heating the butter and oil together, then add the onion, carrot and celery and soften them all for about 5 minutes. Next stir in the rice and, when it's all nicely coated with fat, add salt and boiling water. Put on a tight-fitting lid and cook gently, undisturbed, for 45 minutes.

Meanwhile make the sauce simply by placing all the ingredients (except the cheese) in a pan and whisking them over a medium heat until the butter has melted and the sauce has thickened and come to the boil. Simmer very gently for about 8 minutes, then stir in the grated cheese and set the pan aside while it melts.

Next, about 10 minutes before the rice is ready, heat the oil for the vegetables in a frying-pan and sauté the broccoli for 5 minutes, tossing it around to get it nicely toasted. Then add the shredded leaves and sauté them for 5 minutes or until cooked but still with some 'bite'.

Finally, pile the rice mixture into a large heatproof serving dish, followed by the fried vegetables; pour the cheese sauce over, then sprinkle the remaining grated cheese on top. Place the dish under a pre-heated grill until the topping is golden and bubbling.

VEGETARIAN GOULASH

◆

(Serves 4 people)

This is nicest made with summer vegetables.

2 tablespoons olive oil
2 medium onions, sliced
1 rounded dessertspoon wholemeal flour
1 heaped tablespoon Hungarian paprika
a couple of pinches of cayenne pepper
14 oz tin Italian tomatoes (400 g)
10 fl oz hot water (275 ml), enriched with 1 teaspoon tomato purée
8 oz cauliflower sprigs (225 g) – i.e. half a medium cauliflower head
8 oz new carrots (225 g), cut in chunks
8 oz courgettes (225 g), cut in chunks
8 oz new potatoes (225 g), halved
¹/₂ green pepper, de-seeded and chopped
5 fl oz soured cream or Greek yoghurt (150 ml)
salt and freshly milled black pepper

Pre-heat the oven to gas mark 4, 350°F (180°C).

Start by heating the oil in a flameproof casserole; fry the onions until softened, then stir in the flour, most of the paprika and the cayenne pepper. Cook for a minute, then stir in the contents of the tin of tomatoes, and the water. Bring the sauce up to boiling point, stirring all the time, then add all the vegetables. Season with salt and freshly milled black pepper, cover, then transfer to the pre-heated oven and bake for 30–40 minutes.

Finally stir in the soured cream or yoghurt, scatter the rest of the paprika on top and serve. Brown rice goes well with this, as do green spinach noodles lightly tossed in butter.

THICK ONION TART

◆

(Serves 4–6 people)

The secret of this tart, with its wholewheat cheese pastry, is to cook the onions until they almost caramelise so they form a lovely thick, brown layer over the base. (Illus. opposite p. 288.)

For the pastry
2 oz self-raising flour (50 g)
2 oz wholewheat flour (50 g)
a pinch of salt
¹/₂ teaspoon mustard powder
2 oz margarine (50 g) or butter
1¹/₂ oz Cheddar cheese (40 g), grated
cold water, to mix

For the filling
1¹/₂ lb onions (700 g), chopped fairly small
2 oz butter (50 g)
2 eggs, beaten
4 fl oz double cream (110 g), or natural yoghurt or milk
1 tablespoon grated Cheddar cheese
salt and freshly milled black pepper

Pre-heat the oven, and a baking sheet, to gas mark 4, 350°F (180°C). An 8 inch (20 cm) fluted flan tin, greased.

First make the pastry by sifting the flours, salt and mustard powder into a mixing bowl, then rubbing in the fat until the mixture becomes crumbly. Then stir in the grated cheese, and add enough cold water to make a dough that leaves the bowl clean. Wrap the dough in a polythene bag and leave to rest in the fridge for 30 minutes. Meanwhile you can be preparing the filling.

Melt the butter in a thick-based saucepan, then add the chopped onions, stir to get them well coated in the butter, and cook them (uncovered) over a medium heat for about 30 minutes until they have reduced and turned a deep brown. Give them a stir from time to time to prevent them catching on the bottom of the pan and, if at the end of the time they haven't turned almost mahogany-brown, turn the heat up and cook for a further 10 minutes.

Then roll out the pastry to line the flan tin, prick the base with a fork, place it on the pre-heated baking sheet, and bake in the centre of the oven for 15 minutes. After that remove from the oven and brush the inside of the pastry case with a little beaten egg (from the filling), and return to the oven for another 5 minutes.

Then spread the onions all over the base of the flan, whisk the beaten eggs together with the cream and some seasoning, and pour as much of this mixture over the onions as possible (depending on how much the onions have reduced, there may be a tiny spot left over – though probably not). Finally sprinkle the cheese over the top, return the flan to the oven and bake for 30 minutes till the filling is puffy and golden-brown.

CABBAGE LEAVES STUFFED WITH RICE

◆

(Serves 2 people)

You can make all sorts of stuffings for cabbage leaves if you follow this basic recipe – you could use lentils or chopped nuts or whatever ingredients happen to be handy.

1 smallish head of spring cabbage
12 oz ripe tomatoes (350 g), peeled and chopped
salt and freshly milled black pepper
For the stuffing
long-grain brown rice measured to the 5 fl oz (150 ml) level in a measuring jug
boiling water measured to the 10 fl oz (275 ml) level in a measuring jug
2 tablespoons olive oil
1 medium onion, chopped
1 green pepper, de-seeded and finely chopped
2–3 spring onions, finely chopped
a pinch of cayenne pepper

Cook the rice first of all: heat the oil in a saucepan and fry the onion and green pepper in it for 5 minutes, then add the rice, give it a stir, and pour in the boiling water. Season with salt, cover and simmer for about 45 minutes or until all the liquid has been absorbed and the grains are tender. Turn the cooked rice into a bowl and leave it to cool a little.

Meanwhile prepare the cabbage, discarding the tough outer leaves, then carefully peeling off about six or seven whole leaves. In each one of these make a V-shaped cut with a sharp knife to snip out the hard stalky bits. Next chop up the heart of the cabbage and bring a large saucepan of water to the boil. Blanch the whole leaves and chopped cabbage, separately, by cooking them in the boiling water for 5 minutes.

Then drain the cabbage in a colander, rinse in cold water and drain again. Shake off as much moisture from the leaves as you can and wrap them in a cloth or piece of kitchen paper to dry.

Now heat the oven to gas mark 4, 350°F (180°C). Then add the chopped spring onions and the chopped cabbage to the cooled rice, with a generous pinch of cayenne and some salt and pepper.

Now take a heaped tablespoon of the rice-and-chopped-cabbage mixture and wrap it in one of the prepared leaves – squeezing gently until you have a neat, firm package.

Fill and roll the remaining cabbage leaves with the rest of the stuffing, then pack the parcels closely together in a casserole. Season with salt and pepper, pour the chopped tomatoes over the parcels, cover and bake for 1 hour in the oven.

DOLMADES (STUFFED VINE LEAVES)

---- ◆ ----

(Serves 6 people as a first course or 4 as a lunch dish)

This is one of the nicest vegetarian dishes I know. If you live in an area where there are Greek or Cypriot shops, you should be able to get hold of some vine leaves. If not, use raw spinach leaves or the blanched inside leaves of young spring cabbage.

12 fresh large vine leaves, approx. 2 oz (50 g) in weight
long-grain rice measured to the 3 fl oz (75 ml) level in a measuring jug
boiling water measured to the 6 fl oz (170 ml) level in a measuring jug
1½ tablespoons olive oil
1 small onion, chopped
1 oz pine nuts (25 g)
1 lb tomatoes (450 g), peeled and chopped, or 14 oz tin tomatoes (400 g)
2 teaspoons tomato purée
1½ teaspoons dried oregano
1 tablespoon chopped fresh mint
1 tablespoon chopped fresh parsley
¼ teaspoon ground cinnamon
3 small cloves garlic, crushed
juice of ½ lemon
salt and freshly milled black pepper

Bring a frying-pan of water to boiling point, then add the vine leaves all in one bunch and blanch them for about 1 minute, turning the bunch over after 30 seconds. Then empty them into a colander, rinse under cold running water and, when drained, spread out each leaf flat – vein side uppermost.

For the filling, cook the rice in double its volume of boiling salted water until tender. Heat the oil in a frying-pan and fry the onion and pine nuts to colour them, then tip in the cooked rice together with one-third of the tomatoes, the tomato purée, ½ teaspoon of oregano, the mint, parsley, cinnamon and 2 cloves of crushed garlic. Stir well, cook for a couple of minutes, then, removing the pan from the heat, add the lemon juice, salt and pepper.

Now spoon a dessertspoonful of the rice mixture onto the stalk end of a vine leaf and fold the leaf over once, squeezing and pressing the filling to a sausage-shape. Then tuck in the sides of the leaf and continue to roll up to make a tight, neat, cylindrical parcel.

When all the vine leaves are filled, spoon half the remainder of the tomatoes into the base of a small flameproof casserole or heavy saucepan. Now pack the dolmades in tightly and spoon the remaining tomatoes, garlic and oregano on top. Add a seasoning of salt and pepper. Now press a suitably-sized plate over the dolmades to prevent them unrolling during cooking, cover the casserole with a lid, and simmer very, very gently on top of the stove for 2 hours.

Serve the dolmades hot or cold with the juices spooned over them.

HAZELNUT AND VEGETABLE BURGERS
♦

(Serves 4 people)

Many of the so-called beef burgers of today taste of anything but beef – and those that include TVP (Textured Vegetable Protein) can be a very rubbery consistency. By contrast, these made with nuts and vegetables are simple, honest and quite delicious.

2 medium carrots, grated
2 celery stalks, finely chopped
1 medium onion, finely chopped
2 tablespoons finely chopped cabbage
2 tablespoons brown breadcrumbs
2 oz hazelnuts (50 g), ground
2 tablespoons wheatgerm
a couple of pinches of cayenne pepper
a pinch of ground mace
1/2 teaspoon dried or 1 teaspoon chopped fresh mixed herbs
1 egg
1 tablespoon tomato purée
1 tablespoon natural yoghurt
salt and freshly milled black pepper
For the coating
1 egg, beaten
approx. 4 oz dry wholewheat breadcrumbs (110 g)

These are quite simple to make. Having done the chopping, grating and grinding, put all the ingredients (down to and including the herbs) in a bowl and mix well. In another bowl place the egg, tomato purée and yoghurt and whisk, then add this mixture to the vegetable mixture and season to taste.

Next form the mixture into eight small patties. Cover and chill for a few hours in the refrigerator. This will help to firm up the patties and prevent them breaking during cooking.

Shortly before you are ready to cook the burgers, heat the oven to gas mark 4, 350°F (180°C). Then dip each one into the beaten egg first, then into the wholewheat breadcrumbs, and place on a well-oiled baking sheet. Bake for 15 minutes, then turn the burgers over with care and bake for a further 15 minutes.

Serve with a home-made tomato sauce or Greek yoghurt, and brown pilau rice.

CURRIED NUT ROAST

◆

(Serves 4 people)

This is a perfect recipe to serve to anyone who feels that vegetarian food might be boring – it's never failed to please. Meat-eaters are always amazed that anything that doesn't contain meat can taste so good!

8 oz hazel or Brazil nuts or walnuts (225 g), finely chopped
2 medium onions, finely chopped
1 medium green pepper, de-seeded and finely chopped
cooking oil
3 oz wholewheat breadcrumbs (75 g)
1 clove garlic, crushed
1 teaspoon dried or 2 teaspoons chopped fresh mixed herbs
1 tablespoon mild curry powder or 1 heaped teaspoon hot Madras curry powder
8 oz tomatoes (225 g), peeled and chopped
1 egg, beaten
salt and freshly milled black pepper

Pre-heat the oven to gas mark 7, 425°F (220°C).

A 7 inch (18 cm) square cake tin, greased.

Begin by gently frying the onions and chopped pepper in a little oil until they're softened – about 10 minutes.

Meanwhile, mix the nuts and breadcrumbs together in a large bowl, adding the garlic, herbs and curry powder. Then stir in the onions, pepper and tomatoes, mix very thoroughly and season. Now add the beaten egg to bind the mixture together. Finally, pack the mixture into the prepared tin and bake for 30–40 minutes until golden.

This can be served hot with *Spiced pilau rice* (see page 275), yoghurt, mango chutney, or a *Fresh tomato sauce* (see page 329). It's also very good served cold with a salad.

PROVENÇAL VEGETABLE STEW (RATATOUILLE)

◆

(Serves 4 people)

This famous French recipe is best made in the autumn when the vegetables needed for it are cheap and plentiful.

2 large aubergines
3 medium courgettes
2 medium onions
2 red or green peppers
4 large tomatoes or 14 oz (400 g) tin Italian tomatoes, well drained
2 cloves garlic, crushed
4 tablespoons olive oil
1 tablespoon chopped fresh basil
salt and freshly milled black pepper

This can be a most attractive dish – but not if it ends up mushy. So to avoid this, make sure you don't cut up the vegetables too small (they must retain their individuality), and also make sure you get rid of the excess moisture in the courgettes and aubergines by draining at the start.

Begin, then, by wiping the aubergines and cutting them into 1 inch (2.5 cm) slices, then cut each slice in half; the courgettes should be wiped as well and cut into 1 inch (2.5 cm) slices. Now put the whole lot into a colander, sprinkle generously with salt, press them down with a suitably-sized plate and put weights (or other heavy objects) on top of the plate. Let them stand for about 1 hour – the salt will draw out any bitterness along with excess moisture.

Meanwhile chop up the onions roughly, de-seed and core the peppers and chop these up too. Skin the tomatoes (plunging them into boiling water for a couple of minutes is the best way to loosen the skins), then quarter them and take out the seeds.

To cook the ratatouille: fry the onions and garlic in the oil gently in a large saucepan for a good 10 minutes, then add the peppers. Dry the pieces of courgette and aubergine with kitchen paper, then add them to the saucepan. Next add the basil and a seasoning of salt and pepper, stir once really well, then simmer very gently (covered) for 30 minutes. After that time add the tomato flesh (roughly chopped), taste to check the seasoning and cook for a further 15 minutes with the lid off.

MIXED VEGETABLES À LA GRECQUE

◆

(Serves 2 or 4 people)

This is my number one vegetarian dish. It makes an excellent lunch dish with a brown rice salad (page 446) with a herb vinaigrette (page 438), but mostly I serve it as a starter on crisp lettuce leaves with crusty bread to dip into the juices. You can of course vary the vegetables.

6 button onions
2 oz dry weight kidney beans (50 g), soaked and cooked as described on pages 307 and 308
4 oz cauliflower (110 g), broken into 1 inch (2.5 cm) florets
4 oz small to medium mushrooms (110 g), halved
4 tablespoons olive oil
1 medium onion, finely chopped
1 fat clove garlic, crushed
2 tablespoons wine vinegar
1 lb tomatoes (450 g), peeled and quartered, or 14 oz tin Italian tomatoes (400 g)
1 teaspoon dried oregano
1 heaped teaspoon whole coriander seeds, crushed
8 black peppercorns, lightly crushed
juice of 1 medium lemon
2 fl oz water (55 ml) mixed with 1 heaped teaspoon tomato purée
salt and freshly milled black pepper

To serve
2 tablespoons chopped fresh parsley
2 spring onions (including green tops), finely chopped

Heat 2 tablespoons of the olive oil in a heavy-based pan and soften the onion for 5 minutes. Then add the garlic, wine vinegar, tomatoes, oregano, coriander, peppercorns, lemon juice, water and tomato purée, and some salt. Bring to the boil and stir in the button onions. Now cover the pan and simmer for 20 minutes.

Then add the cooked and drained beans, the cauliflower and mushrooms, cover the pan again and simmer for a further 20 minutes, stirring the vegetables round once or twice during the cooking time. After 20 minutes test the vegetables with a skewer: they should be tender but still firm. Taste and check the seasoning.

Pour the contents of the pan into a shallow dish and leave to cool. I think this dish is best left overnight but a few hours will do. To serve, sprinkle the vegetables with the rest of the olive oil, then scatter the chopped parsley and spring onions on top.

SAUTÉED MIXED VEGETABLES

◆

(Serves 4 people)

Kate Bush – whose performances both singing and dancing project a tremendous amount of energy – is a vegetarian. This recipe and the two that follow it are some of her favourites. They were devised by her sister-in-law Judith and make up a complete meal. It has become a firm favourite for supper in my home.

8 oz onions (225 g), roughly sliced
6 oz carrots (175 g), sliced – approx. 3 small carrots
8 oz mushrooms (225 g), sliced
6 oz green peppers (175 g), cut into ½ inch (1 cm) strips – approx. 2 small peppers
12 oz tomatoes (350 g), quartered
2½ tablespoons sunflower seed oil
salt and freshly milled black pepper

Begin by heating the oil in a large saucepan with a lid (or a shallow casserole). Add the onions and soften them for a minute or two before adding the carrots. Cook for a further couple of minutes, then add the mushrooms, green pepper and tomatoes. Stir and season, then put the lid on and, keeping the heat fairly low, leave the vegetables to steam in their own juice for 20–25 minutes.

Note The vegetables can be varied according to season. Curry spices can also be added to this dish while the oil is heating in the pan. A good combination is: 2 crushed cardamom pods; ½ teaspoon crushed cumin seeds; ¼ teaspoon crushed dried chilli; 1 teaspoon chopped fresh root ginger (or ½ teaspoon ground ginger); 1 teaspoon ground turmeric; 1 chopped clove garlic.

Serve the vegetables, spiced or otherwise, with brown rice (see page 274) and the following two side-dishes.

CUCUMBER AND YOGHURT SALAD

◆

This is good to serve with any curry dish, and I also like it at barbecues as a sauce to go with kebabs etc.

4 inches unpeeled cucumber (10 cm), thinly sliced then cut into strips
10 oz natural yoghurt (275 g)
juice of ½ lemon
1 large clove garlic, crushed
1 tablespoon snipped chives
salt

Simply combine all the ingredients in a bowl. Serve with rice and the sautéed vegetables on page 301 plus a sprinkling of toasted seeds (below).

TOASTED SESAME AND SUNFLOWER SEEDS

◆

These can be sprinkled on any vegetarian dish to add crunchiness and extra flavour.

2 oz sesame seeds (50 g)
2 oz sunflower seeds (50 g)
1 dessertspoon soy sauce

In a shallow heatproof dish, mix the two lots of seeds together, then sprinkle in the soy sauce and mix thoroughly. Now spread them out evenly and place the dish under a hot grill to toast them for 4 minutes – shaking the dish a couple of times to even them out. If you don't want to use them straightaway, they keep well in a screw-top jar.

SCONE PIZZA

(Serves 2 people)

This recipe was given to me by a twelve-year-old on a children's TV programme. I know it has proved extremely popular with other children.

4 oz self-raising flour (110 g)

½ teaspoon salt

1 oz margarine (25 g)

2 tablespoons milk mixed with 2 tablespoons water

For the topping

2 tinned tomatoes, well drained and mashed together
with 1 teaspoon tomato purée

2 oz Cheddar or Mozzarella cheese (50 g), grated

½ onion, very finely chopped

3 mushrooms, thinly sliced

1 teaspoon dried oregano

salt and freshly milled black pepper

a few black olives, pitted and chopped (optional)

a few tinned anchovy fillets, drained (optional)

Pre-heat the oven to gas mark 7, 425°F (220°C).

A baking sheet, well-greased.

First of all sift the flour into a bowl, add the salt, then rub in the margarine. Next *gradually* add the milk and water to mix the ingredients to a soft dough – you may not need all the liquid.

Now roll out the dough to a circle approximately ½ inch (1 cm) thick and place it on the baking sheet. Spread it with the mashed tomato, sprinkle the grated cheese on top of that, then decorate with the chopped onion and sliced mushrooms, and season it with the oregano and some salt and pepper. Then pop it into the oven to bake for 15–20 minutes or until golden-brown and bubbling on top. A few chopped olives would make a nice addition to the topping or, for non-vegetarians, you could use a few anchovies.

SEE ALSO

A risotto for spring
Brown rice, lentil and mushroom salad
Buckwheat and vegetable pie
Courgette and cheese quiche
Egg and lentil curry
Hummus bi tahina
Italian bean and pasta soup
Lentil and vegetable moussaka
Minestrone with macaroni
Mushroom and onion quiche
Non-meat loaf
Spiced chick pea cutlets
Vegetarian shepherd's pie

PULSES

◆

With our food there seems to be an inexorable process at work: yesterday's poor-man's diet is today's luxury. It's hard to believe you could once buy oysters, fifty of them, for a shilling; or that the fish-porters at Billingsgate once went on strike because they were getting too much salmon for lunch! The plain fact is, of course, that over the past century our consumption has far outstripped our resources, except in one rather neglected area – pulses (that is to say, the family of beans, peas and lentils). Pulses for thousands of years have been the staple diet of poor countries all over the world, from China to Mexico.

Sadly, that is still their image. It must be rather humiliating to be a bean: a 'bean-feast' was a meal judged fit only for workmen, and if you 'hadn't got a bean' you really had not got anything at all. Yet ancient peoples were far more respectful than we are: some appointed a god in charge of beans, and others never buried their dead without a supply of beans to take them into the other world.

Doubtless it will be pointed out that we still consume beans in Britain in absolutely vast quantities. I recall a cartoon at the time when de Gaulle was objecting to this country joining the Common Market: it showed the General recoiling from a report on how many million tons of baked beans the British consumed in a year. '*Mon Dieu!*' was his reaction. Nowadays, it is true, we can find all kinds of varieties of tinned beans on the supermarket shelf – yet they all contain sugar in differing amounts, or if they don't it is replaced by saccharin. I have still to be given a convincing explanation why any of it is necessary.

NUTRITIONAL VALUE FOR MONEY

◆

I believe that our attitudes to pulses have changed. There is no doubt about their nutritional value: according to a report by the Consumers Association they took four of the top ten places in the list of vegetable proteins. (Vegetable proteins, are, as already mentioned, called 'second-class proteins' because they lack the important amino-acids that are found in meat, fish, dairy foods, etc.; but this is not to undermine their value – the missing amino-acids are found in flour or rice or pasta, so a plateful of beans-on-toast will provide you with the same amount of protein as beefsteak.) The other nutritional benefit of pulses is that they can provide us with a significant percentage of the natural fibre we need for a healthy diet – in fact are one of the foods that are said to help to *reduce* cholesterol levels.

Varieties of Pulses

First let us run through the commoner types of pulse – there are so many varieties it would be tedious to include them all. People who live alongside immigrant communities will doubtless find some pulses not mentioned here, but those described below can be found on some supermarket shelves or in specialised food shops.

ADUKI BEANS

These are tiny, red-brown beans with a little white thread down one side. Because of their size they make perfect partners to brown rice, to give a good protein balance (see the recipe on page 318).

BUTTER BEANS

These are large, flat beans, cream in colour. Boiled on their own (as I remember them at school) they do tend to be dull: but they make a good thick soup, and are useful if haricot beans are unavailable as they respond well to a well-flavoured vinaigrette dressing with lots of chopped shallots and parsley strewn over.

CHICK PEAS

Light brown, nutty-looking beans, which need careful soaking (definitely overnight) and as much as 3 hours' cooking. But they are worth it in my opinion with their lovely nutty flavour. They can be made into cutlets, soups and salads, or puréed with oil and lemon to a paste to make what the Greeks call *Hummus* (page 313).

HARICOT BEANS

There are two main types of haricot bean: the long, thin, shiny-ivory one which the Italians call *fagioli*, sometimes *canellini*. These are delicious in salads, stews, and Tuscan bean and pasta soup; they are also the kind used in France, cooked in the Breton way and served with mutton and lamb. The other type of haricot is the small round one of tinned baked bean fame. I think they are inferior to, and lack the flavour of, their handsomer cousins.

LENTILS

There are in fact over sixty varieties of lentil. But as far as whole lentils are concerned there are three main types that concern us. Most popular are the green-brown variety (as I call them since they're usually a mixture of both colours) that look like little pills. I love their flavour, and if I never had any more meat I'd be content with a plentiful supply of these around. There is a smaller version, sometimes called Chinese lentils, which are more red-brown and also rarer and more expensive. The French *lentils du puys* are slate-grey and, if you can find them, have a very superior flavour. *Split lentils* are literally filleted lentils, with the skins removed and split naturally into two halves. They cook to a mush very quickly and are suitable for thick purées and soups.

RED KIDNEY BEANS

Not surprisingly, these shiny-polished beans are both red and kidney-shaped. They have a delicious flavour, a must for *Chilli con carne* (page 311). They make a good salad and will adapt themselves to any recipe for bean soup. At one time there was a 'scare' about them causing tummy upsets. It was caused, simply and solely, because they were not being cooked properly. Provided they are boiled for at least 10 minutes before soaking, there won't ever be a problem.

SOYA BEANS

Smallish, round, and a pale yellow-cream colour. They need careful soaking and long cooking, and are rather mealy-textured when cooked. For me their flavour and texture are not up to those of white haricots.

SPLIT PEAS

These halved dried peas can be deep green or golden-yellow. I think the green ones are superior in flavour, but both are suitable for thick, warming pea soups, or for purées or cutlets.

WHOLE DRIED PEAS

The ones used to make 'mushy peas'. They are delicious, with more character than tinned or frozen peas. Especially good with pork or boiled bacon, or made into the traditional *Pease pudding* (page 310).

Other varieties of pulses are much rarer over here, though they play an important part in the cooking of other countries. The white, flat *Lima beans* are used in America for soups and salads, and *black-eyed beans* (cream with a 'black eye') are served with ham. In the Caribbean *black beans* are served spiced or in a sauce as a side-dish, as are *Egyptian beans* (round and brown) in the Middle East. The beautiful pale green *flageolets* in France are a high-class variation of the haricot, and quite delicious.

BUYING AND STORING PULSES
———————— ◆ ————————

Although British farmers are experimenting with growing different types of pulse, most of them are imported at the moment. The vegetables are harvested annually and dried in the autumn, so the year's crop usually begins to reach us around November. Obviously one of the big advantages of dried vegetable pulses is that they do store easily and – provided suitable soaking time is taken into consideration – can be used fairly spontaneously.

However, it is wrong to think that, for cooking, pulses keep indefinitely. After about a year they start to harden to such an extent that sometimes no amount of cooking will soften them. Therefore it is important to buy them from somewhere reliable (and if you do get landed with a batch that is more ancient than it should be, take them back and complain). Also if your memory is as bad as mine, place a little sticker on the storage jar – I use large glass ones – to remind you when you actually purchased the contents. I've found that a year or even 18 months can slip by almost unnoticed in the larder.

SOAKING
———————— ◆ ————————

Most, though not all, dried vegetables have to be soaked to replace the moisture lost in the drying process. Overnight soaking may seem a long time: in fact I once mentioned it on a radio programme, and one listener wrote insisting that beans should never be soaked that long or they would be likely to ferment. (Just for the record – I checked with Queen Elizabeth College of Nutrition, who confirmed that they would have to soak under normal conditions for 36–48 hours before fermentation.)

So, if it's convenient, overnight soaking is perfectly all right except for soya beans and red and white kidney beans. For these, you will need to cover with cold water, bring to the boil, boil for 10 minutes, then leave to soak for up to 2 hours depending on the type of bean. You need about 4 pints (2.25 litres) of soaking water for every 8 oz (225 g) of beans.

COOKING
———————— ◆ ————————

Most pulses except split peas and lentils need rather long cooking: 1½–3 hours according to variety. Perhaps the most important rule is *not* to add any salt until the end of the cooking, which is quite logical really: salt draws out moisture, which is the opposite of the exercise, and hardens the skin, so even a small amount of salt in the soaking or cooking water will simply retard the process. Adding salt at the end makes them taste just as good, I find, but you should taste carefully to add just the right quantity.

DIGESTING PULSES

◆

Dried vegetables in the past have acquired a somewhat bad reputation, and are said to cause flatulence. This shouldn't be the case if the beans are properly soaked and carefully cooked. There is some evidence that throwing away the soaking water and using fresh for cooking helps to eliminate the problem. So if you suffer from bean side-effects I suggest you do just that.

ITALIAN BEAN AND PASTA SOUP

◆

(Serves 4–6 people)

This beautiful thick Tuscan peasant soup is rather hefty for a first course, so I suggest you serve it for lunch with just a salad and some cheese to follow.

8 oz dried white haricot beans (225 g)
4 oz small-cut macaroni (110 g)
1 large onion, chopped small
2 tablespoons olive oil
2 cloves garlic, crushed
2¹/₂ tablespoons tomato purée
1 teaspoon dried or 1 dessertspoon chopped fresh basil
salt and freshly milled black pepper
To serve
2–3 oz Parmesan cheese (50–75 g), grated

Place the beans in a saucepan, then add 3 pints (1.75 litres) cold water to them, bring them to the boil, boil for 1 minute, then turn the heat off and let them soak for 2 hours.

Now gently fry the onion in olive oil together with the garlic for about 10 minutes. Then add the tomato purée and basil, stir for a minute, and pour in the beans and the water they were soaking in. Now bring the soup up to simmering point, cover and simmer gently for about an hour. When the time's up season with salt and pepper, then either put half the soup through a sieve or blend in a liquidiser or food processor. Return the puréed half to the pan, bring to simmering point, then add the macaroni and simmer for a further 10–12 minutes, stirring from time to time. Serve the soup with lots of freshly grated Parmesan cheese to sprinkle over.

THICK BEAN AND BACON SOUP
◆

(Serves 6 people)

8 oz dried butter beans (225 g)
2 pints water (1.2 litres)
1 bay leaf
4 oz streaky bacon or offcuts (110 g)
1 oz butter (25 g)
2 tablespoons oil
1 onion, finely chopped
1 leek, cleaned and finely chopped
2 smallish celery stalks, finely chopped
1 large clove garlic, crushed
approx. 5 fl oz milk (150 ml)
2 tablespoons chopped fresh parsley
salt and freshly milled black pepper

First put the butter beans and water in a saucepan and bring them to the boil, then boil for a minute, cover and leave on one side for about an hour. Now add the bay leaf and any bacon rinds you may have to the pan, bring to the boil again, cover and simmer for 45 minutes (removing the bay leaf and rinds at the end).

Meanwhile heat the butter and oil in a large saucepan, add the chopped vegetables, then chop up the bacon small and add that too. Stir to coat everything with butter and oil, and cook over a low heat for about 10 minutes.

Now tip the cooked beans and their cooking liquor into the pan containing the bacon and vegetables, add the garlic, cover and continue simmering for a further 20 minutes or until the beans and vegetables are soft. Then mash them against the sides of the pan with a large fork, and thin down the soup with milk. Reheat, add the chopped parsley, taste to check the seasoning and serve.

THICK PEA SOUP

♦

(Serves 6 people)

Sprinkle crisp fried croûtons of bread over this just before serving.

3¹/₂ pints stock (2 litres), plus a little extra if needed
12 oz dried split peas, yellow or green (350 g)
2 oz butter (50 g)
4 thick rashers bacon, de-rinded and diced
1 medium onion, roughly chopped
1 celery stalk, chopped
1 large carrot, sliced
salt and freshly milled black pepper

First strain 3¹/₂ pints (2 litres) stock into a large saucepan, then bring just up to simmering point, add the split peas, cover and simmer very gently for about 30 minutes (there is no need to soak the split peas first).

Meanwhile, heat 1 oz (25 g) of the butter in another saucepan and add the bacon and prepared vegetables; cook them over a medium heat for about 15 minutes until softened and nicely golden.

Add the softened vegetables to the stock and split peas, season lightly with salt and freshly milled black pepper, then cover and simmer very gently for a further 40–50 minutes.

When the soup is ready, either press the whole lot through a sieve or liquidise in an electric blender. Now return it to the saucepan, taste to check the seasoning, and add a little more stock if it seems to need thinning a bit.

Before serving, melt the remaining butter into it.

PEASE PUDDING

♦

(Serves 6–8 people)

A real old-fashioned pease pudding is sometimes made in a cloth but more conveniently, I think, in a basin like this.

1 lb whole dried peas (450 g), soaked overnight
a generous pinch of thyme
1 bay leaf
1 small onion, quartered
1 oz butter (25 g)
1 large egg, beaten
salt and freshly milled black pepper

Put the peas, herbs and quartered onion together in a saucepan and cover with plenty of cold water. Bring to the boil, cover and boil gently for 2 hours or until the peas are tender (a sign that they are ready is that they start splitting their skins). Then drain the peas in a colander and discard the bay leaf – the onion can stay in.

Now mash the peas to a pulp. Beat in the butter and egg and, when the butter has melted, taste and season with salt and freshly milled black pepper. Pack the pea purée into a well-buttered 2–2½ pint (1.2–1.5 litre) pudding basin. Put a sheet of greased foil over the top and secure with string. Then steam the pudding over boiling water for 1 hour. Uncover and turn it out onto a warmed plate. Cut in wedges like a steamed pudding to serve.

Pease pudding can be served with boiled bacon or boiled beef and any left-overs can be fried in butter the next day.

CHILLI CON CARNE
♦

(Serves 4 people)

This is very often made with minced beef, but I think it's far nicer made with chuck steak cut into very small pieces. It's medium hot as it is, so if you like things hotter or milder you can adjust the quantity of chilli, but this dish should be hot and spicy, and in my opinion cutting down the spiciness simply reduces it to an ordinary stew. So go carefully with the chilli by all means, but don't relegate it out of existence.

8 oz dried red kidney beans (225 g)
1 lb chuck steak (450 g), cut into very small pieces
approx. 1 tablespoon beef dripping or oil
2 medium onions, chopped
1 fat clove garlic, crushed
1 rounded tablespoon flour
2 heaped tablespoons tomato purée
1 pint hot stock (570 ml)
1 level teaspoon crushed dried chilli pepper or chilli powder
1 large green pepper, de-seeded and chopped
salt

First of all start with the beans. Cover them with cold water, bring them to boiling point and boil for 10 minutes. Then turn the heat off and let them soak for an hour. Towards the end of the soaking time, pre-heat the oven to gas mark 2, 300°F (150°C).

Now in a flameproof casserole melt the beef dripping or oil and gently cook the onions and garlic in it for about 6 minutes. Then turn the heat up, add the beef and brown it well, stirring it around a bit.

Next sprinkle in the flour, stir it in to soak up the juices, then combine the tomato purée with the hot stock and add it gradually to the meat and onions.

Now add the chilli, drain the red beans thoroughly, add them, and bring to simmering point. Put a lid on, then transfer the casserole to the oven and cook for about 1½ hours. When the time's up remove the lid, stir in the chopped pepper, cover again and cook a further 30 minutes. Add salt as necessary before serving.

CHILLADAS

(Serves 8 people)

These lightly spiced lentil cakes flavoured with green peppers really are just as good as having meat.

1 lb whole green-brown lentils (450 g)
1½ pints hot water (850 ml)
4 oz butter or vegetable margarine (110 g)
2 onions, finely chopped
2 cloves garlic, crushed
2 carrots, finely chopped
1 large or 2 small green peppers, de-seeded and chopped small
1 teaspoon cayenne pepper
½ teaspoon ground mace
1 teaspoon dried mixed herbs
4 teaspoons tomato purée
salt and freshly milled black pepper
For the coating
1 egg, beaten
dry fine breadcrumbs
groundnut oil for shallow-frying

Wash the lentils and place them in a saucepan with the hot water. Let them come to the boil, then cover and simmer very gently for about an hour or until all the liquid has been absorbed and the lentils are mushy. Towards the end of their cooking time, heat the butter in a frying-pan and soften the onions, garlic and carrots in it for 5 minutes, then add the chopped pepper and cook for a further 5–10 minutes.

Next, season the lentils and tip them into a bowl to mash them to a pulp with a fork – though not too smooth. Now mix in the softened vegetables together with the cayenne, mace, herbs and tomato purée – then divide the mixture and shape it into 24 small rounds. To cook them, dip them first into beaten egg, then into the breadcrumbs, and shallow-fry them in about ¼ inch (5 mm) of groundnut oil till golden on both sides. Drain on kitchen paper, and serve with a home-made tomato sauce (see page 329).

HUMMUS BI TAHINA
♦

(Serves 6 people)

If you want to make the proper authentic version of this you'll need to hunt out some tahina paste, which is available at specialist food shops and health-food shops.

4 oz chick peas (110 g)
juice of 2 lemons
2 fat cloves garlic
4 tablespoons olive oil
5 fl oz tahina paste (150 ml)
cayenne pepper
salt
To garnish
olive oil
chopped parsley

To begin with put the chick peas in a saucepan and cover them well with boiling water, then put on one side to soak for 2 hours.

Next bring them to the boil, cover and simmer gently for approximately 1½–2 hours until the chick peas are tender. Then drain them – reserve the cooking liquid – and put the chick peas into a blender together with the lemon juice, garlic, olive oil and 5 fl oz (150 ml) of the cooking liquid. Switch on and blend, adding the tahina paste to the mixture as the blades revolve. (It will probably be necessary to stop the blender every now and then to push the mixture down into the goblet.) The consistency should be something like a mayonnaise and, if you think it's too thick, add a little more of the cooking liquid. Taste and season with salt and cayenne pepper.

Place in a serving bowl and garnish with a thin layer of olive oil, some chopped parsley and a pinch or two of cayenne pepper. Have plenty of fresh, hot, crusty bread as an accompaniment.

CASSOULET

◆

(Serves 6 people)

Although this was originally a French peasant dish, I think it's particularly good for entertaining in winter because it's all done in advance and doesn't mind waiting in the oven if you want to eat a bit later than planned.

12 oz dried white haricot beans (350 g)
½ shoulder of lamb – the inside half, not the leg half, and ask the butcher to take out the bone for you
1 lb lean belly pork (450 g), boned and cut into strips
8 oz streaky bacon in one piece (225 g)
8 oz garlic sausage in one piece (225 g)
1 sprig thyme
1 small sprig rosemary
a few parsley stalks
1 bay leaf
2 cloves garlic
4 juniper berries
2 medium onions, chopped
5 oz fresh white breadcrumbs (150 g)
salt and freshly milled black pepper

It's not necessary to soak the beans overnight, but wash them well in about two changes of water before placing them in a saucepan with about 3 pints (1.75 litres) of cold water. Bring to simmering point and after about 2 minutes put aside and leave for an hour for the beans to soak in the liquid.

Meanwhile prepare the other ingredients by first of all trimming any really excess fat off the lamb and cutting the meat into very large (2 inch/5 cm) chunks. Then, using a sharp knife, pare the rind as thinly as possible from both the bacon and the pork, and chop the rinds into very small pieces.

Leave the pork slices whole, but chop the bacon into six chunks; also peel and chop the garlic sausage into largish pieces. Now tie in a little bunch the thyme, rosemary, parsley stalks and bay leaf, then skin and crush the cloves of garlic; also crush the juniper berries using either a pestle and mortar or the back of a tablespoon.

When the beans have finished soaking drain them into a colander, throw away the water, then put them in a large saucepan together with the bacon, chopped bacon and pork rinds, garlic sausage, onions, garlic, juniper, bunch of herbs and some freshly milled black pepper, but no salt as there will be some in the bacon. Cover with about 2½ pints (1.5 litres) cold water, bring to simmering point and simmer gently for 1½ hours.

Half-way through the cooking time pre-heat the oven to gas mark 3, 325°F (170°C), and roast the lamb and pork for 45 minutes.

When the meat is cooked the bean mixture will also be ready, so empty the contents of the saucepan into a sieve or colander placed over a bowl, let it drain, reserve the liquid and remove the herbs. Then in a buttered 5 pint (2.8 litre) earthenware casserole arrange half the bean mixture over the base, placing the pieces of lamb and pork on top. Season with salt and freshly milled black pepper, then add the rest of the bean mixture. Now add to the casserole 15 fl oz (425 ml) of the bean cooking liquid, cover the surface entirely with the breadcrumbs and cook in the oven – uncovered – for 1½ hours.

VEGETARIAN SHEPHERD'S PIE

◆

(Serves 4 people)

If you're not a vegetarian shepherd don't worry, I still think you'll find this recipe quite delicious and far better than many of the minced meat versions.

6 oz whole green-brown lentils (175 g)
4 oz dried split peas, green or yellow (110 g)
1 pint hot water (570 ml)
1 oz butter or margarine (25 g)
2 celery stalks, chopped
1 medium onion, chopped
2 carrots, chopped
½ green pepper, de-seeded and chopped
1 clove garlic, crushed
½ teaspoon dried mixed herbs
2 pinches of ground mace
¼ teaspoon cayenne pepper
salt and freshly milled black pepper
For the topping
8 oz tomatoes (225 g), peeled and sliced
1 small onion, chopped
2 oz butter or margarine (50 g)
1½ lb cooked potatoes (700 g)
2 tablespoons top of the milk
3 oz strong Cheddar cheese (75 g), grated

Begin by washing the lentils and split peas, then put them in a saucepan with the hot water and simmer gently, covered, for approximately 45–60 minutes or until the peas and lentils have absorbed the water and are soft. Pre-heat the oven to gas mark 5, 375°F (190°C).

Meantime, melt the butter in a frying-pan, add the celery, onion, carrots and chopped pepper, and cook gently until softened, then add these to the cooked lentil mixture after mashing it a little first. Add the garlic, herbs, spices, and salt and pepper to taste, then spoon the mixture into a large pie-dish (3 pint/1.75 litre) and arrange the sliced tomatoes on top.

Next, prepare the topping by softening the onion in butter in a small pan, then mash the potatoes, add the cooked onion, butter, top of the milk and grated cheese, and mix thoroughly. Season well, then spread on top of the ingredients in the pie-dish. Bake for about 20 minutes or until the top is lightly browned. Home-made tomato sauce (page 329) is a delicious accompaniment.

NON-MEAT LOAF
◆

(Serves 4 people)

This is delicious hot with a home-made tomato sauce or cold with pickles, chutney and salad.

4 oz dried split peas, yellow or green (110 g), picked over and rinsed
6 oz whole green-brown lentils (175 g)
1 pint vegetable stock or water (570 ml)
2 oz butter or margarine (50 g)
1 medium onion, chopped
½ green pepper, de-seeded and chopped
2 carrots, chopped
2 celery stalks, chopped
1 fat clove garlic, crushed
¼ teaspoon cayenne pepper
¼ teaspoon ground mace
1 egg, beaten
1 teaspoon chopped fresh or ¾ teaspoon dried mixed herbs
2 tablespoons chopped fresh parsley
salt and freshly milled black pepper

A 1 lb (450 g) loaf tin, well-greased.

Start by bringing the stock or water to boiling point, stir in the split peas and simmer, covered, for about 5 minutes. Then add the lentils and continue to simmer, with the lid on, for a further 25–30 minutes or until all the liquid has been absorbed and the lentils and peas are soft; then take off the heat.

Now heat the oven to gas mark 5, 375°F (190°C).

Heat the butter in another pan, add all the prepared vegetables and the garlic and fry for 10 minutes or until golden. Now stir the vegetables into the lentil mixture together with the cayenne, mace, beaten egg, herbs and parsley, mix well, then season to taste.

Spoon the mixture into the prepared tin, cover with foil and bake for 40 minutes. When it's cooked, slip a knife around the inside edge of the tin and turn the loaf out onto a warmed serving dish.

SPICED LAMB WITH CHICK PEAS
♦

(Serves 4–6 people)

If you can't get fresh chillies or root ginger for this recipe, you can use 1 level teaspoon of chilli powder and 2 level teaspoons of ground ginger instead.

6 oz chick peas (175 g)
2 lb boned shoulder of lamb (900 g)
4 tablespoons groundnut oil
1 Spanish onion, thinly sliced
1 aubergine, unpeeled and cut into small chunks – approx. 12 oz (350 g) in weight
1 teaspoon ground turmeric
1 teaspoon garam masala
1 lb tomatoes (450 g), peeled and thickly sliced
3 fresh chilli peppers, halved, de-seeded and finely sliced
2 cloves garlic, crushed
2 tablespoons finely chopped mint
1 tablespoon finely chopped fresh root ginger
5 oz natural yoghurt (150 g)

First of all place the chick peas in a saucepan, cover with 2 pints (1·2 litres) boiling water, put a lid on and leave on one side for 3 hours. Then bring to the boil, and boil, covered, for approximately 1 hour or until the peas are really tender, and put them on one side once again.

Next cut the meat into 1 inch (2.5 cm) cubes, trimming off excess fat. Now heat the oil in a thick-based saucepan, add the cubes of meat (a small quantity at a time) and fry over a high heat, removing the meat to a plate, using a draining spoon, when nicely browned.

Then add the onion and aubergine to the pan, stirring them around in the fat, and fry until coloured before adding the turmeric and garam masala. Cook for another minute, then add the tomatoes, chillies, garlic, mint and ginger. Drain the chick peas, reserving the liquid, then return the meat to the pan together with the chick peas and about 15 fl oz (425 ml) of their cooking liquor.

Bring up to simmering point, cover and cook very gently for 30 minutes, then take off the lid and continue cooking for approximately 45 minutes or until the meat is really tender and the sauce thick. Lastly stir in the yoghurt and, when all is well heated through, serve with *Spiced pilau rice* (page 275).

ADUKI BEAN AND BROWN RICE SALAD

♦

(Serves 6 people)

Aduki beans go very well with brown rice, especially in a salad.

4 oz dried aduki beans (110 g), soaked overnight
1 mugful long-grain brown rice
2 mugs boiling water
1 large green pepper, de-seeded and chopped
2 celery stalks, finely chopped
¹/₂ cucumber, diced – leave the peel on
6 spring onions, finely chopped – including the green parts
salt and freshly milled black pepper
For the dressing
4 fl oz olive oil (110 ml)
1 tablespoon wine vinegar
1 fat clove garlic, crushed
1 teaspoon mustard powder
1 teaspoon salt
2 tablespoons finely chopped parsley
To garnish
2 tablespoons finely chopped celery leaves

First put the beans in a saucepan together with the water in which they were soaked (no need to add salt), bring to the boil and cook for 45 minutes–1 hour or until the beans are tender.

Meantime, place the rice with some salt in another saucepan, and add the boiling water. Bring to the boil, cover and simmer very gently for 40 minutes or until the rice is tender and all the water absorbed.

Next, put all the ingredients for the dressing in a salad bowl and whisk together.

Then while the cooked rice and the beans (drained) are still warm, empty them into the salad bowl and mix everything together lightly with a fork. Leave the salad till cold, then add the chopped vegetables, mixing them in lightly. Taste, and season again if it needs it. Serve sprinkled with chopped celery leaves.

LENTIL, BEAN AND ANCHOVY SALAD
◆

(Serves 4 people)

This is a really delicious salad and substantial enough to serve as a main course for lunch.

8 oz dried white haricot beans (225 g)
8 oz whole green-brown lentils (225 g)
salt and freshly milled black pepper
For the dressing
8 tablespoons oil
1 tablespoon wine vinegar
1 tablespoon lemon juice
1 small onion, finely chopped
1 clove garlic, crushed
1 heaped teaspoon made-up mustard
4 tablespoons finely chopped fresh parsley
To garnish
2 oz tin anchovy fillets (50 g)
2 hard-boiled eggs, peeled and chopped
1 oz small black olives (25 g)
a few crisp lettuce leaves

Prepare the beans in advance by putting them in a saucepan and covering with cold water. Bring to boiling point and boil for 2–3 minutes, then remove from the heat and let the beans soak for about an hour. After that boil them again for about another hour until *just* soft.

About 30 minutes before the beans are ready pick over the lentils (there's no need to soak them); wash them and boil in plenty of water until *just* soft.

Meanwhile mix together in a bowl all the ingredients for the dressing and add the oil from the tin of anchovies. Chop the anchovies and put on one side.

When the beans and lentils are cooked, drain them, tip them into a bowl and, while they're still warm, pour in the dressing. Mix well so that they are well coated and leave to cool.

Before serving, taste the salad and season well with salt and freshly milled black pepper, then place some crisp lettuce leaves on four plates and arrange the mixture on top. Finally garnish with the chopped hard-boiled eggs, chopped anchovies and olives.

RED BEAN SALAD

◆

(Serves 4 people)

A red bean salad always looks so good, as the beans are such a lovely colour, and it's always an attractive one to put in amongst other salads to provide a contrast.

12 oz dried red kidney beans (350 g)
For the vinaigrette dressing
1 tablespoon wine vinegar
1 teaspoon mustard
1 teaspoon salt
2 cloves garlic, crushed
6 tablespoons olive oil
freshly milled black pepper
To finish off
1 medium onion, finely chopped
1 green pepper, de-seeded and finely chopped
2 drops Tabasco sauce

First rinse the beans with cold water and then place them in a saucepan. Cover with plenty of water, bring up to the boil, boil for 10 minutes, then turn off the heat and leave them to soak for 2 hours.

Next pour off the water and cover with fresh cold water. Bring them up to the boil and boil gently for about 1¹/₂–2 hours or until the beans are tender.

Meanwhile prepare the vinaigrette by combining all the ingredients in a bowl. Then, as soon as the beans are tender, drain them and toss them in the vinaigrette while they are still warm. Leave them to cool before adding the chopped onion, green pepper and Tabasco.

If possible leave the salad to marinate for several hours before serving on crisp lettuce leaves.

LENTIL AND VEGETABLE MOUSSAKA

◆

(Serves 2 people)

It's quite amazing how versatile the classic Greek moussaka can be: even without any meat it still holds its own against the original. Lentils do bear some resemblance to the minced meat they replace here, notably in their slightly chewy texture.

2 oz whole green-brown lentils (50 g)
4 fl oz water (110 ml)
1 medium aubergine, cut into small cubes
4 tablespoons oil
1 large onion, finely chopped
4 oz red pepper (110 g), finely chopped
1 large clove garlic, crushed
4 tablepoons red wine or dry cider
1 tablespoon tomato purée
1/4 teaspoon ground cinnamon
1 dessertspoon chopped parsley
salt and freshly ground pepper
For the topping
2 eggs
4 tablespoons natural yoghurt
2 tablespoons grated Parmesan cheese
freshly grated nutmeg

Pre-heat the oven to gas mark 4, 350°F (180°C).

A 2 pint (1.2 litre) soufflé or ovenproof dish.

First the lentils need to be cooked in the water at a gentle simmer for 30 minutes or until they are softened and the water has been absorbed – don't add any salt. Next prepare the aubergine cubes by placing them in a colander, sprinkling them with salt and covering with a plate weighted down with a heavy object – scale-weights are ideal. Leave them to drain for 20 minutes or so, then squeeze them dry in a clean tea cloth.

In the meantime, heat 2 tablespoons of the oil in a frying-pan and cook the onion and red pepper together for about 8–10 minutes or until softened. Remove them to a plate, add the remaining oil to the pan and cook the aubergine – which will also take about 10 minutes to soften.

Next add the garlic, cook that for a minute, then return the onion and pepper to the pan. Now mix the wine or cider and tomato purée together with the cinnamon and parsley in a jug and pour this into the vegetable mixture. Stir in the softened lentils, season well with salt and pepper, and stir everything together to combine thoroughly. Spoon the whole lot into the soufflé or ovenproof dish.

Finally beat the eggs together with the yoghurt, Parmesan and a little freshly grated nutmeg, and pour this over the top of the lentil and vegetable mixture. Bake in the oven for 30 minutes or until the top is puffy and golden.

BUCKWHEAT AND VEGETABLE PIE

◆

(Serves 3–4 people)

Buckwheat has a distinctive flavour of its own, and baked in the oven with vegetables and lentils it makes an excellent vegetarian main course.

6 oz roasted buckwheat (175 g)
2 oz whole green-brown lentils (50 g)
1 tablespoon tomato purée
1 oz butter (25 g)
2 tablespoons oil
1 large onion, chopped
1 green or red pepper, de-seeded and chopped
8 oz mushrooms (225 g), sliced if large
1 clove garlic, crushed
1 heaped teaspoon dried oregano
14 oz tin tomatoes (400 g)
1½ oz cheese (40 g), grated – any sort will do
1 oz wholemeal breadcrumbs (25 g)
cayenne pepper (optional)
salt and freshly milled black pepper

Pre-heat the oven to gas mark 5, 375°F (190°C).

First put the lentils in a pan with 4 fl oz (110 ml) of water and simmer them gently for 20–30 minutes or until tender. While that's happening combine the tomato purée with 1 pint (570 ml) boiling water. Melt the butter in a saucepan, add the buckwheat and stir until it is throughly coated with fat. Pour in the liquid, bring up to simmering point, stir once and add some salt, then put the lid on and cook gently for about 10 minutes.

Meanwhile, heat the oil in a frying-pan and cook the onion and green or red pepper in it for 5 minutes to soften but not to colour them. Add the mushrooms and cook gently for a further 5 minutes. Then stir in the garlic and oregano, season with salt and pepper and add the contents of the tin of tomatoes. Stir well and leave to simmer gently without a lid so that the liquid reduces slightly.

Stir the cooked buckwheat and lentils into the vegetable mixture, then transfer the contents of the pan to a lightly-buttered 2½ pint (1·5 litre) pie-dish. Scatter the grated cheese and breadcrumbs over the surface, and a sprinkling of cayenne if you like. Place the dish in the centre of the oven and bake for 20–30 minutes or until the topping is golden and bubbling.

SPICED CHICK PEA CUTLETS

◆

(Serves 3 people)

These spicy little cutlets are good served hot with slivers of raw Spanish onion and some plain Greek yoghurt as a sauce (or, alternatively, a home-made tomato sauce – see page 329).

8 oz chick peas (225 g), soaked overnight
2 tablespoons oil
1 onion, finely chopped
1 small green or red pepper, de-seeded and finely chopped
1 large clove garlic, crushed
1 dessertspoon grated fresh root ginger
1 tablespoon tomato purée
2 tablespoons natural yoghurt
½ teaspoon chilli powder
1 heaped teaspoon ground coriander
1 heaped teaspoon ground cumin
1 dessertspoon lemon juice
salt and freshly milled black pepper
For the frying
1 large egg, beaten
approx. 3 tablespoons white breadcrumbs
groundnut oil

First of all pour the soaked chick peas, together with their water, into a saucepan, then bring them to the boil, cover and simmer for about 30 minutes or until they're absolutely tender. Drain them throughly and mash them to a pulp.

Put the 2 tablespoons oil in a saucepan and gently fry the onion and green or red pepper along with the garlic and grated ginger until softened, then beat them into the mashed chick peas together with all the remaining cutlet ingredients apart from the salt and pepper. Taste before seasoning with salt and pepper. When the mixture is cool enough to handle, form it into twelve patties and coat each one with egg then breadcrumbs. Heat a couple of tablespoons of oil in a frying-pan and fry the patties to a golden-brown colour. Drain well and serve as soon as possible.

SEE ALSO

Brown rice, lentil and mushroom salad　　*Oxtail with haricot beans*
Chick pea salad　　*Smoked bacon and lentil soup*
Haricot bean and salami salad　　*White bean and tuna fish salad*

PASTA AND PANCAKES

◆

PASTA

◆

If I were asked to choose between a meal in a multi-starred French restaurant or with an Italian family at home, without hesitation I'd choose the latter. Marcella Hazan, in one of my favourite Italian cookbooks, describes the experience beautifully. The whole country, she says, shuts down at midday for this two-hour event and 'there probably has been no influence, not even religion, so effective in creating a rich family life, in maintaining a civilised link between the generations, as this daily sharing of a common joy.'

She says so much more, and so could I, about the Italian way of eating. But let me just commend its simplicity: it is never lavish, vulgar or pretentious. The Italians are not a nation who rely heavily on freezers or canned foods, but manage on very little meat and plenty of seasonal vegetables and fruit. Butter is something of a luxury – in my experience served with bread only at breakfast – and in passing it's interesting to note that, despite their rather obese image, the Italians have one of the lowest incidences of heart disease in the world: so perhaps their use of olive oil in place of butter and their enthusiasm for lots of fresh fruit and salads shows that 'preventative' eating need not be as dull as is sometimes suggested.

However this part of the chapter is concerned with just one item that the Italians have made famous, namely pasta, which is one thing that I think should be a permanent resident in any larder or storecupboard. The marvellous thing about pasta is that, with a little imagination, this one basic ingredient can be made into a whole range of different dishes.

WHAT IS PASTA?

When I was a child, just after the war, spaghetti was something that came out of a tin in a bright orange sauce, and was usually served on toast, sometimes with a poached egg on top! Later on it began to appear in the shops in its natural state, though in quite unmanageable packets, as I recall, at least a yard long. In those days it was dismissed, at any rate by the elderly, as 'foreign', but nowadays foreign holidays and a steady flow of cookbooks have helped to establish it on supermarket shelves, in quite a number of its infinite varieties.

Pasta is simply the Italian word for dough, and in particular a dough made from durum (or hard) wheat. When hard wheat is first ground it produces not flour, but semolina, and this is used – with hard wheat flour and water – to produce pasta. The dough is then moulded or stamped into the appropriate shape by machine and (unless it is to be sold immediately as fresh pasta) it is then dried. Once it was dried in the back gardens of Naples by the Mediterranean breezes, but now technology has reproduced this wonder of nature.

EGG PASTA

Most commercial pastas are purely wheat-and-water but sometimes you come across egg pastas, in which eggs have been added to the basic dough (as they are in home-made pasta). Egg pasta is rich, more filling and quite delicious – and if the packet is printed in Italian it will be described as *pasta all'uovo*.

GREEN PASTA (PASTA VERDE)

This is just pasta into which spinach has been worked at the dough-making stage. This is done, I suspect, more for the sake of colour than for flavour, but it does look most attractive in dishes like lasagne.

WHOLEWHEAT PASTA

It's hard to imagine that we, the British, actually export pasta to Italy, but we do! The Italians are now buying wholewheat pasta that's made here. True, it is more 'healthy', which encouraged me to try it in the early days. But I confess its stodginess makes me rather less enthusiastic nowadays.

HOME-MADE PASTA

It is now possible to buy fresh pasta (that is undried) quite extensively, but the quality of this varies enormously. From a good Italian shop the home-made stuffed pastas (like ravioli and tortellini) and sometimes the ribbon noodles or tagliatelle can be excellent. But from other outlets the result is very often a soggy mass when cooked. Let me come clean here – I actually *prefer* dried spaghetti, which can be cooked to the 'al dente' stage, so much more easily than the factory-made 'fresh' pastas.

Failing that, you could make it at home yourself, but be warned – it is very hard work kneading pasta, and then you are faced with a lump of very resilient, elastic dough which needs to be rolled and stretched out to a transparent thinness! It can be difficult, too, to obtain the correct ingredients (although a strong flour will do). If you want to get really serious about home-made pasta you could, of course, invest in a pasta machine. It's a sort of mangle which can be adjusted to different pasta shapes, and it squeezes and presses the pasta out thinly, which does eliminate a lot of hard work. However if, like me, you're not an absolute perfectionist, a good quality packaged pasta will probably suit you well enough.

PASTA SHAPES

There are literally hundreds of different pasta shapes, which may seem a bit daunting. But it needn't be: for one thing, there is no definitive list – manufacturers can and do add further shapes from time to time. And in fact there are only five basic types:

(1) First there are the tiny decorative shapes that go into soups (*pasta in brodo*) and sometimes into puddings: they can be stars, flowers, letters of the alphabet, little animals . . . the list is endless.

(2) Then there are the solid spaghetti-type pastas, long and thin. *Spaghetti* itself is cylindrical and usually about 10 inches (25 cm) long; it has a thinner cousin, called *spaghettini* sometimes referred to as 'quick-cooking'. In this group I would also include the long, noodle varieties – *tagliatelle* which is flat rather than cylindrical, enriched with eggs and sometimes with spinach, and dried in bunches rather than lengths. It too has a thinner cousin, *linguine*.

(3) Next are what I'd call the *macaroni* group or tubular pastas. Some are cut short or curled slightly: some have pointed ends (*penne*), some are ribbed (*rigatoni*).

(4) The fancy shapes – bows, shells, twists, wheels, frills and the rest of them – are intriguing to look at but all taste the same in the end. Like the pastas in groups (2) and (3) above, these are usually served with a sauce.

(5) Finally there are the pastas which are stuffed or can be bought ready-stuffed. The very large sheets of *lasagne*, and big tubular *cannelloni*, are both meant to be stuffed and baked. Ready-stuffed pasta, *ravioli*, are little square packages with a stuffing inside: *tortellini* are similar but curled in shape.

This list is strictly a basic grouping of variations. My own larder collection consists of spaghetti, tagliatelle, a short-cut macaroni for soups, and a standard macaroni. I find I sometimes buy odd shapes but I can't see any particular advantage in them. On the contrary, the cooking time can be rather uncertain if the shape is thick – and beware of pasta 'shells' in which the boiling water can become trapped, only to escape at the table when it's too late!

COOKING PASTA

First let's discuss what pasta *should* be like when cooked. The now-familiar Italian words *al dente* appear frequently on packets and in many recipes to describe the approved texture of cooked pasta. Translated literally they mean 'to the teeth' which clearly suggests that pasta must have some bite to it.

If it's overcooked all the guts will have gone out of it, and you'll only have a soggy, sticky mass. As an experienced pasta consumer I have found that, over the years, I have come to cook pasta in less and less time, and I now give ordinary supermarket spaghetti only 8 minutes' boiling. In the end there's only one way for you to tell, and that's to bite a bit and see if it's to your liking. I find that macaroni, spaghetti and lasagne take 8–10 minutes to cook, but if you're using a thick variety it might need a couple of minutes more. These suggested timings are for dried (packet) pasta. Fresh or home-made pasta is quicker to cook – perhaps just 1 or 2 minutes.

Pasta isn't quite as fattening as some people imagine. Of course if it is baked with a rich ragù and covered in a melted cheese sauce, then it can be extremely high in calories; but served with a fresh tomato sauce (or with any sauce which only calls for 2 tablespoons of olive oil for four people) it can be much lower in calories than many meat dishes.

If you are serving a layered pasta dish or pasta that is stuffed and baked, you'll only need quite a small quantity of pasta. If you are serving spaghetti or any other type of pasta just with a sauce, then you'll need more, and I recommend 8–10 oz (225–275 g) of pasta – dry weight – between two very hungry people for a main course, or 4–6 oz (110–175 g) as a starter.

NOTES ON INGREDIENTS

One of the best reasons for eating pasta is that, in 15 minutes from start to finish, you can provide yourself with a complete meal – and all from a collection of ingredients that are common to most kitchen cupboards. The following are what I'd consider essential items to keep handy.

Olive oil
For pasta I *do* think this is essential. Whereas for other types of cooking I might substitute groundnut oil, with pasta olive oil (Italian for choice) seems a must and well worth the slight extra expense. Buying in bulk – say 5 litres at a time – is a lot cheaper and quite practical if you use it regularly. Personally I find 1 litre at a time serves my purposes quite adequately and this way it never gets stale.

Basil
Tomatoes are one of the principal ingredients of pasta dishes in Italy, and basil has a strong affinity with tomatoes. Dried basil is not suitable for fresh tomatoes, but it certainly is for tomato sauces. At all events it is better than no basil at all.

Parmesan cheese
Grated and sprinkled over soups and pastas, this cheese is used almost like seasoning in Italy. It is a hard cheese, said to need two to three years' ageing to reach maturity (and some of the more expensive ones have had five or more years'). The preservative used in the packaged, ready-grated Parmesan gives the cheese an alien taste, I think, and I go out of my way to buy whole pieces of the cheese in

delicatessens or Italian shops. It keeps beautifully in a sealed polythene bag in the lowest part of the refrigerator, and this way you can grate it as and when you need it.

Tomatoes

Fresh red ripe summer and autumn tomatoes are best in Italian cooking. In the winter months, however, the tinned variety are far superior to the anaemic imported kind, and when it comes to tinned tomatoes I always buy Italian. They really are the best and very useful indeed for all sorts of cooking purposes when fresh tomatoes are out of season. Tomato purée (or tomato paste as it is sometimes called) is very concentrated in flavour. Useful though it would be to make it oneself when there is a glut of tomatoes in the garden, so far as I am aware it is impossible to make it at home.

HOW TO BOIL PASTA

The number one rule is always to have plenty of boiling water. If too little water is used, the pasta clogs together in a mass and some of it may not cook at all. So allow 4 pints (2.25 litres) of water for each 8 oz (225 g) of pasta.

Always add some salt to the water – about 2 teaspoons for 4 pints (2.25 litres) plus a few drops of olive oil, which will help to keep the strands separate. Have the water boiling rapidly and keep the heat high while you add the pasta (if it's spaghetti, you'll need to push it down gradually into the pan and the water will soften it as it goes down). The water should, if the heat is high enough, come to the boil again very quickly; then give the pasta one really good stir, turn the heat down and let it simmer gently for the required time. *Don't* put a lid on – there's no need to and, if you do, you risk having the water boil over.

When the pasta is cooked to your liking, pour it into a colander sitting in the sink and allow most of the water to drain off. If the sauce is to be served separately, then place the colander over the saucepan in which you cooked the pasta (the heat of the pan will help to keep the pasta hot while you serve) and dish up directly in the kitchen. Serve each helping onto a plate that has been nicely warmed – large soup plates would be ideal because that little bit of depth helps to conserve the heat. Speed is now the important factor (*presto pronto!* as the Italians say), because there is nothing worse than eating pasta that is the wrong side of tepid.

TO SERVE SPAGHETTI

Use two instruments (a large spoon and a fork) to extract a quantity of spaghetti, lifting it as high as possible above the colander, and it will separate from the rest with perfect ease.

TO EAT SPAGHETTI

The big mistake here is trying to wind too much onto the fork at once. Select just two or three strands with your fork and coax them over the rim of the plate. Then, holding the fork at a right angle to the plate, simply wind the fork round and round, so that those few strands extricate themselves from the rest and are twisted round the fork in a little bite-sized bundle. Easier said than done, you're thinking? But remember two things – practice makes perfect and the Italians themselves always wear little napkins tucked neatly under their chins.

FRESH TOMATO SAUCE
◆

(Serves 2 people)

This sauce is good to serve with almost any kind of pasta – and it's also useful for using up those slightly over-ripe tomatoes at the end of the season.

1 lb ripe tomatoes (450 g), peeled and chopped
1 tablespoon olive oil
1 small onion, finely chopped
1 clove garlic, crushed
1 teaspoon tomato purée
1 dessertspoon chopped fresh or $\frac{1}{2}$ dessertspoon dried basil
salt and freshly milled black pepper

To peel the tomatoes pour some boiling water over them and let them stand for a minute or two; then you'll find the skins slip off very easily. Chop up the flesh quite small.

Heat the olive oil in a saucepan, and soften the onion and garlic in it for 5 minutes without letting them brown, then add the tomatoes, tomato purée, basil and a seasoning of salt and pepper. Give everything a good stir, then cover the pan and simmer gently for 15 minutes. After that uncover the pan and simmer for a further 10–15 minutes for the sauce to reduce slightly. It can either be served as it is, or liquidised a little first.

Tomato chilli sauce
Make the sauce as above but add $\frac{1}{4}$ teaspoon chilli powder or chopped dried chilli pepper, in which case it would be a good accompaniment to sausages, rissoles or hamburgers as well as an alternative sauce for pasta.

RAGÙ BOLOGNESE

◆

(Serves 4 people)

This is really the all-purpose Italian pasta sauce: it can form the basis of *Lasagne* or *Baked meat and macaroni pie* (see the recipes on pages 332 and 334), or served with spaghetti it is enough for four people.

6 oz lean minced beef (175 g)
3 oz chicken livers (75 g), chopped small
2 rashers unsmoked streaky bacon, de-rinded and finely chopped
1½ tablespoons olive oil
1 small onion, very finely chopped
1 fat clove garlic, crushed
8 oz tin Italian tomatoes (225 g)
2 heaped tablespoons tomato purée
4 tablespoons red wine
1 teaspoon dried or 1 tablespoon chopped fresh basil
salt and freshly milled black pepper

Heat the oil in a thick-based saucepan, then gently soften the onion, bacon and garlic in it for 5 minutes. Now turn the heat up, add the chicken livers and minced beef, and brown them, keeping the ingredients on the move with a wooden spoon. When the meat has browned, pour in the contents of the tin of tomatoes, plus the tomato purée, wine, basil and some seasoning. Put a lid on and simmer gently for 20 minutes, then take the lid off and simmer gently for a further 20–25 minutes to get a nice concentrated sauce.

SPAGHETTI ALLA CARBONARA

♦

(Serves 2 people)

This doesn't have to be spaghetti – you can use tagliatelle or macaroni. It's a very simple dish of pasta with a bacon and egg sauce that tastes far nicer than it sounds.

8 oz spaghetti (225 g)
4 oz streaky bacon (110 g), de-rinded and chopped
2 large eggs, plus 1 extra yolk
1½ tablespoons olive oil
1 tablespoon grated Parmesan cheese
salt and freshly milled black pepper
To serve
extra grated Parmesan cheese

To cook the pasta, place it in a very large saucepan of boiling salted water to which ½ tablespoon of olive oil has been added to prevent the spaghetti sticking together. It will need 8–10 minutes from the time it comes to the boil. Meantime, heat the remaining olive oil in a saucepan and fry the bacon till the fat starts to run. While all this is happening, whisk the eggs and egg yolk in a bowl, adding some freshly milled black pepper and the tablespoon of Parmesan cheese.

As soon as the pasta is cooked drain it in a colander then return it to the hot saucepan – away from the heat though. Now, quickly and deftly, stir in the beaten eggs and the bacon (plus the oil it was cooked in) and keep stirring to coat the pasta with liquid egg, which will soon cook from the heat of the saucepan and turn slightly granular. Serve on really hot plates with lots of Parmesan cheese to sprinkle over.

Note If you would like to vary the above recipe slightly, you could add a chopped onion or a crushed clove of garlic to cook with the bacon. Another nice addition is to beat 2 tablespoons of double cream or fromage frais into the eggs, which gives a lovely creamy finish to the sauce.

LASAGNE AL FORNO

◆

(Serves 6 people)

For me, this is the supreme pasta dish – wafer-thin leaves of green pasta, layered together with a filling of thick ragù Bolognese and surrounded by a nutmeg-flavoured cream sauce, hot and bubbling. It isn't something you can dash off in a hurry but it's a superb dinner-party dish, and once made it's very easy just to pop in the oven and serve without any last-minute fuss.

1 quantity ragù Bolognese (see page 330)
8 oz lasagne verde (green spinach lasagne) (225 g)
olive oil
freshly grated Parmesan, to finish

For the cream sauce
1¼ pints milk (725 ml)
3 oz butter (75 g)
2 oz plain flour (50 g)
3 fl oz double cream (75 ml)
freshly grated nutmeg
salt and freshly milled black pepper

A roasting tin, measuring about 7 × 9½ inches (18 × 24 cm), well-buttered.

First make up the cream sauce by placing the milk, butter and flour in a thick-based saucepan. Put it over a gentle heat and whisk continuously with a balloon whisk until the sauce comes to simmering point and thickens. Now, with the heat as low as possible, continue to cook the sauce for 10 minutes.

To cook the lasagne (8 oz/225 g will be about sixteen sheets, each measuring 7 × 3 inches or 18 × 7.5 cm), have ready a large saucepan of salted, boiling water to which a little oil has been added. Drop in eight sheets, one at a time. If using fresh pasta cook them for 3 minutes or until they float to the top: if they're dried cook them for about 8 minutes – but make sure you don't overcook, or they will be soggy. When cooked transfer them immediately, using a fish slice, to a bowl of cold water (which will prevent them sticking together). Repeat this process with the remaining sheets.

Next sieve the white sauce into a bowl, beat in the cream, season with salt and pepper and grate in about a quarter of a whole nutmeg. Now spread about a quarter of the ragù over the base of the prepared roasting tin. Cover this with approximately a quarter of the sauce, then arrange a single layer of the drained and dried lasagne over the top. Repeat this process, finishing off with a final layer of cream sauce. Cover the top with a good sprinkling of grated Parmesan cheese – and the lasagne is ready for the oven. All this preparation can be done well in advance. When required, bake in a pre-heated oven, gas mark 4, 350°F (180°C), for 30–35 minutes.

SPAGHETTI WITH ANCHOVIES, MUSHROOMS AND OLIVES

◆

(Serves 2 people)

If you like lots of 'gutsy' flavour in food, you'll like this recipe, which should be made with the very best olive oil and served with lots of fresh Parmesan.

8 oz spaghetti (225 g)
3 tablespoons plus 1 teaspoon olive oil
8 oz mushrooms (225 g), thinly sliced
2 onions, thinly sliced
3 rashers lean bacon, de-rinded and roughly chopped
2 cloves garlic, crushed
5 tinned anchovy fillets, snipped in half
2 tablespoons chopped parsley
6 Spanish stuffed green olives, sliced
salt and freshly milled black pepper
To serve
2 tablespoons grated Parmesan cheese

In a heavy-based frying-pan heat the 3 tablespoons of oil, then gently cook the mushrooms, onions and bacon for about 10 minutes, stirring them around occasionally. Then add the garlic, anchovy fillets, parsley and olives and let them heat through. Season to taste.

In the meantime, cook the spaghetti for 8–10 minutes in boiling salted water to which 1 teaspoon of oil has been added. When cooked, drain in a colander, pile it onto a warmed serving dish, pour the savoury mixture on top and sprinkle on the Parmesan cheese.

BAKED MEAT AND MACARONI PIE

———————— ◆ ————————

(Serves 4 people)

The large, ribbed type of macaroni, sometimes called *rigatoni*, or the un-ribbed *penne* are best for this dish. But ordinary macaroni will do.

1 quantity ragù Bolognese (see page 330)
6–8 oz macaroni (175–225 g)
olive oil
1 clove garlic, crushed
2 oz Cheddar cheese (50 g), grated
For the sauce
1¹/₂ oz butter (40 g)
1 oz plain flour (25 g)
15 fl oz cold milk (425 ml)
freshly grated nutmeg
salt and freshly milled black pepper

Pre-heat the oven to gas mark 4, 350°F (180°C).

First make up the white sauce by placing the butter, flour and milk together in a pan over a medium heat and whisking until the sauce starts to bubble and thicken. Stir with a wooden spoon to get right into the corners of the pan, then whisk again thoroughly. Turn the heat down as low as you can and cook the sauce gently for 6 minutes, then grate in a quarter of a whole nutmeg.

Meanwhile cook the macaroni in plenty of boiling salted water (with a few drops of oil added) for 8–10 minutes – make sure you don't overcook it. When cooked, drain it well in a colander, then in a dry saucepan heat 1 tablespoon of olive oil, add the crushed garlic, return the macaroni to the pan and toss it around well.

Next butter a baking dish or casserole, add the macaroni to it, then pour in first the ragù Bolognese followed by the white sauce. Stir everything thoroughly so the macaroni gets properly coated with both sauces. Finally sprinkle the grated Cheddar cheese over the top, then bake in the oven for 30–40 minutes.

MACARONI WITH LEEKS AND BACON
♦

(Serves 4 people)

Again, I think this is nicest made with the larger type of pasta called *penne*, but supermarket macaroni is almost as good. (Illus. opposite p. 289.)

12 oz macaroni (350 g)
3 small leeks, cleaned and chopped
6 oz streaky bacon (175 g), de-rinded and chopped
olive oil
2 oz butter (50 g)
For the sauce
2 oz butter (50 g)
2 oz plain flour (50 g)
1½ pints milk (850 ml)
6 oz Cheddar cheese (175 g), grated
3 fl oz double cream (75 ml)
salt, freshly milled pepper and freshly grated nutmeg
For the topping
2 tablespoons grated Parmesan cheese
1 tablespoon breadcrumbs
2 pinches of cayenne pepper

A 3 pint (1.75 litre) pie-dish, well-buttered.

Start by bringing a large saucepan of water to simmering point, add some salt, a few drops of olive oil and the pasta, then bring back to the boil and cook for 10 minutes exactly. Then turn the pasta into a colander and, to prevent it cooking any further, rinse it under the cold tap.

While the pasta's cooking, melt the butter in a pan and soften the leeks and bacon over a low heat and, in another pan, make the white sauce with the butter, flour and milk and leave it to simmer very gently.

Now turn the pasta, leeks and bacon into the prepared pie-dish and mix them well together. Next stir the grated Cheddar cheese into the sauce, season to taste with salt, pepper and nutmeg and, finally, add the cream. Then pour the sauce over the ingredients in the pie-dish and sprinkle the top with the Parmesan, breadcrumbs and cayenne pepper.

This is a dish which can be prepared well beforehand then, when it's needed, put into an oven pre-heated to gas mark 4, 350°F (180°C), for 30–40 minutes till the top is nicely browned and the sauce bubbling.

Note You can vary this by using all kinds of different ingredients, such as onions or sliced sautéed courgettes in place of leeks. Or by adding 4 oz (110 g) of sautéed sliced mushrooms and using less bacon.

PASTA WITH CREAM AND WILD MUSHROOM SAUCE

◆

(Serves 2 people)

8 oz dried or fresh pasta, any shape (225 g)

For the sauce
¼ oz Italian dried mushrooms (5 g) – available at specialist food shops and delicatessens
10 fl oz hot water (275 ml)
1 tablespoon olive oil
8 oz fresh dark-gilled mushrooms (225 g), thinly sliced through the stalk
1 large clove garlic, finely chopped
¾ oz butter (20 g)
¾ oz flour (20 g)
freshly grated nutmeg
3 tablespoons double cream
salt and freshly milled pepper

To finish
2 heaped tablespoons finely grated Parmesan cheese

You will need a heatproof shallow serving dish.

Place the dried mushrooms in a measuring jug and pour hot water over them to the 10 fl oz (275 ml) level. Place a crumpled polythene bag on top to keep the mushrooms submerged. Leave them for 30 minutes. After 15 minutes heat the oil in a medium frying-pan and cook the fresh mushrooms, turning the heat down low after a couple of minutes' initial cooking. You can also add a little seasoning at this stage.

When the fresh mushrooms have had 15 minutes' cooking the dried ones will be ready. Strain them in a sieve, reserving the soaking water, then rinse them under cold running water. Squeeze out excess water, dry with kitchen paper, and chop quite small.

Add these to the rest of the mushrooms, along with the chopped garlic, with a few more drops of oil if necessary. Stir well, and leave the mushroom mixture to cook slowly for a further 15 minutes. Strain the soaking liquid – use either a coffee filter or a double thickness of kitchen paper in a sieve. You should be left with approximately 8 fl oz (225 ml) of liquid.

Melt the butter in a small saucepan, stir in the flour, and slowly add the mushroom stock, bit by bit, stirring well after each addition, until you have a smooth, glossy sauce. Season with salt, pepper and grated nutmug. Cook the sauce slowly for 5 minutes, then stir in the cream.

Meanwhile, pre-heat the grill. Cook the pasta in boiling water (with a few drops of olive oil and a little salt) for no more than 8 minutes if dried, 2–4 minutes if fresh. While the pasta cooks, stir the mushrooms and their juices into the sauce and check the seasoning.

When the pasta is cooked, strain it quickly in a colander, return it to the saucepan and pour in the sauce. Mix thoroughly and pour everything into the serving dish. Sprinkle the Parmesan cheese over the surface and flash the dish under the grill for about 30 seconds, or until the cheese is golden. Serve immediately with a lettuce salad and some more Parmesan.

PANCAKES

◆

Pancakes turn up all over the world in various forms. Here in England we have our annual ritual of tossing them out of frying-pans for one reason or another! In Russia they turn up as blinis, made with yeast and served topped with soured cream and caviare. The Jews have blinzes, the nicest of which are those stuffed with cream cheese and cinnamon, folded into parcels, then crisply fried. The Chinese make theirs into little parcels called *won-tons* or crunchy rolls stuffed with vegetables. In Brittany almost every other eating-place is a *crêperie*, or pancake-shop, where their *galettes* and *crêpes* can accommodate an apparently limitless selection of ingredients, both sweet and savoury.

To make a pancake is not difficult, but to make a good *thin* pancake takes a bit of practice. A beginner using the recipe below will probably end up with twelve pancakes, but in no time at all they'll be able to get fourteen or even sixteen out of the same mixture.

CHOOSING THE RIGHT PAN

To make perfect pancakes, you need a good heavy frying-pan not more than 7 inches (18 cm) in diameter – that's the inside base measurement. A larger pan would make the batter difficult to spread out and you'd end up with pancakes with ragged edges. The pan needs to be hot and lightly-greased. The idea is simply to lubricate the pan enough to prevent the pancake from sticking. Too much fat will make the pancake fry – which is all wrong. I think that using butter is best – and remember you will need to re-grease and reheat the pan between each pancake.

KEEPING PANCAKES HOT AND REHEATING THEM

Pancakes are best eaten as soon as cooked but they can be made well ahead, laid flat, wrapped and refrigerated, then reheated next day. Reheat them by stacking them onto a warm plate – cover the stack with foil and set the plate in a warm oven. Alternatively (and this is the usual way to keep freshly cooked pancakes warm while you make the rest of the batch) set the foil-covered plate on top of a pan of simmering water. Pancakes also freeze well, stacked between leaves of greaseproof paper and the whole lot wrapped in foil – but use within three months.

BASIC PANCAKES

◆

(Makes 12–14)

This basic batter is one I have arrived at after many experiments: I think it's light, it does *not* need to stand, and (dare I say it?) it is pretty foolproof. (Illus. opposite p. 352.)

4 oz plain flour (110 g)
a pinch of salt
2 large eggs
7 fl oz milk (200 ml) mixed with 3 fl oz water (75 ml)
2 tablespoons melted butter
a little extra butter for cooking the pancakes

First sift the flour and salt into a large mixing bowl, holding the sieve up high to give the flour an airing. Then make a well in the centre of the flour and break the eggs into it. Now start to whisk the eggs (with an electric or any sort of whisk, or even a fork), beginning to incorporate bits of flour from around the edges as you do so. Then start to add small quantities of the milk-and-water mixture gradually – and ignore any lumps because they'll eventually disappear as the whisk gets to them. When all the milk-and-water has been added, slide a rubber spatula around the edge of the bowl to bring any elusive bits of flour into the centre of things. Then whisk once more till the batter is smooth and the consistency of thin cream.

When you're ready to cook the pancakes, add the 2 tablespoons of melted butter to the batter and stir it in. Then melt about a teaspoon of butter in the pan and swirl it all round to get the whole of the pan thoroughly lubricated. Now tip the excess butter onto a saucer (remember that the pan needs to be coated with butter but the pancakes should not be cooked in fat). Next get the pan really hot, then turn the heat down to medium, and to start with do a test pancake to determine whether or not you're using the correct amount of batter. I find 2 tablespoons about right.

As soon as the batter hits the hot pan, tip it around from side to side to get the base evenly coated with batter. It should take only half a minute or so to cook: you can lift the edge with a palette knife to see if it's tinged gold as it should be. If the pancake is thin enough there is no need to turn it over – it will be cooked through (and when it's rolled up with sugar and lemon or a stuffing, the paler coloured inside will not be visible). Just slide each pancake, when it is cooked, out of the pan onto a warm plate. Cover it with foil and put the plate over a pan of simmering water to keep the pancake warm while you cook the next.

Lemon pancakes

Sprinkle each pancake with freshly squeezed lemon juice and caster sugar, fold in half, then in half again to form triangles. Serve sprinkled with a little more juice and extra sections of lemon.

Strawberry jam pancakes

Have some warmed strawberry jam ready, put a dessertspoonful in the centre of each pancake, then roll it up, folding the ends inwards like a parcel. Serve with pouring cream.

Honey or syrup pancakes

Warm some maple syrup or runny honey. Brush each pancake with it, then fold into triangles (as *Lemon pancakes*), and have more syrup or honey in a jug on the table.

Buckwheat pancakes

Buckwheat flour is available from health-food shops, and is used to make several varieties of pancake, most famous of them the Breton *crêpes*. I think the best results of all are obtained by using half buckwheat flour and half plain (as all buckwheat tends to give them a slightly rubbery texture).

CRÊPES SUZETTE
♦

(Serves 4–6 people)

In restaurants, these used to be produced like a cabaret act, which put me off even ordering them. However, made at home, without all the drama, they really are extraordinarily good.

For the crêpes
1 quantity basic pancake batter (see page 338),
flavoured with the grated rind of 1 medium orange
and 1 tablespoon caster sugar

For the sauce
juice of 3–4 medium oranges – you need 5 fl oz (150 ml) altogether
grated rind of 1 medium orange
grated rind and juice of 1 small lemon
1 tablespoon caster sugar
3 tablespoons Grand Marnier, Cointreau or brandy
2 oz unsalted butter (50 g)

Make the pancakes (*crêpes*), stacking them as described on page 337. Ideally they should be thinner than those in the basic recipe, so use only 1³/₄ tablespoons of batter for each *crêpe*. This should give you at least sixteen.

When you have cooked and stacked the *crêpes*, mix together all the sauce ingredients (except the butter) in a bowl, and warm the plates on which the *crêpes* are to be served. Take a large frying-pan – preferably 10 inch (25 cm) – and melt the butter in it, add the sauce ingredients and allow them to heat very gently.

Place the first *crêpe* in the pan, give it time to warm through, then fold it in half and half again, to make a triangle shape. Slide it to the very edge of the pan. Tilt the pan slightly so that the sauce runs back into the centre, then add the next *crêpe*, and continue until they are all reheated, folded and soaked with the sauce.

If you want to be dramatic, you might at this point heat a tablespoon by holding it over a gas flame or resting it on the edge of a hotplate. Then, away from the heat, pour a little liqueur or brandy into the spoon, return it to the heat to warm the spirit, then set light to it. Carry the tablespoon of flames to the table along with the pan, and pour the flames over the *crêpes* before serving.

SPINACH-STUFFED PANCAKES WITH CHEESE SAUCE

———————— ◆ ————————

(Serves 4 people)

In the summer months, instead of using frozen spinach these can be made with 2 lb (900 g) of fresh spinach cooked with butter and salt (no water), in its own steam in a lidded saucepan, for about 5–7 minutes.

1 quantity basic pancake batter (see page 338), made with half wholewheat flour and half plain flour

2 × 8 oz packets frozen spinach (2 × 225 g)

2 oz butter (50 g)

2½ fl oz double cream (60 ml)

For the cheese sauce

2 oz butter (50 g)

1½ oz plain flour (40 g)

15 fl oz milk (425 ml)

2½ fl oz double cream (60 ml)

1½ oz strong Cheddar cheese (40 g), grated

salt, freshly milled black pepper and freshly grated nutmeg

For the topping

1½ oz strong Cheddar cheese (40 g), grated

1 oz Parmesan cheese (25 g), grated

Pre-heat the oven to gas mark 6, 400°F (200°C).

A shallow baking dish or tin, well-buttered.

Allow the spinach to defrost in a colander placed over a plate, so that the excess liquid drains out of it.

Make up twelve pancakes according to the basic recipe and stack them on a plate (there's no need to keep them warm).

Then make up an all-in-one cheese sauce: place the butter, flour and milk in a saucepan and whisk over a medium heat till thickened. Stir in the cream, the cheese, and season with salt, pepper and nutmeg.

Next, press the excess liquid out of the spinach, melt the butter in a saucepan and stir in the spinach followed by the cream. Continue to stir, preferably with a wooden fork, to break up the spinach. Cook gently until the spinach has absorbed the cream and is a nice soft consistency. Now taste it and season with salt, pepper and a little grated nutmeg.

Next, place about a tablespoonful of the spinach mixture on each pancake and roll each up, folding in the ends. Now pack them side by side in the baking dish or tin. Then pour over the prepared sauce, sprinkle with the Cheddar and Parmesan cheeses and bake on a high shelf for 25 minutes or until it's browned and bubbling.

Note This dish can be prepared well in advance and just popped into the oven to reheat 30 minutes before you need it.

PANCAKE CANNELLONI

◆

(Serves 4 people)

This is my own Anglicised version of the famous Italian *Cannelloni al forno*. It is made with pancakes instead of pasta, and works superbly.

1 quantity basic pancakes (see page 338), approx. 12
1 quantity ragù Bolognese (see page 330)
For the sauce
1¹/₂ oz butter (40 g)
1 oz plain flour (25 g)
15 fl oz cold milk (425 ml)
freshly grated nutmeg
salt and freshly milled black pepper
For the topping
2 heaped tablespoons grated Parmesan cheese
a few drops of olive oil

Pre-heat the oven to gas mark 6, 400°F (200°C).

A shallow gratin dish or baking tin, well-buttered.

To make the sauce, place the butter, flour and cold milk together in a saucepan and whisk over a medium heat until the sauce begins to bubble and thicken. Then reduce the heat as low as possible and allow the sauce to cook gently for 6 minutes. Season with salt and freshly milled pepper and a good grating of whole nutmeg.

Now spread the pancakes out, place an equal quantity of ragù Bolognese on each one, roll them up tightly and fold in the ends. Then tuck them side by side into the prepared gratin dish, pour the sauce over, sprinkle with the Parmesan cheese and drizzle about a teaspoon of olive oil over the surface. Bake on a high shelf for 30 minutes.

APPLE AND CINNAMON CRÊPES

◆

(Serves 2–3 people)

These are the French type of pancakes, served flat and made with buckwheat flour; if you can't get any, use wholewheat flour instead. This is a beautiful recipe. Serve it with chilled pouring cream, crème fraîche or Greek yoghurt.

2 oz plain flour (50 g), sifted
1 oz buckwheat flour (25 g)
1 large egg
4 fl oz milk (110 ml) mixed with 2 fl oz (55 ml) water
¼ teaspoon ground cinnamon
¼ teaspoon vanilla essence
2 small Cox's apples, peeled and cored
1½ oz butter (40 g)
To serve
3 tablespoons dry cider
caster sugar
chilled pouring cream

Begin by mixing the flours together in a bowl, then make a hollow in the centre and break the egg into it and whisk it into the flour together with the milk-and-water mixture, added a little at a time.

Beat until you have a perfectly smooth batter, then add the cinnamon and vanilla essence. Next grate the peeled and cored apples straight into the batter.

At this stage put some plates in the oven to warm and also put the cider in a small saucepan to heat.

Now melt a generous piece of the butter in a 7 or 8 inch (18 or 20 cm) frying-pan and, when hot, rotate the pan so that the sides as well as the base are well coated with the butter. Pour off any excess.

Now drop 2 tablespoons of batter into the hot buttery frying-pan and shake and ease the mixture to spread all over the pan base – using a palette knife if necessary.

Cook until the *crêpe* becomes crisp at the edges and is a lovely golden colour underneath, then, using a fish slice, knife or spatula, toss or turn the *crêpe* over and cook the other side until crisp and golden too. Use a little more butter for each new *crêpe*. Serve the *crêpes* flat on warmed plates, sprinkled with a little of the hot cider, some caster sugar and some chilled pouring cream.

Note This quantity of batter should make seven *crêpes*. If you want to keep them warm between cooking and serving, lay them flat on top of each other between two warmed plates either in a warm oven or on top of a saucepan of simmering water.

CHEESE SOUFFLÉ PANCAKES

◆

(Serves 4 people)

I first ate these in Italy where they were called Crespollini Amalfitan and this version is, I think, exactly the same.

1 quantity basic pancakes (see page 338), approx. 12
For the filling
2 oz butter (50 g)
2 oz plain flour (50 g), sifted
4 tablespoons milk, warmed and infused with a bay leaf, a slice of onion and a few peppercorns for 30 minutes
2 oz strong Cheddar cheese (50 g), grated
½ teaspoon mustard powder
2 pinches of cayenne pepper
3 large eggs, separated
salt and freshly milled black pepper
For the topping
1½ tablespoons grated Parmesan cheese
extra butter

Pre-heat the oven to gas mark 6, 400°F (200°C).

A shallow baking dish or tin, buttered.

First make the filling by melting the butter in a saucepan, add the flour and mix to a smooth paste. Then blend in, a little at a time, the flavoured and strained milk and cook over very gentle heat for 5 minutes. Next stir in the grated Cheddar cheese, the mustard powder and cayenne pepper, and add salt and freshly milled pepper to taste.

Now turn the mixture into a bowl, beat the egg yolks, and very carefully incorporate them with the mixture. In another bowl whisk the egg whites to the soft peak stage: stir 1 tablespoon into the cheese sauce, then gently fold in the rest, using a metal spoon.

Now spoon a generous portion of the mixture onto one half of each pancake and fold the other half over like a Cornish pasty. Place them side by side in the buttered baking dish, sprinkle with Parmesan cheese, put a few dabs of butter on top, and bake in the centre of the oven for approximately 10–15 minutes, by which time they will be golden-brown and puffy. These go well with a raw spinach salad (see page 445).

SEE ALSO

Pesto alla Genovese
Roman gnocchi

HERBS

◆

Writing in the sixteenth century the East Anglian farmer Thomas Tusser listed over fifty herbs that he considered *essential* in every kitchen garden, and at one time – in fact until just over 200 years ago – London's Leadenhall had its very own herb market. The fact that it closed down is probably a sad reflection on the decline of the use of herbs in English cooking. And not just cooking, for every cookbook right up to the last century contained its own batch of herbal healing remedies for a whole litany of ailments, from toothache to gout!

I suppose the decline of herbs ran parallel to the decline of our cooking, at the time the industrial revolution enticed people off the land. But now, two centuries later, I think nature is luring us back from our modern technology to consider what the earth gives – fresh natural foods and fresh natural flavours, and not least the enormous variety of fragrant and fresh-tasting herbs. Living in the country I am fortunate enough to have room for a fairly large herb garden, but even in the cities more and more people have recently set up their window-boxes or grow bags to plant a few fresh herbs to enliven their cooking.

Even if that isn't possible, fresh herbs can now be purchased quite widely in shops and supermarkets. There are quite a number of herb farms which send them out by post (which is a slightly extravagant way of acquiring them, since it involves ever-increasing postal charges). But if we keep on pestering those greengrocers who don't yet stock a decent range of fresh herbs, we will eventually get a steadier and more reliable supply of them.

STORING HERBS

For those who have to buy fresh cut herbs, do *not* store them stuck in a jar of water on a window-sill. Sunlight ruins cut herbs, so tie them loosely but securely in polythene bags and park them in the lowest part of the refrigerator (i.e. a vegetable drawer). In this way I have kept cut chives, tarragon and chervil for up to a week, mint for a fortnight, and thyme, sage and rosemary even longer.

FREEZING HERBS

I don't often freeze herbs because I enjoy using them in their right season – but chopped and stored in freezer tubs they can sometimes be useful in winter. One alternative, if you have a garden, is to grow winter chives (often called Welsh onions). They survive the frost and snow quite happily. I have found that the best way to freeze herbs for my own use is actually to make herb butter (either of mixed herbs or individual ones, see page 405). A good way to do this is to press the butter into ice-cube trays, and slip the trays into polythene bags before putting back in the freezer. This makes it very convenient to use just one of two blocks for melting over steaks, fish or vegetables.

CHOPPING HERBS

There are plenty of little gadgets on the market for chopping herbs, but none as good as a sharp knife and wooden chopping board. The trouble with many of these gadgets is that they squash – rather than chop – the herbs and make them mushy (they also require tedious and intricate cleaning afterwards!).

Ideally you need a good-sized cook's knife, with a 7 inch (18 cm) blade that is slightly curved. Arrange the herbs on the chopping board by spreading them out, then rest the blade of the knife horizontally on the board at the edge furthest away from you. Hold the pointed end between the finger and thumb of one hand to steady it, take the handle in the other hand, and make sharp cutting movements swinging the handle towards you as you chop – so that the blade swivels in a fan shape across the herbs, and back again. Your reward, I promise, will be a deliciously aromatic, herb-scented kitchen.

Chives are an exception as they are far more easily snipped with kitchen scissors. I have also heard it said (and I pass it on to you) that basil should have its leaves torn rather than chopped: this apparently is the best way to retain all the fragrant oils.

COOKING WITH FRESH HERBS

In some recipes whole sprigs of herbs are added to the pot at the beginning of the cooking, so that their flavour can truly permeate the food, but this depends entirely on the nature of the dish and the herb itself. There are times (especially when making sauces or soups) when it is far better to add the herb at the very end, just before serving, so that none of the freshness or fragrance is lost. Examples of this would be chives in leek soup, parsley in parsley sauce, and basil in tomato sauce.

DRIED HERBS

Home drying of herbs is something that requires care and expertise, and there are many good books on the subject. However, commercially dried herbs are very useful in the kitchen at certain times of the year. Some cooks despise the use of dried herbs altogether – and I would agree that some herbs like chives, parsley and particularly mint lose all their charm and flavour when dried. Nevertheless there are those that deserve their place in the kitchen, and in my notes on the varieties of herbs below I have indicated which these are.

Basil

In my kitchen basil reigns supreme (appropriately enough, since its name is derived from the Greek word *basileus* for king!). It is used extensively in Italian and Provençal cooking, has a warm pungent scent and – to me – a taste of the sun. It is lack of sun that makes it difficult to grow here if we have a cold summer, yet I've always managed to grow some in a pot on my kitchen window-sill. Provided the white flowers are pinched off all the time, it goes on producing leaves right through until the end of October or even longer with care.

The fresh leaves are quite delicious, chopped and sprinkled over a tomato salad, or added to sauces and soups just before serving. Anything that has tomato in it will be improved with the addition of basil – the two have a great affinity. Dried basil has nowhere near the character and flavour of the fresh leaves – but dried basil is better than no basil at all, and it's fine in soups and sauces through the winter.

Bay Leaves

Bay trees, with their glossy green leaves, can be quite prolific. I have one about 2 feet (60 cm) high, which gives me all the bay leaves I need. Fresh bay leaves, however, can impart a slightly bitter flavour, so this is a herb which is far better used dried. To dry them is easy: just hang a branch in an airy spot and the leaves will dry in a couple of weeks.

They are used, probably more than any other herb, to flavour stocks, sauces, casseroles and marinades. One unusual idea you might like to try is to place a bay leaf in about 2 inches (5 cm) of boiling water, add some salt, then sit a whole prepared cauliflower in the water to cook with the lid tightly closed. When it's tender (after about 10 minutes), drain, melt some butter over the cauliflower, and sprinkle on a little nutmeg.

Chervil

This herb is used quite a lot in French cooking, but rather less in this country where we tend to prefer the more pungent flavour of parsley. Chervil in fact has a more subtle, delicate flavour, and it is quite easy to grow. Along with a few chives and chopped tarragon, it's delicious in an *Omelette aux fines herbes* (page 25). It can be used in sauces too, but (like parsley) should be added at the last moment if it is to make any sort of impression. Chervil is not good dried.

CHIVES

———— ◆ ————

I wouldn't be without my chives – a very easily grown perennial that adds interest to a whole variety of dishes from early April right through to October. Although a member of the onion family, chives have a sweet flavour entirely their own. A catalogue of how to use them would be endless: they turn up in very many dishes all through the *Cookery Course*, but one of my favourite ways of serving them is to add a couple of heaped tablespoons to 5 fl oz (150 ml) of soured cream, and to pour this over halved jacket potatoes.

Don't chop chives – keep them in bunches and use scissors to snip them in small pieces. They can be deep-frozen for the winter: place them in a sieve, pour boiling water over to blanch them, then cool them under a cold tap. Dry them as thoroughly as possible and freeze in sealed polythene bags.

Dried chives don't work at all, but if you can get hold of a clump (or seeds) of Welsh onion, scallion or green onion (which all look like spring onion tops) you'll find these go on all through the winter. Although they have a slightly stronger flavour, they're suitable for any recipe that calls for chives.

CORIANDER

———— ◆ ————

Fresh coriander leaves have become much more widespread, as people have grown better acquainted with Indian and Middle Eastern food, where they are regularly used. Not one of my favourites: I find their pungent flavour too strong – almost soapy!

DILL

———— ◆ ————

This herb is best-known for its use in commercially pickled cucumbers, where the leafy heads and the seeds are used. The seeds have to be planted annually, but grow very easily; the feathery leaves have a sharp, aromatic flavour. Chopped, they are good in sauces for fish, or added to butter to melt over. Dill goes particularly well with soured cream dressings or sauces, and has a great affinity with cucumber: add 2 tablespoons chopped dill to *Cucumber sauce* (page 397), or try the recipe for cucumber cooked with dill on page 358. I find dried dill can be used successfully if you infuse the leaves in warm water for a few minutes, then drain and use as fresh.

FENNEL

◆

Garden fennel is a fern-like green herb with quite a pronounced aniseed flavour (just as strong as that of bulb fennel described in the Vegetable chapter, page 242). It's good in sauces or stuffing for fish. An interesting variation on the *Italian baked fish* recipe (page 108) is to add a dessert-spoon of chopped fennel leaves to the tomato sauce before pouring it over the fish for baking.

GARLIC

◆

I think of garlic (strictly a member of the onion family) as an essential seasoning. I am often teased about my constant use of garlic, but remain unrepentant: you can, if you truly dislike it, always leave it out, but time and again I have heard from other cooks that garlic has often been added to dishes served to garlic-haters and they've been none the wiser! If like me you happen to love it, did you know it's very easy to grow? All you do is separate the cloves (individual sections) from the bulb, and plant them 2 inches (5 cm) deep and about 2 inches (5 cm) apart in early spring. Then in August you can harvest your own crop, which will be firm, juicy and tasting so much better than imported garlic bought from a shop.

One way to crush garlic – a question I'm asked all the time – is to place the clove on a board, set the flat side of a small knife on top and press with your thumb until you have squashed it to a pulp. You could invest in a proper garlic crusher, though these are tiresome things to clean. Probably the best way is with a pestle and mortar: add a little salt as this helps to reduce the garlic to a smooth paste. And one tip for peeling garlic – place the unpeeled clove on a flat surface and simply press it with your thumb. This breaks the skin all over, and it peels away very easily.

LOVAGE

◆

This is a herb that hardly ever crops up in recipes, yet proliferates in (almost dominates) herb gardens. It has a strong flavour which I can only describe as a sort of pungent, aromatic celery. Because its flavour, like that of coriander leaves, is so penetrating it is not a herb I use a great deal.

MARJORAM

───────── ◆ ─────────

There are three different varieties of this plant. Pot marjoram is a perennial herb which is inclined to spread itself all over the space that is allocated to it. Sweet marjoram is a half-hearted perennial (because it won't survive a hard winter). And there is wild marjoram, which in Greece is called rigani and in Italy oregano. I grow the first type, because I'm not organised enough to sow a new batch each year. I use it, along with other herbs, for herb butters, herb omelettes and herb-flavoured dressings for salads. Fresh pot marjoram can be used for any recipe that calls for oregano, but for winter use I would strongly recommend dried oregano.

MINT

───────── ◆ ─────────

Mint comes in a whole range of varieties that can be used for cooking, and when I first started a herb garden I found myself the proud owner of several kinds. However I gradually came to realise that spearmint was the one I used most, and now grow only that. This is the one used for mint sauce, and for cooking new potatoes. When it's being chopped the kitchen is filled with the most fragrant aroma; and a couple of sprigs added to boiling new potatoes will permeate the room with an appetising smell too. In the summer it is, like chives, a herb I use frequently, and it's included in several recipes that follow. One unusual application I discovered in the Amalfi area of Italy is to place fresh mint leaves in the belly of fish before baking, grilling or frying them.

One word of warning about mint: never use it dried – it loses all its flavour and becomes very musty and lifeless.

PARSLEY

───────── ◆ ─────────

What needs to be said about the most universal and widely used herb of all? No garden or window-box should be without it. The leaves can be used to flavour and enliven the appearance of many, many dishes. The stalks may be added to stocks, while sprigs of parsley are the most ubiquitous garnish of the lot. To keep a good supply going, it's best to sow some seeds in late spring and again at the end of summer, as the plant is a biennial. Supermarkets sell chopped parsley in little tubs, which is useful when you only want to use small amounts.

ROSEMARY

———— ♦ ————

The ancient Greeks said that rosemary was good for the brain – a theory that persisted through the centuries (so we find Ophelia presenting it to Hamlet 'for remembrance'). Be that as it may, the Italians love its strong spicy flavour in the kitchen, and make no excuses for using it. The French are more subtle with it, but there' are many countries that hardly use it at all.

There are those who say that rosemary can be unpleasant if it gets stuck between the teeth – but this doesn't happen if the needle-like leaves are stripped from their stems and then chopped before using. It has a strong affinity with both pork and lamb, and can be chopped and sprinkled over joints and chops before baking (you'll find you can make a lovely rosemary-flavoured sauce with the juices left in the tin with some stock and a little wine).

Rosemary grows very easily into a sturdy bush, and can be used fresh all through the winter. Dried rosemary is all right, but I would recommend that it be chopped as finely as possible since it's much more spiky when dried.

SAGE

———— ♦ ————

Sage has always been one of the great healing herbs: its name comes from the Latin *salvere* (to save). Its culinary use is largely despised by the French, but much favoured by the British and Italians. It is a very strongly flavoured herb, so has to be used with caution. Delicious in stuffings for all poultry and pork (see the recipe on page 198), and especially good in pork sausages.

It is easy to grow, though as with mint there are many varieties. I grow the broad leaf sage. This is a herb that does dry well, without losing much flavour at all.

SORREL

———— ♦ ————

Much loved and used for sauces and soups in France, but not so widely known here. Yet it's easy to grow and well worth including in a herb garden. It has leaves similar in appearance to spinach, and indeed tastes like a sharper version of spinach. Because of this sharpness very little of it is needed – a couple of handfuls, about 1½ oz (40 g) is enough to make a delicious soup.

TARRAGON

—————— ◆ ——————

If the king of herbs is basil, then I would like to nominate tarragon as the queen. It's a sophisticated herb, highly prized in French cooking and an essential ingredient in their famous *Sauce Béarnaise* (see page 395). It goes well in veal and poultry dishes, and is often included in mixed herb dishes. It is, however, a strongly flavoured herb, so always be sparing with it. A sprig or two preserved in some white wine vinegar will help to give a subtle flavour of tarragon to salad dressings all through the winter.

You can only grow it from cuttings, and if you buy a plant (one will be enough) do make sure the label says it's French tarragon. There is a Russian variety which grows up to 5 feet (1.5 m) high, but has nowhere near the flavour of the French. Dried tarragon is useful – if you steep it in warm water for a minute or two before using.

THYME

—————— ◆ ——————

A bush of garden thyme will be a good friend to any cook, as it provides fresh leaves all the year round. It has a really strong, warm resinous flavour, and needs to be used sparingly if it is not to overpower other tastes. A teaspoonful of chopped thyme added to a salad dressing is a good idea, and I use little branches of thyme in my stocks and casseroles – and always add some to beef stews. You'll find it in many recipes in the *Cookery Course*, and as it is a herb that dries well, it's useful for flat dwellers and non-gardeners.

GREEN HERB SOUP

—————— ◆ ——————

(Serves 4–5 people)

This soup adapts to any combination of fresh herbs – mint, sage, tarragon, thyme, rosemary, sorrel or any others that are available.

1 oz butter (25 g)
6 thick spring onions (and their green tops), thinly sliced
6 oz potatoes (175 g), scraped and cubed
5 oz outside lettuce leaves or spinach leaves (150 g), de-stalked and shredded
15 fl oz light stock (425 ml)
2 rounded tablespoons chopped fresh herbs

Basic pancakes (see page 338)

5 fl oz single cream (150 ml)
a generous squeeze of lemon juice
salt and freshly milled black pepper

Melt the butter in a medium-sized pan, and stir in the thinly sliced spring onions and the cubed potatoes. Stir and cook over a gentle heat so the vegetables soften gently without browning.

Now stir in the shredded lettuce. Get it all nicely coated with butter. Then add the stock, bring to simmering point, cover and cook gently for about 10 minutes or just long enough for the potatoes to soften.

Next pour the contents of the saucepan into a liquidiser. Add the chopped fresh herbs and the cream and blend until smooth. Return the purée to the pan and reheat, tasting and flavouring with the lemon juice, salt and pepper. Serve hot with crusty wholewheat bread.

CARROT AND TARRAGON SOUP
◆

(Serves 4–6 people)

This is a delicious, summery soup, but it can be made in the winter with two finely chopped leeks instead of the lettuce leaves and some dried tarragon instead of fresh.

12 oz carrots (350 g)
1 small onion
the outside leaves of a lettuce or 2 leeks
2 oz butter (50 g)
2 sprigs fresh or ¼ teaspoon dried tarragon
1½ pints boiling water (850 ml)
1 teaspoon sugar
3 tablespoons double cream
salt and freshly milled black pepper

First wash and scrape the carrots and slice them thinly, then chop the onion and lettuce fairly small. In a thick-based saucepan gently melt the butter and soften the onion in it for a minute or two, then add the carrots and lettuce, stirring to get a good coating of butter. Now put a lid on and let the vegetables gently 'sweat' for 10 minutes. Next, strip the leaves from the tarragon, pop them in, then add the boiling water, the sugar and a seasoning of salt and pepper. When it returns to simmering point, put a lid on and simmer very gently for 25 minutes. Now either liquidise or sieve the soup, taste to check the seasoning and reheat gently, stirring in the cream just before serving.

Note Don't be tempted to use stock, as this detracts from the fresh flavour of the carrots.

Leg of lamb baked with butter and herbs (see page 360)　　353

SPRING SAUCE FOR LAMB
◆

(Serves 6 people)

I always part company with mint sauce if it's made with malt vinegar which completely overpowers the flavour of the lamb, but the following sauce – which my grandmother always served with lamb – is made with wine vinegar diluted with an equal quantity of water, so it's much milder.

2 tablespoons chopped fresh mint
2 spring onions, very finely chopped
2 lettuce leaves, finely chopped
3 tablespoons wine vinegar
3 tablespoons cold water

Simply combine all the above ingredients and place in a sauce-boat for everyone to help themselves.

PESTO ALLA GENOVESE (FRESH BASIL SAUCE)
◆

(Serves 2 people)

This is a sauce which, freshly made, will throw any pasta lover into transports of delight. The flavour of the fresh basil combined with olive oil and garlic is out of this world!

2 oz fresh basil leaves (50 g)
1 large clove garlic, crushed
1 tablespoon pine kernels
6 tablespoons olive oil
1 oz Parmesan cheese (25 g), grated
salt

If you have a blender, put the basil, garlic, pine kernels and olive oil together with some salt in the goblet and blend until you have a smooth purée. Transfer the purée to a bowl and stir in the grated Parmesan.

If you don't have a blender, use a large pestle and mortar to pound the basil, garlic and pine kernels to a paste. Slowly add the salt and cheese followed by the very gradual addition of the oil until you obtain a smooth purée.

The above quantities will make enough sauce for serving with 8–10 oz (225–275 g) of pasta, which is sufficient for two people.

GREEN HERB AND RICE SALAD

◆

(Serves 8 people)

This is an excellent way to serve rice, cold at a buffet party or warm with barbecue food.

brown basmati rice measured to the 12 fl oz (350 ml) level in a measuring jug
24 fl oz boiling water or vegetable stock (700 ml) – double the volume of rice
2 dessertspoons oil
1 teaspoon salt
2 oz prepared spinach leaves (50 g)
8 spring onions, including the green tops
2 heaped teaspoons chopped fresh herbs (thyme, rosemary, sage, marjoram, tarragon)
grated rind of ½ lemon
For the dressing
1 teaspoon rock salt
½ teaspoon black peppercorns
1 clove garlic
1 teaspoon mustard powder
1 tablespoon wine vinegar
5 tablespoons olive oil

Heat the oil in a pan, stir in the rice, then pour in the boiling water or stock. Add the salt, stir once and allow it to come back to the boil. Cover, then reduce the heat to give a bare simmer. Cook gently for 40–50 minutes or until all the liquid has been absorbed and the rice is just tender.

Next chop up the spinach leaves and spring onions very finely, and fork into the rice along with the herbs and grated lemon rind. Cover the pan with a folded cloth and leave aside for 10 minutes.

Make the dressing by crushing the salt, peppercorns and garlic together with a pestle and mortar. Add the mustard, vinegar and olive oil, then shake the whole lot together in a screw-top jar.

Tip the salad ingredients into a bowl, pour the dressing all over and fluff it with a skewer. Serve the salad warm or cold.

POACHED TROUT WITH HERBS

◆

(Serves 4 people)

This is very light and a good recipe for slimmers if the parsley butter isn't used for serving.

4 trout, weighing approx. 6 oz each (175 g), cleaned
salt
6 whole peppercorns
4 bay leaves
1 small onion, cut into rings
1 lemon
1 sprig fresh or 1 teaspoon dried thyme
3 tablespoons finely chopped fresh parsley
4 fl oz dry white wine (110 ml)
2 tablespoons snipped fresh chives
3 oz butter (75 g)

Place the trout in a large frying-pan or a thick-based roasting tin. Now sprinkle a little salt over them and throw in the peppercorns. Next add the bay leaves, one in between each trout. Lay onion rings over the top; cut half the lemon into slices and arrange them here and there. Add the thyme and sprinkle a tablespoon of chopped parsley over everything. Finally add the wine and enough cold water just to cover the fish. Bring it to the boil on top of the stove and let it simmer gently, uncovered, for 6 minutes if the trout are fresh or 20 minutes if they are frozen.

Mix the remaining parsley and chives with the butter in a small basin, then divide the mixture into four portions. When the trout are ready, carefully lift them out with a fish slice, allowing each one to drain for a few seconds, and serve with the parsley butter and the other half of the lemon cut into wedges.

TROUT WITH BUTTER, CREAM AND CHIVES

◆

(Serves 2 people)

This recipe is a good one for anyone who has to work and then prepare a meal quickly – the whole thing takes little more than 30 minutes.

2 medium trout, weighing approx. 6 or 7 oz each (175 or 200 g), cleaned
butter
3 fl oz double cream (75 ml)
1 bay leaf

| 2 tablespoons snipped fresh chives |
| salt and freshly milled black pepper |

Pre-heat the oven to gas mark 7, 425°F (220°C).

First line a roasting tin with foil and brush it with a little melted butter. Then wash the trout and dry them very thoroughly. Now place them in the roasting tin, brush each one with a little melted butter and season with salt and pepper. Bake them, on a high shelf in the oven, for about 10–15 minutes.

While that's happening pour the cream into a saucepan, add the bay leaf and bring it up to boiling point. Then stir in the chives and 1 oz (25 g) butter, season with salt and pepper, and pour this mixture into a warm jug. Serve it with the fish, some buttered new potatoes and a green salad or some fresh cooked spinach.

BAKED MACKEREL WITH HERB STUFFING
◆

(Serves 2 people)

Mackerel need to be very fresh so try to buy bright, stiff-looking fish rather than flabby, tired-looking ones.

| 2 mackerel, cleaned and heads removed |
| 1 oz butter (25 g) |
| 3 large spring onions, chopped |
| 2 oz white breadcrumbs (50 g) |
| grated rind of ¹/₂ lemon |
| 2 teaspoons lemon juice |
| 1 tablespoon chopped fresh parsley |
| 1 tablespoon snipped fresh chives |
| 1 teaspoon finely chopped fresh or ¹/₂ teaspoon dried tarragon |
| ¹/₂ teaspoon dried thyme or a sprig of fresh thyme |
| oil |
| 5 oz natural yoghurt (150 g) |
| salt and freshly milled black pepper |

Pre-heat the oven to gas mark 5, 375°F (190°C).

Wash and dry the mackerel thoroughly. Start by melting the butter and gently frying the chopped spring onions for about 2 minutes, then combine in the breadcrumbs, lemon rind and juice and half the whole quantity of herbs. Season well with salt and pepper and pack an equal quantity of the mixture into the belly of each fish. Brush the fish with oil and season with salt and freshly milled pepper. Place them in a foil-lined baking tin and bake in the top half of the oven for 25 minutes.

Stir the remaining herbs into the yoghurt and season with salt and freshly milled pepper. Pour over the fish and bake for 5 more minutes, then serve with some buttery potatoes and a crisp green salad.

CHICKEN SALAD WITH TARRAGON AND GRAPES

◆

(Serves 4–6 people)

This is the perfect main-course salad for lunch on a warm summer day, with perhaps some brown rice salad to go with it.

1 cooked chicken, approx. 3–3³/₄ lb (1.3–1.7 kg) raw weight
5 fl oz home-made mayonnaise (150 ml) (see page 438)
3 fl oz double cream (75 ml)
1 heaped teaspoon chopped fresh tarragon or ¹/₂ heaped teaspoon dried tarragon, soaked in warm water for 5 minutes, then squeezed dry in kitchen paper
3 spring onions, finely chopped
1 small lettuce
4 oz green grapes (110 g), halved and de-pipped
a few sprigs of watercress
salt and freshly milled black pepper

Remove the skin from the chicken and slice the flesh into longish pieces where possible. Remove all the chicken from the bones and place all the meat in a bowl, seasoning with salt and pepper.

In a separate bowl mix the mayonnaise thoroughly with the cream, adding the chopped tarragon and finely chopped spring onions. Now pour the sauce over the chicken, mix it well so that all the chicken pieces get a good coating, then arrange it on a plate of crisp lettuce leaves and garnish with green grapes and a few sprigs of watercress.

CUCUMBER WITH SOURED CREAM AND DILL

◆

(Serves 2–3 people)

Dill goes well with all cucumber or soured cream recipes. This combines both, and is a marvellous vegetable accompaniment to fish.

1 lb cucumber (450 g), cut into ¹/₂ inch (1 cm) cubes with the skin left on
1¹/₂ oz butter (40 g)

| 2 spring onions, chopped (including the green tops) |
| 1 teaspoon chopped fresh or ¼ teaspoon dried dill |
| 2½ fl oz soured cream (60 ml) or Greek yoghurt |
| 1 dessertspoon lemon juice |
| salt and freshly milled black pepper |

Heat the butter in a smallish pan and stir in the chopped spring onions. Cook for 2 minutes before tipping in the cucumber cubes. Now give them a good stir to coat with the butter, sprinkle with the dill, then cover and cook over a medium heat for about 8 minutes.

Shake the pan now and then to make sure none of the cucumber catches on the base of the pan.

As soon as the pieces are just tender (but still with a bit of 'bite' to them), turn the heat right down to minimum, stir in the soured cream and a little lemon juice, season with salt and pepper, and just let the cream warm through before serving.

Note This is also good made with some small, young courgettes.

PORK CHOPS WITH SAGE AND APPLES
◆

(Serves 4 people)

This is an excellent recipe and a very easy one.

| 4 lean pork chops |
| 3 level dessertspoons very finely chopped fresh or |
| 3 teaspoons dried sage |
| 4 tablespoons dried white breadcrumbs |
| 1 small egg |
| oil |
| butter |
| 2 Cox's apples, cored and sliced into rings but with skins left on |
| 1 medium onion, sliced into rings |
| salt and freshly milled black pepper |

First of all mix the sage and breadcrumbs together and season well with coarsely milled black pepper and salt. Then beat up the egg and dip the pork chops first in the egg, then into the breadcrumb and sage mixture, pressing firmly all round so that the chops get a really good even coating.

Now heat 2 tablespoons of oil and 1 oz (25 g) butter together in a frying-pan and brown the chops quickly on both sides with the fat fairly hot, then lower the heat and let them gently cook through (it will take around 25–30 minutes depending on the thickness of the chops).

While that's happening, melt a little more butter and oil in another frying-pan and fry the apple and onion rings. Drain everything on crumpled greaseproof paper before serving.

LEG OF LAMB BAKED WITH BUTTER AND HERBS

———————— ♦ ————————

(Serves 4–6 people)

This has proved one of the most popular recipes in the *Cookery Course* over the years, and the *Redcurrant, orange and mint sauce* (page 400) is a must to serve with it. (Illus. opposite p. 353.)

1 leg of lamb, approx. 4 lb (2 kg) in weight
3 oz butter (75 g), at room temperature
1 teaspoon finely chopped fresh rosemary
2 tablespoons chopped fresh mint
2 tablespoons chopped fresh parsley
1 teaspoon chopped fresh thyme
1 clove garlic, crushed
salt and freshly milled black pepper
For the gravy
1 dessertspoon plain flour
3 fl oz dry red or white wine (75 ml)
approx. 10 fl oz vegetable stock (275 ml)

Pre-heat the oven to gas mark 5, 375°F (190°C).

Mix the butter, herbs and garlic together, adding a level teaspoon of salt and some freshly milled black pepper. Stab the joint in several places with a skewer, and rub the herb butter all over the upper side (these stabs with the skewer will allow the butter to run into the joint during the cooking).

Now wrap the joint loosely in foil, sealing well. Place it in a meat-roasting tin and cook it for 2 hours, then open out the foil and cook it for a further 30 minutes to brown nicely. With these cooking times the lamb will be slightly pink. If you like it well done give it a little extra time in the foil before opening it out. Remove the joint to a warm serving dish in a warm place while you make the gravy.

Empty the juices from the foil into the roasting tin, then tilt it slightly. You will see the meat juices and the fat separating, so spoon off most of the fat into a bowl and leave the juices in the tin. Now place the tin over a medium heat, and when the juices start to bubble, sprinkle in the flour and work it to a smooth paste using a wooden spoon, then cook it for a minute or so to brown. Now pour in the wine and stock by degrees, stirring continuously and adding just enough stock to make a thin gravy. Taste to check the seasoning, pour into a jug and serve with the lamb.

SOFT, CREAMY CHEESE WITH HERBS

♦

(Serves 4 people)

This can be made with full-fat cream cheese, curd cheese or quark depending on the size of your waist! Perhaps a good compromise might be a half and half mixture of full-fat and curd cheese.

6 oz soft cheese (175 g)
2 spring onions, very finely chopped
2 tablespoons chopped fresh parsley
1 tablespoon snipped fresh chives
1 level teaspoon chopped fresh tarragon
1 level teaspoon chopped fresh thyme
1 clove garlic, crushed
freshly milled black pepper and salt (if it needs it)

Combine all the above ingredients together in a basin, then form the cheese into a round cake-shape, and serve it for lunch with lots of fresh crusty bread and a crisp salad. This can also be used to spread on opened jacket potatoes, or melted over new potatoes or any root vegetable.

SEE ALSO

Aïoli sauce
Buttered new potatoes with parsley, mint and chives
Cabbage with garlic and juniper
Cheese and herb sausages
Fresh tomato sauce
Fresh tomato soup with basil
Fried mustard-and-herb-coated chicken
Garlic butter
Herb butter
Hot herb and garlic loaf
Jacket potatoes with soured cream and chives

Liver in yoghurt and juniper sauce
Marinated mackerel
Mushrooms in hot garlic butter
Pipérade
Rice with herb butter
Roast pork with green butter
Sauce rouille
Sauce tartare
Scotch eggs with fresh herbs
Stuffed jacket potatoes with garlic and herbs
Young carrots with tarragon butter

SPICES AND FLAVOURINGS

◆

Countries have grown rich, gone to war, built empires on spice. It was the trading currency of the medieval world, its value greater than gold and precious metals. So it is curious to find, in medieval cookery books, so many different spices competing (and in such prolific amounts) in a single recipe. In one I have in front of me a humble pike is treated to no less than eight different flavourings. Such abandon with precious spices is commonly supposed to have disguised the taste of not-very-fresh food. And no doubt it did in many cases, but I also think there was an element of status-seeking in it as well. The cookery books that have survived, after all, were those compiled by master-chefs for grand households. When – in the seventeenth century – spices became more widely available and cheaper in England, they began to be used with much more discretion and English cooking consequently improved (the 'best in the world' according to Defoe at the time).

With our conquest of India, the British became even more spice-conscious as exotic curry flavourings were added to the repertoire, along with the already traditional taste of pickles, relishes and preserves. The Victorians in particular were very partial to a whole range of weird and wonderful compounds of spices, which were commercially produced under names like Harvey's Sauce: some of the better ones have survived to the present day (like Worcestershire sauce and tomato ketchup). I have the feeling that we are still suffering a bit from the legacy of the Victorians in this: there is a tendency to prefer to add flavourings to our food in the form of bottled sauces at the table, rather than incorporate them more discriminatingly in the cooking.

However, the range of spices available, even in local supermarkets, is now more impressive. They open up a whole world of recipes, and there is no excuse for our cooking horizons to be bounded by plain fried fish or grilled lamb chops (excellent though they are). All that is required is the confidence to go out and buy them and to experiment – not like a medieval alchemist throwing anything and everything together in a hotch-potch of flavours, but with restraint, allowing the flavour of the spices to enhance and complement the flavour of the food. The recipes in this section (and elsewhere in the book) are designed to demonstrate the balanced use of individual spices in recipes, and the combinations that have been shown to work through experience.

It is impossible to describe the flavour of each spice with any meaning – only testing them for yourself can be any guide – but the list below offers some explanation of their origin and possible uses. An important point to bear in mind when using spices is that ready ground they quickly lose their flavour. I have found it useful to put a little date sticker on each spice jar to check on how long I've had them. After three months or so I find they need to be replaced to ensure they're always used in perfect condition. For the same reason I try to buy them from shops with a large turnover. I have included in this section some equally important seasonings and flavourings which are normally lumped together under the ungainly title of condiments, and whose proper use is vital to good cooking. Garlic, however, is dealt with in the Herbs chapter.

SALT

It's amazing the difference salt makes to food, almost magically bringing out the flavour of a soup or sauce that may have seemed quite bland. Just how much salt you should or should not use has always been a subject for debate: some 'connoisseurs' even suggest that to add additional salt at the table is an insult to the chef. I believe that's nonsense. Each individual's capacity for salt is different, and what may be enough for the chef may not be enough for his diners. At the same time it could be true that adding more salt to food is a matter of acquired habit rather than need (as with sugar), which is why tinned baby foods now do not contain any salt – so at least our babies are not forming the habit! Others argue the health aspect, pointing out that salt – although a mineral essential to life – can in too high quantities exacerbate (not cause) hypertension and high blood pressure, which are themselves contributory factors to heart disease. This, I think, is an argument only for discretion, which is fundamental to all cooking anyway. If you discover that you *have* oversalted a dish with liquid ingredients, you can rescue it by putting in a peeled potato or two, which will absorb some of the salty flavour.

TYPES OF SALT

First of all it's as well to discount the snob element. Since the vogue for kitchen shops there's a lot of rock/sea/Mediterranean/crystal salt around. My advice is never to buy it from fancy packets. It is true that pure, unrefined salt is better than refined because it's saltier and you need less, but you can buy it from chemists, delicatessens and health-food stores without paying for the packaging.

Basically there are two kinds of salt. For cooking and the table there is common salt mined from rocks or extracted from sea water. The other kind is saltpetre, which comes out of the earth and is used for curing and pickling. The sea salt I use comes from Maldon; it is packaged in ordinary boxes and, although it may be too expensive to use exclusively for cooking, I think it's essential for the table and especially good with chips, sautéed potatoes, fritters and other deep-fried foods. Unlike other unrefined salts – such as crystal salt which needs to be crushed first with a pestle and mortar – Maldon comes in tiny flakes and at table can easily be crushed between the fingers. Now there are some excellent salt-mills available, but do invest in a good quality wooden one – acrylic ones never seem to work for long.

For everyday use the bulk of our salt comes from rock-deposits in Cheshire. Our so-called 'table salt' is very finely grained and has a chemical (magnesium carbonate) added to make it free-running. Personally I use what is termed 'cooking salt', which has fractionally larger grains, is cheaper and available at supermarkets. Even for the table I can't see the point of paying more for finer grains, particularly using a salt-cellar and spoon rather than a sprinkler.

PEPPER

◆

Pepper in my opinion is the most important spice in the kitchen. The one way in which beginners can instantly improve the character and flavour of their cooking and eating is to invest in a pepper mill. *Freshly milled* pepper has a fragrance and flavour that the dusty ready-ground stuff cannot approach. This is partly due to the fact that any spice once ground immediately starts to lose its essential flavour, and partly to the fact that most pepper-pots find their way to the table containing ready-ground 'white' pepper. Both black and white pepper come from the berries of the same tree, called *Piper nigrum*, but let us see where the difference lies.

BLACK PEPPER

Black peppercorns are the whole immature berries. The berries themselves are made up of a white inner kernel and a black outer husk. The white is the hottest part of the berry and when used on its own is distinctly fiery. It is the black outer part that has the aromatic fragrance that really enhances the flavour of food. And this part is included in black pepper, where the berries are gathered while still green, then dried whole in the sun until they turn black.

I always use this, freshly milled, in my cooking. There is a school of thought that objects, aesthetically at any rate, to finding black speckles in a white sauce. I can only say that, knowing what they are, all my family and friends have grown quite used to them and don't give it a second thought. (Curious, isn't it, that everyone expects grated nutmeg to look brown and speckled on food and raises no objection, perhaps because there is no such thing as white nutmeg?)

WHITE PEPPER

For this the berries are allowed to mature fully before they are harvested. The husks are then split and discarded, and the white kernels are dried to become white peppercorns.

Stored whole, the dried berries will retain their taste and aroma almost indefinitely. But by the time they have been powdered to dust in a factory, stored in a shop and lain about in a pepper-pot it is not surprising the result bears no comparison to the fresh and delicate flavour you can keep locked up in your pepper mill (and unlike salt-mills, pepper-mills do work).

GREEN PEPPERCORNS

This variety of pepper has only reached us in the last few years. These are the young, soft berries harvested before they have even developed separate husks and kernels. They are not dried, but retain their moisture and are preserved in small tins or jars. Deliciously aromatic – but still with a peppery fragrance.

CAPSICUMS

Under this heading come a bewildering variety of the pepper family – red, green, chilli, sweet, paprika, cayenne. Not least are they bewildering because at times their power (i.e. lethal or mild) can only be identified by one means, and that is by tasting.

FRESH CHILLIES

These look like small fresh green peppers: sometimes they are long, finger-thin and somewhat crooked and at other times they are shiny-smooth like small rounded carrots. Treat them with respect for the reason above. If they are hot, take the precaution of discarding the really hot seeds and core, and use just the chopped flesh, which is less ferocious (a little chilli powder can always be added to increase the hotness, but there is little that can be done to subdue it afterwards). However, provided this warning is observed, fresh chillies – plentiful where there are immigrant communities – really give an authentic taste to Indian dishes and curries.

WHOLE OR CRUSHED DRIED CHILLIES; CHILLI POWDER

Whole dried chillies are useful when there are no fresh ones available. Again, exercise caution. A good compromise is to remove the seeds and use only the outer paper-like casing. Crushed dried chillies (skins and seeds) are good for a dish like chilli con carne, but should be used more sparingly than powdered ones, being definitely more pungent. Chilli powder is the most widely available chilli for the kitchen, but if stored too long it will lose some of its character, if not heat. All the above are used mostly in curries and chilli sauces. Sometimes, however you will find a spice labelled 'chilli con carne seasoning': this is usually a blend of half chilli and half ground cumin, so is 50 per cent less powerful. I think chilli con carne tastes better with pure chilli.

CAYENNE PEPPER

The difference between this and chilli powder is not always clear, because both can be made from varieties of the same capsicum family. Cayenne is finer and more suitable for sprinkling on food. It is also a very fiery spice, so caution is needed, but it certainly adds zest to smoked fish pâtés in particular and cheese dishes, cheese scones and biscuits (for a cheese topping on any baked dish, mix some grated cheese with breadcrumbs and a couple of good pinches of cayenne pepper).

TABASCO SAUCE

This is a commercially prepared chilli sauce: very hot, only the merest drop or two is needed at any one time. It is used in much the same way, and in the same dishes, as cayenne pepper.

PAPRIKA

A spice made from the ground seeds of sweet peppers (pimentoes as they are sometimes called). It has the flavour of sweet pepper too, and none of the penetrating hotness of chilli. Of all ground spices paprika seems to lose flavour the fastest, so buy in small quantities, and if you haven't used it all after a few months, start again. I actually only use paprika for Hungarian goulash and *Chicken paprika* (page 380), and always buy Hungarian in preference to Spanish. If you see the words 'hot' or 'mild' on a jar, don't take too much notice because it is never a hot spice (to give an edge to it in a goulash I add just a pinch of chilli).

MUSTARD
—————— ♦ ——————

Commercially speaking, mustard has run riot recently. Where once the supermarket stocked only the familiar canary-yellow dry English mustard powder, nowadays the shelves display at least half a dozen – often more – imported varieties or at least home-made imitations of them. They are even turning up in tourist gift shops in pretty pottery jars. Wider choice is always to be welcomed of course, but personally I have always preferred my mustard to be pungent and, well, mustardy, which is why I still think our own home-grown mustard from East Anglia qualifies as the best. But what are its rivals, and how do they differ from it?

ENGLISH MUSTARD

This is made basically – as it has been for over 200 years – by the milling and blending of two different mustard seeds, the brown (confusingly sometimes called black) and the white (sometimes known as yellow). It is the brown seed that provides the pungency; the white, flavour: but both only come to life when the resulting powder is mixed with water (see below). It is now possible also to buy English mustard ready made-up – which is fine if the lid is replaced firmly and quickly each time, as mustard exposed to the air loses its kick very rapidly.

DIJON MUSTARD

This is the main mustard of France. It is the nearest to our own, though less ferocious. As the name implies it is made in and around Dijon in Burgundy, and there are any number of local variations. In some the mustard seed is mixed with spices and the acid juice of unripe grapes (verjuice), in others with diluted vinegar; yet others are blended with various white wines of the region. Like nearly all foreign mustards it comes not in powder form but already made-up, since it contains liquid. If you are ever in Burgundy look out for an excellent one called Temeraire, but in any case buy *genuine* Dijon mustard rather than pale English imitations.

BORDEAUX MUSTARD

This is what we tend to call French mustard over here. It is much darker, and because it also contains the husk of the mustard seed, it is milder and distinctly aromatic. Packed as it is with vinegar, sugar, spices and tarragon it can tend to compete with rather than enhance the flavour of some food, and it should be used very selectively.

Among the other mustards that adorn our shelves, one might take note of the sweet-sour *German mustard*, dark and not dissimilar to the Bordeaux; it goes admirably with German sausage but otherwise should be used with discretion. *American mustard* is much the same colour as ours, but is positively sweet and strictly for hot dogs. *Moutarde de Meaux* is a whole-grain mustard that has become fashionable of late. I find it rather over-rated and lacking 'bite'. For most requirements in cooking (as opposed to using it as a condiment) our English mustard, and Dijon, are more than adequate.

HOW TO MAKE MUSTARD

It's amazing, but even a simple little task like mixing mustard needs a bit of thought. It is the essential oils in mustard that give it its power and pungency, but these are not developed in the whole mustard seed or in the dry milled powder. What is needed for the flavour to emerge is a chemical reaction brought on by the addition of a little water, and even then it needs a good 10–15 minutes for the flavour to develop fully (so always make up mustard well in advance of using it). The water, too, must be cold – hot water can cause a rather different reaction, which may provide a bitter flavour.

Mustard is a very good emulsifier. Apart from the flavour it can add, it does a good stabilising job in something like mayonnaise, and can provide a slight thickening to vinaigrette or to *Cumberland sauce* (see the recipe on page 399).

Vinegar

———— ♦ ————

Originally sour wine (which is the precise meaning of the French *vin aigre*), but now the name embraces all similar sour liquids: wine vinegar, cider vinegar, malt vinegar and so on. It is created by an entirely natural process in which alcohol is turned into acetic acid. The bacteriological processes need not concern us overmuch, but the differences between various vinegars – and their uses – are most important.

WINE VINEGAR

Like the wine it is made from, this can be either red or white. The best comes from Orleans in France, where it is produced slowly and in oak casks – so look out for that name on the label when you're buying. This is the vinegar to use where it is important that the flavour does not dominate or overwhelm other ingredients, for instance in salad dressings or sauces.

MALT VINEGAR

In England vinegar has traditionally been made from beer rather than wine. The resulting malt vinegar is dark coloured and powerfully flavoured. Indeed in cooking it can only too often be a flavour-killer, masking everything it comes into contact with. It is best confined to pickling and chutneys where it is reduced and mellows with keeping. And of course malt vinegar is essential with that old English classic, fish and chips!

CIDER VINEGAR

Self-evidently made from cider. Healthy it may be (as some food theorists maintain), but it has its own distinctive taste, and is not an automatic substitute for other vinegars. Use it only where a recipe actually specifies it.

DISTILLED VINEGAR

This is colourless, strong and popular in Scotland. Because it is stronger (up to 12 per cent acetic acid) it has excellent preserving powers, and is used for pickling especially in recipes like a red tomato chutney when it is important to keep the rosy colour of the tomatoes.

FLAVOURED VINEGARS

Vinegars containing fruit, herbs or spices can be bought in some shops. Their uses are limited and, anyway, you can quite easily make your own. Tarragon vinegar, for instance, is made simply by steeping a bunch of tarragon in wine vinegar for a time, then straining the liquid if necessary. Fruit vinegars have to be used with great discretion. Introducing raspberry or blackcurrant flavours became the height of fashion not so long ago – but the results were not always very edible.

ALLSPICE

It is not, as the name would suggest, a combination of spices. Bought whole (which is to be recommended) it looks like a smoother version of peppercorns, but is in fact the dried berry of an evergreen. It got its name because it is supposed to have the flavour of three spices: nutmeg, cloves and cinnamon. However, the flavour is not really like any of these. It is used in pickling quite a lot, also for marinades for dishes like soused herring or mackerel. If a recipe calls for ground allspice, it is best to grind it with a pestle and mortar yourself as and when you need it.

CAPERS

I have included capers – not strictly a spice – here because I look on them as such important store-cupboard ingredients. A few capers can jazz up many otherwise ordinary dishes, like plain grilled fish, or sprinkled on pizzas or to add an extra dimension to sauces. I have seen caper bushes, with their very pretty pink flowers, growing out of the rocks along the Amalfi coast in Italy, where they are used extensively in the local cooking – especially *Salsa verde* (see page 402). What they are in fact are the buds of the plant, picked and pickled. Even once the jar is opened they keep their sweet-sharp flavour for some time, provided they remain covered by the pickling liquid. Ideally this should be white wine vinegar, though unfortunately some

British firms subject them to our lethal malt vinegar, from which their flavour never quite recovers even when you rinse them under the cold tap. In Italian shops, particularly in London, capers can be bought loose.

CARAWAY SEEDS

These, with their nutty toasted flavour, are not much favoured in our cooking nowadays except in old-fashioned seed cake (loved or hated, depending on one's upbringing – I well remember a schoolfriend trying to pick out all the seeds before eating it!). In Austria and Germany they are used quite a lot in various types of sausage, goulash and cabbage dishes.

CARDAMOM

An eastern spice, the sun-dried pods are pale green-grey, revealing inside the tiny, black, highly aromatic seeds. It is quite expensive, as spices go, but a little goes a long way. One pod crushed and added (add both pod and seeds) to pilau rice will impart a delicious flavour, recognisable even to those unfamiliar with the look of cardamom. It is used widely in curry dishes, occasionally in sweet recipes, and should never be bought ready-ground.

CINNAMON

This is a spice made from the inner bark of a tree belonging to the laurel family, which is what the pale brown and hollow cinnamon sticks look like. Break pieces off to add in cooking, then extract them, like bay leaves, at the end. British cooks are familiar with it as a pudding spice and for use in cakes (for this it must be bought ready-ground as it's impossible to grind it at home). It is worth noting that its strength can vary enormously, so shop around for a brand that is reliable and buy in small quantities. One of the best flavour tips I've picked up is from Greek cookery, where a hint of cinnamon is often used in savoury dishes. A little added to the meat in a moussaka gives the dish an authentic Greek flavour, and I've even taken to adding it to shepherd's pie.

CLOVES

———— ♦ ————

Cloves look like tiny wooden nails, and their aroma is dark, pungent and exotic. Those who were subjected to the highly concentrated 'oil of cloves' as a toothache remedy understandably find their flavour intolerable, but for others cloves can enhance all sorts of dishes, from mince pies and Christmas pudding to bread sauce and baked gammon. Unlike other spices, ground cloves seem to taste stronger than whole ones (perhaps because so little is needed, one tends to add too much). A little ground cloves always goes into my spiced red cabbage. Others like the flavour of cloves in an apple pie – where I think just two or three whole ones are better than adding ground cloves, although consumers have to be diligent in seeking them out!

CORIANDER

———— ♦ ————

I'm particularly fond of coriander: the tiny, round seeds crush easily and give off an aromatic, almost scented flavour sometimes said to be reminiscent of roasted orange peel (in fact Margaret Costa in her *Four Seasons Cookbook* suggests tying the crushed seeds in muslin and adding them to the fruit for marmalade). Coriander turns up in the cooking of countries all over the world. In India it is an important curry spice and the leaves – quite different in flavour – are used a great deal as a herb. Spanish, Portuguese, Arab, Turkish and Greek cuisines all rely on coriander: in fact any recipe *à la grècque* includes it. A lovely way to serve olives with aperitifs is to toss them first in a mixture of crushed coriander seeds, crushed garlic and a little vinaigrette dressing. Coriander quickly loses flavour once ground. Buy it whole, it's so easy to do yourself.

CUMIN

———— ♦ ————

Although this turns up in quite a few Mexican and Moroccan dishes, it is a spice I associate with curries. It looks like – and indeed is – long, tiny seeds, which are very easy to grind with a pestle and mortar. Sometimes whole seeds are added to pilaus and, with their strong piquant flavour, they are an essential curry spice.

371

CURRY POWDER AND GARAM MASALA

Curry powder – that is to say a ready-made blend of powdered Indian spices – is always to hand in my kitchen, though by no means always for curries. I sprinkle it onto cheesy biscuits, into sauces, and even like to add some to kedgeree. Unfortunately there is no uniformity amongst commercial curry powders, and some are a good deal hotter than others. The secret is to know your brand of curry powder, and to try and use a little of a hot one rather than a lot of a mild one. Sometimes Indian recipes call for garam masala, which is a blend of spices usually added at the end of cooking a curry.

CURRY PASTE

This can be used instead of curry powder and is particularly useful for marinades and kebabs. It is a blend of spices preserved in oil with sometimes a smaller amount of vinegar added. Like curry powder these pastes can be of varying strength – from very hot to fairly mild. They are particularly useful for marinating or coating as in the recipe for *Indian kebabs* (see page 377).

GINGER

One of the most widely used spices of all, which comes to us to use fresh, dried, powdered, preserved in syrup and crystallised: a very versatile spice. In this country we are partial to ginger in our gingerbread, cakes, puddings and pickles – not forgetting the ginger beer which in its heyday came in those beautiful stoneware bottles, now collectors' items. If you can get hold of fresh root ginger, it really does add a clean fresh taste, as well as spiciness, to curries. It looks just like a knobbly, misshapen root and it can be stored wrapped in cling film in the vegetable drawer of a refrigerator for several days, or in the freezer wrapped in freezer-foil and unpeeled. (Elizabeth David says that, peeled and sliced, it stores well in a small jar of sherry.)

Lumps of dried ginger are used in making up pickling spices for chutneys and pickles. Preserved ginger is expensive, though less so if you buy it in plain jars (some supermarkets have good stocks around Christmas): chopped up it adds a touch of luxury sprinkled with some syrup over ice cream, or added to rhubarb fool – in fact ginger has a great affinity with rhubarb – or adorning the top and inside of a preserved ginger cake. Ginger is most commonly found, and used, in its powdered form: check that it is spicy and fresh-tasting, and not musty and stale.

JUNIPER

—— ♦ ——

These are purple-black, rather wrinkled berries, most notorious as a basic ingredient in gin. But juniper is very much a cooking spice as well, especially with game and pork dishes (perhaps because it grows wild in hill-country where animals and birds feed on the autumn-ripened berries). For cooking, the berries are dried and always crushed before use. Their flavour seems to have a special sympathy with garlic, and if you want to try out juniper for the first time, I suggest you try the cabbage recipe on page 235, which is really delicious. Juniper berries are not as widely available as some other spices, sadly. So the more we pester our suppliers for them, the more plentiful they'll become.

MACE AND NUTMEG

—— ♦ ——

These two spices belong together, because they come from the same source.

MACE

This is part of the outer covering of the nutmeg – resembling a thick-meshed cage – which is removed and dried to become brittle and pale orange in colour. It is sold either in pieces (blades) or ready-ground. With a stronger, much more concentrated flavour than nutmeg it has to be used with care. Ready-ground it can eventually get stale, but that is a built-in handicap because the brittleness of the spice makes it impossible to grind at home. It has been used extensively in English cooking in the past, for such recipes as potted meats and fish pâtés. If it is not available, nutmeg can always be used instead.

NUTMEG

Another favourite of mine: I always keep it within arm's reach in the kitchen, in a special compartment in its own grater. It's always been a popular spice in this country – eighteenth-century gentlemen wore miniature graters containing a nutmeg on a chain round their necks, so they could grate some over their hot mulls and toddies at a moment's notice. It's said to be good for sleep and to increase the potency of alcoholic drinks – but I leave you to judge that for yourselves!

It is an important spice for cakes and puddings: all milk puddings should have a dark, caramelised nutmeg crust, and it gives an attractive freckled effect to egg custards and custard tarts. Although the French rarely use it, the Italians accord it great importance – and rightly so, as it contributes a subtle flavouring to cheese dishes, vegetables like spinach, creamy white sauces, meat fillings for ravioli and so on. If I had the power I would ban the sale of ground nutmeg as it's quite useless. If your local grocer or supermarket does not stock whole nutmegs, try a chemist.

MIXED SPICE

—————— ♦ ——————

Usually a made-up combination of ground nutmeg, cinnamon, cloves and allspice. Most useful for puddings and cakes, but buy it in small quantities and shop around a little for one you like, as they can vary quite a lot in composition.

SAFFRON

—————— ♦ ——————

The most expensive spice of all. It comes from the dried stigmas of a variety of crocus, and is used for its deep yellow colouring as well as for flavour. Being so costly it's as well that very little – just a few strands – is needed to colour and flavour something like a Spanish paella or an Italian risotto. It is also used in the South of France in fish stews and soups, and turns up here in Cornish saffron cake. If a recipe calls for it and you don't have any, a teaspoonful of turmeric will give you the authentic colour (though obviously a different flavour). To use saffron, crush it and mix with a small amount of water or stock before adding it to the other ingredients.

TURMERIC

—————— ♦ ——————

This is a spice originating from a plant of the ginger family, and it is a bright orange-yellow colour. For all its flamboyance it's a mild spice, and is used freely in curries where its colour is more robust than its flavour (I also add turmeric to rice for the same reason). It can only be bought ready-ground (be careful with it: it can stain hands and clothes rather badly).

VANILLA

————— ◆ —————

There is a marked difference between pure vanilla essence and vanilla flavour essence. The former is extracted from vanilla pods (from a species of climbing orchid): the latter is made from a substitute.

Whole dried vanilla pods, long, thin, dark and rather wrinkled, are useful to have in the kitchen. I think the flavour they provide is better than from essence; if you have time, warm the milk (for, say, a custard) and allow the vanilla pod to infuse into it for a short while. A single pod will last for ages, and can be wiped and dried after use, then stored in a jar for the next time. Another tip is to keep a pod buried in the jar containing caster sugar – then when you make a custard or a sweet sauce, the sugar will already have its own vanilla flavouring.

BRAISED STEAK WITH GREEN PEPPERCORN SAUCE

————— ◆ —————

(Serves 2 people)

This has a lovely piquant flavour. If possible try to get two whole slices of braising steak, but failing that cubes of steak will do.

12 oz–1 lb braising steak (350–450 g)
1 tablespoon beef dripping
1 large onion, sliced
4 fl oz dry white wine or dry cider (110 ml)
1 sprig thyme
1 clove garlic
1 heaped teaspoon plain flour
1 teaspoon tomato purée
3 teaspoons green peppercorns
salt and freshly milled black pepper

Pre-heat the oven to gas mark 2, 300°F (150°C).

Start by melting the dripping in a frying-pan till it is nice and hot, then pop the pieces of steak in and sear them till brown on both sides. Then remove them to a casserole, with the aid of a draining spoon. Now to the fat left in the pan add the onion slices, and brown these, then spoon them over the meat. Next spoon off any excess fat from the pan – tilting it to one side will help – and to the juices that remain add the wine; bring it up to simmering point, at the same time scraping the base and sides of the pan.

Pour the wine over the meat, and add the thyme and garlic (crushed slightly) and a little seasoning. Cover the casserole, then braise the steak in the oven for 2 hours. After that, pour all the juices and the garlic clove into the goblet of a liquidiser and (keeping the onions and meat warm meantime) add the flour, tomato purée and 2 teaspoons of the green peppercorns to the juices. Blend at top speed until smooth, then pour the sauce into a saucepan with the remaining teaspoon of peppercorns. Bring up to simmering point, and pour it over the meat before serving.

Note This could be braised on top of the stove over a very low heat, provided it is covered with foil under a well-fitting lid.

STEAK AU POIVRE
◆

(Serves 2 people)

In restaurants this is sometimes served swimming in a sickly cream and brandy sauce. Personally I think the combined flavours of the peppercorns and the steak need nothing else but a glass of wine to rinse out the pan at the end.

2 entrecôte (sirloin) or rump steaks, 6–8 oz each (175–225 g) in weight
2 heaped teaspoons whole black peppercorns
2 tablespoons olive oil
1 clove garlic, crushed
5 fl oz red wine (150 ml)
salt

First crush the peppercorns very coarsely with a pestle and mortar (or use the back of a tablespoon on a flat surface). Pour the olive oil into a shallow dish, add the crushed garlic, then coat each steak with the oil and press the crushed peppercorns onto both sides of each steak. Then leave them to soak up the flavour in the dish, covered in a cool place, for several hours – turning them over once in that time.

When you're ready to cook, pre-heat a thick-based frying-pan (without any fat in it) and when it's very hot sear the steaks quickly on both sides. Then turn down the heat and finish cooking them according to how you like them (a medium-rare entrecôte will take about 6 minutes and should be turned several times during the cooking). One minute before the end of the cooking time pour in the wine, let it bubble, reduce and become syrupy. Then sprinkle a little salt over the steaks and serve immediately with the reduced wine spooned over. These are delicious served with *Gratin dauphinois* (page 256) or jacket potatoes and a green salad.

INDIAN KEBABS

◆

(Serves 4 people)

These spicy kebabs are first marinated in a spicy yoghurt mixture before grilling.

1½ lb fillet end of leg of lamb (700 g), cut into cubes
2 tablespoons olive oil
1 medium onion
4 firm tomatoes
1 small green pepper
2 teaspoons mild curry powder
2 teaspoons curry paste
juice of 1 large lemon
5 oz natural yoghurt (150 g)
1 inch piece fresh root ginger (2.5 cm)
salt and freshly milled black pepper

First of all – 4 hours or so before you cook – place the cubes of lamb in a wide shallow dish, season with salt and pepper, then pour in the olive oil. Leave the meat to soak up the oil for about 2 hours, turning the pieces over once or twice.

Cut the onion into quarters, split the quarters into pieces and add these to the meat: also cut the tomatoes into quarters and the de-seeded pepper into 1 inch (2.5 cm) pieces and add these to the marinating meat. Now in a small basin mix the curry powder, curry paste, lemon juice and yoghurt together and pour this mixture over the meat, etc. Stir and mix everything around well, then leave for another 2 hours in a cool place.

To cook the kebabs, pre-heat the grill, then peel and slice up the piece of ginger. Now onto four long flat (rather than rounded) skewers, thread the meat, onion, tomato and pepper alternately with a little slice of ginger here and there. Pack everything up tightly together, and grill the kebabs under the grill for about 15 minutes, turning them frequently and basting occasionally with the marinade. Serve on *Spiced pilau rice* (see page 275) with the juices spooned over. These are even more special if cooked over hot charcoal.

BEEF CURRY WITH WHOLE SPICES

◆

(Serves 3 people)

A simple but wonderful recipe this, where the distinctive flavours of the spices seem to come through individually.

1½ lb chuck steak (700 g), cut into cubes
2 level teaspoons coriander seeds, crushed
1 teaspoon cumin seeds, crushed
2 cardamom pods, crushed
groundnut oil
2 large onions, sliced
2 cloves garlic, crushed
2 fresh green chilli peppers, de-seeded and chopped
1½ inch piece fresh root ginger (4 cm), grated or very finely chopped
1 level tablespoon ground turmeric
2 fl oz hot water (55 ml)
1 tablespoon grated creamed coconut
5 oz natural yoghurt (150 g)
salt

Begin by dry-roasting the crushed spices in a frying-pan for about 5 minutes over a gentle heat to draw out the flavours. Then brown the cubes of meat in oil in a flameproof casserole, and transfer them to a plate. Add the onions to the pan and fry them for about 5 minutes, before adding the garlic and all the spices, including the chillies and ginger. Continue to cook for a further 5 minutes before returning the meat to the pan.

Next mix the water with the creamed coconut, whisking with a fork, then gradually stir in the yoghurt, and add some salt. Cover the casserole and keep the heat at the lowest possible simmer for 2 hours, stirring everything around a few times.

After 2 hours, take the lid off and continue to cook for a further 15 minutes to reduce the sauce slightly. Serve this with pilau rice, Indian pickles and mango chutney.

Note If you can't get fresh root ginger, use a dessertspoon of ground ginger.

SPICED CHICKEN

◆

(Serves 6 people)

This is such a simple recipe it hardly seems possible it can taste so good.

6 chicken breasts on the bone (with skins intact) or other chicken portions
1 level dessertspoon ground ginger
1 level dessertspoon ground turmeric
1 level teaspoon Madras curry powder
1 clove garlic, crushed
1¹/₂ tablespoons groundnut oil
2 medium onions, chopped small
5 oz natural yoghurt (150 g)
5 fl oz single cream (150 ml)
salt and freshly milled black pepper
a few sprigs of watercress, to garnish

A few hours before you want to eat, arrange the pieces of chicken in a large shallow casserole with a lid (or a meat-roasting tin covered with foil – the chicken pieces must be side-by-side in a single layer).

Season the chicken with salt and pepper, then mix the powdered spices together and sprinkle approximately 1 heaped teaspoonful over the chicken. Now put a little piece of the crushed garlic onto each section of chicken, then drizzle 1 tablespoon oil over and, using your hands, rub the spices, oil and garlic into the chicken flesh. Pierce each portion with a skewer in several places, so that the flavours can penetrate. Leave the chicken (covered) in a cool place for several hours.

When you're ready to cook, pre-heat the oven to gas mark 4, 350°F (180°C). Place the casserole in the oven (uncovered) for 30 minutes. Meanwhile fry the onions in the rest of the oil over a low heat for 10 minutes to soften, and mix the remaining spices together with the yoghurt and cream.

When the 30 minutes are up, take the chicken pieces out of the oven, spoon the onion over them, then pour the yoghurt mixture all over. Put on the lid (or cover with foil) and return the chicken to the oven for another 30–45 minutes – or until the pieces are tender – basting with the juices once or twice during the cooking.

Garnish with a few sprigs of watercress, and serve with spiced rice and mango chutney.

Note There are always rather a lot of juices left over with this dish, but this is unavoidable – so just spoon a little over the chicken before you serve and discard the rest.

CHICKEN PAPRIKA

◆

(Serves 4 people)

This is nice served with some brown rice or well-buttered noodles and a crisp green salad. (Illus. opposite p. 384.)

approx. 3 lb chicken (1.3 kg), quartered
groundnut oil
2 medium onions, chopped
1 dessertspoon plain flour
2 good pinches of cayenne pepper
1 heaped tablespoon paprika (preferably Hungarian) plus a little extra
1 lb tomatoes (450 g), peeled and chopped, or 14 oz (400 g) tin Italian tomatoes
5 fl oz chicken stock (150 ml)
1 medium green pepper, de-seeded and cut into small strips
5 fl oz soured cream (150 ml)
salt and freshly milled black pepper

Pre-heat the oven to gas mark 3, 325°F (170°C).

Begin by heating a little oil in a frying-pan and gently frying the chicken joints to a golden colour. Then use a draining spoon to transfer them to a casserole, and season them with salt and pepper.

In the oil left in the pan fry the onions gently for about 10 minutes to soften. Now stir the flour, cayenne and paprika into the pan, with a wooden spoon, to soak up the juices before adding the chopped tomatoes. Stir them around a bit, then add the stock.

Bring everything up to simmering point, then pour over the chicken in the casserole, put a lid on and bake in the oven for 45 minutes. After that stir in the chopped pepper, replace the lid and cook for a further 30 minutes. Just before serving spoon the soured cream all over, mixing it in just to give a marbled effect, then sprinkle on a little more paprika.

MARINATED PORK WITH CORIANDER

◆

(Serves 3 people)

The Greeks call this traditional dish Afelia. If you have time to leave the meat to steep overnight and for the flavours to develop so much the better.

1 pork fillet, cut into bite-sized cubes
3 tablespoons olive oil plus extra for frying
juice of 1 lemon
10 fl oz dry white wine or dry cider (275 ml)
2 heaped teaspoons coriander seeds, crushed
1 fat clove garlic, crushed
salt and freshly milled black pepper

Place the pieces of pork in a shallow dish and season them with salt and freshly milled pepper. Now pour the 3 tablespoons of oil over the pieces of meat, followed by the juice of the lemon and 2 tablespoons of the white wine. Sprinkle in the crushed coriander seeds and the garlic, and mix everything together. Cover the dish with a cloth and leave it all to marinate overnight – or as long as possible – stirring now and then.

To cook the pork, melt a little more oil in your largest frying-pan and when it's fairly hot add the cubes of pork and cook them over a medium heat, turning them and keeping them on the move. When they have browned a little, pour in the rest of the white wine, let it bubble and reduce to a syrupy consistency. The pork will take approximately 10–15 minutes to cook altogether. Serve with a little rice and a salad.

MOUSSAKA

◆

(Serves 4 people)

The small amount of cinnamon gives it a really authentic Greek flavour.

1 lb minced lamb or beef (450 g)
3 medium aubergines, cut into rounds about ¹/₂ inch (1 cm) thick
8 oz onions (225 g), sliced
2 cloves garlic, chopped
olive oil
2 tablespoons tomato purée
3 fl oz red or white wine (75 ml)
1 teaspoon ground cinnamon
1 tablespoon chopped fresh parsley
salt and freshly milled black pepper
For the topping
3 oz butter (75 g)
3 oz plain flour (75 g)
1 pint milk (570 ml)
2 oz Cheddar cheese (50 g), grated
freshly grated nutmeg
2 eggs

Pre-heat the oven to gas mark 4, 350°F (180°C).

Sprinkle the aubergine slices with salt and put them in a colander. Then place a plate on top of them and a heavy weight on top of that, and leave them for 30 minutes. This is to drain off some of their excess moisture. Meanwhile fry the onions and chopped garlic in some oil (preferably olive oil) for about 5 minutes, then add the minced meat to the pan to brown – stirring it to break up any lumps. In a basin mix together the tomato purée, wine, cinnamon and parsley, season it all with salt and pepper, then pour the mixture over the onions and meat when it has browned. Stir well, and leave on a gentle heat to simmer for about 20 minutes.

Now back to the aubergines: heat some olive oil in another frying-pan, dry the aubergine slices in kitchen paper, then fry each one to a golden-brown on both sides. When they are browned leave them on kitchen paper to drain (aubergines eat up cooking oil!). When the aubergines are done, take a casserole and arrange some of them in it. Spread part of the meat mixture on top, followed by another layer of aubergines – until everything is incorporated.

Next make up the topping for the moussaka. Melt the butter in a saucepan and stir in the flour until smooth, then add the milk gradually, stirring vigorously with each addition until you have a smooth white sauce. Next stir in the grated cheese, followed by a seasoning of salt, pepper and freshly grated nutmeg. Allow the sauce to cool, then whisk up the eggs, first on their own and then into the sauce. Pour the sauce over the meat and aubergines, then bake (uncovered) for an hour until the top is fluffy-golden. This is nice served with pilau rice (page 275) with the addition of 1 tablespoon pine nuts and 1 tablespoon currants for a quantity for 4 people.

GUACAMOLE

◆

(Serves 4 people)

This recipe is originally from Mexico. If you like spicy food, it makes an ideal first course.

2 large tomatoes
2 medium avocados
juice of 1 medium lemon
¹/₂ medium onion, grated
1 clove garlic, crushed
¹/₂ teaspoon chilli powder
a dash of Tabasco sauce
salt and freshly milled black pepper

Skin the tomatoes to start with – if you pop them in a basin, pour boiling water over them and leave for a few minutes, you'll find the skins slip off quite easily. Then cut the tomatoes into quarters, scoop out and discard the seeds, and chop the flesh into fairly small pieces.

Now halve the avocados and remove their stones. Place each half skin-side up on a wooden board and, with a sharp knife, make an incision down the centre of the skin of each one. Peel the skins off. Chop up the avocado flesh and transfer it to a fairly large mixing bowl, and straightaway pour the lemon juice over it to help stop it discolouring. Now with a teaspoon scrape off from the under-side of the skins all that very green avocado flesh still clinging to them: this is what gives the guacamole a really good green colour. Add this to the bowl, then mash all the avocado with a large fork almost to a purée (it doesn't matter if there are a few little lumps).

Now add the tomatoes, grated onion and garlic to the avocado, season with salt and pepper, and finally stir in the chilli powder and Tabasco. Taste it at this stage to check the seasoning (it does need a fair amount of salt to bring out the flavour) and add more chilli if you think it needs it. Cover the bowl with cling film and keep in a cool place – ideally in the lowest part of the refrigerator – until needed.

Serve in individual dishes with some hot crusty bread, large croûtons or slices of thin toast.

Note Don't make this too far ahead, because avocado does tend to discolour. If that happens just give the guacamole a good stir – the taste won't be affected.

SAUTÉED CAULIFLOWER WITH CORIANDER
♦

(Serves 2 people)

Cauliflower florets, just tossed in oil and fried quickly, seem to retain their crunchiness and flavour – which they can so easily lose when cooked with water.

1 smallish cauliflower
1 small clove garlic
1 level teaspoon whole coriander seeds
2 tablespoons olive oil
1/2 onion, finely chopped
1/2 oz butter (10 g)
salt and freshly milled black pepper

First prepare the cauliflower, by separating it into fairly small florets (about an inch/2.5 cm long, including the stalk). Wipe them but don't wash them – they'll be cooked anyway at a fairly high temperature.

Next chop the peeled clove of garlic finely and crush the coriander seeds with a pestle and mortar (or use the end of a rolling-pin and a small bowl).

Now heat the oil in your largest frying-pan till really hot, then add the cauliflower. After a minute or two toss the pieces over by shaking the pan and add the coriander seeds and onion and continue to cook the cauliflower for about 5–7 minutes, seasoning it with a sprinkling of salt and pepper.

Finally add the butter and chopped garlic to the pan and cook for a further minute – by which time the cauliflower will have turned an attractive nutty-golden colour, but still retain some bite. Serve straightaway.

SPICED PEARS IN RED WINE

◆

(Serves 6 people)

For this you need to get hold of really hard pears. After long cooking they will turn a lovely glazed dark red colour, and look most attractive.

6 large hard pears
1 pint red wine (570 ml)
4 oz sugar (110 g)
2 whole cinnamon sticks
1 vanilla pod
1 rounded dessertspoon arrowroot
15 fl oz whipped cream (425 ml)

Pre-heat the oven to gas mark ½, 250°F (130°C).

Peel the pears but leave the stalks on them, then lay them in a large casserole. Then in a saucepan bring the red wine, sugar and cinnamon to the boil, add the vanilla pod to the mixture and pour the whole lot over the pears. Cover the casserole, and bake very slowly for about 3 hours, turning the pears over half-way.

After the 3 hours transfer the pears to a serving bowl to cool, and pour the liquid back into a saucepan (you can discard the vanilla pod and cinnamon sticks now).

In a cup mix the arrowroot with a little cold water till you have a smooth paste, then add this to the saucepan with the liquid. Bring to the boil, stirring till the mixture has thickened slightly to a syrup.

Then pour it over the pears, allow to cool a little and baste each pear with a good coating of the syrup.

Place in the fridge to chill thoroughly, and serve with whipped cream or perhaps a mixture of half whipped cream and half Greek yoghurt.

Note This also works very well with dry cider, which transforms the pears into a glazed amber colour.

Chicken paprika (see page 380)

SEE ALSO

Baked lamb with coriander
Baked marrow with tomatoes and coriander
Buttery kedgeree
Chicken with whole spices
Chilli con carne
Chilli eggs
Creamed potatoes with nutmeg
Creamy chicken curry
Crisp cinnamon flan
Curried lambs' kidneys
Curried nut roast
Curried ox kidneys
Damson (or plum) and cinnamon crumble
Egg and lentil curry
Eliza Acton's vegetable mulligatawny
Fried mustard-and-herb-coated chicken
Gingernuts
Honey and spice cake
Hungarian goulash
Linzertorte
Paprika liver
Peppered liver
Pork kidneys in chilli sauce
Red cabbage and coriander salad
Rhubarb and ginger crumble
Saffron rice
Sautéed mixed vegetables
Spiced apple and onion sauce
Spiced apple and raisin crumble
Spiced fig pudding with rum butter
Spiced green tomato sauce
Spiced lamb with chick peas
Spiced pilau rice
Spiced plum or damson chutney
Vegetarian goulash

Home-made mayonnaise (see page 438)

SAUCES

◆

It's the one subject that strictly divides us from our cousins on the other side of the English Channel, *sauces*. In France there are literally hundreds: over here (according to the French) we have only one, and that's custard. Of course we do have more than one, but the chauvinists are for ever arguing that the quality of our meat, fish and game is so superior that it has no need of clever sauces to enhance the flavour! Be that as it may, every honest cook will have to admit that – superior meat or not – the British are tireless consumers of bottled commercial ketchup, salad creams, gravy powders, instant packet sauces and even tinned custard.

It seems to me it's not so much that we despise sauces, but rather that as a nation we have never properly acquired the techniques of making them. So, when a housewife hurries out to the supermarket to buy her packet cheese sauce or gravy mix, what is it she's afraid of making at home? There may be an understandable fear of the unknown (for without experience how can anyone *know* anything), but usually there are more practical barriers – like the age-old problem of:

LUMPS

The very first thing to know, if you're going to master the art of sauce-making, is that lumps simply *don't matter*. If a sauce goes lumpy all you do is whisk the lumps out of it or pass it through a sieve – that's precisely what sieves are for. You can even pop the offending sauce into a liquidiser, if there's one handy. This is not to say that a lump-free sauce isn't preferable in the first place: but don't let the problem cause you a moment's concern.

What you have to remember about a sauce where the basic ingredients are flour, liquid and fat is (a) that flour and liquid, combined directly together, will always go lumpy and (b) that if the flour is thoroughly blended with some fat first, that will never happen. If you have not sufficiently blended the fat with the flour, then simply whisk or sieve the lumps out.

CURDLING

Another headache, when it comes to the more advanced butter-and-egg based sauces, is curdling. But again it needn't be a problem. In the first place a beginner (or indeed anyone who's not an absolute purist) can use a little stabiliser – such as cornflour – to help things along. Or, if the sauce has curdled, it *can* be remedied. With egg yolk sauces such as hollandaise the remedy is to use a fresh egg yolk and start again, adding the curdled ingredients to it. With proper custard a teaspoon of cornflour will prevent curdling happening in the first place.

BASIC SAUCE INGREDIENTS
◆

Let's begin by examining the basic ingredients of a sauce and what they are doing in it.

FLOUR

In a basic white sauce and all the others that are derived from it flour is what thickens the liquid. As we have already seen (page 36), little granules of starch are present in wheat flour, and when these become wet and hot they burst as boiling point is reached: the granules collapse and spread, becoming gelatinous. Whisking then distributes this throughout and the sauce is thus thickened. (In this context I have found that self-raising flour is more inclined to go lumpy than plain flour, so I don't use it for sauces.)

CORNFLOUR

This is pure starch separated from the rest of the flour, which does the thickening job very efficiently. But unfortunately it does not make a sauce with either the character or creamy texture that comes from white flour. Although I never make sauces with cornflour, I find it very useful for adding to egg-based sauces (especially 'proper' custard) to prevent the eggs from curdling – but only in a *small* amount so as not to affect the flavour.

ARROWROOT

This is an edible starch which comes not from corn but from a plant root grown in the West Indies, which is ground down to a fine powder. As a thickening it is excellent for making a glaze for, say, a fruit flan because, unlike cornflour, it will thicken fruit juices and keep them clear and transparent at the same time. To use it for a glaze for a flan, you need about 1 rounded teaspoon for every 5 fl oz (150 ml) of liquid, and it has to be added to a little cold water first before being mixed with your liquid and being brought up to boiling point (at that stage remove it from the heat straightaway, as over-boiling can cause it to liquify and lose its thickening power).

LIQUID

The liquid base for a sauce can be almost anything: light home-made chicken or bone stock, the stock from boiling vegetables (especially if the sauce is to be served with those vegetables), sometimes milk, other times a mixture of milk and stock. Both wine and cider are particularly good for gravies or sauces to accompany meat or fish.

Whenever expert cooks continually disagree on a finer point of cookery it usually means it's not that important. So it is with the question of the temperature of liquid being added to a sauce. There are those who swear it must be hot, and those who insist it should be cold: in my humble opinion it doesn't matter one scrap. If it happens that the liquid you're adding is hot from the stock-pot, fine. On the other hand, if it's cold milk from the fridge, that's fine too. But one exception I must state now – and this is when you are making an *all-in-one sauce* (see page 391): for this the liquid you start off with should be *cold*.

BUTTER AND OTHER FATS

Butter is what makes a sauce creamy and rich, and as a rule is added in the same proportion as the flour. For extra creaminess the amount of butter can be increased, or else cream or soured cream added. Soured cream needs careful attention, though, because boiling can cause it to curdle: whereas ordinary cream *won't* hurt if it comes to the boil. Dripping, pork fat and lard are sometimes used in place of butter to make a brown roux.

BASIC WHITE SAUCES
◆

WHAT IS A ROUX?

To make a classic béchamel 'white' sauce, the first process is to combine melted butter with an equal quantity of flour. The result is called a *roux*: the basis into which the required amount of liquid is worked to make the finished sauce.

In this cookery course we need never actually bother with the word roux, because when a recipe requires an equal quantity of butter and flour mixed together, it will say that. However, roux is the term used in French classic cookery to describe the base of three different types of sauce: *roux blanc* (white base), *roux blond* (pale-cream roux), and *roux brun* or brown roux where the fat and flour are allowed to go on cooking longer – up to 30 minutes – to brown and give the finished sauce a nutty flavour. It is quite a tricky operation to perfect, rarely needed except in advanced cooking.

You may have heard that it is possible to make up a batch of butter-and-flour and store it in the refrigerator ready for use. But it will only keep for about four weeks (and anyway only takes a few seconds to mix) so I don't really see the point. I know I can never tell how much I might need in the space of four weeks – if any.

HOW LONG SHOULD A SAUCE BE COOKED?

White sauces, when they're first made, can have a rather 'raw' flavour – which means that not all the starch granules have burst and disintegrated into the sauce. For that reason they have to be 'cooked', that is to say left over the gentlest possible heat for about 6–10 minutes. During this cooking process a thin layer of skin may form on the surface. I find this can usually be whisked back into the sauce quite happily, but you can actually prevent this skin forming by keeping back 1 or 2 tablespoons of liquid and 'floating' it on top at the end, without stirring it in. Then whisk it in normally after the sauce has cooked.

KEEPING A SAUCE WARM

The only acceptable way to keep a sauce warm, or reheat it, is to place the saucepan in another larger saucepan or pot of gently simmering water (to provide heat all round and not just underneath). It is also a good idea to cover it with cling film, allowing the film to sit right on top of the sauce and adhere to it. This stops a skin forming.

BASIC WHITE SAUCE: TRADITIONAL METHOD

♦

We've considered the basic ingredients: now they have to be combined correctly. Here are the standard proportions for a pouring sauce – badly-made sauces are often too thick and pasty, so do measure the quantities carefully.

For 1 pint (570 ml)
1½ oz plain flour (40 g), sifted
2 oz butter (50 g)
1 pint milk or half milk, half stock (570 ml)
salt and freshly milled black pepper

For 15 fl oz (425 ml)
1 oz plain flour (25 g), sifted
1½ oz butter (40 g)
15 fl oz milk or half milk, half stock (425 ml)
salt and freshly milled black pepper

The basic procedure is to (a) melt the butter over a medium heat, (b) stir in the flour off the heat, and (c) back on the heat, add the liquid bit by bit until it has all been incorporated and the sauce is smooth and glossy.

So begin by having the liquid ready in a measuring jug, then melt the butter in a small saucepan very gently – it must not brown or it will affect the flavour and colour of the finished sauce. Take it off the heat as soon as the butter has melted and stir in the sifted flour. Stir to form a smooth glossy paste, then return the saucepan to a medium heat and start to add the milk – about 1 fl oz (25 ml) at a time – stirring quite vigorously with a wooden spoon as you pour, to incorporate each bit of liquid thoroughly before adding the next. If you're conscientious about the stirring you won't get any lumps: if you do, then either whisk them away with a wire or rotary whisk or sieve the finished sauce.

When all the milk has been incorporated, turn the heat to its lowest possible setting and let the sauce cook for 6–10 minutes. Then taste and season as required.

Note I always use freshly milled black pepper because I don't mind the little dark speckles, but if you do then use freshly milled white. For extra creaminess beat in an extra knob of butter at the end or else a couple of tablespoons of thick cream.

BÉCHAMEL SAUCE

◆

(Serves 4–6 people)

When a plain white sauce is called for, you can give it extra flavour by *infusing* the milk beforehand for about 30 minutes. For this you need:

For 15 fl oz milk (425 ml)
1 small piece of carrot
¹/₂ smallish onion
2 inch piece of celery (5 cm)
6 whole black peppercorns
1 blade mace
¹/₂ bay leaf

Place the above ingredients in a saucepan with the 15 fl oz (425 ml) of milk, and then bring it to the boil very slowly. After that, remove from the heat and allow it to infuse for 20 minutes. Then strain the milk into a jug and proceed to make the sauce following the method described above. Alternatively you can let it cool for 45 minutes, and carry on with the all-in-one method following.

White wine sauce
Infuse the ingredients above in 10 fl oz (275 ml) of dry white wine instead of milk. Use the strained liquid to make up a sauce with 1¹/₂ oz (40 g) butter and 1 oz (25 g) flour, then finish off by adding 5 fl oz (150 ml) single or double cream, depending on how creamy you want it.

BASIC WHITE SAUCE: ALL-IN-ONE METHOD

♦

This speeded-up version is even easier than using a packet! All you need is a balloon whisk (or a coil wire or rotary whisk) and a wooden spoon. It is suitable for all sauces except those where a vegetable has to be 'sweated' in butter first. *But* the liquid you add to this one must be cold: the dreaded lumps will form if the flour goes straight into hot liquid.

1½ oz butter (40 g)
1 oz plain flour (25 g), sifted
15 fl oz cold milk or half milk, half stock (425 ml)
salt and freshly milled pepper

Simply place all the ingredients in a saucepan, put the saucepan on a medium heat and whisk until the sauce starts to bubble and thicken. Then stir with a wooden spoon, to get right into the corners of the pan, and whisk again thoroughly. Turn the heat down as low as possible and cook the sauce gently for 6 minutes.

Those first three recipes above are the basis for a whole range of sauces; on their own they would be rather dull of course, but so many other ingredients can be used for flavouring. Here are three variations on the all-in-one method, bearing in mind that the infused milk or stock must be cooled for a minimum of 45 minutes before use (if you're in a hurry, use the traditional method). Cream is used here to add a touch of luxury, but if not available it can be replaced by the same quantity of milk.

MUSTARD SAUCE

◆

(Serves 4–6 people)

This is a good sauce which is often served with herrings.

10 fl oz milk (275 ml)
1 small onion, halved
1¹/₂ oz butter (40 g)
1 oz plain flour (25 g), sifted
2 rounded teaspoons mustard powder
5 fl oz stock (150 ml)
1 teaspoon lemon juice
salt and cayenne pepper

Bring the halved onion and the milk slowly to the boil, then remove from the heat and let it infuse until cooled. Now place the strained infused milk together with the butter, flour, mustard powder and stock in a saucepan, and bring to the boil, whisking continuously. Then cook the sauce gently for 5 minutes. Taste and season with salt, cayenne and lemon juice.

MORNAY SAUCE

◆

(Serves 6–8 people)

This is a basic cheese sauce which can be used in a wide variety of dishes. Grated Gruyère cheese could be used instead of Cheddar here, for a spot of refinement.

10 fl oz milk (275 ml)
10 fl oz single cream (275 ml), or use all milk
1 level teaspoon mustard
1 oz plain flour (25 g), sifted
1¹/₂ oz butter (40 g)
2 oz strong Cheddar cheese (50 g), grated
1 oz Parmesan cheese (25 g), grated
a pinch of cayenne pepper
¹/₂ teaspoon lemon juice
salt and freshly milled black pepper

Place the first five ingredients in a saucepan and whisk over the heat till smooth and thickened. Now add the cheeses, stir to melt them in, then cook the sauce *gently* for 5 minutes. Season to taste with salt, pepper, cayenne and lemon juice. This is excellent poured over cauliflower or broccoli, and finished under the grill with more cheese on top. It is also good poured over baked fish (in which case a cooking liquid could be used). Sprinkle over more cheese and pop it under the grill.

Spinach and cheese sauce
This is a delicious, colourful sauce to pour over halved hard-boiled eggs on a bed of brown rice, or to accompany any grilled or fried fish. Cook 8 oz (225 g) fresh spinach leaves as on page 260, then place them in a liquidiser with a cheese sauce made with 2 oz (50 g) butter, 1 oz (25 g) plain flour, 10 fl oz (275 ml) milk, 3 oz (75 g) grated cheese, and 2 tablespoons double cream. Liquidise until you have a pale green, speckled sauce. Season with salt, pepper and freshly grated nutmeg, and reheat before serving.

PARSLEY SAUCE
◆

(Serves 4–6 people)

I like parsley sauce best with baked fish cutlets of various kinds: it's also very good with boiled gammon.

15 fl oz milk (425 ml)
1 tablespoon single cream
1¹/₂ oz butter (40 g)
³/₄ oz plain flour (20 g), sifted
3 tablespoons finely chopped parsley
1 teaspoon lemon juice
salt and freshly milled black pepper

Place the first four ingredients in a saucepan, and whisk them over the heat till smooth and thickened. Then cook for 5 minutes, add the parsley and lemon juice, and season to taste.

Note For extra flavour you can infuse the milk with the parsley stalks first – but let it get absolutely cold before using it for the all-in-one method.

BUTTER SAUCES

♦

HOLLANDAISE SAUCE

♦

(Serves 6 people)

This adaptation of one of the famous French butter sauces goes particularly well with vegetables, like fresh artichokes or new season's asparagus. See page 34 for a simpler version of this sauce.

For the reduction
2 tablespoons white wine vinegar
3 tablespoons water
1 slice onion
1 blade mace
1/2 small bay leaf
6 black peppercorns
For the sauce
1 tablespoon water
3 egg yolks
6 oz unsalted butter (175 g), at room temperature
lemon juice to taste
salt and freshly milled black pepper

Place the first six ingredients together in a small saucepan and simmer gently (uncovered) until the mixture is reduced to about 1 tablespoon – keep your eye on it because it can boil away before you know it! Then strain the reduced mixture into a bowl, add a further tablespoon of water and a little seasoning. Whisk in the egg yolks.

Next place the bowl over a pan of *barely* simmering water, and add 1/2 oz (10 g) of the butter, whisking until it has melted and the mixture has thickened slightly. Carry on adding lumps of butter – approximately 1/2 oz (10 g) at a time – and allow the butter to melt and the mixture to thicken before adding any more.

When all the butter is in, carry on whisking and cooking gently for a further 2 minutes. Then remove the bowl from over the water, taste, and add lemon juice and seasoning as required. If the mixture curdles (which it will only do if overheated) place a fresh egg yolk in a clean bowl and gradually whisk in the curdled mixture to bring it back.

SAUCE BÉARNAISE

◆

(Serves 6 people)

This is one of the great French butter sauces. It is tricky to make because it can curdle or – if you really overheat it – even scramble! However, if you're careful, and add a little mustard powder to help stabilise it, you should have no problems. It is delicious with any plain meat or fish, and especially with *Bœuf en croûte* (page 516).

For the reduction
1 tablespoon coarsely chopped fresh or ¹/₂ teaspoon dried tarragon
1 tablespoon coarsely chopped fresh parsley
1 tablespoon chopped shallot or spring onion
6 black peppercorns, crushed
2 tablespoons white wine vinegar
5 fl oz dry white wine (150 ml)
For the sauce
3 egg yolks
1 teaspoon mustard powder
1 tablespoon water
1 oz butter (25 g), at room temperature
6 oz butter (175 g), melted
salt

Start off in a small saucepan by boiling the herbs, shallot, peppercorns, wine vinegar and white wine together until the mixture has reduced by about a third – in other words there should be about 3 tablespoons of slightly syrupy liquid left.

Now whisk the egg yolks and mustard together in the top of a double saucepan. Strain the vinegar mixture through a fine sieve onto the egg yolks, add the water and beat over hot (but not boiling) water, using a wire whisk. Next beat in the solid butter, about ¹/₂ oz (10 g) at a time, then gradually add the melted butter, a drop at a time – still whisking after each addition until all the butter is in and the sauce has thickened. Taste and season with salt and keep warm over the hot water till needed.

OTHER SAVOURY SAUCES

———————— ♦ ————————

BUTTERY ONION SAUCE

———————— ♦ ————————

(Serves 4–6 people)

A lovely sauce, this one, to serve with roast lamb in the late autumn when the mint has finished.

2 oz butter (50 g)
1 large onion, chopped small
¾ oz plain flour (20 g), sifted
10 fl oz milk (275 ml)
5 fl oz vegetable stock (150 ml)
salt, pepper and a scraping of nutmeg

Since the onion needs to 'sweat' in the butter first to release its juices, it is best to use the traditional white sauce method in this recipe.

Start off by melting 1½ oz (40 g) of the butter in a saucepan then, keeping the heat very low, allow the onion to cook for about 10 minutes without colouring. Stir it around from time to time. Then add the flour and stir to a smooth paste.

Now gradually incorporate the milk and stock, a little at a time, whisking or stirring vigorously after each addition till you have a smooth sauce. Turn the heat down to its absolute minimum setting, and let the sauce cook for 6 minutes. Season with salt, pepper and a scraping of nutmeg – and finish off by stirring in the remaining ½ oz (10 g) butter just before serving.

Leek cream sauce
A delicious sauce to serve with a boiled bacon joint; this can be made by using the previous recipe, replacing the onion with 2 medium leeks, cleaned and chopped.

CELERY SAUCE

♦

(Serves 4–6 people)

For serving with chicken or boiled bacon, this sauce is ideal.

6 oz celery stalks (175 g), cut into ¼ inch (5 mm) pieces
1½ oz butter (40 g)
¾ oz plain flour (20 g), sifted
5 fl oz milk (150 ml)
1 teaspoon lemon juice
salt, pepper and freshly grated nutmeg

First place the celery in a saucepan and pour boiling water on it, add some salt and simmer for 10 minutes. Then drain the celery (reserving the cooking liquid) and, in the same saucepan, melt the butter and gently sweat the celery in it for a further 10 minutes with the lid on. Then uncover, stir in the flour until smooth, and gradually beat in the milk and 5 fl oz (150 ml) of the reserved liquid, a little bit at a time. Cook for 2 minutes, then liquidise the sauce to a purée. Sieve it as well, as sometimes there are fibrous bits of celery that refuse to be liquidised, then return it to the saucepan to reheat, and season with salt, pepper, lemon juice and a sprinkling of nutmeg.

CUCUMBER SAUCE

♦

(Serves 4–6 people)

This is the sauce to serve with fish, say fillets of brill or even salmon if the season (and the price) are right.

1 firm young cucumber
2 fl oz dry white wine (55 ml)
1½ oz butter (40 g)
1 oz plain flour (25 g), sifted
5 fl oz single cream (150 ml)
½ teaspoon lemon juice
salt and freshly milled black pepper

Pare off the peel of the cucumber, preferably with a potato peeler as it is important (for the colour of the sauce) to leave some of the green. Then divide the cucumber in half and liquidise one half together with the white wine (this should yield about 10 fl oz/275 ml of liquid). Chop the other half of the cucumber into small dice and sweat them gently with the butter in a covered saucepan for 10 minutes. Stir in the flour, beat till smooth, then add the cucumber liquid and cream – bit by bit – whisking all the time until you have a smooth sauce. Cook gently for about 5 minutes, taste, and season with salt, pepper and lemon juice.

SPICED APPLE AND ONION SAUCE

◆

(Serves 4 people)

An apple sauce – with a little onion added – goes well with most pork dishes. If you don't like cloves, you can leave them out of this recipe.

½ oz butter (10 g)
½ medium onion, finely chopped
1 medium cooking apple, peeled, cored and thinly sliced
1 large Cox's apple, peeled, cored and thinly sliced
2 cloves
2 tablespoons water or dry cider
1 dessertspoon sugar
a little freshly grated nutmeg

Begin by melting the fat in a thick-based saucepan, soften the chopped onion in it for 5 or 6 minutes, then add the slices of apple. Give them a good stir before adding the cloves and the water (or cider) and sugar. Stir again, cover the saucepan and leave the apples to cook down to a fluff (about 10 minutes). When they're cooked remove the cloves, beat the apples down to a smooth sauce, grate in a little nutmeg and pour into a jug to serve.

TRADITIONAL BREAD SAUCE

◆

(Serves 5–6 people)

This is my favourite sauce for serving with roast turkey, chicken or pheasant. It is fragrant, light and creamy. I find quite a lot of resistance to it because people have rarely tasted the real thing. When they do, they are soon converted!

3 oz freshly made white breadcrumbs (75 g) – a 2-day-old white loaf with the crusts removed will be stale enough to grate, but the best way to do this is in a liquidiser, if you have one

1 medium onion
15 cloves
1 bay leaf
6 black peppercorns
15 fl oz milk (425 ml)
2 oz butter (50 g)
2 tablespoons double cream
salt and freshly milled black pepper

A couple of hours before you need the sauce, cut the onion in half and stick the cloves in it. How many cloves you actually use depends on you, but I, personally, like a pronounced flavour; if you really don't like cloves, you can use some freshly grated nutmeg instead. Place the onion studded with the cloves, plus the bay leaf and the 6 black peppercorns in a saucepan with the milk. Add some salt, then bring everything up to boiling point. Take off the heat, cover the pan and leave in a warm place to infuse for 2 hours at least – or longer won't matter.

When you're ready to make the sauce, remove the onion and reserve it; discard the bay leaf and peppercorns. Stir the breadcrumbs into the milk and add 1 oz (25 g) of the butter and some salt. Leave the saucepan on a very low heat (stirring now and then) until the crumbs have swollen and thickened the sauce, approximately 15 minutes. Now replace the clove-studded onion and again leave the saucepan in a warm place until the sauce is needed.

Just before serving, remove the onion, beat in the remaining butter and the cream, and taste to check the seasoning.

CUMBERLAND SAUCE

◆

(Serves 8 people)

This is, perhaps, my favourite English sauce – delicious at Christmas with hot or cold gammon or tongue, and it stores in a screw-top jar for up to two weeks in a refrigerator. Remember some commercial red-currant jellies are not entirely authentic – go for a make that guarantees a high fruit content on the label.

1 medium lemon
1 medium orange
4 large tablespoons authentic redcurrant jelly
4 tablespoons port
1 heaped teaspoon mustard powder
1 heaped teaspoon ground ginger

First, thinly pare off the rinds of both the lemon and the orange (either with a very sharp paring knife or a potato peeler), then cut them into very small strips, about ½ inch (1 cm) in length and as thin as possible. Boil the rinds in water for 5 minutes to extract any bitterness, then drain well.

Now place the redcurrant jelly in a saucepan with the port and melt, whisking them together over a low heat for about 5 or 10 minutes. The redcurrant jelly won't melt completely, so it's best to sieve it afterwards to get rid of any obstinate little globules.

In a serving bowl mix the mustard and ginger with the juice of half the lemon till smooth, then add the juice of the whole orange, the port and redcurrant mixture and finally the strips of orange and lemon peel. Mix well – and it's ready for use. Cumberland sauce is always served cold.

REDCURRANT, ORANGE AND MINT SAUCE

◆

(Serves 8 people)

No-one can believe such a good sauce as this can be so simple to make. It is absolutely perfect for the delicate flavour of lamb in the peak of summer.

4 tablespoons authentic redcurrant jelly (one with a high fruit content)
grated rind of 1 orange
1½ tablespoons chopped fresh mint

Place the jelly in a small basin, break it up with a fork, then mix in the orange rind and the mint – and that's it. It must be one of the quickest sauces in the world, and it's absolutely delicious.

BITTER ORANGE SAUCE

◆

(Serves 4 people)

The bitterness of Seville oranges gives a delicious edge to this sauce which is one of my favourites to serve with duck. If they're out of season and you're using sweet oranges, add a tablespoon of lemon juice to the orange juice to give it sharpness.

2 fairly small Seville oranges
1 level tablespoon plain flour

| 10 fl oz stock made from the duck giblets (275 ml) – |
| see chicken giblet stock, page 65 |
| 3 heaped teaspoons brown sugar |
| 4–5 tablespoons port |
| salt and freshly milled black pepper |

First of all, take off the outer rinds of the oranges with a peeler or zester, then cut the rinds up finely into very thin shreds. Pop them into some boiling water and blanch for 5 minutes, then drain well. Next, squeeze the juice from the oranges and keep it on one side.

When the duck is cooked, transfer it to a serving plate to 'relax' and keep warm, then spoon out the excess fat from the roasting tin and sprinkle the flour into the juices that remain. Stir it in well to form a paste and cook over a medium heat for a couple of minutes to brown slightly – as you do this, scrape the base and sides of the tin with a wooden spoon. Next add the stock gradually, stirring to make a smooth sauce, then add the sugar. Cook for a minute or two more before adding the orange juice and rind and a seasoning of salt and pepper. Just before serving, stir in the port, then pour the sauce over the duck and serve straightaway.

MORELLO CHERRY SAUCE

♦

(Serves 4 people)

This is another sauce that is deceptively simple, a perfect partner for duck. It is made with morello cherry jam and, as always, it must be a good make with a high fruit content.

| 6 oz morello cherry jam (175 g) |
| 5 fl oz red wine (150 ml) |

Simply combine the jam and the wine in a saucepan, and simmer without a lid for 10 minutes. This is enough for four people and can be made well in advance and reheated just before serving.

SPICED GREEN TOMATO SAUCE

♦

(Serves 4 people)

If you're likely to have a crop of tomatoes that will never ripen, fear not, because this sauce is a real winner and really delicious with good pork sausages and lots of creamy mashed potato.

½ onion, chopped
½ green pepper, de-seeded and chopped
½ fresh green chilli pepper, de-seeded and chopped
1 tablespoon oil
1 lb green tomatoes (450 g), coarsely minced or very finely chopped (you needn't peel them)
1 large clove garlic, crushed
½ teaspoon whole cumin seeds, crushed
salt and freshly milled black pepper

Using a thick-based saucepan, fry the onion, green pepper and chilli in the oil over a low heat for about 10 minutes. Now add the tomatoes, garlic, crushed cumin seeds and seasoning, and bring to simmering point. Cover and simmer for 15 minutes with the lid on and for a further 10 minutes without the lid, which will allow some of the excess liquid to reduce.

Note This sauce also goes very well with some fleshy fish, such as turbot or mackerel.

ITALIAN GREEN SAUCE (SALSA VERDE)

◆

(Serves 2 people)

This is a strong-flavoured, quite garlicky sauce, which does wonders for plain mackerel fillets or some grilled trout.

4 tinned anchovy fillets, drained
1 tablespoon capers
1 level teaspoon mustard powder
1 small clove garlic, crushed
1½ tablespoons lemon juice
6 tablespoons olive oil
2 tablespoons chopped fresh parsley
1 tablespoon chopped fresh or 1 teaspoon dried basil
salt and freshly milled black pepper

To start with chop the anchovy fillets as small as possible and crush them to a paste in a mortar (if you haven't a mortar a small bowl and the end of a rolling-pin will do).

Put the capers in a small sieve and rinse them under cold running water to remove the vinegar they were preserved in. Dry them on kitchen paper and chop them as minutely as you can and add them to the anchovies.

Next add the mustard, garlic, lemon juice and some freshly milled black paper and mix well. Now add the oil, mix again and check the taste to see how much salt to add.

Just before serving, sprinkle in the chopped herbs and again mix thoroughly so that all the ingredients are properly combined.

Note This behaves rather like a very thick vinaigrette and, before each serving, always needs to have another mix.

AVOCADO SAUCE

◆

(Serves 4–6 people)

This pale green pistachio-coloured sauce is delicious with cold salmon in the summer or for use as a dip with lots of thin slivers of raw vegetables.

1 medium avocado
1 tablespoon lemon juice
1 clove garlic, crushed
5 fl oz soured cream (150 ml) or Greek yoghurt
salt and freshly milled black pepper

Scrape the avocado flesh away from the skin into a bowl, making sure you scrape away the very green bit next to the skin as this is important for the colour of the sauce. Then mash it to a purée together with the lemon juice, garlic and seasoning and combine it with the soured cream, mixing thoroughly until you have a smooth, pale green, creamy sauce. Cover the basin tightly with cellophane wrap to stop the avocado discolouring and chill in the refrigerator till needed. Do make this sauce the same day as it's required, since it tends to discolour if left too long.

GRAVY

◆

I see from the *Oxford Dictionary* that gravy is supposed to be 'the fat and juices which exude from flesh in cooking' or a dressing for meat and vegetables made from these. Well, if you were roasting a baron of beef in the eighteenth century no doubt enough juices would exude from it to provide sufficient gravy. Nowadays our more modest joints need a little help with the gravy, if there's to be enough to go around.

First of all I would like to say quite emphatically that commercially produced gravy mixes, highly flavoured beef extracts, meat cubes or stock cubes are *not* needed. Their chemical flavours will not enhance the meat at all: on the contrary they only compete with it. So what is needed? Quite simply the meat-roasting tin containing its fat and juices – or the pan in which the meat has been browned. The additional liquid can be wine, dry cider, stock or even water. There are two ways to make gravy:

DEGLAZING METHOD

This is useful when just a little thin gravy is required. Most of the fat (if any) is spooned out of the pan, then with a wooden spoon you scrape off all the crusty bits that cling to the base and sides of the pan (this is deglazing). Then to these and the juices, add wine, stock or water: boil briskly for a few seconds to form a sauce.

GOOD OLD-FASHIONED GRAVY

For this – the familiar slightly thick gravy that goes with a roast joint – the principles are as follows. First make sure you're using a good thick-based roasting tin or cast-iron gratin dish (see page 11), then when the meat comes out of the oven, lift it onto a plate and leave it to 'relax' before carving (see page 140). Now tilt the roasting tin, and you will see quite clearly the actual meat juices down in the corner and the fat, separately, settling on top of the juices. Take a large tablespoon and spoon most of the fat off into a bowl – leaving behind 1–2 tablespoons, depending how much gravy you need.

Now place the roasting tin over direct heat (turned fairly low), and when the juices start to sizzle sprinkle in some plain flour – about 1 level tablespoon to each 10 fl oz (275 ml) of liquid to be used. Next, with a whisk quickly work the flour into the fat, using circular movements all over the base of the tin. Then when you have a smooth paste, begin to add the liquid gradually, keeping up the vigorous whisking all over the base of the tin. Carry on like this until all the liquid has been added and you have a smooth sauce (if it's too thick, add a little more liquid). If you have already added too much liquid by mistake, just boil briskly for a minute or two and the sauce will reduce and thicken again. Taste and season the sauce, and add a few drops of gravy browning if it needs it. Before serving, pour the gravy into a warm jug.

INSTANT GRAVY

There will be times when you want to make some gravy from scratch, without the benefit of any meat juices. All you need do for this is melt 1 oz (25 g) of dripping or lard in a small saucepan and fry ½ finely chopped onion in it. Keep the heat high and let the onion turn really brown. Then stir in 1 oz (25 g) of plain flour and gradually whisk in 15 fl oz (425 ml) of stock (or hot water flavoured with ½ teaspoon of Worcestershire sauce and 1 dessertspoon of mushroom ketchup). Simmer for 5 minutes and season to taste, adding a few drops of gravy browning if it needs it.

NOTES ON GRAVY INGREDIENTS

Stock
Can be meat or chicken giblet or vegetable stock – potato water and so on. If you are just using boiling water enrich it with a few drops of Worcestershire sauce and a dessertspoon of mushroom ketchup.

Wine

Can be useful for gravies if there's some around. Just a couple of tablespoons can really enrich the flavour. Dry cider is a good alternative, and much more economical.

Gravy browning

Commercial gravy browning is simply a concentrated caramel (burnt sugar). It doesn't have the chemical flavours of gravy-mixes and is invaluable for enhancing the colour of gravy. If you don't have, or don't want to use gravy browning, then slice ½ onion and place it in the meat-roasting tin along with the meat: it will turn jet black and caramelise during the roasting, and colour the gravy for you.

Flour

I always use plain flour for gravy, having found in the past that self-raising tends to go lumpy.

FLAVOURED BUTTERS

◆

These can be used instead of sauces for all sorts of dishes. They are a lot quicker to make and add interest to something plain.

HERB BUTTER

◆

(Serves 6 people)

You can serve this with chops, steaks or fish or with hot cooked vegetables such as carrots, new potatoes, courgettes or cauliflower. You could also stir some into a vegetable soup or a sauce at the last minute. This is a good way of storing fresh herbs if you have a freezer.

6 oz butter (175 g), at room temperature
4 tablespoons chopped fresh parsley
1½ tablespoons snipped fresh chives
1 teaspoon chopped fresh tarragon or thyme
1 large clove garlic, crushed
1 dessertspoon lemon juice
salt and freshly milled black pepper

Combine all the above ingredients together. Store, covered with foil, in the refrigerator in 2 oz (50 g) portions.

Anchovy Butter

◆

(Serves 6 people)

This can be served spread on wholemeal toast sprinkled with cayenne pepper. You can also serve it melted over plain grilled fish fillets.

5 oz unsalted butter (150 g), at room temperature
2 oz tin anchovy fillets in oil (50 g)
1 clove garlic, crushed
¼ teaspoon anchovy essence
½ teaspoon grated onion
1 teaspoon lemon juice
cayenne pepper

First drain the anchovy fillets, then pat them as dry as possible with some kitchen paper. Then place the butter in a bowl and beat it with a wooden spoon till it's light and creamy – then add the anchovies after pounding them to a pulp. Stir in the garlic, anchovy essence, onion and lemon juice, then taste it and season with cayenne pepper (it should be fairly piquant). Now pile the butter into a bowl, cover and chill for an hour or two before serving.

Note You can make this by just placing everything in a liquidiser and blending until smooth – only if you do, use fewer anchovies (about three-quarters of the above) as liquidising seems to make them taste stronger.

Hot Lemon Butter

◆

(Serves 4–6 people)

This can be served as a quick accompaniment to asparagus, globe artichokes or fish.

4 oz salted butter (110 g)
1 tablespoon lemon juice
grated rind of ½ lemon
salt and freshly milled black pepper

Heat the butter, lemon juice and rind in a small saucepan. As soon as the butter melts and starts to sizzle, season with the salt and pepper and serve it very hot.

BRANDY BUTTER

◆

(Serves 6 people)

3 oz unsalted butter (75 g), at room temperature
3 oz caster sugar (75 g)
1¹/₂ tablespoons brandy
1 teaspoon lemon juice

Make sure that the butter is at room temperature before you begin, then beat, using a wooden spoon, until white and creamy.

Add the sugar a little at a time and beat well after each addition. Continue until all the sugar is in, then gradually work in the brandy a few drops at a time, still beating. Lastly, beat in the lemon juice and, when everything is thoroughly amalgamated, transfer the butter to a suitable dish and chill for 2–3 hours before serving.

SWEET SAUCES

◆

PROPER CUSTARD SAUCE

◆

(Serves 4 people)

Packet custard is very popular, but if you want to serve a pudding for a special occasion a *real* custard with it is incomparably nicer. I'm afraid I do admit to cheating a little here, by using 1 teaspoon of cornflour. But in my experience, it saves an awful lot of anxiety by stabilising the sauce and preventing it from curdling.

10 fl oz double or single cream (275 ml)
3 egg yolks
1 level teaspoon cornflour
1 level tablespoon caster sugar
2 drops vanilla essence

First heat the cream in a small saucepan up to boiling point; and while it's heating thoroughly blend the egg yolks, cornflour, sugar and vanilla together in a small basin. Then pour the hot cream in – stirring all the time – and return the mixture to the saucepan. Heat very gently (still stirring) until the sauce has thickened, which should only take a minute or two.

If it does overheat and start to look granular, don't worry. If you remove it from the heat and continue to beat it *will* become smooth again as it cools

– because the small addition of cornflour does a very efficient stabilising job. Serve the custard warm or, with a hot pudding or pie, chilled.

SAUCE SABAYON

(Serves 4 people)

This is a sweet sauce for serving with hot puddings like a Spotted Dick or light lemony sponge. It's also very good with a bread and butter pudding.

3 large egg yolks
2 oz caster sugar (50 g)
5 fl oz dry white wine (150 ml)

Start by placing a small saucepan of water on a low heat, and heat the water to just below simmering point.

Now put the egg yolks and sugar into a pudding basin and whisk until the mixture starts to thicken. Next sit the basin over the saucepan of simmering water and, keeping the heat low and continuing to whisk, add the wine slowly, a little at a time. When you've added all the wine, continue whisking until the egg yolk has cooked and thickened to a fairly thick fluffy sauce. Serve the sauce warm from a warmed jug or serving bowl.

Note This could be made with dry cider instead of wine, in which case it would go very well with an apple pudding.

PORT WINE SAUCE

(Serves 6 people)

This puts any steamed pudding into the dinner-party class and is especially good with the raisin pudding on page 601.

grated rind of 1 Seville orange (but an ordinary orange will do)
5 fl oz water (150 ml)
2 oz caster sugar (50 g)
1 oz unsalted butter (25 g)
1 teaspoon plain flour
5 fl oz ruby or tawny port (150 ml)
¹/₂ nutmeg, freshly grated
1 tablespoon Seville orange juice

Begin by gently boiling the orange rind, water and sugar in a thick-bottomed saucepan for 15 minutes.

Meanwhile, mix the butter into the flour and divide it up into about 6 pieces, adding them to the syrup at the end of the cooking time, followed by the port, nutmeg and orange juice. Boil the mixture for 1 minute over a gentle heat, stirring continuously, then serve immediately.

Note The sauce can be prepared in advance, except for the butter and flour part, which should be added just before serving.

RUM OR BRANDY SAUCE

◆

(Serves 4–6 people)

I always think a pouring sauce is best with a rich Christmas pudding – I happen to prefer it with rum, but if you would rather use brandy the quantities are the same. If you prefer *Brandy butter* the recipe is on page 407.

2 oz butter (50 g)
2 oz plain flour (50 g), sifted
15 fl oz milk (425 ml)
2 oz caster sugar (50 g)
2–3 tablespoons rum or brandy

First of all slowly melt the butter in a small saucepan. Now work the flour into the melted butter, using a wooden spoon, until the mixture is fairly smooth. Then gradually add the milk and stir well after each addition to keep the mixture free from any lumps.

When all the milk is added and you have a smooth creamy sauce, stir in the sugar, and let it cook over a very low heat for 10 minutes, stirring it slowly all the time to prevent it sticking. Then add the rum, and taste to check if more rum is needed before serving (here I have given the minimum quantity – I always like it fairly boozy!).

BUTTERSCOTCH SAUCE

◆

(Serves 6 people)

People never fail to drool over this lovely, thick, butterscotch sauce – delicious poured over ice cream just by itself, or with chopped bananas or fresh sliced peaches.

2 oz butter (50 g)
3 oz soft brown sugar (75 g)
2 oz granulated sugar (50 g)
5 oz golden syrup (150 g) – approx. one-third of a 1 lb (450 g) tin
4 fl oz double cream (110 ml)
a few drops of vanilla essence

First of all, place the butter and both the soft brown and granulated sugars in a medium-sized, thick-based saucepan together with the syrup. Heat slowly, and once the ingredients have completely melted and the sugar dissolved and formed a liquid continue to heat gently for about another 5 minutes. Then turn off the heat underneath the saucepan.

Now gradually stir the double cream into the sauce, followed by a few drops of vanilla essence. Stir for a further 2 or 3 minutes, or until the sauce is absolutely smooth.

That's it; serve it hot or cold. If you want to keep it, it will store well for several weeks in a cool place in a screw-top jar.

SEE ALSO

Aïoli sauce
Baby broad beans in parsley sauce
Braised celery with cheese and onion sauce
Chicken in barbecue sauce
Chicken with lemon sauce
Coeurs à la crème
Cranberry and orange relish
Deep-fried sprats in mustard sauce
Eliza Acton's English salad sauce
Fresh tomato sauce
Home-made mayonnaise
John Tovey's quick hollandaise sauce
Pesto alla Genovese (fresh basil sauce)
Ragù Bolognese
Redcurrant jelly
Roast stuffed goose with prunes in Armagnac
Sauce rouille
Sauce tartare
Spiced fig pudding with rum butter
Spring sauce for lamb
Tomato chilli sauce
Trout with caper sauce
Yoghurt seafood sauce

CHEESE

◆

Cheese is one of the very few foods which has the distinction of providing one complete course of a meal on its own, without any other preparation or adornment. This makes it one of the best friends of a harassed hostess: an imaginative cheese board with a small selection of water biscuits, crisp celery and some tart apples is a very good alternative to a dessert when you're pushed for time. But a good cheeseboard can be something of an adventure too. Over the centuries the art of cheese-making has produced an incredible range of textures and flavours, and over the last few years more and more of them have become available in our shops. So try to offer guests a good variety, say some Stilton, Cheddar, Brie or Camembert, and perhaps a goat's cheese. With a little bit of experimenting you can come up with all kinds of different combinations of your own.

In this section we are also concerned with the uses of cheese in cooking – and they are many. Cheese is used in sauces, pastry, fondues, omelettes, for toasting, gratining (i.e. browning the top of a dish under the grill after sprinkling with grated cheese), grating onto soups or pasta, in salads and in cheesecakes. Here, too, care must be taken to choose the right kind of cheese for the right kind of cooking. So first of all let's look at the various methods of cheese-making and the results they produce.

CHEESE-MAKING

◆

All cheese is made from milk – mostly cow's milk, sometimes goat's and occasionally ewe's – and the basis of all cheese-making is the separation of the solids (curds) from the liquids (whey) in the milk. From then on a whole variety of processes may take place, depending on the nature of the finished cheese – cutting, stirring, scalding, salting, moulding, pressing, ripening and so on.

There are literally thousands of different cheeses, the character of each one dependent not only on its method of production but also on unique local conditions, such as the nature of the grazing for the dairy herds. However, broadly speaking, one can distinguish certain 'families' of cheese:

411

SOFT PASTE CHEESES

These are the ones with the floury (unwashed) rinds and very soft creamy centres, of which Brie and Camembert are perhaps the most famous. Slightly firmer, but similar in texture, are those cheeses whose rinds are regularly washed while they're ripening (to keep the moisture needed for fermentation): Pont l'Evêque is a well-known example. Also in the category of 'soft paste' come the goat's cheeses, although in practice the range of textures in goat's cheese is huge.

BLUE-VEINED CHEESES

These are cheeses which have been injected with a penicillium mould, which creates the characteristic blue veins. Unlike other cheeses they ripen from the inside out and have to be perforated with special needles to aerate them and encourage the mould. In France Roquefort is the prince of the blue cheeses, in England Stilton.

PRESSED UNCOOKED CHEESES

These cheeses are bandaged with a cloth, placed in a mould, then kept under pressure for up to 24 hours. Most of our English cheeses are of this kind, though the degree of pressing (and therefore the texture) varies. Caerphilly, for instance, is a lightly pressed cheese while Cheddar is hard-pressed.

HARD-PRESSED COOKED CHEESES

To make these cheeses the curds are 'cooked' at 140°F (60°C) before being put into moulds and very firmly pressed. During the maturing period (up to six months) fermentation occurs internally, creating the holes which are characteristic of such cheeses as Gruyère and Emmenthal.

In addition to these four 'families' of cheese, we can also buy processed cheese, which has little connection with the natural cheeses from which it is processed. The product is made by grinding down a cheese (e.g. Cheddar), mixing it to a paste, flavouring it, then packing it into small portions – and I can't see much point in it.

Finally there is a group of cheeses generally known as fresh unfermented cheeses, sometimes (incorrectly) called cream cheeses; these are soft cheeses, which are made from naturally soured milk, whole or skimmed milk, or cream. Their fat content, and their flavour, varies a great deal. They have varied uses in cooking – cheesecakes, for instance, or cheese spreads or salads – but they should all be used as fresh as possible.

SOFT CHEESES

There is a bewildering array of so-called soft cheeses in the shops now, most coming labelled in different categories: *full fat* (very rich and fattening!), or *medium fat* (lighter but still with a discernible creaminess), or *low fat* which provides a mild lactic cheesy flavour without the smooth creaminess of the fattier cheeses.

They also come in a variety of names. There is the familiar *cream cheese* and *curd cheese*, then there is the German *quark*, and from France *fromage frais*, and from Italy *Mascarpone* (these last four being medium to low fat cheeses), then low fat *cottage cheese*, and *skimmed milk cheese* with only traces of fat. All can be used in recipes that call for soft cheese: which one you use depends on your calorie-counting or your taste. Fromage frais, incidentally, is a good substitute for cream in cooking, can be spooned over desserts instead of cream, and can often be bought ready flavoured with fruit in the same way as yoghurt. The medium fat fromage frais is best, in my opinion, and to stabilise it for cooking, use rice flour or cornflour as for yoghurt (see page 488).

COTTAGE CHEESE

This is made from pasteurised skimmed milk. The regulations state that it must contain less than 2 per cent milk fat, and it is therefore often recommended for those on a diet, though on its own the flavour is really rather bland.

CURD CHEESES

These have a more pronounced flavour, and the curds are formed by the natural action of lactic acid in milk. The fat content of curd cheese varies depending on the degree, if any, to which the milk has been skimmed.

CREAM CHEESES

As the name suggests these are made from cream (single and double) rather than milk, and as a result they have a higher fat content. In this country cream cheeses are sold unripened; they have a buttery texture and a rich, faintly acid flavour.

FARMHOUSE OR FACTORY?
———————— ♦ ————————

Some years ago I spent a delightful day on a farm – Chewton Dairy farm at Chewton Mendip to be precise – watching a real expert assessing and grading Cheddar cheese. Just by pressing his thumb on top of one and gauging the amount of 'bounce' under pressure, he could tell both the age and quality of a cheese. In his grandfather's day, he said, this test was carried out by standing on the huge cheeses and bouncing from one to the other! He then proceeded to insert a cheese iron into the

Cheddar, to twist it sharply then withdraw it, extracting a small quantity of cheese from the centre. The 'bloom' on the back of the iron told him the smoothness and fat content of the cheese, and then by rubbing a small piece of the cheese between thumb and forefinger he could check the texture. A good cheese, I was informed, should 'feel like a well-nourished dairy-maid'!

This farm is one of only a few which continue to make traditional Cheddars. A small quantity of Cheshire cheese, and even less of Lancashire, is also still made on farms. Altogether about 10 per cent of our English cheese is 'farmhouse' and it's the best you can buy. It is made from the finest quality milk that the dairy herds produce and is well-matured – always worth looking out for. Elsewhere in the British Isles not a few independent producers have sprung up – almost a cottage industry – producing small amounts of local cheeses. The rest of our cheese is now made in factories – or 'creameries' as they prefer to be called. Modern economics have made this inevitable and even in France, where they are particularly choosy about their cheese, the same trend is happening. Factory cheese, however, is subject to the same stringent standards of classification as farmhouse, and can be excellent.

GRADING

In the case of farmhouse cheese, the very finest quality cheese is graded and labelled as *superfine*, and good quality cheese as *fine*. The equivalent grades for factory-made cheeses are *extra selected* and *selected*. In both cases, the rest of the cheese which is saleable in spite of having some fault is simply called *graded*.

BUYING AND STORING CHEESE

♦

Since most of us buy our cheese in relatively small quantities – either pre-packed or sliced off a whole cheese – the complex business of caring for a whole cheese (damp wrapping, polishing, and humidity control) need not concern us too much, though there are some shopkeepers and restaurateurs who could certainly do some homework on the subject.

It is best, wherever possible, to buy cheese from a specialist cheese shop or market stall, where the supplier can advise you which ones are at their best and very often are happy to give you slivers to taste before you buy.

If you are buying portions from larger cheeses, look out for any that are cracked or look sweaty: it means they have been exposed to shop temperature for too long and are in the process of drying out. In the case of soft paste cheese, check that they are springy to the touch and (unless you want to eat them immediately) not *too* runny.

At home the best place to store your cheese is at the bottom of the refrigerator or, failing that, some other *cool* place. At all events wrap each piece tightly in foil, with no little tears or gaps to let the air in (cling film is not as suitable as foil as it exposes the cheese to too much light). Those china cheese dishes or domes, however attractive they may be, are not the place to store cheese since they offer no protection from the air.

Most cheeses, however, have best flavour and texture if they are brought to room temperature about 1 hour before eating.

BRITISH CHEESES

There are – if you don't include the elusive Blue Vinney (said to be made secretly in Dorset) and the very local Yorkshire cheeses – ten major British cheeses. All are made from cow's milk, and their very names are evocative of the dairy pastures where, for the most part, they are still produced.

CHEDDAR

One of the most imitated of cheeses, and understandably so: we import Cheddars from all kinds of places like New Zealand and Ireland, but the original English Cheddar is still the best – and in particular Farmhouse Cheddar, which is well-matured (anything up to nine months) and stronger than the mild, younger Cheddars that are widely available. A good Cheddar cheese should look amber yellow and fresh, without a greasy shine, and it should feel firm but not hard. Its clean and mellow flavour makes it very suitable for cooking, toasting, topping, for cheese sauces or simply for serving with pickled onions and beer for a ploughman's lunch.

CHESHIRE

Said to be the oldest of English cheeses, it comes in red, white or blue – very patriotic! The red Cheshire, which has been artificially coloured, is milder than the white, which ideally should be flaky and slightly salty (though this will depend on its age). Both red and white Cheshire are good melting cheeses. The blue-veined variety (sometimes artificially produced, sometimes not) has a distinctive ripe, salty flavour.

DOUBLE GLOUCESTER

A bright orange (artificially induced) colour, but with a mature, creamy and delicate taste. It's best eaten, I think, just with biscuits and celery. It is called 'double' because when it's whole it's twice the size of a single Gloucester (which is not sold now anyway). The variety which includes chives is known as Cotswold cheese.

CAERPHILLY

Another eating, rather than cooking, cheese. It's a quick ripener, ready for eating after only two weeks, which makes it white, mild and semi-soft.

WENSLEYDALE

From Yorkshire as the name implies, this comes in two varieties. The young white Wensleydale is mild and very slightly salty; the blue-veined Wensleydale has been allowed to mature for some six months, is soft and flaky in texture and rich, almost sweet, in flavour.

LANCASHIRE

A white mild cheese, with a fairly soft and crumbly texture which is supposed to make it 'spreadable', but certainly makes it an excellent toasting cheese.

DERBY

Mild, hard and honey-coloured when at its best, which is at about four to six weeks. A standard variation is the sage Derby, which is flavoured with chopped sage leaves and coloured green with spinach.

LEICESTER

This is red and crumbly with a medium-strong flavour when it has fully matured after three months. It's good for toasting.

STILTON

Named after the village on the Great North Road where it was sold to coach travellers, who spread its fame all over the country. A whole Stilton is 9 inches high and 8 inches across (23 × 20 cm) with a crinkly brown rind. The habit of spooning the cheese out of the centre and then pouring port in to keep it moist still persists. In my opinion this ruins the flavour and texture of the cheese, which really ought to be firm and creamy white with a clean network of blue veins. It is far better to slice Stilton horizontally and to keep it wrapped, in the fridge. At full maturity (six months) Stilton should be rich and mellow with a sharp, salty aftertaste. The young version, white Stilton, has not developed a mould and is mild and crumbly.

DUNLOP

It might be described as the national cheese of Scotland, where indeed it is mainly found nowadays. It is a smooth, creamy white cheese with a mild, occasionally slightly sourish flavour. It is named after the town of Dunlop in Ayrshire.

416

Anchoïade (see page 459)

CONTINENTAL CHEESES

Once you could only find these – or at least a reasonable selection of them – at specialised cheesemongers or delicatessens, but nowadays many supermarkets carry quite an adventurous stock of them. They are always worth trying out for yourself, so here's a list (by no means exhaustive) of some you might come across.

FRANCE

France is *the* country for cheese-making: there are many hundreds of cheeses which are purely local specialities (and if you're ever in a particular region, do ask to sample the local cheese – it may be the only chance you ever get!). Some of course have become world famous. Of the soft paste cheeses *Brie* is widely exported in its traditional disc shape, with a downy white rind and a faintly straw-coloured interior. It should be springy to the touch, creamy and fairly mild in flavour. Farmhouse or unpasteurised Brie is the best of all. Rather tangier and fruitier is the famous *Camembert*, which to me is the very essence of the rich dairy lands of Normandy. Also worth trying, if you want a stronger spicy soft cheese, is its neighbour *Livarot* or, from the Alsace region, *Munster*.

The greatest of the French blue-veined cheese (called *bleus*) is *Roquefort*, a ewe's milk cheese. To qualify for the name, the cheese has to mature only in the humid natural caves of Roquefort. Rather expensive, it's often used in recipes for quiche or salad dressing, but really deserves to be eaten on its own for its strong, distinctive taste to be appreciated. Other French *bleus* are available over here, such as *Bleu de Bresse* which is somewhat milder than Roquefort.

A proper catalogue of French pressed cheeses would be almost endless, but amongst those that find their way over here I'd mention *Saint-Paulin* from Brittany, mild and velvety and useful in cooking (also *Port Salut* which is a Saint-Paulin relative, made in a local monastery). *Reblochon* from the Savoy region is also mild and creamy; *Cantal* from the pastures of the Auvergne is a firm, nutty-flavoured cheese.

Goat's cheeses (or *chèvres*) can be absolutely delicious and they come in all shapes and sizes. *Saint-Maure* for example is cylindrical, firm to the touch and full-flavoured. *Valençay* is shaped like a sawn-off pyramid, its rind is dusted with charcoal, and it tastes mild and slightly nutty. *Banon* (from Provence) is disc-shaped and comes wrapped in chestnut leaves. The tiny round *Crottins* are exceptionally good.

SWITZERLAND

Best known of the Swiss cheeses are the hard, cooked varieties. The yellow-amber *Gruyère*, with its pock-marking of little holes, has a distinct fruit flavour. So does the ivory-coloured *Emmenthal*, which has a slightly firmer, oilier texture and rather larger holes. Both are good melting and toasting cheeses, and the basis of several traditional fondue recipes.

Dried fruit salad with yoghurt and nuts (see page 491)

HOLLAND

Both the semi-hard Dutch cheeses, the firm yellow *Gouda* and the mild red-rinded *Edam*, have long been familiar over here. We can now buy mature Gouda which is a good melting cheese, and Edam, while not a cheese for connoisseurs, is a good friend of slimmers, having fewer calories than most other hard cheeses.

ITALY

The Italian repertoire of cheeses is extensive, and the Italians make good use of their cheeses in cooking. *Parmesan,* a hard brittle cheese, is indispensable for grating over soups, pasta and other dishes. It is widely sold here ready-grated, but don't ever buy it because it has lost a good deal of its flavour: so try to get hold of a whole piece of it and grate it yourself when needed – it keeps very well in a sealed polythene bag. *Pecorino* is another hard cheese used in the same way, but with a stronger, saltier taste. *Mozzarella,* a very white soft cheese (occasionally found made from buffalo's milk) comes in little plastic bags to keep it moist. It is the traditional cheese for cooking on pizza, with a nice elastic texture, and when really young and fresh it is delicious with a little olive oil in a salad with ripe tomatoes and fresh basil. For the end of a meal creamy *Bel Paese* and pungent, almost runny, blue *Gorgonzola* make a good contrast.

GREECE

Greek cheeses, unfortunately, are usually only to be found in Greek or Cypriot shops in Britain, but *Feta* (soft ewe's milk cheese) is delicious, when very fresh, in a salad; and the hard salty *Kefalotyri* is excellent fried.

CHEESE AND ONION QUICHELETS
———————— ♦ ————————

(Makes 10)

The name sounds odd but it describes these little cheese tarts perfectly. Serve them on picnics or car journeys or at buffet parties when you need food that can be picked up easily.

For the pastry
2 oz wholewheat flour (50 g)
2 oz self-raising flour (50 g)
1 oz margarine (25 g)
1 oz lard (25g)
salt and freshly milled black pepper
cold water, to mix

For the filling
¹/₂ oz butter (10 g)
1 onion, finely chopped
1¹/₂ oz strong Cheddar cheese (40 g), grated
3 fl oz milk or cream (75 ml)
1 large egg, beaten
¹/₄ teaspoon mustard powder
cayenne pepper

Pre-heat the oven to gas mark 4, 350°F (180°C).

First make up the pastry: sift the flours together and add some seasoning, then rub in the fats until the mixture is crumbly; add enough cold water to make a dough that leaves the bowl clean. Place the dough in a polythene bag and leave to rest in the fridge for 30 minutes. Then roll out the dough and, using a 3¹/₄ inch (8 cm) plain cutter, cut out rounds. Use the rounds to line a patty tin.

Next, for the filling, melt the butter in a small saucepan and soften the onion in it over a low heat for 10–12 minutes. Leave to cool, then put a little onion in the base of each tartlet and a little grated cheese on top. Now whisk together the milk, egg and mustard powder and season to taste, then spoon some of the liquid carefully into each tartlet.

Bake in the centre of the oven for about 30 minutes, then top with a light sprinkling of cayenne pepper. These little tarts can be served hot or cold.

PAN-FRIED PIZZA

(Serves 2–4 people)

This is an extremely quick and easy way to make a pizza, without having to bother with making a yeast bread dough.

For the base
8 oz self-raising flour (225 g)
¹/₂ teaspoon salt
freshly milled black pepper
¹/₂ teaspoon dried oregano
4–5 tablespoons olive oil

For the topping
4 generous tablespoons tomato purée
14 oz tin Italian tomatoes (400 g), drained and chopped
approx. 5 oz Mozzarella cheese (150 g), cut into small slices
1 dozen black olives, pitted and chopped
2 oz mushrooms (50 g), thinly sliced
1 teaspoon dried oregano
1³/₄ oz tin anchovy fillets in oil (45 g), drained (oil reserved) and cut in half lengthways

First sift the flour, salt, freshly milled black pepper and oregano into a bowl. Make a well in the middle and pour in 2 tablespoons of olive oil, then 4 tablespoons of water. Now mix to a soft, though not sticky, dough – you may find you have to add a further tablespoon or so of water to get the right consistency. Prepare a floured surface, turn the dough out onto it and knead lightly. Now roll out a round to fit the base of a 9–10 inch (23–25 cm) frying-pan.

Next heat 1 tablespoon of olive oil in the pan, place the circle of dough in the pan and cook over a low heat for about 5 minutes or until the base is lightly brown.

Have ready an oiled plate and turn the pizza base out onto it. Then, after heating a further 1 tablespoon of oil in the pan, slide the pizza base back in, and cook the reverse side for 5 minutes.

During this time, spread the tomato purée over the surface of the pizza base, together with the drained tomatoes. Next scatter over the slices of cheese, chopped olives, mushrooms and oregano. Finally, arrange the anchovy fillets on top in a criss-cross pattern and drizzle on the oil from the tin.

To see if the under-side of the pizza base is cooked you can lift up a corner with a palette knife and have a look. When it's cooked, transfer the pan to a pre-heated grill for 2 or 3 minutes to melt the cheese and heat the topping. Serve straightaway with a mixed salad.

Note This can also be made successfully with 85 per cent plain wheatmeal flour.

CHEESE AND HERB SAUSAGES

◆

(Serves 3–4 people)

This is adapted from a traditional Welsh recipe called Glamorgan sausages. They really are lovely – we like them served with fried broccoli and red tomato chutney.

5 oz fresh white or wholewheat breadcrumbs (150 g)
1 medium onion, grated
4 oz strong Cheddar cheese (110 g), grated
1 teaspoon dried or 2 teaspoons chopped fresh mixed herbs
³/₄ teaspoon mustard powder
1 egg yolk
salt and freshly milled black pepper
For coating and frying
¹/₂ oz breadcrumbs (10 g)
¹/₂ oz Parmesan cheese (10 g), grated
1 egg white, lightly beaten
oil

Place the breadcrumbs in a large mixing bowl together with the grated onion, Cheddar and herbs; add the mustard powder and a seasoning of salt and pepper. Then add the egg yolk and stir to bind the mixture together. Now divide it into twelve or fourteen small portions and, using your hands, roll each piece into a sausage shape, squeezing it to hold it together.

Before frying them, mix the breadcrumbs reserved for coating with the Parmesan cheese and dip each sausage first into the egg white and then into the breadcrumb and cheese mixture and coat evenly.

Fry in hot shallow oil till crisp and golden. Drain on crumpled kitchen paper before serving.

ROMAN GNOCCHI

◆

(Serves 3–4 people)

These are little fingers made with cheese and semolina, then baked in the oven with butter. Simple, inexpensive but really good. They *can* be served with a fresh tomato sauce, but I don't think they need it. I would serve these as a lunch dish with salad and good bread.

10 fl oz milk (275 ml)
5 oz semolina (150 g) – the coarse type is best
10 fl oz water (275 ml)
freshly grated nutmeg
3 oz butter (75 g)
5 oz Parmesan cheese (150 g), grated
2 eggs, beaten
salt and freshly milled black pepper

Put into a saucepan the milk, semolina and water together with a good grating of nutmeg and a little salt and pepper, and bring it all to the boil, stirring all the time. Let the mixture boil for about 4 minutes (still stirring) until it is thick enough to stand a spoon up in. Then remove the pan from the heat and beat in 1 oz (25 g) of the butter, 3 oz (75 g) of the Parmesan cheese and both the beaten eggs. Check the seasoning, then spread the mixture in a small Swiss roll tin or something similar (approximately 11 × 7 inches/28 × 18 cm), lined with oiled greaseproof paper. Leave to cool or refrigerate – overnight if possible.

When you're ready to cook the gnocchi, pre-heat the oven to gas mark 6, 400°F (200°C).

Then cut the cheese and semolina mixture into 'fingers' (you should get about 24 to 27) or use a 2 inch (5 cm) pastry cutter for round shapes, and peel away the greaseproof paper. Place them, slightly overlapping, in an 11½ inch (29 cm) shallow buttered gratin dish, then dot the top of the gnocchi with the remaining 2 oz (50 g) of butter and bake for 10 minutes.

Then baste the gnocchi with the melted butter and sprinkle the remaining 2 oz (50 g) of Parmesan over them. Replace the dish on an upper shelf of the oven and bake for a further 30 minutes or until the whole thing is golden-brown and bubbling nicely. You might think this seems too much butter, but when serving it should be soaked in melted butter. Not for slimmers or the health-conscious, but wonderful.

SPINACH AND CREAM CHEESE QUICHE

◆

(Serves 4–6 people)

Fresh spinach would be best for this quiche, but 1 lb (450 g) of frozen spinach (so long as it's well drained) would do as an alternative.

wholewheat shortcrust pastry made with 3 oz wholewheat flour (75 g) and 3 oz self-raising flour (75 g) with 3 oz fat (75 g) (see page 497)

For the filling
2 lb fresh spinach (900 g)

1 oz butter (25 g)
8 oz cream cheese (225 g)
5 fl oz milk (150 ml)
3 eggs, beaten
2 tablespoons grated Parmesan cheese
freshly grated nutmeg
a squeeze of lemon juice
salt and freshly milled black pepper

Pre-heat the oven to gas mark 4, 350°F (180°C), and pop in a baking sheet.

First make the pasty and use it to line a 10 inch (25 cm) flan tin. Prick the pastry base all over with a fork, and bake on the pre-heated baking sheet for 15 minutes. Remove the flan tin from the oven and brush the pastry all over with some of the beaten egg from the filling ingredients. Return the flan tin to the oven and cook for a further 5 minutes to allow the egg to set.

Set the flan tin on one side, but leave the baking sheet in the oven and increase the heat to gas mark 5, 375°F (190°C).

Now prepare the filling. First wash the spinach, discarding any coarse stalks or damaged leaves. Drain the leaves thoroughly and place them in a heavy-based saucepan together with the butter and some salt and pepper (there is no need to add any water). Cover and cook the spinach for about 7 minutes, giving the pan a shake occasionally, until the spinach collapses down into the butter.

Then drain the spinach thoroughly in a colander, pressing out any excess moisture. Now place the cream cheese in a bowl and beat it, gradually adding the milk followed by the remaining beaten eggs, the Parmesan cheese and a seasoning of salt, pepper and nutmeg. Chop up the drained spinach with a sharp knife, and stir it into the cream mixture, adding a squeeze of lemon juice and (if it needs it) a little more seasoning.

Pour the whole mixture into the flan case and place the flan tin on the hot baking sheet in the upper part of the oven. Bake for 40 minutes, or until the filling is puffy and golden on top.

Note This is also very nice made with a cheese shortcrust pastry, using 3 oz (75 g) each of wholewheat and self-raising flours, 3 oz (75 g) of fat and 2 oz (50 g) grated Cheddar cheese.

WELSH RAREBIT SOUFFLÉ

◆

(Serves 3 people)

This, if you've got the time, is a Welsh rarebit with a difference. It's rich golden-brown, light and puffy.

6 slices bread (cut medium thick) from a small loaf

For the topping
½ oz butter (10 g)
½ oz plain flour (10 g)
6 tablespoons milk
1 teaspoon French mustard
a dash of Worcestershire sauce
a little cayenne pepper
2 eggs, separated
1 oz strong Cheddar cheese (25 g), grated
1 oz Parmesan cheese (25 g), grated
salt and freshly milled black pepper

First melt the butter in a small saucepan, blend in the flour and cook for a minute or two before adding the milk very gradually, stirring all the time. Let the mixture bubble for 2 minutes, take the saucepan off the heat and stir in the mustard, Worcestershire sauce, a little cayenne, some salt and freshly milled pepper. Next beat the egg yolks, stir them into the sauce and leave it on one side to cool for a minute.

Now toast the bread on one side. Then beat the grated cheeses into the sauce mixture. Whisk the egg whites until stiff and, using a metal spoon, carefully fold them into the cheese mixture. Cover each slice (on the untoasted side) liberally with the cheese mixture. Pop the slices under a medium grill and when the tops are golden-brown, light and puffy, serve at once.

TOASTED CHEESE WITH ALE
♦

(Serves 4 people)

This is a lovely sort of toasted cheese, good for a really speedy supper.

4 thick slices bread
cayenne pepper

For the topping
8 oz strong Cheddar cheese (225 g), grated
2 oz butter (50 g)
1 tablespoon mustard powder
4 tablespoons brown ale
salt and freshly milled black pepper

First melt the butter in a saucepan. Then add the mustard, brown ale, grated cheese and some seasoning and, with a wooden spoon, stir continuously until the mixture looks creamy and the cheese has almost melted – but it's important that you don't let the mixture boil.

Then remove the saucepan from the heat and quickly toast the bread slices on both sides until they're nice and crisp. Pour the cheese mixture over each piece of toast, sprinkle with cayenne pepper, then place them under the grill until hot and bubbling. Serve immediately with, perhaps, some more brown ale to drink with it.

FILLETS OF SOLE GRATINÉS

◆

(Serves 4 people as a starter or 3 as a main course)

This, like all the best recipes in the world, is unbelievably simple and tastes really good. You can use Dover sole, lemon sole or even plaice fillets.

6 fillets of sole
8 oz stale breadcrumbs (225 g)
3 oz Cheddar cheese (75 g), grated
2 tablespoons chopped fresh parsley
melted butter
salt and freshly milled black pepper
To garnish
6 lemon or lime quarters

Pre-heat the grill to its highest setting.

Mix the breadcrumbs, grated cheese and parsley with 4 oz (110 g) melted butter. Line the grill pan with foil and paint the foil with a little more melted butter. Lay the sole fillets on it and season them with salt and freshly milled black pepper, cover them with the breadcrumb mixture and pour over a little more melted butter. Cook under the hot grill for about 5 minutes until the crumbs have turned a rich brown and the fish is cooked. Serve garnished with quartered lemons or limes to squeeze over. Good with tiny new potatoes dressed with melted butter and chives, and some fresh shelled peas.

GREEK SALAD

◆

(Serves 2–3 people as a lunch dish)

This should, authentically, have crumbled pieces of Greek Feta cheese mixed in with the salad ingredients, but white Stilton would be an alternative.

6 oz Feta cheese (175 g), chopped in small pieces
6 ripe, firm tomatoes, cut in quarters then in eighths
½ small young cucumber or 1 whole ridge cucumber, cut into ⅛ inch (3 mm) thick slices, the slices then halved
1 medium onion, cut in thin rings, then the rings halved
2 oz small firm black olives (50 g)
4 tablespoons olive oil (Greek if possible)
salt and freshly milled black pepper
To garnish
1 small lemon, quartered

Simply mix the cheese, tomatoes, cucumber, onion and olives together in a salad bowl. Season with salt and freshly milled black pepper, then pour the oil all over everything just before serving. Garnish with lemon quarters for squeezing over the salad.

DUTCH OMELETTE
◆

(Serves 1 person)

This is an omelette made with Dutch Gouda cheese, which is placed in the centre then melted under a hot grill so that the omelette itself is finally wrapped round a lovely, creamy, stretchy mass of cheese. It is also excellent with Italian *Bel Paese*.

2 large fresh eggs
2 oz Gouda cheese (50 g)
1 tablespoon snipped chives or very finely chopped spring onion tops
1 oz butter (25 g)
salt and freshly milled black pepper

Pre-heat the grill to a high heat.

Break the eggs into a small basin and, using a fork, mix them lightly together, season, and add the snipped chives. Now cut the cheese, with a sharp knife, into thin slices.

Then over a fairly high heat melt the butter in a 7 inch (18 cm) frying-pan. When the butter starts to froth, swirl it round so that the pan base and sides are well coated, then pour in the eggs. Quickly lay the cheese slices down the centre of the omelette and, after cooking the base of the omelette for a few seconds, transfer the pan to the hot grill. Leave it there until the cheese just melts (it will overcook if left too long).

Have a hot plate ready and fold the omelette into three: tilt the pan, flip the edge of the omelette nearest you over the centre part, then roll that over the far side of the omelette and turn the whole lot over again and out onto a plate.

Eat the omelette absolutely immediately with some crusty bread and a garlicky salad.

ALPINE EGGS

◆

(Serves 3 people)

This is a recipe I have given many times before, but I don't apologise for including it here again because it never fails to please and is the quickest supper dish for any number of people – including one.

6 large fresh eggs
12 oz Cheddar or Lancashire cheese (350 g), grated
approx. 1 oz butter (25 g)
salt and freshly milled black pepper
To garnish
1 dessertspoon snipped fresh chives

Pre-heat the oven to gas mark 4, 350°F (180°C).

Butter a shallow oval baking dish quite generously, then cover the base with half the grated cheese. Now carefully break the eggs on to the cheese, season well with salt and freshly milled black pepper, then sprinkle the rest of the cheese over the eggs, covering them completely.

Dot with a few flecks of butter here and there, then bake in the centre of the oven for 15 minutes, by which time the cheese will be melted and bubbling, and the eggs just set. Just before serving sprinkle the chives over, and serve with crusty fresh bread and a crisp green salad.

Note For a special occasion serve Alpine eggs as a first course. Use individual 3 inch (7.5 cm) ramekin dishes (buttered) with 1 egg per person and 2 oz (50 g) grated Gruyère cheese per person. Prepare and cook in exactly the same way as above.

CHEESE TARTLETS WITH MUSHROOM PÂTÉ

◆

(Makes about 24)

These are made with a really crisp cheese pastry and filled with a mushroom and onion pâté.

427

For the pastry
4 oz wholewheat flour (110 g)
4 oz self-raising flour (110 g)
a pinch of salt
1 teaspoon mustard powder
2 oz margarine (50 g)
2 oz lard (50 g)
3 oz Cheddar cheese (75 g), grated
cold water, to mix
For the filling
1 oz butter (25 g)
1 small onion, finely chopped
6 oz flat mushrooms (175 g), finely chopped
2 eggs
4 fl oz milk (110 ml)
freshly grated nutmeg
1 tablespoon grated Parmesan cheese
salt and freshly milled black pepper

Begin by making the pastry: sift the flours, salt and mustard into a large mixing bowl, add the bran remaining in the sieve, rub in the fats until the mixture is crumbly, stir in the cheese, and add sufficient water to make a dough that leaves the bowl clean. Wrap the pastry in a polythene bag and chill it in the refrigerator for about 30 minutes.

Now melt the butter in a small pan and sauté the onion in it until soft – about 5 minutes. Then stir in the mushrooms and continue to cook gently, uncovered, for 30 minutes, stirring occasionally. The mixture should now have formed a sort of paste. Taste and season.

Pre-heat the oven to gas mark 5, 375°F (190°C), and put a baking sheet in near the top.

Next, on a floured board, roll out the pastry fairly thinly and use a 3 inch (7.5 cm) cutter to cut out pastry rounds. Ease these into greased 2½ inch (6 cm) patty tins, prick the bases, then put on the baking sheet in the oven and cook for 5 minutes.

Now beat the eggs lightly, take the pastry out of the oven and brush each tart with a little egg, then return to the oven for a further 5 minutes.

Now whisk the milk, some seasoning and nutmeg into the beaten eggs. Put a little of the mushroom and onion mixture in the base of each tartlet and, very carefully, pour on some of the egg mixture. Sprinkle with Parmesan, and return to the oven for 30 minutes until the mixture is set. Finally, leave in the patty tins to cool for about 15 minutes.

Note For individual quiches for six people for a light lunch dish, this recipe can be adapted by multiplying all the ingredients × 1½ and made into six 3 inch (7.5 cm) quiches.

BROCCOLI CHEESE SOUFFLÉ

◆

(Serves 4 people)

This always looks so beautiful. It's a pale green colour with a golden-brown crust.

1 lb fresh broccoli (450 g)
1 oz butter (25 g)
2 tablespoons plain flour
5 fl oz milk (150 ml)
2 oz Cheddar cheese (50 g), grated
a pinch of cayenne pepper
freshly grated nutmeg
2 large eggs
2 extra egg whites
salt and freshly milled black pepper
1 tablespoon grated Parmesan cheese

Pre-heat the oven to gas mark 6, 400°F (200°C).

A 1³/₄ pint (1 litre) soufflé dish, well-buttered.

If you've never made a soufflé before, don't worry because this is a fairly easy one, and no soufflé is ever *all that* difficult once you've mastered the art of whipping egg whites to the right stage and, having got them to the right stage, the art of folding them in properly.

Having turned on the oven, take a large meat-roasting tin, big enough to hold the soufflé dish, then fill it with 1¹/₂ inches (4 cm) of hot water and put that in the oven to pre-heat as well.

Now start to prepare the broccoli by trimming off the very stalky bits, then place the rest in a saucepan with a little salt and about 6 fl oz (175 ml) of boiling water. Put a lid on and simmer it gently for about 10–15 minutes or until the broccoli has softened and most of the water has disappeared.

Now drain the broccoli well, then transfer to a largish mixing bowl and, using a large fork, mash it to a pulp. Get it as pulp-like as possible, but don't worry too much about getting rid of all the fibrous pieces of stalk.

Next melt the butter in a saucepan and stir in the flour. Then when it's smooth gradually add the milk, stirring vigorously after each addition. When all the milk is in you should have a thick glossy paste and now you can mix in the Cheddar cheese, keeping the pan over the lowest heat possible. After that, empty the cheese mixture into the bowl containing the broccoli pulp, then mix everything together thoroughly. Do a bit of tasting, add salt if it needs it and also some freshly milled pepper, a pinch of cayenne and about a quarter of a whole nutmeg, freshly grated.

Now for the egg bit. Separate the eggs, add the two yolks to the broccoli mixture and mix them in fairly thoroughly. (All this, by the way, can be done well in advance.) For the four whites, take a very large mixing bowl – making sure it's completely dry and free from grease, and you'll need a whisk which is the same. Whisk the egg whites until they stand up in peaks when you lift the whisk, but be careful not to overdo it, or they'll start to flop a bit and go watery.

As soon as they're ready carefully fold into the broccoli mixture first just 1 tablespoon of egg white to loosen it, then carefully fold in the rest, using a metal spoon. Turn the bowl round as you fold, adding about a quarter of the mixture at a time. (When you're folding the egg whites in, the most important thing to remember is that you don't want to lose all the air you've whisked into them.)

Now spoon the mixture into the prepared soufflé dish, sprinkle with a dusting of Parmesan cheese, place the dish in the roasting tin, and cook the soufflé for 30–35 minutes. When it's done, it should be nicely risen and beginning to crack on the surface – but be careful not to overcook; it should be soft and moist inside. And, needless to say, serve immediately.

Note This is equally good made with 1 lb (450 g) cooked cauliflower or courgettes mashed to a pulp. And, if you were so inclined, you could also use 85 per cent wheatmeal flour instead of white.

ORANGE CHEESECAKE
◆

(Serves 8 people)

This is unbelievably easy, it doesn't need any cooking and can be made well in advance.

For the base
4 oz wheatmeal biscuits (110 g), crushed to fine crumbs with a rolling-pin
2 oz butter (50 g)

For the filling
1¹/₂ lb cream cheese (700 g)
grated rind of 1 orange, boiled in water for 5 minutes, then drained
2 oz caster sugar (50 g)
3 fl oz frozen concentrated orange juice (75 ml), thawed

For the topping
fresh orange segments or strawberries (optional)

Begin by melting the butter in a saucepan, but do not let it brown.

Then stir in the biscuit crumbs and mix well. Now press the mixture into a lightly-oiled 8 inch (20 cm) cake or flan tin with a loose base and leave in a cool place, or in the refrigerator, to harden a little.

When it has firmed, beat the cream cheese, orange rind and sugar together very thoroughly, add the thawed orange juice and continue beating until you have a smooth mixture, then pour it into the biscuit-lined tin. Cover with foil and chill thoroughly.

If you wish, the cheesecake can be decorated with segments of fresh orange (carefully peeled, skinned and well drained) or, in the summer, whole strawberries make it particularly delicious – but don't decorate with either fruit until just before serving or it will soak into the filling.

Note If you like, the wheatmeal biscuits can be chocolate coated.

CURD CHEESECAKE WITH FRUIT TOPPING
◆

(Serves up to 12 people)

This large cheesecake will serve up to twelve people. Use whatever fruit is in season – in summer the nicest topping is a mixture of 8 oz (225 g) strawberries and 4 oz (110 g) each of redcurrants and raspberries.

For the base
8 oz wheatmeal biscuits (225 g), crushed into crumbs
4 oz butter (110 g)
For the filling
1½ lb curd cheese (700 g)
3 eggs
6 oz sugar (175 g)
1 teaspoon vanilla essence
For the topping
10 fl oz double cream (275 ml), whipped
fresh fruit (as above)
icing sugar

Pre-heat the oven to gas mark 2, 300°F (150°C).

A 9 inch (23 cm) tin about 2–3 inches (5–7.5 cm) deep with a loose base.

Gently melt the butter in a small saucepan, without letting it brown, then stir the crushed biscuits into it. Transfer the biscuit mixture into the cake tin and press it down evenly all over to form a base.

Now combine the curd cheese, eggs and sugar together in a mixing bowl and beat to form a smooth, thick cream – an electric mixer is best for this. Then mix in the vanilla essence and pour the mixture over the biscuit base, smoothing it out evenly.

Cook the cheesecake for 30 minutes on the centre shelf, then turn the oven off and leave it to get quite cold in the oven. It should then be chilled for at least 2 hours, or preferably overnight. To turn the cheesecake out of the tin, rinse a clean dishcloth in hot water: hold it around the tin for a few seconds, then push up the base very gently. Just before serving, top the cake with the whipped cream, the fresh fruit and a dusting of icing sugar.

Note The base for this also tastes very good made with 4 oz (110 g) finely crushed shortbread biscuits and 4 oz (110 g) ground hazelnuts.

FRESH LEMON CHEESECAKE WITH FROSTED GRAPES

♦

(Serves 6–8 people)

This is fresh-tasting and lighter than the other cheesecake recipes given in this book, and looks attractive with clusters of frosted grapes on top.

For the base
4 oz digestive biscuits (110 g), crushed into crumbs
2 oz butter (50 g)
For the filling
12 oz cottage cheese (350 g)
¹/₂ oz powdered gelatine (10 g)
2 large egg yolks
2¹/₂ oz caster sugar (60 g)
grated rind and juice of 2 lemons
5 fl oz double cream (150 ml)
For the topping
1 egg white
4 oz seedless grapes (110 g)
caster sugar

An 8 inch (20 cm) flan tin or sponge tin with a loose base, lightly-oiled.

First prepare the base of the cheesecake by melting the butter in a small saucepan, then mix the melted butter with the biscuit crumbs in a bowl. Spoon the mixture into the prepared tin and press it well down all over as evenly as possible.

Now put the gelatine, along with 3 tablespoons cold water, into a small cup and stand this in a small saucepan of barely simmering water. Leave it for about 10 minutes or until the gelatine looks clear and transparent. Then put it on one side.

Now put the egg yolks, sugar and cheese in a liquidiser, blend for about 1 minute, then add the lemon juice and rind plus the gelatine (pour the gelatine through a strainer). Blend again until everything is thoroughly mixed and the mixture absolutely smooth. Now whip up the cream until you get a 'floppy' consistency, pour this into the liquidiser and blend again for just a few seconds. Next pour the whole mixture over the biscuit base, cover with foil and chill for a minimum of 3 hours.

Meanwhile whisk up the egg white. Break the grapes into little clusters of two or three grapes each and dip each bunch first in the egg white, then in a saucer of caster sugar. Leave them spread out on greaseproof paper for a couple of hours before using them to decorate the cheesecake.

CŒURS À LA CRÈME

◆

(Serves 4 people)

This lovely cream mixture was originally served in heart-shaped dishes (hence the name). But small ramekins will do for the less romantic! It is lovely for serving with soft summer fruits, ideally a mixture of raspberries and redcurrants.

8 oz unsalted cream cheese (225 g)
10 fl oz soured cream (275 ml)
2 level tablespoons caster sugar
2 large egg whites
To serve
fruit of your choice, such as raspberries and redcurrants
4 tablespoons double cream

Quite simply combine the cream cheese, soured cream and sugar thoroughly in a mixing bowl. Then whisk the egg whites until they are stiff and fold them carefully into the cream mixture. The whole lot now needs to be drained – overnight – in a cool place, and this is done by placing the mixture in a suitably-sized square of muslin, and placing this in a sieve over a bowl. When it has drained completely, pile the mixture into small dishes or ramekins, arrange your fruit on top, then pour a tablespoon of cream over each serving.

SEE ALSO

A risotto for spring
Asparagus and cheese tart
Baked spinach with brown rice and cheese
Braised celery with cheese and onion sauce
Brown rice and vegetable gratin
Cheese sauce
Cheese savouries
Cheese soufflé
Cheese soufflé pancakes
Cream cheese and herb filling for vol-au-vents
Cream cheese with herbs
Eggs Florentine
Eggs and leeks au gratin
Gougère with cheese
Gratinée of ham and eggs
Home-made curd cheese
Italian stuffed aubergines
Omelette savoyarde
Richmond maids of honour
Scone pizza
Spinach-stuffed pancakes with cheese sauce
Wholewheat cheese-crusted scones

SALADS AND DRESSINGS

♦

I think it would be true to say that salads in this country were not all they should have been for a very long time: largely, I suspect, for the same reason our vegetable cooking lacked imagination – namely that our meat and fish were so good and plentiful that any other additions to the table took second place. Over a hundred years ago, a Victorian food writer described our lack of skill with salads as 'a defect in our national character'. He put it down to our obsession with pickles, and I think he had a point. Perhaps our delicious chutneys and pickles *are* to blame for that all-too-familiar sight a few years ago: wet lettuce leaves, tomato quarters and perhaps a radish presented alone and undressed, with only a bottle of the dreaded factory-made salad cream for company.

Well, times have changed and so have salads. They have been enlivened by a much wider knowledge of and interest in good food. Now recipes from around the world, and the ingredients needed to make them, are part and parcel of culinary life.

SALAD DRESSINGS

♦

The two most widely used salad dressings are mayonnaise and vinaigrette, and indeed most other dressings are derived in some way from these two. It's the job of a good dressing to complement a salad rather than disguise it, and that's why the right ingredients are so important. This needs to be emphasised because the lack of them is the reason why so many dressings in so many restaurants are abysmal. So let's have a look first at the essential ingredients.

VINEGAR

As far as I'm concerned, *malt vinegar* should never find its way anywhere near a salad – its strong taste is too overpowering for delicate salad vegetables (I'm not decrying it: for pickling onions or sprinkling over fish and chips I wouldn't use anything else!). Salads need the much milder *wine vinegar*, preferably the kind made by the slow Orleans method (see page 368). *Cider vinegar* is also suitable for dressings and is less expensive.

One vinegar I've grown fond of in recent years is the Italian *balsamic vinegar*, which is made from the boiled-down must of a certain type of grape and aged in wood for at least ten years. It is dark and pungent and slightly less of it is needed, but it makes a wonderful vinaigrette.

You can also make your own *flavoured vinegars* by adding sprigs of fresh herbs to steep in the vinegar. Tarragon is perhaps the best herb to use – and this is also a good way of conserving it for the winter, when a few drops of tarragon vinegar will give a dressing a nostalgic summery flavour.

OIL

Olive oil

Olive oil is obviously the best choice, though its cost seems to get increasingly prohibitive. What few people realise, though, is the enormous saving that can be made by buying olive oil in bulk. It can be widely bought in 3, 4 or 5 litre cans (or polythene packs) which will save you pounds if you've been in the habit of buying small bottles from supermarket shelves.

The best-quality olive oil comes straight from freshly cold-pressed ripe olives – this is called 'first pressing'. After that, there is usually a second pressing where the olives are heated in order to extract every last drop. The first pressing gives a fruity but mild taste: the second a stronger, often rather harsh one (sometimes if the olives were over-ripe it is too strong, and the oil has to be what one might call de-flavoured).

The only way to find an olive oil that suits you is to experiment. I have found that a good Italian or Provençal olive oil is what I personally like best, though I've also had very good Greek olive oil made from olives from the Calamata region. All these can be widely purchased at specialised food shops – indeed in many supermarkets.

Groundnut oil

This is always my second choice for salad dressings and, in fact, for mayonnaise it is my first choice. It is rich without having a pronounced flavour, but you do need to hunt around for it in specialised food shops or delicatessens. Maybe it will become more widely available if we keep nagging retailers for it!

Sunflower oil and soya oil

These and all other culinary oils can be used in salad dressings. These are strictly a matter of personal preference: when used for cooking some of them have a quite distinctive flavour, but when used cold are much milder and do not compete with the other flavours in a dressing. They are, for the most part, more economical than olive oil but can never, in my opinion, compare with it for use in salads.

Other nut oils in the repertoire are *hazelnut oil*, *walnut oil* and *sesame oil* which are all worth experimenting with but need to be used with discretion. Sometimes their flavour is too strong, especially sesame, so it's a good idea to start by blending a little with a groundnut oil to dilute the flavour. For me a fruity olive oil is always first, but with a little walnut oil added makes a very good dressing, especially if the salad contains chopped walnuts.

LEMONS

Lemon juice, if liked, can be used instead of vinegar in a dressing. I once had a lovely salad in Greece made from olives, tomatoes, cucumber and Feta cheese, with fresh lemon juice squeezed straight on with a drizzle of olive oil. The combination was just right for that salad, though on the whole I have to admit that wine vinegar is preferable.

VINAIGRETTE DRESSING

The recipe I give, let me say straightaway, is a guideline rather than a rule. Not only do individual tastes differ, but the ingredients can vary too. Sometimes a sharper dressing is what's required, sometimes a milder one. However I usually stick to the old saying: 'Be a counsellor with the salt, a miser with the vinegar, and a spendthrift with the oil.' This is good advice – the most common fault (especially in restaurants) is over-enthusiasm with the vinegar; and even worse I think, is the addition of sugar to counteract it. Anyway, my version is as follows:

VINAIGRETTE DRESSING
— ♦ —

1 level teaspoon salt (English rock salt, crushed, is best for this)
1/2–1 clove garlic (according to taste)
1 rounded teaspoon mustard powder
1 tablespoon wine or balsamic vinegar
freshly milled black pepper
6 tablespoons olive oil

I like to start off with a pestle and mortar: first of all crush the flakes of rock salt to a powder, then add the peeled garlic and pound that together with the salt – which will immediately bring out its juices and turn it into a smooth paste. Next add the mustard powder, vinegar and some freshly milled pepper, and mix thoroughly until the salt dissolves. Finally add the olive oil, and just before dressing the salad, pour everything into a screw-top jar and shake vigorously to get it thoroughly blended.

I think salad dressings should be made as fresh as possible. So if you happen to have some left over, use it the next day but don't keep it any longer. For notes on how to dress a salad, see page 443.

Note There are any number of variations on this theme.

Vinaigrette with herbs

Add a teaspoon each of chopped fresh chives, tarragon, parsley, basil, chervil or mint (or half a teaspoon of oregano or thyme) or whatever herbs you have to hand. Chop them small and stir into the vinaigrette: it will look rather thick but will spread itself out beautifully once you toss it into the salad.

Vinaigrette with lemon

If you require an especially tart dressing to counteract the richness of whatever the salad is to be served with, use lemon juice instead of vinegar. This is especially good for a green salad to serve with fish, or for a salad to accompany an outdoor barbecue where lemons are squeezed over the meat as well.

MAYONNAISE

No commercially made mayonnaise, or short cut home-made version, can beat the thick, shining, wobbly texture of a proper mayonnaise you make yourself (see photo opposite page 385). For me, it's one of the true luxuries of the kitchen. Making mayonnaise for the first time can be a daunting experience, but *only* if the process is not explained properly. The following method is the traditional one and, I can assure you, pretty foolproof if you follow the instructions to the letter. At first it may seem a bit stupid to be adding the oil literally drop by drop, and you'd be forgiven for thinking you're going to be there all night. The temptation to add more will be great. Don't, because the fact is, this method actually only takes 7 minutes from start to finish (yes . . . I've timed myself with a stopwatch).

HOME-MADE MAYONNAISE
— ◆ —

(Makes 10 fl oz/275 ml)

2 large egg yolks
1 clove garlic, crushed
1 heaped teaspoon mustard powder
1 level teaspoon salt
freshly milled black pepper
10 fl oz groundnut oil (275 ml)
white wine vinegar

A 1½ pint (850 ml) basin, an electric mixer (or balloon whisk if you need the exercise), plus a damp tea cloth for standing the basin on to keep it steady.

Begin by putting the egg yolks into the basin, then add the crushed garlic and sprinkle in the mustard powder, salt and a few twists of freshly milled pepper: mix all these well together. Now with the groundnut oil in a jug in one hand, and your mixer or whisk in the other, add *one* drop of oil to the egg mixture, and whisk that in. However daft it sounds, this is the key to success – whisking each drop of oil in thoroughly, before adding the next. It's *not* going to take all day, because in a few minutes – after you've added several drops of oil – the mixture will begin to thicken. At that stage – and only then – you can begin to add the oil in larger drops (when the mixture has started thickening, the critical point is past).

When about half the oil is in, add about a teaspoon of vinegar to thin the mixture down. Now you can begin pouring the oil in a thin, steady trickle – whisking the whole time. When it's all in, taste and season with salt and pepper and, if it needs it, a little more vinegar.

Curdling occurs if you add the oil too fast at the beginning. If that happens, don't despair. Simply put a fresh egg yolk into a clean basin, add the curdled mixture to that (drop by drop), then carry on with the remainder of the oil as if nothing had happened.

Mayonnaise should be stored in a screw-top jar in a cool place – the bottom of the fridge if you like – for no longer than a week.

Instant mayonnaise

For a quick (though not so thick) version of mayonnaise: place 2 *whole* eggs in a food processor or liquidiser and blend with the mustard, salt, pepper and garlic (same quantities as in the previous recipe). Then, with the motor turning, pour in all the oil in a steady stream. Taste and add vinegar at the end. This is actually better for a home-made tartare sauce (see below).

Mayonnaise forms the basis for a number of other sauces, as below.

Aïoli sauce

This is one of the best-known, and is often served with fish or vegetables in the South of France. Follow the method above precisely, using 4 cloves of garlic instead of 1 (or more if you're a garlic addict!).

Sauce tartare

A proper, home-made sauce tartare served with plain grilled or fried fish is an absolute delight. Stir into the finished mayonnaise 2 heaped tablespoons finely chopped gherkins, 2 heaped tablespoons chopped capers, and 2 level teaspoons chopped parsley (or 1 level teaspoon chopped tarragon).

Sauce rouille

This is sometimes spread on baked croûtons of French bread and eaten with fish soups, or else stirred into the soup itself. It's also good served with any fried fish, or used as a dip for fried prawns for a first course. Make up the classic mayonnaise as on pages 438–9, adding 2 crushed cloves garlic, 2 dessertspoons lemon juice (instead of the vinegar), 1 teaspoon tomato purée and ¹/₂ teaspoon cayenne pepper (or more depending on how much kick you want to give it).

ELIZA ACTON'S ENGLISH SALAD SAUCE

◆

(Serves 4–6 people)

This sauce made with fresh cream and some cooked egg yolks makes a lovely dressing for potato, or for any other vegetable salad; it's good served with cold chicken, eggs or even fish; and with a little curry powder added it is ideal for a macaroni salad. The recipe comes from *Modern Cookery for Private Families* (modern, that was, in 1845).

3 eggs
1 tablespoon cold water
2 pinches of cayenne pepper
¹/₄ teaspoon salt
5 fl oz double cream (150 ml)
4 teaspoons white wine vinegar

Bring the eggs to the boil in plenty of cold water (they must be completely covered) and give them 9 minutes exactly from the time it starts boiling. Then run them under the cold tap to cool them – and stop them cooking any further. Peel away the shells and the whites, and place the *yolks only* in a mixing bowl.

Add the tablespoon of cold water and pound the yolks to a smooth paste with a wooden spoon. Then add a couple of pinches of cayenne plus the salt, and stir in the cream, bit by bit, mixing it smoothly as you go. When it's all in, add the vinegar and taste to check the seasoning. If you think the mixture's far too runny at this stage, don't worry. Cover the bowl and leave it for a couple of hours in the refrigerator, after which time it will have thickened (it should, in any case, have the consistency of thickish cream rather than mayonnaise).

SALAD INGREDIENTS AND THEIR PREPARATION

◆

LETTUCE

I could never recommend one particular kind of lettuce, because I like to ring the changes in my salads, and each variety has a different charm of its own. However I do have firm opinions on how a lettuce should be treated, whatever the variety.

First of all I've found the best way to store lettuces is to remove the root but otherwise leave them whole, and enclose them in a polythene bag in the lowest part of the fridge. I believe washing should be avoided if possible, as once the leaves are wet it is so difficult to get them dry again. What I prefer to do is take a damp piece of kitchen paper and wipe each leaf, removing any specks of dust (and crawly things) – this way the lettuce leaves remain dry and can more easily be coated with dressing. Now I realise many people will not agree with me here and will want to wash the leaves: in that case plunge the separated leaves briefly into cold water and place them in a salad basket, then either hang them up after a good shaking or else swing the basket round and round out-of-doors. Finish off by drying the leaves carefully with kitchen paper. Never use a knife when you prepare lettuce, because cutting tends to brown the edges of the leaves. Breaking up the leaves too soon can cause them to go limp quickly, so always leave them whole, if possible, until you're ready to serve the salad (and even then use your hands rather than a knife).

OTHER SALAD LEAVES

The salad repertoire has been greatly extended of late by the now regular appearance in shops of what has been called 'designer lettuce', leaves of different varieties and hues which often come ready mixed in salad packs. One of the nicest is *Curly endive* (or *Frisée*) with its lacey, curled stalks and leaves. For dashing colour *Radiccio* is a bright red lettuce with white stalks, while *Lollo rosso* looks like a green multi-layered can-can skirt edged with dark red. *Oak leaf* does not belie its name with a green centre and reddish almost mahogany-coloured edges, and *Lambs' lettuce* (or *Salade du Mâche*) too has the appearance of dark green leaves in the shape of lambs' tongues.

It is true that a salad made with a mixture of these can look most attractive, but sometimes the washed, pre-packed products can be found to have lost much of their perkiness. In the end I admit to preferring crisp fresh leaves of cos, such as Little Gem, or cabbage lettuce as a base for a salad – with perhaps just a few other leaves for looks. As a green salad a mixture of lettuce, watercress and finely chopped shallots or spring onions takes a lot of beating.

CHINESE LEAF

This looks like a cross between a cabbage and a head of celery – thick white ribs edged with a green leaf. It is marvellous for winter salads when imported lettuces are thin and travel-weary. Just slice it whole, horizontally, as and when you need it, storing the rest in a polythene bag. The very stalky bits at the base, in fact, are delicious lightly fried and served as a vegetable.

CHICORY

These are tight little buds of very crisp leaves (sometimes white, sometimes a reddish colour). Since light spoils the leaves they are usually wrapped in tissue paper, and are best kept in this until needed. They can be braised and cooked as a vegetable, but I think are best sliced horizontally and used to give a salad extra crunchiness. The leaves are slightly bitter tasting and therefore need a well-flavoured dressing.

BEETROOT

This is a salad vegetable that suffers either from having no flavour if it's served alone, or from being totally overpowered by malt vinegar. I prefer to buy it cooked, chop it up with a generous sprinkling of raw shallot or onion and serve it in a vinaigrette dressing. If you want to cook it yourself, it needs washing before boiling with root, skin and a little of the stalk intact (as it's important not to let any of the juice 'bleed' out). It's ready when the skin slips off easily. The time it will take depends on size – anything from 30–60 minutes over a gentle simmer.

CABBAGE

Most varieties of cabbage make good salad ingredients if the stalks are removed and the leaves are very finely shredded. See *Red cabbage and coriander salad* on page 449.

FENNEL

A bulbous-looking vegetable, similar in texture to celery but with a distinctive aniseed flavour. Sliced raw and separated into strips in a salad it responds beautifully to a well-flavoured olive oil dressing or some very garlicky mayonnaise.

CUCUMBER

There's nothing nicer than a firm, young cucumber eaten the day it's picked with its flower still intact at the end. However, if you're obliged to buy a plastic-wrapped one, do try to feel whether the stalk end is soft – if it is, that cucumber's past its peak. I never peel cucumbers because, as with many other vegetables, I like the appearance and flavour of the skins. If you prefer to peel them, use a potato peeler (which will only pare off the outer skin). Ever since I discovered them on holiday in

Greece I've loved the crunchiness of *ridge cucumbers*. These are shorter and fatter than ordinary cucumbers with little prickles along the ridges. The tough skins usually have to be peeled.

SPRING ONIONS

Finely chopped (including most of the green parts as well) these are the best onions for salads – or whole, to be taken on picnics and dipped in salt. Welsh onion – which resembles the green part of spring onion – grows happily in our herb bed through the winter, too. It has a stronger flavour than chives but, finely chopped, it makes an excellent winter substitute for chives.

WATERCRESS

I love watercress in a green salad, and now that it can be bought ready picked-over and vacuum-packed, it saves such a lot of time (even if it is a little more expensive). Inside the unopened pack, watercress will keep for about 5 days, but once exposed to the air it wilts extremely quickly. For this reason, if you use it for a salad or garnish, don't put it on until the last moment. Watercress bought in bunches should be first picked over and de-stalked, then stored upside down with the leaves submerged in cold water – but do dry them well before adding to a salad.

THE WELL-DRESSED SALAD

I really wouldn't suggest that the French have the last word on everything in the kitchen, but when it comes to dressing a salad properly, we can certainly learn from them. In Italy a haphazard sprinkling of some vinegar, followed by the same oil with no particular regard for proportions, has killed off many a salad I would have otherwise enjoyed there. (I once read of the owner of a taverna on one of the Greek islands who, with the aid of a sprinkler fixed to the top of a bottle, could aim the dressing for a salad from a distance of four tables away!). In England we have a chemical-tasting oddity called salad cream which often lurks amongst the naked ingredients – or worse, is sometimes presented to you in a plastic sachet to squeeze over!

The French, on the other hand, dress their salads with a lot of care – and care is the operative word. A green salad will be given a wide bowl, with ample room for tossing, so that each leaf will be coated and glistening. A tomato salad will be presented on a wide, shallow plate so that the slices don't overlap each other and become damp and woolly. The tradition at eighteenth-century French dinner parties was for the salad to be dressed at table by the hands of the most beautiful lady present. And therein lies the secret of the well-dressed salad – not looks, but *hands*. I'm convinced this is the only way to dress a leafy green salad really well.

So a few points to remember: always have a roomy bowl with space to toss the salad well, sprinkle in a little dressing at a time – never pour it so that one leaf gets totally drenched, and toss the leaves with your hands gently and carefully, so they get evenly coated but never soggy. Use *only* enough dressing to achieve this: if you finish up with pools at the bottom of the bowl, you have failed.

GREEN SALAD

The nicest green salads are the simplest, those with the least ingredients: crisp, dry lettuce leaves, perhaps with some watercress, or a mixture of salad leaves which can now be purchased in sealed packets, a little finely chopped spring onion (or shallot) and a plain vinaigrette dressing. Another nice addition is some small cubes of firm but ripe green avocado.

TOMATO SALAD

A tomato salad needs careful preparation and, properly made, it makes a good starter before a meal served with some crusty French bread and fresh butter. Choose firm but ripe tomatoes. Pour some boiling water over them and in a minute or two the skins will slip off very easily.

Never prepare a tomato salad too far in advance, because once you slice tomatoes they go a bit woolly. Another important point is that you should use a large flat plate for them – or else smaller individual plates – because the slices shouldn't overlap, another thing that causes sogginess.

For my tomato salad I like to sprinkle on some very finely chopped raw shallot or spring onion and lots of chopped fresh parsley and perhaps a mere trace of sugar – and some fresh basil leaves torn into small pieces and scattered over combine wonderfully with the flavour of the tomatoes. Do not dress the salad until the last minute before serving. If the tomatoes are really well-flavoured they need only be sprinkled with fine olive oil, crushed rock salt and freshly milled pepper. If they need some added flavour, use a made-up vinaigrette.

GREEN WINTER SALAD

◆

(Serves 4–6 people)

Crisp chicory and Chinese leaves with winter lettuce and an avocado make a delicious salad for the winter months when there is a shortage of fresh greens.

1 small lettuce
1 head chicory
1/2 head Chinese leaf
1 small onion
1 ripe avocado
For the dressing
2 cloves garlic
1 level teaspoon salt
1 level teaspoon mustard powder
1 1/2 tablespoons wine vinegar
4 1/2 tablespoons olive oil

Select only the crispest leaves of the lettuce, wipe them and arrange them in a salad bowl. Discard any bruised leaves and the hard stalk of the chicory, then slice it directly into the bowl in about 1/4 inch (5 mm) slices (separating the slices). Now slice the Chinese leaf in the same way, chop the onion fairly finely, and add them too. The avocado should be cut from top to bottom, opened up and the stone removed. Now cut each half in half again, and with a sharp knife you should find the skin will peel away whole if the avocado's ripe. Then chop the flesh into 3/4 inch (2 cm) squares and add to the salad. Toss it well.

Then make up the dressing. Place the peeled garlic cloves, salt and mustard powder in a mortar and crush to a paste. Next stir in the wine vinegar, followed by the oil, then transfer to a screw-top jar and shake vigorously to amalgamate everything. Pour the dressing over the salad, mix to give it all a good coating and serve.

RAW SPINACH AND WATERCRESS SALAD

◆

(Serves 4 people)

This salad is a meal in itself. If you're a vegetarian, replace the bacon with chopped walnuts and add 1 tablespoon walnut oil to the dressing.

8 oz young spinach leaves (225 g)
1 bunch watercress
2 hard-boiled eggs, peeled and chopped
4 rashers bacon, grilled until crisp
For the dressing
4 tablespoons dry sherry
3 tablespoons olive oil
3 tablespoons wine vinegar
1 teaspoon lemon juice
salt and freshly milled black pepper

Wash the spinach and watercress leaves thoroughly first, and discard the stalks and any damaged leaves. Then dry them carefully in a clean tea towel (or salad basket) – do this a few hours ahead of time if you can, to be sure of getting them quite dry.

To make the dressing, whisk the first four ingredients together in a basin, using a fork, or shake them together in a screw-top jar, then taste and season to your liking.

To make the salad, tear the spinach leaves into manageable pieces and place in a salad bowl with the watercress leaves. Pour the dressing over and toss the leaves thoroughly. Then garnish with the chopped eggs and the bacon crumbled into small pieces, and eat straightaway.

RICE SALAD

◆

(Serves 4–6 people)

This can, of course, also be made with white rice – in which case the rice needs to be cooked for just 15 minutes.

long-grain brown rice (preferably basmati) measured to the 10 fl oz (275 ml) level in a measuring jug
1 pint boiling water (570 ml)
1 dessertspoon olive oil
3–4 tablespoons vinaigrette dressing (see page 437)
3 spring onions, very finely chopped
2 inch piece unpeeled cucumber (5 cm), finely chopped
2 large tomatoes, peeled and finely chopped
1/2 red or green pepper, de-seeded and finely chopped
1 red dessert apple, cored and chopped, with the skin left on
1 oz currants (25 g)
1 oz walnuts (25 g), finely chopped
salt and freshly milled black pepper

Heat the oil in a saucepan, then stir in the rice to get the grains nicely coated. Add some salt, pour the boiling water over and bring back to the boil. Stir once, place the lid on and simmer the rice gently for 40 minutes or until all the liquid has been absorbed (tilt the pan slightly to check if there's any water left). Now empty the rice into a salad bowl, fluff it up with a fork and then pour the dressing over while it's still warm.

Leave it to get cold, then mix in all the other ingredients, adding a little more dressing if you think it needs it, and tasting to check the seasoning. Keep in a cool place until needed.

BROWN RICE AND TUNA FISH SALAD
♦

(Serves 3–4 people)

Serve this summery lunchtime salad on crisp lettuce leaves, and have some lemon quarters to squeeze over and some cayenne pepper on the table.

long-grain brown rice measured to the 8 fl oz (225 ml) level in a measuring jug
boiling water measured to the 16 fl oz (450 ml) level in a measuring jug
1 oz butter (25 g)
7 oz tin tuna fish (200 g)
2 inch piece unpeeled cucumber (5 cm), finely chopped
1 tablespoon drained capers
1 tablespoon chopped fresh parsley
1 teaspoon grated lemon rind
a few drops of Tabasco sauce
salt and freshly milled black pepper
For the dressing
3 tablespoons olive oil
1 dessertspoon wine vinegar
1 teaspoon mustard powder
juice of 1/2 lemon
To serve
lettuce leaves
lemon quarters
cayenne pepper

Melt the butter in a medium-sized pan, then stir in the rice so that it gets nicely coated with butter. Add the boiling water and 1/2 teaspoon salt, stir once only, then cover and simmer gently for 40 minutes. When the time's up, check that the rice is tender and there is no water left in the pan. Now tip the cooked rice into a wide shallow bowl and fluff it up with a skewer.

Next, in a screw-top jar, combine the dressing ingredients by shaking vigorously, pour all over the rice while it is still warm, then leave to cool.

Meanwhile drain the tuna in a sieve set over a bowl, and break the fish into small flakes. When the rice is cool, add the tuna (plus 1 tablespoon of its oil), together with all the remaining ingredients. Mix thoroughly, taste and season well.

NEW POTATO SALAD WITH MINT AND CHIVES

◆

(Serves 4–6 people)

This potato salad is so good it's almost best to eat it on its own.

2 lb small new potatoes (900 g)
2 sprigs mint
1 quantity vinaigrette dressing (see page 437)
3 tablespoons chopped fresh mint
2 tablespoons chopped fresh parsley
2 tablespoons snipped fresh chives
8 medium spring onions, very finely chopped
salt and freshly milled black pepper

Wash the potatoes but *don't* scrape them (there's a lot of flavour in the delicate skins of new potatoes). Place them in a saucepan with salt and the mint sprigs, then pour onto them enough boiling water to come about half-way up. Put on a tight-fitting lid and simmer them until tender, being very careful not to overcook. About 20–25 minutes should be enough: test them with a skewer – they should be tender but firm. Overcooking will make them watery and mushy.

Drain them in a colander, then put them in a salad bowl. Chop them roughly with a knife, and pour on the dressing while they're still warm. Mix thoroughly. When the potatoes have cooled, mix in the chopped herbs and spring onions. Taste and season, and keep the salad in a cool place until needed.

Mince pies (see page 502)

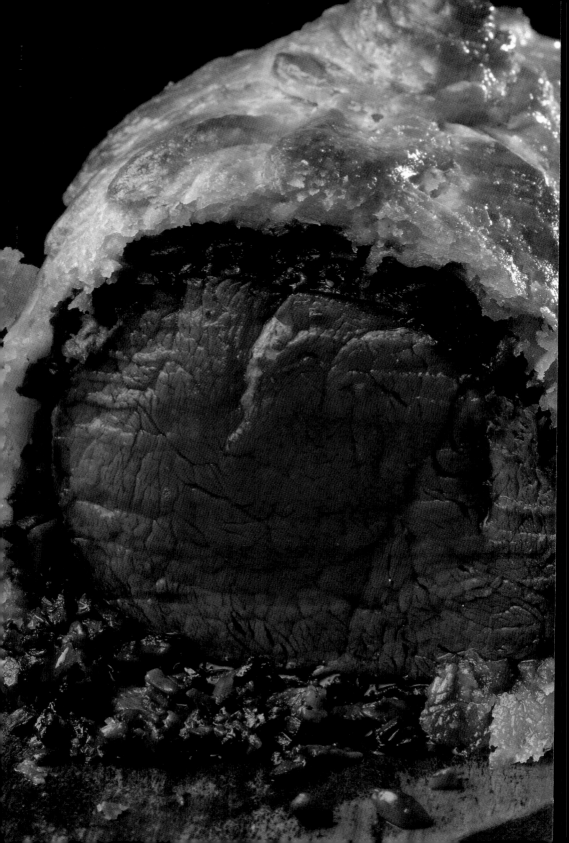

RED CABBAGE AND CORIANDER SALAD

◆

(Serves 6–8 people)

This is an ideal winter salad and a good one for help-yourself parties.

8 oz red cabbage (225 g)
1 medium Cox's apple
1 onion, finely chopped
2 celery stalks, finely chopped
For the dressing
½ teaspoon coriander seeds, crushed
1 clove garlic
½ teaspoon salt
½ teaspoon mustard powder
freshly milled black pepper
2 tablespoons olive oil
2 tablespoons wine vinegar
2½ oz natural yoghurt (60 g)

First of all crush the coriander seeds and place them in a dry frying-pan over a medium heat for 5–10 minutes, shaking them around, to allow the heat to draw out their flavour. Meanwhile cut the cabbage into quarters; remove the ribby parts, then shred the rest as finely as possible directly into a large mixing bowl. Then grate the apple (leaving the skin on) into the cabbage, and add the chopped onion and celery. Stir it around and get everything evenly distributed before making the dressing.

For the dressing, crush the garlic together with the salt, mustard powder and some pepper with a pestle and mortar (or in a basin using the end of a rolling-pin), then pour in the oil and vinegar. Give it a good stir, then add the yoghurt and crushed coriander. Now mix vigorously with a fork to amalgamate everything, pour the dressing onto the salad and toss well.

Note You can make and dress this salad well in advance as it keeps well in a polythene box stored in the refrigerator.

CHINESE BEANSPROUT SALAD WITH SOY DRESSING

◆

(Serves 4–6 people)

This is a very bright and beautiful salad to look at and the unusual dressing makes it really different.

Bœuf en croûte (see page 516)

8 oz fresh beansprouts (225 g)
1 small red pepper, de-seeded and chopped
approx. 6 inch piece unpeeled cucumber (15 cm), diced
1 small onion, thinly sliced and separated into rings
½ bunch watercress
For the dressing
½ teaspoon ground ginger
½ small onion, finely chopped
6 fl oz olive oil or, for economy, groundnut oil (175 ml)
2 fl oz red wine vinegar (55 ml)
2 fl oz cold water (55 ml)
2 tablespoons soy sauce
1 small celery stalk, chopped
2 teaspoons tomato purée
2 teaspoons lemon juice
salt and freshly milled black pepper

In a good roomy bowl combine the beansprouts, chopped pepper, diced cucumber and sliced onion. Pick over the watercress, selecting the best leaves, and add them to the salad. Cover the bowl with cling film and chill in the refrigerator while you make up the dressing. For this, all you do is simply place all the dressing ingredients in a liquidiser, and blend until smooth. Taste, and season the dressing as required.

For this salad I would suggest you serve the dressing separately in a jug, for people to help themselves.

Note If you don't have a liquidiser, then combine the dressing ingredients by shaking them together in a screw-top jar.

FOUR STAR SALAD
◆

(Serves 4 people)

This salad is a meal in itself. The 'stars' in question here are avocado, French garlic sausage, mushroom and lettuce, with a lovely, garlicky, soured cream dressing.

8 oz French garlic sausage (225 g), in one piece
1 medium lettuce
4 oz small pink-gilled mushrooms (110 g)
2 ripe avocados
4 spring onions, finely chopped
For the dressing
5 fl oz soured cream (150 ml)
2 cloves garlic, crushed

| 2 tablespoons mayonnaise |
| 1 teaspoon mustard powder |
| 2 tablespoons olive oil |
| 1 tablespoon wine vinegar |
| 1 tablespoon lemon juice |
| salt and freshly milled black pepper |

Begin by combining the soured cream with the garlic, mayonnaise and mustard powder. Then mix together the oil, vinegar and lemon juice and gradually add these to the soured cream mixture, tasting and seasoning with some salt and pepper.

Now slice the garlic sausage into ¹/₂ inch (1 cm) slices and then cut these slices into ¹/₂ inch (1 cm) strips. Next break up the lettuce leaves and arrange them in a salad bowl: wipe and thinly slice the mushrooms (don't take the skins off) and add these to the lettuce pieces. Finally prepare the avocados by removing the stones and peeling them, then cutting them into ¹/₂ inch (1 cm) cubes. Add these to the lettuce and mushrooms with the strips of garlic sausage.

Mix it all together gently, then add the dressing and toss again very gently. Sprinkle the chopped spring onions all over the surface and serve straightaway. This is nice served with *Home-made granary bread* which can be made by following the *Quick and easy wholemeal bread* recipe (page 43), using half wholewheat flour and half multigrain flour.

CHICK PEA SALAD
◆

(Serves 4–6 people)

Chick peas are nutty and slightly crunchy in a salad but you have to plan this one in advance because they must be soaked (see page 305).

| 8 oz chick peas (225 g), soaked overnight |
| 8 oz haricots verts (thin green string beans) (225 g) |
| 5 fl oz garlic-flavoured mayonnaise (150 ml) (see pages 438–9) |
| 1³/₄ oz tin anchovy fillets in oil (45 g), drained and finely chopped |
| 6 spring onions, finely chopped |
| 2 tablespoons capers, drained and chopped |
| 2 tablespoons finely chopped parsley |
| 1 dozen black olives, pitted and halved |
| lemon juice to taste |
| salt and freshly milled black pepper |
| *To serve* |
| a few crisp lettuce leaves |

Bring the chick peas to the boil and simmer until tender (about 1¼ hours). Don't salt the water though, or the chick peas will never soften! The topped and tailed green beans will need 3 or 4 minutes in boiling salted water, then tip them into a colander, rinse them with cold water, drain well and cut each bean in half.

Combine the mayonnaise, anchovy fillets, spring onions, capers, chopped parsley and a good seasoning of salt and pepper. Then fold the well drained and cooled chick peas with the green beans and black olives into the mayonnaise mixture. Taste, and add a little lemon juice and more seasoning if necessary. Serve piled on a bed of crisp lettuce leaves.

HARICOT BEAN AND SALAMI SALAD
♦

(Serves 2 people)

Not simply a side-salad this one, but a pretty substantial lunch (or supper) dish on its own. The haricot beans I recommend for this are the long, thin variety (rather than the small 'baked bean' type).

8 oz dried haricot beans (225 g)
1 small onion stuck with 2 cloves
a few parsley stalks
1 bay leaf
1 clove garlic, crushed
¼ teaspoon dried thyme or a sprig of fresh thyme
2 oz Italian salami (50 g), finely diced
1 small onion, chopped
2 tablespoons chopped fresh parsley
freshly milled black pepper
For the dressing
1 clove garlic
1 heaped teaspoon salt
1 teaspoon mustard powder
1 tablespoon red wine vinegar
5 tablespoons olive oil

First place the beans in a saucepan, add about 4 pints (2.25 litres) cold water, cover with a lid and bring to the boil. Then turn off the heat and leave the beans to soak for 1 hour. After that, add the onion stuck with cloves, the parsley stalks, bay leaf, garlic, thyme and a few twists of pepper (but *no* salt). Bring the beans back to the boil and simmer gently, uncovered, for 1–1½ hours or until tender.

While the beans are cooking, prepare the dressing. Crush the garlic in the salt (with a pestle and mortar), and then mix in the mustard powder and some pepper, followed by the vinegar and the oil. Transfer the dressing to a screw-top jar and shake vigorously to blend the ingredients. (If you have neither a pestle and mortar nor a garlic press, place the peeled clove on a hard surface and crush it with the flat blade of a knife.)

When the beans are cooked, drain them and discard the onion, bay leaf and parsley stalks. Tip the beans into a large bowl. Pour over the dressing, then add the diced salami, chopped onion and parsley – mix gently to avoid breaking the beans. Taste and season, and leave to cool before serving.

Note If you can't get Italian salami, use another kind.

BROAD BEAN SALAD
◆

(Serves 2 people)

I devised this recipe when I had a glut of broad beans in the garden – now it's a firm favourite.

1½ lb young broad beans (700 g), the weight before shelling
2 rashers lean bacon, de-rinded
4 spring onions, finely chopped
1 tablespoon chopped fresh herbs (I use a mixture of tarragon, marjoram and parsley)
For the dressing
1 level teaspoon crushed rock salt
1 dessertspoon lemon juice
1 dessertspoon wine vinegar
4 dessertspoons oil
1 small clove garlic, crushed
1 teaspoon mustard powder
freshly milled black pepper
To serve
lettuce leaves

First cook the bacon until it's really crisp, then drain it well and crumble it into very small pieces. Next make the dressing by dissolving the salt in the lemon juice and vinegar for a few minutes, then shake with the rest of the ingredients in a screw-top jar to get everything thoroughly amalgamated.

Now cook the shelled beans in a very little salted water for about 5 minutes – it's very important not to overcook them or they'll lose their colour and go mushy. Drain them thoroughly and toss them in the dressing while they're still warm. When they're cool, toss in the finely chopped spring onions, the bacon and the chopped herbs. Serve the salad on some crisp lettuce leaves.

SALADE NIÇOISE

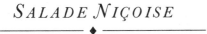

(Serves 4–6 people)

This is a favourite summer lunch dish in our house, served with *Hot herb and garlic loaf* (see page 460), but it also makes a nice refreshing and light first course.

1 lettuce
vinaigrette dressing with garlic and herbs (see pages 437–8) – you won't need the full quantity
12 oz firm ripe tomatoes (350 g), peeled, de-seeded and quartered
½ small young cucumber, peeled and cut in smallish chunks
1 tablespoon finely chopped onion or spring onions
4 oz cooked new potatoes (110 g), sliced
4 oz cooked French beans (110 g)
2 hard-boiled eggs, peeled and quartered
7 oz tin tuna fish (200 g), well drained
1¾ oz tin anchovy fillets in oil (45 g), well drained
2 oz black olives (50 g)
1 tablespoon chopped fresh parsley

First arrange lettuce leaves around the base of a large salad bowl and sprinkle on a little vinaigrette dressing. Then arrange the tomatoes and cucumber in layers with a little more dressing, then add the onion, slices of potatoes and French beans. Now place the quartered hard-boiled eggs on top with the tuna fish, which should be broken up into chunky flakes. Finally decorate the salad with the anchovy fillets, making a latticed effect (or whatever you like), then sprinkle on the black olives, the chopped fresh parsley and the rest of the dressing. Serve as soon as possible.

SEE ALSO

Aduki bean and brown rice salad
Chicken salad with tarragon and grapes
Cucumber and yoghurt salad
Greek salad
Lentil, bean and anchovy salad
Red bean salad

BARBECUES AND PICNICS

◆

Eating out of doors is a bit of a hit-and-miss affair in this country for obvious reasons (such as getting only one week of sunshine in any one summer, for instance). If that sounds tongue in cheek, it's meant to because I feel the whole subject of outdoor eating in Britain should be approached with a sense of humour and with a certain flexibility.

Not that I'm a pessimist. Each spring I look at patio furniture in glossy magazines, and I dream dreams. These include candle-lit geraniums, the sizzling of charcoal-cooked food, the tinkle of ice-filled glasses, and all the rest. Such dreams never include the Suffolk winds that blow the smoke back in the direction of the guests, their eyes getting steadily redder, their coughs louder. Nor do they include what to do with fifty sausages (that fitted so well on the barbecue) having to go eight at a time under the grill in the kitchen because it's pouring! Even the most enthusiastic books on barbecues finish up with realistic advice, including among the recommended accessories bug-repellent sprays and burn lotions.

As picnickers, too, we display the same kind of grim, resolute determination. In French films picnics are all about rivers and willows and punts, or fields of red poppies and buzzing bees. In Britain the hot tarmac of the zoo car-park will do, or a patch of grass with four lanes of traffic on either side. I have even seen a man and his wife, in a remote part of the Lake District, clad in sou'westers eating their lunch with plates perched on the car bonnet as the rain bucketed down! We all have our funny picnic stories, I'm sure. Nevertheless eating outdoors *is* fun and, if only to avoid eating in those motorway cafés, picnics are necessary.

EATING AL FRESCO

◆

The number one requirement for food in the open air is that it should have lots of gutsy flavour. Delicate, subtle dishes can easily lose their identity outside. Simple food – and lots of it – is the best, I've found: even the humble British banger is quite transformed with a smoky, crispy, barbecued skin. Remember, too, that appetites mysteriously increase out of doors and people can eat more if the food is simple than if it's very rich.

BARBECUES

♦

If you're planning to improvise your own barbecue – or at the other end of the scale have ambitions for a built-in garden barbecue – then you should refer to one of several specialised books on the subject. For those of us in the middle who are content with a ready-made barbecue, however, there is a wide range of equipment and accessories to suit every taste and occasion. Basically there are only two kinds of barbecue: the brazier-type with a shallow bowl, where the air flows *over* the burning charcoal, and the grill-type with built-in air vents, where the air flows up and through the charcoal. All manner of attachments can be bought – hoods, spits, windshields, warming ovens – but none of these affects the basic operation.

CHARCOAL

This is the commonest form of fuel, and comes either in pre-formed briquettes (which are more efficient) or as lumpwood (which is cheaper). Hardwood can be used for large barbecues, but is quite impractical for the normal commercial makes.

LAYING THE FIRE

On the brazier type of barbecue I think it is a good idea to line the bowl first with a sheet of aluminium foil (shiny side upwards), which will help to reflect the heat. Cover with a generous layer of charcoal, making sure it covers the whole area rather than just the centre and is not packed too tightly.

LIGHTING UP

At home we use a commercial barbecue fuel to get the charcoal alight – but it needs to be done with care. Sprinkle some all over the charcoal, then *wait* for a few minutes for it to get absorbed. Special barbecue fire-lighters (broken up into smaller pieces and scattered among the charcoal) can be used, but don't start cooking until all the pieces are completely burned out, or the smoke will include some unpleasant fumes. In any case it is pointless to start cooking before the charcoal is properly and evenly alight, and that can take anything from 20 to 30 minutes. At night you can easily tell because the charcoal will glow pink: during the day the pieces will start to turn white.

COOKING ON CHARCOAL

Try to set your barbecue where it will get sufficient draught but is not directly in the wind. Most barbecues have a grill that can be adjusted to different heights above the fire, which will control the speed of cooking, but sooner or later fat from the food will drop onto the coals and make them flare up. So have a jug of water handy and sprinkle a little onto the fire with your hands – just enough to douse the flame, but not so much that you stop the coals burning.

For that extra smoky flavour you can add small chips of aromatic wood to the fire (such as hickory or apple wood), but these chips should be well soaked in water before use, unless you buy specially prepared packets of 'smoke chips'. Fresh herbs, such as rosemary, also add an interesting flavour to the smoke: these should be sprinkled on the fire towards the end of the cooking.

EQUIPMENT

Experience has taught me that implements with very long handles are what are called for in tending barbecue food! Long-handled tongs and fork (for turning the food) will keep your hands a safe distance from the heat and a pair of gloves will give added protection. For kebabs, thread the meat etc. onto *flat* skewers rather than round ones (which tend to turn themselves without turning the meat).

BARBECUE FOODS

Almost anything can be barbecued, it would seem. I have a friend who has an annual barbecue featuring barbecued whole salmons. And I once received a letter from a viewer of my TV cookery series, asking me to inform her (a) how long it would take to barbecue a suckling pig and (b) how many would it serve? I'm afraid that adventurous lady has my admiration but failed to get a very satisfactory reply – our own attempts at barbecuing are rather more modest.

My advice to anyone starting out is to think of a barbecue in the same terms as a grill and to follow the same principles as for grilling sausages, chops, steaks, kebabs etc. Large chicken joints on the bone can be tricky, as the outside gets scorched before the inside is cooked. So the thing to do is either to use smaller joints or else part-cook the chicken in a conventional oven and finish off on a barbecue.

Fish barbecue well, in particular whole fresh mackerel, fish steaks and cutlets, and fish kebabs (see page 109). Brush all barbecue items with a little oil before they go onto the heat, and if they have to be marinated, baste them with the marinade juices while they are cooking.

AMERICAN HAMBURGERS

(Serves 2–3 people)

In this country the word hamburger conjures up all sorts of dubious images of frozen and packaged discs of meat and greasy griddles. The real hamburger is something else: 100 per cent pure ground beef cooked, if possible, over charcoal to give it a charred, smoky crispness at the edges with a juicy medium-rare centre. All it needs then is a jacket potato brimming with soured cream and chives, and a selection of relishes and ketchup. This recipe will make four 4 oz (110 g) hamburgers to serve in large buns, or three larger burgers (which may need a few more minutes' cooking, depending on how you like them).

1 lb chuck steak, about 80 per cent lean meat and 20 per cent fat (450 g)
2 level teaspoons salt
coarsely milled black pepper
a little oil

To prepare the meat you can either pass it through the fine blade of the mincer twice (which tenderises it) – ask the butcher to do it for you – or you can grind the meat finely in a food processor.

To make the hamburgers, place the meat in a bowl and sprinkle in the salt and a good seasoning of coarsely milled black pepper.

Mix this in thoroughly, then divide the mixture into four portions. Take each portion in your hands and shape it into a ball, then place the ball on a flat surface and press to flatten it into a hamburger shape about ¾ inch (2 cm) thick.

Now brush each hamburger with very little oil and grill under a pre-heated grill set to high, or over hot charcoal, giving them 4–6 minutes on each side depending on how you like them. Serve in bap rolls (toasted on cut side only), and spread with slivers of raw or fried onion and relishes or tomato ketchup.

CEVAPCICI (YUGOSLAV KEBABS)

◆

(Serves 3–4 people)

These are delicious little minced sausages threaded onto skewers.

8 oz chuck steak (225 g)
8 oz lean belly pork or spare rib (225 g)
2 cloves garlic, crushed
1 teaspoon paprika
cayenne pepper
1 tablespoon finely chopped fresh mint
salt and freshly milled black pepper
For the sauce
approx. 4 inch piece cucumber (10 cm), chopped into small cubes
5 oz natural yoghurt (150 g), Greek for preference
2 teaspoons chopped fresh mint
1 clove garlic, crushed

First the meats should be put through the finest blade of the mincer or chopped finely in a food processor. Then place them in a mixing bowl along with the garlic, paprika, a pinch of cayenne and a good seasoning of salt and pepper. Stir in the chopped mint and mix thoroughly to amalgamate everything. If possible, leave the mixture in a cool place for a while to allow the flavours to develop, then mould the mixture into about nine little sausage shapes, about 2 inches (5 cm) in length. Thread these onto skewers – the flat kind are best – and cook over hot charcoal or under a pre-heated grill for 10–20 minutes, turning them frequently.

Serve them with the yoghurt sauce, made by simply combining all the sauce ingredients in a bowl with salt and freshly milled black pepper to taste.

ANCHOÏADE

(Serves 3–4 people)

This is a delicious snack with all the flavours of Provence to serve out of doors, either as a first course at a barbecue or for lunch, or else on small croûtons to serve with drinks before a meal. (Illus. opposite p. 416.)

1³/₄ oz tin anchovy fillets in oil (45 g)
8 black olives
1 small onion, finely chopped
1 ripe tomato, peeled and chopped
a few drops of wine vinegar
1 large or 2 small cloves garlic, crushed
2 heaped teaspoons tomato purée
1 rounded teaspoon dried oregano or 2 teaspoons chopped fresh marjoram
1 tablespoon chopped fresh parsley
freshly milled black pepper
8 × 1 inch (2.5 cm) baked croûtons of French bread cut diagonally (see page 98)
olive oil
chopped fresh basil, to garnish

Begin by pounding the anchovies (with their oil) to a pulp, either using a pestle and mortar or a basin and the end of a rolling-pin. Then pit the olives, chop their flesh up finely and add this to the anchovy mixture along with the chopped onion, tomato and a few drops of wine vinegar. Stir thoroughly, then add the crushed garlic, tomato purée, oregano, parsley and some freshly milled pepper, and stir again.

Then spread the mixture generously on the croûtons. All this can be done in advance. Then to finish off, pour a few drops of oil over each slice, place them under a pre-heated medium grill for 5 minutes to heat through, and sprinkle with chopped basil before serving.

HOT HERB AND GARLIC LOAF

♦

This is perfect for a barbecue or party when lots of salads are being served.

1 French stick loaf
For the herb butter
3 oz butter (75 g), at room temperature
2 cloves garlic, crushed
2 tablespoons chopped fresh herbs (parsley and chives with a little tarragon and thyme if available) or 1½ teaspoons dried mixed herbs

Pre-heat the oven to gas mark 6, 400°F (200°C).

First mix the butter, garlic and herbs together. Using a sharp knife, make diagonal incisions along the loaf, as if you were slicing it – but not slicing right through. The loaf should stay joined at the base. Now spread each slice with butter on both sides (it's easiest to do this with your hands) and spread any remaining herb butter along the top and sides of the loaf. Wrap the loaf in foil and bake it in the oven for about 10–15 minutes, and serve hot. Or if you have the space, you could heat it through by placing it on the barbecue, turning it over several times.

ITALIAN STUFFED AUBERGINES

♦

(Serves 3 or 6 people)

These are good to serve as a first course at a barbecue for six people or for lunch in the garden on a hot day for three people with a salad and cold drinks.

3 medium aubergines
olive oil
1 onion, chopped
1 large clove garlic, crushed
2 teaspoons chopped fresh or 1 teaspoon dried basil
6 tinned anchovy fillets, drained and chopped

approx. 6 oz Italian Mozzarella cheese (175 g), cut in thin slices
3 largish tomatoes, sliced
1½ tablespoons capers, drained and roughly chopped
salt and freshly milled black pepper

Trim the green stalks from the aubergines and slice them in half lengthways. If you have a grapefruit knife use that, or otherwise a teaspoon, to get out the pulpy centres of the aubergines leaving a shell not less than ¼ inch (5 mm) thick. Sprinkle the shells liberally with salt and leave upside down to drain for 45 minutes. Meanwhile chop the pulp.

Now heat 2 tablespoons of the oil in a saucepan and gently fry the onion until softened. Stir in the chopped pulp, crushed garlic and half the basil. Season with salt and pepper and cook over a low heat for about 10 minutes, stirring now and then. After this stir in the chopped anchovies.

Next wipe the aubergine shells with kitchen paper and arrange them in a small oiled roasting tin or baking dish. Spoon the onion/pulp mixture into the shells, then arrange alternate slices of cheese and tomato on top of each aubergine half and sprinkle with the chopped capers. Finally sprinkle with the remaining basil and dribble a little more olive oil over each. Season and bake (uncovered) at gas mark 4, 350°F (180°C), in the top of the oven for 40 minutes.

MUSTARD-GLAZED LAMB CUTLETS
◆

(Serves 4 people)

These are best of all barbecued, but still taste very good grilled and they provide a special supper dish in moments.

8 lamb cutlets, trimmed of most of the fat
2 tablespoons made-up mustard (English or Dijon)
3 rounded tablespoons demerara sugar
salt and freshly milled black pepper

Pre-heat the grill to a high setting.

Wipe the cutlets first with some absorbent kitchen paper to dry them, season them with salt and pepper, then spread both sides of each cutlet with mustard. Now dip them in sugar, making sure they get an even coating, and grill them for about 5 minutes on each side – or more or less, depending on their thickness.

Note Loin chops can be cooked in the same way but need approximately 10 minutes each side.

LAMB KEBABS

◆

(Serves 4 people)

These are perhaps the nicest barbecue food of all but, if the weather is against you, fear not – they still taste good when grilled indoors.

1½ lb fillet end of leg of lamb or pieces from a boned-out shoulder (700 g)
6 small bay leaves
2 cloves garlic, crushed
2 teaspoons dried oregano
1 medium onion
1 small green or red pepper, de-seeded
juice of 1 large lemon
6 tablespoons olive oil
8 small mushrooms
4 small tomatoes, halved
salt and freshly milled black pepper

To serve
1 large lemon, quartered

Start by preparing the meat: cut it into small bite-sized pieces (leaving some of the fat on the cubes as this helps to keep them juicy). Place the meat in a bowl, and then season it with salt and freshly milled black pepper. Now add the bay leaves (snipped in half), crushed garlic and oregano. Peel the onion and cut it into quarters, then separate the quarters into layers and add these to the meat together with the green or red pepper cut into ½ inch (1 cm) pieces.

Pour over the lemon juice, followed by the olive oil, and leave the meat to marinate (covered with a cloth) for several hours or overnight, stirring the ingredients and turning the meat cubes over now and then.

When you are ready to grill the kebabs, get your charcoal hot (or pre-heat your grill), then take a skewer – preferably a flattened one rather than a twisted or round one – and start by threading one mushroom and half a tomato (rounded end towards the handle of the skewer), then alternate a piece of meat, half a bay leaf, a piece of onion and a piece of pepper. Load the other skewers in the same way.

When everything is threaded onto the skewers, finish off each one with the other half of the tomato and another mushroom. Push gently at both ends, because it's important for everything to be packed as tightly as possible. Grill the kebabs, basting them from time to time with the oil marinade and turning them over. They'll take about 15–20 minutes to be charred nicely on the outside and pink and juicy within. Serve with the lemon quarters.

PORK SPARE RIBS IN BARBECUE SAUCE

◆

(Serves 4 people)

Pork spare ribs (the actual rib bones) or lean belly pork slices are both good coated and flavoured with a barbecue sauce.

12 pork spare ribs
For the sauce
1 clove garlic
3 tablespoons dry white wine or dry cider
6 tablespoons soy sauce
1 rounded tablespoon tomato purée
1 teaspoon mustard powder
1 level tablespoon soft brown sugar
a few drops of Tabasco sauce
freshly milled black pepper

First crush the garlic in a bowl, and pour in the wine (or cider) and soy sauce. Then stir in the tomato purée, followed by the mustard powder and sugar. Next add a few drops of Tabasco, then give it all a good stir and season with pepper – no salt is needed.

Leave the sauce a few moments for the flavours to develop, then when the meat is ready to be cooked, brush each side generously with the barbecue sauce. Grill or barbecue the meat for about 15 minutes on each side, basting now and then with the extra sauce.

PICNICS AND FOOD FOR TRAVELLING

◆

When it comes to picnics nothing will budge me an inch from my keep-it-simple philosophy. In Edwardian days it was all very well, when butler, maid, bar and fully-equipped hamper could be transplanted into the country. And if you're very rich, I suppose you can still pick up a Henley or an Ascot hamper from one of the smart London food establishments (though whether the contents will warrant the price is debatable). For less grand affairs I feel many people go wrong by trying to transport the sort of meal they would eat at home: it just doesn't taste the same on squashy paper plates with plastic knives and forks in sizes fit only for four-year-olds.

Rough outdoor living demands rough outdoor food. Some of the nicest picnics I've had have been in Italy – crusty bread, chunks of salami, ripe plum tomatoes, cheese, olives, pickled pimentoes, peaches and huge black cherries, and of course quantities of something Italian to drink. All we had to pack on these occasions was pepper and salt, an insulated dish for butter, knives, plates and glasses. No cooking was involved, you will note. Even in this country you can approximate this kind of ready-made picnic by stopping at a chain-store with a good food department and buying bread, pork pies, salads in tubs, good fruit and a cake.

However, if you're not pushed for time and want to plan and prepare a picnic, all the recipes in this section will serve you well out of doors or, if there's a last minute change of weather, inside.

EQUIPMENT

For me, real plates, cutlery and glasses (even if not particularly elegant) are infinitely preferable to anything in the plastic line. We have some thick chunky glasses which may not look very sophisticated but are far nicer – especially if you're drinking wine – than paper cups. In fact the only 'special' equipment I have is a Thermos flask and a wide Thermos jug (for soup in cold weather), and an insulated butter dish (if you put very cold butter in it, it keeps cool all day), and an insulated bag with a little freezer pad (which also keeps things cool when it is frozen and placed inside). Oh, and some other important items: salt and pepper mills and a corkscrew!

To keep things like cakes and rolls fresh, I think the best thing is to wrap them first in greaseproof paper, then in foil and place them in plastic bags. Polythene boxes are all right, but in our house by the time we've found the right lid to fit the right box, there's no time for a picnic.

PICNIC FOODS

French bread
This is excellent for picnics, sliced diagonally, split, buttered and filled with slices of strong Cheddar cheese and sliced raw onion, then sandwiched together again.

Bap rolls
These are delicious filled with the following mixture (for six people): mash 6 boiled eggs while they're still warm with a good knob of butter, 4 teaspoons mayonnaise, salt and pepper. Stir in 2 heaped tablespoons of very finely chopped spring onion.

Crusty rolls
Buy garlic sausage or salami in one piece, so that you can slice it more thickly. Fill the rolls with this plus some thin slices of (drained) dill pickled cucumbers or drained Italian pickled pimentos.

Garlic butter
If you mash a clove of garlic into 8 oz (225 g) butter along with 2 tablespoons of chopped parsley, then chill it well and place in an insulated butter dish, this will be lovely to spread on French bread or rolls.

Rice or potato salad
These are handy salads to take on a picnic, because they are dressed beforehand, but you do need a polythene box with a tight-fitting lid.

Crunchy things are nice at picnics – for instance, radishes and crisp spring onions. Firm tomatoes are a good idea, but it goes without saying that they should be taken whole: never slice them or put them in sandwiches, they're too soggy (and that goes for cucumbers too). Some of my favourite picnic recipes are included in this chapter but other parts of the book also contain several that are suitable for travelling.

Let me mention a few (these, and others, are listed at the end of this chapter). *Boeuf en croûte* is rather extravagant perhaps, but left to cool, then cut in slices, it's a super idea for a special picnic. *Sausage rolls* or *cheese and onion quichelets* are picnic perennials that never fail. *Quick wholewheat pizza*, cut into sections and wrapped carefully, tastes marvellous in the open air. *Mustard-and-herb-coated chicken* needs no plates or knives and forks, so is good for car journeys. *Cold chicken pie* should be taken in the tin it was cooked in, double wrapped, then cut when you arrive. *Date, apple and walnut loaf* is a moist cake with a crunchy crust.

SCOTCH EGGS WITH FRESH HERBS

◆

(Makes 4)

Scotch eggs are marvellous for travellers or picnickers. Take spring onions to go with them and, if you've got plates, some chutney.

4 eggs
8 oz sausagemeat (225 g)
2 spring onions, finely chopped
1 teaspoon finely chopped fresh thyme
3 teaspoons snipped fresh chives
1 tablespoon finely chopped fresh parsley
seasoned plain flour
1 small egg, beaten
toasted breadcrumbs
salt and freshly milled black pepper
oil for deep-frying

Hard-boil the eggs by covering them in cold water, bringing it to the boil, simmering gently for 9 minutes and cooling them under cold running water. Next mix the sausagemeat with the spring onions and herbs and season well. Then shell the cooled eggs and coat each one with some seasoned flour. Divide the sausagemeat into four portions and pat each piece out on a floured surface to a shape roughly 5 × 3 inches (13 cm × 7.5 cm). Now place an egg in the centre of each piece and carefully gather up the sausagemeat to cover the egg completely. Seal the joins well, and smooth and pat into shape all over. Next coat them one by one, first in beaten egg and then thoroughly and evenly in the breadcrumbs.

Now heat 1½ inches (4 cm) of oil in a deep frying-pan up to a temperature of 350–375°F (180–190°C). (If you don't have a thermometer, you can easily test the temperature by frying a small cube of bread – if it turns golden-brown within 1 minute the oil is hot enough.) Put the eggs into the oil and fry for 6–8 minutes, turning frequently until they have turned a nice brown colour. Drain on crumpled greaseproof paper.

When they're absolutely cold, wrap in cling film and store in the lower part of the fridge.

BACON AND EGG PIE

◆

(Serves 4–6 people)

A home-made bacon and egg pie makes a very good and easily transportable picnic dish, I find. Alternatively, it's nice served warm after the 'picnic' if the weather wasn't up to scratch!

4 large eggs
6 rashers lean streaky bacon, de-rinded
5 fl oz milk (150 ml)
salt and freshly milled black pepper
For the shortcrust pastry
6 oz plain flour (175 g)
3 oz lard (75 g)
a pinch each of salt and freshly milled black pepper
cold water, to mix

Pre-heat the oven (and a baking sheet) to gas mark 6, 400°F (200°C).

An 8 inch (20 cm) flan tin, rimmed if possible and 1½ inches (4 cm) deep.

Hard-boil three of the eggs – which I do by putting them in a saucepan, covering them with cold water, bringing to the boil and simmering gently for 9 minutes. Cool them quickly by running cold water from the tap over them. Then, while they're cooling, grill (or fry) the bacon gently until the fat begins to run, and make up the shortcrust pastry (see page 497). Leave it to rest wrapped in a polythene bag in the fridge for 20 minutes, then divide the pastry in half, and roll out one half to line the flan tin.

Peel the hard-boiled eggs and chop them quite small, chop the bacon fairly small too and arrange them both in the flan. Season with freshly milled pepper and a very little salt. Beat the remaining egg together with the milk, then pour the mixture over the contents of the pie. Roll out the rest of the pastry to form a lid, dampen the edges and seal well all round, using any trimmings to decorate. Make a small hole in the centre of the pastry, brush the top with milk, then put on the baking sheet on a high shelf in the oven and bake for 10 minutes. After that reduce the heat to gas mark 4, 350°F (180°C), and bake for a further 30 minutes.

Little bacon and egg pies
Alternatively you can make individual pies in 2½ inch (6 cm) patty tins, using 3 inch (7.5 cm) and 3½ inch (9 cm) cutters.

For eleven to twelve little pies you'll need: the quantity of pastry as above, 2 hard-boiled eggs, 4 rashers back bacon, 1 egg and 4 fl oz (110 ml) milk beaten together.

Use the larger rounds of pastry to line the patty tins, divide the chopped eggs and bacon between the pies, then pour in the egg-and-milk mixture, and top with the smaller pastry rounds. Brush the tops with any left-over egg-and-milk mixture, and bake on a pre-heated baking sheet in the oven at gas mark 6, 400°F (200°C), for 10 minutes, then reduce the heat to gas mark 5, 375°F (190°C), and cook for a further 25 minutes.

SPANISH TORTILLA
◆

(Serves 2–4 people)

This is an omelette which is as nice served cold as it is hot – and excellent therefore for taking on a picnic, where you can cut it into wedges.

4 large eggs
2 medium potatoes, cut into small dice
1 medium onion, chopped
1 small green pepper, de-seeded and chopped
2 oz piece Spanish chorizo or similar sausage (50 g), cut into small dice
3 tablespoons olive oil
salt and freshly milled black pepper

Begin by heating 2 tablespoons of the oil in a frying-pan, add the potatoes and cook them for 8–10 minutes (stirring them from time to time) until they're evenly browned. Then add the onion, pepper and sausage. Stir well and carry on cooking for another 6–8 minutes.

Now beat the eggs and season them well with salt and pepper, and pour them into the frying-pan over the vegetable mixture. Cook over a medium heat for 3 minutes or so, drawing the cooked egg into the centre of the pan with a palette knife and letting the liquid egg run into the gaps. When the omelette is firm – but still slightly moist – turn it upside down onto a plate. Then heat the remaining tablespoon of oil in the pan and slide the omelette back into the pan (other side up). Cook it for a further 3 minutes. You can of course serve this straightaway; otherwise leave to get cold, cover and keep in a cool place until needed. If you find the classic Spanish way of turning the omelette difficult, you can pre-heat the grill before you start and grill the top side till golden.

MEAT LOAF

◆

(Serves 6–8 people)

This is a good idea for a picnic as, once cold, it can be cut into firm slices. However, it's also very good served hot with a *Fresh tomato sauce* (see page 329).

1 lb lean minced beef (450 g) – from a reliable butcher
8 oz minced pork or pork sausagemeat (225 g)
2 medium onions, minced
1 small green pepper, de-seeded and finely chopped
1 dessertspoon tomato purée
1 fat clove garlic, crushed
2 slices white bread from a large loaf
3 tablespoons milk
1 level teaspoon dried mixed herbs
2 tablespoons chopped fresh parsley
1 egg, beaten
salt and freshly milled black pepper

Pre-heat the oven to gas mark 5, 375°F (190°C).
A 2 lb (900 g) loaf tin.
Put the minced beef in a large mixing bowl with the pork, onions, chopped pepper, tomato purée and garlic and give everything a thorough mixing, seasoning well with salt and freshly milled pepper. Cut the crusts off the bread, soak it in the milk, then squeeze the excess milk out of it and add it to the rest of the ingredients, along with the mixed herbs

and parsley. Now give the mixture another thorough mixing, and finally stir in the beaten egg to bind it.

Press the mixture into the 2 lb (900 g) loaf tin, spreading evenly, then bake it in the oven for 1¼ hours. When it's cooked it will have shrunk and begun to come away from the sides of the tin. Allow it to get cold in the tin, wrap it in a double sheet of foil and take it to the picnic wrapped in a cloth or in an oblong plastic box.

Note Meat loaf is delicious served cold with pickles and salad. It also goes very well sliced and put into sandwiches or rolls.

ALL-IN-ONE BANANA AND WALNUT LOAF

◆

This is an extremely easy cake, ideal for picnics as it has a pronounced flavour.

3 oz soft margarine or very soft butter (75 g)
4 oz caster sugar (110 g)
1 large egg, beaten
8 oz plain flour (225 g)
2 level teaspoons baking powder
4 medium bananas, peeled
grated rind of 1 orange
grated rind of 1 lemon
2 oz walnuts (50 g), roughly chopped

Pre-heat the oven to gas mark 4, 350°F (180°C).

A loaf tin, base measuring 3½ × 7½ inches (9 × 19 cm), greased, with the base lined with greaseproof paper, also greased.

Start off by placing the margarine, sugar and the beaten egg in a large mixing bowl, then sift in the flour and baking powder. In another bowl slice the bananas and mash them to a pulp with a fork.

Now, use an electric mixer to whisk the sugar, fat, egg and flour together until they are thoroughly combined – don't worry if the mixture looks rather dry at this stage.

Next add the orange and lemon rinds, followed by the mashed bananas and chopped walnuts, and whisk again thoroughly. Then transfer the mixture to the prepared tin and level the top off.

Bake on the centre shelf of the oven for 50–55 minutes, until the loaf is golden, well-risen and springs back when pressed with a finger. Leave to cool in the tin for 10 minutes, then loosen around the edges and turn out onto a wire cooling tray to finish cooling. This cake is nice sliced and spread with butter.

HONEY AND SPICE CAKE

◆

This cake has a tangy citrus flavour and a sharp lemon icing, and tastes sensational in the open air.

3 oz clear, runny honey (75 g)
8 oz plain flour (225 g)
1 level teaspoon ground ginger
1 level teaspoon ground cinnamon
¼ teaspoon ground cloves
3 oz caster sugar (75 g)
finely grated rind of 1 small orange
finely grated rind of 1 small lemon
4 oz butter (110 g)
1 large egg, beaten
1 level teaspoon bicarbonate of soda
2 oz finely chopped mixed candied peel (50 g)
For the icing
6 oz sifted icing sugar (175 g)
1 tablespoon lemon juice
To decorate
6 pieces crystallised ginger, chopped

Pre-heat the oven to gas mark 3, 325°F (170°C).

One 7 inch (18 cm) square tin or 8 inch (20 cm) round tin, lightly-buttered.

First of all weigh a cup or small basin on the scales, then weigh the 3 oz (75 g) of honey into it. Now place the basin into a saucepan containing barely simmering water and warm the honey a little, but be careful: it mustn't be too hot, just warm.

Next sift the flour and spices into a large mixing bowl, then add the sugar and the orange and lemon rind. Now add the butter in small pieces, then rub it lightly into the flour, using your fingertips, until the mixture becomes crumbly. Next, lightly mix in the beaten egg, using a large fork, followed by the warm honey. Then in a small basin, mix the bicarbonate of soda with 3 tablespoons of cold water, stir until dissolved, then add it to the cake mixture and beat, quite hard, until the mixture is smooth and soft. Then, finally, stir in the mixed peel and spoon the mixture into the prepared tin, spreading it out evenly.

Bake the cake just above the centre of the oven for about 50 minutes or until well-risen and springy to the touch. Cool it for 10 minutes, then turn it out onto a wire rack to get quite cold.

Meanwhile prepare the icing by sifting the icing sugar into a bowl, then add 2 tablespoons of warm water along with the lemon juice and mix to a thin consistency that will coat the back of a spoon. If you don't think it's thin enough add a little more water. Now place the cake on a wire rack, with a large plate underneath, and pour the icing all over, letting it run down and coat the sides a bit. Then decorate the top with chopped ginger and store in an airtight tin.

SEE ALSO

Asparagus and cheese tart
Boeuf en croûte
Cheese and onion quichelets
Cheese tartlets with mushroom pâté
Cold chicken pie
Cornish pasty pie
Date, apple and walnut loaf
Fish kebabs
Indian kebabs
Mustard-and-herb-coated chicken
Omelette savoyarde
Quick wholewheat pizza
Sausage rolls
Shoulder of lamb with rice and kidney stuffing
Spinach and cream cheese quiche

CREAM, ICE CREAM AND YOGHURT

◆

Since the western world has become involved in a seemingly endless dialogue on fats and their contribution to the causes of coronary disease, cream (along with butter, oils and other fatty foods) has inevitably come in for quite a battering. It goes without saying, however, that this chapter is not an invitation to everyone to eat lashings of cream regardless: moderation is always the last word. The fact is that cream is a natural food, and an ingredient to be used (with restraint) in cooking. I would, for instance, rather have just one ice cream per year made from (guess what!) ice *cream*, than dozens made from synthetic, over-sweetened non-milk fat. For those who are forbidden cream, or are cutting down on their calories, then I would recommend they replace it with home-made yoghurt (see page 487) – which is utterly delicious and very different from the commercially made kinds. There are of course an increasing number of substitutes now on the market (see below). But I confess that much as I enjoy *crème fraîche* or Greek yoghurt, I am never going to forego entirely the luxury of our native double cream.

CREAM

◆

Without being too scientific about the subject, let's first consider the difference between the various types of cream. Butterfat is the name given to small globules present in milk, though not visible to the naked eye. Each one of these is surrounded by a layer made up of some of the other solid components in the milk. These little globules tend to gather together and rise to the surface of the milk, forming a layer. This layer is then skimmed off to become cream or butter. The best pouring cream of all is the unpasteurised, thick, buttercup-yellow cream from Jersey cows.

The various types of cream are graded according to the amount of butterfat they contain. Thus *double cream* has to contain no less than 48 per cent butterfat, *single cream* no less than 18 per cent, and *half cream* no less than 12 per cent.

WHIPPING (OR READY-WHIPPED) CREAM

This must contain not less than 35 per cent butterfat. This, in fact, is the minimum requirement for whipping ability, which is the reason why single cream is unsuitable for whipping.

CLOTTED CREAM

This has the highest butterfat content of all (55 per cent), and the clotting is achieved by a special treatment. The milk is scalded at a temperature of 180°F (82°C) and allowed to cool overnight before being skimmed. It is, as anyone who has had a holiday in the West Country knows, a real luxury.

There are of course other types of cream available: for instance, *UHT* (*ultra heat treated*) *cream*, packed in foil-lined containers, which keeps much longer than fresh cream, and *sterilised cream*, marketed in glass bottles, which lasts even longer. However, the treatment that these products undergo to ensure their long life does affect their flavour. Unless there is absolutely no alternative, it is my opinion they are not worth using.

SOURED (OR CULTURED) CREAM

This is single cream (not less than 18 per cent butterfat) which, when commercially made, is heated and then inoculated with a culture. The temperature is controlled, and when the acidity reaches a certain level, clotting takes place. In Russia and some northern European countries cream was allowed to sour naturally for use in cooking, and many people have asked me if it is possible to sour cream at home. It's not, unfortunately, because all our bottled milk and cream is pasteurised, but it is possible to simulate it.

If you can't get soured cream you can simulate it by adding 1 teaspoon of lemon juice to 5 fl oz (150 ml) of single or double cream, depending on how creamy you want it. Leave it for half an hour or so, and it will have begun to thicken. Another, quicker, way is simply to combine in equal quantities cream (single or double) and natural yoghurt, which also cuts down the calories.

Soured cream is particularly useful in recipes, giving them a distinctive flavour (sharper than cream, but creamier than yoghurt). When you're buying it, it's important to look carefully at the date stamp and make sure the expiry date is as far off as possible. Soured cream becomes more acid the older it gets. It *will* keep for about a week in the refrigerator, but bear in mind the flavour will be that much sharper.

CRÈME FRAÎCHE

This is the French equivalent of our double cream. Before the days of pasteurisation, when cream was kept the natural ferments in it would begin to sour it and make it taste faintly sharp. What the French do is to re-introduce a ferment after pasteurisation, so that the cream tastes livelier than the blander pasteurised product (and in turn puts more of a kick into the classic creamy sauces).

It is sometimes possible to buy it in Britain. But failing that there are various ways to produce an approximate resemblance to crème fraîche –

the easiest being to mix together equal parts of double cream (whipped to the floppy stage) and natural yoghurt (Greek for a richer consistency or skimmed milk yoghurt for a lighter one).

BUTTERMILK

This used to be the liquid left over from milk that had been churned into butter: it was left aside to sour naturally and then used in baking. Today it is made commercially with a culture, but it can still be used as a raising agent in the making of scones and soda bread.

EGGS EN COCOTTE WITH SOURED CREAM AND ASPARAGUS

◆

(Serves 6 people)

This is a lovely way to make a little asparagus go a long way, and its delicate flavour is just right with soft creamy eggs.

8 oz asparagus (225 g)
6 large fresh eggs
10 fl oz soured cream or Greek yoghurt (275 ml)
1 oz butter (25 g)
6 heaped teaspoons freshly grated Parmesan cheese
salt and freshly milled black pepper

Pre-heat the oven to gas mark 4, 350°F (180°C).
Six 3½ inch (9 cm) ramekin dishes, well-buttered.

Steam the asparagus (see page 228) for just 4 minutes – it needs to be only half-cooked. Then when it's cool enough to handle, chop it into 1 inch (2.5 cm) lengths and arrange the pieces in the bases of the dishes – making sure each one gets its fair share of the tips, but also reserving six for the garnish.

Now carefully break an egg into each little dish, season it with salt and freshly milled black pepper, then gently spoon approximately a tablespoon of soured cream over each egg, spreading it out with a knife so that it covers the top completely.

Dot them with flecks of butter and sprinkle each one with a teaspoon of Parmesan cheese and place an asparagus tip in the centre (all this can be done well in advance if you like).

To cook, pour about an inch (2.5 cm) of boiling water into a meat-roasting tin, place the dishes in it, pop the whole lot in the oven and bake for about 15–18 minutes. Bear in mind, however, that the eggs will go on cooking in the heat from the dishes on the way to the table. Serve with buttered wholemeal bread and chilled white wine.

LEEK AND SOURED CREAM FLAN

◆

(Serves 4–6 people)

This flan has a very crisp, cheese, wholewheat pastry and makes a very good lunch dish with a salad.

For the pastry
3 oz self-raising flour (75 g)
3 oz wholewheat flour (75 g)
a pinch of salt
³/₄ teaspoon mustard powder
1¹/₂ oz lard (40 g)
1¹/₂ oz margarine or butter (40 g)
2 oz Cheddar cheese (50 g), finely grated
cold water, to mix
For the filling
3 lb leeks (1.3 kg), trimmed with 1¹/₂ inches (4 cm) of green left on, then sliced thinly
2 oz butter (50 g)
1 clove garlic, crushed
5 fl oz soured cream (150 ml)
2 tablespoons double cream
1 large egg, beaten
2 oz Cheddar cheese (50 g), grated
salt and freshly milled black pepper

A 10 inch (25 cm) loose-based flan tin, greased.

To make the pastry, sift the flours, salt and mustard into a large bowl, then rub in the fats until the mixture resembles fine breadcrumbs. Now stir in the cheese, and add enough cold water to make a dough that leaves the bowl clean. Pop the pastry into a polythene bag and leave to rest in the fridge for 30 minutes.

Meanwhile pre-heat the oven to gas mark 4, 350°F (180°C), and put in a baking sheet to pre-heat as well. Roll out the pastry and line the flan tin, using any surplus pastry to reinforce the sides and base, carefully smoothing it into place. Prick the base all over with a fork, then bake the flan case in the centre of the oven on the baking sheet for 15 minutes. After that, remove from the oven and brush all over with a little beaten egg (from the filling ingredients). Return to the oven for 5 minutes more, then remove and turn the heat up to gas mark 5, 375°F (190°C).

Now for the filling. Melt the butter in a large pan, add the leeks and garlic, and some seasoning. Cover and cook gently, without browning, for 10–15 minutes until they're sufficiently reduced to fill the flan case comfortably. Drain in a colander and return to the pan. Meanwhile combine the creams with the beaten egg and stir this into the leek mixture, seasoning to taste. Spread the mixture over the pastry case, sprinkle with the cheese and bake in the centre of the oven for 40 minutes, until brown and crispy.

PORK CHOPS WITH CREAM AND MUSHROOMS

◆

(Serves 6 people)

This recipe is one of the most popular ones I've ever given. It's excellent for a dinner party because it doesn't need last minute attention.

6 large pork chops, trimmed of excess fat
2 oz butter (50 g)
2 teaspoons chopped fresh or 1 level teaspoon dried thyme
12 oz mushrooms (350 g)
juice of 1 large lemon
1½ tablespoons plain flour
5 fl oz double cream (150 ml)
salt and freshly milled black pepper

Pre-heat the oven to gas mark 4, 350°F (180°C).

Place a large double sheet of cooking foil on a meat-roasting tin, bearing in mind it must be large enough to wrap the chops in.

Now in a frying-pan, brown the chops nicely on both sides in butter, and then transfer them onto the foil. Season each one with salt and freshly milled black pepper and a little thyme.

Now chop the mushrooms roughly and fry them in the same pan in which the meat was browned, adding a little more butter if you think it needs it. Then pour in the lemon juice, let it bubble for a minute, then sprinkle in the flour and stir with a wooden spoon until you have a rather soggy-looking mushroom mixture. Don't worry – it always looks awful at this stage.

Spoon the mixture over the pork chops, some on each, then spoon a little of the double cream over each one. Now wrap up loosely in foil, sealing it very securely, and bake them for 1 hour. Serve the chops with the delicious juices poured over. Since this is very rich, keep the accompanying vegetables fairly simple. A sprig or two of watercress beside each chop gives extra colour.

Note When this is cooked the cream takes on a slightly curdled appearance, but this doesn't in any way spoil the delicious flavour.

EIGHTEENTH-CENTURY CREAMED APPLE FLAN

───────────── ◆ ─────────────

(Serves 6 people)

This recipe is a nostalgic one for me as it's one of the first I tried after some research at the British Museum into eighteenth-century British cooking, and it prompted me to do a whole lot more!

For the pastry
4 oz plain flour (110 g), sifted
1 oz margarine or butter (25 g)
1 oz lard (25 g)
cold water, to mix
For the filling
4 large cooking apples, peeled, cored and sliced
2 tablespoons water
2 oz butter (50 g)
2 tablespoons caster sugar
3 digestive biscuits, crushed into crumbs with a rolling-pin
grated rind of 1 small lemon
2 tablespoons brandy
freshly grated nutmeg
3 egg yolks
2¹/₂ fl oz double cream (65 ml)

Pre-heat the oven to gas mark 4, 350°F (180°C).

An 8 inch (20 cm) flan tin, lightly-greased.

Make up the pastry by rubbing the fats into the sifted flour until the mixture resembles breadcrumbs. Then add enough water to make a dough that leaves the bowl clean. Pop the pastry in a polythene bag and leave to rest in the fridge for 20 minutes or so, then roll it out and use to line the flan tin. Prick the base all over with a fork, and bake for 20 minutes.

Meanwhile put the sliced apples in a saucepan with the water and cook until they are pulpy. Transfer them to a large mixing bowl and beat until you have a smooth purée. Then whisk in the butter and the caster sugar, followed by the biscuit crumbs, lemon rind, brandy and a good grating of nutmeg. Combine everything thoroughly and leave the mixture to cool.

Next whisk the egg yolks together with the cream – don't over-do it, you just want to thicken it slightly. Then when the apple mixture has cooled, stir the eggs and cream into it. Pour the whole lot into the partly cooked flan case, then bake in the oven for a further 30 minutes.

Note You can, if you like, substitute cider for the brandy.

PHEASANT WITH CREAM AND APPLES

◆

(Serves 2 people)

A hen pheasant is best for this recipe, which will only serve two, but you can, of course, double or treble the list of ingredients for more people.

1 plump young pheasant (oven-ready)
1 oz butter (25 g)
1 tablespoon oil
¹/₂ onion, chopped small
3 medium Cox's apples
approx. 6 fl oz dry cider (175 ml)
5 fl oz double cream (150 ml)
salt and freshly milled black pepper

First, heat the butter and oil together in a casserole. Then season the pheasant with pepper and salt and brown in the hot fat, turning it frequently so it browns evenly all over. Add the onion and let it soften gently while you quarter, core, and peel the apples. Slice them, not too thinly, and stir them into the casserole. Then add the cider, turn the bird onto its side and cover the casserole. Cook over a very low heat for about 1 hour or so, remembering that half-way through the cooking time you will have to turn the bird onto its other side.

Then, when the bird is cooked, remove it to a warmed serving dish. Simmer the apples remaining in the casserole until almost all the liquid has evaporated. Stir in the cream and season with salt and freshly milled black pepper. Heat gently, then pour the apples and cream over the pheasant and serve.

PLUM AND SOURED CREAM FLAN

◆

(Serves 4–6 people)

Since I've been writing recipes, this is one I've found to be most popular with everyone who makes it.

shortcrust pastry made with 6 oz (175 g) flour and 3 oz (75 g) fat (see page 497)
For the filling
1¹/₄ lb dessert plums (575 g)
10 fl oz soured cream (275 ml)
1 oz caster sugar (25 g)
3 egg yolks

¹/₂ teaspoon ground mixed spice
1 teaspoon ground cinnamon
2 oz demerara sugar (50 g)

Pre-heat the oven, and a baking sheet, to gas mark 6, 400°F (200°C).
A 10 inch (25 cm) fluted flan tin, greased.

Roll out the shortcrust pastry and line the flan tin. For the filling, halve the plums and remove the stones. Now beat the soured cream together with the caster sugar, egg yolks and mixed spice, then pour this into the flan case and arrange the plums over the top (flat side up). Place the flan on the baking sheet and bake for 20 minutes.

Then mix the cinnamon with the demerara sugar and sprinkle it all over the top. Bake for a further 20 minutes, turning the heat right up to gas mark 8, 450°F (230°C), for the final 5 minutes so that the top can brown nicely. Serve warm or cold.

ENGLISH RHUBARB FOOL
◆

(Serves 4 people)

Rhubarb fool has always been one of my favourite English puddings. You'll find all manner of recipes for it – but it's best of all when it's made with a proper custard, like this one.

2 lb rhubarb (900 g), washed and cut into chunks
2 oz caster sugar (50 g)
1 teaspoon ground ginger
For the custard
8 fl oz double cream (225 ml)
1 teaspoon cornflour
1 tablespoon caster sugar
3 egg yolks
2 drops pure vanilla essence
To decorate
4 pieces preserved ginger, cut into tiny chunks

First of all put the chunks of rhubarb together with the caster sugar into a saucepan, then sprinkle in the ground ginger. Cover the saucepan and cook the rhubarb very gently for 15–20 minutes, stirring frequently (you want the rhubarb to be tender but not mushy). Then place the cooked rhubarb in a sieve over a bowl to drain off some of the juice.

Meanwhile make the custard. Bring the double cream up to boiling point in a small saucepan. Mix the cornflour, sugar, egg yolks and

479

vanilla essence together in a basin until smooth. Pour the boiling cream into the mixture, whisk thoroughly, then return the whole lot to the saucepan and back onto a medium heat. Carry on whisking until it has thickened, then immediately pour the custard into a bowl to cool (if it looks a little granular you can get it smooth again by beating).

Now mash the drained rhubarb until smooth and combine it evenly with the custard. Pour this mixture into four serving dishes (stemmed glasses look nice), top with pieces of preserved ginger, cover with cling film and chill slightly before serving.

RICH LEMON CREAM WITH FROSTED GRAPES

♦

(Serves 12 people)

This is the very nicest lemon dessert I've ever come across. It serves about twelve people, so is very good for a party. For a smaller quantity, use a 6 inch (15 cm) tin, 1 level dessertspoon gelatine, 1 egg yolk and half the remaining ingredients.

5 fl oz milk (150 ml)
4 level tablespoons caster sugar
grated rind and juice of 4 lemons
1 level tablespoon powdered gelatine
1 egg yolk
1¼ pints double cream (725 ml)
4 large egg whites
To decorate
4 oz white grapes (110 g)
1 egg white
caster sugar

An 8 inch (20 cm) round cake tin, lightly-oiled.

Place the milk, sugar, grated lemon rind, gelatine and egg yolk together in a blender or liquidiser. Blend for half a minute at top speed, then pour the mixture into a small saucepan and stir over a very gentle heat for 3 or 4 minutes until fairly hot but *not* boiling. Now return the mixture to the liquidiser and whizz round again, adding the lemon juice and 10 fl oz (275 ml) of the cream. When all is thoroughly blended, pour the mixture into a bowl, cover with foil and chill, stirring occasionally until the mixture is syrupy.

Whip the remaining cream lightly until it just begins to thicken, then in another very large bowl whisk the egg whites until stiff and carefully fold them into the lemon mixture, followed by the cream. Pour the mixture into the tin, cover and chill until firm.

Squidgy chocolate log (see page 548)

To make the frosted grapes, first of all whisk up the egg white. Then break the grapes into clusters of two or three grapes each and dip each bunch first in the egg white, then in a saucer of caster sugar. Leave them spread out on greaseproof paper for a couple of hours before using them.

Before serving, dip the cake tin for a moment in hot water, and turn the lemon cream over onto a plate. Decorate with the frosted grapes and serve the cream cut in slices rather like a cake.

CRÈME CARAMEL

◆

(Serves 4–6 people)

My husband Michael always makes this at home. It turns out in a pool of lovely dark toffee caramel, and is soft and creamy within. If you are feeling really wicked serve it with some chilled Jersey pouring cream – ecstasy!

5 fl oz milk (150 ml)
10 fl oz single cream (275 ml)
4 large eggs
1½ oz soft brown sugar (40 g)
pure vanilla essence
For the caramel
4 oz granulated or caster sugar (110 g)
2 tablespoons water, tap hot

Pre-heat the oven to gas mark 2, 300°F (150°C).

A 1½ pint (850 ml) soufflé dish.

First make the caramel. Put the granulated (or caster) sugar in a medium-sized saucepan and heat. When the sugar begins to melt, bubble and darken, stir and continue to cook until it has become a uniform liquid syrup, about two or three shades darker than golden syrup. Take the pan off the heat and cautiously add the water – it will splutter and bubble quite considerably but will soon subside. Stir and, when the syrup is once again smooth, quickly pour it into the base of the dish, tipping it around to coat the sides a little.

Now pour the milk and cream into another pan and leave it to heat gently while you whisk together the eggs, brown sugar and a few drops of vanilla essence in a large bowl. Then, when the milk is steaming hot, pour it onto the egg and sugar mixture, whisking until thoroughly blended. Then pour the liquid into the dish and place it in a large roasting tin. Transfer the tin carefully to the oven, then pour hot water into it to surround the dish up to two-thirds in depth. Bake for 1 hour. Cool and chill the crème caramel, until 1 hour before you're ready to

From top: **Wholewheat shortbread; Shortbread biscuits; Gingernuts; Whole oat crunchies; Scottish shortbread**
(see pages 567–72)

serve it. Free the edges by running a knife around before inverting it onto a serving plate.

CRÈME BRÛLÉE

◆

Crème brûlée has its origins in England – it was invented at Trinity College, Cambridge, where it was known as Burnt Cream. This could be called a cheat's version, but really it isn't. It has merely been adapted to help those who (like me) have never had a domestic grill that is suitable for fast caramelising of sugar. So here the caramel is made separately and simply poured over.

1 pint double cream (570 ml)
6 egg yolks
4 level teaspoons cornflour
2 tablespoons caster sugar
a few drops pure vanilla essence
For the caramel
4 oz granulated sugar (110 g)

Six ramekins, 3 inches (7.5 cm) in diameter.

You need to start the recipe the day before, so that the custard can be well chilled and firm. Heat the cream until it reaches boiling point, and while it's heating blend the egg yolks, cornflour, caster sugar and vanilla essence in a bowl. Then pour the hot cream in, stirring all the time with a wooden spoon, then return the mixture to the saucepan. Heat very gently (still stirring) until the sauce has thickened – which should only take a minute or two. (If it does overheat, don't worry – if you remove it from the heat and continue to beat it *will* become smooth again as soon as it cools.) Divide the custard between the ramekins and leave to cool. Cover each dish with cling film and refrigerate overnight.

About an hour before serving make the caramel. Place the granulated sugar in a heavy pan, then place the pan over a very low heat to dissolve the sugar gently and caramelise it (to get all the sugar to melt, just shake and tilt the pan from side to side, but don't stir). When all the sugar has dissolved and you have a clear syrup (about 10–15 minutes) remove the pan from the heat and pour immediately over the custards, covering the surface of each one. Now just leave them for a few minutes for the caramel to harden. Before eating the crème brûlée, tap the surface of the caramel with a spoon to crack and break it up.

Note To remove any hardened caramel from your pan, fill it with hot water and bring it to the boil.

VANILLA ICE CREAM
◆

You can of course buy electric ice cream gadgets and sorbetières, but I don't think they're worth the extra expense. The freezing compartment of the fridge will do, provided it is turned down to its coldest setting about half an hour before you start to freeze the ice cream.

10 fl oz double cream (275 ml)
10 fl oz single cream (275 ml)
4 egg yolks
3–4 drops pure vanilla essence
2 slightly rounded teaspoons custard powder
1¹/₂ oz caster sugar (40 g)

1 freezer-proof polythene box, approximately 1¹/₂ pints (850 ml) capacity, with lid.

First of all whip the double cream until it reaches the 'floppy' stage but isn't too thick, then pop it into the fridge to chill. At the same time put the polythene box into the freezer to chill as well.

Now make the custard by first pouring the single cream into a saucepan and then heating it up to boiling point. While that's happening beat together the egg yolks, vanilla essence, custard powder and sugar until absolutely smooth. Next pour the hot cream onto this mixture, whisking with a fork as you pour. Now return the custard to the pan and continue to whisk it over a medium heat until it has thickened and come up to boiling point again. (Ignore any curdled appearance, which may come about if you don't keep stirring and have the heat too high. The custard powder will stabilise it provided you beat it off the heat: poured into a bowl it *will* become quite smooth again.)

Now place the bowl of custard in a bowl of cold water, and stir it now and then until absolutely cold. Then fold in the chilled whipped cream. Pour the whole lot into the chilled polythene box, cover and freeze for a couple of hours or until it is just beginning to set. At the same time place a mixing bowl in the freezer to chill, then as soon as the mixture does begin to set, tip it into the chilled bowl and whisk (with an electric hand whisk or a rotary whisk) very thoroughly. Then return the ice cream to the polythene box, put it back in the freezer (covered) and leave until frozen (about 3 hours). Before serving, remove the ice cream to the main body of the fridge for 45 minutes to get a smooth, not-so-hard texture.

PRALINE ICE CREAM

◆

1 quantity vanilla ice cream (see page 483)

For the praline
2 oz caster sugar (50 g)
2 oz unblanched almonds (50 g)

Place the sugar and almonds together in a pan over a low heat, and leave them until all the crystals of sugar have completely dissolved to a liquid. Cook until the liquid has turned a rich brown colour. Then pour this mixture onto a well-oiled baking sheet, spreading the almonds out in a single layer. Leave the mixture to cool and become brittle, then, using a palette knife, lift it off the baking tray onto a flat surface. Break it up with a few bashes from a rolling-pin, then crush it fairly finely with the rolling-pin.

Stir the crushed praline thoroughly into the ice cream about half an hour before serving. You can, if you like, make the praline at any time and store it wrapped in foil in the fridge.

Note If you are short of time, the praline is also good just sprinkled over ice cream.

BLACKCURRANT ICE CREAM

◆

(Serves 6–8 people)

I think blackcurrants make the very nicest ice cream, smooth, rich and velvety. However this same recipe works very well with loganberries, or even raspberries, if you prefer.

1 lb blackcurrants (450 g)
6 oz sugar (175 g)
5 fl oz water (150 ml)
10 fl oz double cream (275 ml)

A 1³/₄ pint (1 litre) freezer-proof polythene box with a lid and a nylon sieve (a metal one can discolour the fruit).

There's no need to take the stalks off the blackcurrants; just pile them – about one-third of a pound (150 g) at a time – into the sieve set over a mixing bowl, and mash like mad with a wooden spoon until you have extracted all the pulp and only the stalks, pips and skins are left in the sieve.

Loganberries or raspberries should be sieved in the same way.

Now place the sugar and water in a saucepan over a medium heat, stir until all the sugar crystals have dissolved, then let it come to the boil, and boil for 3 minutes exactly. Then remove from the heat and stir the syrup into the fruit pulp. Whip the cream until it *just* begins to thicken. Be careful not to overwhip – it mustn't be thick, just floppy. Fold the cream into the fruit mixture until thoroughly blended. Pour it into the polythene box, and freeze in a freezer or in the ice-making compartment of a refrigerator turned to its coldest setting.

As soon as the mixture begins to set (about 3 hours) turn it out into a bowl and beat thoroughly. Then return it to the freezer (in the box) until set – about another 3 hours. Remove to the main part of the fridge about an hour before serving.

Note This ice cream should be eaten within 3 weeks.

BLACK FOREST GÂTEAU
◆

(Serves 6–8 people)

Poor old Black Forest gâteau has suffered a wave of popularity among catering suppliers and freezer centres. For this reason it's worth reminding ourselves of what it should taste like by making the real thing. This one is light and squidgy, as the recipe contains no flour.

6 large eggs
5 oz caster sugar (150 g)
2 oz cocoa powder (50 g), sifted
For the filling and topping
10 fl oz double cream (275 ml)
1 level tablespoon caster sugar
1 lb tin (or jar) morello cherries (450 g)
1 or 2 tablespoons Kirsch or rum
2 oz plain chocolate (50 g)

Pre-heat the oven to gas mark 4, 350°F (180°C).

Two 8 inch (20 cm) sandwich tins, oiled with groundnut oil and the bases lined with greaseproof paper, also oiled.

Start off by separating the eggs and placing the whites in a clean grease-free bowl. Put the yolks in another bowl and whisk them with the caster sugar until they just begin to pale and thicken (be careful not to thicken them too much, though). Now fold in the sifted cocoa powder.

Next, with a clean whisk, beat the egg whites until stiff but not too dry. Stir a heaped tablespoon of the egg white into the chocolate mixture to loosen it up a little bit. Then, using a metal spoon, carefully and gently fold in the rest of the egg white (trying not to lose any air). Divide the mixture equally into the prepared sandwich tins and bake them near the centre of the oven for about 15–20 minutes. They won't appear to be cooked exactly, just set and slightly puffy, and when they're taken out of the oven they will shrink (but that's normal). Leave the cakes to cool in the tins, but turn them out while they're still faintly warm and strip off the base papers.

Now whip the cream with the tablespoon of caster sugar until it is a floppy, spreadable consistency. Next empty the tin of cherries into a sieve set over a bowl and combine 2 tablespoons of the juice with the Kirsch or rum. Sprinkle this over the cake layers and, using a palette knife, spread about a third of the whipped cream over one cake.

Then slice the cherries and de-pip them (if they have any pips). Leave about a dozen whole ones for the decoration. Now arrange the sliced cherries all over the cake spread with cream. Next, carefully place the other cake on top and cover the entire cake with the remaining cream, again using a palette knife. Finish off by arranging the whole cherries around the edge, then grate the chocolate and sprinkle it all over.

YOGHURT

◆

It's hard to believe that yoghurt – once a rather obscure substance to be found only in equally obscure health-food shops – has now become one of our staple snacks. There appears to be no limit to the flavours of the month which turn up on the supermarket shelves; but it is just this that disappoints me about the many commercial brands. Despite all the invention which has been lavished on the sweetened flavoured varieties, they have failed to come up with a true *natural* yoghurt that bears much resemblance to what yoghurt should taste like. Let's look at the reasons for this.

WHAT IS YOGHURT?

It is a substance made from milk (whole, skimmed, evaporated or dried) which is first sterilised by heating to 190–221°F (88–105°C), then cooled to 106–114°F (41–45.5°C) and inoculated with a specially prepared culture. It is then incubated at a warm temperature until the acidity reaches a certain level and clotting takes place. After that it is cooled again, and is ready to eat or be stored.

In the Balkans and the Middle East yoghurt is made naturally from whole milk. This is boiled in open containers, which enable the milk to evaporate and reduce down to about two-thirds, or even half, its original volume. When it is made into yoghurt it is therefore thick, with a natural layer of cream on the surface. It also has a natural sweetness, like the sweetness of fresh milk, which it only loses as it ages and grows more acid. Commercially produced yoghurt is usually made with skimmed (low fat) milk and then thickened by the addition of powdered skimmed milk, rather than by reducing. So it doesn't have the creaminess of home-made natural yoghurt and the time taken in distribution means that it is fairly acid by the time it reaches our homes.

It is now possible to get close to the original when we buy Greek yoghurt. Because it is packed in tubs it doesn't have that lovely thick skin on its surface, but it *is* much richer and finer than the skimmed milk natural yoghurt.

HOME-MADE YOGHURT

I have already hinted that flavour is one reason for making your own yoghurt at home, but there are others. For one thing it is a great saving on the household bill (especially if you have a family that likes yoghurt), since the cost of making it at home is a third or a quarter of the shop version. You can also be sure that the ingredients you use – and the flavours you add – are pure and natural. And equally important, it is so easy.

After quite a number of hit-and-miss yoghurt-making sessions (involving airing cupboards, warm blankets and the like) I was lucky enough to come across a method of making it at home – adapted by a man called Peter Bradford from the various methods he had studied in the Middle East – which involves just three items of equipment; a milk saver to prevent the milk boiling over, a cooking thermometer, and a wide-necked insulated jar. These items of equipment can now be purchased at good kitchen shops and many branches of Boots.

No electricity is needed, no warm cupboards and, best of all, after the initial stages, no effort on your part. The process works all by itself! The only ingredients required are 1 pint (570 ml) of milk and 1 teaspoon of natural yoghurt (as a 'starter' on the first occasion). This is the method:

Place 1 pint (570 ml) of milk in a fairly large, wide saucepan along with the milk saver (basically a small glass disc). Bring it up to the boil, then let it simmer very gently for about 30 minutes, or until the milk has reduced to about 14 fl oz (400 ml), or roughly two-thirds of its original volume. Now tip the reduced milk into a clean jug and place the jug in a bowl of cold water. Let the milk cool for 5 minutes, then place a clean dry thermometer in the milk. If you're using a special yoghurt kit thermometer, wait until the mark reaches the red line: if you're using an ordinary cooking thermometer, wait until the temperature falls to 120°F (49°C). Now place 1 teaspoon of natural unsweetened yoghurt – a commercial brand will be all right – in the insulated jar, add a little of the milk, stir well, then add the rest of the milk, still stirring. Next place the lid on the jar, and leave it like that for not less than 6 hours (or longer won't hurt). Unscrew the lid, and inside you will have almost 15 oz (425 g) of delicious natural yoghurt for the price of 1 pint (570 ml) of milk. Replace the inner lid and store in the refrigerator.

Some important points

Everything must be as clean as possible. And when you are washing out the jar before use, make sure it isn't still warm from the washing water: it must be room temperature.

Never use sweetened or flavoured yoghurt as a starter: it must be natural yoghurt (you can use the low-fat variety). If you're making yoghurt continuously, you can in fact set aside 1 teaspoon of the previous batch to start the next, but every three months or so it is best to start with commercially made yoghurt (as this will have the right balance of culture). Home-made yoghurt can be made with long-life, skimmed or even powdered milk, but I think whole fresh milk makes the best.

HOME-MADE CURD CHEESE

This can be made from fresh yoghurt simply by placing a nylon sieve over a bowl and lining the sieve with a double piece of gauze. This is the method:

Tip the freshly-made yoghurt into the nylon bag (or sieve) and allow the whey – the liquid content – to drain into the bowl beneath, leaving just the curd, or solid content, in the bag. After about 6 hours you will have a soft, creamy curd cheese which can then be used in exactly the same way as any other curd cheese or cottage cheese. You can, for instance, add some seasoning, garlic and fresh chopped herbs to it. I like it eaten Greek-fashion, chilled as a dessert with a spoonful of runny honey poured over.

COOKING WITH YOGHURT

There are many recipes throughout the *Cookery Course* which make use of yoghurt. It does have a tendency to separate when subjected to heat and cooking, but this in no way affects the flavour (and myself, I'm not the least bothered about the slightly granular appearance). If, however, you want to stabilise yoghurt for cooking, blend 1 teaspoon rice flour or cornflour with a little cold water, mix this with 5 oz (150 g) of yoghurt, and simmer it for 10 minutes, stirring all the time.

SERVING YOGHURT

Yoghurt with honey and wheatgerm
Serve thick yoghurt well chilled in stemmed glasses, with runny honey dribbled over the top and a generous sprinkle of wheatgerm.

Yoghurt with muesli
Place 2 tablespoons of muesli per person in bowls, cover completely with 2 tablespoons of thick yoghurt, and top with runny honey.

Home-made fruit yoghurt
For the best results, use equal quantities of thick yoghurt and chopped fruit – strawberries, raspberries, blackcurrants or loganberries are all good. Add enough caster sugar or honey to sweeten according to your taste.

Dried fruit yoghurt
This is nicest of all made with prunes or dried apricots (or a mixture of both). Soak 4 oz (110 g) of apricots or prunes – or 2 oz (50 g) of each – overnight. Add 2 tablespoons of brown sugar and cook them for 10 minutes. Drain well in a sieve, then chop the flesh of the fruit and combine it with 10 oz (275 g) of thick yoghurt.

YOGHURT SEAFOOD SAUCE
◆

(Serves 4–6 people)

This is a lovely, piquant but very easy sauce for shellfish – for instance, *Avocado and fresh crab salad* on page 90.

2 rounded tablespoons mayonnaise (see page 438)
4 tablespoons natural yoghurt, about 5 oz (150 g)
1 tablespoon tomato purée
1 tablespoon Worcestershire sauce
2 level teaspoons horseradish sauce
2 tablespoons lemon juice
1 clove garlic, crushed
cayenne pepper
salt

This recipe is unbelievably easy, because all you do is combine all the above ingredients with a seasoning of salt and a pinch of cayenne, and stir well to blend them together thoroughly. Store, covered, in a cool place until needed. For slimmers this can be made entirely with Greek yoghurt and no mayonnaise.

CHILLED YOGHURT AND CUCUMBER SOUP
◆

(Serves 6–8 people)

This deliciously light and subtle soup is incredibly easy and quick to make. However it *does* need some fresh British cucumbers and not the rather tasteless imported ones.

1 medium, firm, young cucumber
5 oz natural yoghurt (150 g)
2¹/₂ fl oz soured cream (60 ml)
1 small clove garlic, crushed
1 teaspoon lemon juice
a little milk
1 level teaspoon chopped fresh mint
a few slices of lemon, cut very thinly
salt and freshly milled black pepper

First of all peel the cucumber thinly with a potato peeler so as to leave some of the green, then slice it. Reserve a few slices to garnish the soup, then place the rest in a liquidiser along with the yoghurt, soured cream and crushed garlic. Switch on and blend at the highest speed until smooth. Add a seasoning of salt and pepper and lemon juice, then pour the soup into a tureen and if it seems to be a little too thick, thin it with some cold milk. Now stir in the chopped fresh mint, cover with foil or with a lid and chill very thoroughly for several hours before serving.

To serve, ladle the soup into individual soup bowls and float a few thin slices of cucumber and a thin slice of lemon on each one.

CUCUMBER RAITA

◆

(Serves 4 people)

This is a side dish for curries. The idea is that the coolness of the yoghurt and the cucumber will counteract the hotness of the curry and so it does – much more effectively than cold drinks.

2 oz peeled cucumber (50 g)
5 oz natural yoghurt (150 g)
1 spring onion, finely chopped
¹/₂ clove garlic, crushed
salt and freshly milled black pepper
To serve
2 pinches of cayenne pepper
1 pinch of cumin seeds

First slice the cucumber thinly, then cut the slices in half, put into a basin and sprinkle with salt. Leave it for an hour, by which time a lot of the liquid will have been drawn out of it, so drain off the liquid and dry the cucumber in some kitchen paper.

Now combine the cucumber, yoghurt, spring onion and garlic, mixing them thoroughly. Season with salt and freshly milled pepper. Pour the mixture into a serving bowl, sprinkle with cayenne and cumin, cover and chill thoroughly before serving.

DRIED FRUIT SALAD WITH YOGHURT AND NUTS

◆

(Serves 4–6 people)

If you're wholefood-minded, you'll love this, which is full of good natural things. In the first edition of this book it had some sugar in it, but I have come to the conclusion it tastes *better* without it. (Illus. opposite p. 417.)

4 oz prunes (110 g)
4 oz dried apricots (110 g), separated
4 oz dried figs (110 g) – cut out the hard stalk ends
4 oz large raisins (110 g), separated
grated rind and juice of 1 orange
15 oz natural yoghurt (425 g)
2 oz hazelnuts (50 g), chopped and toasted

The night before, place the four dried fruits in a deep 2¹/2 pint (1.5 litre) bowl and cover with 1¹/4 pints (725 ml) cold water. Make quite sure *all* the fruit is immersed and leave to soak overnight.

The next day, drain off 3 fl oz (75 ml) of the water, then place the fruits and the remaining water in a small pan. Cover and bring to simmering point, and leave to simmer gently for about 10 minutes or until all the fruit feels tender when tested with a skewer. Next stir in the orange rind and juice, then tip the whole lot into a shallow serving bowl to cool. Cover with cling film and chill. Serve the salad spooned into dishes with the yoghurt and nuts handed round separately.

SEE ALSO

Chocolate and soured cream cake filling
Coeurs à la crème
Cream puffs
Creamed potatoes with soured cream and chives
Cucumber and yoghurt salad
Gratin dauphinois
Jacket potatoes with soured cream and chives
Liver in yoghurt and juniper sauce
Simple Stroganoff
Soured cream soda bread
Sweetbreads with soured cream and onion sauce
Vegetarian goulash

PASTRY

◆

Of all the cooking skills pastry-making, it seems, is the one that causes most problems. Pondering on why this should be, I think I detect two main reasons: first there are too many conflicting and confusing rules, and secondly pastry-making is one of those skills that needs to be *taught*. It's not an instinct you're either born with or not – it's a technique that needs proper explanation and a little bit of patience and practice. Unfortunately practice is rarely something that is allowed for in cooking. People spend money on driving lessons or learning a foreign language, but when it comes to food, if it doesn't work the first time, it's a 'wicked waste'.

PASTRY PSYCHOLOGY

Yes, there is a sort of psychology involved. Attitude is the word I think sums it up, your attitude towards pastry-making. Once you've been shown how to do it, you must be bold and self-assertive! Go to it with confidence – I almost think that pastry dough can sense anxiety and then start to play up! True, you need to be light-handed, but in this chapter you'll learn how to be light-handed. Also true, pastry must not be overhandled, and overhandling is a symptom of nervousness: just as people who lack confidence insist on stirring, prodding or peeping at things, so it is with pastry. So approach this subject with a confident attitude, and I'm sure perfect pastry is just a few pages away.

PASTRY PERVERSITY

Although there is a set of basic rules for making pastry, there will always be those infuriating people who appear to break or ignore the rules and still turn out perfect pastry. Well . . . other people's cooking often tastes better than your own, if only because you haven't had to do it. If you are a beginner, don't be side-tracked away from the basic ground rules: a hundred and one versions from friends and family will only confuse you.

There are quite a number of different pastries: shortcrust, quick flaky, and suet crust will suit most purposes for beginners, while choux and proper puff pastry are for slightly more advanced cooks.

SHORTCRUST PASTRY

———— ♦ ————

What is shortcrust? There is no such thing – in answer to an eight-year-old who once asked me – as longcrust. Short in this context actually means friable or easily crumbled, so the shorter the pastry the crumblier it is. It is the most useful and versatile of all pastries (the kind that crops up in your apple pies or jam tarts), and once this one is mastered the various other kinds will be relatively easy to learn.

FLOUR

Ordinary *plain flour* is best for shortcrust pastry. *Self-raising flour* is used by some people, but I think it produces a more 'cakey' texture, being slightly aerated: the finished pastry is softer, less crisp than with plain flour. Air, however, is a vital ingredient, and all flour must be sifted. Sifting is done not only to disperse the lumps, but also to give the flour an airing – so the higher you hold your sieve over the bowl, the further the flour travels and the more air it incorporates. (Because I always sift white flour, I never pay the extra money for superfine or supersifted flours: the ordinary 'own-brand' in a reliable supermarket is perfectly good, so sifting yourself saves money.)

Wholewheat flour can also be used for shortcrust. Because this flour is coarse-textured, the pastry can sometimes seem heavy or difficult to roll. Therefore to combine the flavour of the wholewheat with a lightness of texture, I use the proportion of half wholewheat flour to half white self-raising.

SALT

I have included a generous pinch of salt in many pastry recipes. For my own part I only use it in savoury ones, in which case I season with salt *and* freshly milled pepper.

FATS

The choice of fat will determine the flavour as well as the texture of your pastry, and here any differences of opinion can probably only be resolved in the end by personal taste, and the type of recipe the pastry is intended for (for instance, to me in a bacon-and-egg pie or a Cornish pasty lard seems to give the 'right' flavour). Below are my own comments on different combinations.

All margarine

This means block, not soft margarine which is not suitable. It gives a fairly flaky texture, but cooked at a high temperature, gas mark 7, 425 °F (220 °C), it has a pronounced margarine flavour.

All butter

This produces the crunchiest, crispest shortcrust, but although the flavour is good it is also rich and rather more fatty. So I wouldn't choose this for a recipe with a rich, creamy filling. Butter is also a little more difficult to rub in.

All lard

This makes a shorter and flakier pastry, but it does have a distinctive flavour which is good for savoury recipes and not so good for sweet. Because lard reaches room temperature more quickly than butter or marge, if too soft it can be more difficult to rub in. All lard pastry also needs less water for mixing.

Half butter: half lard

This is very easy to rub in and handle. The pastry has a good texture with the right amount of crispness, and a good flavour.

Half margarine: half lard

Again easy to rub in and roll out – and my personal favourite for most of my own pastry-making. A few experiments will soon reveal your own preferences.

As a rule fat should be used at room temperature. If it is too cold, it will be inconvenient to rub in: if it is too warm, it will be already slightly oily and the additional heat of your hands will make it too soft to rub in correctly (this will only worry you in a heat-wave or a particularly hot kitchen, in which case don't take it out of the fridge too soon). Fat removed from the refrigerator and left in a cool place for 2 hours before it's needed is generally about right.

LIQUID

Cold water, as cold as possible in fact, is best for shortcrust pastry. The amount you use can vary enormously, because (as we discovered with bread) different flours absorb different amounts. It is best to add a little at first, and a little more as you need to. What you are aiming for in the end is a dough that's smooth without any dryish bits or cracks in it, moist enough to incorporate all the flour and fat and leave the bowl fairly cleanly. Remember that too much water will produce a hard crust, and too little will make the dough difficult to roll out – but having said that, you will find it easy enough to get the right balance.

SHORTCRUST PASTRY – BASIC PRINCIPLES

(1) *Making the dough: keeping cool*
It is true everything should be as cool as you can manage for pastry-making, because if the ingredients – and your hands – are too warm the fat becomes too soft, even oily, and it coats more flour grains than it should. The flour is then unable to absorb enough water and the pastry will be too crumbly. However, don't be put off if your kitchen is typically hot and steamy. Open a window and make the pastry as near to the window as possible.

(2) *Rubbing in*
Once the flour is sifted into a bowl, you then divide the fat into smallish lumps and add them to the flour. Start off with a knife and 'cut' the fat into the flour. Then use your finger-tips only: start to lift the pieces of fat up with the flour and rub them gently through your fingers. Now it's well known that light hands make good pastry – that means, in a word, be as *gentle* as you can. Keep lifting your hands high above the bowl and let in the air and, therefore, lightness. Although this process is called 'rubbing in', I'd prefer to call it 'mingling in', which is nearer what it should be.

(3) *Mixing*
We've established that coolness is important, so here speed is what is needed. The less you handle it, the less likely the warmth of your hands will affect it. Once the fat has been evenly distributed and the mixture looks crumbly, you can start to add the water. Run the cold tap for a minute to get it really cold, half-fill a jug and sprinkle in the water all over about 1 tablespoon at a time – you should need 3–4 tablespoons, but it is impossible to be precise because different flours have different absorption levels. Use a round-bladed knife to start to mix to a dough, and finish off with your hands to bring it all together, adding more water – perhaps only the merest trace – till you have enough. (*Sprinkling* the water all over brings it together more quickly than pouring it into the centre and having to work the wet out towards the dry edges.)

(4) *Resting*
It's a bore, but if you don't want your pastry to break as you roll it out or shrink while it is cooking, you must allow it at least 20–30 minutes before you roll it out. Why? Because, as we discovered with bread, the gluten in the flour reacts to water and develops in time, becoming more pliable and elastic (and so easier to roll and less likely to shrink). Wrap the dough carefully in foil or a polythene bag, and leave it to rest in the refrigerator to keep it cool – this covering is important, to prevent the pastry acquiring a tough skin which will break and crack as you start to roll it out.

495

(5) *Rolling*

What you need for this is a flat surface, a table-top, laminated work surface or a proper pastry board. Also the length of the rolling-pin is important: the longer it is, the more evenly it will roll (I find the 18 inch/45 cm one ideal, and without handles it is far easier to control). A flour dredger is not an expensive item and will sprinkle flour lightly and evenly. Place the dough on a lightly floured surface, and first shape it with your hands (to a round, or oblong, or whatever your final shape must be). But do this speedily – the less your warm hands come into contact with the pastry the better it will be. Give the rolling-pin a dusting of flour, and start to roll with both hands positioned flat at each end of the pin, keeping the pressure even and being *gentle*. Save all your aggressions for making bread dough! If the pastry starts sticking to the pin, dust the pin (rather than the pastry) with more flour.

Don't turn the pastry over while you're rolling: it is totally unnecessary and the pastry you've rolled out will only shrink back and possibly break. When you are rolling a specific shape, always revolve the pastry rather than the rolling-pin. To roll out to a round shape, all you do is keep giving the pastry a quarter-turn after each rolling. Any shape should be rolled fractionally larger than you actually require to line a tin.

(6) *Transferring pastry to a tin*

The best way is to place the rolling-pin at either end of the pastry, and lightly roll the pastry round the pin, then transfer it to the waiting tin – place the tip of the pastry over one edge of the tin and unroll. Now start to ease the pastry gently into position to line the tin (what you need to keep in mind at this stage is that it is better for the pastry to shrink at the lining stage than to be stretched (otherwise it will shrink in the oven). So ease back any overlapping bits into the tin, leaving yourself as little to trim off as possible. Take care, as well, to press it into position firmly so that no air can be trapped underneath.

CUTTING OUT

Whenever you need to cut out tartlets or pastry shapes, remember to dust the edge of the cutter with flour first. Then place it on the pastry and give it a sharp *tap*. It's very tempting to want to twist the cutter, but my advice is don't, unless you want your round tartlet shapes to turn out oval.

BAKING BLIND

Baking something 'blind' means cooking the pastry on its own in the oven, before the filling goes in. There is a tendency, when this is done, for the base to balloon up during the cooking if there is any air trapped under the pastry. Various remedies for this are used, like lining papers and baking beans to weight the pastry down – but if you have lined the tin with the pastry properly (see above) these things are redundant. And an extra precaution is to prick the base all over with a fork to release any trapped air (no, the filling won't run through the holes, because as the pastry sets they'll close up again). I also brush the base with some beaten egg which acts as a kind of moisture-proof coating and helps to keep the pastry crisp before the filling goes in. A final way of making sure is simply to open the oven after 7–8 minutes, have a look and, if the pastry is puffing up, press it back down and prick it once more.

OVEN TEMPERATURES

These will vary according to the recipe, but most need a pre-heated oven (gas mark 5–7, 375–425°F, 190–220°C). A pre-heated baking sheet, too, is essential for anything that needs a crisp base, as this will conduct the heat more efficiently under the tin.

BAKING TIN, TRAYS, ETC.

I cannot stress enough that metal is so much better a conductor of heat than either glass or porcelain. I admit those white fluted porcelain dishes look extremely pretty and many women's magazines show tempting pictures of quiches and flans made in them. But alas, what looks good from the outside is often watery and soggy within – so for crisp, evenly cooked pastry, use metal.

Note So far I have been setting out my own personal notes on ingredients and preferences. These are not rigid rules and I myself often feel like ringing the changes, so in the following recipes, the type of fat you use is up to you. If you're a vegetarian, for instance, you will obviously want to use vegetable fat or margarine: similarly any recipe for shortcrust pastry can easily be changed to wholewheat shortcrust.

BASIC SHORTCRUST PASTRY
♦

Since confusion regularly arises over the term '4 oz of shortcrust pastry' (does it mean 4 oz total weight of pastry, or shortcrust made with 4 oz flour?) I have given the required quantities of flour *and* fat. Thus the recipe below is for '6 oz of shortcrust pastry'.

4 oz flour (110 g)
1 oz margarine (25 g), at room temperature
1 oz lard (25 g), at room temperature
a pinch of salt
cold water, to mix

Sift the flour and salt into a large mixing bowl, holding the sieve up as high as possible to give the flour an airing. Then cut the fat into small cubes and add them to the flour. Now, using your fingertips, lightly and gently rub the pieces of fat into the flour – lifting your hands up high as you do this (again to incorporate air) and being as quick as possible.

When the mixture looks uniformly crumbly, start to sprinkle roughly 2 tablespoons of water all over. Use a round-bladed knife to start the mixing, cutting and bringing the mixture together. Carefully add more water as needed, a little at a time, then finally bring the mixture together with your hands to form a smooth ball of dough that will leave the bowl clean. (If there are any bits that won't adhere to it, you need a spot more water.) Now rest the pastry, wrapped in foil or polythene, in the refrigerator for 20–30 minutes before rolling out.

For *wholewheat pastry*, follow the method above, using 2 oz (50 g) of wholewheat flour and 2 oz (50 g) of white self-raising flour.

Clearly these quantities will vary with each recipe – i.e. you may find you need 8 oz (225 g) of flour and 4 oz (110 g) of fat – but generally speaking the proportion of fat is always half that of flour.

DEEP FRUIT PIES

These are made in the traditional deep, oval, rimmed pie-dishes and only have a crust over the top with a steam-hole in the centre, about the size of a 10p piece. The advantage with this type of pie is that you retain all the juices of the fruits, leaving the top crust crisp and separate.

Making a pastry lid

When you are making a classic pie that has a single crust on top, you should roll out the pastry to approximately 1 inch (2.5 cm) larger than the rim of the pie-dish. Then cut a 1 inch (2.5 cm) strip all round and, after you have dampened the rim of the pie-dish with water, fix this strip all round it – you'll probably have to join up several pieces. Next dampen the pastry rim and transfer the lid to sit comfortably on top of the pie. Using a sharp knife, trim any excess pastry off, then, using the blunt side of the knife and your thumb, press the two edges firmly together and knock the edges all round to make a layered effect. Then flute the edges by using your thumb to make an impression and the broad blade of the knife to draw in the edges of the pastry. Then make a steam-hole and decorate with leaves etc.

Decorations

To make pastry leaves out of any left-over trimmings, simply cut small leaf shapes and on them incise the veins of real leaves using the blunt side of a small kitchen knife. Usually a pie has a steam-hole in the centre of the lid and what you can do to decorate that is make up a pastry rose with more of the trimmings. Roll up a long strip to make the centre of the flower, then cut small rounds of pastry in half to form the petals. Stick these round the centre of the pie lid (using some beaten egg). Bake the rose on the baking sheet next to the pie and pop it in position over the steam-hole before sending it to the table.

APPLE AND BLACKBERRY PIE

◆

(Serves 4 people)

This is best of all made with wild blackberries, which seem to have twice as much flavour as the cultivated kind.

For the shortcrust pastry
6 oz plain flour (175 g)
1½ oz lard (40 g)
1½ oz margarine or butter (40 g)
a pinch of salt
cold water, to mix

For the filling
1 lb cooking apples (450 g) – 4 medium apples
8 oz blackberries (225 g), washed
3 oz sugar (75 g)

To glaze
milk and caster sugar

Pre-heat the oven to gas mark 7, 425°F (220°C).

A 1½ pint (850 ml) rimmed pie-dish.

Start by making the pastry (see page 497), then leave it to rest while you peel and slice the apples straight into the pie-dish. Then sprinkle in the blackberries and the sugar.

Now roll out the pastry, about 1 inch (2.5 cm) larger than the pie-dish, then cut out a 1 inch (2.5 cm) strip to fit the edge of the dish. Dampen the edge, then fit on the strip of pastry, pressing it firmly, and dampen that too. Then press the rest of the pastry over that to form a lid, knock up and flute the edges and make a steam-hole in the centre. And if you have time make some decorative leaves with the pastry trimmings (see page 498).

Now brush the pastry with milk and sprinkle on a light dusting of caster sugar. Place the pie on a baking sheet on a high shelf and bake for 10 minutes, then reduce the heat to gas mark 5, 375°F (190°C), and continue baking for a further 30 minutes. Then, using a skewer, take out a piece of apple from the centre to test if it's cooked – if it still feels very firm, give it another 5 minutes. Serve hot with chilled pouring cream to mingle with the juices.

Note If you want a larger pie to serve eight people use a 3 pint (1.75 litre) pie-dish and a pie-funnel, and double all the ingredients.

Alternative fillings for deep fruit pies

Here are three different fillings, bearing in mind that the pastry method and cooking times are as in the previous recipe.

English gooseberry pie
For this you'll need 2 lb (900 g) young green gooseberries, 6 oz (175 g) caster sugar and a 1½ pint (850 ml) pie-dish.

Fresh cherry pie
1½ lb (700 g) fresh cherries, 3 level tablespoons demerara sugar, ½ teaspoon ground cinnamon and a 1½ pint (850 ml) pie-dish.

Damson plum pie
1½ lb (700 g) damsons or damson plums, 4 oz (110 g) sugar and a 1½ pint (850 ml) oval pie-dish.

BASIC DOUBLE-CRUST FRUIT PIE

The quantities for the recipe below are for any basic fruit pie with a double crust using either plain or wholewheat shortcrust. That is to say the pastry for a 9½ inch (24 cm) enamel pie-plate is always 8 oz (225 g) flour and 4 oz (110 g) fat. The filling is usually 1½ lb (700 g) fruit.

SPICED APPLE AND RAISIN PIE
◆

(Serves 6 people)

For the pastry
4 oz wholewheat flour (110 g)
4 oz self-raising flour (110 g)
2 oz margarine or butter (50 g)
2 oz lard (50 g)
a pinch of salt
cold water, to mix

For the filling
1½ lb Bramley apples (700 g)
1 oz soft brown sugar (25 g)
¼ teaspoon ground cloves
½ teaspoon ground cinnamon
¼ whole nutmeg, grated

3 oz raisins (75 g)	
2 tablespoons water	
To glaze	
milk and caster sugar	

Pre-heat the oven to gas mark 6, 400°F (200°C).

A 9½ inch (24 cm) enamel pie-plate.

First quarter, core and peel the apples, then slice them thinly into a saucepan and mix them with the sugar, spices and raisins. Next sprinkle in the water and cook gently (with a lid on) for about 10 minutes or until the apples are soft and fluffy. Then empty the mixture into a bowl to cool.

Next make up the pastry (see page 497) and leave it to rest while you pre-heat the oven – putting in a baking sheet – and lightly grease the pie-plate.

Roll out a *little more* than half the pastry to a round, then transfer it to line the plate, pressing it gently and firmly all round. Now spoon in the filling, then roll out the other half of the pastry to form a lid. Dampen the bottom layer of pastry round the edge with water, then fix the lid into position, pressing it very firmly all around. Trim, flute the edges all round and decorate as explained on page 498. Make a hole in the centre (or just snip the pie along the centre with a pair of scissors to make holes) for the steam to escape.

Brush with milk next, then sprinkle on a dusting of caster sugar, which will give a nice crisp sugared surface when the pie is baked. Place the pie on the baking sheet and bake for 30 minutes.

Alternative double-crust pie fillings

To get the correct balance of filling, I find it's always best to cook it a little first as the ripeness and sharpness in fruit varies. You can then gauge just the right amount of sugar. Also I've found that cooking the fruit first allows you to get rid of some of the excess juice, e.g. with rhubarb or plums. Alternatively, as with apples, water can be added to make a moister filling.

Apple pie

For the very best flavour use 1 lb (450 g) Bramleys and 8 oz (225 g) Cox's, 1 oz (25 g) sugar and 2 tablespoons water.

Rhubarb pie

A little ginger always brings out the flavour of rhubarb, so place 2½ lb (1.25 kg), cut in chunks, in a saucepan with 1 rounded teaspoon ground ginger and 3 oz (75 g) dark brown sugar but *no* water. Then cook gently, stirring now and then, for about 10 minutes and drain well in a sieve set over a bowl before using.

Summer fruits pie

A delicious combination: 12 oz (350 g) raspberries, 4 oz (110 g) redcurrants, 4 oz (110 g) blackcurrants, 5 oz (150 g) caster sugar. Place the fruits and sugar in a saucepan and cook, very gently, for just 4 minutes, then drain in a sieve set over a bowl.

OTHER SHORTCRUST PIES AND TARTS

Shortcrust pastry can be used to enclose other fillings apart from fruit. Home-made mincemeat is vital for mince pies during the festive season, and other traditional recipes include tarts made with lemon curd and syrup. Using all lard, shortcrust is an ideal casing for a savoury pastry pie.

MINCE PIES

(Makes 3 dozen)

One tip I may be able to pass on, as a result of years of fraught Christmas preparations – that is, to invest in at least four tins which make a dozen tarts each. It's infuriating when a tin only holds nine and it's impossible to place them both on the same shelf. What I now do is bake two dozen, a dozen on each shelf, changing over at half-time, and prepare another two dozen while they're cooking. (Illus. opposite p. 448.)

For the pastry
12 oz plain flour (350 g)
3 oz lard (75 g)
3 oz margarine or butter (75 g)
a pinch of salt
cold water, to mix

For the filling
1¹/₂ lb mincemeat (700 g) (see page 621)

For the top
milk and icing sugar

Pre-heat the oven to gas mark 6, 400°F (200°C).

For the normal 2¹/₂ inch (6 cm) patty tins you'll need one fluted 3 inch (7.5 cm) pastry cutter, and one fluted 2¹/₂ inch (6 cm) cutter.

Make up the pastry (see page 497) and allow it to rest for 20–30 minutes. Then roll half of it out to about ¹/₈ inch (3 mm) thick and cut it out into three dozen 3 inch (7.5 cm) rounds, gathering up the scraps and re-rolling again. Then do the same with the other half of the pastry, this time using the 2¹/₂ inch (6 cm) cutter.

Now grease the patty tins lightly and line them with the large rounds; fill these with the mincemeat (not too much – only to the level of the edges of the pastry).

Now dampen the edges of the smaller rounds of pastry with water and press them lightly into position to form lids, sealing the edges. Brush each one with milk and make about three snips in the top with a pair of scissors.

Bake near the top of the oven for 25–30 minutes until they're a light golden-brown. Then cool them on a wire tray and sprinkle with sifted icing sugar. Store the cooled mince pies in an airtight tin and warm them slightly before serving.

LANCASTER LEMON TART

♦

(Serves 4–6 people)

This is a first cousin of a Bakewell tart, using home-made lemon curd instead of jam, which I think goes very well with the flavour of almonds.

For the pastry
3 oz plain flour (75 g)
³/₄ oz lard (20 g)
³/₄ oz margarine or butter (20 g)
a pinch of salt
cold water, to mix

For the filling
3 rounded tablespoons lemon curd (see page 544)
3 oz butter (75 g), at room temperature
3 oz caster sugar (75 g)
1 egg, beaten lightly
1 oz ground almonds (25 g)
4 oz self-raising flour (110 g)
grated rind and juice of 1 large lemon
1 oz whole almonds (25 g), peeled and halved

Pre-heat the oven to gas mark 6, 400°F (200°C).

A 7 or 8 inch (18 or 20 cm) enamel pie-plate, lightly-greased.

First make up the pastry (see page 497), allowing it to rest. Then roll it out and line the pie-plate, fluting the edges, then spread the lemon curd all over the pastry.

Now cream the butter and sugar together till pale and fluffy, then gradually beat in the egg about a teaspoonful at a time. Gently and carefully fold in the ground almonds and flour, followed by the lemon juice and grated rind.

503

Now spread this mixture evenly over the lemon curd, smoothing it out with a palette knife. Then sprinkle the halved almonds over the surface. Bake it, on a baking sheet, in the centre of the oven for 15 minutes, then reduce the heat to gas mark 2, 300°F (150°C), and continue cooking for a further 25–30 minutes.

This can be served either warm or cold with cream.

LEMON MERINGUE PIE
♦

(Serves 6 people)

This is one sweet dish, with its three distinct elements, that needs a careful balance of textures and quantities. The filling has to be lemony enough, neither too stiff nor too oozy. The meringue should be wafery crisp on the outside and soft and marshmallowy within. This recipe is so light it literally melts in the mouth.

For the pastry
4 oz plain flour (110 g)
1 oz margarine or butter (25 g)
1 oz lard (25 g)
a pinch of salt
cold water, to mix

For the filling
grated rind and juice of 2 large lemons
10 fl oz cold water (275 ml)
3 level tablespoons cornflour
2 oz caster sugar (50 g)
2 large egg yolks
1¹/₂ oz butter (40 g)

For the meringue
2 large egg whites
4 oz caster sugar (110 g)

Pre-heat the oven to gas mark 5, 375°F (190°C).

The best dish for this recipe is a deep enamel pie-plate with sloping sides and a rim, measuring 6 inches (15 cm) at the base and 8 inches (20 cm) at the top.

Start by making up the pastry (see page 497) and chilling it in the fridge for 20 minutes. Then roll it out to a round about ¹/₃ inch (8 mm) larger all round than the rim of the tin. Cut away a narrow ¹/₃ inch (8 mm) strip all round, dampen the rim of the tin with water and fix this pastry strip on it all round, pressing down well. Next dampen the pastry strip and transfer the pastry round to line the tin –

making sure you don't trap any air underneath it. Then flute the edge of the pastry and prick the base all over with a fork. Bake on a high shelf of the oven for 20–25 minutes or until cooked through.

Remove the pastry case from the oven, and immediately lower the heat to gas mark 2, 300°F (150°C), for the meringue.

Next the filling. Measure the cold water into a jug and spoon the cornflour and sugar into a bowl. Add enough of the measured water to mix the cornflour to a smooth paste, then pour the rest of the water along with the grated lemon rind into a small saucepan. Bring this up to the boil, then pour it onto the cornflour paste and mix till smooth.

Transfer the mixture back to the saucepan and bring back to the boil. Then simmer gently for 1 minute – stirring all the time to prevent it from catching. Remove the pan from the heat and beat in the egg yolks, lemon juice and finally the butter. Pour the lemon mixture into the pastry shell and spread it out evenly.

Finally the meringue. For this use a large roomy bowl and in it whisk the egg whites till they form stiff peaks. Beat in a quarter of the caster sugar at a time until it is all incorporated, then spread the meringue mixture all over the filling. Use a broad-bladed knife to spread the meringue to the very edge of the pastry rim, so it seals the top completely. (With your knife you can also make a few decorative swirls.) Cook in the oven for 45 minutes, until the meringue has turned pale beige and is crisp on the outside and squashy within. Serve warm or cold.

WHOLEWHEAT TREACLE TART
♦

(Serves 6 people)

I think the crunchiness of wholewheat pastry, and wholewheat breadcrumbs too, make a nicer treacle tart than the traditional version.

For the pastry
2 oz wholewheat flour (50 g)
2 oz self-raising flour (50 g)
1 oz lard (25 g)
1 oz margarine or butter (25 g)
a pinch of salt
cold water, to mix
For the filling
4 oz wholewheat breadcrumbs (110 g)
5 tablespoons golden syrup and 1 tablespoon black treacle or 6 tablespoons darker syrup
To glaze
milk

Pre-heat the oven to gas mark 5, 375°F (190°C).

An 8 inch (20 cm) fluted flan tin with a loose base, lightly-greased.

Make the pastry (see page 497) and allow it to rest for 20–30 minutes. Then roll it out thinly and line the flan tin with it, cutting off the pastry trimmings and keeping them on one side.

If you place the tinned treacle and syrup in the pre-heating oven for about 10 minutes, with the lids removed, you will find it easier to pour.

Measure out the warmed treacle and syrup into a bowl, and stir in the breadcrumbs quite thoroughly before pouring the whole lot into the prepared pastry case.

Now roll out the pastry trimmings and cut strips long enough to make a criss-cross pattern all over the surface of the tart. Then brush the strips and edges lightly with milk and place the tart on a baking sheet in the oven. Bake it for about 30–35 minutes. Serve still warm with some chilled whipped cream.

CORNISH PASTY PIE

◆

(Serves 6 people)

I find Cornish pasties often have too much pastry and not enough filling. However, the traditional filling of steak, potato and turnip is so delicious I now make one big pie using this filling – which is also a lot quicker than making individual pasties.

For the pastry
12 oz plain flour (350 g)
6 oz lard (175 g)
salt and freshly milled pepper
cold water, to mix
For the filling
1¼ lb chuck steak (575 g)
1 large onion, finely chopped
1 level teaspoon dried mixed herbs
1 medium to large potato
1 medium to large turnip
1 tablespoon water
salt and freshly milled pepper
To glaze
beaten egg

Pre-heat the oven to gas mark 6, 400°F (200°C).

A well-greased baking sheet or a well-greased 10 inch (25 cm) fluted metal quiche tin – see recipe.

Make the pastry first (see page 497), adding a little salt and pepper to season it, then pop it into a plastic bag and leave it in the fridge for 10–15 minutes. Meanwhile, slice the meat into very thin strips about 2 inches (5 cm) long (it's important to keep them very thin in order that they cook in the time given).

Place the meat in a mixing bowl, with the chopped onion and mixed herbs. Then peel the potato and turnip and slice these as thinly as possible too (the slicing edge of a four-sided grater does this thin slicing job in moments).

Now, if you are using a quiche tin, roll out half the pastry, large enough to line the tin with about 1/2 inch (1 cm) overlapping. Then layer the filling ingredients in it (in any order). Season well with salt and pepper as you go, and finally sprinkle in 1 tablespoon of water.

Roll out the other half of the pastry, dampen the edge all round, then fit it over the top of the pie. Then seal the edges, folding them inwards and pressing gently to make a rim just inside the edge of the tin. Make a steam-hole in the centre (about the size of a 10p piece), brush the surface with beaten egg, and bake the pie on a baking sheet, on a high shelf, for 15 minutes. Then turn the heat down to gas mark 4, 350°F (180°C), and continue to cook on the centre shelf for a further 1 1/2 hours. This is still very good eaten cold, so it's a good idea for a picnic.

Instead of using a quiche tin, you could simply roll out two 11 inch (28 cm) diameter rounds of pastry and place one on the baking sheet. Layer the ingredients (as above) on it but leave 1 inch (2.5 cm) all round the edge. Now place the other pastry round on top and seal the edge by turning the bottom piece inwards all the way round, then make deep diagonal cuts with the edge of a teaspoon handle all the way round the edge. Then proceed as above.

QUICHES AND OPEN TARTS

For years I've been experimenting with this type of recipe to eliminate – for ever – the problem of the soggy pastry base that seems to plague so many people, myself included. I'm happy to announce that the problem seems largely solved by (a) pre-baking the pastry case, (b) *always* using a baking sheet underneath the tin, (c) painting the inside of the pre-baked pastry shell with beaten egg and allowing it to rest for 5 minutes in the oven before the filling goes in. I have already said (but will stress again) that the container must be *metal*, not porcelain or glass.

QUICHE PASTRY
◆

4 oz plain flour (110 g)
1 oz lard (25 g)
1 oz margarine or butter (25 g)
a pinch of salt
cold water, to mix

This will be enough for a lightly-greased 8 inch (20 cm) quiche or flan tin with fluted edges and a removable base, or if you like a deeper quiche, use a 7¹/₂ inch (19 cm) tin that is 1¹/₂ inches (4 cm) deep.

Make up the pastry, then rest it for 20–30 minutes in a polythene bag in the fridge. Meanwhile, pre-heat the oven to gas mark 4, 350°F (180°C), with a baking sheet placed on the centre shelf.

Then roll out the pastry and line the tin with it, easing any overlapping pastry back into the sides if you can. Be careful to press firmly on the base and sides, then prick with a fork all over. Bake the pastry case for 15 minutes on the centre shelf, then remove it from the oven and paint the inside of it, all over, with some of the beaten egg to be used in the filling ingredients, and pop it back into the oven to set for a further 5 minutes.

Now add the filling and bake for a further 30–40 minutes until the quiche is set in the centre and has turned golden-brown and looks puffy. The best way to add filling is to arrange the filling ingredients over the base of a pre-cooked quiche. Then whisk the eggs first, then whisk with the cream (if you do this in a jug you can pour half the mixture onto the quiche, take it to the oven, then pour the rest in when it's safely on the shelf – it avoids spilling *en route*).

Note An alternative and excellent pastry to use for a quiche is the cheese pastry in the *Thick onion tart* recipe on page 293.

Fillings for quiches
Double cream is best of all, but you can happily use single cream, milk or natural yoghurt (Greek yoghurt is especially good). For economy 2 eggs are sufficient, but for a firmer set and extra richness an extra egg yolk is required.

MUSHROOM AND ONION QUICHE
◆

This is made with what the French called *duxelles*, a paste made with chopped mushrooms and onion (see page 248). For extra flavour add ¹/₄ oz (5 g) dried Italian mushrooms, soaked and finely chopped, as the rest of the filling goes in.

8 oz flat mushrooms (225 g), chopped very, very small
1 medium onion, chopped very small
1 oz butter (25 g)
2 large eggs, plus 1 extra yolk
10 fl oz double cream (275 ml)
freshly grated nutmeg
salt and freshly milled black pepper

Heat the butter in a saucepan and soften the onion in it for 5 minutes or so. Now stir in the chopped mushrooms and let it all cook gently (uncovered) for 30 minutes or until most of the juice has evaporated – giving it a stir quite often. Transfer the filling to the tart with a draining spoon, and arrange it evenly over the base.

Beat the eggs thoroughly, then whisk the cream into them and season with salt, pepper and a small grating of nutmeg. Pour this mixture over the filling, put the flan on the baking sheet in the oven and bake for 35–40 minutes, or until the centre is set and the filling golden and puffy.

Serve straight from the oven, if possible (though this does reheat quite well).

COURGETTE AND CHEESE QUICHE
◆

8 oz courgettes (225 g)
2 oz cheese, preferably Gruyère (50 g), grated
1 small onion, finely chopped
1 oz butter (25 g)
2 large eggs, plus 1 extra yolk
10 fl oz single or double cream (275 ml) or half cream and half yoghurt
1 tablespoon grated Parmesan cheese
salt and freshly milled black pepper

Slice the courgettes fairly thinly. Soften the onion in the butter in a frying-pan for 5 minutes, then add the courgettes and brown them a little, turning them frequently. Now transfer both onions and courgettes to the pastry case, sprinkle the grated Gruyère over them, and proceed as in the previous recipe (sprinkling the Parmesan over the top before baking).

SMOKED SALMON TART

—— ◆ ——

6 oz smoked salmon (175 g), chopped – offcuts are fine
2 large eggs, plus 1 extra yolk
10 fl oz double cream (275 ml)
freshly grated nutmeg
a pinch of cayenne pepper
salt and freshly milled black pepper

Simply arrange the smoked salmon evenly over the base of a pre-cooked quiche pastry, then beat up the eggs and cream with a seasoning of salt, freshly milled black pepper and a little freshly grated nutmeg. Pour in the filling and dust the surface with no more than a generous pinch of cayenne. Bake as above.

Note For a *Kipper tart*, use the recipe above but instead of the smoked salmon use 8 oz (225 g) of skinned, chopped kipper fillet.

CLASSIC QUICHE LORRAINE

—— ◆ ——

For this classic cream and bacon tart the ingredients are:

8 rashers smoked streaky bacon, grilled till crisp and chopped small
3 oz Gruyère cheese (75 g), grated
2 large eggs, plus 1 extra yolk
10 fl oz double cream (275 ml)
salt and freshly milled black pepper

The method and timing are exactly the same as above. Simply place the cheese and bacon in the pre-cooked pastry case, and pour in the cream and egg filling, adding pepper but not too much salt (as there is some already in the bacon).

SUET CRUST PASTRY

—— ◆ ——

If you've never tried this pastry, then it's a must next time you make steak and kidney pie. Because it is made with shredded beef suet it has the best possible flavour for a beefsteak pie. But more than that – it is beautifully easy to make since there is no rubbing-in. It is resilient and easy to roll out, and it is deliciously light and crusty.

Important note Suet crust is always made with self-raising flour because, suet being a heavy fat, the pastry needs a raising agent to aerate it and make it lighter. And as it is made with self-raising flour, it follows that suet crust should always be rolled out and used *immediately* – because once the raising agent in the flour becomes damp it will begin to lose its raising power. This pastry can't be made in advance, but it is easy so this should not be a problem.

BUTCHER'S SUET

This can be used, but it's tedious separating suet from skin and membrane and grating it finely. Packet suet is quite pure, with a coating of flour (or rice flour) to separate the grains.

BASIC SUET CRUST PASTRY
◆

These quantities will be enough to top a 1½ pint (850 ml) rimmed pie-dish. For a 2½ pint (1.5 litre) pie-dish use 12 oz (350 g) self-raising flour and 6 oz (175 g) suet.

8 oz self-raising flour (225 g)
4 oz shredded suet (110 g)
salt and freshly milled black pepper (for a savoury crust)
cold water, to mix

Sift the flour into a bowl, then sprinkle the suet in, season with salt and pepper and just mix it in lightly with your hands to distribute it evenly. Now sprinkle in some cold water (you'll find you need more for this pastry than for shortcrust). Begin mixing with a round-bladed knife, and then use your hands at the end to bring it all together to a smooth elastic dough that leaves the bowl clean. Suet crust should be left for 5 minutes, then rolled out immediately. You should always roll it out rather more thickly than shortcrust, approximately ½ inch (1 cm) thick.

BEEFSTEAK AND KIDNEY PIE

◆

(Serves 4 people)

Suet crust pastry made with shredded beef suet is perfect for steak and kidney pie, as the beef flavour in the pastry complements it so well.

1 quantity suet crust pastry (see page 511)

For the filling
1¹/₂ lb chuck steak (700 g), cut in 1 inch (2.5 cm) cubes
6 oz ox kidney (175 g), chopped
2 medium onions, roughly chopped
1 tablespoon beef dripping
1¹/₂ tablespoons plain flour
¹/₂ teaspoon dried mixed herbs
¹/₂ teaspoon Worcestershire sauce
2 teaspoons mushroom ketchup
15 fl oz beef stock (425 ml)
8 oz dark-gilled mushrooms (225 g), sliced
salt and freshly milled black pepper

A 2 pint (1.2 litre) pie-dish.

In a large saucepan fry the chopped onions in the dripping for a few minutes, then add the cubes of steak and the kidney. Continue to cook (stirring now and then) till the meat is nicely browned, then add the flour and stir it in well. Add the herbs next, followed by the Worcestershire sauce and the ketchup: season with salt and pepper and gradually stir in the stock. Finally add the mushrooms, bring the whole lot to simmering point, and simmer gently for about 2 hours or until the meat is tender. Check the seasoning and pour everything into the pie-dish. Pre-heat the oven to gas mark 7, 425°F (220°C).

Mix the pastry to a smooth elastic dough, and roll it out on a lightly floured surface to a shape about 1 inch (2.5 cm) larger than the rim of the pie-dish. Now cut a 1 inch (2.5 cm) strip all round, dampen the edge of the pie-dish and press this pastry strip on. Then dampen the strip and lay the pastry lid on top, pressing it down and sealing it around the edge. Flute the edge, make a small steam-hole in the centre, and bake in the oven for 30–40 minutes, until the pastry is golden-brown.

Note To make a pie for six people, use a 3 pint (1.75 litre) dish, and the ingredients will be 2¹/₂ lb (1.25 kg) chuck steak, 12 oz (350 g) ox kidney, 8 oz (225 g) mushrooms, 2 tablespoons flour, 1 pint (570 ml) stock; and for the pastry: 12 oz (350 g) self-raising flour, 6 oz (175 g) shredded suet.

Meringues (see page 577)

BEEFSTEAK AND KIDNEY PUDDING

◆

(Serves 4 people)

Properly made, I think this is one of the glories of real British cooking! For notes on steaming see page 597.

For the suet crust pastry
12 oz self-raising flour (350 g)
6 oz shredded suet (175 g)
salt and freshly milled black pepper
cold water, to mix
For the filling
1 lb chuck steak (450 g)
8 oz ox kidney (225 g)
2 level tablespoons well-seasoned flour
1 medium onion, sliced
cold water
Worcestershire sauce
salt and freshly milled pepper

A 2 pint (1.2 litre) pudding basin.

Make up the pastry to form an elastic dough that leaves the bowl clean, keep a quarter of it (for a lid), roll the rest out and line the well-buttered pudding basin with it. Next chop the steak and the kidney into fairly small cubes, toss them in the seasoned flour, then add them to the pastry-lined basin. Pop the slices of onion in here and there, then add enough cold water to reach almost to the top of the meat and sprinkle in a few drops of Worcestershire sauce and season.

Roll out the pastry lid, dampen its edges and put it in position on the pudding. Seal well and cover with a double sheet of foil – pleated in the centre to allow room for expansion while cooking – secure with string, and place it in a steamer over boiling water. Steam for 5 hours, topping up the boiling water half-way through.

OLD ENGLISH RABBIT PIE

◆

(Serves 4–6 people)

This is a really delicious pie, good for a dinner party – and if you can get hold of a wild rabbit for it so much the better.

Rich bread and butter pudding (see page 587)

For the suet crust pastry
12 oz self-raising flour (350 g)
6 oz shredded suet (175 g)
salt and freshly milled black pepper
cold water, to mix

For the filling
1 rabbit, approx. 3 lb (1.3 kg) in weight, cut into joints
2 medium onions, chopped fairly small
1 medium cooking apple, peeled, cored and sliced
8 oz unsmoked streaky bacon (225 g), in one piece
1 bay leaf
10 fl oz dry cider (275 ml)
15 fl oz stock or water (425 ml)
4 oz pitted prunes (110 g), chopped (weighed after the stones have been removed)
1¹/₂ oz plain flour (40 g) and 1¹/₂ oz butter (40 g), worked to a paste
¹/₂ whole nutmeg, grated
salt and freshly milled black pepper

Pre-heat the oven to gas mark 7, 425°F (220°C).

A 2¹/₂ pint (1.5 litre) pie-dish.

Wash the rabbit joints first of all, and place them (apart from the ribs, which don't carry much meat) in a large saucepan. Tuck in the onions and apple amongst the meat. Now remove the rind from the bacon, chop the meat up into 1 inch (2.5 cm) cubes and add that to the saucepan along with the bay leaf, a little salt and some freshly milled pepper. Pour in the cider and the stock, bring to simmering point, skim off any bits of scum, then put a lid on and leave to simmer gently for about an hour or until tender.

When they're cooked remove the rabbit pieces together with the bacon, apple and onion (with a draining spoon) and transfer them to the pie-dish, sprinkling in the chopped prunes as well. Now add the butter-and-flour mixture to the stock in the saucepan, adding it in tiny (peanut-size) pieces, stir them round over a medium heat to melt and thicken the sauce. Sprinkle in the nutmeg and when the sauce reaches simmering point pour it over the rabbit.

Now make up the suet crust pastry. Mix the flour, ¹/₂ teaspoon salt, pepper and suet together, then add enough cold water to form a fairly soft, elastic dough that leaves the bowl cleanly. Roll the dough out to a shape 1 inch (2.5 cm) wider than the top of the pie-dish, and cut a 1 inch (2.5 cm) wide strip all round. Dampen the rim of the dish and press this strip around it. Now dampen the rim of the pastry, and place the pastry lid in position on top, pressing well all round to seal the edges, which can be decorated with fluting if you like. Make a small hole for steam to escape, then bake for 30 minutes or until golden-brown.

QUICK FLAKY PASTRY
◆

This pastry is surely heaven-sent. It's uncomplicated, no trouble to roll out and handle, and tastes really crisp and flaky. That doesn't sound like the flaky pastry you've heard about? Probably not – the advanced version certainly calls for time and effort, which few of us can spare (though if you do have the time, there is a recipe for puff pastry on page 520). In this one, a much higher percentage of fat than in shortcrust is *grated* directly into the flour, so eliminating the repeated processes of rolling out, folding over and half-turning which make the traditional flaky pastry so time-consuming. The results, I'm quite certain, will speak for themselves. You can make this pastry with butter which will give a richer result, or equally well with block margarine.

QUICK FLAKY PASTRY
◆

8 oz plain flour (225 g)
6 oz butter or block margarine (175 g)
a pinch of salt
cold water, to mix

Take the fat hard from the fridge, weigh out the required amount, then wrap it in a piece of foil and return it to the freezing compartment of the refrigerator for 30–45 minutes. Meanwhile sift the flour and salt into a mixing bowl.

When you take the margarine out of the freezer hold it in the foil, dip it into the flour, then grate it on a coarse grater placed in the bowl over the flour. Keep dipping the fat down into the flour to make it easier to grate. At the end you will be left with a lump of grated fat in the middle of the flour, so now take a palette knife and start to distribute it into the flour – don't use your hands – just keep trying to coat all the pieces of fat with flour until the mixture is crumbly. Now add enough water to form a dough that leaves the bowl clean, using your hands to bring it all gently together. Pop the dough into a polythene bag and chill it for 30 minutes – this time in the main body of the fridge.

SAUSAGE ROLLS WITH QUICK FLAKY PASTRY

◆

(Makes about 24)

These are our once-a-year treat at home at Christmas, with some crunchy pickled onions and celery.

1 quantity quick flaky pastry (see page 515)
1 egg, beaten with 1 tablespoon milk
For the filling
1 lb good pork sausagemeat (450 g)
1 medium onion, grated
1 teaspoon sage

Pre-heat the oven to gas mark 7, 425°F (220°C).

Make up the pastry as on page 515, and leave it to rest in the refrigerator for 30 minutes. Mix the sausagemeat, onion and sage together thoroughly in a mixing bowl, then on a floured surface roll out the pastry to form an oblong (as thin as you can). Cut this oblong into three, then divide the sausagemeat mixture also into three, making three long rolls the same length as the pastry (if it's sticky sprinkle on some flour).

Place one roll of sausagemeat onto one strip of pastry. Brush the beaten egg mixture along one edge, then fold the pastry over and seal it as carefully as possible. Lift the whole thing up and turn it, so that when you put it down the sealed edge is underneath. Press lightly, then cut into individual rolls each about 2 inches (5 cm) long. Snip three V-shapes in the top of each roll with scissors, and brush with beaten egg. Then repeat all this with the other portions of pastry and meat.

Place all the rolls on a baking sheet and bake high in the oven for 20–25 minutes. Store the cooled sausage rolls in a tin, and warm them slightly before serving.

BŒUF EN CROÛTE

◆

(Serves 6 people)

Fillet steak is overwhelmingly expensive, but for a very special occasion it does make a most attractive and delicious main course, wrapped in pastry with a mushroom stuffing. (Illus. opposite p. 449.)

For the quick flaky pastry
6 oz plain flour (175 g)

4 oz margarine or butter (110 g)
cold water, to mix
For the filling
1³/₄ lb thick end fillet steak (800 g)
a little brandy
2 oz butter (50 g)
1 Spanish onion
12 oz mushrooms (350 g)
freshly grated nutmeg
1 egg, beaten
salt and freshly milled black pepper

Pre-heat the oven to gas mark 5, 375°F (190°C).

First of all make up the pastry as on page 515, pop it into a polythene bag and chill in the body of the fridge for 30 minutes. Meanwhile you can be trimming the meat, removing any excess fat and bits of sinew. Brush it all over with some brandy, rub ¹/₂ oz (10 g) of butter over it, place it in a roasting tin and cook for 40 minutes (basting it now and then with the juices). Then remove from the oven and leave to get quite cold.

Chop the onion and mushrooms as finely as possible, then melt the remaining butter in a small saucepan. Stir the onion into it, allow it to cook for 5 minutes, then stir in the mushrooms and continue to cook the mixture over a gentle heat (without a lid) for about 20–25 minutes, so that the juices will be drawn out of the mushrooms and onion and evaporate, leaving you with a concentrated mixture. The final mixture *mustn't* be too liquid. Season it then with salt, pepper and a grating of nutmeg.

When both the meat and mushroom mixture are ready, pre-heat the oven to gas mark 8, 450°F (230°C). Take the pastry from the fridge and roll it out to a rectangle approximately 14 × 10 inches (35 × 25 cm). Trim the edges (keep the trimmings for decoration), then spread half the mushroom and onion mixture over the centre. Place the fillet on top and the rest of the mixture on top of that: pat it down into a good shape. Now brush the edges of the pastry with beaten egg, and wrap the pastry like a parcel around the meat – if necessary brush the edges at each end and fold them over again.

Place the whole lot on a baking sheet, brush all over with beaten egg (including any decorations you have added), and bake in the oven for a further 30 minutes. This should be served cut into thick slices, together with some gravy made with the meat juices left in the roasting tin and some red wine.

ECCLES CAKES

♦

(Makes about 18–20)

These spicy currant pastries are, predictably, a northern delicacy – which are never better than when home-made.

1 quantity quick flaky pastry (see page 515)
For the filling
3 oz butter (75 g)
5 oz soft brown sugar (150 g)
5 oz currants (150 g)
1 teaspoon ground cinnamon
1/2 teaspoon freshly grated nutmeg
grated rind of 1 large orange
2 oz finely chopped mixed candied peel (50 g)
To glaze
milk and caster sugar

A greased baking sheet.

Make up the pastry as described on page 515, then wrap it in a piece of foil and place it in the freezing compartment of the fridge for 30 minutes.

Meanwhile, prepare the filling by first melting the butter in a small saucepan. Then take it off the heat and stir in all the filling ingredients quite thoroughly and leave it to cool.

Next turn the dough out onto a lightly floured surface. Roll it out to about 1/8 inch (3 mm) thick, then using a plain 3 1/2 inch (9 cm) cutter, cut the pastry into rounds. Put a teaspoon of filling onto each round, then brush the edge of half the circle of pastry with water, and bring the other side up to seal it. Then bring the corners up to the centre and pinch to seal well. Now turn your sealed pastry parcel over, so that the seam is underneath, then gently roll it flat to about 1/4 inch thick (5 mm) and pat it into a round shape. Place all the parcels on the greased baking sheet and gash each one diagonally across three times, using a sharp knife. Now brush them with milk and sprinkle with caster sugar and bake them in the oven pre-heated to gas mark 7, 425°F (220°C), for about 15 minutes or until golden-brown. Then transfer them to a wire rack to cool.

PUFF PASTRY

———————— ♦ ————————

Some time ago I had almost given up on traditional puff pastry. It wasn't that I couldn't make it well, it was just that I couldn't spare the *time* to make it well! All that long resting and rolling never seemed to fit in with the rest of my life, and I would either leave it too long in the fridge (so that I couldn't roll it), or I would be impatient and not leave it long enough.

Then, a few years ago, my friend John Tovey showed me his method, which takes 30 minutes flat. Because his is the best I've ever tasted (invariably light and crisp), I no longer persevere with any of the other methods. His recipe follows, but first some general points about puff pastry.

WHAT IS PUFF PASTRY?

It is the pastry used for vol-au-vents, sausage rolls, mince pies, jam puffs, and toppings for savoury and fruit pies. Unlike shortcrust or suet crust pastries, both of which can be described as granular in texture, puff pastry is made up of a number of thin layers (although they're close together, they are in fact quite separate). This is achieved by layering the fat into the flour, rather than rubbing it in. The dough is also folded (more layering), and after folding sealed at the edges, so that air is trapped inside. During the baking the expansion of steam forces the layers up, and the pastry rises (hence the French name for puff pastries, *mille feuilles* or thousand leaves).

Finally, here are a few points to bear in mind when making puff pastry:

(1) Always use strong white flour, as this provides more elasticity than ordinary plain flour.

(2) The fat should be at room temperature when making the pastry, but the finished pastry should be thoroughly chilled before using (preferably overnight). The best combination of fat to use is half margarine and half lard.

(3) Allow the pastry to come back to room temperature before rolling out for use.

(4) Once rolled and cut out, the pastry should be allowed to chill again (15–20 minutes) before going into the oven.

(5) Dampen the baking sheet with cold water – to create a steamy atmosphere in the oven which encourages the pastry to rise.

(6) The oven *must* be hot: gas mark 8, 450°F (230°C). Use the shelf just above the centre of the oven.

WARNING!

Having assembled a quantity of beautifully layered puff pastry, remember that the trimmings you have left after rolling out and cutting will not be layered together laterally. So re-rolled trimmings will not rise up and layer in quite the same way as the pastry from the first rolling. I think it is best to keep the trimmings (in a polythene bag in the fridge) for later use as a pie crust or for *Richmond maids of honour* (see page 523).

As most of the recipes here use half the basic quantity, when you make it divide it into two and freeze one portion – it freezes beautifully.

JOHN TOVEY'S ROUGH PUFF PASTRY

♦

This, unlike my quick flaky pastry on page 515, is the real thing – perfect, puffy, flaky layers, which are very light and crisp.

1 lb strong plain flour (450 g), sifted with a pinch of salt
8 oz margarine (225 g), cut into ½ oz (10 g) pieces (i.e. 16 pieces)
8 oz lard (225 g), cut into ½ oz (10 g) pieces
10 fl oz iced water (275 ml), less 1 tablespoon
1 tablespoon lemon juice

Sift the flour and salt into a bowl, then add the pieces of fat. Now just flick them around to get them all coated with flour, but don't 'work' the pastry yet or attempt to mix them in. Make a well in the centre and pour in the iced water mixed with the lemon juice. Take a palette knife and make cuts across and across, turning the bowl around as you go so that you gently bring all the ingredients together. Work quickly, and as soon as you have a reasonable lump of mixture, turn it out onto a floured board – along with all the loose flour that's left.

Now, using your hands, lightly and gently shape the mixture into a brick shape, then take a large, long rolling-pin and (holding it right at the ends) make three quick depressions widthwise. Then, still keeping your hands at the ends of the pin (the pressure should not be directly over the pastry) roll the brick shape into an oblong roughly 13 inches (33 cm) long and 8 inches (20 cm) wide.

Fold one-third over to the centre, then the other third over that. Use your pin to press the edges firmly and trap the air. Now rest the pastry for 5 minutes, then lift it and flour the board. Give the pastry a quick quarter-turn and make three depressions again. Repeat the whole process three more times, remembering to keep your board and pin well floured throughout. Wrap the pastry in foil or polythene and chill well before using, preferably overnight.

Note Before attempting to roll the pastry out for use, do make sure you allow it to come back to room temperature.

VOL-AU-VENTS

Traditional vol-au-vents are rather fiddly things to make: they require a certain thickness of pastry to make room for the fillings, and then quite a bit of the soggy centre has to be scraped out and wasted. John Tovey has come up with the brilliant idea of simply baking small rounds of pastry, halving them, and sandwiching them together with a filling. The results are far crisper, with less pastry and more filling – a lighter, tastier product altogether.

BASIC VOL-AU-VENTS

♦

(Makes 12)

½ quantity (1 lb/450 g) John Tovey's rough puff pastry (see page 520)

milk or beaten egg

Pre-heat the oven to gas mark 8, 450°F (230°C).

Roll the pastry out to about ⅛ inch (3 mm) thick as evenly as possible, then using a 3½ inch (9 cm) fluted cutter cut out twelve rounds. Place these on a damp baking sheet, and leave them to rest for 10 minutes in a cool place or in the fridge. Brush each one with a little milk or beaten egg, and bake on a high shelf in the oven for 10–15 minutes.

When they are a good rich golden colour, remove them from the oven and transfer to a wire cooling tray. Slice each one in half horizontally (making sure you keep them in pairs, ready for re-assembling). If there is any uncooked pastry in the centre, scrape it out – but there should be only very little.

If you use the hot mushroom filling (see the following recipe) you can fill and serve the vol-au-vents straightaway, or else warm them through and fill when you are ready. For cold fillings such as the cream cheese one on page 522, fill and sandwich them together just before serving.

You can serve the vol-au-vents as a lunchtime snack with a salad (two per person) or as a first course (one to two per person). For buffet parties, or for serving with drinks, you can make small, bite-sized versions, using a 2 inch (5 cm) cutter. Remember that they shrink in width during cooking.

Note For the hot vol-au-vents, a little melted butter brushed over the surface before serving gives them a lovely sheen.

HOT MUSHROOM AND BACON FILLING

◆

8 oz mushrooms (225 g), roughly chopped
2 rashers back bacon, de-rinded and chopped
2 oz butter (50 g)
½ medium onion, chopped fairly small
1 oz flour (25 g)
8 fl oz single cream (225 ml)
freshly grated nutmeg
salt and freshly milled black pepper

Melt the butter gently in a pan, and soften the onion and bacon in it for about 5 minutes. Then stir in the mushrooms and cook over a gentle heat for about 6 more minutes, stirring now and then. Next sprinkle in the flour, and stir well to soak up all the juices. Add the cream, a little at a time, stirring well after each addition. Cook the mixture for about 5 minutes (still giving it the odd stir). Taste and season with as much salt, pepper and nutmeg as you think it needs. Finally spoon the filling onto the warm vol-au-vents and sandwich them together.

CREAM CHEESE AND HERB FILLING

◆

6 oz cream cheese (175 g)
2 cloves garlic, crushed
2 tablespoons finely chopped parsley
2 tablespoons snipped chives
salt and freshly milled black pepper

Simply mash the ingredients together, blending them thoroughly. Taste to check the seasoning, then use the mixture to sandwich the cold vol-au-vents together (being fairly generous with the filling) just before serving.

CREAM PUFFS

◆

(Makes 12)

These are a sweet 'afternoon tea' version of the basic vol-au-vent recipe.

½ quantity (1 lb/450 g) John Tovey's rough puff pastry (see page 520)
a little milk
2 tablespoons granulated sugar

For the filling
6 heaped teaspoons strawberry jam (or any other flavour)
5 fl oz whipped cream (150 ml)

Pre-heat the oven to gas mark 8, 450°F (230°C).

Roll and cut the pastry as in the vol-au-vents recipe on page 521. Brush each round on one side with milk, place it milk-side down on a saucer of granulated sugar, then bake on a baking sheet (sugar-side uppermost) to get a nice, sugary, crusty topping. Bake on a high shelf in the oven for 10–15 minutes, then split them, cool and sandwich together with jam and whipped cream. If you don't want to bother with a sugar-crusted topping, leave them plain and simply dust them with icing sugar before serving.

RICHMOND MAIDS OF HONOUR
♦

(Makes about 16)

These little puff pastry cheese cakes were said to have been created by the maids of honour at Richmond Palace in the sixteenth century.

¼ quantity (8 oz/225 g) John Tovey's rough puff pastry (see page 520)
a little icing sugar
For the filling
8 oz curd cheese (225 g)
1½ oz caster sugar (40 g)
grated rind of 1 lemon
1 oz ground almonds (25 g)
1 rounded tablespoon currants
1 large egg and 1 egg yolk
a little apricot jam

Pre-heat the oven to gas mark 6, 400°F (200°C).

Start by rolling out the pastry to ⅛ inch (3 mm) thick, then using a 3¼ inch (8 cm) fluted cutter cut out little circles and place them in tartlet tins.

Combine the cheese, caster sugar, lemon rind, ground almonds and currants in a bowl, then beat the egg and egg yolk together and add this as well. Mix, very thoroughly, with a fork until everything is evenly blended. Next, spoon the merest trace of jam into the base of each pastry case, and fill each one about two-thirds full with the cheese mixture. Bake them in the centre of the oven for about 25–30 minutes, by which time the mixture will have puffed right up and turned a lovely golden-brown.

Take them out of the oven and transfer them onto a wire rack to cool. Don't worry as you see the centres starting to sink down because that's absolutely correct and normal. When they're cool they'll look nice with a faint dusting of icing sugar sifted over.

CRÈME PATISSIÈRE
♦

(Makes 15 fl oz/425 ml)

This delicious custard cream makes an alternative – almost better – filling than fresh cream for all kinds of pastries.

15 fl oz milk (425 ml)
1 vanilla pod
5 egg yolks
4 oz caster sugar (110 g)
2 level tablespoons plain flour
1 level tablespoon cornflour
½ oz butter (10 g)

Pour the milk into a pan, and pop in the vanilla pod. Bring to the boil, then take the pan off the heat and leave for the milk to infuse. Whisk the egg yolks together with the caster sugar in a bowl, until the mixture is thick and creamy-coloured. Then gradually whisk in the flour and the cornflour.

Remove the vanilla pod from the milk, and pour the infused milk into the egg yolk mixture – stirring vigorously as you pour. Return the whole lot to the rinsed-out pan and bring to the boil over a medium heat (still stirring all the time). Simmer for 3 minutes and continue to beat briskly. As the mixture thickens lumps may form, but these will eventually beat out.

Take the pan off the heat, and finally beat in the butter. Transfer the cream to a bowl, and cover closely with a buttered sheet of greaseproof paper over the surface, to prevent a skin forming. Leave to get cold – but use the cream within 2–3 days.

Note After the cream has thickened you could add a little liqueur!

RICH FLAN PASTRIES
♦

I like a light, crunchy, nutty-flavoured pastry for 'special' open fruit flans. When making either of the two recipes that follow, I use 6 oz (175 g) plain flour which makes enough pastry to line an 8 inch (20 cm) flan tin and also make a lattice-work top.

CRISP CINNAMON FLAN
♦

(Serves 6 people)

6 oz plain flour (175 g)
1 teaspoon ground cinnamon
3 oz butter (75 g)
3 tablespoons caster sugar
3 egg yolks
For the filling
1 lb blackcurrants, gooseberries or loganberries (450 g)
2 tablespoons granulated sugar
1 rounded teaspoon arrowroot
To glaze
a little caster sugar

Pre-heat the oven to gas mark 6, 400°F (200°C).

An 8 inch (20 cm) flan tin, lightly-greased.

First prepare the pastry. Sift the flour with the cinnamon into a mixing bowl, then rub in the fat, stir in the sugar and use the egg yolks in place of liquid to mix the pastry to a dough. Pop it into a polythene bag and chill for an hour in the fridge before using.

Meanwhile prepare the filling by sprinkling the sugar over the fruit in a saucepan and heating gently until the juice begins to run. Then mix the arrowroot with enough cold water to make a smooth paste, mix this with the fruit and simmer till thickened.

To make the flan, roll out three-quarters of the pastry and line the flan tin with it, pricking the base with a fork. Now fill with the fruit mixture and arrange the remaining pastry in a lattice pattern over the top. Brush the top with cold water, dust with a little caster sugar, then bake on a baking sheet for 10 minutes. Reduce the heat to gas mark 5, 375°F (190°C), and cook for a further 35 minutes. Serve (warm or cold) with whipped cream.

LINZERTORTE

◆

(Serves 6 people)

This is a famous Austrian torte named after the town of Linz. The rich pastry flan is made with ground hazelnuts. If you can't get hold of cranberry jelly, redcurrant could be used.

6 oz plain flour (175 g)
3 oz hazelnuts (75 g), ground
2 oz icing sugar (50 g), sifted
finely grated rind of 1 lemon
¹⁄₄ teaspoon ground cinnamon
freshly grated nutmeg
4 oz butter (110 g)
2 egg yolks
For the filling
12 oz cranberry jelly (350 g)
2 teaspoons lemon juice
a little icing sugar

Pre-heat the oven to gas mark 5, 375°F (190°C).

A 9 inch (23 cm) round, fluted flan tin with a removable base, well-buttered.

First combine the flour, ground hazelnuts, icing sugar, lemon rind, cinnamon and a few gratings of whole nutmeg in a bowl, then rub in the butter until the mixture is crumbly. Stir in the egg yolks and form the mixture into a dough. Weigh a 5 oz (150 g) piece of the pastry dough and put it on one side. Roll out the rest on a floured surface to a 10 inch (25 cm) round. Place this in the base of the tin and, using your fingers, gradually ease the dough up the side of the tin so that it stands up above the edge. Smooth the base out with your hands.

Next, for the filling, mix the jelly with the lemon juice and spoon all but 2 tablespoons onto the pastry, smoothing it out evenly to the edge. Use the rest of the dough to make a lattice-work pattern on the top, with strips about ¹⁄₃ inch (¹⁄₂–1 cm) wide. Then go round the pastry edge with a fork, turning it over inside the edge of the tin to give about a ¹⁄₂ inch (1 cm) border all round.

Bake on a high shelf for 30 minutes, or until the pastry is golden-brown. Then, as soon as the flan comes out of the oven, use the reserved jelly to fill up the squares formed by the lattice. Sift icing sugar over the top and serve it warm or cold with whipped cream.

CHOUX PASTRY

———— ◆ ————

This is the light, crisp, airy pastry which is used to make éclairs, profiteroles, or savoury gougères. It puffs up in the oven until it is eventually set by the heat of the cooking. The airiness, in fact, is caused because choux has a high water content which during the cooking process is turned into steam, which forces the pastry shell outwards, and gives it some volume.

What's so good about choux is that it doesn't call for any particular pastry skills (like lightness of hand or careful rolling). Of course some people make hard work of it by recommending that it always has to be piped through piping bags. But personally – quite apart from the fact that piping requires experience and a steady hand – I find it a wasteful method; and I'm convinced that a freshly baked golden profiterole looks so much crustier if it's spooned, rather than piped, onto a baking sheet.

My own advice on choux pastry can be summarised as follows:

(1) Try to use strong plain flour, which (with its higher gluten content) gives crisper results than ordinary soft plain flour.

(2) Raising the oven temperature during the cooking, I have found, gives really crisp, well-risen choux.

(3) Choux pastry doesn't keep well, and it is best eaten as soon as possible. It will stay crisp for up to 4 hours, though I prefer to have mine ready just 2 hours before it is needed.

(4) Fillings, if put in too far in advance, make the pastry soggy. So it is advisable to fill the cakes, buns or whatever as near as possible to the time they are to be eaten.

BASIC CHOUX PASTRY

———— ◆ ————

5 fl oz cold water (150 ml)
2 oz butter (50 g), cut into small pieces
2½ oz strong plain flour (60 g)
1 teaspoon sugar (only for sweet choux pastry, otherwise use a seasoning of salt and pepper)
2 eggs, well beaten

Pre-heat the oven to gas mark 6, 400°F (200°C).

First of all, put the water in a medium-sized saucepan together with the pieces of butter, and leave on one side while you weigh out the flour.

As you are going to need to 'shoot' the flour quickly into the water and melted butter, fold a sheet of greaseproof paper to make a crease, then open it up again. Sift the flour straight onto the square of greaseproof. If the end product is going to be sweet, add the sugar to the flour; if it is to be savoury, season the flour well with salt and pepper instead.

Next, place the saucepan of water and butter over a moderate heat, and stir with a wooden spoon. As soon as the butter has melted and the mixture comes up to the boil, turn off the heat immediately as too much boiling will evaporate some of the water, then tip the flour in – all in one go – with one hand, while you beat the mixture vigorously with the other (you can do this with a wooden spoon, though an electric hand whisk will save you lots of energy).

Beat until you have a smooth ball of paste that has left the sides of the saucepan clean (probably this will take less than a minute). Then beat the beaten eggs in – a little at a time and mixing each addition in thoroughly before adding the next – until you have a smooth glossy paste.

At this stage grease a baking sheet lightly, then hold it under cold running water for a few seconds, and tap it sharply to get rid of excess moisture (this will help create a steamy atmosphere, which in turn helps the pastry to rise). Your choux pastry is then ready for any of the following recipes.

PROFITEROLES
◆

(Makes about 18)

Profiteroles – little choux buns filled with cream and covered in a chocolate sauce – make a rather special ending to a dinner party.

1 quantity choux pastry (see page 527)
For the filling
10 fl oz double cream (275 ml), whipped thick
For the chocolate sauce
8 oz plain chocolate (225 g)
3 tablespoons water

Pre-heat the oven to gas mark 6, 400°F (200°C).
A large baking sheet, greased and dampened.
Place teaspoons of choux pastry on the baking sheet, and then bake in the pre-heated oven for 10 minutes. After that, increase the heat to gas mark 7, 425°F (220°C), and bake for a further 15–20 minutes until the choux buns are crisp, light and a rich golden colour. Pierce the side of each one (to let out the steam), then cool them on a wire rack.

To make the chocolate sauce, melt the chocolate together with the water in a basin fitted over a saucepan of simmering water, stirring until you have a smooth sauce (see my note on chocolate, page 575).

Just before serving, split the choux buns in half, fill each one with a teaspoon of whipped cream, then join the halves together again. Pour the melted chocolate over them and serve immediately.

Note Don't be tempted to put the cream in too far in advance, because this tends to make them soggy.

CHOCOLATE AND HAZELNUT CHOUX BUNS

◆

(Makes 8 or 9)

These lovely, light, airy choux buns are filled and topped with a squidgy chocolate mousse mixture and coated with chopped nuts.

1 quantity choux pastry (see page 527)

For the mousse filling
6 oz plain chocolate (175 g)
3 large eggs, separated

For the topping
2 level tablespoons chopped, toasted hazelnuts

The mousse filling should be made several hours in advance. Melt the chocolate in a heatproof bowl set over a pan of barely simmering water. Then beat the egg yolks into the chocolate and allow the mixture to cool. Whisk the egg whites to the soft peak stage. Stir 1 tablespoon of the egg white into the chocolate mixture to loosen it, then carefully fold in the remainder. Cover the bowl and chill in the refrigerator for about 3 hours.

Pre-heat the oven to gas mark 6, 400°F (200°C). Place rough dessertspoons of the choux pastry on a greased and dampened baking sheet and bake, on a high shelf, for 10 minutes. Then increase the heat to gas mark 7, 425°F (220°C) for a further 20–25 minutes until the buns are nicely brown and puffy. Pierce the side of each one and cool on a wire cooling tray.

It's best not to put in the filling until about an hour before serving. All you do is slice the choux buns horizontally, but not quite in half, then place a spoonful of the chocolate mousse inside, spread a little over the top using the back of the spoon, and finally, sprinkle each one with chopped hazelnuts.

COFFEE ÉCLAIRS

◆

(Makes 8 or 9)

You can, of course, make these as the choux buns in the preceding recipe, but if you want to serve the classic éclair shape you'll need to use a piping bag.

1 quantity choux pastry (see page 527)
For the filling
1 tablespoon instant coffee powder
1 tablespoon caster sugar
2 teaspoons boiling water
10 fl oz double cream (275 ml)
For the icing
2 teaspoons instant coffee powder
1 tablespoon boiling water
5 oz icing sugar (150 g), sifted

Pre-heat the oven to gas mark 6, 400°F (200°C).

Spoon the choux pastry into a large nylon piping bag, fitted with a plain ½ inch (1 cm) piping nozzle. Pipe the mixture onto greased and rinsed baking sheets in lengths just over 3 inches (7.5 cm).

Bake the éclairs on a high shelf for 10 minutes, then increase the heat to gas mark 7, 425°F (220°C), for a further 10 minutes. Remove them from the oven to a wire cooling tray and make a slight hole in the side of each one.

For the filling, dissolve the coffee and sugar in the boiling water. Beat the cream till thickened and add the coffee mixture to it, stirring to blend it evenly. Now wash and dry the piping bag and nozzle thoroughly; spoon the coffee cream into it. Slit the éclairs along one side, pipe in the cream and carefully press the tops gently back over the cream.

Next prepare the icing. In a small basin dissolve the coffee in the boiling water, sift the icing sugar into it and stir. It should now be the consistency of thick cream. Finally, dip the tops of the éclairs into the icing and let the excess drip back into the bowl before returning each one to the wire rack.

Note As an alternative filling for choux buns, profiteroles or éclairs you could use the *Crème patissière* on page 524. For a coffee flavour, add 1 dessertspoon instant coffee dissolved in 1 teaspoon warm water, and for a chocolate filling combine the cream with 2 oz (50 g) melted plain chocolate.

GOUGÈRE WITH CHEESE

♦

(Serves 2 people)

This is a ring of cheese-flavoured choux pastry, crisp on the outside and slightly squidgy inside. It is nice served with a salad for a lunch dish.

1 quantity choux pastry (see page 527)
2¹/₂ oz Cheddar cheese (60 g), grated
¹/₂ teaspoon mustard powder
a good pinch of cayenne pepper
1 egg, beaten
salt and freshly milled black pepper

Pre-heat the oven to gas mark 6, 400°F (200°C).

Make the choux paste in exactly the same way as outlined on page 527 – seasoning with salt and pepper instead of adding sugar – except that immediately after you have added the beaten eggs, also add 2 oz (50 g) of the cheese, the mustard and the cayenne pepper.

Now spoon dessertspoons of the mixture onto a greased and ready-dampened baking sheet, so that they touch each other and form a circle that is approximately 7 inches (18 cm) in diameter.

Brush the choux circle with some beaten egg, then sprinkle the remaining grated cheese all round the top. Bake in the pre-heated oven for 10 minutes, then increase the heat to gas mark 7, 425°F (220°C), and cook for a further 20–25 minutes. Serve it hot and puffy, straight from the oven.

Note To make this recipe extra special, you could use Swiss Gruyère cheese instead of Cheddar.

SEE ALSO

Bacon and egg pie
Caramelised apple flan
Cheese and onion quichelets
Eighteenth-century creamed apple flan
Flaky fish pie
Plum and soured cream flan
Spinach and cream cheese quiche
Thick onion tart

CAKES

◆

One of the cheapest ways to add a touch of luxury to our everyday eating, I think, is to indulge in a little home baking now and then. Some of the chief contributors to the boredom of our modern synthetic diet are those dull factory-made cakes and flavourless biscuits which come so prettily wrapped on our supermarket shelves. Eating of course is for sustenance – but surely for enjoyment too: and hasn't the sheer blandness of mass production taken away some of the joy?

If you have never done any home baking, or have lapsed for some time, I do hope you'll revive the art. There's so much personal pleasure in it and a sort of wholesomeness about a kitchen filled with the aroma of baking – a lovely way to make your family feel spoiled.

I've never believed, as some people seem to, that you either have a gift for cake-making or you don't. Confidence is the key and nothing can shake one's confidence like having a failure with a cake into which so much care has gone. So perhaps the first thing we ought to do is to try to understand what is actually happening when a cake is being baked – because any interference with this process could end in the failure we all want to avoid!

WHAT HAPPENS WHEN YOU BAKE A CAKE?

◆

When fat and sugar are mixed together – the process is called creaming –little bubbles of air are being trapped in the mixture, each one surrounded by a film of fat (which is why the mixture changes colour during creaming as the trapped air creates a foam). It is this air which produces the lightness in the finished cake, but unless beaten egg is added to the mixture the fat would collapse and the air escape during cooking. The egg white conveniently forms a layer around each air bubble, and as the temperature of the cake rises in the heat of the oven this layer coagulates and forms a rigid wall round each bubble, preventing it from bursting and ruining the texture of the cake.

During the baking the bubbles of air will expand and the cake will 'rise'. At the same time the stretchy gluten in the flour – which has formed an elastic network round the air bubbles – will stretch until, at a higher temperature, it loses its elasticity and the shape of the cake becomes fixed.

But until that moment is reached the expansion process must be allowed to continue uninterrupted. Which is why a) the cake should be baked as soon as it is mixed and b), even more importantly, the oven door should *never* be opened in the early stages of cooking: the temperature will drop suddenly and the air in the cake will stop expanding and actually contract. The whole structure of the cake will then sink back because there's nothing to prop it up. So, remember, never look at a cake until three-quarters of the cooking time has elapsed.

CAKE TINS

Here we have another possible cause of failure. There are so many differing sizes of cake tin available, and even a ½ inch (1 cm) difference all round can often upset both the timing of a recipe and the finished size of the cake. It is therefore *important* to use the correct sized tin. In my recipes I usually try to keep to 7 or 8 inch tins (which metrically are approximately 18 or 20 cm – the difference in volume is minimal). These are fairly standard sizes, though some manufacturers come up with some very strange alternatives in the name of metrication.

SPONGE SANDWICH TINS

To get a properly risen cake it is most important to use a sponge tin that is at least 1 inch (2.5 cm) deep. The cause of many a flat sponge cake is a sponge tin that is too shallow.

LOAF TINS

These too come in a confusing array of sizes, and again I have kept all my recipes to two sizes – either the 2 lb (900 g) capacity loaf tin, or else a slightly narrower tin with a base measurement of 7½ inches (19 cm) by 3½ inches (9 cm).

NON-STICK SURFACES

Normally I use non-stick bakeware simply as an extra aid, never relying on it exclusively. In practice I use it as I would normal bakeware, greasing and lining it by the traditional method. I just find this more reliable.

CAKE INGREDIENTS

PLAIN FLOUR

Unless yeast is used in a recipe (e.g. *Hot cross buns* on page 53) ordinary soft flour is always best for cake recipes requiring plain flour. This has a lower protein content than strong flour, and therefore produces that finer, shorter texture suitable for cakes, biscuits and scones.

SELF-RAISING FLOUR

On those occasions when a raising agent is called for, it is usually more convenient to use a self-raising flour since this has a standard amount of raising agent already added to it. From time to time a recipe might need rather more (or less) raising power, in which case plain flour plus the appropriate quantity of baking powder is used.

WHOLEWHEAT FLOUR

Nowadays most food scientists are agreed about the lack of fibre in our diet, and even the commercial giants are replacing the bran which was milled out of the flour in the first place (thus we see 'bran' finding its way into countless breakfast cereals, biscuits and cakes). To meet the problem at home you can, if you wish, switch over completely to wholewheat flour in baking. I'm delighted to report that most of my wholewheat experiments with cakes have been very successful, which I hope some of the following recipes will prove.

BAKING POWDERS

These are normally a mixture of bicarbonate of soda and another acid-acting chemical, like cream of tartar. Very often, though, one needs far less raising power than these mixtures give – which explains why some recipes require bicarbonate of soda on its own. Sometimes one needs an extra lift, as when baking with wholewheat flour or when using the all-in-one method (see page 541), and more baking powder is required.

FATS

Flavour-wise it is said you can't beat butter in baking. And certainly for purists that's probably true – I see one leading chain-store proudly advertises 'made with all butter' on its cake wrappings! My own opinion is that margarine – now it has improved so much in flavour – is very good for baking, and with the advent of soft margarine and the all-in-one method of making sponges (see the recipes), I actually hardly ever use butter for baking. Very occasionally I use lard, as in the *Marmalade cake* recipe (see page 551).

Fats should usually be at room temperature for cake-making. Allow 1 hour to soften butter, block margarine and lard. Soft or whipped margarines can be used straight from the fridge (although in practice I usually allow half an hour at room temperature).

SUGAR

I believe caster sugar is worth paying the extra for in baking (especially for sponges), since it does give a finer texture. Some people manage successfully to make granulated sugar into caster sugar in a liquidiser and to save money, but be warned; if you over-do it you can finish up with a powdery 'icing' sugar and won't have saved anything! In wholefood cakes, soft brown sugar (or sometimes demerara) can be used and indeed is preferable.

EGGS

As discussed on page 21, eggs for all cooking purposes should be at room temperature. If they are too cold or used straight from the fridge, they curdle more easily. So remember to remove them from the fridge a couple of hours before beginning baking.

AIR

Yes, another all-important ingredient. Air means lightness in your cakes, and to incorporate it you need (i) large and roomy mixing bowls, and (ii) always to sift the flour, holding your sieve up high to give the flour a good airing on its way to the bowl. Careful folding with a metal spoon, which cuts cleanly into the mixture, enables you to retain the precious air incorporated at the mixing stage.

WHAT WENT WRONG?

◆

I hope you're not reading this section because things *have* gone wrong! It's really here to try to prevent that happening, or at least to reassure you.

HIT OR MISS

One of the primary reasons why cakes sometimes fail is the recipe itself. It might be wrong or simply too vague, like some of grandma's hand-me-downs which never mention details like tin sizes or oven temperature. Be suspicious of any recipe that does not offer you all the information you need. But if it is precise, then follow it precisely: if it calls for an 8 inch (20 cm) square tin and you've only got a 6 inch (15 cm) round tin, it *does* matter.

OVER-ANXIETY

It is always tempting to take a peep in the oven to see how your creation is getting on. As I mentioned before, impatient cooks are inviting disaster.

CURDLING

If you are using a creaming method (see page 538), it can sometimes happen that the beaten eggs are added to the sugar-and-fat mixture too quickly, causing the whole mixture to separate. This 'breaking up' means that some of the air incorporated at the creaming stage will escape and the finished cake will be slightly heavier. For beginners the way to avoid this is to add the beaten eggs just a teaspoonful at a time, whisking preferably with an electric hand whisk. If it does curdle, don't worry: the cake won't be as light but it's not a disaster.

FRUIT SINKING

This is usually a fault in the recipe. It means the mixture is too slack (too liquid) to hold the fruit. Fruit cakes need a larger proportion of flour in order to hold the fruit evenly. Glacé cherries and other sugar-coated fruit should be rinsed and dried (and chopped if large) before adding to a cake mixture. Both the size of the fruit and sugar coating can cause sinking.

OVER-BROWNING

Sometimes the top of a cake becomes brown before the centre is cooked. To prevent this, check the cake three-quarters of the way through the cooking time and, if necessary, fit a protective circle of double greaseproof paper (with a hole about the size of a 50p piece in the centre) over the top of the cake.

But above all don't be daunted. Always remember the good things that go into a home-made cake, and even if the finished product does happen to have sunk a bit, it will still taste delicious.

Notes on Preparation
◆

LINING TINS

Where a recipe asks you to line a tin, always do so. It may seem like an extra bother, but it only takes a few moments and it makes turning out the cake far easier. Greaseproof paper is used in most cases, but for delicate cakes like sponges I use silicone paper (from good stationers) for a base lining, as it *never* sticks. Remember to allow an extra couple of inches (5 cm or so) so that the lining paper extends above the rim of the tin.

For a round tin

Cut a strip of paper slightly longer than the circumference of the tin, and fold back about an inch (2.5 cm) along its length. Snip this at intervals with scissors, cutting at a slight angle right up to the fold. Grease the tin, then press the paper around the sides. You will find the snipped edge will overlap on the base of the tin to give a snug fit. Finally, cut a circle of paper – using the tin as a template – to fit over the snipped paper at the base.

For a square tin
Cut a piece of paper to size by measuring the length and width of the tin and adding twice its depth. Centre the tin on the paper, then make four cuts from the paper's edge right up to the corners of the tin. Grease the tin and fit the paper inside, folding and overlapping at the corners. Then add a base paper, again using the tin as a template.

GREASING TINS

In my experience so-called non-stick tins sometimes do! So I recommend that you always grease cake tins regardless. The best thing is to use some of the same sort of fat as is used for the cake mixture. Smear it evenly all over the inside of the tin, making sure you get into the corners.

FLOURING TINS

Some recipes state that the tins should also be lightly dusted with flour. This is unnecessary unless for some reason the cake needs to be extra crisp at the edges.

COOLING AND STORING CAKES

———— ♦ ————

All cakes have to be completely cooled on a wire cooling rack (which allows air to circulate around them) before storing.

For storage, cake tins are definitely better than plastic boxes, because metal is non-porous. However carefully you wash plastic, smells linger on. The previous occupant of a plastic container can taint the next, and mould can develop. Also never store cakes and biscuits in the same tin, as the moisture from the cake will make the biscuits soggy. For short-term storing an aluminium foil wrapping can be used, but if you're storing a rich fruit cake for a longer period, then use a double layer of greaseproof paper on the inside and foil on the outside – because the acid in the fruit can corrode the foil if it comes into direct contact with it and a mould will develop.

FREEZING CAKES

———— ♦ ————

Cakes freeze very well especially those cakes, like say sponges, which are to be eaten as though they were freshly baked. Some cakes, however, have to mature – like Dundee cakes – and this process is better in a storing-tin than in a freezer.

SOME DIFFERENT METHODS OF CAKE-MAKING

◆

CREAMING

This is the term used when a cake is made with butter or block margarine (soft or whipped margarines are unsuitable). It means that the fat and sugar are beaten together till creamy and pale: the eggs are then beaten into this mixture, bit by bit. This method is explained in the *Classic Victoria sponge* recipe (page 539).

RUBBING-IN

A cake made by this method starts off with the fat being rubbed into the flour – exactly the same as for shortcrust pastry. Butter, block margarine and lard can all be used. It is a very easy method – see the *Marmalade cake* recipe (page 551).

BOIL-AND-BAKE

In recipes of this kind the fat and liquid are boiled together before the flour is added. Again, a very straightforward method, as in the *Sticky date cake* recipe (page 550).

ALL-IN-ONE

Exactly as the name suggests, these cakes are mixed all in one go. All the ingredients go into the bowl together and the mixing is done in seconds. Soft margarine is tailor-made for this method.

SPONGE CAKES

◆

I have to admit that since soft margarine came onto the market and sponge cakes can be made simply by combining all the ingredients in the bowl at once, I very rarely make the classic Victoria sponge, which is a lot more work. However, there will probably always be those who prefer cakes made with butter for that bit of extra flavour. Anyway, for those who are new to cake-making or those who would like to experiment, here are my own notes on the differences between the various methods of sponge-making:

CLASSIC (VICTORIA) SPONGE

This provides a good buttery flavour and, if skilfully made, should have a light texture; but it is not quite as moist or light-textured as an all-in-one sponge, especially after storing. It is also richer and fattier.

ALL-IN-ONE SPONGE MADE WITH SOFT MARGARINE

The texture of this is very light – it really melts in the mouth – and its flavour is slightly less rich than the Victoria made with butter.

ALL-IN-ONE SPONGE MADE WITH BUTTER

The all-in-one method can be used with soft butter that has been brought up to room temperature and whipped a little before adding to the rest of the ingredients. It isn't as light in texture as the soft margarine version, but the bonus is its richer buttery flavour.

WHOLEWHEAT ALL-IN-ONE SPONGE

I have found that wholewheat flour sometimes works well in an all-in-one mix with the addition of 2½ teaspoons baking powder. I say sometimes, because *some* British wholewheat flours seem to cause the sponge to sink, whereas imported American, Canadian or 'blended from more than one country' brands work better, due to their gluten content. You might find it safer to use 85 per cent wheatmeal flour plus 1 teaspoon baking powder.

WHISKED FATLESS SPONGE

This is extremely light in texture, but the absence of fat can give a hint almost of rubberiness. This one must be eaten as fresh as possible: it can become stale by the next day.

There are of course other, rather more complicated sponge recipes, such as a Genoese or an oil-based sponge. But as this is essentially a basic cookery course I have not included them here. Recipes for them can be found in *Delia Smith's Book of Cakes* (Coronet Books).

CLASSIC VICTORIA SPONGE
— ♦ —

I find a 4 oz (110 g) mixture (i.e. 4 oz or 110 g each of flour, sugar and butter to 2 eggs) gives just the right depth and balance between cake and filling, if 7 inch (18 cm) tins are used. However, if you like your sponges to have more depth, you can increase this mixture to 6 oz (175 g) each of flour, sugar and butter and use 3 eggs; and these quantities can also be used for 8 inch (20 cm) tins. Allow an extra 5–10 minutes' cooking time.

4 oz butter (110 g), at room temperature
4 oz caster sugar (110 g)
2 large eggs
a few drops pure vanilla essence
4 oz self-raising flour (110 g), sifted
To finish
jam and sifted icing sugar

Pre-heat the oven to gas mark 3, 325°F (170°C).

Two 7 inch (18 cm) sponge tins at least 1 inch (2.5 cm) deep, greased, and the bases lined with greaseproof paper.

In a medium-sized mixing bowl, cream the butter and sugar together until you get a pale, fluffy mixture that drops off the spoon easily (an electric hand whisk speeds this up considerably, but a wooden spoon will do). Then in a separate jug or bowl beat the eggs together thoroughly, then add them a little at a time, beating well after each addition. For a beginner I recommend just a teaspoonful at a time: if you add it like this, just a little at a time and beating after each addition, the mixture won't curdle.

When the eggs have been incorporated, stir in a few drops of vanilla essence, then take a metal spoon (which will cut and fold the flour in much better than a wooden spoon). Have the flour in a sieve resting on a plate, then lift the sieve high above the bowl and sift about a quarter of the flour onto the mixture. Then replace the sieve on the plate, and lightly and gently fold the flour into the mixture (if you beat the flour in, you'll lose some precious air). Then repeat until all the flour is incorporated. Lifting the sieve high above the bowl will ensure the flour gets a good airing before it reaches the mixture.

Now that the flour has been added you should have a mixture that will drop off the spoon easily when you tap it on the side of the bowl (this is what is called a good 'dropping' consistency). If the consistency is not right, add 1–2 teaspoons of hot water.

Now divide the mixture equally between the two tins – if you want to be very precise you could place both tins on balance scales (I've never bothered, though, because I don't mind if one sponge is fractionally larger than the other). Place them on the centre shelf of the oven, and they'll take about 25–30 minutes to cook. When they are cooked the centres will feel springy when lightly touched with a little finger tip and no imprint remains.

When you are satisfied that the sponges are cooked, remove them from the oven, then after about 1 minute turn them out onto a wire cooling tray, loosening them around the edges with a palette knife first. Then carefully peel off the base papers and leave the cakes to cool completely before sandwiching them together with jam and sifting a little icing sugar over the surface.

Note A wholewheat Victoria sponge can be made using 4 oz (110 g) wholewheat flour plus 1 teaspoon baking powder.

ALL-IN-ONE SPONGE

◆

For me this is the best sponge of all, and should work even if you've never made a cake before in your life.

4 oz self-raising flour (110 g), sifted
1 teaspoon baking powder
4 oz soft margarine or butter (110 g), at room temperature
4 oz caster sugar (110 g)
2 large eggs
2–3 drops pure vanilla essence
To finish
lemon curd or jam (with fresh cream; optional) and sifted icing sugar

Pre-heat the oven to gas mark 3, 325°F (170°C).

Two 7 inch (18 cm) sponge tins, no less than 1 inch (2.5 cm) deep, lightly-greased and lined with greaseproof paper (also greased) or silicone paper.

Take a large roomy mixing bowl, and sift flour and baking powder into it, holding the sieve high to give the flour a good airing. Then simply add all the other ingredients to the bowl, and whisk them – preferably with an electric hand whisk – till thoroughly combined. If the mixture doesn't drop off a wooden spoon easily when tapped on the side of the bowl, then add 1 or 2 teaspoons of tap-warm water, and whisk again.

Now divide the mixture between the two prepared tins, level off and bake on the centre shelf of the oven for about 30 minutes. When cooked leave them in the tins for only about 30 seconds, then loosen the edges by sliding a palette knife all round and turn them out onto a wire cooling rack. Peel off the base papers carefully and, when cool, sandwich the cakes together with lemon curd or jam (or jam and fresh cream), and dust with icing sugar.

All-in-one chocolate sponge
Add 1 tablespoon of cocoa powder to the basic ingredients. Omit the vanilla essence.

All-in-one coffee and walnut sponge
Add 2 oz (50 g) of finely chopped walnuts, plus 1 tablespoon of instant coffee powder mixed with 1 dessertspoon of hot water, to the basic ingredients. Omit the vanilla essence. For filling and topping use *Coffee cream mousseline* (page 545).

All-in-one orange or lemon sponge

Add the grated rind of a medium orange or lemon, plus 1 dessertspoon of the juice, to the basic ingredients. Omit the vanilla essence.

All-in-one orange or lemon layer cake

Use 6 oz (175 g) flour, margarine and sugar to 1½ teaspoons baking powder and 3 large eggs, together with the orange or lemon flavour as above, in two 7 inch (18 cm) tins. Bake for 30 minutes, then when the cakes are cold, slice each one carefully in half horizontally. Use a lemon or orange curd filling (page 544) to sandwich the four layers together, and dust with icing sugar.

WHISKED FATLESS SPONGE

♦

This is a very good recipe for those attempting to cut the fat content in their diet – and one or two slices will not contain a great deal of egg.

3 large eggs
3 oz caster sugar (75 g)
3 oz plain flour (75 g), sifted
½ teaspoon baking powder
To finish
a little caster sugar, jam and sifted icing sugar

Pre-heat the oven to gas mark 4, 350°F (180°C).

Two 7 inch (18 cm) sandwich tins, liberally brushed with melted fat and the bases lined with greaseproof paper (also greased).

First separate the eggs; placing the whites in a very large grease-free bowl and the yolks in a separate one. Now add the sugar to the yolks and whisk, either with an electric hand whisk or by hand, until the mixture is very pale and fluffy and has thickened – about 5 minutes with an electric whisk. Now wash and dry the whisk very thoroughly and use it to beat the whites until stiff but not dry.

Next with the aid of a large metal spoon fold the egg whites into the yolk-and-sugar mixture alternately with the sifted flour and baking powder, starting and finishing with egg whites. Then spoon an equal quantity of the mixture into the prepared tins and bake in the centre of the oven for 20–25 minutes. The sponges are cooked when they feel firm and springy in the centre and have begun to shrink slightly away from the sides of the tins.

Leave to cool in the tins for 3 minutes, then have ready a sheet of greaseproof paper, sprinkled with a little caster sugar. Turn the cakes out onto this before transferring to a wire rack to finish cooling. Then sandwich them together with jam, and dust the top with icing sugar.

Note It's important to eat a fatless sponge as fresh as possible.

LEMON CURD BUTTERFLY CAKES

♦

(Makes 12–13 cakes)

These little sponge cakes are baked in small paper baking cases, which can usually be bought at good stationers.

6 oz self-raising flour (175 g)
a pinch of salt
4 oz soft margarine (110 g), at room temperature
4 oz caster sugar (110 g)
2 large eggs
1 dessertspoon lemon juice
grated rind of 1 lemon
For the filling
1 quantity lemon curd (see page 544)

Pre-heat the oven to gas mark 5, 375°F (190°C).

A patty tin, greased, and some paper baking cases.

First of all make up the filling, and leave to get quite cold.

To make the cakes, combine all the ingredients together in a bowl and beat till absolutely smooth (1–2 minutes). Then, using a spoon, drop an equal quantity of the mixture into the paper cases, and sit the cases in the patty tin – give it two or three light taps to settle the cake mixture. Then bake on the shelf just above the centre of the oven for 15–20 minutes or until the cakes are well risen and golden. Then remove them to a wire rack and leave to cool.

When they're cool, take a sharp knife and cut the top off each at an angle in a circle about ¹/₂ inch (1 cm) from the edge of the cake, so that you remove a cone-shaped round, leaving a cavity in the centre. Cut each cone in half (top to bottom) and set aside. Fill the cavity of each cake with the lemon curd then sit the two cone-shaped pieces of cake on top like butterfly wings.

SPONGE TOPPINGS AND FILLINGS

♦

These are an important part of a finished sponge, and while jam in the centre and icing sugar on top are delicious, there are a great many possible alternatives. What starts out as an ordinary sponge can be made into something really special.

One of the little campaigns that runs through my cooking is to try to reduce the amount of sugar in recipes, wherever possible and desirable. Consequently I have avoided those sticky sweet icings and butter creams (which taste even worse made with margarine) in this section. Instead here are several delicious alternatives, that aren't too much bother and taste far better. Quantities are for the standard sponge recipes on the previous pages.

FRESH LEMON CURD

♦

Home-made lemon curd is so easy a child can make it, and it is a beautifully fresh-tasting filling. The quantity here is enough to sandwich a layer cake.

grated rind and juice of 1 large, juicy lemon
3 oz caster sugar (75 g)
2 large eggs
2 oz unsalted butter (50 g)

Place the grated lemon rind and sugar in a bowl. In another bowl whisk the lemon juice together with the eggs, then pour this mixture over the sugar. Add the butter cut into little pieces, and place the bowl over a pan of barely simmering water. Stir frequently till thickened – about 20 minutes. Then cool the curd and use it to sandwich the sponges together, spreading it thickly. If you want to make this ahead, store in a clean dry jar with a screw-top lid. It is best eaten within a week.

Note For *orange curd* replace the lemon with 1 large orange.

COFFEE CREAM MOUSSELINE

— ◆ —

This is a soft, fluffy, not-too-sweet creamy filling; it goes very well with the *Coffee and walnut sponge* on page 541.

2¹/₂ oz caster sugar (60 g)
4 tablespoons water
2 large egg yolks
5 oz unsalted butter (150 g), at room temperature
1 tablespoon instant coffee powder dissolved in
1 tablespoon hot water

Place the sugar and water together in a small saucepan and slowly bring it to the boil – keep an eye on it and make sure the sugar has dissolved completely before it comes to the boil. Then let it simmer gently for about 10-15 minutes or until the mixture forms a 'thread' when pressed between thumb and forefinger (to do this take some on a teaspoon, cool it a little, and dip your finger in cold water before testing). If you have a cooking thermometer the temperature should be between 218°F (103°C) and 220°F (105°C).

Now whisk the egg yolks in a bowl (place the bowl on a damp tea towel to steady it), then pour the sugar syrup onto the egg yolks in a steady stream, whisking all the time. Then whisk the butter in, about 1 oz (25 g) at a time, till you have a smooth fluffy cream. Now whisk in the dissolved coffee, and use the cream to sandwich the cake and to decorate the top (along with some walnut halves perhaps). This fills and tops a 7 or 8 inch (18 or 20 cm) sponge.

CHOCOLATE AND SOURED CREAM FILLING

— ◆ —

This has a sophisticated, dark bitter chocolate flavour and is not at all sweet (should you want it sweeter, add 1 dessertspoon of caster sugar).

5 oz plain dessert chocolate (150 g)
5 fl oz soured cream (150 ml)

Break the chocolate into a basin fitted over a pan of barely simmering water, add the soured cream too, and stir – keeping the heat low until the chocolate has melted. Then remove the pan from the heat and as soon as the mixture has cooled, spread it over the centre and top of a 7 or 8 inch (18 or 20 cm) chocolate sponge. A few walnuts or hazelnuts are nice for decoration.

CHOCOLATE FUDGE FILLING AND TOPPING

◆

This makes enough to fill and top a 7 or 8 inch (18 or 20 cm) cake.

3 oz granulated sugar (75 g)
3 fl oz evaporated milk (75 ml)
4 oz unsweetened cooking chocolate or plain dessert chocolate (110 g)
1½ oz butter or soft or hard margarine (40 g)
2 drops pure vanilla essence

To start with combine the sugar and evaporated milk in a heavy saucepan. Place the pan over a low heat and allow the sugar to dissolve, stirring frequently. When all the granules of sugar have melted, bring the mixture to the boil and simmer very gently for 6 minutes – this time without stirring.

Take the pan off the heat, stir in the chocolate (broken into small pieces) and keep stirring until the chocolate has melted. Finally stir in the butter and vanilla essence.

Now transfer the mixture to a bowl, cool, then cover with cling film and chill for a couple of hours until it has thickened to a spreadable consistency.

FAMILY CAKES

◆

In the section that follows I have selected some of my own favourite cake recipes, and have attempted at the same time to cover a variety of cake-making methods.

OATMEAL PARKIN

◆

One of the fascinating things about this traditional northern recipe is that it's nothing out of the ordinary when it's freshly made – but if kept in an airtight tin it matures to a lovely chewy consistency. One week's keeping is enough, but two weeks' is even better! It is also worth tracking down the darker syrup available as this gives an even better flavour than the mixture of golden syrup and black treacle.

5 oz dark syrup (150 g), or 4 oz golden syrup (110 g)
plus 1 oz black treacle (25 g)
3 oz margarine (75 g)
3 oz soft brown sugar (75 g)
6 oz medium oatmeal (175 g)
3 oz self-raising flour (75 g), sifted
1¹/₂ teaspoons ground ginger
a pinch of salt
1 small egg, beaten
1 dessertspoon milk

Pre-heat the oven to gas mark 1, 275°F (140°C).

One 6 inch (15 cm) square cake tin, lightly-greased.

First weigh a saucepan on the scales, then weigh the syrup or syrup and treacle into it. Then add the margarine and sugar to the saucepan and place it over a gentle heat until the margarine has melted down. Don't go away and leave it unattended, as for this one you do not want it to boil.

Meanwhile measure the oatmeal, flour and ginger into a mixing bowl, add a pinch of salt, then gradually stir in the warmed syrup mixture until everything is thoroughly blended. Next add the beaten egg and lastly the milk. Now pour the mixture into the prepared tin and bake in the centre of the oven for about 1¹/₂ hours or until the centre feels springy to the touch.

Then cool the parkin in the tin for 30 minutes before turning out. Don't worry too much if the parkin sinks slightly in the middle – it sometimes happens in Yorkshire too, I'm told.

DATE, APPLE AND WALNUT LOAF

◆

A very easy and deliciously wholesome cake – which I particularly like to make for a picnic or a packed lunch.

4 oz soft margarine (110 g)
6 oz soft brown sugar (175 g)
2 eggs, lightly beaten
4 oz wholewheat flour (110 g)
4 oz plain flour (110 g)
a pinch of salt
1¹/₂ teaspoons baking powder
1 small cooking apple, peeled, cored and roughly chopped
4 oz walnuts (110 g), roughly chopped
3 oz pitted dates (75 g), roughly chopped
3 or 4 tablespoons milk

Pre-heat the oven to gas mark 4, 350°F (180°C).

A loaf tin with base measurements of 3¹/₂ × 7¹/₂ inches (9 × 19 cm), well-buttered.

Put the margarine, sugar, eggs, flours, salt and baking powder into a large mixing bowl (sifting the flours in), then whisk them together with an electric hand whisk until thoroughly combined. Next add the apple, followed by the walnuts and pitted dates. Finally add the milk, then mix it all well before transferring the mixture to the prepared tin. Spread it out evenly, then bake for 1 hour or until the loaf feels springy in the centre and a skewer inserted in the middle comes out clean.

Let the cake cool for a minute or two in the tin, then turn it out onto a wire tray. Store in an airtight tin as soon as cold.

Note Chopped prunes (the sort you don't soak) can be used for a change instead of apples.

SQUIDGY CHOCOLATE LOG

◆

This is a cake that has no flour in it – so it's extremely light and moist. It's also a bit wicked, with its chocolate mousse and whipped cream filling!

6 large eggs, separated
5 oz caster sugar (150 g)
2 oz cocoa powder (50 g)

For the filling
8 oz plain chocolate (225 g)
2 tablespoons water
2 large eggs, separated
8 fl oz double cream (225 ml)

To finish
icing sugar

Pre-heat the oven to gas mark 4, 350°F (180°C).

A tin 11½ × 7 inches (29 × 18 cm) and about 1 inch (2.5 cm) deep, oiled and the base lined with silicone paper.

Begin by making the chocolate filling. Break the plain chocolate in pieces into a basin and add the water. Now place the basin over a saucepan of barely simmering water and wait for the chocolate to melt. After that, remove from the heat and beat it with a wooden spoon until smooth. Next beat the 2 egg yolks, first on their own, then into the warm chocolate mixture. Let it cool a bit then whisk the egg whites till stiff and fold them into the chocolate mixture. Cover the bowl and chill in the refrigerator for about an hour.

Meanwhile you can get on with the cake. First place the egg yolks in a basin and whisk until they start to thicken, then add the caster sugar and continue to whisk until the mixture thickens slightly – but be careful not to get it *too* thick. Now mix the cocoa powder into the egg yolk mixture, then, using a clean whisk and bowl, beat up the egg whites to the soft peak stage. Next carefully cut and fold the egg whites into the chocolate mixture – gently and thoroughly – then pour the mixture into the prepared tin.

Bake the cake on the centre shelf for 20–25 minutes until springy and puffy. When the cake is cooked, remove it from the oven but leave it in the cake tin to cool (it will shrink quite a bit as it cools but don't worry, that's normal).

Then when the cake is quite cold, turn it out onto an oblong of greaseproof paper which has been liberally dusted with icing sugar. Peel away the cake tin lining paper from the bottom of the cake (which is now facing upwards), then spread the chocolate mousse filling over the cake. Next whip the cream softly and spread it over the chocolate filling. Finally, gently roll up the cake to make a log shape. This will serve eight people and, although it's unlikely that there will be any left, you can cover any remaining cake with an upturned basin and keep it in the refrigerator. As an alternative, an 11 oz (300 g) tin of sweetened chestnut purée (*crème de marrons*) can replace the chocolate mousse.

Note During the rolling up, the cake will crack, but this is quite normal and looks most attractive. (Illus. opposite p. 480.)

STICKY DATE CAKE

◆

This is an example of what I call 'boil-and-bake'. There's no sugar in it, but the boiled condensed milk gives a lovely dark toffee flavour.

4 oz raisins (110 g)
8 oz pitted dates (225 g), chopped
6 oz sultanas (175 g)
4 oz currants (110 g)
10 oz margarine (275 g)
10 fl oz water (275 ml)
14 oz tin condensed milk (400 g)
5 oz plain flour (150 g)
5 oz wholewheat flour (150 g)
a pinch of salt
³/₄ teaspoon bicarbonate of soda
1 generous tablespoon chunky marmalade

Pre-heat the oven to gas mark 3, 325°F (170°C).

An 8 inch (20 cm) square cake tin, greased and lined.

Place all the fruits in a saucepan, together with the margarine, water and condensed milk and bring to the boil. Stir frequently to avoid sticking. Simmer the mixture for exactly 3 minutes and stir occasionally. Now transfer the mixture to a large mixing bowl and let it cool for approximately 30 minutes. While it's cooling, weigh the flours and sift them into a bowl together with the salt and bicarbonate of soda. (When sifting wholemeal flour, you frequently find small quantities of bran left in the sieve; these can be tipped onto the already sifted flour.)

When the fruit mixture has cooled stir into it the flour, salt and bicarbonate of soda and add a good round tablespoon of marmalade. Now spoon the mixture into the prepared tin and bake the cake on the centre shelf of the oven for 2¹/₂ hours. This cake does get rather brown on top if not protected. You should therefore cover it from the beginning of the cooking with a double square of greaseproof paper (with a hole the size of a 50p piece in the centre).

After removing the cake from the oven let it cool in the tin for 5 minutes before turning it out on a wire tray. This is quite a large cake which will keep well for several weeks in an airtight tin and, I think, even improves with keeping. If you prefer, you could make this in two 1lb (450 g) loaf tins and halve the cooking time.

MARMALADE CAKE

◆

This delicious cake has a tendency to crumble, but if you wrap it in foil and store for a couple of days you will find it cuts very nicely then.

8 oz plain wholewheat flour (225 g), sifted
3 level teaspoons baking powder
4 oz dark soft brown sugar (110 g)
4 oz soft margarine (110 g)
grated rind of ½ large lemon
grated rind of ½ large orange
1 level teaspoon ground mixed spice
4 oz mixed dried fruit (110 g)
5 fl oz milk (150 ml)
1 teaspoon cider vinegar or wine vinegar
1 rounded tablespoon chunky marmalade
For the topping
1 tablespoon demerara sugar

Pre-heat the oven to gas mark 4, 350°F (180°C).

A loaf tin 7½ × 3½ inches (19 × 9 cm), greased and the base lined with lightly-greased greaseproof paper.

In a large mixing bowl combine the flour, baking powder and sugar, then rub the fat into the dry ingredients until the mixture resembles coarse breadcrumbs. Next add the grated lemon and orange rinds, the mixed spice and dried fruit. Stir everything together well, then add the milk a little at a time, followed by the vinegar. Stir until all the ingredients are evenly distributed, and finally stir in the marmalade. You should now have a good dropping consistency, so that when you tap a spoonful of the mixture on the side of the bowl, it drops off easily (you can adjust this with a touch more milk if necessary).

Spread the mixture evenly in the prepared tin and sprinkle the top with the demerara sugar. Bake in the centre of the oven for 1¼ hours or until the cake has shrunk slightly from the sides of the tin and feels firm in the centre. Leave to cool in the tin for 10 minutes before turning out onto a wire cooling rack.

TRADITIONAL DUNDEE CAKE

◆

This is a really good fruit cake for those who don't like the heavy, rich sort (see the following recipe). It does have an excellent flavour and a light crumbly texture.

5 oz butter (150 g), at room temperature
5 oz caster sugar (150 g)
3 large eggs
8 oz plain flour (225 g), sifted
1 teaspoon baking powder
milk (if necessary)
6 oz currants (175 g)
6 oz sultanas (175 g)
2 oz glacé cherries (50 g), rinsed, dried and cut into halves
2 oz mixed whole candied peel (50 g), finely chopped
2 tablespoons ground almonds
grated rinds of 1 small orange and 1 small lemon
2 oz whole blanched almonds (50 g)

Pre-heat the oven to gas mark 3, 325°F (170°C).

A 7–8 inch (18–20 cm) round tin, greased and lined with greaseproof paper.

Put the butter and sugar in a mixing bowl and beat with a wooden spoon until light and fluffy – or an electric mixer will do this much more quickly.

Whisk the eggs separately then, a little at a time, beat them into the creamed butter and sugar. Next, using a large tablespoon, carefully *fold* in the flour and baking powder. Your mixture needs to be of a good, soft dropping consistency so, if it seems too dry, add a dessertspoon of milk.

Now carefully fold in the currants, sultanas, cherries, mixed peel, ground almonds and orange and lemon rinds. Then spoon the mixture into the prepared cake tin, smoothing it out evenly with the back of the spoon. Next arrange the whole almonds in circles on top of the mixture, but do this carefully and lightly; if they are pressed in they will sink during the baking.

Place the cake in the centre of the oven and bake for 2–2¹/₂ hours or until the centre is firm and springy to the touch. Let it cool before taking it out of the tin. This cake keeps very well in an airtight tin and tastes all the better if kept for a few days before cutting.

RICH FRUIT CAKES

◆

My recipe is the one I always make for a 'celebration' cake. It is more or less my mother's recipe and I have made it for Christmas, birthdays and weddings. It is very rich and if you prefer a fruit cake with a lighter, crumblier texture I recommend the *Traditional Dundee cake* above.

Rich fruit cakes are best made about eight weeks before they are needed, but if you can't manage this, it's not a disaster: they just *taste* better if they mature a little.

The recipe which follows is for an 8 inch (20 cm) round cake or a 7 inch (18 cm) square one – just the right size for Christmas – and I have given the directions for a simple and *quick* decoration using almond paste and royal icing.

RICH FRUIT CAKE
◆

1 lb currants (450 g)
6 oz sultanas (175 g)
6 oz raisins (175 g)
2 oz glacé cherries (50 g), rinsed and finely chopped
2 oz mixed whole candied peel (50 g), finely chopped
3 tablespoons brandy
8 oz plain flour (225 g)
1/2 teaspoon salt
1/4 teaspoon freshly grated nutmeg
1/2 teaspoon ground mixed spice
8 oz unsalted butter (225 g)
8 oz soft brown sugar (225 g)
4 large eggs
2 oz almonds (50 g), chopped – the skins can be left on
1 dessertspoon black treacle
grated rind of 1 lemon
grated rind of 1 orange

Pre-heat the oven to gas mark 1, 275°F (140°C).

An 8 inch (20 cm) round cake tin, or a 7 inch (18 cm) square tin, greased and lined with greaseproof paper.

The night before you make the cake, place all the dried fruit and peel in a bowl and mix in the brandy. Cover the bowl with a cloth and leave to soak for at least 12 hours.

It is quite a good idea before you measure the treacle to place the tin in the warming drawer of the oven, so that it melts a little which makes things easier.

Sift the flour, salt and spices into a large mixing bowl, and in a separate bowl cream the butter and sugar together until the mixture's light and fluffy (this in fact is the most important part of the cake, so don't cut any corners). Next beat up the eggs and – a tablespoon at a time – add them to the creamed mixture, beating thoroughly after each addition. If it looks as if it might start to curdle, you can prevent this happening by adding a little of the flour.

When all the egg has been added, fold in the flour and spices (fold, don't beat). Now stir in the fruit and peel that has been soaking, the nuts, the treacle and the grated lemon and orange rinds.

Spoon the mixture into the prepared cake tin, and spread it out evenly with the back of a spoon. (If you are not going to ice the cake, at this stage you can arrange some blanched almonds over the surface – but do it lightly, or else they disappear forever into the cake!)

Tie a band of brown paper around the outside of the tin, and cover the top of the cake with a double square of greaseproof paper (with a hole in the middle approximately the size of a 50p piece). Bake the cake on the lower shelf of the oven for 4¼–4¾ hours, and don't open the door to peek at it until at least 4 hours have passed.

When the cake is cold, wrap it well in double greaseproof paper and store in an airtight tin. I like to 'feed' it at odd intervals with brandy during the storage time. To do this, strip off the lining papers, make a few holes in the top with a thin darning needle and pour a few teaspoons of brandy in to soak into the cake. Repeat at intervals for a week or two.

CHRISTMAS CAKE

◆

For a basic and uncomplicated icing, I've chosen a layer of almond paste topped with a semi-rough royal icing, decorated with an almond paste flower (in this case a poinsettia). Ideally the cake should be almond iced at least seven days before the royal icing is put on – to give it a chance to dry out. Otherwise the almond oil may seep through and discolour the royal icing. The thick 'snowy' icing in this recipe, however, should keep the oil at bay even if you (like me) find that sometimes you still have the cake decorating to do on Christmas Eve!

an 8 inch (20 cm) round cake or a 7 inch (18 cm) square cake, made from the rich fruit cake recipe (see page 553)
For the almond paste *
1 lb ground almonds (450 g)
8 oz caster sugar (225 g)
8 oz icing sugar (225 g)
2 eggs
2 egg yolks – reserve the whites for the royal icing (see below)
½ teaspoon almond essence
1 teaspoon brandy
1 teaspoon lemon juice
red, green and yellow food colouring
* Part of this is used to ice the cake, the rest is used to model the flower decorations

For the royal icing
4 large egg whites – combine three but keep one separate
approx. 1 lb 2 oz icing sugar (500 g), sifted
1 teaspoon glycerine

To make the almond paste, begin by sifting the two sugars into a large bowl and stirring in the eggs and egg yolks. Put the bowl over a pan of barely simmering water and whisk for about 12 minutes until the mixture is thick and fluffy. Then remove the bowl from the heat and sit the base in a couple of inches of cold water.

Next whisk in the essence, brandy and lemon juice and carry on whisking until the mixture is cool. Stir in the ground almonds and knead to form a firm paste. Weigh out 6 oz (175 g) of the paste and reserve this (in a bowl covered with cling film) for making the flower decoration.

Divide the rest of the paste in half and roll out one piece into a shape approximately 1 inch (2.5 cm) larger than the top of the cake (your working surface should be kept dusted with some sifted icing sugar so that the paste doesn't stick to it). Brush the top of the cake with some of the egg white for the icing, then invert the cake to sit centrally on the almond paste and with a palette knife press the paste up around the edge of the cake. Now turn the cake the right way up and brush the sides with egg white.

Roll out the other half of the paste into a rectangle and trim it so that it measures half the circumference of the cake by twice the height of the cake (use a piece of string to measure this). Now cut the paste rectangle in half lengthways, and lightly press the two strips onto the sides of the cake. Smooth over the joins of the paste with a knife, then smooth again with a rolling-pin, and leave the cake covered with a clean cloth to dry out.

To make the almond paste poinsettia, take out the paste reserved for decoration. Now using a skewer (so as not to overdo it) colour yellow a small piece about the size of a walnut. Divide the remaining paste in half, colouring one half of it green, the other red. Cut out two templates in stiff paper or card to resemble poinsettia leaves: one with smooth edges for the inner circle of red leaves and one with serrated edges for the outer circle of green leaves. Roll out both colours of paste to about 1/8 inch (3 mm) thick, then with the aid of the templates cut out six red leaves and six green. Trace a suggestion of veins on the surface with the back of the knife. Let the leaves dry, face upwards over a rolling-pin (so that they curve). Model the yellow paste into some small pea-sized balls and leave everything to dry overnight.

To make the royal icing, place the three egg whites in a grease-free bowl. Then stir in the icing sugar, a spoonful at a time, until the icing falls thickly from the spoon. At that point, stop adding any more sugar and whisk with an electric mixer for 10 minutes or until the icing stands up in stiff peaks, then stir in the glycerine. Now spoon half the icing into a screw-top jar and put aside in the fridge. Beat about 2 teaspoons more egg white into the remaining half of the icing.

Next use a dab of icing to fix the cake to a 10 inch (25 cm) cakeboard, then spread about two-thirds of the remainder on top of the cake. Work the icing back and forth to get rid of any tiny air bubbles, then take a clean plastic ruler and, holding it at each end, glide it once over the surface of the cake to give a smooth finish.

Hold the ruler vertically and remove any surplus icing from the top edges of the cake, then spread the remaining icing onto the sides of the cake. Keeping your ruler vertical, turn the cake round in one sweep to smooth the sides – a turntable is ideal for this, but two plates set base to base will also do the job. Now leave the cake for 24 hours for the icing to dry.

To finish off, mark the centre of the cake with a 3¼ inch (8 cm) plain circular cutter, then, taking your reserve icing from the screw-top jar, spread it thickly outside the marked circle. Use a broad-bladed knife to 'spike' the icing into snow-like peaks. At the edge, bring the peaks over and down to give the effect of hanging snowy icicles. Lastly lay the green almond paste leaves in the centre of the cake, then the red leaves on top of them to form a poinsettia. Place the small yellow 'berries' in the centre, fixing them in place with a little icing. Set the whole effect off with red ribbon, tied in a bow around the cake.

QUANTITIES AND COOKING TIMES FOR DIFFERENT SIZES OF RICH FRUIT CAKE

	6 inch (15 cm) round or 5 inch (13 cm) square	9 inch (23 cm) round or 8 inch (20 cm) square	11 inch (28 cm) round or 10 inch (25 cm) square
currants	8 oz (225 g)	1¼ lb (575 g)	2 lb (900 g)
sultanas	3 oz (75 g)	8 oz (225 g)	12 oz (350 g)
raisins	3 oz (75 g)	8 oz (225 g)	12 oz (350 g)
glacé cherries, rinsed and finely chopped	1½ oz (40 g)	2½ oz (60 g)	4 oz (110 g)
mixed candied peel, finely chopped	1½ oz (40 g)	2½ oz (60 g)	4 oz (110 g)
brandy	3 tablespoons	4 tablespoons	6 tablespoons
plain flour	4 oz (110 g)	10 oz (275 g)	1 lb (450 g)
salt	a pinch	½ teaspoon	½ teaspoon
freshly grated nutmeg	¼ teaspoon	½ teaspoon	½ teaspoon
ground mixed spice	¼ teaspoon	¾ teaspoon	1 teaspoon
unsalted butter	4 oz (110 g)	10 oz (275 g)	1 lb (450 g)
soft brown sugar	4 oz (110 g)	10 oz (275 g)	1 lb (450 g)

	6 inch (15 cm) round or 5 inch (13 cm) square	9 inch (23 cm) round or 8 inch (20 cm) square	11 inch (28 cm) round or 10 inch (25 cm) square
eggs	2	5	8
almonds, chopped	1¹/₂ oz (40 g)	2¹/₂ oz (60 g)	4 oz (110 g)
black treacle	1 teaspoon (rounded)	1 tablespoon	1¹/₂ tablespoons
grated lemon rind	¹/₂ lemon	1 large lemon	2 lemons
grated orange rind	¹/₂ orange	1 large orange	2 oranges
cooking times (approx.)	3¹/₂ hours	4³/₄ hours	5¹/₂ hours

The size of your cake will obviously depend on the number of people you need to cater for. You may need more than one tier for a very special occasion such as a wedding. As a guide, I estimate that the 8 inch (20 cm) cake on page 553 would be sufficient for between 25 and 40 people. The easiest way for me to give you the ingredients and cooking times for the different sizes of cake is in the table opposite and above. The method in all cases is the same as on pages 553–4.

ALMOND PASTE FOR DIFFERENT SIZES OF RICH FRUIT CAKE

The ingredients in the table on page 558 differ slightly from my quick almond paste on page 554, and to fix this paste to the cake I use apricot jam instead of egg white. In this case, I think it is essential to let the almond-iced cake dry for at least a week before applying any royal icing, especially if the iced cake is going to be kept a while before being eaten. If you are going to ice it and eat it very soon afterwards, two days' drying will be enough.

Mix all the dry ingredients together first, then stir in the almond essence, lemon juice, sherry, and egg yolks and combine everything to form a stiff paste. Transfer the paste to a pastry board (dusted with icing sugar) and knead it into a ball. Try not to handle it *too* much – the heat of your hands might make it oily. Warm the apricot jam and brush it over the top and sides of the cake. Now take about half the paste and roll it out to a shape approximately 1 inch (2.5 cm) larger than the top of the cake. Invert the cake on the paste shape and trim the edges if you need to.

Next roll out the rest of the paste into an oblong which is half the circumference and twice the height of the cake (use some string or a tape measure to get these measurements), then cut the oblong in half lengthways. Roll up one strip. Lightly place one end against the side of the cake and unroll the paste, pressing firmly to the cake as you go.

ALMOND PASTE FOR DIFFERENT SIZES OF RICH FRUIT CAKE

	6 inch (15 cm) round or 5 inch (13 cm) square	9 inch (23 cm) round or 8 inch (20 cm) square	11 inch (28 cm) round or 10 inch (25 cm) square
ground almonds	8 oz (225 g)	1 lb (450 g)	1¹/₂ lb (700 g)
icing sugar, sifted	4 oz (110 g)	8 oz (225 g)	12 oz (350 g)
caster sugar	4 oz (110 g)	8 oz (225 g)	12 oz (350 g)
almond essence	2 drops	¹/₂ teaspoon	1 teaspoon
lemon juice	¹/₂ teaspoon	1 teaspoon	2 teaspoons
sherry or brandy	1 dessertspoon	1–2 tablespoons	2–3 tablespoons
egg yolks	3	5	8
apricot jam (warmed and sieved)			

Repeat with the other strip to complete the sides of the cake and press the joins together. Turn the cake the right way up, even the surfaces with a rolling-pin and store in a double sheet of greaseproof paper for at least a week before applying royal icing.

ROYAL ICING FOR DIFFERENT SIZES OF RICH FRUIT CAKE

If your cake is in tiers, then in order to support the weight of one tier on top of another, you are going to need *three* layers of this hard-set icing. If it is only one tier, then a single layer with the quantities given in the table on page 559 will be all right (you can also add 2–3 teaspoons of glycerine to give a softer texture, if preferred). The cake boards for a tiered cake in each case need to be 2–3 inches wider than the width of the cake itself. Useful items of equipment would be a turntable, palette knife and plastic icing scraper.

Place the egg whites in your largest bowl (and make sure it is grease-free), then stir in the sifted icing sugar, two spoonfuls at a time. When it is all stirred in, take an electric mixer and whisk at top speed for about 10 minutes, by which time the icing should be standing up in peaks at least 2 inches (5 cm) high. As soon as you reach this stage, cover the bowl with a damp cloth to prevent the icing drying out.

Use a little icing to stick the cake to the board, then place the board on the turntable and give the cake one coat of icing – using one-third of the quantity. Ice the top of the cake first, and then the sides with the aid of the palette knife. Get the sides smooth with a plastic scraper, and the top with a palette knife dipped into hot water and shaken. Smooth the icing right up to the edge of the board too. Store the rest of the icing in a plastic container, and leave the cake to dry overnight. Then give it two more coats, leaving each to dry overnight.

ROYAL ICING FOR DIFFERENT SIZES OF RICH FRUIT CAKE

	6 inch (15 cm) round or 5 inch (13 cm) square	9 inch (23 cm) round or 8 inch (20 cm) square	11 inch (28 cm) round or 10 inch (25 cm) square
icing sugar, sifted	1 lb (450 g)	1½ lb (700 g)	2 lb (900 g)
egg whites	2–3	4	6

DECORATION

Even for a special occasion cake, I find the simpler the design the better, keeping piping to an absolute minimum and using roses made from modelling paste. These roses can be tinted in various colours and offset by gold or silver paper leaves. Finish off with satin ribbon tied around the cake or around each tier.

MODELLING PASTE ROSES

◆

2 oz lard (50 g)
2 tablespoons lemon juice
2 tablespoons water
1½ lb icing sugar (700 g), sifted
food colouring (according to your design)

Heat the lard and lemon juice with the water until the fat melts. Then stir in 8 oz (225 g) of the icing sugar, and cook over a very low heat until the sugar dissolves and turns a semi-opaque colour (about 2 minutes). Then remove the pan from the heat and stir in the rest of the sugar which will eventually give you a mixture the consistency of dough.

Turn it out onto a working surface dusted with icing sugar, knead for a few seconds, then divide it in half and work in whatever colours you have chosen. Add the colour with a skewer in *small* drops until you arrive at the right shade. The paste should be stored in a plastic bag.

When you're ready, roll out the paste and cut out some small, circular shapes the size of a 10p piece, and some slightly smaller than £1 coins. Make up the roses, curving the circular pieces around and pinching them gently into shape. Leave them to dry on a tray overnight.

Arrange the roses how you like, with some gold or silver paper leaves here and there, sticking them on to the cake with small amounts of icing. To neaten the edges of the cake at the base and top, you could pipe a tiny row of beads (using an icing bag fitted with a large, plain, no. 1 nozzle). Alternatively, you can use a no. 17 leaf nozzle, piping all around the top edge of the cake and then around the side, using the corner of the cake as the 'stem' for the leaves. Finally tie bands of ribbon in place around the cake or around each of the tiers.

WEDDING CAKES

———— ♦ ————

A beautiful, tiered wedding cake can be much easier to make than you think, provided that you use a hard royal icing to give you firm enough bases to support the separate tiers. Don't worry if you feel your flat icing is not all it should be, because in our design the surfaces are hidden beneath flowers – so any unevenness is concealed. The edges – always tricky – will have just enough piping to camouflage any mistakes, and the ribbon will disguise any lack of smoothness on the sides.

Most wedding cakes will be an amalgam of two tiers (a 6 inch/15 cm and a 9 inch/23 cm cake, or a 9 inch/23 cm and an 11 inch/28 cm) or of three tiers (6, 9 and 11 inch cakes) depending on the number of guests you have to cater for. As a guide the cakes will feed the following numbers: 6 inch (15 cm) cake, approximately 20 people; 9 inch (23 cm) cake, approximately 45 people; and the 11 inch (28 cm) cake approximately 75 people.

The base boards for each tier need to be slightly larger than the cake. Thus the 11 inch (28 cm) cake needs a 14 inch (35 cm) board, the 9 inch (23 cm) cake an 11 inch (28 cm) board, and the 6 inch (15 cm) cake an 8 inch (20 cm) board. The larger cakes will need a thinner board on top to support the cake and the columns above it. Thus the 11 inch (28 cm) cake has an 8 inch (20 cm) board on it and the 9 inch (23 cm) cake a 6 inch (15 cm) board. The flower sprays are placed on top of these and the top of the cake has matching flowers in a small silver vase. If you, too, want to decorate the cake with fresh flowers, stick the supporting columns firmly in place on the thin boards, then give them to your florist with instructions for matching the colours. You will also need a cake base or stand. This can be hired from most hire firms. Accessories such as decorating nozzles etc. can be obtained from Twitters, 81 Hoe Street, Walthamstow, London E17 4SA (*tel:* 081-520 0525/0893).

SEE ALSO

All-in-one banana and walnut loaf
American brownies
Black Forest gâteau
Chocolate and hazelnut choux buns
Coffee éclairs
Cream puffs
Curd cheesecake with fruit topping
Eccles cakes
Fresh lemon cheesecake with frosted grapes
Honey and spice cake
Linzertorte
Orange cheesecake
Richmond maids of honour
Strawberry shortcake

SCONES AND BISCUITS

◆

In the days when households had such things as 'baking' days, bread and cakes would be baked in batches to last a week or even longer. The kitchen range was brought up to heat and kept topped up all day, and not an inch of space or minute of fuel time was wasted. Girdle cakes or crumpets used the heat on the top of the stove, scones fitted in alongside the bread, and biscuits were dried out at the end of the day as the heat died down in the range. The results, I'm sure, must have been enough to feed an army.

Nowadays few of us have the time or inclination to bake on such an organised scale, and inevitably the main casualties have been those items which form the subject of this chapter. We have come to rely very largely on bakeries and supermarkets for our scones and biscuits, but we are paying very dearly for this convenience (as a quick comparison between the weight and prices of almost any packet of biscuits will confirm). Yet this branch of baking is the easiest of all, using ingredients that most people keep regularly in their storecupboard. I hope the recipes in this section will inspire you to re-discover some of the pleasures of 'batch' baking, and save lots of money at the same time!

HOW TO BAKE PERFECT SCONES

◆

The modern scone seems to have evolved from something rather similar to the girdle cake (see the recipe on page 564): it was only when raising agents were introduced to flour that scones began to be oven-baked and well-risen as we know them today. And that straightaway brings me to one of the most persistent queries I get from readers: why don't their scones ever rise to a proper height?

Now some problems are difficult to answer specifically, particularly when you can't see what people are doing wrong. But on the subject of scones I can nearly always put them right by suggesting that perhaps they are rolling the dough out too thinly – the major cause of failure. The dough for a perfect scone would never be rolled out to anything less than 3/4 inch (2 cm). And there's another minor cause for concern which can be tracked down to the rolling too – that's scones which emerge uneven in shape. This is caused by uneven pressure on the rolling-pin, which tends to make the dough (and therefore the scones) slanted. Hardly a disaster; in fact it can be quite appealing by giving them that home-made air in contrast to the clinical perfection of the shop-bought variety!

PLAIN SCONES

(Makes about 12)

Eat these with butter, home-made jam and, if you can get it, whipped untreated Jersey cream or clotted cream.

8 oz self-raising flour (225 g)
1¹/₂ oz butter or margarine (40 g), at room temperature
1¹/₂ tablespoons caster sugar
a pinch of salt
5 fl oz milk (150 ml)
a little extra flour

Pre-heat the oven to gas mark 7, 425°F (220°C).

A baking sheet, greased.

First of all, sift the flour into a bowl and rub the butter into it rapidly, using your fingertips. Next stir in the sugar and salt, then take a knife and use it to mix in the milk little by little. Now flour your hands a little and knead the mixture to a soft dough – adding a drop more milk if it feels at all dry.

Then turn the dough out onto a floured pastry board and roll it out to a thickness of not less than ³/₄ inch (2 cm) using a lightly floured rolling-pin. Take a 1¹/₂ or 2 inch (4 or 5 cm) pastry cutter (either fluted or plain) and place it on the dough, then tap it sharply so that it goes straight through the dough – don't twist it or the scones will turn out a peculiar shape! After you have cut out as many scone shapes as you can like that, knead the dough trimmings together again and repeat until you have used it all.

Then place the scones on the greased baking sheet, dust each one with a little extra flour and bake near the top of the oven for 12–15 minutes. When cooked the scones will have turned a crisp golden-brown. Cool on a wire rack and eat them slightly warm, still crisp on the outside and soft and light inside. In fact, always eat scones as fresh as possible as they can go stale very quickly. They freeze well, but still eat them within a month.

WHOLEWHEAT FRUIT SCONES

◆

(Makes 7 or 8)

It took several tests and a few brick-like results before I got the right combination of ingredients for these, and I think it is most important to have the oven really hot before you bake them in order to raise them properly.

3 oz wholewheat flour (75 g)
3 oz self-raising flour (75 g)
1 teaspoon baking powder
½ teaspoon ground cinnamon
1 oz soft brown sugar (25 g)
1 oz butter or margarine (25 g), at room temperature
1½ oz mixed dried fruit (40 g)
1 large egg
2–2½ tablespoons milk
extra milk and wholewheat flour

Pre-heat the oven to gas mark 8, 450°F (230°C).

A baking sheet, well-greased.

In a mixing bowl sift the flours and combine with the bran left in the sieve, the baking powder, cinnamon and sugar. Rub in the fat and mix in the dried fruit. Beat the egg with 2 tablespoons of milk and add this, mixing it to a smooth dough with a palette knife. If you need to, add more milk.

Next roll out the dough to ¾ inch (2 cm) thick and, using a 2½ inch (6 cm) cutter, cut out the scones. Place them on the baking sheet, brush the tops with milk and dust them with wholewheat flour. Bake on a high shelf in the oven for 15–20 minutes. Serve warm, spread with butter.

WHOLEWHEAT CHEESE-CRUSTED SCONES

◆

(Makes 6 to 8)

If you can't think of anything for a quick snack lunch or late supper, these are quick to make and quite irresistible served warm and spread with butter. For a lighter variety use 6 oz (175 g) white self-raising flour and omit the baking powder.

3 oz wholewheat flour (75 g)
3 oz self-raising flour (75 g)
1 teaspoon baking powder
¹/₂ teaspoon mustard powder
¹/₂ teaspoon salt
2 good pinches of cayenne pepper
1 oz butter (25 g), at room temperature
3 oz strong Cheddar cheese (75 g), finely grated
1 large egg
2–3 tablespoons milk

Pre-heat the oven to gas mark 7, 425°F (220°C).
A baking sheet, well-greased.

First sift the flours into a mixing bowl, add the bran remaining in the sieve, the baking powder, mustard, salt and a good pinch of cayenne pepper. Mix them together well, then rub in the butter – using your fingertips – until the mixture is all crumbly. Now mix in most of the grated cheese, leaving about 1 tablespoon.

Next, in a small bowl, beat the egg together with 2 tablespoons of milk. Add this to the mixing bowl to make a soft dough – what you are after is a smooth dough that will leave the bowl clean, so add just a few more drops of milk if it is too dry.

Now roll out the dough on a floured surface to a thickness of about ³/₄ inch (2 cm) and use a 2¹/₂ inch cutter (6 cm) to cut out the scones. Place the scones on the baking sheet, brush the tops with milk, then sprinkle the remaining grated cheese over the top of each scone, with a faint dusting of cayenne. Bake on a high shelf for 15–20 minutes, cool them slightly on a wire tray, and serve warm.

WHOLEWHEAT GIRDLE CAKES
◆

(Makes about 25)

Unlike oven-baked scones, girdle cakes are cut quite thin and cooked on top of the stove. Traditionally cooked on a heavy iron girdle, they can now be made in a thick-based, heavy frying-pan (though iron girdles are still available at good kitchen shops).

4 oz wholewheat flour (110 g)
4 oz self-raising flour (110 g)
1 teaspoon baking powder
3 oz caster sugar (75 g)
¹/₂ teaspoon ground mixed spice
4 oz butter or margarine (110 g), at room temperature
3 oz mixed dried fruit (75 g)

| 1 large egg |
| a little milk, if necessary |
| butter, for greasing |

Begin by sifting the dry ingredients (except the fruit) together into a mixing bowl, add any bran remaining in the sieve, then rub in the butter until the mixture becomes crumbly. Then add the fruit and mix it in thoroughly. Next beat the egg lightly, add it to the mixture, and mix to a dough (if it seems to be a little too dry, you can add a spot of milk).

Transfer the dough onto a lightly floured surface and roll out to a thickness of about 1/4 inch (5 mm). Then, using a 2 1/2 inch (6 cm) plain cutter, cut the dough into rounds – re-rolling and cutting the trimmings until you have used all the dough.

Now lightly grease your pan and heat it over a medium heat, then cook the girdle cakes, a few at a time, for about 3 minutes on each side. If they look as if they are browning too quickly, turn the heat down because they must be cooked all through and still be fairly brown and crisp on the outside. Serve warm with lots of butter and perhaps some home-made jam.

CRUMPETS

(Makes about 12)

Although you can buy quite good crumpets, I do think they're fun to make – especially on a cold snowy day when everyone's housebound. Once upon a time you could buy special crumpet rings, but egg cooking rings will do equally well provided you grease them really thoroughly.

| 10 fl oz milk (275 ml) |
| 2 fl oz water (55 ml) |
| 1 teaspoon caster sugar |
| 1 tablespoon dried yeast |
| 8 oz strong plain flour (225 g) |
| 1 teaspoon salt |
| butter, for greasing |

A thick-based frying-pan and some egg cooking rings.

First of all heat the milk and water together in a small saucepan till they are hand-hot. Then pour into a jug, stir in the sugar and dried yeast and leave it in a warm place for 10–15 minutes till there is a good frothy head on it.

Meanwhile sift the flour and salt into a mixing bowl, make a well in the centre and, when the yeast mixture is frothy, pour it all in. Next use a wooden spoon to work the flour into the liquid gradually, and beat well at the end to make a perfectly smooth batter. Cover the basin with a tea towel and leave to stand in a warm place for about 45 minutes – by which time the batter will have become light and frothy.

Then to cook the crumpets: grease the insides of the egg rings well, and grease the frying-pan as well before placing it over a medium heat. Arrange the rings in the frying-pan, and when the pan is hot spoon 1 tablespoon of the crumpet batter into each ring. Let them cook for 4 or 5 minutes: first tiny bubbles will appear on the surface and then, suddenly, they will burst leaving the traditional holes. Now take a spoon and fork, lift off the rings and turn the crumpets over. Cook the crumpets on the second side for about 1 minute only. Re-grease and reheat the rings and the pan before cooking the next batch of crumpets.

Serve crumpets while still warm, generously buttered. If you are making crumpets in advance then reheat them by toasting lightly on both sides before serving.

BISCUITS

The origins of the biscuit are described in the word itself. 'Twice-cooked' it means in French, and that goes back to the days when bakers were in the habit of putting slices of newly-baked bread back into the cooking oven, so that they dried out completely. The result was something like a rusk, and was used as ships' biscuits for long voyages.

For a long time housewives continued to dry their biscuits with a second baking: the practice only died out at the beginning of the last century, but when it did the quality and variety of biscuits improved no end. There's almost no limit to the kind of biscuit that can be easily baked at home today. Here are some favourites using a range of basic biscuit ingredients.

SHORTBREADS

One thing that distinguishes the several 'rules' about making shortbread that have been handed down is their conflicting advice. Thus one old Scottish cookbook of mine suggests that it should be 'browned to taste'; a more modern one recommends no colouring at all on the surface. There is a consensus that butter – and only butter – should be used: yet I have a friend who makes hers with margarine and I have to admit that it tastes very good.

For my part I would say that shortbread mixture should *not* be overcooked: it ought to be a pale golden colour and not golden-brown. And I certainly think that the mixture shouldn't be over-worked, because the heat in your hands can turn the fat oily. To overcome this the method I now use involves beating the fat with a wooden spoon to soften it, then gradually working it into the other ingredients. This way it is only handled at the end. When it is mixed, you can then either just pat and spread the dough straight into a prepared tin, or else roll out the dough and cut the biscuits out. Some say the latter method makes the shortbread tough because it involves extra handling, but I've not found this.

SHORTBREAD BISCUITS
◆

(Makes about 15)

4 oz butter or margarine (110 g), at room temperature
2 oz caster sugar (50 g)
6 oz plain flour (175 g), sifted
extra caster sugar, for dusting

Pre-heat the oven to gas mark 2, 300°F (150°C).
A baking sheet, lightly-greased.
Begin by first beating the butter with a wooden spoon to a soft consistency, then beat in the sugar followed by the sifted flour. Still using the wooden spoon, start to bring the mixture together, then finish off with your hands to form a paste. Now transfer this to a board lightly dusted with caster sugar, then quickly and lightly roll it out to about 1/8 inch (3 mm) thick (dusting the rolling-pin with sugar if necessary). Use a 3 inch (7.5 cm) fluted cutter to cut the biscuits out, then arrange them on the baking sheet and bake on a highish shelf in the oven for 30 minutes. Cool the biscuits on a wire rack, dust them with some caster sugar, and store in an airtight tin to keep them crisp. (Illus. opposite p. 481.)

SCOTTISH SHORTBREAD
◆

(Makes 12 wedges)

This shortbread is made in one piece in a tin, then cut into wedges after baking. The addition of fine semolina gives it a crunchier texture. (Illus. opposite p. 481.)

6 oz butter or margarine (175 g), at room temperature
3 oz caster sugar (75 g)
6 oz plain flour (175 g), sifted
3 oz fine semolina (75 g)
icing sugar, for dusting

Pre-heat the oven to gas mark 2, 300°F (150°C).

An 8 inch (20 cm) fluted flan tin with a loose base.

First of all beat the butter in a bowl with a wooden spoon to soften it, then beat in the sugar followed by the sifted flour and the semolina. Work the ingredients together with the spoon, pressing them to the side of the bowl, then finish off with your hands till you have a dough that doesn't leave any bits in the bowl.

Next transfer the dough to a flat surface and roll it out lightly to a round (giving it quarter turns as you roll), then transfer the round to the tin. Lightly press the mixture evenly into the tin, right into the fluted edges (to make sure it's even you can give it a final roll with a small glass tumbler). Now you *must* prick the shortbread all over with a fork or it will rise up in the centre while it's baking.

Bake the shortbread for 1–1¼ hours on the centre shelf, then using a palette knife mark out the surface into twelve wedges while it's still warm. Leave it to cool in the tin, then remove the rim of the tin, cut the shortbread into wedges, dust with icing sugar and store in an airtight tin.

Strawberry shortcake

In the summer a round of shortbread made as above and left whole can be spread with whipped cream or fromage frais, and topped with strawberries just before serving. This makes a really delicious pud for a summer dinner party, or tea in the garden.

WHOLEWHEAT SHORTBREAD

◆

(Makes 12 wedges)

This is similar to the previous recipe, but I've used half wholewheat flour for more of a wheaty flavour, and ground rice in place of semolina for crunchiness. (Illus. opposite p. 481.)

6 oz butter or margarine (175 g), at room temperature
2 oz caster sugar (50 g)
3 oz wholewheat flour (75 g), sifted
3 oz plain flour (75 g), sifted
2 oz ground rice (50 g)
a little extra sugar, for dusting

Pre-heat the oven to gas mark 2, 300°F (150°C).

An 8 inch (20 cm) fluted flan tin with a removable base, lightly-greased.

Start by beating the butter in a bowl with a wooden spoon to soften it, then beat in the sugar followed by the flours and ground rice. Work them together as much as you can with the wooden spoon, then finish off with your hands lightly and quickly. Now roll out the dough to approximately an 8 inch (20 cm) round, giving it quarter turns as you roll. Transfer it to the tin and press it evenly into the edges. If it seems uneven on top, just roll lightly over the surface with a glass tumbler.

Now prick the dough all over to prevent it rising, then bake it for 1 hour 10 minutes on a high shelf. Remove the shortbread from the oven, mark it into twelve portions while it's still warm and dust with sugar. Then cool it in the tin, remove the portions and store them in an airtight tin.

OAT BISCUITS

Oats have long been used in Scotland and the north of England for biscuit-making: they give a lovely crunch to the biscuit as well as a characteristic nutty flavour. Prepared oats come in a variety of forms, all of them suitable for baking.

Oatmeal

This means that the oats have been milled, in the same way as wheat is milled into flour. Oatmeal comes in different grades, most commonly as *fine* or *medium* (either of which can be added to bread dough or used for biscuits – see the *Oatmeal biscuits* recipe on page 570), or *coarse* which is often used for porridge.

Oat flakes

These are also known as *rolled oats* and are the husked grains which have been rolled mechanically into flakes. Very good for porridge and biscuits.

Whole oats

Also referred to as *jumbo oats*, these are flakes as well, but large and coarse. They also have more of a nutty flavour and are excellent for biscuits.

Quick cooking oats

These so-called 'instant oats' have been treated in some way and are not really suitable for baking.

WHOLE OAT CRUNCHIES

(Makes 12)

These are the quickest and easiest biscuits I've ever made: they have a nice crunchy, toffee taste. If you can get hold of jumbo oats from a health-food shop so much the better, otherwise all ordinary porridge oat flakes will do. (Illus. opposite p. 481.)

2 oz whole (jumbo) oats (50 g)
2¹/₂ oz porridge oats (60 g)
3 oz demerara sugar (75 g)
4 oz margarine or butter (110 g)

Pre-heat the oven to gas mark 5, 375°F (190°C).

A shallow baking tin measuring 11 × 7 inches (28 × 18 cm), well-greased.

First weigh out the oats and sugar, place them in a bowl and mix them together as evenly as possible. Then gently melt the margarine in a saucepan – only just melt it, be careful not to let it brown. Next pour the melted margarine into the bowl with the oats and sugar and mix until everything is well and truly blended.

Now all you have to do is to tip the mixture into the prepared tin and to press it out evenly all over using your hands.

Bake on the centre shelf of the oven for 15 minutes or until a nice pale gold colour. Then remove the tin from the oven and cut the mixture into twelve portions while it's still warm. Leave it in the tin until cold and crisp before storing the biscuits in an airtight tin.

OATMEAL BISCUITS

(Makes 24)

I think it's really nice to be able to offer home-made biscuits with cheese and these are lovely with some Stilton or strong Cheddar and crisp celery.

6 oz wholewheat flour (175 g)
2 oz medium oatmeal (50 g)
4 teaspoons soft brown sugar
1 teaspoon baking powder
¹/₂ teaspoon salt
¹/₄ teaspoon hot curry powder
4 oz butter or margarine (110 g), at room temperature
approx. 1 tablespoon milk

Pre-heat the oven to gas mark 4, 350°F (180°C).

A baking sheet, lightly-greased.

Simply combine all the dry ingredients together in a bowl, then rub the fat evenly in. Add just enough milk to give you a slightly wetter dough than you would require normally (say, for shortcrust pastry) – since this pastry is prone to breaking, a little extra moisture is deliberately used to help to hold it together.

Next, turn the dough out onto a floured working surface and roll out to about 1/8 inch (3 mm) thick. Use a 2¾ inch (7 cm) cutter to cut out the biscuit rounds – re-rolling the trimmings and adding a drop of milk if the dough happens to become a little dry.

Place the biscuits on the baking sheet and bake them for 15–20 minutes until firm and lightly browned. Leave them to cool on the baking sheet for 5 minutes before transferring them to a wire rack to cool. Store in an airtight tin.

OTHER BISCUITS

I am including here three more of my favourite recipes that come into this category. The first one, for *American brownies*, calls for some explanation. Since the first edition of this book I have received more queries about this recipe than for any other – the reason being that I had not made it clear enough what brownies are exactly. So please read the introduction before you write.

AMERICAN BROWNIES

◆

(Makes 15 squares)

Brownies are squidgy, nutty chocolate bars; they are not cakes and therefore do not have the texture of a cake. They are supposed to be moist and chewy, but because of their moistness people tend to think they haven't cooked them long enough. So if this appeals to you, and you want to be really self-indulgent, here goes.

4 oz butter (110 g)
2 oz American unsweetened chocolate (available at specialised food shops) or plain dessert chocolate (50 g)
2 eggs, beaten
8 oz granulated sugar (225 g)
2 oz plain flour (50 g), sifted
1 teaspoon baking powder
¼ teaspoon salt
4 oz chopped nuts (110 g) – these can be walnuts, almonds, hazelnuts or Brazils or a mixture

Pre-heat the oven to gas mark 4, 350°F (180°C).

A baking tin measuring 7 × 11 inches (18 × 28 cm), well-greased and lined with greaseproof paper. Bring the paper up a good 2 inches (5 cm) above the rim of the tin.

First of all melt the butter and the chocolate (broken up into small pieces) together in the top of a double saucepan (or else place in a basin fitted over simmering water on a very low heat). Away from the heat, stir all the other ingredients into the butter and chocolate mixture thoroughly, then spread all this in the lined tin.

Bake in the oven for 30 minutes, until the mixture shows signs of shrinking away from the side of the tin, and the centre feels springy. A knife inserted in the centre should come out cleanly (but don't overcook – it will firm up as it cools). Then leave the mixture in the tin to cool for 10 minutes before dividing into approximately fifteen squares and transferring them to a wire rack to finish cooling.

GINGERNUTS

◆

(Makes 16)

These are, like most biscuits, extremely simple to make at home and you'll wonder why you ever bought them! (Illus. opposite p. 481.)

4 oz self-raising flour (110 g)
1 slightly rounded teaspoon ground ginger
1 teaspoon bicarbonate of soda
1½ oz granulated sugar (40 g)
2 oz margarine (50 g)
2 tablespoons golden syrup

Pre-heat the oven to gas mark 5, 375°F (190°C).

One large (or two small) baking sheet(s), lightly-greased.

Begin by sifting the flour, ginger and bicarbonate of soda into a mixing bowl, add the sugar, then lightly rub in the margarine until the mixture is crumbly. Next add the syrup and mix everything together to form a stiff paste.

Now divide the mixture into sixteen pieces about the same size as each other, and roll each piece into a little ball. Place them on the baking sheet(s), leaving plenty of room between them because they spread out quite a bit while they're cooking. Then simply flatten each ball slightly with the back of a spoon and bake just above the centre of the oven for 10–15 minutes, by which time they will have spread out and cracked rather attractively. Cool on the baking sheet(s) for 10 minutes, then transfer to a wire rack to finish cooling, and store in an airtight tin.

CHEESE SAVOURIES

♦

(Makes about 30)

I like to make batches of these, cut out quite small, to serve with drinks at a party. They can be sprinkled with different toppings to vary the flavours.

2 oz wholewheat flour (50 g)
¼ teaspoon salt
a pinch of cayenne pepper
1 twist freshly milled black pepper
2 oz Cheddar cheese (50 g), grated
2 oz Parmesan cheese (50 g), grated
2 oz butter (50 g), at room temperature
Optional toppings
garlic salt, celery salt, mild curry powder or cayenne pepper

Pre-heat the oven to gas mark 5, 375°F (190°C).

A baking sheet, lightly-greased.

First of all sift the flour and salt into a mixing bowl, and add the cayenne and black pepper. Next add the two cheeses along with the butter and rub the mixture to the crumbly stage, then bring the mixture together – it shouldn't need any liquid, but if it does add just a drop of milk.

Now roll out the dough to a thickness of about ⅛ inch (3 mm), then use a 1 or 1½ inch (2.5 or 4 cm) cutter to cut out the biscuits. Arrange them fairly close together on the baking sheet, sprinkle the selected topping (if any) on them, then bake on a high shelf in the oven for 10– 12 minutes, before removing to a wire rack to cool and crisp. Store them in an airtight tin.

SEE ALSO

Scone pizza

FRUITS AND PUDDINGS

◆

My philosophy on puddings and sweet dishes goes something like this: since most of us seem to be engaged in an on-going battle with the good things of life and too many calories, the only practical way to maintain a balance is to treat myself to a really delicious pudding just once a week. Since I so often find the desserts, even in the best restaurants, are a let-down I prefer to ensure that this once-a-week treat is home-made: then I *know* it will be as special as I want it to be.

When I first began testing recipes for publication I quickly learned one thing, and that is that too much sugar kills flavour. Therefore I have always kept sugar to a minimum in my recipes, and since the first edition of the *Cookery Course* I have in fact continued to reduce sugar in many of my recipes. It's amazing how when you eat less of it, the less you want. If your palate is not addicted to sugar, all sorts of natural ingredients begin to reveal their own sweetness. If you were to adopt this philosophy you would find a special pleasure in eating something really *wicked* once in a while! Before we begin the recipes, just a word about ingredients.

GELATINE

Cold mousses, soufflés and jellies need flavourless gelatine to get them to set. One detail worth paying close attention to is to make sure your gelatine has dissolved properly: failure to do so is perhaps the commonest cause of problems.

There are two kinds of gelatine. One (not very widely available) is transparent leaf gelatine. The other is powdered gelatine, which comes in packets of ½ oz (10 g) each. This amount of powdered gelatine is usually enough to stiffen 1 pint (570 ml) of liquid (or use three sheets of gelatine per pint).

The best way to dissolve gelatine is to sprinkle it into a cup or small basin containing 3–4 tablespoons of some hot or cold liquid. Stir it, and when the gelatine has soaked up the liquid place the cup in a pan of barely simmering water and leave until it has dissolved completely and turned transparent. To test this, dip a teaspoon in, turn it over and you'll soon see if there are any undissolved granules. It's important not to let the liquid boil – so keep the heat under the pan gentle, and before you use it pass the gelatine through a strainer, to extract any bits of skin that may have formed. Another tip (that appears on the back of some packets) is that you should sprinkle the gelatine granules onto the liquid, and not the other way round.

CREAM

Only double cream (or whipping cream) is suitable for whipping. Take care, though, because over-whisking can cause the cream to take a curdled appearance, so that it won't fold into anything (untreated Jersey cream is very prone to this). So if you have to fold cream into anything, beat it only to the thickened 'floppy' stage. For piping it has to be stiffer: beat it until stiff peaks are left when you lift the whisk from the cream (but again, don't over-do it).

CHOCOLATE

Oh dear, what have they done to chocolate? The cocoa solids in chocolate have been gradually eroded: so-called cooking chocolate has only traces in it, while some brands of plain dessert chocolate have between 30 and 37 per cent. Luckily one supermarket chain has a De-Luxe chocolate with a 51 per cent cocoa content. If you're going to eat chocolatey desserts, then I do think they should taste genuine rather than synthetic.

When you cook chocolate, bear in mind that overheating, or leaving it near the heat too long, makes it granular, when other ingredients are added, and the chocolate loses all its gloss. But if you deal with it carefully you'll never have any problems. Just break the chocolate up into small squares, place them in a basin fitted over a pan of barely simmering water (if it's boiling too fast turn the heat out, so that you just have very hot water), and the chocolate will melt round the edge. Then stir it with a wooden spoon, and in 3–5 minutes it will all have melted and become smoothly liquid.

COLD PUDDINGS
◆

SUMMER PUDDING
◆

(Serves 6 people)

Maybe the reason why this pudding is such a favourite is because we only have these particular fruits for a short time each year – anyway in our house it's become a sort of annual event. Do try to get a well-made white loaf though: the texture of sliced white is most unsuitable.

1 lb raspberries (450 g)
8 oz redcurrants (225 g)
4 oz blackcurrants (110 g)
5 oz caster sugar (150 g)
7–8 medium slices white bread from a large loaf

A 1½ pint (850 ml) pudding basin, lightly-buttered.

Separate the redcurrants and blackcurrants from their stalks by holding the tip of each stalk firmly between finger and thumb and sliding it between the prongs of a fork – pushing the fork downwards, so pulling off the berries as it goes. Rinse all the fruits, picking out any raspberries that look at all musty.

Place the fruits with the sugar in a large saucepan over a medium heat and let them cook for about 3–5 minutes, only until the sugar has melted and the juices begin to run – don't overcook and so spoil the fresh flavour. Now remove the fruit from the heat, and line the pudding basin with the slices of bread, overlapping them and sealing well by pressing the edges together. Fill in any gaps with small pieces of bread, so that no juice can get through when you add the fruit.

Pour the fruit and juice in (except for about two-thirds of a cupful), then cover the pudding with another slice of bread. Then place a small plate or saucer (one that will fit exactly inside the rim of the bowl) on top, and on top of that place a 3 lb or 4 lb (1.3 kg or 1.8 kg) weight, and leave in the refrigerator overnight.

Just before serving the pudding, turn it out on to a large serving dish and spoon the reserved juice all over, to soak any bits of bread that still look white. Serve cut into wedges, with a bowl of thick cream on the table.

PAVLOVA

◆

(Serves 6 people)

This is a delicious pudding from Australia, which is very difficult to make if you don't have the right recipe but dead easy if you do! Served with sharp fruits to counteract the sweetness of the meringue, it is truly one of the greats.

3 large fresh egg whites
6 oz caster sugar (175 g)
For the topping
10 fl oz cream (275 ml), whipped
12 oz soft fruits (350 g) – raspberries, strawberries and redcurrants mixed
a little icing sugar

Pre-heat the oven to gas mark 2, 300°F (150°C).

A lightly-oiled baking sheet, lined with silicone paper, which peels off very easily.

I never make this with the traditional cornflour and vinegar, since side-by-side comparisons have revealed very little difference.

Place the egg whites in a large clean bowl and have the sugar measured and ready. Now whisk the egg whites until they form soft peaks and you can turn the bowl upside down without them sliding out (it's very important, though, not to over-beat the eggs because, if you do, they will start to collapse). When they're ready, start to whisk in the sugar, approximately 1 oz (25 g) at a time, whisking after each addition until all the sugar is in.

Now take a metal tablespoon and spoon the meringue mixture onto the prepared baking sheet, forming a circle about 8 inches (20 cm) in diameter. Then spoon round blobs next to each other so that they join up to form a circle all around the edge. Now, using the tip of a skewer, make little swirls in the meringue all round the edge, lifting the skewer up sharply each time to leave tiny peaks.

Now place the baking sheet in the oven, then immediately turn down the heat to gas mark 1, 275°F (140°C), and leave it to cook for 1 hour. Then turn the heat right off but *leave* the Pavlova inside the oven until it's completely cold. I always find it's best to make a Pavlova in the evening and leave it in the turned-off oven overnight to dry out. It's my belief that the secret of successful meringues of any sort is to let them dry out completely, which is what this method does perfectly.

To serve the Pavlova, lift it from the baking sheet, peel off the paper and place it on a serving dish. Then just before serving, spread the whipped cream on top, arrange the strawberries, etc., on top of the cream and dust with a little sifted icing sugar. Serve cut into wedges.

Note Of course, this can be made with just one kind of fruit – for instance strawberries. In the winter, when there are no soft fruits available, sliced bananas and chopped preserved ginger, or slices of fresh mango with passion fruit are good.

MERINGUES

If you simply want to make meringues (see the photo opposite page 512), use the recipe above, only spoon dessertspoonfuls of the mixture (using two spoons to shape them) onto a baking sheet – the cooking time is the same. When they are cool, sandwich them together with whipped cream.

STRAWBERRIES IN RASPBERRY PURÉE

(Serves 4–6 people)

This is one of the simplest and most delicious sweet dishes I know and proves it's not always necessary to spend hours in the kitchen to make something spectacular.

1 lb firm strawberries (450 g)
8 oz raspberries (225 g)
2½ oz icing sugar (60 g), sifted
5 fl oz double cream (150 ml), whipped

Hull the strawberries, but don't wash them – just gently wipe them with a piece of damp kitchen paper. The raspberries should then be pressed to a pulp through a nylon sieve, and mixed with the icing sugar. Now arrange the strawberries in a bowl (a glass one would show off the attractive colour of this dish), and sit the bowl on some ice-cubes which you have arranged in the bottom of another bowl.

Mix the raspberry purée into the strawberries, then just before serving top with the whipped cream.

CARDINAL PEACHES

◆

(Serves 6 people)

These look and taste stunning served in stemmed glass dishes – a really fresh and fragrant way to end a meal.

6 large, ripe peaches
1¹/₂ tablespoons caster sugar
1 vanilla pod
12 oz raspberries (350 g)
2–3 oz icing sugar (50–75 g)
1 tablespoon flaked almonds, toasted

First wash the peaches and place them, whole and unpeeled, in a large saucepan. Pour in just enough water to cover them, add the caster sugar and the vanilla pod, bring it up to simmering point, then put a lid on and simmer gently for about 10 minutes. Then drain the peaches, and when they're cold slip the skins off.

Meanwhile sprinkle the raspberries with icing sugar and leave them for 20 minutes. Then press them through a nylon or hair sieve to make a purée. Now place the peaches in a bowl and pour the raspberry purée over. Cover with cling film and chill thoroughly for several hours. To serve them, place on one large serving dish or in six individual dishes and sprinkle with flaked almonds.

FRESH FRUIT SALAD

◆

(Serves 8 people)

Any fresh fruit salad may be varied according to whatever fruits are in season but this one seems to have just the right balance. If you don't have rum – or don't like it – you can replace it with fresh orange juice.

2 oranges
8 oz black grapes (225 g)
1 pineapple
2 Cox's apples
2 Comice pears
2 bananas
For the syrup
4 oz caster sugar (110 g)
10 fl oz water (275 ml)
juice of 1 lemon
6 tablespoons rum

Begin by making the syrup. To do this, place the sugar and water in a small pan, and let the sugar dissolve over a gentle heat. Then bring to the boil and simmer for a minute, remove from the heat and add the lemon juice, then tip into a serving bowl to cool. When cold, add the rum.

Now prepare the fruits. Peel the oranges and divide into segments, then add all the segments to the syrup in the bowl, and toss well. Rinse and drain the grapes, then cut each one in half and remove the pips before adding to the syrup. Slice the top off the pineapple and cut away the sides and the base: then slice the pineapple across and cut the slices into segments, and add to the syrup. The apples and pears need to be cored but leave the peel on, and slice directly into the syrup. Leave the bananas till last – they discolour the quickest – and peel and slice straight into the bowl. When all the fruit is in, toss everything well, cover the bowl with cling film and chill in the fridge before serving.

DRIED FRUIT JELLY

◆

(Serves 6 people)

This is cool and light and is good after a rich meal. It goes beautifully served with home-made natural yoghurt (see page 487) or Greek yoghurt.

4 oz prunes (110 g)
4 oz dried apricots (110 g)
2 oz sugar (50 g)
1 small piece cinnamon stick
1 strip orange rind
juice of 1 orange
1 level tablespoon powdered gelatine

Start this off the night before by putting the prunes and dried apricots to soak in a pint (570 ml) of cold water. Then, when you are ready to make the jelly, pour the fruits (and the water they were soaked in) into a saucepan, adding the sugar, cinnamon and orange rind, and simmer gently for 20 minutes. Next fit a sieve over a bowl, pour the fruits into it and let them drain thoroughly. Then pour the liquid into a measuring jug, and add the orange juice and enough water to make it up to a pint (570 ml). At this stage taste to check there's enough sugar.

Now put 3 tablespoons of the liquid into a small bowl, sprinkle in the gelatine and, when it has absorbed all the liquid, fit the bowl over a saucepan of barely simmering water. Stir now and then, and when the gelatine has dissolved and become transparent, strain it back into the rest of the mixture, mixing it in thoroughly.

Take the stones out of the prunes and chop all the flesh of the fruits roughly and arrange in the base of a 2 pint (1.2 litre) mould. Pour the gelatine mixture over the fruit and leave in a cool place to set.

TRADITIONAL TRIFLE

◆

(Serves 6–8 people)

This is a real trifle made with proper custard – a bit extravagant but well worth it.

5 trifle sponge cakes
raspberry jam
8 oz frozen raspberries (225 g) – no need to defrost
2 fl oz sherry (55 ml)

2 small bananas, peeled and sliced thinly

For the custard
10 fl oz double cream (275 ml)
3 egg yolks
1 oz caster sugar (25 g)
1 level teaspoon cornflour

To decorate
10 fl oz double cream (275 ml)
2 oz flaked almonds (50 g), lightly toasted

Break the sponge cakes in pieces and spread a little raspberry jam on each piece. Then put them into a large glass bowl and sprinkle the raspberries and sherry over them, giving everything a good stir to soak up the sherry.

To make the custard, heat the double cream in a small saucepan. Blend the egg yolks, sugar and cornflour together thoroughly in a basin, and when the cream is hot, pour it over the egg mixture stirring the whole time. Return the custard to the saucepan and stir over a very low heat until thick, then remove it and allow to cool.

Slice the bananas, sprinkle them in amongst the raspberries and pour the custard over. Whip up the cream and spread it on the top. Decorate with the flaked almonds. Cover and chill for 3 or 4 hours before serving.

APRICOT HAZELNUT MERINGUE
◆

(Serves 6 people)

A light and delicious – and rather special – sweet. Again, the sharpness of the apricots counteracts the sweetness of the meringue, which has a lovely nutty flavour. You can buy ready-ground hazelnuts at wholefood shops and delicatessens, or if you're grinding your own, brown them first in the oven (gas mark 4, 350°F, 180°C) for 10 minutes and grind them in a food processor or liquidiser.

3 large egg whites
6 oz caster sugar (175 g)
3 oz ground hazelnuts (75 g)

For the filling
4 oz dried apricots (110 g), soaked overnight
juice of 1 small orange
1 small strip orange rind
¹/₂ inch cinnamon stick (1 cm)
1 tablespoon soft brown sugar
2 teaspoons arrowroot
To finish
10 fl oz double cream (275 ml)
a few whole toasted hazelnuts

Pre-heat the oven to gas mark 5, 375°F (190°C).

Two 7 inch (18 cm) sandwich tins, lightly-oiled and the base lined with silicone or greaseproof paper, also lightly-oiled.

First whisk the egg whites in a bowl until they form stiff peaks, then whisk in the caster sugar, a little at a time. Then, using a metal spoon, lightly fold in the ground hazelnuts. Now divide the mixture equally between the two tins and level them out. Bake the meringues on the centre shelf of the oven for 20–30 minutes. Leave them in the tins to cool for 30 minutes before turning out (the surface will look uneven, but don't worry). When they're cooled, loosen round the edges, turn them out onto wire racks and strip off the base papers.

While the meringues are cooking, you can prepare the apricot filling. Drain the soaked apricots in a sieve over a bowl, then transfer the apricots to a small saucepan and add the orange juice, rind, cinnamon and sugar plus 2 tablespoons of the soaking water. Simmer gently for 10–15 minutes until they are tender when tested with a skewer, then remove the cinnamon stick and orange rind. Mix the arrowroot with a little cold water and add this to the apricot mixture, stirring over a fairly low heat, until the mixture has thickened. Then leave it to get quite cold.

To serve the meringue: whip the cream, then carefully spread the cold apricot mixture over one meringue, followed by half the whipped cream. Place the other meringue on top, spread the remaining cream over that and decorate the top with some whole toasted hazelnuts.

RICH CHOCOLATE MOUSSE

◆

(Serves 2 people)

This one is definitely amongst my top ten favourite puds. It can be made for any number of people if you remember to use 1 egg and 2 oz (50 g) of chocolate per person. Do make sure the chocolate you use has a high percentage of cocoa solids.

4 oz plain dessert chocolate (110 g)
2 eggs, separated
To serve
1 tablespoon rum or brandy
2 heaped teaspoons whipped cream
grated chocolate and/or chopped, toasted nuts

Two stemmed wine glasses or ramekins.

Melt the chocolate as described on page 575. When it is smooth and liquid, remove it from the heat. Beat the egg yolks and add them to the chocolate while it's still hot, beating thoroughly (this cooks the egg yolks slightly).

Now leave the mixture to cool for about 15 minutes. Then beat up the egg whites – not too stiffly, just to the soft peak stage – then fold them into the chocolate mixture. Next spoon the mixture into the glasses, cover each one with foil or cling film and chill until firm (about 2 hours).

When you're ready to serve, make a few holes in the top of each mousse (using a small skewer or darning needle) and spoon some rum or brandy over the surface to soak in. Then top with a blob of whipped cream and some grated chocolate or chopped nuts. This mousse is very nice served with *langue de chat* biscuits.

Chocolate orange mousse
Add the grated rind and the juice of ½ orange to the chocolate at the melting stage.

COLD CHOCOLATE ORANGE SOUFFLÉ

◆

(Serves 4–6 people)

I have a weakness for anything 'chocolatey' and this is one of my most favourite chocolate puddings.

¹/₂ oz powdered gelatine (10 g)
grated rind and juice of 1 large orange
2 eggs, separated
3 whole eggs
3 oz caster sugar (75 g)
7 oz good quality plain chocolate (200 g)
2 fl oz water (55 ml)
3 fl oz double cream (75 ml), lightly beaten until floppy but not thick
To decorate
5 fl oz double cream (150 ml), whipped
1 tablespoon grated chocolate

Start off by soaking the gelatine in the orange juice in an old cup, then place it in a pan of barely simmering water until it has dissolved and become completely transparent.

While that is happening, place the 2 egg yolks, 3 whole eggs and the sugar in a largish mixing bowl and place this over another pan of barely simmering water. Now, using an electric hand or rotary whisk, whisk until the mixture has become thick and creamy, which should be in approximately 10 minutes. Then remove the mixing bowl from the heat and place another bowl over the hot water and break the chocolate into it, add the 2 fl oz (55 ml) water and stir until the chocolate has melted and become a smooth liquid. Remove it from the heat, stir in the grated orange rind, and leave it to cool for about 15 minutes. Now stir and fold the chocolate mixture into the egg mixture along with the gelatine, which should be put through a strainer.

Now whisk the egg whites – not too stiffly, just to the soft peak stage – and fold them into the mixture gently and carefully. Finally, fold in the whipped cream.

Next pour the mixture into a straight-sided 2 pint (1.2 litre) soufflé dish, cover and chill for several hours. Serve decorated with blobs – or piped rosettes – of cream and sprinkle with a little grated chocolate.

CARAMELISED APPLE FLAN

♦

(Serves 4–6 people)

This is from a French recipe called *Tarte Tatin* – it's baked, chilled and then served upside down.

shortcrust pastry, made with 4 oz plain flour (110 g) and 2 oz butter (50 g) (see page 497)

For the filling
4 oz dark soft brown sugar (110 g)
1 teaspoon ground cinnamon
1 lb Bramley apples (450 g), peeled, cored and thinly sliced
1 lb Cox's apples (450 g), peeled, cored and thinly sliced

Pre-heat the oven to gas mark 4, 350°F (180°C).

An 8 inch (20 cm) cake tin, brushed with melted butter, with a circle of greaseproof paper, also brushed with melted butter, covering the base.

Begin by covering the base of the prepared tin with brown sugar, pressing it down evenly and well. Now sprinkle on the cinnamon, and then arrange the sliced apples neatly, the Cox's first, making sure they're pressed well down.

Roll out the pastry to a thickness of approximately ¹/₂ inch (1 cm) and cut out a circle that will fit the top of the tin. Cover the apples with the pastry, pressing it down gently. Place in the centre of the oven for 40 minutes until the pastry is golden.

When the tart is quite cold, loosen it round the edges, cover with a plate and carefully turn it all upside down, then remove the tin and the greaseproof paper. As this always reminds me of Provence, I like to serve it with crème fraîche.

HOT PUDDINGS

If there is a gap in the repertoire of Haute Cuisine then it is surely in the area of what I'd call 'proper puddings'. You'd have thought it would have taken a really exotic dish to get a Frenchman beside himself with admiration for the cooking of any other country but his own: yet at the end of the seventeenth century M. de Valbourg, a French traveller in England, wrote this:

Ah! What an excellent thing is an English pudding! It is manna that hits the palate of all sorts of people, better than that of the wilderness.

But our puddings didn't stop there: throughout the eighteenth century and into Victorian times the British pudding was unsurpassed. George I (Pudding George – hence the nursery rhyme about Georgy-Porgy) was particularly partial to the boiled variety, and later Prince Albert became a champion of our puddings. Up at the Palace the royal chefs were very busy creating new temptations for the royal palate: Queen's pudding, Windsor pudding, Empress pudding, Albert pudding. If he had lived 150 years later how much more ecstatically would that nice Frenchman have written: 'To come at pudding time is to come in the most lucky moment in the world!'

Nowadays of course he'd be hard pushed to find a traditional pudding on a restaurant menu. It has become a casualty of affluence and our national preoccupation with dieting and calorie-counting. However, our memories are not so easily dimmed as one might imagine, and people's eyes often light up at the mention of something steamy, curranty or syrupy. It would seem to me the height of irony if our figure-conscious generation should be the one that lets the traditional pudding die of neglect – even as it continues to push up the sales of confectionery, bars of chocolate, synthetic packaged desserts and artificial ice creams.

SOME NOTES ON HOT PUDDING INGREDIENTS

Flour

Self-raising flour must be used in all suet and sponge recipes. Plain flour plus baking powder can be used, but self-raising is preferable because it already contains just the right balance of raising agent. When an all-in-one sponge method is used an extra amount of raising agent is needed.

Fats

I find packet shredded suet is actually better, as well as more convenient, for suet puddings than butcher's suet because it is shredded to exactly the right size and is completely free of skin and membrane.

Dried fruits

One tip I can pass on when buying dried fruits, and that is always buy it in cellophane packets or else loose. The important thing is to be able to *see* what you're buying. Those enclosed cardboard packets only too often carry last season's dried fruit with a very dry and musty look to it.

Pudding spices

The ground spices used in puddings can go stale and lose their strength if they're stored too long. So buy them in small quantities, and better discard any you have had for as long as a year. Nutmeg really should be *freshly grated* at all times: once ground its fragrance vanishes extremely quickly.

Candied peel

The same tendency is to be found with this. Buy your candied peel whole and you'll find it has a great deal more flavour than the ready-cut peel (and only cut the peel as and when you need it). It will keep almost indefinitely in a screw-top jar, so it is worth buying in a stock of it when it's readily available at Christmas time. If at other times it is not to be found at your local shops or supermarket, you will probably be able to get some at a specialised food shop or health-food store.

Chocolate
This can be tricky to work with if not handled carefully. As I mentioned before use 'proper' chocolate rather than 'cooking' chocolate and follow the instructions on page 575.

RICH BREAD AND BUTTER PUDDING
◆

(Serves 4–6 people)

Never fear if you have some stale bread that needs using up. This is a light delicious pudding with a lovely dark toasted nutmeg crust. (Illus. opposite p. 513.)

8 slices bread from a small loaf, buttered
$^1/_2$ oz candied lemon or orange peel (10 g), finely chopped
2 oz currants (50 g)
10 fl oz milk (275 ml)
2$^1/_2$ fl oz double cream (60 ml)
2 oz caster sugar (50 g)
grated rind of $^1/_2$ small lemon
3 eggs
freshly grated nutmeg

Pre-heat the oven to gas mark 4, 350°F (180°C).

A 2 pint (1.2 litre) enamel baking dish (one of the oblong kind), well-buttered.

Cut each slice of buttered bread in half – leaving the crusts on. Now arrange one layer of buttered bread over the base of the baking dish, sprinkle the candied peel and half the currants over, then cover with another layer of the bread slices and the remainder of the currants.

Next, in a glass measuring jug, measure out the milk and add the double cream. Stir in the caster sugar and lemon rind, then whisk the eggs, first on their own in a small basin and then into the milk mixture. Pour the whole lot over the bread, sprinkle over some freshly grated nutmeg, and bake in the oven for 30–40 minutes. Serve warm.

APPLE AND ORANGE CRUNCH

♦

(Serves 4 people)

I like this crunchy pudding served with *Proper custard sauce* (page 407) or, failing that, a thick pouring cream.

4 oz butter (110 g)
approx. 12 thinnish slices bread from a small brown or white loaf
3 medium cooking apples, peeled and sliced thinly
½ rind and all the juice of 1 small orange
3 oz demerara sugar (75 g)

Pre-heat the oven to gas mark 4, 350°F (180°C).
A 1½ pint (850 ml) baking dish, well-buttered.

Melt the butter in a saucepan over a low heat. Cut the crusts off the bread slices, and spread six or seven on both sides with melted butter, using a pastry brush. Place them in the well-buttered baking dish, covering the base and sides as a lining. Press them down firmly, then sprinkle in a layer of sliced apple, a little grated orange rind and juice, and a layer of sugar. Carry on like this until all the apple is used, but keep back a tablespoon of sugar. Brush melted butter on the other slices of bread and press them on top. Sprinkle on the remaining sugar and add any melted butter left.

Bake the pudding for 45 minutes or until the top is crisp, golden and crunchy and the apples inside are soft.

LEMON SURPRISE PUDDING

♦

(Serves 4 people)

In this pudding the 'surprise' is that after it is cooked you'll find that underneath the light sponge topping there's a delicious pool of lemony sauce.

2 oz butter (50 g)
4 oz caster sugar (110 g)
rind and juice of 2 large lemons
2 eggs, separated
2 oz self-raising flour (50 g), sifted
5 fl oz milk (150 ml)

Pre-heat the oven to gas mark 4, 350°F (180°C).
1½ pint (850 ml) deep baking dish, buttered.

First beat the butter, sugar and lemon rind together until well softened (it won't go light and fluffy because there's more sugar than butter). Then beat in the egg yolks, a little at a time. Next fold in the flour, alternately with the milk and lemon juice. Finally whisk the egg whites and fold them in as well (the mixture will look a bit curdled at this stage, but that's normal). Pour the mixture into the baking dish and bake in the centre of the oven for 40–45 minutes or until golden-brown. It's usual to serve this pudding hot from the oven, but as a matter of fact it's just as nice served cold.

CHOCOLATE AND WALNUT PUDDING

◆

(Serves 4 people)

This is a pudding popular with children, as when it's cooked it's surrounded with its own pool of chocolate sauce.

2 oz caster sugar (50 g)
1/2 teaspoon ground cinnamon
2 oz fine semolina (50 g)
1 teaspoon baking powder
2 oz cocoa powder (50 g)
1 oz butter (25 g), melted
2 eggs, beaten
1/4 teaspoon pure vanilla essence
1 oz walnuts (25 g), finely chopped
3 oz dark soft brown sugar (75 g)
10 fl oz hand-hot water (275 ml)
icing sugar

Pre-heat the oven to gas mark 4, 350°F (180°C).
A 1³/₄ pint (1 litre) deep, oval baking dish, buttered.
Start by sifting the first four ingredients and 1 oz (25 g) of the cocoa powder into a mixing bowl and, in a separate bowl, whisk together the melted butter, eggs and vanilla essence. Then stir this into the dry ingredients together with the chopped walnuts and pour this mixture into the buttered baking dish.
Now mix together the brown sugar and remaining cocoa powder and, with a fork, gradually whisk in the hot water, then pour this all over the pudding (you may think this sounds unusual, but it's correct).
Place the pudding in the pre-heated oven and bake for 30 minutes or until the pudding has risen and is firm in the middle. Before serving sprinkle the top with some icing sugar.

ELIZA ACTON'S RICH RICE PUDDING

———————— ♦ ————————

(Serves 4 people)

Tinned rice pudding might be convenient, but it bears no resemblance to the proper kind, which always has a dark caramelised skin on top, covering just the right amount of creaminess and stickiness inside.

4 oz short-grain rice (110 g)
1½ pints milk (850 ml)
3 oz caster sugar (75 g)
2 oz butter (50 g)
3 eggs
grated rind of ½ lemon
freshly grated nutmeg

Pre-heat the oven to gas mark 2, 300°F (150°C).

For this you'll need a 2 pint (1.2 litre) baking dish, well-buttered.

First put the rice into a saucepan, add the milk and bring it slowly almost to simmering point, then let it cook very gently until the rice is practically tender, which should take about 10 minutes.

Next add the sugar and butter and stir until they have dissolved and melted. Now take the saucepan off the heat and let the mixture cool a little, then stir in the eggs – well beaten – with the lemon rind.

Pour the mixture into the baking dish, sprinkle on some freshly grated nutmeg and bake for 30–40 minutes – or longer if you prefer a thicker consistency. Serve with pouring cream.

Note This rice pudding when cooked separates into a layer of creamy rice with a layer of rice custard on top. If you prefer it not to separate, after the 10 minutes' initial cooking carry on cooking gently (without boiling) until the mixture has thickened. Then continue as above.

HOT CHOCOLATE RUM SOUFFLÉ

———————— ♦ ————————

(Serves 4 people)

If you were feeling really wicked you could serve a hot chocolate sauce with this as well as the cream! Just melt 3 oz (75 g) good chocolate with 2 tablespoons cream over hot water.

4 oz plain chocolate (110 g)
2 tablespoons rum
4 egg yolks
6 large egg whites

> ### To serve
> **10 fl oz double or single cream (275 ml)**
>
> **icing sugar**

Pre-heat the oven and a baking sheet to gas mark 6, 400°F (200°C).

A 2 pint (1.2 litre) soufflé dish, well-buttered.

Break the chocolate into a mixing bowl, add the rum and place the bowl over a saucepan of water that has just boiled and leave it until the chocolate is soft, then beat, using a wooden spoon, until it's smooth.

In a small basin whisk the egg yolks thoroughly and stir them into the chocolate. In another bowl – and making sure your beater is clean and dry – whisk the egg whites until stiff, then fold them gently and carefully into the chocolate mixture, using a metal spoon. Next pour it all into the prepared soufflé dish and bake, on the baking sheet, for approximately 20 minutes or until the soufflé is puffy and springy to touch.

Serve straight from the oven, dusting the top with some sifted icing sugar and with the cream in a jug to pour over separately. (It's much better to serve pouring cream with this rather than whipped cream.)

QUEEN OF PUDDINGS
◆

(Serves 4 people)

This, with a cloud of meringue on top, is probably one of the lightest and most mouthwatering puddings ever invented.

> **1 pint milk (570 ml)**
>
> **¹/₂ oz butter (10 g)**
>
> **4 oz fresh white breadcrumbs (110 g)**
>
> **2 oz caster sugar (50 g), plus 1 teaspoon**
>
> **grated rind of 1 small lemon**
>
> **2 eggs**
>
> **3 level tablespoons raspberry jam**

Pre-heat the oven to gas mark 4, 350°F (180°C).

You'll need a generously buttered 1¹/₂ pint (850 ml) oval pie-dish.

First pour the milk into a saucepan and bring to the boil. Remove from the heat and stir in the butter, breadcrumbs, 1 oz (25 g) of the sugar and the lemon rind, and leave for 20 minutes to allow the breadcrumbs to swell.

Now separate the eggs, beat the yolks and add them to the cooled breadcrumb mixture. Pour it all into the pie-dish and spread it out evenly. Bake in the centre of the oven for 30–35 minutes, or until set.

Meantime, in a small saucepan melt the jam over a low heat and, when the pudding is ready, remove it from the oven and spread the jam carefully and evenly all over the top.

Next beat the egg whites until stiff, then whisk in 1 oz (25 g) of caster sugar and spoon this meringue mixture over the pudding. Finally, sprinkle a teaspoon of caster sugar over it all and bake for a further 10–15 minutes until the topping is golden-brown.

Note If you want to serve eight people, double the ingredients, use a 3 pint (1.75 litre) baking dish and give both stages a fraction more cooking time.

CIDER BAKED APPLES WITH TOASTED MUESLI

♦

(Serves 4 people)

This is a very simple recipe, but really delicious when the first Bramley apples come into season.

4 medium Bramley apples
10 fl oz dry cider (275 ml)
a little butter
4 tablespoons muesli

Pre-heat the oven to gas mark 5, 375°F (190°C).

Begin by wiping and coring the apples – if you have an apple corer this is quite a simple job. Next, with a sharp knife, cut just through the skin around the centre of each apple.

Pour the cider into a shallow baking tin, then lightly grease each apple – wiping them with a buttered piece of kitchen paper is a good way of doing this. Now stand the apples upright in the cider.

Bake them for about 40 minutes or until they're tender when tested with a skewer, and baste them occasionally with the cider during the cooking time.

After 15 minutes put the muesli in the oven in an uncovered baking dish so that it will heat through and have a slightly toasted appearance.

When the apples are cooked, place them on top of the muesli, pour the juices over and serve with some cold pouring cream.

Note There is no need to add sugar to the apples if the muesli is sweetened.

TRADITIONAL APPLE CHARLOTTE

♦

(Serves 4 people)

This is a real apple charlotte, moulded in a basin, so that when it's turned out the outside is crisp and buttery with the apples cooked to a pulp inside.

1 lb apples (450 g) – half Bramley and half Cox's if possible
1 tablespoon caster sugar
4 oz butter (110 g)
6 slices bread from a large loaf, about ¼ inch (5 mm) thick with crusts removed
1 egg yolk

A 1 pint (570 ml) pudding basin.

Peel, core and thinly slice the apples first of all, rinse them in cold water and put them in a saucepan with the sugar and 1 oz (25 g) of the butter. Cook them over a low heat until they are soft enough to beat into a purée. Beat them and leave on one side to cool.

Meanwhile melt the remaining 3 oz (75 g) of butter gently, and cut each slice of bread into rectangles. Next brush each piece of bread with melted butter (both sides), being careful not to leave any unbuttered patches, then line the pudding basin with approximately three-quarters of the bread (or as much as you need). Don't leave any gaps between the pieces – overlap them and press firmly.

When the apple purée has cooled, beat the egg yolk into it and fill the lined basin with the mixture. Finally seal the top with overlapping slices of the remaining bread. Place a suitably-sized ovenproof plate on top of the pudding and weigh it down with a 2 lb (900 g) scale-weight. Meanwhile pre-heat the oven to gas mark 6, 400°F (200°C).

After 30 minutes place the basin (with the weight still on it) in the oven to bake for 35 minutes. Then, with an oven cloth, remove the plate and weight, and bake the pudding for another 10 minutes to brown on top. Leave the pudding to settle in the basin for a minute after removing from the oven, then carefully invert it onto a warmed plate to serve.

BAKED APPLE AND ALMOND PUDDING

♦

(Serves 4–6 people)

Since this recipe was given to me many years ago by the proprietor of the Sign of the Angel in Laycock, it has become really popular with readers of the *Cookery Course* as I know from their many letters.

1 lb cooking apples (450 g), peeled, cored and sliced
2 oz soft brown sugar (50 g)
4 oz butter (110 g), at room temperature
4 oz caster sugar (110 g)
2 large eggs, beaten
4 oz ground almonds (110 g)

Pre-heat the oven to gas mark 4, 350°F (180°C).

A buttered pie-dish approximately 1½ pint (850 ml) capacity.

Place the apples in a saucepan with the brown sugar and approximately 1 tablespoon water, simmer gently until soft, and then arrange them in the bottom of the prepared pie-dish.

In a mixing bowl, cream the butter and caster sugar until pale and fluffy and then beat in the eggs a little at a time. When all the egg is in, carefully and lightly fold in the ground almonds. Now spread this mixture over the apples, and even out the surface with the back of a tablespoon. Then bake on a 'highish' shelf in the oven for exactly 1 hour.

This pudding is equally good served warm or cold – either way it's nice with some chilled pouring cream. It will keep in the refrigerator for 3 or 4 days.

FRUIT CRUMBLES

Crumbles are a good all-round family sweet dish, which can be varied not just by using fruits in season, but also by ringing the changes with the crumble topping. Whatever problems you may have with your pastry-making technique, you're absolutely safe with a crumble because there is no resting or rolling-out involved.

BASIC CRUMBLE TOPPING
◆

(Serves 6 people)

8 oz plain or wholewheat flour (225 g)
3 oz butter (75 g), at room temperature
3–4 oz soft brown sugar (75–110 g), according to taste

Pre-heat the oven to gas mark 4, 350°F (180°C).

Place the flour in a large mixing bowl, then add the butter and rub it into the flour lightly, using your fingertips. Then when it all looks crumbly, and the fat has been dispersed fairly evenly, add the sugar and combine that well with the rest.

Now sprinkle the crumble mixture all over the fruit in a pie-dish or shallow gratin dish, spreading it out with a fork. Place the crumble on a high shelf in the oven and bake it for 30–40 minutes or until the top is tinged with brown.

VARIATIONS ON THE CRUMBLE TOPPING

(1) Instead of all flour use 4 oz (110 g) wholewheat flour and 4 oz (110 g) jumbo or porridge oats.
(2) Instead of all flour, use 4 oz (110 g) wholewheat flour and 4 oz (110 g) unsweetened muesli.
(3) For a nut crumble topping, use 6 oz (175 g) wholewheat flour and 3 oz (75 g) chopped nuts. You will need to use only 3 oz (75 g) of soft brown sugar with the 3 oz (75 g) of butter.

SPICED APPLE AND RAISIN CRUMBLE

◆

(Serves 6 people)

2 lb Bramley apples (900 g), peeled, cored and sliced
3 oz raisins (75 g)
1 oz soft brown sugar (25 g)
1 level teaspoon ground cinnamon
1/4 teaspoon ground cloves
2 tablespoons water

Pre-heat the oven to gas mark 4, 350°F (180°C).

A 3 pint (1.75 litre) pie-dish or a 9–10 inch (23–25 cm) shallow gratin dish.

Place the sliced apples, raisins, sugar and spices in a saucepan, sprinkle with the water, then cook gently until the apples are soft and fluffy. Spoon the mixture into the pie-dish and sprinkle with any of the crumble toppings above. Use a fork to even it out, but don't press it down at all. Cook for 30–40 minutes until the topping is tinged with brown.

Alternative crumble fillings

All the recipes that follow are cooked at the same temperature as the recipe above and are all cooked in the same size pie-dish or gratin dish. They all serve six people.

Rhubarb and ginger crumble

Use 2 lb (900 g) rhubarb, 3 oz (75 g) soft brown sugar and 1 level teaspoon ground ginger.

Cut the rhubarb into chunks, then place in a saucepan together with the sugar and ginger. Cook over a gentle heat (covered) for 15 minutes, stirring to get the uncooked pieces at the top down into the heat. Try not to overcook it, though – it should be chunky, not mushy. When it's cooked, drain off about half the juice, then transfer the fruit to a pie-dish, sprinkle with a crumble topping (see pages 594–5), and bake for 30–40 minutes.

Gooseberry crumble

Use 2 lb (900 g) gooseberries and 6 oz (175 g) caster sugar.

Just top and tail the gooseberries, place them in the dish, and sprinkle in the caster sugar. Top straightaway with one of the crumble mixtures (see pages 594–5), and bake on the centre shelf of the oven for 40–45 minutes.

Damson (or plum) and cinnamon crumble

Use 2 lb (900 g) damsons or plums, 4–6 oz (110–175 g) demerara sugar and 1 teaspoon ground cinnamon.

Wash the damsons or plums, then place them whole in the pie-dish. Sprinkle them with the sugar and cinnamon, then spread with a crumble topping (see pages 594–5). I think the nut crumble mixture is the nicest for this. Bake for 30–40 minutes until the topping is tinged with brown.

Note Plums should be stoned and halved, but damson stones are easier left for the diners to extract!

Dried fruit crumble

For this you can use any combination of dried fruits: prunes, apricots, figs, raisins etc. You need 1 lb (450 g) mixed dried fruits, the rind and juice of 1 large orange and 2 oz (50 g) demerara sugar.

Soak the fruit overnight in a deep bowl, covered with about 1¼ pints (725 ml) of water. Next day drain off 5 fl oz (150 ml) of the water, then place the rest of the water, the fruit and the sugar in a saucepan, bring to simmering point and simmer for 10 minutes or until the fruit is tender. Then stir in the orange juice and rind, pour the whole lot into the pie-dish and top with the basic or the oat crumble (see pages 594–5), and bake for 30–40 minutes.

Mincemeat and apple crumble

Use 8 oz (225 g) Bramley apples, 8 oz (225 g) Cox's apples and 1 lb (450 g) mincemeat.

Peel, core and slice the apples and mix with the mincemeat. (No sugar is needed as the mincemeat and apples provide enough sweetness.) Spoon into the base of a 3 pint (1.75 litre) baking dish, top with crumble mixture (see pages 594–5) and bake for 30–40 minutes.

BLACKCURRANT CRUMBLE
◆

(Serves 4–6 people)

1 lb blackcurrants (450 g)
2 tablespoons caster sugar
For the crumble topping
8 oz plain flour (225 g)
3 oz butter (75 g)
3–4 oz light soft brown sugar (75–110 g)

Pre-heat the oven to gas mark 4, 350°F (180°C).

I think this particular crumble is nicest baked in a shallow 9 inch (23 cm) fluted ceramic dish (or something similar).

Strip the blackcurrants from their stalks, arrange them in the dish, sprinkle with the sugar, and top with the crumble topping (made as on page 594). Press it down firmly and evenly. Bake for 30–40 minutes.

Raspberry crumble
This is made in the same way as the blackcurrant crumble, but with 1 instead of 2 tablespoons of caster sugar sprinkled over the fruit.

STEAMED PUDDINGS

A steamed pudding is far easier to make and serve than most people seem to think. The mixing makes little demand on your time, needs no particular skill, and once the pudding is on the stove it requires very little attention. Extra steaming does no harm at all: so if you want to serve it an hour later than planned, say, it will be just as good.

Steamer
Not a very costly piece of equipment but, I think, an essential one (see page 11). Over the years it will earn its keep, even if it's only for making your own Christmas puddings. Modern steamers are made to fit most sizes of saucepan. Because the pudding cooks only in the steam that rises from the water boiling in the saucepan underneath, there's no

danger here of the water itself bubbling in to swamp the pudding. Filled three-quarters full, the water should not need topping up for most steaming recipes – but if it does look like getting a bit low, always top up with boiling water. I should add that one of the beauties of steaming is, if you possess more than one steamer (I find I need four at Christmas!), you can steam two puddings over one pan of water – change the position of the steamers over at half-time.

An alternative form of steaming, if you don't have a steamer, is to sit the pudding basin on a small upturned plate or perhaps a wad of crumpled foil inside a saucepan (so it can sit above the water-line). The saucepan is then filled with boiling water but *only* up to a third of its capacity. There are snags: if the heat is too high, the water can boil up too fiercely and into the pudding – and it is liable to boil away rather more quickly than with a steamer. The answer is to keep a vigilant eye on it.

Lids

Whether you are using a steamer or a saucepan, it is essential to have a well-fitting lid, to prevent the steam escaping and the water drying up completely. Inevitably *some* steam will escape, but it won't be a problem if your lid fits properly.

Coverings

Old-fashioned boiled puddings were sometimes made directly inside pudding-cloths. Nowadays china pudding basins are much more convenient, and whereas once even these would be covered with greaseproof paper and linen cloth, today modern foil does the job on its own. The basin should be covered with double foil for extra strength, and this should be pleated in the centre (to allow room for expansion when the pudding is cooking). Before placing the foil over the basin, butter the side that will come into contact with the pudding – to prevent it sticking – then tie the foil all around the edge of the basin as tightly as you can with string. And if you can make a little handle with the string at the same time, it will make it easier to lift the basin out of the saucepan at the end.

Pressure-cooking puddings

A pressure cooker is ideal for steaming puddings, as it cuts the steaming time considerably. If you own one, the manufacturer's instruction booklet will explain the general principles. But first a couple of important points.

The preparation of the pudding is the same as for ordinary steaming, and the basins are covered and tied down in a similar way. Place the trivet inside the pressure cooker, add 1½ pints (850 ml) of water and bring this up to simmering point. Then lower the pudding in, to stand on the trivet, and put the lid on but leave the vent open – so that the pudding gets 15 minutes' gentle steaming before the pressure is brought up (keep the heat very low for this, to prevent too much steam escaping, thus reducing the correct water level inside). Then after 15 minutes, start the pressure at low (5 lb/2.25 kg) and give the pudding 35 minutes if the ordinary steaming time was 1½ hours, or 1 hour if the ordinary steaming time was 2–3 hours.

CHRISTMAS PUDDING
◆

For two puddings in 2 pint (1.2 litre) basins, or four in 1 pint (570 ml) basins.

This has proved to be one of the most popular recipes I've ever produced and if you're making it for the first time, I hope you'll agree. I actually prefer to eat our puddings around Christmas-time rather than keep them for the following year when they don't taste as good. Made in October or November they are perfect by Christmas (nevertheless still wonderful if you have to make them at the last minute!).

8 oz shredded suet (225 g)
4 oz self-raising flour (110 g), sifted
8 oz white breadcrumbs (225 g), grated from a stale loaf
1 heaped teaspoon ground mixed spice
½ teaspoon grated nutmeg
¼ teaspoon ground cinnamon
1 lb soft brown sugar (450 g)
8 oz sultanas (225 g)
8 oz raisins (225 g)
1¼ lb currants (575 g)
2 oz mixed peel (50 g) – finely chopped whole candied and citron peel if available
2 oz almonds (50 g), blanched, skinned and chopped
1 apple, peeled, cored and finely chopped
grated rind of 1 orange and 1 lemon
4 eggs
4 tablespoons rum
5 fl oz barley wine (150 ml)
5 fl oz stout (150 ml)

Put the suet, flour, breadcrumbs, spices and sugar in a bowl, mixing in each ingredient thoroughly before adding the next. Then gradually mix in all the dried fruit, peel and nuts and follow these with the apple and the orange and lemon rind.

In a different bowl beat up the eggs, and mix the rum, barley wine and stout into them. Empty all this over the dry ingredients – and then stir very hard indeed (it's vital this mixing, so recruit some help if necessary). You may find you need a bit more stout – it's not possible to be exact with the liquid quantities, but the mixture should be of a good dropping consistency (that is, it should fall from the spoon when tapped sharply against the side of the bowl).

After the mixing, cover the bowl with a cloth and leave it overnight. The next day, grease two (or four) pudding basins and pack the mixture into them right to the top. Cover each basin with a square of greaseproof paper, with a square pudding cloth on top. Tie these round the rims of the bowls with string, then tie the corners of the cloth together on top.

Steam the puddings for 8 hours – keeping an eye on the water now and then to make sure it doesn't boil away. When cooked and cooled, remove the paper and cloths and replace with a fresh lot. Store in a cool dry place and, when ready to eat, steam for 2 hours.

ST STEPHEN'S PUDDING
◆

(Serves 4–6 people)

This pudding was sent to me by a television viewer in East Anglia and is a very good alternative pudding for those who prefer a less rich pudding for Christmas. I also often serve it at dinner parties.

4 oz breadcrumbs (110 g)
2 oz self-raising flour (50 g), sifted
2 oz soft brown sugar (50 g)
3 oz shredded suet (75 g)
a pinch of salt
4 oz seedless raisins (110 g)
2 medium cooking apples
grated rind of 1 lemon
1 egg
3 tablespoons milk

A 2 pint (1.2 litre) pudding basin, well-greased.

In a large mixing bowl first combine all the dry ingredients, then add the raisins, the apples (peeled and then grated) and the grated lemon rind. Stir thoroughly to combine everything well. Now beat the egg into the milk and stir the whole lot into the mixture.

Pack the mixture into the pudding basin, cover the basin tightly with a sheet of greaseproof paper, then with a sheet of foil, and secure with string. Steam the pudding for 2 hours. Serve with *Proper custard sauce* or with *Brandy butter* (page 407).

STEAMED RAISIN PUDDING

---◆---

(Serves 4 people)

This is a very special steamed pudding, suitable for a dinner party but so easy to make. Don't worry about the absence of sugar – the raisins provide enough sweetness.

2 oz white breadcrumbs (50 g)
2 oz self-raising flour (50 g), sifted
4 oz shredded suet (110 g)
8 oz prepared stoned raisins (225 g)
1/8 teaspoon salt
1/2 nutmeg, grated
1/2 teaspoon ground ginger
1/8 teaspoon ground mace
1 oz whole mixed candied peel (25 g), finely chopped
grated rind of 1 orange
3 eggs
3 tablespoons brandy

You will need a 1½ pint (850 ml) pudding basin, well-buttered.

In a large bowl mix together the breadcrumbs, flour and suet. Add the raisins, making sure there are none stuck together. When these ingredients are well mixed, add the salt, nutmeg, ginger, mace, candied peel and orange rind and again mix thoroughly.

Now in a small basin beat the eggs well and add them and the brandy to the mixture and stir for at least 5 minutes to amalgamate everything thoroughly and evenly. Pack the pudding basin with the mixture, cover with greaseproof paper and foil, and tie down with string. Steam for 4 hours, making sure that the saucepan doesn't boil dry. When ready to serve, loosen the pudding all round the sides with a palette knife and turn out onto a heated dish. Serve with the *Port wine sauce* on page 408.

SPICED FIG PUDDING WITH RUM BUTTER

◆

(Serves 6 people)

2 oz self-raising flour (50 g), sifted
6 oz fresh white breadcrumbs (175 g)
4 oz shredded suet (110 g)
8 oz dates (225 g), pitted and chopped
6 oz dried figs (175 g), chopped
3 oz raisins (75 g)
2 oz preserved ginger (50 g), chopped
½ teaspoon ground mixed spice
generous quantity of freshly grated nutmeg
grated rind and juice of 1 orange
2 large eggs
2 tablespoons brandy

You'll need a generously buttered 1½ pint (850 ml) pudding basin.

Place the measured flour, breadcrumbs and suet in a mixing bowl. Add the fruits, spices and the orange rind and mix together very thoroughly.

Next beat the eggs with the brandy and orange juice and add this to the mixture, stirring well to make sure all the ingredients are thoroughly mixed, then pack the mixture into the basin. Cover with a double piece of buttered foil, pleated in the middle, and tie it under the rim of the basin with string. Steam the pudding over boiling water for 4 hours.

This is delicious served with some ice-cold rum butter made as follows. Take 4 oz (110 g) unsalted butter and into it gradually beat 4 oz (110 g) dark soft brown sugar until you have a pale cream mixture. Then beat in – a little at a time – 2–3 tablespoons of rum and chill the butter for several hours.

WHOLEWHEAT TREACLE SPONGE

◆

(Serves 4 people)

This is much lighter than it actually sounds and it's lovely served on a cold day with extra warmed syrup poured over.

2 tablespoons golden syrup
4 oz wholewheat flour (110 g), sifted
2½ teaspoons baking powder
2 large eggs

4 oz soft brown sugar (110 g)

4 oz soft margarine (110 g)

You'll need a 1¹/₂ pint (850 ml) pudding basin, well-buttered.

Begin by putting the golden syrup in the base of the pudding basin.

Next place all the remaining ingredients in a bowl and beat well for 2 or 3 minutes until thoroughly mixed. Now spoon this mixture on top of the golden syrup and, using the back of the spoon, spread it out evenly. Cover this with a double piece of buttered foil, pleated in the middle (to allow for expansion) and press down over the rim of the basin and tie round with string. Cut off any extra foil about an inch (2.5 cm) from the string.

Place in a steamer over boiling water and steam for 1¹/₂ hours. Make sure that the saucepan does not boil dry or the water go off the boil and, when necessary, use *boiling water* to top up. When cooked, turn onto a warmed plate and serve hot with custard or extra syrup.

Note If using a pressure cooker the cooking time will be 20 minutes' steaming and 45 minutes at 5 lb (2.25 kg) pressure.

SEE ALSO

Apple and blackberry pie
Apple and cinnamon crêpes
Apple pie
Basic pancakes
Blackcurrant ice cream
Black Forest gâteau
Brown rice pudding with prunes and apricots
Chocolate and hazelnut choux buns
Cœurs à la crème
Coffee éclairs
Crème brûlée
Crème caramel
Crêpes Suzette
Crisp cinnamon flan
Curd cheesecake with fruit topping
Damson plum pie
Dried fruit salad with yoghurt and nuts
Eighteenth-century creamed apple flan
English gooseberry pie
English rhubarb fool
Fresh cherry pie

Fresh fruit and mint vinaigrette
Fresh lemon cheesecake with frosted grapes
Lemon meringue pie
Lemon soufflé omelette
Linzertorte
Mince pies
Old-fashioned bread pudding
Orange cheesecake
Plum and soured cream flan
Praline ice cream
Profiteroles
Rhubarb pie
Rich lemon cream with frosted grapes
Spiced apple and raisin pie
Spiced pears in red wine
Squidgy chocolate log
Strawberry shortcake
Summer fruits pie
Vanilla ice cream
Wholewheat treacle tart
Zabaglione

PRESERVING

♦

The British have always been particularly good at preserving and pickling (just as we have excelled at smoking and curing). We have always been fortunate in this country to be able to grow a wide range of fruits and vegetables, beyond our immediate needs, and so have mastered the arts of storing up produce for the dreary winter months. We even exported our enthusiasm abroad – to India, for example – and came back with all manner of chutneys. You can still see the legacy of this passion at our local flower show – and doubtless at shows all over the country – where multi-coloured mountains of neatly labelled jars stand awaiting inspection and judgement.

Perhaps the necessity to preserve food is no longer so pressing, but the pleasure remains. There's no doubt that strawberry jam spread on a crumpet or fresh-baked scone does bring the memory of a sunny June into the greyness of January, and some dark, spicy plum or damson chutney served with cold ham can remind us that the fruitfulness of autumn can be savoured throughout the year. Some shop-bought jams do now have a high fruit content but even they somehow never capture the fresh flavour of home-made jam. Commercial pickles and chutney are blandly uniform and somehow fail to evoke any such pleasurable dream. All this combined with soaring prices in the shops provides good reasons for making these items at home. And anyone who cares about real food and real flavour won't grudge the time spent on preserving, when a spoonful of faintly sharp and fruity damson jam can put bread-and-jam into the luxury class, or some spicy home-made plum sauce can utterly transform a modest meal of bangers and mash.

GENERAL EQUIPMENT

♦

Contrary to what you might think, preserving at home does not call for a whole battery of special equipment. Below is a list of the general items which will come in very useful.

PRESERVING PANS

A heavy-gauge aluminium preserving pan is a good investment – it's large, sturdy, and will last a lifetime. Its biggest asset is its size, since it will hold more than most family-sized saucepans. It is also very wide and open at the top which means (in the case of chutney-making) the vinegar can reduce more effectively. Perhaps I ought to emphasise 'open' here, because I recall one distressed reader phoning the paper I worked for, saying she had been simmering her chutney for a whole day and it still hadn't reduced. On phoning her back I discovered she had used a large saucepan, instead of a preserving pan, and because I hadn't said otherwise in the recipe, she had kept the lid on! Don't let the lack of a preserving pan stop you from making jams and pickles, but don't ever put the lid on your saucepan.

JARS AND LIDS

Ideally, preserving jars are what you need to make life simple, since they seal down with their own proper lids, and can be bought in a variety of sizes. If you take care of them they do last a lifetime, but for economy, if you get into the habit of saving up all the jars that come into your possession, you'll soon build up quite a collection. At the time of writing most of these are of 1 lb (450 g) capacity, which works well for most things (except pickled onions), so I have kept to this size as a guideline in most recipes. But it's really not important – other sizes of jar can be used; if each one is filled to capacity, then any left-overs can be stored in small jars or used up quickly. You must bear in mind that the vinegar in pickles and chutneys can corrode metal, so for these plastic coated lids are essential.

Warning
Never use paper or cellophane covers for pickles and chutneys. They are fine for jams, but vinegar will evaporate during long storage if the jars aren't completely airtight (which paper covers never are). This is why chutney shrinks and dries out when covered with paper.

All jars and lids for preserving must be washed in warm, soapy water, rinsed thoroughly in warm water, then well dried with a clean towel. As an extra precaution I always place the jars in a moderate oven for 5 minutes, and pour the contents in while the jars are very hot. If you want to use for something else a jar that once contained pickled onions, soak it overnight in cold water with a teaspoonful of bicarbonate of soda stirred in. This should remove any evidence of pickled onions by the next day!

GAUZE

In my early days of cooking I used to get infuriated when cookery books demanded muslin bags to hold the spices, because I never had such a thing as muslin lying around. However, I then discovered that ordinary gauze from the chemist was perfect for the job of holding spices for pickles (or pips for jam-making).

WAXED PAPER DISCS

Circles of waxed paper are placed over chutneys and jams (wax-side down) to provide a seal. These can be made from the waxed paper found in breakfast cereal packets, or bought from stationers ready-made.

INGREDIENTS FOR PRESERVING

The vital point to remember is that all ingredients like fruit and vegetables for preserving must be sound. Anything that looks damaged or decayed in the slightest way should not be used.

CHUTNEY-MAKING

Chutney is derived from a Hindu word, and in fact reveals the origin of this particular form of preserving – namely India. In the first place, chutneys were attempts to reproduce in Britain the exotic recipes brought back by our Indian traders in the eighteenth and nineteenth centuries: but these efforts very soon brought forth a large range of home-grown preserves – of which piccalilli is one of the best-known examples. Our own native fruits, like plums, damsons and unripe tomatoes, proved excellent for this form of preserving, which involves slow simmering in vinegar.

A chutney is ready when the vinegar has reduced sufficiently. The way to tell this is to make a channel with a wooden spoon right across the surface of the chutney. If the spoon leaves a channel imprinted for a few seconds – without it being filled with vinegar – then the chutney is ready.

STORING CHUTNEYS

All chutneys should be stored for *at least three months* before using. This causes them to mature and mellow in flavour (freshly made chutney is too harsh and vinegary). A cool, dark place is usually recommended for storage, and in these days of central heating I have found under the bed in the spare bedroom as good a place as any! Failing that, a covered cardboard box in the garage or garden shed will do.

SPICED PLUM OR DAMSON CHUTNEY

(Makes about 6 lb/2.75 kg)

When the preserving season comes around, this plum chutney is an automatic choice with us. You can also make it with damsons, stewed in their own juice first to remove the stones. Picking out the damson stones does take time, I fear, but the result is the very best chutney of all!

3 lb plums (1.3 kg) – the small dark ones are best
1 lb cooking apples (450 g)
3 largish onions
3 cloves garlic
2 heaped teaspoons ground ginger
1 lb seedless raisins (450 g)
1 lb dark soft brown sugar (450 g)
1 lb demerara sugar (450 g)
2 pints malt vinegar (1.2 litres)
2 tablespoons salt
2 small cinnamon sticks
1 oz whole allspice berries (25 g)
1 dessertspoon whole cloves

A preserving pan (or very large pan), a 12 inch (30 cm) square piece of gauze (which can be brought from chemists), some string and six 1 lb (450 g) preserving (Kilner) jars or jars with plastic-lined screw-top lids.

First of all wash and dry the plums, then slit them down the natural line of the fruit with a sharp knife and remove the stones – putting the halved plums into the pans as you go. Next core and mince the apples (with the peel left on) and add them to the pan, then peel and mince the onions and add them as well.

Now crush the garlic and add that, followed by the ginger and raisins, the sugars and the vinegar. Sprinkle in the salt and stir everything thoroughly. The cinnamon, allspice berries and cloves should be wrapped in the gauze and tied loosely to form a little bag, which should then be tied onto the handle of the pan and suspended into the middle of the rest of the ingredients.

Bring everything to the boil, then lower the heat and let the chutney simmer very gently for 2–3 hours, stirring it occasionally and rather more often towards the end to prevent it sticking to the bottom. When almost all the vinegar has disappeared and the chutney has thickened to a soft consistency, it's ready. It *will* thicken more when it has cooled, so be careful not to overcook it (and remember the narrower the top of the pan, the longer the chutney will take to reduce).

While it is still warm, pour it into the jars (washed, dried and put into a moderate oven to warm through first). Cover with waxed discs and seal down with a screw lid. Label when cold and store in a cool, airy cupboard. Leave to mellow for at least 3 months before eating.

Note You can use a food processor instead of a mincer.

GREEN TOMATO CHUTNEY
◆

(Makes about 8 lb/3.6 kg)

Originally I thought this was a good recipe for using up all those stubborn green tomatoes that never seemed to ripen, but now we all love this chutney so much I don't even want half my tomatoes to ripen – just so I'll be able to make plenty.

2½ lb green tomatoes (1.25 kg)
2 lb onions (900 g)
2½ lb cooking apples (1.25 kg)
1 lb seedless raisins (450 g)
6 large cloves garlic, crushed
½ tablespoon cayenne pepper
½ tablespoon salt
2 level dessertspoons ground ginger
1 lb 6 oz soft brown or demerara sugar (625 g)
1 oz pickling spice (25 g)
3 pints genuine malt vinegar (1.75 litres)

A small preserving pan, eight 1 lb (450 g) preserving jars, a mincer, string and some gauze.

Wash the tomatoes and cut them into quarters; peel the onions and quarter them; quarter and core the apples, leaving the peels on and keeping them in water to prevent browning.

Using the medium blade of a mincer, mince the tomatoes and place them in the pan; next mince the onions, then the raisins followed by the apples (don't worry if they have now turned brown), adding them all to the pan. Now add the garlic, the cayenne, salt, ginger and sugar, blending everything thoroughly. Next tie the pickling spice in a small piece of double-thickness gauze and attach it to the handle so that it hangs down into the other ingredients.

Now pour in the vinegar, bring to simmering point, remove any scum from the surface, then let it simmer very gently for about 3½ hours without covering. Stir now and then, especially towards the end, to prevent sticking. It's ready when the vinegar has been almost absorbed, the chutney has thickened to a nice soft consistency and the spoon leaves a trail. Do be careful not to overcook, and remember it does thicken up quite a bit as it cools.

Pour the hot chutney into hot jars, filling them as full as possible. Cover with waxed sealing discs and seal with a tight lid at once. Label the jars when the chutney is cold.

Note A food processor can be used in place of the mincer.

OLD DOWERHOUSE CHUTNEY
$\blacklozenge$

(Makes 8 lb/3.6 kg)

This is a very old recipe given to me hand-written on a yellowing page from a cookbook belonging to someone's great-grandmother. In fact I got the name wrong in the first edition, and have been corrected by several readers. It is an extremely good recipe, anyway.

1½ lb plums, preferably Victorias (700 g)
8 oz green or red tomatoes (225 g), whatever's available
8 oz onions (225 g)
1½ lb cooking apples, weighed after coring and quartering (700 g) – about 2 lb (900 g) to start with
1 lb stoned raisins (450 g)
4 oz preserved ginger (110 g) – the sort that's preserved in syrup
¼ oz garlic (5 g), finely chopped
1 pint malt vinegar (570 ml)
1½ lb demerara sugar (700 g)
1½ tablespoons cooking salt
¼ oz whole dried chilli peppers (5 g)

A preserving pan or very large saucepan, a small square of gauze, some string and eight 1 lb (450 g) jars.

First, pick over the plums and wash them, then cut them in half, remove the stones and cut the halves into two (or if very large into three). Then chop the tomatoes roughly into not-too-small pieces, and place both plums and tomatoes into a preserving pan.

Now pass the onions, apples, raisins and preserved ginger through the coarse blade of a mincer, or chop them finely in a food processor, and add these to the pan together with the chopped garlic, vinegar, sugar and salt. Tie the chillies in the gauze with string and suspend them from the handle of the pan. Now cook the chutney very slowly for about 1–1½ hours, or until most of the liquid has evaporated and you've given it the 'channel' test as described on page 606. Also, have a few good stirs during the cooking – and especially towards the end to prevent the mixture sticking to the base of the pan.

Pot the chutney when it is still hot into hot jars. Seal with waxed discs and tight lids. Label the jars when the chutney is cold.

SWEET PICCALILLI
◆

(Makes about 5 lb/2.25 kg)

There's nothing like a few home-made pickles and chutneys for brightening up left-over meat, sausages or other winter economy dishes. When there are no runner beans left, this one can be made with frozen string beans (sometimes called *haricots verts*).

2 medium cauliflowers, divided into 1 inch (2.5 cm) florets
1 lb small onions (450 g), quartered and cut across
2 pints malt vinegar (1.2 litres), plus 5 tablespoons
¹/₂ whole nutmeg, grated
¹/₂ teaspoon ground allspice
1 cucumber, peeled, cut into ¹/₄ inch (5 mm) rounds, then each round quartered
1 lb runner beans (450 g), cut into largish slices
12 oz caster sugar (350 g)
2 cloves garlic, crushed with 3 teaspoons salt
2 oz mustard powder (50 g)
1 oz ground turmeric (25 g)
6 level tablespoons plain flour
3 tablespoons water

A large saucepan and five 1 lb (450 g) jars.

First place the cauliflower florets, onions and 2 pints (1.2 litres) vinegar together in a large saucepan, then add the nutmeg and allspice and bring to the boil. Cover and simmer for 8 minutes. Now take the lid off and stir in the cucumber, runner beans and sugar. Crush the garlic in the salt and stir this in as well. Bring the mixture up to simmering point again, cover and cook for a further 5 minutes. The vegetables should still all be slightly crisp – so don't go away and forget them.

Now set a large colander over a large bowl and pour the contents of the saucepan into it and leave it all to drain (reserving the vinegar). Mix the mustard powder, turmeric and flour together in a bowl. Gradually work in the additional 5 tablespoons of vinegar and the water to make a fairly loose paste. Next add a ladleful of the hot vinegar liquid, drained from the vegetables, stir and transfer the blend to a saucepan.

Bring to the boil, whisking with a balloon whisk, and gradually adding the remaining hot vinegar. Boil gently for 5 minutes, then transfer the vegetables from the colander to the large bowl, and pour over the sauce. Stir well to mix, then spoon the piccalilli into washed, dried and warmed screw-top jars. Keep for three months before eating.

Note If you get lumps in the sauce, whisk with a rotary whisk to disperse them.

VICTORIA PLUM OR DAMSON KETCHUP

◆

(Makes 3¹/₂ pints/2 litres)

This is delicious served with cold meats or sausages and will keep indefinitely. Use bottles that have contained shop-bought ketchup or you can buy the old-fashioned type 'pop' bottles from good kitchen shops.

8 lb plums or damsons (3.6 kg)
8 oz currants (225 g)
1 lb onions (450 g), chopped small
2 pints distilled white vinegar (1.2 litres)
2 oz coarse salt (50 g)
1 lb demerara sugar (450 g)
Tie the following spices in a piece of gauze
6–8 dried chilli peppers
1 tablespoon black peppercorns
1 tablespoon mustard seeds
¹/₂ oz dried root ginger (10 g), crushed a bit first
¹/₂ oz whole allspice berries (10 g)
2 cloves garlic

First slit the plums with a sharp knife and remove the stones, then place the fruit in a large pan and add the currants, onions and the bag of spices. Add half the vinegar, bring to the boil and simmer gently, uncovered, for about 30 minutes or until the mixture is soft.

Now remove the bag of spices, place the contents of the pan in a liquidiser and blend until perfectly smooth – if necessary sieve as well. Then rinse out the pan and return the purée and bag of spices to it, adding the salt, sugar and the remaining vinegar. Bring to simmering point and cook gently, uncovered, for 1¹/₂–2 hours or until the ketchup has reduced to approximately 3¹/₂ pints (2 litres). Stir now and then to prevent sticking.

In the meantime prepare the containers by boiling the bottles and their tops. When the ketchup is ready pour it into the bottles while they're still hot, filling them to within an inch (2.5 cm) of the top. Put on the tops immediately but screw them only half-way and if you're using the 'pop' type bottles push the top in but leave the lever up.

Next place the bottles in a larger deep pan (standing them on an upside down, heatproof plate) and add warm water to within 1¹/₂ inches (4 cm) from the tops. Bring the water to the boil and after 10 minutes transfer the bottles to a wooden surface and complete the sealing.

PICKLING

———— ◆ ————

I'm afraid I have neither the stamina nor the patience to endure long pickling sessions (especially with onions). So I always use the method in the recipe below, which cuts out the normal salting and brining process. The results are excellent, except that the vegetables pickled in this way do need to be eaten within three months. I actually find that no hardship – a batch made in October ensures a good supply for Christmas, and after that another batch can be made. The whole thing takes about 45 minutes from start to finish. (Those who require longer-keeping pickles should salt the onions first. Layer the peeled onions and sprinkle salt over each layer and then all over the top. Leave them overnight and the next day rinse off the salt, dry the onions with a clean cloth and proceed as below.)

QUICK PICKLED ONIONS

———— ◆ ————

In this recipe I put the spices in with the onions, which gives them a lovely, hot spicy flavour. Just the thing to serve with strong Cheddar cheese, real bread, real ale or real home-made sausage rolls (see page 516). You can preserve shallots similarly.

4³/₄ lb pickling onions (2.1 kg)
1 oz pickling spice (25 g)
3¹/₄ pints malt vinegar (1.8 litres)

Four 1³/₄ pint (1 litre) preserving jars (or the equivalent).

Peel the onions – preferably while you listen to some good music on the radio to take your mind off the job. Then pack the jars half-full with the onions and sprinkle a level dessertspoon of pickling spice into each jar. Then fill up each jar with more onions, followed by another dessertspoon of pickling spice.

Now pour the vinegar over the onions, right up to the top so that it covers them completely, and fix on the lids. Store in a cool, dark place for at least 8 weeks but not more than 3 months (see above) before eating.

Note If you don't have proper preserving jars, any other jars will do, provided they have plastic-coated lids. Paper covers will *not* do – see the notes on jars, page 605.

PICKLED RED CABBAGE

♦

This, again, is made by a quick no-salting method; and the cabbage keeps perfectly crisp for up to four months.

1½ lb red cabbage (700 g), cleaned and shredded
1 oz pickling spice (25 g)
1¾ pints malt vinegar (1 litre)
1 level tablespoon coriander seeds

Five 1 lb (450 g) preserving jars.

Place the pickling spice in a saucepan with the vinegar, cover with a lid, and bring to simmering point very slowly over a gentle heat. Then remove the pan from the heat, and allow the vinegar to infuse the spicy flavours for about 4 hours.

After that strain the vinegar into a large mixing bowl (reserving the spices), stir in the red cabbage and the coriander seeds, and mix thoroughly. Now spoon this mixture into the prepared jars, making sure each jar has enough vinegar to come right up to the top. Extract some pieces of red chilli (or whole ones) from the pickling spices, and place them amongst the red cabbage. Seal down the jars and store for about 2 months before opening.

JAM AND MARMALADE MAKING

♦

The great advantage of home-made jams is that they are pure, made from fruit and sugar only – unlike some of their shop-bought cousins which often list several other ingredients as well. It is true you *can* buy the more expensive brands which proudly display the fact that they contain no preservative or colouring, but (being an avid jam label studier) I have rarely come across a jam – or a marmalade – that is made only from fruit and sugar, whatever the price. The answer, both in terms of quality and economy, is to make them at home and add a touch of luxury to everyday eating.

WHAT IS JAM?

Essentially it's preserved fruit. The fruit, if it is in good condition and slightly under-ripe, contains in its cell walls a natural setting agent called pectin. This, together with the natural acid from the fruit, is released when the fruit is boiled with sugar. As the mixture boils, the sugar concentrates and all three (sugar, acid and pectin) combine to form a mass that eventually reaches 'setting point'.

INGREDIENTS

Fruit

First of all, this should be dry since the water content in damp fruit will dilute the pectin and the acid, and render them less active. Very dusty fruit should be wiped with damp kitchen paper, but normally the boiling process will effectively purify the fruit. Research has shown that slightly under-ripe fruit contains a lot more pectin and fruit acid than over-ripe fruit (which should be avoided). With fruits that contain less acid than others, this deficiency is made up by adding lemon juice.

Sugar

The proportion of sugar to fruit varies according to the type of fruit used. For me, the really sharp fruits – like damsons or loganberries – make the best jams because they are not overpowered by the sweetness of the sugar. In other words, the fruit flavour is stronger. This is also why I believe the bitter Seville oranges make the best marmalade: tasting of oranges rather than sugar. I don't find that special preserving sugar is essential, and in fact never use it because it's so much more expensive.

EQUIPMENT

The equipment for jam-making is the same as that outlined at the beginning of the chapter, except you will find some recipes advise the use of jam thermometers. These are clipped to the side of the preserving pan, and when the mixture reaches 220°F (104°C) setting point should be reached. However, I must say I have never had much success with thermometers, perhaps because the steam caused by fast-boiling makes it impossible to see the temperature clearly (and if you take the thermometer out, the temperature marking drops immediately). I would recommend you use the 'cold plate' test: see page 615.

Jars

They need the same treatment as outlined on page 605, except that in this case the coverings can be cellophane discs kept in place by elastic bands. These are sold in packets, which also contain the waxed discs. Many people say cellophane is the best covering, though it must be admitted that proper lids are a lot more convenient when you start to eat the jam!

IMPORTANT POINTS FOR JAM-MAKING

(1) Tough-skinned fruits should be simmered and softened before the sugar is added, as the sugar has a hardening effect.

(2) Soft-skinned fruits (like strawberries) that tend to disintegrate when

cooked should be soaked in sugar first to harden them – and so help to keep the fruit in the finished jam whole.

(3) The sugar must be dissolved completely before the jam is boiled, otherwise it will be difficult to set and the finished jam will be sugary. To test if the sugar has dissolved, dip a wooden spoon in, turn it over, and if no sugar crystals are visible on the liquid that coats the spoon, it has indeed dissolved. (But be sure to stir well and try this test two or three times.) To speed up the dissolving process, you can warm the sugar in a bowl in the oven before adding it.

(4) Never try to make jam in too large quantities. It will take far too long to come to the boil, and then will not boil rapidly enough to produce a good set.

(5) *How to test for a set.* When you start to cook the fruit place about four small plates in the freezing compartment of the fridge. Then, when you have boiled the jam for the given time, remove the pan from the heat, and place a teaspoonful of the jam onto one of the chilled plates. Allow it to cool for a few seconds, then push it with your finger: if a crinkly skin has formed on the jam, then it has set. If it hasn't set, boil it again for another 5 minutes and then do another test.

(6) Ignore any scum that rises to the surface while the jam is boiling. If you keep skimming it off, you'll find you have no jam left! Instead, wait until you have a set, then remove the jam from the heat and stir in a small lump of butter which will disperse the scum.

(7) After the jam has set, allow it to settle for 15 minutes (specially necessary for jam containing whole fruit – such as strawberry or damson or even chunky marmalade – to prevent the fruit rising to the top when it's poured into the jar). Then pour into dry, clean, warmed jars, filling them as far up to the neck as possible. Then immediately place a waxed disc over the surface, and tie down straightaway with cellophane covering (to do this, wipe the cellophane with a damp cloth and place it on the jar damp side up). Wipe the jars with a hot damp cloth.

(8) Don't put the labels on until the jam is cold, since the heat will prevent them sticking properly and they will very soon peel off.

(9) Store in a cool, dry, and preferably dark, place. Too much light is not good for storage, while a damp or steamy atmosphere can cause mould to develop on the surface of your jam.

(10) If things go wrong. . . . If the jam hasn't set after cooling and potting, tip it all back into the pan and boil again, adding the juice of a small lemon. If a mould develops on the surface, remove it plus about 1/2 inch (1 cm) of the jam underneath. The rest of the jam will not be affected.

(11) There is no need to use commercially produced pectin. It's expensive and shouldn't ever be necessary.

STRAWBERRY JAM

◆

(Makes 6 lb/2.75 kg)

The way to keep strawberries whole in jam is to cover them with the sugar and leave them overnight. The sugar will then draw out the juices and firm the fruit.

4 lb slightly under-ripe dry strawberries (1.8 kg)
3 lb sugar (1.3 kg)
juice of 2 large lemons
½ oz butter (10 g)

Six 1 lb (450 g) jars, a preserving pan with a lightly-buttered base, and four small plates chilled in the ice-making compartment of the refrigerator.

Hull the strawberries and wipe with some damp kitchen paper, then layer them in the preserving pan, sprinkling them with the sugar as you go. Leave them like this overnight, by which time the sugar should have almost dissolved.

To make the jam, place the pan over a lowish heat just to melt the rest of the sugar and draw some of the juice out of the strawberries – don't stir too much, just shake the pan now and then to keep the fruit as whole as possible. When the sugar has completely dissolved, add the lemon juice, turn up the heat and as soon as the jam is really bubbling, time it for 8 minutes and then remove it from the heat. Spoon a little onto a chilled plate, allow it to cool, then push with your little finger: if it forms a crinkly skin, it's set. If not, boil it up for a further 3–4 minutes. Repeat the test, removing the pan from the heat three or four times if necessary until you have a set.

Then remove from the heat, stir in a small lump of butter to disperse any scum, and allow the jam to settle for 15 minutes before pouring it into dry clean jars (heated in a moderate oven for 5 minutes). Seal immediately with waxed discs and tie down while still warm. Label when cold.

Note Try not to wash strawberries or attempt to make jam after it has rained heavily and the fruit is wet – it must be as dry as possible. If you are forced to wash the fruit, dry it and spread it out on clean tea cloths to dry further before using. Any extra moisture will dilute the pectin and make setting more difficult.

LOGANBERRY JAM
◆

(Makes 5 lb/2.25 kg)

You can make this in any quantity, using 1 lb (450 g) of sugar for each pound of loganberries.

3 lb loganberries (1.3 kg), preferably under-ripe
3 lb granulated sugar (1.3 kg)
½ oz butter (10 g)

Pre-heat the oven to gas mark 4, 350°F (180°C).

Five 1 lb (450 g) jars, washed, dried and heated in the oven for 5 minutes, and four small plates in the freezer compartment of the fridge to get them really cold.

Pick over the fruit, discarding any stalks or leafy bits, then put them into a pan. Don't wash them as the heat from the cooking will purify them. Place the pan on a fairly low heat – don't stir at all, just leave it on the heat until the juices start to run.

Then, gently, shake the pan from side to side, to get the top loganberries down to the bottom; or you can stir, but be careful and try not to break the fruit too much – it's nice to get some whole fruits in the finished jam. Now leave it to cook very slowly for about 30 minutes or until the fruit is cooked and all the berries are tender.

While all that's happening – in fact as soon as you've put the fruit on to cook – tip the sugar into a bowl and place it in the pre-heated oven. When the fruit is cooked, add the hot sugar, tipping the pan and stirring gently. Then leave it again on a low heat for a further 15 minutes or so until the sugar has dissolved completely – it's very important no sugar crystals should be left or the finished jam will go sugary. The way to test this is by coating the back of a wooden spoon with the mixture and you will be able to see if the sugar hasn't dissolved.

As soon as it has dissolved, turn the heat right up as high as it will go, and boil the jam rapidly for 10 minutes. Then remove it from the heat, spoon a little onto one of your cooled plates, and when it's cool push the jam with your little finger. If a crinkly skin has formed, it's set. If not boil it rapidly again for 5 minutes, test again and carry on like this until the jam has set.

Ignore any scum while the jam is boiling, but as soon as it's set, add a little knob of butter which will get rid of most of it (you can skim off any that's left with a slotted spoon). Leave the jam for 15 minutes to settle, then pour it into the hot jars, filling them right to the top. Cover straightaway with waxed discs, and seal with tight-fitting lids or cellophane. Label the jars when the jam is cold.

Damson jam

Use 2¼ lb (1 kg) of sugar to 3 lb (1.3 kg) of fruit. Simmer the fruit in 15 fl oz (425 ml) of water until soft, then proceed as for *Loganberry jam* above.

Plum jam

Use 2 lb (900 g) stoned, halved fruit and 1½ lb (700 g) sugar. Simmer the fruit in 8 fl oz (225 ml) of water until tender, then proceed as for *Loganberry jam* above.

Blackcurrant jam

Use 2 lb (900 g) of fruit simmered in 1 pint (570 ml) of water until tender. Add 2½ lb (1.25 kg) of sugar and continue as for *Loganberry jam* above.

SEVILLE ORANGE MARMALADE

◆

(Makes 6 lb/2.75 kg)

I find it hard to make in one go larger quantities than are given in the recipe below.

2 lb Seville oranges (900 g)
4 pints water (2.25 litres)
1 lemon
4 lb granulated sugar (1.8 kg), warmed
½ teaspoon butter

Six 1 lb (450 g) jars, a 9 inch (23 cm) square of gauze, string, and three or four saucers.

Begin by measuring the water into a preserving pan, then cut the lemon and oranges in half and squeeze the juice out of them. Add the juice to the water, and place the pips and any bits of pith that cling to the squeezer on the square of muslin (laid over a dish or cereal bowl first). Now cut the orange peel into quarters with a sharp knife, and then cut each quarter into thinnish shreds. As you cut add the shreds to the water and any pips or spare pith you come across should go onto the muslin. The pith contains a lot of pectin so don't discard any and don't worry about any pith and skin that clings to the shreds – it all gets dissolved in the boiling.

Now tie the pips etc. up loosely in the muslin to form a little bag, and tie this onto the handle of the pan so that the bag is suspended in the water. Then bring the liquid up to simmering point, and simmer gently, uncovered, for 2 hours or thereabouts until the peel is completely soft – test a piece carefully by pressing it between your finger and thumb. At this point pop the saucers into the freezing compartment of the fridge.

Next remove the bag of pips and leave it to cool on a saucer. Then pour the sugar into the pan and stir it now and then over a low heat, until all the crystals have melted (check this carefully, it's important). Now increase the heat to very high, and squeeze the bag of pips over the pan to extract all of the sticky, jelly-like substance that contains the pectin. As you squeeze you'll see it ooze out. You can do this by placing the bag between two saucers or using your hands. Then stir or whisk it into the rest.

As soon as the mixture reaches a really fast boil, start timing. Then after 15 minutes spoon a little of the marmalade onto one of the cold saucers from the fridge, and let it cool back in the fridge. You can tell – when it has cooled – if you have a 'set' by pushing the mixture with your little finger: if it has a really crinkly skin, it is set. If not, continue to boil the marmalade and give it the same test at about 10-minute intervals until it does set.

After that remove the pan from the heat (if there's a lot of scum, most of it can be dispersed by stirring in half a teaspoon of butter, and the rest can be spooned off). Leave the marmalade to settle for 20 minutes.

In the meantime the jars (washed, rinsed and dried first) should be heated in a moderate oven for 5 minutes. Pour the marmalade, with the aid of a funnel or a ladle, into the jars and cover with waxed discs and seal while still hot. Label the jars when quite cold.

QUICK BRAMBLE JELLY
♦

(Makes 1 lb/450 g)

This is not a jelly that will keep for long – perhaps only a month – but if you've been for a long walk in the autumn and returned with a harvest of brambles from the hedgerows, this recipe is so easy and quick to make and it does taste delicious spread on hot crumpets or scones.

1 lb ripe blackberries (450 g)
6 fl oz water (175 ml)
1 lb granulated sugar (450 g)
juice of 1 lemon

A 1 lb (450 g) jar, a large nylon sieve and a piece of chemist's gauze about 14 inches (35 cm) square.

Wash the blackberries and place in a thick-based saucepan with the water, then stew them very gently with a lid on for about 20–25 minutes. Now and then give them a good mash to reduce them to pulp and squeeze as much juice out of them as possible. After that add the sugar and lemon juice to the pan and allow the sugar to dissolve completely, with the heat still low. There must not be any whole granules of sugar left. This takes about 10–15 minutes. Now turn the heat right up and boil fairly rapidly for 8 minutes, stirring now and then to prevent sticking.

Meanwhile warm a large bowl and a 1 lb (450 g) jam jar in the oven – get them nice and hot – and then place the sieve, lined with the gauze, over the bowl and pour the blackberry mixture into the lined sieve. Then, using a wooden spoon, get all the liquid through as quickly as possible, squeezing the remaining pulp as much as you can – but do be quick as the jelly sets if you take too long. Now pour the jelly into the warmed jar, cover with a waxed disc, cool and tie down.

Note If it begins to set before you've had a chance to pour it into the jar, just reheat it gently.

REDCURRANT JELLY
♦

(Makes 2 lb/900 g)

One preserve that has suffered bitterly from commercialism is redcurrant jelly: so often it is sickly sweet and the flavour of the redcurrants is lost amongst other ingredients. Luckily I've found an extremely easy recipe for making it from Eliza Acton's *Modern Cookery for Private Families* (1840). Her name for it was 'Superlative Redcurrant Jelly'.

2 lb redcurrants (900 g)
2 lb sugar (900 g), warmed

1 packet gauze from the chemists, 1 large nylon sieve and two 1 lb (450 g) jars, washed, dried and heated in a moderate oven for 5 minutes.

The first easy thing is that there's no need to go through the tedious business of stripping the currants from the stalks. Just place the washed fruit – stalks and all – in a preserving pan, bring slowly to the boil, and stir and press the redcurrants to break down the fruit and release the juice. As soon as the fruit is cooked (about 10 minutes), add the warmed sugar, stir until absolutely dissolved, then bring the mixture up to a rapid boil, and boil for 8 minutes.

Meanwhile place a large nylon sieve over a bowl and line it with a double layer of gauze. Then, when the 8 minutes are up, tip the whole lot into the sieve and let it drip through. If you don't mind not having a completely clear jelly, you can press to extract as much as possible. Then pour the jelly into warmed jars, cover with waxed discs and tie down.

Note This makes 2 lb (900 g), but the process is exactly the same for a larger quantity.

HOME-MADE CHRISTMAS MINCEMEAT
◆

(Makes 6 lb/2.75 kg)

I give you a warning here. Once you've tasted home-made mincemeat in mince pies, you'll never again be able to revert to shop-bought!

1 lb cooking apples (450 g), peeled, cored and finely chopped
8 oz shredded suet (225 g)
12 oz raisins (350 g)
8 oz sultanas (225 g)
8 oz currants (225 g)
8 oz whole mixed candied peel (225 g), finely chopped
12 oz soft dark brown sugar (350 g)
grated rind and juice of 2 oranges
grated rind and juice of 2 lemons
2 oz whole almonds (50 g), cut into slivers
4 teaspoons ground mixed spice
1/2 teaspoon ground cinnamon
1/2 nutmeg, grated
6 tablespoons brandy

Just mix all the ingredients, except for the brandy, together in a large bowl very thoroughly. Then cover with a cloth and leave for 12 hours. Place the mincemeat, loosely covered with foil, in a cool oven, gas mark 1/4, 225°F (120°C), for 3 hours. This process slowly melts the suet which coats the rest of the ingredients, and prevents fermentation taking place if too much juice seeps from the apples during storage. Then allow it to get quite cold, stir in the brandy and spoon into clean dry jars. Cover with waxed discs, then seal.

VEGETARIAN MINCEMEAT

◆

(Makes 3–4 lb/1.3–1.8 kg)

This recipe first appeared in the *Food Aid Cookery Book* and was given to me by David Sulkin. It's not just for vegetarians – it is also extremely good for the health conscious as it contains no animal fat and no added sugar. It will keep for up to a year.

8 oz dried bananas (225 g)
8 oz dried apricots (225 g)
8 oz raisins (225 g)
5 oz sultanas (150 g)
1/2 teaspoon ground mixed spice
1/4 teaspoon ground ginger
1/4 teaspoon ground cloves
1/4 teaspoon nutmeg, freshly grated
2 1/2 oz fresh orange or tangerine peel (60 g)
1 lb apples (450 g), finely grated including peel
juice of 1 lemon
8 oz creamed coconut (225 g)
4 fl oz brandy (110 ml)
3 tablespoons concentrated apple juice

First separate the dried bananas and chop them into pieces about 1/4 inch (5 mm) thick. Then chop the apricots and add to the bananas along with the raisins, sultanas and spices.

Now chop the orange peel into small pieces and boil it in 4 fl oz (110 ml) of water for 5 minutes (this will kill the toxins in the peel and soften it). Then drain it in a sieve and set aside to cool.

Add the grated apples to the dried fruit mixture. As you do this, sprinkle a little lemon juice on now and then to stop them going brown. Next grate the creamed coconut into the bowl, then add the cooled peel, brandy and concentrated apple juice. Stir to mix everything thoroughly. Then pack into clean, dry jars and store either in the fridge or in a very cool place until needed. Use as conventional mincemeat.

UNCLE BILLY'S TOFFEE

◆

(Makes about 1 1/4 lb/575 g)

For years my Uncle Billy (from Wales) cherished the secret of his home-made toffee – which is the best I've ever tasted, I swear. Then he relented, and I can pass on to you the recipe for this buttery, chewy delicacy!

1 lb soft brown sugar (450 g)
12 oz salted butter (350 g)
1 teaspoon malt vinegar
5 fl oz water (150 ml)

A shallow tin 7½ inches (19 cm) square, lightly-oiled.

First take your very largest saucepan – toffee tends to boil over if it doesn't have much room, so a 4¼ or 5 pint (2.5 or 3 litre) one would be ideal. Put all the ingredients in the saucepan, and bring them *slowly* to the boil over a low heat (about 10–15 minutes), stirring occasionally. When the sugar has completely dissolved, turn the heat up a little, insert a cooking thermometer and let the mixture bubble away (without stirring) until the temperature reaches 250°F (130°C) – which will take about 10 minutes. Then pour it into the prepared tin and leave to set.

When it has set, turn the toffee out onto a board and break it up with a small hammer (or other heavy object), then store the pieces in a polythene bag tied at the neck.

Note If you do not possess a cooking thermometer, test the toffee by dropping a teaspoonful into a saucer of cold water: if it sets immediately into a soft, pliable ball, the toffee is ready.

SEE ALSO

Lemon curd

LEFT-OVERS

$\blacklozenge$

Here, at the very end of the *Cookery Course*, it seemed appropriate to look at what to do with left-overs. However well we plan, and however meticulous we are, we all have food left over at times and it would be criminal not to put it to good use. A recent study in one American city showed that about 15 per cent of the food bought in most households was thrown away – all of it perfectly usable meat, bread and so on. A far cry from the traditional 'Vicarage mutton' which Dorothy Hartley quotes as being served 'hot on Sunday, cold on Monday, hashed on Tuesday, minced on Wednesday, curried on Thursday, broth on Friday, cottage pie on Saturday'.

That must have been quite some joint! But there's a lot to be said for the idea, with the price of meat being what it is. At home, when we do have a joint I like to buy a decent cut, so that it can provide two or three meals. The same goes for poultry or the end of a bacon joint – there's always something that can be made from it.

So here are a few ideas – even for left-over stale bread, which, if you don't own a freezer, can become an enormous problem. Quite simply, make it into an old-fashioned bread pudding, which will disappear in seconds.

SALMON AND CAPER FISH CAKES

$\blacklozenge$

(Serves 2–3 people)

Sometimes a whole salmon – or even a middle cut – can yield some left-overs. But these fish cakes are so good that you can even use some tinned red salmon to make them.

For the fish cakes
8 oz salmon (225 g)
8 oz creamed mashed potato (225 g)
2 tablespoons chopped fresh parsley
2 dessertspoons capers, drained and chopped
2 small gherkins, chopped
2 hard-boiled eggs, peeled and chopped small
1 tablespoon lemon juice
freshly grated nutmeg

2 pinches of cayenne pepper
salt and freshly milled black pepper

For the coating and shallow-frying
1 egg, beaten
approx. 3 oz dry white breadcrumbs (75 g)
groundnut oil and butter

To garnish
watercress and lemon quarters

In a large mixing bowl combine all the ingredients for the fish cakes together thoroughly, then taste and season as required with salt and pepper. (If the fish and potatoes are freshly cooked, you will need to chill the mixture at this stage for an hour or two to get it nice and firm.)

When you're ready to cook, lightly flour a working surface, turn the fish mixture out onto it and form it into a long roll 2–2½ inches (5–6 cm) in diameter. Cut the roll into twelve round fish cakes. Pat each cake into a neat flat shape, and dip each one first into beaten egg and then in the dry white breadcrumbs. Now shallow-fry the cakes in equal quantities of oil and butter until golden-brown on both sides. Drain on crumpled kitchen paper and serve immediately. If you like you can cook cod or other fish for this recipe – and it is also nice to mash the potato with 1 dessertspoon of mayonnaise.

RISSOLES

(Serves 2–3 people)

This recipe is my standard one, but in fact the ingredients are by no means invariable. I like to vary them slightly. For something really spicy (with either lamb or beef) I add ¼ teaspoon of chilli powder and half a green or red pepper very finely chopped or minced. For a Middle Eastern flavour to your rissoles, try adding ½ teaspoon of ground cumin plus ½ teaspoon ground coriander. Or for an Indian influence, add 1 level teaspoon of curry powder, ½ teaspoon of ground ginger and ½ teaspoon ground turmeric. Whichever combination you choose, home-made rissoles are quite delicious, especially with creamy mashed potatoes and home-made chutney.

| 8 oz cooked lamb or beef (225 g) |
| 1 small onion |
| 1½ oz fresh breadcrumbs (40 g) |
| ¼ teaspoon ground cinnamon |
| 2 level tablespoons chopped parsley |
| 1 clove garlic, crushed |
| 1 small egg, beaten |
| salt and freshly milled black pepper |

| *For the coating and shallow-frying* |
| seasoned wholewheat flour |
| oil |

Either mince both the onion and the meat through the finest blade of a mincer, or else chop them finely in a food processor. Then place them in a mixing bowl and add the rest of the ingredients. Now just mix and mix until everything is thoroughly blended. Divide the mixture into six portions, and shape each into a round cake shape with your hands. Then coat each rissole all over with some seasoned wholewheat flour.

All this can be done in advance, and the rissoles can be covered and chilled in the fridge. When you're ready to cook, heat some oil in a frying-pan (just enough to cover the base) and when it's very hot fry the rissoles for 5 minutes on each side.

SPECIAL COTTAGE PIE

♦

(Serves 4 people)

This is 'special' because it has a topping of potatoes and leeks which really adds an extra dimension.

| 1 lb minced cooked beef (450 g) |
| 2 medium onions, chopped |
| 1 large carrot, chopped very small |
| 1 oz beef dripping (25 g) |
| ½ teaspoon ground cinnamon |
| ½ teaspoon dried mixed herbs |
| 1 tablespoon chopped fresh parsley |
| 1 level tablespoon plain flour |
| 1 tablespoon tomato purée |
| 10 fl oz hot beef stock (275 ml) |
| salt and freshly milled black pepper |

| *For the topping* |
| |
| 2 lb potatoes (900 g) |

2 medium leeks, cleaned and chopped
2 oz butter (50 g)
1 oz Cheddar cheese (25 g), grated

Pre-heat the oven to gas mark 6, 400°F (200°C).

First of all fry the onions in the dripping until they are soft, then add the carrot and minced meat, continuing to cook for about 10 minutes until the meat and carrot have browned a little. Now season with salt and pepper and add the cinnamon, mixed herbs and parsley. Stir in the flour, mix the tomato purée with the hot stock, add to the meat mixture and bring to simmering point.

To make the topping: boil the potatoes in salted water and cook the leeks gently in the butter. When the potatoes are done, cream them and then stir in the cooked leeks together with their butter and season to taste with salt and pepper.

Put the meat mixture into a well-greased baking dish, spread the potato mixture over the top, sprinkle on the grated cheese and bake for about 25 minutes or until the top is crusty and golden. If you want to use fresh mince for this, give it 20 minutes' initial cooking instead of 10.

BAKED STUFFED COURGETTES

◆

(Serves 2 people)

This is a Greek-inspired recipe, very good for using up a little left-over lamb.

4 large courgettes
1 tablespoon oil
12 oz ripe tomatoes (350 g), peeled and chopped
1 dessertspoon tomato purée
salt and freshly milled black pepper
For the stuffing
white or brown long-grain rice measured to the 3 fl oz (75 ml) level in a measuring jug
2 tablespoons oil
1 medium onion, finely chopped
1 clove garlic, crushed
6 oz minced cooked lamb (175 g)
1 heaped tablespoon chopped fresh parsley
1/4 teaspoon ground cinnamon

Pre-heat the oven to gas mark 4, 350°F (180°C).

Wipe the courgettes, but don't peel them. Cut each one widthways into three pieces, then using a small knife, flat skewer, or apple corer, hollow out the centre of each piece. You should then end up with twelve hollowed-out little barrel shapes. Now, sprinkle the insides with salt and leave them to drain for about 30 minutes.

While that is happening, cook the rice in double its volume of boiling salted water, until all the water has been absorbed and each grain is separate (this will take about 15 minutes for white rice, 40 minutes for brown). Heat the 2 tablespoons oil in a frying-pan, soften the chopped onion in it for 5 minutes, then stir in the garlic followed by the minced lamb and, finally, the rice. Stir well so that everything gets a good coating of oil. Then sprinkle in the parsley and cinnamon and some salt and pepper and remove the pan from the heat.

Now wipe the insides of the courgettes with kitchen paper and fill each one with the stuffing, packing it in as tightly as possible. As each one is filled, lay it in a casserole and, when they're all in, tuck any left-over stuffing in between them. Sprinkle another tablespoon of oil all over.

Next beat the tomatoes to a pulp, stir in the tomato purée, season with salt and pepper, and pour the mixture all over the courgettes. Bake with a lid on the casserole for 45 minutes and for a further 15–30 minutes without the lid until the courgettes are tender. Serve with extra rice and perhaps a green salad.

GRATINÉE OF HAM AND EGGS
◆

(Serves 3–4 people)

This is a good recipe for using up the remains of a bacon joint.

6 oz boiled bacon (175 g), cut into ½ inch (1 cm) cubes
brown basmati rice measured to the 10 fl oz (275 ml) level in a measuring jug
1 pint boiling water (570 ml)
1½ tablespoons olive oil
2 medium onions, roughly chopped
For the cheese sauce
¾ oz plain flour (20 g)
¾ oz butter (20 g)
8 fl oz milk (225 ml)
1 oz strong Cheddar cheese (25 g), grated
salt and freshly milled black pepper
For the topping
2 hard-boiled eggs, peeled and sliced

1 oz strong **Cheddar cheese (25 g)**, grated

1 tablespoon breadcrumbs

cayenne pepper

In a small flameproof casserole, heat the olive oil and fry the onions for 5 minutes. Then add the bacon cubes, stir in the rice, season with a little salt and pour in the boiling water. Simmer gently – with a lid on – for 45 minutes or until the water is absorbed and the rice tender.

While that's happening, put the flour, butter and milk in a saucepan, then – whisking continuously – bring to simmering point, by which time the mixture will have thickened. Add a seasoning of salt and freshly milled black pepper and simmer for 6 minutes. Remove from the heat and stir in the grated cheese.

A few minutes before the rice is cooked, turn on the grill. When the rice is ready, tip it into a shallow gratin dish and fluff it gently with a skewer. Then place the sliced eggs over the top and pour on the cheese sauce. Next sprinkle on the grated cheese and the breadcrumbs and add a dusting of cayenne pepper. Place the dish under a heated grill and serve when the top is brown and bubbly. This is nice served with fried cabbage or broccoli.

BUBBLE AND SQUEAK

◆

(Serves 2 people)

An old-fashioned favourite for using up left-over potatoes and cabbage or you could, of course, use Brussels sprouts.

1 small cabbage

1 lb cooked potatoes (450 g)

1 oz butter (25 g)

1 heaped tablespoon seasoned flour

salt and freshly milled black pepper

beef dripping, for frying

First cut the cabbage into quarters, remove the hard stalk and shred the rest. Wash it thoroughly, then plunge it into fast-boiling water, put a lid on and boil for about 6 minutes. Then transfer the cabbage to a colander and let it drain thoroughly (by putting a plate with a weight on it on top).

Mash the potatoes with the butter and a good seasoning of pepper (preferably with an electric hand whisk). When smooth mix the potatoes with the drained cabbage, then take tablespoons of the mixture and shape them into round cakes. Dust these with seasoned flour, then fry them in hot dripping to a good, crisp, golden-brown on both sides. Drain on crumpled greaseproof paper, and serve straightaway.

Note This can be made in one large cake by simply spooning the mixture into a hot frying-pan and smoothing it out and turning it over with the help of a plate. Serve it cut in wedges. Lovely with cold cuts, especially gammon.

CREAMY CHICKEN CURRY

◆

(Serves 4 people)

This is good for either left-over chicken or turkey. It has a fairly mild curry flavour but you can 'hot it up' if you like by adding a little more curry powder.

1 lb cooked chicken (450 g), cut into 1 inch (2.5 cm) pieces
2 tablespoons groundnut oil
1 large onion, roughly chopped
2 celery stalks, chopped
1 large green pepper, de-seeded and chopped
1 heaped tablespoon plain flour
1 rounded teaspoon Madras curry powder
1 level teaspoon ground ginger
1 level teaspoon ground turmeric
1 clove garlic, crushed
1 pint chicken stock (570 ml)
2 tablespoons double cream
salt and freshly milled black pepper

In a large flameproof casserole heat up the oil and soften the onion in it for 5 minutes, then add the chopped celery and green pepper and soften these for 5 minutes more. Next add the prepared chicken pieces and toss them around with the other ingredients.

Now stir in the flour, curry powder, spices and crushed garlic, and continue to stir to soak up the juices. Next, gradually add the stock, a little at a time, stirring well after each addition. Season with salt and pepper, put a lid on and simmer very gently for 20–25 minutes or until the vegetables are just tender. Remove the curry from the heat, stir in the cream and serve with *Spiced pilau rice* (see page 275) and mango chutney.

HAM CROUQUETTES

‡

(Serves 4 people)

This is obviously a good way to use up left-over ham, but it's also worth buying some ham just to make them.

12 oz cooked ham (350 g)
1 large onion
2 slices wholemeal bread, soaked in a little milk and then squeezed out
1 clove garlic, crushed
1 tablespoon chopped parsley
2 teaspoons Dijon mustard
1 egg, beaten
plain flour
salt and freshly milled black pepper
olive oil, for frying

Mince the cooked ham, using the coarse blade of your mincer, and put the onion through the mincer also. Then, in a large mixing bowl, combine the ham and onion. Break up the soaked bread and stir this in, together with the garlic, parsley and mustard. Season with pepper, but be sparing with the salt – as the ham may be salty. Add the beaten egg and stir thoroughly.

Now mould the mixture into eight large – or twelve smallish – croquettes or rolls, pressing firmly to bind them together. Sprinkle some flour onto a pastry board and roll each croquette in it so that they're all lightly dusted with flour. Shallow-fry them in olive oil to a light brown colour. Fried eggs make a nice accompaniment.

OLD-FASHIONED BREAD PUDDING

◆

(Serves 4 people)

This is a lovely spicy cross between a cake and a pudding – perfect for using left-over bread.

8 oz bread (225 g) – it doesn't matter whether this is brown or white but cut off the crusts
10 fl oz milk (275 ml)
2 oz butter (50 g), melted
3 oz soft brown sugar (75 g) – if you don't have any brown sugar, you can use white
2 level teaspoons ground mixed spice
1 egg, beaten
6 oz mixed dried fruit (175 g) – currants, raisins, sultanas, candied peel
grated rind of ½ orange
freshly grated nutmeg

Pre-heat the oven to gas mark 4, 350°F (180°C).

A 2–2½ pint (1.2–1.5 litre) baking dish, buttered.

Begin by breaking the bread into suitably-sized pieces and place them in a bowl. Pour over the milk, then give the mixture a good stir and leave it for about 30 minutes so that the bread becomes well soaked with the milk.

Now add the melted butter, the sugar, mixed spice and beaten egg. Using a fork, beat the mixture well, making sure that no lumps remain, then stir in the mixed fruit and orange rind. Next spread the mixture in the prepared baking dish and sprinkle over some freshly grated nutmeg. Bake in the pre-heated oven for about 1¼ hours. This is nice served with hot custard but some people are particularly partial to eating it cold.

SEE ALSO

Rich bread and butter pudding
Turkish stuffed peppers

INDEX

◆

Bold numbers refer to the photographs.

Aduki beans 305
  and brown rice salad 318
Aïoli sauce 86, 87, 439
All-in-one banana and
  walnut loaf 469–70
All-in-one sponge cakes 539,
  541–2
Allspice 369
Almond
  and apple pudding 593
  paste 554, 555, 557–8
Alpine eggs 427
American brownies 571–2
American hamburgers 457–8
Anchoïade 459–60, **opp. 416**
Anchovy(ies)
  anchoïade 459–60, **opp. 416**
  butter 406
  lentil and bean salad 319
  with pizza and mozzarella
  57
  with spaghetti 333
Anthony's chopstick chicken
  204–5
Apple(s)
  baked apple and almond
  pudding 593
  and blackberry pie 499
  with braised pork 173–4
  with braised red cabbage
  236
  caramelised apple flan
  584–5
  charlotte, traditional 593
  and chestnut stuffing 199
  cider baked, with toasted
  muesli 592
  and cinnamon crêpes 343
  date and walnut loaf 465,
  547–8
  18th-century creamed apple
  flan 477
  and mincemeat crumble
  596–7
  with Normandy pork 173
  and orange crunch 588
  with pheasant and cream
  478
  pie, double-crust 501
  with pork chops and sage
  359–60
  sauce 147
  spiced apple and onion
  sauce 147, 398
  spiced apple and raisin
  crumble 595–6
  spiced apple and rasin
  pie 500–1
  stuffing 203
  tomato and celery cream

  soup 82
Apricot(s)
  with brown rice pudding
  283
  hazelnut meringue 581–2
Arbroath smokies 121, 124–5
Arrowroot 387
Artichokes 243–5
  and carrot soup 80–1, 245
  cream soup 81
  globe 243–4
  Jerusalem 244–5
  starter 86
Asparagus 86, 227–8
  and cheese tart 92–3
  with eggs en cocotte 474
  as a starter 86
  steaming 228
Aubergines 228–9
  baked, with tomatoes 229
  Italian stuffed 460–1
  moussaka 381–2
Avocado
  chilled avocado soup 70
  with creamed chicken 186
  in four star salad 450–1
  and fresh crab salad 90
  guacamole 382–3
  mousse with prawns and
  vinaigrette 89–90
  sauce 86, 87, 403
  as a starter 86
  vinaigrette 88–9

Bacon 151
  with cabbage 235, **opp. 225**
  with cauliflower and garlic
  238–9
  and egg pie 466–7
  faggots and peas 212–13
  with halibut 114
  with macaroni and leeks
  335, **opp. 289**
  with mashed swedes 263
  and mushroom filling 522
  and ox liver hotpot 213–14
  pot roast 152–3
  quiche Lorraine 510
  smoked bacon and lentil
  soup 78
  spaghetti alla carbonara 331
  thick bean and bacon soup
  309
Baking powder 534
Banana and walnut loaf,
  all-in-one 469–70
Baps 464
  breakfast 51
Bara brith 52–3
Barbecue sauce

  with chicken 190
  pork spare ribs in 463
Barbecues 455–63
Barley 284
Basil 327, 347
  with fresh tomato soup 80
  sauce (pesto alla Genovese)
  354
Bay leaves 347
Bayonne ham 86
Beans 229–31, 304–8
  aduki beans and brown rice
  salad 318
  baby broad beans in parsley
  sauce 230–1
  broad bean salad 453–4
  cassoulet 314–15
  chilli con carne 311–12
  haricot bean and salami
  salad 452–3
  Italian bean and pasta soup
  308–9
  lentil and anchovy salad 319
  oxtail with haricot beans
  222–3
  purée of broad beans 231
  red bean salad 320
  thick bean and bacon soup
  309
  white bean and tuna fish
  salad 91
  varieties 305–6
Beansprout salad with soy
  dressing, Chinese 449–50
Béarnaise sauce 395
Béchamel sauce 390
Beef 139–45, 164–9
  accompaniments to 141
  American hamburgers
  457–8
  in beer 164
  bœuf Bourguignonne 167
  bœuf en croûte 465, 516–17,
  opp. 449
  bœuf en daube 142–3
  boiled beef and dumplings
  144–5
  braised in Guinness, with
  pickled walnuts 177–8
  braised meatballs with
  peppers and tomatoes
  176–7
  braised steak and onions in
  stout 168
  braised steak with green
  peppercorn sauce 375–6
  cevapcici 458–9
  chilli con carne 311–12
  Cornish pasty pie 506–7
  curry with whole spices 378

  cuts, 139–40, 159–60
  English pot-roast 143–4
  Hungarian goulash 166
  meat loaf 468–9
  pot-roasting 139
  rissoles 625–6
  roasting 140–1
  simple Stroganoff 165–6
  special cottage pie 626–7
  steak and kidney pie 511–12
  steak and kidney pudding
  512–13
  steak au poivre 376
  stewed shin, with mushroom
  dumplings 168–9
  stock 64–5
Beetroot 442
  chilled consommé 64
Beurre manié 161
Biscuits 566–73
  oat 569–71
  shortbreads 566–9
Black beans 306
Black butter 106–7
Blackberry
  and apple pie 499
  quick bramble jelly 619–20
Blackcurrant
  crumble 597
  ice cream 484–5
  jam 618
  vinegar 369
Black-eyed beans 306
Black Forest gâteau 485–6
Bleu de Bresse cheese 417
Bloater paste 124
Bloaters 124
Bœuf Bourguignonne 167
Bœuf en croûte 465, 516–17,
  opp. 449
Bœuf en daube 142–3
Bradenham ham 151
Brandy butter 407
Brandy sauce 409
Bread and rolls 35–54
  baking 42
  bap rolls 464
  bara brith 52–3
  breakfast baps 51
  chapattis 52
  croûtons 73, 85, 98
  crusty rolls 464
  French 464
  hot herb and garlic loaf 460
  muffins 50–1
  oatmeal 46–7
  plain white 44–5
  poppy seed rolls 47–8
  quick and easy wholemeal
  43–4

Bread and rolls – *contd.*
  quick wheatmeal rolls 48–9
  soured cream soda 45–6
  tins 12
Bread and butter pudding 587,
  opp. 513
Bread pudding, old-fashioned
  632
Bread sauce 398–9
Brie cheese 417
Broad beans 229–31
  in parsley sauce, baby 230–1
  purée of 231
  salad 453–4
Broccoli 231–3
  cheese soufflé 429–30
  Chinese stir-fried 232–3
  fritters 233
Brownies, American 571–2
Brussels sprouts 233–4
Bubble and squeak 629–30
Buckling, smoked 121, 124
Buckwheat 285
  flour 285
  pancakes 339
  and vegetable pie 322
Butter, flavoured 405–7
  anchovy 406
  black 106–7
  Brandy 407
  Garlic 248–9, 465
  green 149
  herb 237, 246, 275, 405, 460
  hot lemon 244, 406
  rum 602
  tarragon 237
Butter beans 305
  thick bean and bacon soup
  309
Butter sauces 394–6
Buttered leeks 245
Buttered new potatoes with
  parsley, mint and chives
  258–9
Butterfly cakes, lemon curd
  543
Buttermilk 474
Butterscotch sauce 409–10
Buttery kedgeree 280–1
Buttery onion sauce 396

Cabbage 234–6, 442
  bubble and squeak 629–30
  fried, with bacon 235, **opp.
  225**
  with garlic and juniper
  235–6
  leaves, stuffed with rice 295
  red 236
    braised, with apples 236
    and coriander salad 442,
    449
    pickled 613
Caerphilly cheese 416
Cakes 532–60
  boil-and-bake 538, 547–8
  Christmas 554–9
  cooling and storing 537
  family 546–52
  freezing 537
  fruit 551–9
  ingredients 533–5
  sponge 538–46
  tins 533, 536–7
  wedding 560
  see also Biscuits; Cheesecake;
    Scones; Shortcake

Calabrese 231–2
  Chinese stir-fried 232
Calves' liver 206
Calves' sweetbreads with
  soured cream and onion
  sauce 223–4
Camembert cheese 417
Candied peel 586–7
Cannelloni pancake (al forno)
  342
Cantaloupe/musk melon 87
Caper(s) 369–70
  with baked fish and soured
  cream 113
  with potted haddock 128
  and salmon fish cakes 624–5
  sauce, with trout 119–20
Capsicums 365–6
Caraway seeds 370
Carbonnade de bœuf à la
  flamande 164
Cardamom 370
Cardinal peaches 578–9
Carrot(s) 237
  and artichoke soup 80–1,
  245
  and tarragon soup 353
  young, with tarragon butter
  237
Casseroles 158–78
  browning meat 161
  cuts 159–60
  equipment 11, 163–4
  lamb's tongue 220–1
  principles of 160–2
  stock for 63
  thickening 161
Cassoulet 314–15
Cauliflower 232, 238–9
  cheese soufflé 430
  with garlic and bacon
  238–9
  sautées, with coriander
  232, 238, 383–4
Cayenne pepper 366
Celery 239–41
  braised, with cheese and
  onion sauce 240–1
  sauce 397
  tomato and apple cream
  soup 82
Cevapcici 458–9
Chapattis 52
Charcuterie 86
Charantais melons 87
Cheddar cheese 413–14, 415
Cheese 411–34
  Alpine eggs 427
  and asparagus tart 92–3
  with baked spinach and
  brown rice 261
  blue veined 412
  British 415–16
  broccoli cheese soufflé 429–
  30
  cœurs à la crème 433
  Continental 417–18
  cottage 413
  and courgette quiche 509
  courgettes and tomatoes au
  gratin 242
  cream 413
  curd 413
  Dutch omelette 426–7
  eggs and leeks au gratin 29
  fillets of sole gratinés 425
  goats (chèvres) 417

  with gougère 531
  Greek 418
  Greek salad 425–6
  hard-pressed cooked 412
  and herb sausages 421
  Italian 418
  making 411–13
  with minestrone 71–2
  mornay sauce 392–3
  Mozzarella with pizza 57
  and onion quichelets
  418–19, 465
  and onion sauce 240–1
  pan-fried pizza 419–20
  Parmesan 327
  pressed uncooked 412
  Roman gnocchi 421–2
  sauce 291–2, 341–2, 628–9
  savouries 573
  shortcrust pastry 423
  skimmed milk 413
  soft 412–13
  soft creamy, with herbs 361
  soft paste 412
  with soupe à l'oignon 72–3
  soufflé 31
  soufflé pancakes 344
  spinach and cream cheese
  quiche 422–3
  and spinach sauce 261, 393
  tartlets with mushroom pâté
  427–8
  toasted, with ale 424–5
  Welsh rarebit soufflé 423–4
  wholewheat cheese-crusted
  scones 563–4
Cheesecake 430–3
  curd, with fruit topping
  431–2
  fresh lemon, with frosted
  grapes 432–3
  orange 430–1
Cherries
  Black Forest gâteau 485–6
  fresh cherry pie 500
  Morello cherry sauce 197, 401
Chervil 347
Cheshire cheese 415
Chestnut and apple stuffing
  199
Chick peas 305
  hummus bi tahina 313
  salad 451–2
  spiced cutlets 323
  with spiced lamb 316–17
Chicken 179–95
  Anthony's chopstick 204–5
  in barbecue sauce 190
  broilers 181
  categories of 180–1
  chill-fresh 180
  cold chicken pie 192–3, 465
  coq au vin 186–7
  creamed, with avocado 186
  creamy chicken curry 630
  free-range 180
  fried mustard-and-herb-
  coated 194–5, 465
  frozen 179–80, 182
  with grape stuffing 193–4
  jointing and boning 182–3
  with lemon sauce 189–90
  New York dressed 180
  paprika 366, 380, **opp. 384**
  in the pot (poule au pot)
  188–9
  poussins 181

  salad with tarragon and
  grapes 360
  spiced 379
  stock 65–6
  stuffing 184–5
  traditional roast, with
  stuffing 184–5
  with whole spices 191–2
Chicken liver
  pâté 98–9, **opp. 160**
  with risotto and mushrooms
  278–9
Chicory 442
Chilladas 312–13
Chilli(es) 365–6
  con carne 306, 311–12, 366
  eggs 32
  in guacamole 382–3
  sauce, with pork kidneys
  219–20
  tomato sauce 329
Chinese
  beansprout salad 449–50
  leaf 442
  mushroom sauce 69, 84
  stir-fried green vegetables
  232–3
Chives 348
  with buttered new potatoes
  258–9, **opp. 256**
  with creamed potatoes 252
  with jacket potatoes 254, 348
  with new potato salad 448
  with trout and cream 356–7
  winter (Welsh onions) 345
Chocolate
  all-in-one sponge 541
  American brownies 571–2
  fudge filling and topping
  546
  and hazelnut choux buns
  529
  mousse, rich 583
  orange mousse 583
  orange soufflé, cold 583–4
  profiteroles 528–9
  in puddings 575, 587
  rum soufflé, hot 590–1
  and soured cream filling 545
  squidgy chocolate log 548–9,
  opp. 480
  and walnut pudding 589
Cholesterol 19
Choux buns, chocolate and
  hazelnut 529
Choux pastry 527–31
Christmas cake 554–9
Christmas mincemeat, home-
  made 621
Christmas pudding 599–600
Chutney 606–11
  green tomato 608
  old Dowerhouse 609
  spiced plum or damson
  606–7
  sweet piccalilli 610
  Victoria plum ketchup 611
Cider
  baked apples with muesli
  592
  with braised pork 173–4
  in casseroles 161
  vinegar 368, 435
Cinnamon 370
  and apple crêpes 343
  crisp cinnamon flan 525
  and damson crumble 596

Cinnamon – *contd.*
  in moussaka 381–2
Cloves 371
Cod 107
Cod's roe
  smoked 123
  taramasalata 93–4
Cœurs à la crème 423–4
Coffee
  cream mousseline filling 542,
    545
  éclairs 530
  and walnut sponge 541–2
Coley 107
Coq au vin 186–7
Coquilles St Jacques 131
Coriander 348, 371
  with baked lamb 157
  with baked marrow 247
  with marinated pork 380–1
  and red cabbage salad 449
  with sautéed cauliflower
    383–4
Cornflour 387
Cornish pasty pie 265, 506–7
Corn-on-the-cob 241
Cottage pie, special 626–7
Country pâté 97, **opp. 160**
Courgettes (zucchini) 241–2
  baked stuffed 627–8
  and cheese quiche 509
  cheese soufflé 31
  fritters 242
  and tomatoes au gratin 242
Cream 472–82
  clotted 473
  and egg sauce 125–6
  with Normandy pork 173
  with pheasant and apples
    478
  with poached egg and
    watercress 28
  with pork chops 476
  rich lemon cream with
    frosted grapes 480–1
  smoked fish 96
  with trout and chives 356–7
  whipping 472, 575
  and wild mushroom sauce
    336–7
  see also Ice cream; Soured
    cream
Cream cheese 413
  cœurs à la crème 433–4
  and herb filling 522
  with herbs 361
  and spinach quiche 422–3
Cream puffs 522–3
Creamed apple flan, 18th-
  century 477
Creamed chicken with
  avocado 186
Creamed parsnips 250
Creamed potatoes 252
Crème brulée 482
Crème caramel 481–2
Crème fraîche 472, 473–4
Crème patissière 524
Crêpes 337, 339
  apple and cinnamon 343
  Suzette 339–40
Croquettes, ham 631
Croûtons 85
  anchoïade on 459–60
  with beef in beer 164–5
  large 98
  with soupe à l'oignon 72–3

Crudités 86–7
Crumbles 593–7
Crumpets 565–6
Cucumber 442–3
  raita 490–1
  sauce 348, 397–8
  with soured cream and dill
    358–9
  and yoghurt salad 302
  and yoghurt soup, chilled
    489–90
Cumberland sauce 368, 399–400
Cumin 371
Curd cheese 413
  cheesecake with fruit topping
    431–2
  home-made 488
  Richmond maids of honour
    523–4
Curly endive (frisée) 441
Curried lambs' kidneys 217
Curried nut roast 298
Curried ox kidneys 218–19
Curry 372
  beef, with whole spices 378
  creamy chicken 630
  eggs and lentil 26–7
Custard cream *see* Crème
  patissière
Custard in rhubarb fool 479–80
Custard sauce, proper 407–8

Dabs 107
Damson
  and cinnamon crumble 596
  jam 618
  ketchup 611
  plum pie 500
  spiced damson chutney
    606–7
Date
  apple and walnut loaf 465,
    547–8
  sticky date cake 549–50
Derby cheese 416
Dill 348
  with cucumber and soured
    cream 358–9
Dogfish 106
Dolmades 296
Double Gloucester cheese 417
Dover sole 102, 105
  baked fillets with mushroom
    stuffing 112
  grilling 104
Duck 195–7
  roast 196–7
  sauces for 197
  stuffing 196
Dumplings
  with boiled beef 144–5
  mushroom, with beef 168–9
  parsley, with Irish stew 171
Dundee cake, traditional
  551–2
Dunlop cheese 416
Dutch omelette 426–7
Duxelles 248, 508
Dwarf beans (haricots verts)
  230

Eccles cakes 518
Éclairs, coffee 530
Edam cheese 418
Eel, smoked 122
Eggs 18–34, 535
  Alpine 427

bacon and egg pie 466–7
baked (en cocotte) 24
  beating whites 21–2
  boiled and hard-boiled 22–3
  cheese soufflé 31
  chilli 32
  en cocotte with soured cream
    and asparagus 474
  and cream sauce 125–6
  Florentine 262
  frying 24
  gratinée of ham and 628–9
  John Tovey's quick
    hollandaise sauce 34
  and leeks au gratin 29
  and lentil curry 26–7
  mayonnaise 86
  omelettes 24–6, 33–4, 426–7
  pasta 325
  pipérade 30
  poached, with cream and
    watercress 28
  poaching 23
  Scotch, with herbs 465–6
  scrambling 23
  spaghetti alla carbonara 331
  Spanish tortilla 468–9
  zabaglione 33
  see also Omelettes; Quiches
Egyptian beans 306
Eliza Acton's
  English salad sauce 440
  rich rice pudding 590
  vegetable mulligatawny
    75–6
Emmenthal cheese 417
English gooseberry pie 500
English pot-roast 143–4
English rhubarb fool 479–80
Equipment 9–17
  baking 11–12
  barbecue 457
  cake tins 533, 536–7
  casseroles 11, 163–4
  electric slow cooker 163
  food processor 17
  frying pans 11, 24
  jam-making 614
  liquidiser 17
  pancakes 337
  pastry 11, 497
  picnic 464
  preserving 604–5
  pressure cookers 163–4,
    598–9
  saucepans 9–11
  steamers 11, 597–8

Faggots and peas 212
Fagioli 305
Fats 40, 493, 534, 586
Fennel 242–3, 349, 442
  braised 243
Feta cheese 418
  in Greek salad 425–6
Fig pudding with rum butter,
  spiced 602
Filo parcels, spinach 290
Finnan haddock 121, 124
Fish 101–37
  baked fillets with mushroom
    stuffing 112
  baked, with soured cream
    and capers 113
  barbecuing 457
  batter 108
  fisherman's pie 110

flaky fish pie 111
  in foil en papillote 104
  freshwater 119–21
  garlicky fish soup 83
  Italian baked 108–9, 349,
    opp. 160
  kebabs 109
  methods of cooking 102–4
  oily 114–18
  preparing 102
  shellfish 129–37
  smoked 121–9
  smoked fish creams 96
  smoked fish pâté 95
  smoked fish pie 126–7, **opp.
    192**
  stock 67
  white 105–14
Fish cakes
  kipper 127–8
  salmon and caper 624–5
Fisherman's pie 110
Flageolets 306
Flaky fish pie 111
Flaky pastry, quick 515–18
Flan pastry 525–6
Flounders 107
Flour 35, 37–8, 40, 387, 493,
  533–4, 586
Forcemeat stuffing 203
Four star salad 450–1
French bread 464
  croûtons 72–3, 85, 98,
    459–60
  hot herb and garlic loaf 460
  soupe à l'oignon 72–3
Frittata 25
Fritters
  broccoli 233
  courgette 242
Fromage frais 413
Fruit
  cold puddings 575–82
  crumbles 594–7
  deep pies 498–500
  double-crust pies 500–2
  fresh, with mint vinaigrette
    88
  fresh fruit salad 579
  for jams and marmalade 614
  summer fruits pie 502
  summer pudding 575–6
  topping for curd cheesecake
    431–2
  vinegars 369
  yoghurt 489
Fruit cakes 551–9
  almond icing 554, 555, 557–8
  Christmas cake 554–9
  decorations 559
  rich 552–4
  royal icing 554, 555–6, 558–
    9
  traditional Dundee 551–2
  wedding 560
Fruit, dried
  crumble 596
  jelly 580
  for puddings 586
  salad with yoghurt and nuts
    491, **opp. 417**
  yoghurt 489
  wholewheat scones 563

Galettes 285, 337
Gammon 151–4
  baked 152

Gammon – *contd.*
  baked sugar-glazed whole
    153–4
Garam masala 372
Gardener's soup 77
Garlic
  butter 248–9, 465
  with cabbage and juniper
    235–6
  with cauliflower and bacon
    348–9
  hot herb and garlic loaf 460
  jacket potatoes stuffed with
    herbs and 255
Garlicky fish soup 83
Gazpacho, chilled Spanish
  78–9
Gelatine 574
Ginger 372
  and rhubarb crumble 596
Gingernuts 572, **opp. 481**
Girdle cakes 561
  wholewheat 564–5
Globe artichoke 243–4
  sauces for 244
Gnocchi, Roman 285, 421–2
Goose 202–4
  roast stuffed 202–4
Gooseberry crumble 596
Gooseberry pie, English 500
Gorgonzola cheese 418
Gouda cheese 418
  in Dutch omelette 426–7
Gougère with cheese 531
Goulash
  Hungarian 161, 166, 366
  vegetarian 293
Grapes
  with chicken salad 358
  frosted, with lemon
    cheesecake 432–3
  frosted, with rich lemon
    cream 480–1
  stuffing, with chicken 193–4
Gravy 403–5
  browning 405
  deglazing 404
Greek salad 425–6
Green herb and rice salad 355
Green herb soup 352–3
Green peppercorns 365
  sauce, with braised steak
    375–6
Green salad 444
Green sauce, Italian 402–3
Green tomato chutney 608
Green tomato sauce 401–2
Green winter salad 444–5
Gruyère cheese 417
  with soupe à l'oignon 72–3
Guacamole 382–3

Haddock 107
  Arbroath smokies 121,
    124–5
  buttery kedgeree 280–1
  Finnan 121, 124
  golden cutlets 125
  potted with capers 128
  smoked 107, 124–5
  smoked, with cream and
    egg sauce 125–6
  smoked fillets 125
Hake 107
Halibut 107
Ham 151–4
  baked sugar-glazed 153–4

Bayonne 86, 151
Bradenham 151
croquettes 631
cuts 151
gratinée of egg and 628–9
Parma (prosciutto) 86, 151
Suffolk cured 151
Wiltshire cured 151
York 151
Hamburgers, American 457–8
Haricot beans 305
  cassoulet 314–15
  Italian bean and pasta soup
    308–9
  lentil and anchovy salad 319
  with oxtail 222–3
  and salami salad 452–3
Haricots verts 230
Hazelnut(s)
  apricot meringue 581–2
  and chocolate choux buns
    529
  Linzertorte 526
  oil 436
  and vegetable burgers 297–
    8
Heart 209
Herbs 345–61
  with baked leg of lamb 360–
    1, **opp. 353**
  cheese and herb sausages
    421
  and cream cheese filling 522
  dried and fresh 346
  freezing 345–6
  green herb and rice salad
    355
  green herb soup 352–3
  herb butter 237, 246, 275,
    405
  hot herb and garlic loaf 460
  jacket potatoes stuffed with
    garlic and 255
  mustard-and-herb-coated
    chicken 194–5, 465
  with poached trout 356
  with Scotch eggs 465–6
  with soft, creamy cheese 361
  stuffing, with mackerel 357–
    8
  with vinaigrette 438
Herrings 114–15
  grilling 104
  smoked 123–4
  soused 115–16
  see also Bloaters; Buckling;
    Kippers
Hollandaise sauce 394
  John Tovey's quick 34, 244
Honey
  pancakes 339
  and spice cakes 470–1
  with yoghurt and wheat-
    germ 488
Honeydew melons 87
Horseradish 141
Hot cross buns 53–4, **opp. 128**
Hotpot 138
  Lancashire 170
  ox liver and bacon 213–14
Hummus bi tahina 305, 313
Hungarian goulash 166, 366
Huss 106

Ice cream 472, 483–5
  blackcurrant 484–5
  praline 484

vanilla 483
Icing
  almond 554, 555, 557–8
  modelling paste roses 559
  royal 554, 555–6, 558–9
Indian kebabs 377
Irish stew with parsley
  dumplings 171, 284
Italian
  baked fish 108–9, 349, **opp.
    161**
  bean and pasta soup 308–9
  green sauce (salsa verde)
    402–3
  salamis 86
  stuffed aubergines 460–1

Jam 613–20
Jelly
  dried fruit 580
  quick bramble 619–20
  redcurrant 620
  see also Jam
Jerusalem artichokes 244–5
  and carrot soup 245
John Tovey's
  quick hollandaise sauce 34
  rough puff pastry 520–1
  tomato, apple and celery
    cream soup 82
Juniper 373
  with cabbage and garlic
    235–6
  and yoghurt sauce 213

Kebabs
  fish 109
  Indian 377
  lamb 462
  Yugoslav (cevapcici), 458–
    9
Kedgeree, buttery 280–1
Ketchup, Victorian plum or
  damson 611
Kidney(s) 207–9
  curried lamb's 217
  curried ox 218–19
  in fresh tomato sauce 215–
    16
  in jacket potatoes 218
  lamb's in red wine 214–15,
    opp. 224
  pork, in chilli sauce 219–20
  pork, in mushroom and
    onion sauce 216–17
  and rice stuffing, with lamb
    156
  steak and kidney pie 511–12
  steak and kidney pudding
    512–13
Kippers 121, 123
  fish cakes 127
  grilled 123
  jugged 123–4
  marinated fillets 128–9
  tart 510

Lamb 154–7, 170–2
  accompaniments to 155
  baked, with coriander 157
  cassoulet 314–15
  cuts, 154, 160
  Indian kebabs 377
  Irish stew with parsley
    dumplings 171
  kebabs 462
  Lancashire hotpot 170

leg of, baked with butter and
  herbs 360–1, **opp. 353**
moussaka 381–2
mustard-glazed cutlets
  461–2
ragout of 172
rissoles 625–6
shoulder of, with rice and
  kidney stuffing 156–7
spiced, with chick peas
  317–18
spring (mint) sauce for 354
stuffed breast of 155–6
Lambs' hearts 209
Lambs' kidney(s) 208
  curried 217
  in fresh tomato sauce
    215–16
  in jacket potatoes 218
  in red wine 214–15, **opp.
    224**
Lambs' lettuce (salade du
  mâche) 441
Lambs' liver 207
  paprika 211
  peppered 210–11
  . in yoghurt and juniper sauce
    213
Lambs' sweetbreads 210
Lambs' tongues 209
  casserole 220–1
Lancashire cheese 416
Lancashire hotpot 170
Lancaster lemon tart 503–4
Lasagne 326
  al forno 332
  ragù Bolognese 330
Leek(s) 245
  buttered 245
  cream sauce 396
  and eggs au gratin 29
  onion and potato soup 69–70
  with macaroni and bacon
    335, **opp. 289**
  and soured cream flan 475–6
  special cottage pie 626–7
  and turnips boulangère 265
Left-overs 624–32
Leicester cheese 416
Lemon
  all-in-one layer cake 542
  all-in-one sponge 542
  cheesecake with frosted
    grapes, fresh 432–3
  curd butterfly cakes 543
  fresh lemon curd 544
  hot lemon butter 244, 406–7
  Lancaster lemon tart 503–4
  meringue pie 504–5
  pancakes 339
  rich lemon cream with
    frosted grapes 480–1
  in salad dressing 437
  sauce, with chicken 189–90
  soufflé omelette 33–4
  surprise pudding 588–9
  with vinaigrette 438
Lemon sole 105
Lentils 306
  bean and anchovy salad 319
  brown rice and mushroom
    salad 281–2
  buckwheat and vegetable pie
    322
  chilladas 312–13
  eggs and lentil curry 26–7
  non-meat loaf 316–17

Lentils – *contd.*
  smoked bacon and lentil soup 78
  split 306
  and vegetable moussaka 320–1
  vegetarian shepherd's pie 315–16
Lettuce 441
  with braised peas 260
Lima beans 306
Linzertorte 526
Liver 206–7, 210–14
  chicken liver pâté 98–9, **opp. 160**
  faggots and peas 212–13
  ox liver and bacon hotpot 213–14
  paprika 211
  peppered 210–11
  in yoghurt and juniper sauce 213
Loganberry jam 617
Lollo rosso 441
Lovage 349

Macaroni 326
  and baked meat pie 330, 334
  with leeks and bacon 335, **opp. 289**
  with minestrone 71–2
  ragù Bolognese 330
Mace 373
Mackerel
  baked, with herb stuffing 357–8
  grilling whole 104
  marinated 116–17
  smoked 121, 122–3
  smoked pâté 94–5, 123
Maids of honour, Richmond 523–4
Mange tout 245–6
  stir-fried 246
Marinade, marinated
  beef 142–3
  kipper fillets 128–9
  mackerel 116–17
  mushrooms 92
  pork with coriander 380–1
  soused herrings 115–16
Marjoram 350
Marmalade 613–15
  cake 550–1
  Seville orange 618–19
  see also Jam; Jelly
Marrow 246–7
  baked, with tomatoes and coriander 247
Mascarpone cheese 413
Mayonnaise 438–40
  aïoli sauce 439
  egg 86
  home-made 244, 438–9, **opp. 385**
  instant 439
  sauce rouille 440
  sauce tartare 439
Meat 138–78
  baked meat and macaroni pie 334
  browning 161
  casseroles and braised dishes 158–78
  loaf 468–9
  roasting and pot-roasting 138–57

roasting tins 11
see also Beef; Lamb; Pork; Veal
Meatballs, braised with peppers and tomatoes 176–7
Melons 86, 87
Meringue 577, **opp. 512**
  apricot hazelnut 581–2
  lemon pie 504–5
  pavlova 576–7
  queen of puddings 591–2
Mince pies 502–3, **opp. 448**
Mincemeat
  and apple crumble 596–7
  home-made Christmas 621
  vegetarian 622
Minestrone with macaroni 71–2
Mint 350
  with buttered new potatoes 258–9, **opp. 256**
  with new potato salad 448
  redcurrant and orange sauce 400
  spring sauce for lamb 354
  vinaigrette with fresh fruit 88
Morello cherry sauce 197, 401
Mornay sauce 392–3
Mortadella sausage 86
Moules à la marinière 130–1
Moussaka 381–2
  lentil and vegetable 320–1
Mousse
  avocado, with prawns and vinaigrette 89–90
  chocolate orange 583
  rich chocolate 583
Mousseline, coffee cream 545
Mozzarella cheese 86, 418
  with pizza 57, 419–20
Muesli
  home-made 284, 286
  toasted, with cider-baked apples 592
  with yoghurt 488
Muffins 50–1
Mulligatawny soup, Eliza Acton's 75–6
Mushroom(s) 247–9
  and bacon filling 522
  brown rice and lentil salad 281–2
  Chinese mushroom soup 69, 84
  dumplings, with beef 168–9
  Duxelles 248, 508
  in four star salad 450–1
  in hot garlic butter 248–9
  marinated 92
  and onion quiche 508–9
  and onion sauce with pork kidneys 216–17
  pâté with cheese tartlets 427–8
  with pizza and pepperoni 56
  with pork chops and cream 476
  with rice 275
  with risotto and chicken livers 278–9
  with spaghetti and anchovies 333
  stuffing with baked fish fillets 112
  wild mushroom sauce with pasta 336–7
Mussels 129–31

with garlic stuffing 131
moules à la marinière 130–1
Mustard 366–8
  -glazed lamb cutlets 461–2
  -and-herb-coated chicken 194–5, 465
  sauce 392
  sauce with deep-fried sprats 118

Non-meat loaf 316–17
Normandy pork with cream and apples 173
Norwegian red fish 107
Nut roast, curried 298
Nutmeg 373–4
  with creamed potatoes 252

Oatmeal 285, 569
  biscuits 570–1
  bread 46–7
  parkin 546–7
  traditional porridge 285, 286–7
Oats 285, 569–71
  biscuits 569, 570–1
  flakes/rolled 285, 560
  quick cooking 569
  whole/jumbo 569
  whole oat crunchies 570
Offal *see* Kidneys, Liver, etc.
Ogen melons 87
Oil 436–7
  olive 327
Old Dowerhouse chutney 609
Olives
  with pizza and Mozzarella 57
  with spaghetti 333
  with Spanish pork 174–5
Omelettes 24–6
  Dutch 426–7
  aux fines herbes 25, 347
  lemon soufflé 33–4
  open-faced 25
  Savoyarde 26
  tortilla/frittata 25
  see also Eggs
Onion(s) 249
  braised steak and 168
  buttery onion sauce 396
  and cheese quichelets 418–19, 465
  and cheese sauce 240–1
  crisp-fried onion rings 249
  leek and potato soup 69–70
  and mushroom quiche 508–9
  and mushroom sauce 216–17
  pork and sage stuffing 198–9
  quick pickled 612
  rice 275
  shallots 249
  soup à l'oignon gratinée 72–3, **opp. 129**
  and soured cream sauce 223–4
  spring 443, 465
  spring with braised peas 260
  spiced apple and onion sauce 398
  thick onion tart 293–4, **opp. 288**
  tripe and 224–5
Orange
  all-in-one layer cake 542
  all-in-one sponge 542
  and apple crunch 588

bitter orange sauce 197, 400–1
cheesecake 430–1
chocolate orange mousse 583
chocolate orange soufflé 583–4
and cranberry relish 202
fresh orange curd 544
redcurrant and mince sauce 400
Seville orange marmalade 618–19
Ossobuco 175–6
Ox kidneys 208
  curried 218–19
Ox liver 207
  and bacon hotpot 213–14
Ox sweetbreads 210
Oxtail 209
  with haricot beans 222–3
Ox tongue 209
  cold pressed 221–2

Pancakes 337–44
  apple and cinnamon crêpes 343
  basic 338–9, **opp. 352**
  buckwheat 339
  cannelloni 342
  cheese soufflé 344
  crêpes Suzette 339–40
  honey or syrup 339
  lemon 339
  reheating 337–8
  spinach-stuffed, with cheese sauce 340–1
  strawberry jam 339
Paprika 366
  chicken 380, **opp. 384**
  liver 211
Parkin, oatmeal 546–7
Parma ham (prosciutto) 86
  with minestrone 71–2
Parmesan cheese 327, 418
Parsley 350
  with buttered new potatoes 258–9, **opp. 256**
  dumplings 171
  sauce 393
  sauce, with broad beans 230–1
Parsnips 249–50
  baked 250
  creamed 250
Pasta 324–37
  in brodo 326
  with cream and wild mushroom sauce 336–7
  egg 325
  fresh tomato sauce for 329
  green (pasta verde) 325
  home-made 325
  Italian bean and pasta soup 308–9
  pesto alla Genovese 354
  ragù Bolognese 330
  shapes 326
  wholewheat 325
  see also Lasagne; Spaghetti; etc.
Pastry 492–531
  baking blind 496–7
  cheese shortcrust 423
  choux 527–31
  equipment 11, 497
  filo 291
  glazing 111
  puff 519–24

Pastry – *contd.*
  quiche 507–10
  quick flaky 515–18
  rich flan 525–6
  shortcrust 493–8
  suet crust 510–14
Pâté 85, 94–100
  chicken liver 98–9, **opp. 160**
  country 97, **opp. 160**
  croûtons served with 85
  mushrooms 427–8
  pork (rillettes de Tours)
    99–100, **opp. 160**
  smoked fish 95
  smoked fish creams 96
  smoked mackerel 94–5, 123
Pavlova 576–7
Peaches, cardinal 578–9
Pearl barley 284
Pears in red wine, spiced
    384–5
Peas 259–60
  braised, with lettuce and
    spring onions 260
  with faggots 212
  non-meat loaf 316–17
  pease pudding 310–11
  split 306
  thick pea soup 310
  vegetarian shepherd's pie
    315–16
  whole dried 306
  see also Chick peas
Pease pudding 306, 310–11
Pecorino cheese 418
Penne (pasta) 326
Pepper 364–6
  black 364, 376
  capsicums 365–6
  cayenne 366
  chicken paprika 380
  chillies 365–6
  green peppercorn sauce
    375–6
  green peppercorns 365
  paprika 366
  peppered liver 210–11
  steak au poivre 376
  white 365
Pepperoni with pizza and
    mushrooms 56
Peppers
  with braised meatballs
    176–7
  paprika 210
  with rice 275
  Turkish stuffed 282–3
Pesto alla Genovese 354
Pheasant with cream and
    apples 478
Piccalilli, sweet 610
Pickling 612–13
  quick pickled onions 612
  red cabbage 613
Picnics 455, 463–71
Pig's liver 207
  faggots and peas 212
Pipérade 30
Pizza 55–60
  dough 55
  with Mozzarella, anchovies
    and olives 57
  pan-fried 419–20
  with pepperoni and
    mushrooms 56
  pissaladière 59–60
  quick wholewheat 58–9, 465

scone 302–3
Plaice 104, 107
Plum
  and cinnamon crumble 596
  damson plum pie 500
  jam 618
  and soured cream flan 478–9
  spiced plum chutney 606–7
  Victoria plum ketchup 611
Poppy seed rolls 47–8
Pork 145–51, 173–5
  accompaniments to 147
  apple sauce with 147
  braised, with apples and
    cider 173–4
  braised meatballs 176–7
  casserole and braised 160,
    173–5
  cassoulet 314–15
  cevapcici 458–9
  chops with cream and
    mushrooms 476
  chops with sage and apples
    359–60
  cuts 145–6, 160
  faggots and peas 212
  loin of pork Dijonnaise 150–
    1, **opp. 193**
  marinated, with coriander
    380–1
  meat loaf 468–9
  Normandy, with cream and
    apples 173
  pâté 99–100
  roast, with green butter
    149
  roasting 146–7
  sage and onion stuffing
    198–9
  sausages braised in red wine
    178
  smoked cured pork loin 151
  Spanish, with olives 174–5
  spare ribs in barbecue sauce
    463
  stuffed pork tenderloin
    148–9
  see also Bacon; Ham
Pork kidneys 208
  in chilli sauce 219–20
  in mushroom and onion
    sauce 216–17
Porridge, traditional oatmeal
    285, 286–7
Port Salut cheese 417
Port wine sauce 408–9
Pot barley 284
Potato(es) 251–9
  boulangère 245, 255–6
  bubble and squeak 629–30
  buttered new, with parsley,
    mint and chives 258–9,
    opp. 256
  chips 253–4
  creamed with nutmeg 252
  creamed with soured cream
    and chives 252
  crunchy roast 252–3
  gratin dauphinois 256–7
  jacket 254–5
  kidneys in 218
  with soured cream and
    chives 252
  stuffed with garlic and
    herbs 255
leek and onion soup 69–70
new 258

new potato salad with mint
    and chives 448
  punchnep 265, 266
  punchnep soup 76–7
  salad 465
  sauté potatoes Lyonnaise
    257–8
  sauté potatoes Niçoise 258
  special cottage pie 626–7
Pot-roasting 139
  bacon 152–3
  beef 139
  English pot-roast 143–4
Poultry *see* Chicken; Duck;
    Goose; Turkey
Praline ice cream 484
Prawns 134–5
  with avocado mousse 89–90
  spiced, with tomatoes 135
Preserving 604–23
  chutneys 606–11
  equipment 604–5, 614
  ingredients 606
  jam and marmalade making
    613–20
  pickling 612–13
  mincemeat 621–2
Profiteroles 528–9
Prosciutto (Parma ham) 86
Provençal vegetable stew
    299
Proteins 289, 304
Prunes
  in Armagnac 147, 202–4
  with brown rice pudding
    283
Puddings 574–603
  cold 575–85
  hot 585–603
  Christmas 599–600
  crumbles 593–7
  pressure-cooking 598–9
  steamed 597–603
Puff pastry 519–24
Pulses 304–23
Punchnep 265, 266
Punchnep soup 76–7

Queen of puddings 591–2
Quichelets, cheese and onion,
    418–19, 465
Quiches 507–10
  courgette and cheese 509
  Lorraine 510
  mushroom and onion 508–9
  spinach and cream cheese
    422–3

Rabbit pie, old English 513–14
Radicchio 441
Ragù Bolognese 330
Raisin
  spiced apple and raisin
    crumble 595–6
  spiced apple and raisin pie
    500–1
  steamed raisin pudding
    600–1
Raita, cucumber 490–1
Raspberry(ies)
  crumble 597
  purée, strawberries in 578
  vinegar 369
Ratatouille 299
Ravioli 326
Reblochon cheese 417
Red cabbage *see* Cabbage

Redcurrant jelly 620
  in Cumberland sauce 399–
    400
  orange and mint sauce 400
Red kidney beans 306
  chilli con carne 311–12
  salad 320
Rhubarb
  English rhubarb fool 479–
    80
  and ginger crumble 596
  pie 501
Rice 268–83
  Arborio 271
  Basmati 271, 272
  brown 269–70
  and aduki bean salad
    318
  with baked spinach and
    cheese 261–2
  lentil and mushroom
    salad 281–2
  pudding, with prunes
    and apricots 283
  and tuna fish salad 447–8
  and vegetable gratin
    291–2
  buttery kedgeree 280–1
  cabbage leaves stuffed with
    295
  Carolina 271
  dolmades 296
  Eliza Acton's rich rice
    pudding 590
  grain sizes 269
  and green herb salad 355
  with herb butter 275
  and kidney stuffing 156
  with mushrooms 275
  onion 275
  Patna 271
  with peppers 275
  perfect 274–5
  risotto 271, 272, 277–80
  saffron 276
  salad 446–7, 465
  spiced pilau 275
  stock for 63
  Turkish stuffed peppers
    282–3
  wild 270
Rice flakes 272
Rice flour 272
Richmond maids of honour
    523–4
Rigatoni 326
Rillettes de Tours 99–100,
    opp. 160
Risotto 271, 277–80
  with chicken livers and
    mushrooms 278–9
  alla Milanese 272, 277,
    opp. 257
  for spring 279–80
Rissoles 625–6
Rolls *see* Bread
Roman gnocchi 421–2
Roquefort cheese 417
Rosemary 351
Roux 388
Rum
  butter 602
  hot chocolate rum soufflé
    590–1
  sauce 409
Rye 284
Runner beans 230

Sabayon sauce 408
Saffron 374
  rice 276
Sage 351
  with pork chops 359–60
  pork and onion stuffing 198–9
Saint-Paulin cheese 417
St Stephen's pudding 601
Salad dressing 435–40
  Eliza Acton's English salad sauce 440
  lemons 437
  mayonnaise 435, 438–40
  oil 436–7
  soured cream 450–1
  soy 449–50
  vinaigrette 437–8
  vinegar 435–6
Salads, 435–54
  aduki beans and brown rice 316
  avocado and fresh crab 90
  broad bean 453–4
  brown rice and tuna fish 447–8
  brown rice, lentil and mushroom 281–2
  chick pea 451–2
  chicken, with tarragon and grapes 360
  Chinese beansprout, with soy dressing 449–50
  cucumber and yoghurt 302
  dried fruit, with yoghurt 491
  four star 450–1
  fresh fruit 579
  Greek 425–6
  green 444
  green herb and rice 355
  green winter 444–5
  haricot bean and salami 452–3
  lentil, bean and anchovy 317
  new potato 448
  Niçoise 454
  potato 465
  raw spinach and watercress 445–6
  red bean 318
  red cabbage and coriander 449
  rice 446–7, 465
  taramasalata 93–4
  tomato 86, 444
  white bean and tuna fish 91
Salami, Italian 86
  and haricot bean salad 452–3
Salmon 120–1
  and caper fish cakes 624–5
  foil-baked fresh 120
  smoked 121, 122
  smoked salmon tart 510
Salmon trout (sea trout) 121
Salsa verde 402–3
Salt 39, 363–4, 493
Saucepans 9–11
Sauces, savoury 386–403
  aïoli, 86, 87
  apple 147
  for artichokes 244
  avocado 86, 87, 403
  barbecue 190
  basic ingredients 387–8
  basic white 388–91
  basil (pesto alla Genovese) 354

béarnaise 395
béchamel 388, 390
bitter orange 197, 400–1
bread 398–9
butter 394–6
buttery onion 396
caper 119–20
celery 397
cheese 291–2, 341–2, 628–9
cheese and onion 238–9
chilli 219–20
cream and egg 125–6
cream and wild mushroom 336–7
cucumber 397–8
Cumberland 399–400
curdling 386–7
for duck 197
Eliza Acton's English salad 440
green peppercorn 375–6
hollandaise 394
Italian green (salsa verde) 402–3
leek cream 396
lemon 189–90
lumps, getting rid of 386
Morello cherry 401
mornay 392–3
mushroom and onion 216–17
mustard 118, 392
parsley 230–1, 393
quick hollandaise, John Tovey's 34, 244
ragù Bolognese 330
redcurrant, orange and mint 400
rouille 440
soured cream and onion 223–4
spiced apple and onion 147, 398
spiced green tomato 401–2
spinach and cheese 261, 393
spring sauce for lamb 354
stock for 63
tabasco 366
tartare 107, 439
tomato 215–16, 329–30
tomato chilli 329
white wine sauce 390
wild mushroom 336–7
yoghurt and juniper 213
yoghurt seafood 489
Sauces, sweet 407–10
  butterscotch 409–10
  chocolate 528–9
  custard 407
  port wine 408–9
  rum or brandy 409
  sabayon 408
Sausage rolls 465
  with quick flaky pastry 516
Sausages
  braised in red wine 178
  cheese and herb 421
  French garlic 450–1
  haricot bean and salami salad 452–3
  Mortadella 86
  pepperoni, with pizza 56
  salami 86
Scallops 131–4
  cream soup 132–3
  in the shell 133–4

Scampi (Dublin Bay prawns) 134
Scone pizza 302–3
Scones 561–4
  plain 562
  wholewheat cheese-crusted 563–4
  wholewheat fruit 563
Scotch broth 74–5, 284
Scotch eggs with fresh herbs 465–6
Scottish shortbread 567–8
Seafood sauce with yoghurt 489
Semolina 285
Sesame oil 436
Sesame, toasted seeds 302
Shallots 249
Shellfish 129–37
Shortbread 566–9
  biscuits 567, **opp. 481**
  Scottish 567–8, **opp. 481**
  strawberry shortcake 568
  wholewheat 568–9
Shrimps 134
Skate 106
  with black butter 106–7
Smoked
  bacon and lentil soup 78
  bloaters 124
  buckling 121, 124
  cod's roe 123
  cured pork loin 151
  eel 122
  fish 87, 121–1
  fish creams 96
  fish pâté 95
  fish pie 126–7, **opp. 192**
  haddock 124–5
  herrings 123–4
  kippers 121, 123–4, 127–9, 510
  mackerel 122–3
  mackerel pâté 94–5
  salmon 121, 122
  salmon tart 510
  sprats 124
  trout 122
Soda bread, soured cream 45–6
Sole 104, 105
  Dover 102, 104
  fillets of sole gratinés 425
  goujons of 105–6
  lemon 105
  witch 105
Sorrel 351
Soufflé
  broccoli cheese 429–30
  cheese 31
  cheese soufflé pancakes 344
  cold chocolate orange 583–4
  hot chocolate rum 590–1
  hot crab 135–7
  lemon soufflé omelette 33–4
  Welsh rarebit 423–4
Soups 61, 67–84
  carrot and artichoke 80–1
  carrot and tarragon 353
  chilled avocado 70
  chilled beet 71
  chilled beetroot consommé 71
  chilled Spanish gazpacho 78–9
  chilled yoghurt and cucumber 489–90
  Chinese mushroom 69, 84

Eliza Acton's vegetable mulligatawny 75–6
  gardener's 77
  garlicky fish 83
  green herb 352–3
  Italian bean and pasta 308–9
  leek, onion and potato 69–70
  minestrone 71–2
  punchnep 76–7
  scalloped scream 132–3
  Scotch broth 74–5
  smoked bacon and lentil 78
  soupe à l'oignon gratinée 72–3, **opp. 129**
  stocks 61–7
  thick bean and bacon 309
  thick pea 310
  tomato, apple and celery cream 82
  turkey 66
  vichyssoise 70
  watercress cream 73–4
Soured cream 473
  with baked fish and capers 113
  and chocolate filling 545
  cœurs à la crème 433–4
  with creamed potatoes 252
  with cucumber and dill 358–9
  dressing 450–1
  with eggs en cocotte and asparagus 474
  with jacket potatoes 254
  and leek flan 475–6
Soy dressing 449–50
Soya beans 306
Soya oil 436
Spaghetti 326
  with anchovies, mushrooms and olives 333
  alla carbonara 331
  ragù Bolognese 330
Spanish gazpacho, chilled 78–9
Spanish pork with olives 174–5
Spanish tortilla 468
Spices 362–85
  beef curry with whole 378
  chicken with whole 191–2
  honey and spice cake 470–1
  mixed 374
  pudding 586
Spiced
  apple and onion sauce 147, 398
  apple and raisin crumble 595–6
  apple and raisin pie 500–1
  chick pea cutlets 323
  chicken 379
  fig pudding with rum butter 602
  green tomato sauce 264, 401–2
  lamb with chick peas 317–18
  pears in red wine 384–5
  pilau rice 275
  plum and damson chutney
  rum or da
  606–7   matoes 135
Prawns with to
  nach 260–2
  rown rice and
  cheese 263–4

Spinach - *contd.*
 and cheese sauce 261, 393
 and cream cheese quiche
  422–3
 eggs Florentine 264
 filo parcels 291
 pancake stuffed with 340–1
 pasties 290
 raw spinach. and watercress
  salad 445–6
Split peas 306
 non-meat loaf 316–17
 vegetarian shepherd's pie
  315–16
Sponge cakes 538–46
 all-in-one 539, 541–2
 classic Victoria 538, 539–40
 toppings and fillings 544–6
 whisked fatless 539, 542–3
Sponge pudding, wholewheat
 treacle 602–3
Sprats 117
 deep-fried, in mustard sauce
  118
 smoked 124
Spring onions 443, 465
 with braised peas 260
Spring sauce for lamb 354
Starters 85–94
Steak *see* Beef
Stilton cheese 416
Stock 61–7
 brown beef 64
 for casseroles 161
 chicken carcass 66
 chicken giblet 65–6
 duck 197
 fish 67
 for gravy 404
 light beef 64
 pressure-cooked beef 64–5
 pressure-cooked chicken 66
 for sauces, casseroles or rice
  63
 shellfish 67
 turkey carcass 66
 turkey giblet 66
 see also Soups
Strawberries in raspberry
 purée 578
Strawberry jam 616
 pancakes 339
Strawberry shortcake 568
Stroganoff, simple 165–6
Stuffed
 aubergines, Italian 460–1
 breast of lamb 155–6
 cabbage leaves 295
 courgettes 627–8
 jacket potatoes 255
 peppers, Turkish 282–3
 pork tenderloin 148–9
 roast goose 202–4
 spinach-stuffed pancakes
  341–2
 tomatoes, Turkish 264–5
 vine leaves (dolmades) 296
Stuffing
 apple 203
 chestnut and apple 199
 for chicken 184–5
 for duck 196
 forcemeat 203
 garlic 131
 grape 193–4

herb, with mackerel 357–8
 mushroom 112
 pork, sage and onion 198–9
 rice and kidney 156
 for turkey 198–9
Suet crust pastry 510–14
Sugar, 39–40, 535, 614
Summer fruits pie 502
Summer pudding 575–6
Sunflower seeds, toasted 302
Swedes 263
 mashed, with crispy bacon
  263
Sweetbreads 210
 with soured cream and
  onion sauce 223–4
Syrup pancakes 339

Tabasco sauce 366
Tagliatelle 326
Taramasalata 93–4
Tarragon 352
 butter with young carrots
  237
 and carrot soup 353
 with chicken salad 360
 vinegar 369, 436
Tartare sauce 107, 439
Tarte tatin 584
Thyme 352
Toffee, Uncle Billy's 622–3
Tomato sauce
 chilli 329
 chilli eggs in 32
 fresh 329
 kidneys in fresh 215–16
 spiced green 264, 401–2
Tomato(es) 263–5, 465
 apple and celery cream soup
  82
 with baked aubergines 229
 with baked marrow 247
 with braised meatballs 176–
  7
 in casseroles 161
 and courgettes au gratin 242
 fresh tomato soup with basil
  80
 gardener's soup 77
 green tomato chutney 264,
  608
 with pasta 328, 329
 for picnics 465
 pipérade 30
 salad 86, 444
 with spiced prawns 135
 Turkish stuffed 264–5
Tongue 209
 cold pressed ox 221–2
 lamb's tongue casserole
  220–1
Tortellini 326
Tortilla, Spanish 25, 468–9
Treacle
 wholewheat treacle sponge
  602–3
 wholewheat treacle tart
  505–6
Trifle, traditional 580–1
Tripe 210
 and onions 224–5
Trout 119
 brown 119
 with butter, cream and
  chives 356–7

with caper sauce 119–20
 poached, with herbs 356
 rainbow 119
 smoked 122
Tuna fish
 and brown rice salad
  447–8
 and white bean salad 91
Turbot 107
Turkey 197–202
 carcass and giblet stock 66
 cranberry and orange relish
  with 202
 left-over 198
 soup 66
 stuffings 198–9
 traditional roast 200–1
Turkish stuffed peppers 282
Turkish stuffed tomatoes
 264–5
Turmeric 374
Turnips 265–7
 buttered 266
 glazed baby 266–7
 and leeks boulangère 265
 punchnep 265, 266
 punchnep soup 76–7

Uncle Billy's toffee 622–3

Vanilla 375
 ice cream 483
Veal
 kidneys 208
 ossobuco 175–6
Vegetables 226–67
 and brown rice gratin 291–2
 and buckwheat pie 322
 in casseroles 162
 Chinese stir-fried green
  232–3
 crudités 86–7
 and hazelnut burgers 297–8
 and lentil moussaka 320–1
 mixed à la Grecque 300
 mulligatawny, Eliza Acton's
  75–6
 provençal stew 299
 sautéed mixed 301
 see also individual vegetables;
  salads
Vegetarian dishes 288–303
 goulash 293
 mincemeat 622
 shepherd's pie 315–16
Vichyssoise 70
Victoria plum ketchup
 611
Victoria sponge, classic 538,
 539–40
 wholewheat 540
Vinaigrette 87, 244, 437–8
 avocado 88–9
 with avocado mousse and
  prawns 89–90
 fresh fruit and mint 88
 with herbs 438
 with lemon 438
Vinegar 368–9, 435–6
 balsamic 435
 cider 435
 flavoured 436
 wine 435
Vine leaves 296
Vol-au-vents 521–2

Walnut(s)
 and banana loaf, all-in-one
  469–70
 and chocolate pudding 589
 and coffee sponge 541–2
 date and apple loaf 465,
  547–8
 oil 436
 pickled, with braised beef
  177–8
Watercress 443
 cream soup 73–4
 with poached eggs and cream
  28
 and raw spinach salad 445–
  6
Wedding cakes 560
Welsh rarebit soufflé 423–4
Wensleydale cheese 416
Wheat 36–8, 284–5
Wheat bran 285
Wheatgerm 285
 with yoghurt and honey
  488
Wheatmeal flour 37
Wheatmeal quick rolls 48–9
White bean and tuna fish
 salad 91
White sauce, basic 388–91
White wine sauce 390
Whitebait 117
Whiting 107, 125
Wholegrain cereals 284–5
Wholewheat
 cheese-crusted scones 563–4
 cheese savouries 573
 flakes 285
 flour 37, 493, 534
 fruit scones 563
 girdle scones 564–5
 grains 284
 pasta 325
 pastry 493, 498
 quick pizza 58–9, 465
 shortbread 568–9, **opp. 481**
 sponge cakes 539, 540
 treacle sponge 602–3
 treacle tart 505–6

Yeast 38–9, 40
Yoghurt 472, 486–91
 chilled yoghurt and
  cucumber soup 489–90
 with creamed potatoes 252
 cucumber raita 490–1
 and cucumber salad 302
 dried fruit 489
 with dried fruit salad 491
 home-made 487–8
 home-made curd cheese from
  488
 home-made fruit 489
 with honey and wheatgerm
  488
 Indian kebabs marinated in
  377
 and juniper sauce 213
 with muesli 488
 seafood sauce 489
York ham 151
Yorkshire pudding 141–2
Yugoslav kebabs 458–9

Zabaglione 33
Zucchini *see* Courgettes